Standardization under EU Competition Rules and US Antitrust Laws

NEW HORIZONS IN COMPETITION LAW AND ECONOMICS

Series Editors: Steven D. Anderman, *Department of Law, University of Essex, UK* and Rudolph J.R. Peritz, *New York Law School, USA*

This series has been created to provide research based analysis and discussion of the appropriate role for economic thinking in the formulation of competition law and policy. The books in the series will move beyond studies of the traditional role of economics – that of helping to define markets and assess market power – to explore the extent to which economic thinking can play a role in the formulation of legal norms, such as abuse of a dominant position, restriction of competition and substantial impediments to or lessening of competition. This in many ways is the *new horizon* of competition law policy.

US antitrust policy, influenced in its formative years by the Chicago School, has already experienced an expansion of the role of economic thinking in its competition rules. Now the EU is committed to a greater role for economic thinking in its Block Exemption Regulations and Modernisation package as well as possibly in its reform of Article 102. Yet these developments still raise the issue of the *extent* to which economics should be adopted in defining the public interest in competition policy and what role economists should play in legal argument. The series will provide a forum for research perspectives that are critical of an unduly-expanded role for economics as well as those that support its greater use.

Titles in the series include:

Intellectual Property and Antitrust
A Comparative Economic Analysis of US and EU Law
Mariateresa Maggiolino

A Legal Theory of Economic Power
Implications for Social and Economic Development
Calixto Salomão Filho

Collective Dominance and Collusion
Parallelism in EU and US Competition Law
Marilena Filippelli

Cartels, Competition and Public Procurement
Law and Economic Approaches to Bid Rigging
Stefan Weishaar

The Chinese Anti-Monopoly Law
New Developments and Empirical Evidence
Edited by Michael Faure and Xinzhu Zhang

Standardization under EU Competition Rules and US Antitrust Laws
The Rise and Limits of Self-Regulation
Björn Lundqvist

Standardization under EU Competition Rules and US Antitrust Laws

The Rise and Limits of Self-Regulation

Björn Lundqvist

Associate Professor of Competition Law, Copenhagen Business School, Denmark

NEW HORIZONS IN COMPETITION LAW AND ECONOMICS

Edward Elgar

Cheltenham, UK • Northampton, MA, USA

Published by
Edward Elgar Publishing Limited
The Lypiatts
15 Lansdown Road
Cheltenham
Glos GL50 2JA
UK

Edward Elgar Publishing, Inc.
William Pratt House
9 Dewey Court
Northampton
Massachusetts 01060
USA

A catalogue record for this book
is available from the British Library

Library of Congress Control Number: 2013958017

This book is available electronically in the ElgarOnline.com Law Subject Collection, E-ISBN 978 1 78195 486 7

MIX
Paper from
responsible sources
FSC® C013056
FSC
www.fsc.org

ISBN 978 1 78195 485 0

Typeset by Columns Design XML Ltd, Reading
Printed and bound in Great Britain by T.J. International Ltd, Padstow

Contents

Figures

Table of cases

A. EU CASES AND CASES FROM MEMBER STATES

(i) EU cases

(ii) Cases from the Member States

Germany

The Netherlands

UK

(iii) Decisions by the EU Commission

B. US CASES

(i) US court cases

(ii) FTC cases and briefs

(iii) U.S. International Trade Commission (ITC) Decisions

1. R&D collaborations, technology standardization agreements and patent pools: antitrust problems or efficient solutions to antitrust problems?

When interviewed, a representative for the world's leading equipment supplier and network service operator of mobile and fixed phone and telecommunications stated that the two most important outputs of research are patents and technology standards.[1] The representative for the telecommunications firm went on to say that technology standardization is never an end in itself because consumers' requirements and competitors' positions need to be taken into consideration and balanced against each other.[2] The firms that combine forces in the standardization committees change over time but collaboration remains essential since the processes in the technical committees are usually consensual.[3] In fact, the negotiation of compromises in the technical committees of standard-setting organizations permits a feedback loop into research activities. Technical committees create platforms where competitors can communicate, negotiate and collaborate about the development and the standardization of the technology.[4]

In relation to intellectual property rights, the members of these technical committees are these days conscious of the patent or IP 'ecosystem' that is linked to suggested standards. They often file patent applications before the

---

1 Rudi Bekkers et al., 'Case studies on the interface between research and standardisation, and case studies on patent pools as a coordination mechanism' (INTEREST consortium Priority 8 No. Contract 503 594, EU 6th Specific Targeted Research Project, 2006), 53. [The document is on file with the author.]

2 Ibid. 55.

3 Ibid.

4 Ibid.

initial meeting when discussing which technologies to standardize.[5] The intellectual property rights that are the result of this process are placed in technology pools[6] or utilized as bargaining chips when negotiating cross-licence or licence agreements, or used as the basis for court cases in the furious patent and standards wars taking place at the moment.[7]

In some industries, for example, the telecom industry or in the IT sector, it is clear that competitors, to a certain degree jointly in collaboration, govern the development and direction of the relevant technology. They not only collaborate when setting the standard, but actually agree on what technology to develop in the first place. In other words, they often conduct (joint) R&D with the aim of creating a dominant technology in consortia or fora. Such consortia, which aim not only to

---

[5] Claudia Tapia, *Industrial Property Rights, Technical Standards and Licensing Practices (FRAND) in the Telecommunications Industry* (Carl Heymanns Verlag – eine Marke von Wolters Kluwer Deutschland GmbH 2010), 90 et seq. and 241 et seq.

[6] Collaborations where licensors agree that their industrial intellectual property rights should be licensed in a bundle, or through a vehicle for licensing third parties, are often called patent pools, even though neither US nor EC antitrust laws restrict these forms of collaborations only to patentees (see discussion infra under Chapters 3.5 and 3.6). Indeed, copyrights are allowed to enter patent pools as essential intellectual property rights for the relevant artistic or technology development so a better name for patent pools would be technology pools. However, since the term 'patent pool' has gained such acceptance, both the terms, i.e. 'technology pool' and 'patent pool', will be used as synonyms in this book. In principle, copyrights do not foreclose in the same manner as patents and should therefore not represent essential parts of a technology. Indeed, copyright protects material should not, in principle, be part of patent pools. However, regarding copyright protected software, the intertwined development of the law and the software technology has created legal protection under copyright laws that in practice work similarly to patents. Hence, from a practical standpoint copyright protected software can be essential for a technology. However, rather than allowing for copyrights to be included in technology pools, the legislator should limit the ambit of copyright law. Cf. Hanns Ullrich, 'Patent Pools: Approaching a Patent Law Problem via Competition Policy', in Claus-Dieter Ehlermann and Isabela Atanasiu (eds), *European Competition Law Annual 2005: The Interaction Between Competition Law and Intellectual Property Law* (Hart Publishing, 2007), 311 et seq.

[7] See R. Bekkers et al., 'Case studies on the interface between research and standardization, and case studies on patent pools as a coordination mechanism', (INTEREST consortium Priority 8 No. Contract 503 594, EU 6th Specific Targeted Research Project, 2006), 131, describing the history of the 3G mobile telecommunication technology where the patent pools were rebranded as 'patent platforms'.

develop a technology jointly, but also to implement that technology as a *de facto* or *de jure* standard, seem to be more prevalent in these industries than others, while they have started to multiply also in other industries. Certain standards in the IT sector are examples of standards developed in *consortia* and/or out of joint R&D.[8] For example, VGA and SXGA analog computer display standards (VESA), digital transmission standards such as the digital subscriber line or DSL (DSLForum), and internet-related developer standards such as HTML were developed out of consortia. Moreover, the Advanced Access Content System Licensing Administrator (AACS LA) digital rights management for high-definition videodisk standards (adopted into both HD-DVD and Blu-Ray standard), and also the CD-ROM, HD-DVD and Blu-Ray standards were developed in the consumer electronic (audiovisual) industry and might be regarded as derived from joint standard efforts of consortia akin to R&D collaborations.[9] Many of these standards originated from various consortia efforts, and they were later accepted, *de facto*, as standards by stakeholders or agreed upon (*de jure*) in more formal standard-setting organizations.

Moreover, some argue that in the telecommunications sector there have also been incidences of consortia efforts based on joint R&D with the aim of creating and implementing global standards, for example the push-to-talk technology.[10]

---

[8] Stacy Baird, 'The Government at the Standard Bazaar', (2007) 18 *Stanford Law & Policy Review*, 35, 50 et seq., stating that video standards such as the VGA and SXGA analog computer display standards (VESA), digital transmission standards such as digital subscriber line or DSL (DSLForum), internet related developer standards such as HTML (W3C), XML, SOAP and the OpenCable Application Platform (OCAP) are all derived from consortia. See also Marcus Glader, 'Open Standards: Public Policy Aspects and Competition Law Requirements', (2010) 6 *European Competition Journal*, 611, 623 et seq.

[9] Ibid.

[10] Claudia Tapia, *Industrial Property Rights, Technical Standards and Licensing Practices (FRAND) in the Telecommunications Industry* (Carl Heymanns Verlag – eine Marke von Wolters Kluwer Deutschland GmbH, 2010), 84, with references in fn. 392. It may furthermore be argued that the very early telecom network technologies NMTS and GSM were developed in consortia and that there was a form of standard or technology wars in which different EU Member State governments were also involved in promoting the technologies developed by national champions. Cf. Maurits Dolmans, 'Standards For Standards', (2002) 26 *Fordham International Law Journal*, 163, 181, and Rudi Bekkers et al., 'Case studies on the interface between research and standardisation, and case studies on patent pools as a coordination mechanism', (INTEREST consortium Priority 8 No. Contract 503 594, EU 6th Specific Targeted Research Project, 2006). 121.

Under the R&D or the 'pre-standardization phase', competitors may conduct joint or unilateral R&D within selected technology avenues. Standard-setting in this regard may be regarded as a form of collective innovation.[11] Recent novel empirical research carried out by Justus Baron and Tim Pohlmann shows that firms with substitutable R&D programs or patent portfolios are more likely to be member of the same pre-standardization consortium.[12] Indeed, through upfront R&D coordination under the consortium, firms that have the same business model can coordinate R&D and better anticipate technology selection decision in SDOs.[13] Initially, several technical solutions or ideas may be discussed and even pitted against each other in contests. Inputs from competitors are taken into consideration and hopefully consensus is reached around one solution. Simultaneously, R&D is conducted. Thus, before and during the negotiations over technical specifications within committees or groups under formal SDOs, stakeholders conduct R&D unilaterally or jointly in fora or consortia. They return to the R&D table for more research, and then re-join again in the technical committee to negotiate the width and depth of the soon to be standardized technologies. The patent applications filed before the initial meetings may be amended or redrafted.[14] Also, after the implementation of successful standards, firms pursue the strategy of obtaining patents essential under the standard agreed upon.

In the end, during the pre-standardization phase, they create, not only a defined technology for interoperability, but also complementary and blocking patents, while agreeing on a technology standard. In fact, the Baron and Pohlmann research, based on a database including all ICT standards issued between 1992 and 2009, shows that consortia have been formed for all standards with an unusually high number of patent

---

[11] Josef Drexl, 'Anti-competitive Stumbling Stones on the Way to a Cleaner World: Protecting Competition in Innovation Without a Market', (2012) 8 *Journal of Competition Law & Economics*, 507, 534.

[12] Justus Baron and Tim Pohlmann, 'Who Cooperates in Standard Consortia – Rivals or Complementors' (2013) 9 *Journal of Competition Law & Economics*, 905, 921, 928.

[13] However, the research show that R&D specific or technology specialisets firms are not members of the pre-standardization consortia. Ibid.

[14] Cf. general discussion regarding this and also divisional and continuations in Dietmar Harhoff et al., 'The Strategic Use of Patents and its Implications for Enterprise and Competition Policies', in, final report to the Commission in Tender for NO ENTR/05/82, (8 July 2007), 94 et seq.

holders.[15] These efforts also continue after the standard is set. 'Downstream' consortia or patent pools are used to promote, maintain and enforce existing standards.[16]

Indeed, antitrust authorities, as well as antitrust scholars, are well aware that such collaborations are taking place continuously in (primarily) the network-driven industries.[17] This represents a form of 'coopetition' between competitors, collaborating in defining and, in some sense, pricing the technology, while opening up the opportunity for single firms to add essential patents under the standard.

The rise of standards is an implicit consequence of a need for more and more products to interact. Interoperability between products and services is today more needed than before, and these organizations have sprung from the market (bottom-up) need of firms to collaborate. Compatibility and interoperability are clearly at least perceived as increasingly essential to many industries. A simplified 'standardization business model' of the business strategies played out in some network-driven industries, such as the telecommunications industry, could be depicted as follows (Figure 1.1):

Under the model, competitors negotiate and agree on standards while conducting unilateral, joint or outsourced R&D. They *de facto* agree on a research path which will, in the end, result in similar innovations, and, hence, overlapping and complementary patents and, *de facto* or *de jure* technology standards. A technology standardization agreement, in turn,

---

[15] Justus Baron and Tim Pohlmann, 'Who Cooperates in Standard Consortia – Rivals or Complementors' (2013) 9 *Journal of Competition Law & Economics*, 905, 912.

[16] Ibid., 910.

[17] For example, R&D joint ventures have been an accepted form of collaboration under both US and EU antitrust laws for decades. The US antitrust policy was that R&D ventures should be judged under the Rule of Reason even before the dawn of the Chicago school economics. See US Department of Justice, *Antitrust Guide Concerning Research Joint Ventures* (1980), 3 et seq. For early EU policy, see, e.g., the 1968 notice concerning agreements, decisions and concerted practices in the field of cooperation between enterprises, OJ C 75/3, 27.07.1968, 3, where the Commission stated, inter alia, that pure R&D cooperations generally do not restrict competition, i.e., they are per se legal, on the condition that the parties are free to pursue their own R&D. See also Commission, *Report on Competition Policy* 1971, 46. There are different forms of collaboration that mirror different forms of technology standards. Compatibility standards will mainly be discussed in this thesis. For a definition of different standards, see Chapter 2.4.

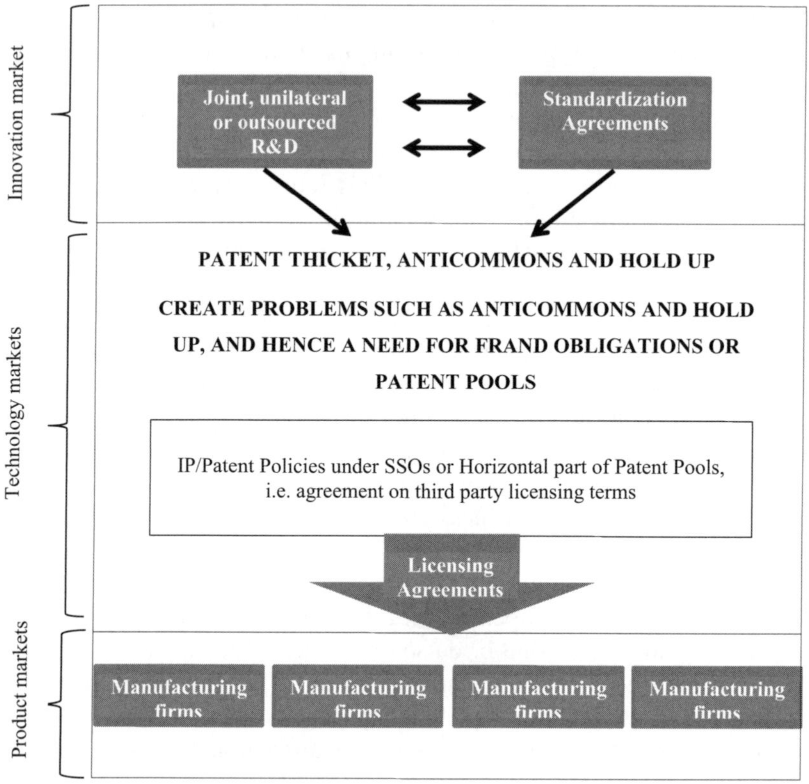

Figure 1.1 Standardization business model

results in similar or joint follow-on R&D after the standard is set. This is one outcome of the collaborative innovation model under standard setting.

The proliferation of overlapping, blocking and complementary patents, especially under successful, or expected to be successful, *de facto* or *de jure* technology standards, may create 'patent thickets',[18] the problem of 'anticommons',[19] and the existence of individual patentees (PAEs) holding standard essential patents (SEPs). Thus, individual patentees holding

[18] For the definition of the 'patent thicket', see Carl Shapiro, 'Navigating the Patent Thicket: Cross Licenses, Patent Pools and Standard Setting', in Adam Jaffe et al. (eds), *Innovation Policy and the Economy* (MIT Press, 2001), 119 et seq.

[19] For a definition of the 'tragedy of the anticommons', see Michael Heller & Rebecca Eisenberg, 'Can Patents Deter Innovation? The Anticommons in Biomedical Research', (1998) 280 *Science*, 698, 698 et seq. See also Micheal Heller,

SEPs will be able to 'hold up' competitors and product producing firms from utilizing the technology on the product markets.[20] The patent thicket, which relates to the problem of access to multiple existing patent-protected technologies, may hinder exploitation of the technology in product market and subsequent innovative work, e.g. follow-on innovations.[21] Interestingly, the thickets seem mostly prevalent under standards, which, of course, is logical. Successful standards are both the result of and the cause for R&D and patent application efforts.

'The Tragedy of the Anticommons: Property in the Transition from Marx to Markets', (1998) 111 *Harvard Law Review*, 621, 660 et seq.

[20] Recently the problem of patent 'hold up' under industrial standards, and the terms on which essential patents should be made available, have been addressed not only in the academic literature (see Chapter 4 infra) but also confronted several courts in Europe and the United States. The paramount litigation was all part of the global feud between Qualcomm and Nokia, leading in the end to complaints by both Nokia and Qualcomm to the US International Trade Commission (ITC) and by Nokia to the EU Commission. Regarding Nokia's complaint over Qualcomm to ITC in September 2007, see Press Release http://www.usitc.gov/ext_relations/news_release/2007/er0918ee1.htm, accessed 3 April 2011. For Qualcomm's complaint over Nokia in July 2006, see http://www.usitc.gov/ext_relations/news_release/2006/er0707dd3.htm, accessed 3 April 2011. See also EC Commission's Memo/Press Release, MEMO/07/389, dated 1 October 2007 'Commission initiate formal proceedings against Qualcomm'. On the joint complaint of Nokia, Ericsson, Texas Instruments, Broadcom, NEC and Panasonic, the EU Commission started an investigation into whether Qualcomm was abusing its dominance based on patent rights included in the 3G system since it did not license these rights on Fair, Reasonable, and Non-Discriminatory (FRAND) terms. See also Qualcomm's suit against Nokia for patent infringement, Qualcomm Inc. v. Nokia Corp. 466 F.3d 1366 (Fed. Cir. 2006). See furthermore, Broadcom v. Qualcomm Inc. 501 F.3d. 297 (3rd Cir 2007). Interestingly, it seems that Nokia and Qualcomm settled their differences during the summer of 2008. See Matt Richtel, 'In Settlement, Nokia Will Pay Royalties to Qualcomm' in *New York Times* 24 July 2008, http://www.nytimes.com/2008/07/24/technology/24qualcomm.html?_r=1&scp=1&sq=nokia%20qualcomm&st=cse., accessed 3 April 2011.

[21] For the mosaic description, see Hanns Ullrich, 'Patent Pools: Approaching a Patent Law Problem via Competition Policy', in Claus-Dieter Ehlermann & Isabela Atanasiu (eds), *European Competition Law Annual 2005: The Interaction Between Competition Law and Intellectual Property Law* (Hart Publishing, 2007), 322. Regarding patent thicket, see Carl Shapiro, 'Navigating the Patent Thicket: Cross Licenses, Patent Pools and Standard Setting', in Adam Jaffe et al. (eds), *Innovation Policy and the Economy* (MIT Press, 2001), 119 et seq.

To be able to produce products under standardized technologies, vertically integrated firms (often large multinationals) need to access SEPs. Due to the problems of gaining access to the SEPs held by certain technology-only firms, or, as they are sometimes called, patent assertion entities (PAEs), SDOs have recently developed IP or patent policies that generally stipulate that their members should, first, acknowledge and present potential SEPs when the standard is developed and, furthermore, should agree to give access to SEPs on fair, reasonable and non-discriminatory (FRAND) terms.

Firms that have agreed on the standard and the IP/patent policies with the FRAND terms will be able to collect FRAND royalties for SEPs. They might furthermore agree to use the definition of the standardized technology or agree on a new definition of the relevant technology for the creation of a patent pool. The early modern patent pool cases from the mid 90s are examples of pools derived from standardized technologies.[22] They represent one-stop-shops with a packet of licences for one combined royalty rate. The pool may then be utilized to collect royalties, which are then transferred to the standard or technology pool essential patentees. Firms not agreeing on the patent pool terms may very well pursue a unilateral strategy, trying to obtain bilateral licence agreements, either under the FRAND royalty regimes or supra-FRAND royalty schemes, depending on whether the firm is a member of the relevant SDO or not.

Notwithstanding the clear interlink between these forms of collaboration – joint R&D, technology standardization agreements (including FRAND patent policies or intellectual property arrangements), and cross-licence or joint licensing under similar terms, or even under technology pools – are considered detached from each other under antitrust law and IP law, both in the United States and in the European Union.[23] Each form of collaboration is examined separately to identify potential micro-economic efficiencies and its likely pro- or anti-competitive effects.[24] The overall strategy and the rather clear overlaps between these forms of collaboration are neither addressed nor analysed.

---

[22] Rudi Bekkers et al., 'Emerging Ways to Address the Reemerging Conflict between Patenting and Technological Standardization', (2012) 21 *Industrial and Corporate Change*, 901, 910 et seq.

[23] Hanns Ullrich, 'Patent Pools – Policy and Problems', in Josef Drexl (ed), *Research Handbook on Intellectual Property and Competition Law* (Edward Elgar, 2008), 160 et seq.

[24] Ibid.

Moreover, the interface between these forms of collaboration and the unilateral conduct of individual patentees are not entirely appreciated.

Correspondingly, these forms of collaborations and conduct have, with a few exceptions, been analysed separately in the scholarly antitrust discussion. Both jurists and economists focus either on R&D collaborations,[25] technology standard-setting activities,[26] or patent pool.[27] Only rarely has the interaction between these forms of collaborations attracted any interest, and then either the interface between R&D and standard setting,[28] the interface between technology standard setting and patent pools, or unilateral conduct has been discussed.[29] The broader spectrum has received surprisingly little treatment in the legal and economic literature.[30]

This book attempts to fill that void. Its purpose is to consider how the standardization process, (i.e. the agreements entered into and actions of firms conducted, *before, while and after* a technology is developed, with the aim of providing an omnipresent technology structure for a market,

---

25 See footnotes to the text, infra Chapters 2.7 and 4.2.4.

26 See footnotes to the text, infra Chapter 4.

27 See footnotes to the text, infra Chapter 5.

28 See footnotes to the text, infra Chapter 4.2.4.

29 See footnotes to the text, infra Chapter 5.5.

30 For exceptions, see generally Rudi Bekkers et al., 'Patent pools and non assertion agreements: Coordination mechanisms for multi-party IRP holders in standardisation', in EASST 2006 Conference 2006. This document is on file with the author.]; Rudi Bekkers et al., 'Case studies on the interface between research and standardisation, and case studies on patent pools as a coordination mechanism', in (INTEREST consortium Priority 8 No. Contract 503 594, EU 6th Specific Targeted Research Project, 2006). [The document is on file with the author.]; Gil Ohana et al., 'Disclosure and negotiation of Licensing Terms Prior to Adoptation of Industry Standards: Preventing another Patent Ambush', (2003) 24 E.C.L.R, 644; Michael Schallop, 'The IPR Paradox: Leveraging Intellectual Property Rights to Encourage Interoperability in the Network Computing Age', (2000) 28 *AIPLY Quarterly Journal*, 195; Nari Lee, 'Patented Standards and the Tragedy of Anti-commons', (2006) *Teollisoikeudellisia Kirjoituksia VII*; Hanns Ullrich, 'Patente, Wettbewerb, under technische Normen: Recht- und ordnungspolitische Fragestellungen', (2007) 10 *GRUR* 2007, 817; John Barton, 'Antitrust Treatment of Oligopolies with Mutual Blocking Patent Portfolios', (2002) 69 *Antitrust Law Journal*, 851; Maurits Dolmans, 'Standards For Standards', (2002) 26 *Fordham International Law Journal*, 163; Mark Lemley, 'Intellectual Property Rights and Standard-Setting Organizations', (2002) 90 *California Law Review*, 1889; and also, generally, Hanns Ullrich, 'Patent Pools – Policy and Problems', in Josef Drexl (ed), *Research Handbook on Intellectual Property and Competition Law* (Edward Elgar, 2008), 139 et seq.

i.e. standards) is regulated under United States antitrust laws and European Union competition rules, respectively and comparatively. The current focus on single firms' use of patents to exclude competition, e.g. patent and FRAND ambush will be discussed at length in Chapter 6 of the book. However, the question asked initially is whether the forms of collaboration making up the standardization process should be explicitly and implicitly exempted and promoted under US antitrust and EU competition law, as they are today, or whether they would benefit from a heightened and more intense legal (antitrust) scrutiny. Has the self-regulation of markets, i.e. the standardization process, gone too far? Are these forms of collaboration more of an antitrust problem in themselves than the problems they are designed to resolve?

Apart from an introductory chapter this book is divided into seven chapters. First, the multitude of different standards that exist and their effect on competition is discussed. A theme running through this book is that competition policy should be different depending on what sort of standard and what markets are being standardized. Some standards have very marginal potential anti-competitive effects, while other standards may restrict both dynamic and static competition. Secondly, the notion of strategic patenting in different industries is analysed. The new form of industry structure derived from strategic patenting and the proliferation of standards and patents is presented. I discuss the PAEs and why these are considered to hold-up certain industries.

I also introduce the notion of 'IP Banks', the new form of multinationals. IP Banks are firms that neither produce nor innovate; they only manage and cultivate large portfolios of intellectual property rights. However, they are not PAEs or patent trolls, but rather the old multinationals that seem to be progressing into having, as their core business activity, the creation of standards, the control of technology and the preservation of IPR portfolios, including trade marks, rather than R&D or for that matter the production of goods. Many products bear their trade marks, but the production of goods and even R&D is to a large extent outsourced to other firms, or, in the case of R&D, to universities and clusters of R&D-only firms connected to them. The production is conducted by manufacturing firms often situated in South East Asia. The IP Banks drive or chaperone the industry while being 'technology hubs' due to their activity in standard-setting organisations. They assign firms to conduct joint R&D or manufacture, but the IP Banks make profit by aligning their patent portfolios with the successful standards.

Several multinationals could be viewed to have a business strategy as the one depicted above, or at least to migrate towards it. Interestingly, the EU Commission in it recent merger decision regarding the purchase by

Micrsoft of Nokia's hand set business indirectly discuss this business strategy when analysing what Nokia will become by retaining all SEPs and near-SEPs in the telecom industry, but stop being a manufacturer of hand-sets.[31] It seems clear that the Commission was and is clearly worried about this development.[32]

The next part of the book, Chapter 3, starts with a description and discussion of the governance and institutional structure of standard setting/development organizations. What internal and external rules exist to regulate these organizations, and what kind of regulations should govern the SSOs? As a background to that discussion, the deregulation of drafting public technical specifications to SSOs is discussed. The so-called New Approach, under which the EU de-regulated technical specifications to SSOs, is analysed. The conclusion is that while standards today originate from firms' reaction to the need for standards of interoperability, standards, at least under the EU system, historically originated from public efforts to regulate the technical specifications of goods.

Thereafter, in Chapter 4, agreement on technology (standards), pre-standardization agreements, joint R&D with a focus on creating standards, and SDOs' IP policies are scrutinized in light of competition law. The United States regulation of the National Collaborative Research and Production Act (NCRPA) will be analysed. After its latest amendment, the NCRPA encompasses not only joint R&D, but also the conduct of Standard Development Organizations (SDOs), and 'standard-setting activities'. Standard-setting activities encompass IP arrangements. The equivalent EU competition law regulations will be discussed. The rules governing the exemption, under EU competition law, of standardization agreements are analysed. The R&D block exemption and the latest Horizontal Guidelines mirror the latest developments under US antitrust law, while being slightly more lenient.

---

[31] Commission decision 4 December 2013, Case No COMP/M.7047 – Microsoft/Nokia, 34 *et seq*, http://ec.europa.eu/competition/mergers/cases/decisions/m7047_20131204_20310_3495212_EN.pdf. Accessed 26 February 2014.

[32] EU Competition Commissioner Joaquin Almunia also warned Nokia of becoming a patent troll. In my view Nokia will not become a patent troll, rather a IP Bank. See Don Reisinger, 9 December 2013, 'EU to Nokia: Don't become a "patent troll"', http://news.cnet.com/8301-1035_3-57614945-94/eu-to-nokia-dont-be-a-patent-troll/. Accessed 27 February 2014.

After standard-setting activities have been discussed, the antitrust treatment of SDO connected patent pools is scrutinized in Chapter 5. The antitrust regulations for patent pools have certainly changed over the years and, even though patent pools today are treated leniently compared to only 25 years ago, technology pools are clearly more regulated than IP arrangements between members under SDOs. The difference between IP Policies and patent pools is hence discussed. Therefore, an effort has been made in this part of the book to compare the regulation of patent pools to the IP arrangements SEP holders may enact under standards.

Abuse of dominance or monopolization will be discussed in the succeeding chapter. When may holders of SEPs be considered to be monopolizing or abusing their dominant market position? It seems now that a holder of a SEP patentee may face an accusation of abuse when, for example, making use of injunctions, or by not giving access to SEPs on FRAND terms. The main issue, in fact, is whether holders of the SEP are obliged under competition rules or antitrust law to grant access to such patents on FRAND terms? Furthermore, it seems that a general consensus is building up that FRAND commitments, under competition law, run with the SEPs when they are assigned or transferred. Thus, are SEPs only proprietary rights in the US and EU? In other words, an SEP implies a right for its holder to have FRAND terms only, not to exclude violators.

In the same chapter, I also discuss the US developments. In the US, under the current intellectual property law doctrine, the *eBay* case[33] implies that injunctions are not available, at least not for PAEs, when trying to prevent infringers of SEPs. The Supreme Court in *eBay* seems to imply that even public policy considerations should be taken in these circumstances. Some cases seem even to state that the doctrines of patent misuse, estoppel, and/or waiver imply that conducting a patent or FRAND ambush, and thus deceiving an SSO, render the SEPs in fact unenforceable all together. Under competition law, Sherman Act sec. 2 may be applicable when a patentee deceives an SSO,[34] while according to *Rambus* the plaintiff still needs to show an anti-competitive effect under US Antitrust law. The US case law development seems contradictory and needs to be analysed, otherwise the rather absurd conclusion would be that antitrust law is more patentee friendly than US IP law.

---

33 eBay Inc. v. MercExchange, L.L.C., 547 U.S. 388 (2006).

34 Broadcom v. Qualcomm Inc. 501 F.3d. 297 (3d Cir. 2007).

Standards have different antitrust effects depending on what kind of standard is being scrutinized. At the end of the book, I will present the somewhat novel idea that product/technology design standardization agreements with its adjoining collaborations must, first, be assessed in their entire context and, secondly, benefit from a more intense antitrust scrutiny. Other kinds of standards, such as interoperability network standards, need a different, more lenient, antitrust scrutiny, while performance standards seldom have any anti-competitive effect at all. Interoperability standards, as well as other basic virtual technologies, are today developing into an infrastructure not only for the high-tech industry but also our virtual society. These standards need to be selected with care, and must thus be scrutinized under different policy objectives. Their collusive anti-competitive effects may be less serious but the potential anti-competitive effects of individual patentees holding up access to these standards by refusing to enter licence agreements for their SEPs are great.

I argue that requirements for deciding whether a standard should be considered anti-competitive, both in reference to the standard agreement and the structure and governance of the SSO, need to depend on the sort of standard being evaluated and the sort of markets the standard will affect. Requirements for open access to the decision-making process and good governance, i.e. transparent and undistorted procedure, should be enforced especially when deciding basic or interoperability standards, where the relevant market(s) being standardized cannot hold more than one such standard. The pro-competitive effects of such collaborations are great and collusive effects of such standards must thus be tolerated, while product design standards, on the other hand, should be scrutinized under different requirements. Indeed, a product standard agreement, where competitors agree on limit competition to only take place under one sort of product or technology in a market that may harbour and benefit from competition between several different products or technologies, should not be scrutinized much differently from other forms of horizontal collaboration. Parties to a product standard agreement may easily facilitate collusive agreements on price and output with a standard which exclude competing technologies on a market that would be able to facilitate several technologies. Competitors colluding to limit competition by substitute for competition by imitation is potentially restricting competition if they cannot show that the collaboration would render considerable efficiencies.

It seems clear, from the discussion regarding Art 102 and the Sec. 2 Sherman Act, that some of the violations discussed at the moment (e.g. patent ambush) could be addressed under both the intellectual property law system and the competition law system. US law treats the issue of injunctions, for example, under intellectual property law rather than under antitrust law.

Indeed, standardization should benefit from its own guidelines under competition law and intellectual property law in the US and EU, where the issues of anti-competitive agreement and monopolization are addressed.

The intellectual property law perspective of the collaborations and problems raised in this book will not be discussed in detail or exhaustively. Nonetheless, some intellectual property law solutions will be presented at the end of the book. It is clear that the problems which R&D collaborations, technology standardization agreements, and patent pools aim to solve originate from the unprecedented increase in legal protection of intellectual property that has taken place since the beginning of the 1980s.[35] There are intellectual property law solutions to the problems now dealt with in the form of exemptions under competition law,[36] and, as stated at the conclusion of this book, these intellectual property law solutions are to be preferred. However, since it seems impossible to

---

[35] Even though the proliferation problem is global, it seems to originate in the United States. See, e.g., the survey made by Jaffe regarding the increase in US patent applications. The increase in applications began in the middle of the 1980s and has increased by approximately 6 per cent each year since then, cf. Adam Jaffe, 'The U.S. Patent System in Transition: Policy Innovation and the Innovation Process', (2000) 29 *Elsevier Research Policy* 531, 536 et seq. According to Jaffe, even though the number of applications grows, the number of innovations does not necessarily grow by the same magnitude, or at all. It seems as if foreign applications are increasing steadily in every patent jurisdiction implying that inventors today apply for protection in more jurisdictions than before. See Adam Jaffe and Josh Lerner, *Innovation and its Discontents* (Princeton University Press 2004), 170 et seq. See also Levang, noting that there are (were) three million pending patents for 'expressed sequence tags' (EST) of DNA in the USA: Bradley Levang, 'Evaluating the Use of Patent Pools for Biotechnology: A Refutation to the USPTO White Paper Concerning Biotechnology Patent Pools', (2002-2003) 19 *Santa Clara Computer & High Tech Law Journal*, 229, 232 with references. See also generally FTC, *To Promote Innovation: The Proper Balance of Competition and Patent Law and Policy* (FTC 2003), Chapters 4 and 5. See http://www.ftc.gov/os/2003/10/innovationrpt.pdf, accessed 3 April 2009. Joseph Farrell and Robert Merges, 'Incentives to Challenge and Defend Patents: Why Litigation won't Reliably Fix Patent Office Errors and Why Administrative Patent Review Might Help', (2004) *Summer Berkeley Technology Law Journal*, 943, 944 et seq.

[36] See discussion, infra, in Chapter 4.

introduce IP law solutions, competition law solutions are also presented.

Unfortunately, given the need for delimitation, neither the vertical part of patent licensing agreements nor the merger regulations of joint ventures will be discussed.[37]

[37] For the Commission Regulation (EC) No 772/2004 of 27 April 2004 on the application of Art. 81(3) of the EC Treaty to categories of technology transfer agreements, OJ L 123, 27.04.2004, 11 et seq., hereinafter the TTBER. See, e.g., generally Lars Kjölbye and Lucas Peeperkorn, 'The New Technology Transfer Block Exemption Regulation and Guidelines', in Claus-Dieter Ehlermann and Isabela Atanasiu (eds), *European Competition Law Annual 2005: The Interaction Between Competition Law and Intellectual Property Law* (Hart Publishing 2005), 161 et seq.; Steven Anderman, 'Technology Transfer and the IP/Competition Interface', in Claus-Dieter Ehlermann & Isabela Atanasiu (eds), *European Competition Law Annual 2005: The Interaction between Competition Law and Intellectual Property Law* (Hart Publishing, 2005), 211, 213 et seq.; Steven Anderman and John Kallaugher, *Technology Transfer and the New EU Competition Rules* (Oxford University Press 2006), 1 et seq; Pat Treacy, 'Intellectual Property Transactions and Block Exemtions – The Future', (2005) 11 *Computer and Telecommunications Law Review*, 191; Erik Vollebregt, 'The New Technology Transfer Block Exemption: From Straightjacket to Moving Targets', (2004) 10 *Computer and Telecomunications Law Review*, 123; Frank Fine, 'The EU's New Antitrust Rules For Technology Licensing: A Turbulent Harbour For Licensors', (2004) 29 *European Law Review*, 766; Frank Fine, *The EC Competition Law on Technology Licensing* (Sweet & Maxwell Ltd 2006); Marc Hansen and Omar Shah, 'The New EU Technology Transfer Regime – Out of the Straightjacket into the Safe Harbour?', (2004) 25 *European Competition Law Review*, 465; Joel Smith, 'EC: Competition – Revised Technology Transfer Block Exemption Rules in Force', (2004) 26 *European Intellectual Property Review*, 113; Pat Treacy and Thoams Heide, 'The New EC Technology Transfer Block Exemption Regulation', (2004) 26 *European Intellectual Property Review*, 414; Maurits Dolmans & Anu Piilola, 'The New Transfer Block Exemption: A Welcome Reform, After All', (2004) 27 *World Competition*, 351; Cyril Ritter, 'The New Technology Transfer Block Exemption under EC Competition Law', (2004) *Legal Issues of Economic Integration;* Steven de Schrijver and Mel Marquis, 'Licensing Technology in the EU after the Big Bang: the New Technology Transfer Block Exemption Regulation and Guidelines', (2004) *Business Law Review* 161; Hanns Ullrich, 'IP-Antitrust in Context: Approaches to International Rules on Restrictive Uses of Intellectual Property Rights', (2003) 48 *Antitrust Bulletin*, 837.

2. The proliferation of IPRs and the rise of standards

2.1 NETWORK EFFECTS AND INTEROPERABILITY

It has been claimed that the information economy is populated with temporary monopolies. Hardware and software firms hold monopolies today knowing that a new technology will emerge that will topple their technology and, thus, overtake their monopoly position. In comparison, the industrial economy was, and still is, populated by stable oligopolies. The central difference between these two economies is that they have fundamentally different approaches to being successful: the driver in industrial economics is economy of scale, while the driver for the information economy is network effect.[1]

Network effects are now an old idea.[2] We all know what it is, and can point to certain networks. The term was invented at the time of Microsoft and Intel's great success and was a way to describe Wintel's success on the PC market compared to the suffering of Apple. As Wintel's share on the PC market grew, users found Wintel more and more attractive and

---

[1] Several researchers have discussed this. See Carl Shapiro and Hal R. Varian, *Information Rules* (Harvard Business School Press 1999), 173 et seq. See also Neil Gandal, 'Compatibility, Standardization, and Network Effects: Some Policy Implications', (2002) 18 *Oxford Review of Economic Policy*, 80; Michael Katz and Carl Shapiro, 'Systems Competition and Network Effects', (1994) 8 *Journal of Economic Perspective*, 93; Mark Lemley and David McGowan, 'Legal Implications of Network Economic Effects', (1998) 86 *California Law Review*, 479; Michael Schallop, 'The IPR Paradox: Leveraging Intellectual Property Rights to Encourage Interoperability in the Network Computing Age', (2000) 28 *AIPLY Quarterly Journal*, 195

[2] For definitions of network industries and tipping, see Michael Katz and Carl Shapiro, 'Systems Competition and Network Effects', (1994) 8 *Journal of Economic Perspective*, 93, 105 et seq.; Mark Lemley and David McGowan, 'Legal Implications of Network Economic Effects', (1998) 86 *California Law Review* 479, 500 et seq.; and Mark Lemley, 'Intellectual Property Rights and Standard-Setting Organizations', (2002) 90 *California Law Review*, 1889, 1896 et seq.

eventually the market 'tipped' to the advantage of Wintel. Network effects or network externalities imply that demand drives the economy. The value of a network or a technology (a standard) depends on the demand for the same. Other things being equal, it is better as a consumer or customer to be connected to a bigger network than a smaller network.[3]

Some economists argue that monopoly power in these cases is desirable. They argue that the drawbacks of monopoly power, which a proprietary standard entails, can be offset by the economic efficiencies derived from large networks.[4] Having a single standard results in a large network and is a desirable outcome. It is argued that the substantial investment into the development and promotion of a technology, which will only become the dominant standard on a market for a short time, will only be undertaken if firms have the prospect of (true) monopoly profits.[5]

Large networks may however require interoperability and right to access. Interoperability as a term implies many things, and is used in many settings. First, the success of the new virtual infrastructure networks, or platforms, such as the internet and the telecommunication technologies, is based on interoperability between competing firms' products. Interoperability is the linking of systems, networks or services so that they work together successfully.[6] Competing firms' products can use the same virtual infrastructure. Furthermore, different technologies on these platforms must also interoperate. In fact, the demand for interoperability also restricts and eliminates the consequences of network effects, while interoperability between technologies (perhaps due to the standard-setting process that has decided on this) may prevent one technology for becoming the *de facto* standard, and thus gaining a monopoly position. Secondly, interoperability implies that products today need to interact more and more. There are interfaces between different

---

[3] Ibid.

[4] Susanne Scotchmer, *Innovation and Incentives* (MIT Press 2004), 296 et seq., 289 et seq. See also Kamiel J. Koelman, 'An Exceptio Standardis: Do We Need an IP Exemption for Standards', (2006) 7 *IIC*, 823, 239 et seq., making reference to Scotchmer.

[5] Ibid.

[6] Claudia Tapia, *Industrial Property Rights, Technical Standards and Licensing Practices (FRAND) in the Telecommunications Industry* (Carl Heymanns Verlag – eine Marke von Wolters Kluwer Deutschland GmbH 2010), 9 fn 22, with references.

products, and producers need to agree on the technology of these interfaces.[7]

Network effects and interoperability lie at the heart of standard setting. A standard can both prevent network effects and be a vehicle to create said effects. Moreover, standards create interoperability. In general, firms try to achieve interoperability or compatibility by connecting their products to a standard.[8] This inevitably put limits on competition policy. To create the virtual infrastructure or interoperability, the standard-setting procedure needs to be an open venture where firms negotiate and collaborate on technology, while conducting unilateral, and sometimes, collaborative R&D.[9] Such a procedure creates the 'best' technology, while other forms of procedure for creating the 'best' technology (such as competition) may create suboptimal results because then a *de facto* technology will, due to network effects, be implemented. Such technology may gain its monopoly position due to network effects, while being neither the 'best' technology nor a suitable organization structure for a market with only one firm providing the entire response to a demand.[10] Furthermore, by including several firms in the standard-setting process, monopolies are prevented, both on the downstream technology market and the downstream product markets, to the benefit of oligopolies or more competitive markets. Indeed, collective standard-setting procedures may have clear pro-competitive effects, while preferring standard-setting over competition in network markets still implies that rivalry is limited and the idea of temporary monopolies is disregarded.

---

[7] Ibid. See specifically, Michael Schallop, 'The IPR Paradox: Leveraging Intellectual Property Rights to Encourage Interoperability in the Network Computing Age', (2000) 28 *AIPLY Quarterly Journal*, 195.

[8] Claudia Tapia, *Industrial Property Rights, Technical Standards and Lincesing Practices (FRAND) in the Telecommunications Industry* (Carl Heymanns Verlag – eine Marke von Wolters Kluwer Deutschland GmbH 2010), 7 with references.

[9] Josef Drexl, 'Anti-competitive Stumbling Stones on the Way to a Cleaner World: Protecting Competition in Innovation without a Market', (2012) 8 *Journal of Competition Law & Economics*, 507, 534.

[10] The old war between VHS and Betamax standards is claimed to have achieved an outcome where the lesser quality standard (VHS) still won the standard war and became the global standard. However, there is research that claims that VHS on the whole was a better product and technology. Cf. Julian Christ and André Slowak, 'Why Blue-Ray v. HD-DVD is not VHS v. BETAMAX: The Co-evolution of Standard Setting Consortia', (2009) *FZID Discussion Papers*, Universität Hohenheim, 4 et seq. with references.

Theoretically, collective innovation and oligopolies are promoted on the behalf of short-lived monopolies.

Moreover, today firms in collaboration create interoperability or the virtual infrastructure, not governments. It seems that governments neither have the technical capacity, knowledge nor the ability to decide on technologies for global standards. Instead, firms' heightened ability to create standards is inevitable, given the development of global entrepreneurial activity. Global standards are the prerogative of global firms. This also implies a restriction of competition policy.

To what extent can competition law agencies or courts review the selection of a technology to become a standard? Possibly, the agencies and courts have very little room to do this, while they do have an ability to chaperone the procedure to establish the standards. Misuse of the standard process may very well constitute competitive harm, while the selection of technology is out of reach for the courts.

2.2 PATENT MANAGEMENT STRATEGIES

In some industries, mostly related to the 'new' economy or industries with complex products and technology which requires interoperability, there has been a proliferation of patents and patent applications.[11] There are several reasons for this proliferation.[12]

First, generally, the technology in, for example, the semiconductor, telecommunications or biotech business is such that, in light of the low thresholds enforced under patent law[13], there was and still is a large

---

[11] Dietmar Harhoff et al., 'The Strategic Use of Patents and its Implications for Enterprise and Competition Policies', in final report to the Commission in Tender for NO ENTR/05/82, (8 July 2007), 72 et seq, and 86 et seq. FTC, *To Promote Innovation: The Proper Balance of Competition and Patent Law and Policy* (FTC 2003), 24.

[12] See B.H. Hall et al, A Study of Patent Thickets (UK Intellectual Property Office 2013), 8, 17 et seq, listing six reasons contributing to the growth of patent thickets: (i) strengthening of patent rights in the US; (ii) cumulative nature of science and the extension of technology, (iii) shifts in the degree of technology opportunitiy in various key technologies; (iv) strategic patenting and the increase of PAEs; (v) lack of resources and misaligned incentives at patent offices; and (vi) growth in trade of high technology products.

[13] Ibid It should be acknowledged that especially under US patent law, there has lately been a move from the Courts to try to make the requirements to obtain a patent more rigorous. Cf., e.g. KSR Int'l Co. v. Teleflex, Inc., 550 U.S. 398 (2007)

number of patentable incremental innovations in what is essentially a small step in the development of the technology or the science.[14] The technologies are complex and therefore the innovation becomes cumulative, yet again the low thresholds for obtaining patents increase the complexity rather then create easy structures of ownership for technology. For example, a computer programme may include millions of lines of code that constitute potentially hundreds of thousands of patentable innovations. This creates, or at least has the potential to create, mosaics of intellectual private property over single technologies in these industries.[15]

Secondly, 'defensive patenting' and 'strategic patenting'[16] have been, and are, common strategies for vertically integrated firms in the network industries with complex technologies.[17] In the IT, telecommunications, consumer electronics and to some extent pharmaceutical/biotech industries, it seems that defensive patenting is the general business model, where firms try to increase the size of their patent portfolios by filing large numbers of patents.[18] They use these patents to fend off accusations of infringement. The sheer magnitude of patents may give firms an incentive to apply for even more, since only by possessing several patents will a firm be able to fend off infringement claims. Hence, a firm that knowingly intrudes on another inventor's patent, will want to obtain other

---

[14] FTC, *To Promote Innovation: The Proper Balance of Competition and Patent Law and Policy* (FTC 2003), 25 et seq. with references.

[15] Hanns Ullrich, 'The Interaction between Competition Law and Intellectual Property Law – An Overview', in Claus Dieter Ehlermann and Isabela Atanasiu (eds), *European Competition Law Annual 2005: The Interaction between Competition Law and Intellectual Property Law* (Hart Publishing, 2007), 143 et seq., regarding the fragmentation of property knowledge under patent law.

[16] Dietmar Harhoff et al., 'The Strategic Use of Patents and its Implications for Enterprise and Competition Policies', in final report to the Commission in Tender for NO ENTR/05/82, (8 July 2007).

[17] B.H. Hall et al, A Study of Patent Thicket (UK Intellectual Property Office 2013), 8, 17 et seq John Barton, 'Antitrust Treatment of Oligopolies with Mutual Blocking Patent Portfolios', (2002) 69 *Antitrust Law Journal*, 851, 854. Barton states that patents became bargaining chips in, e.g., the semiconductor industry where some firms explicitly and publicly had a policy to obtain blocking patents of interest to other firms. For network industries and the concept of 'tipping', see Michael Katz and Carl Shapiro, 'Systems Competition and Network Effects', (1994) 8 *Journal of Economic Perspective*, 93, 105 et seq.

[18] Dietmar Harhoff et al., 'The Strategic Use of Patents and its Implications for Enterprise and Competition Policies', in final report to the Commission in Tender for NO ENTR/05/82, (8 July 2007), 11.

patents and surrounding patents in order to strengthening its bargaining position in future negotiations and patent infringement claims. It 'floods' the technology or the biotech markets with patents.[19] If accused of infringement, it may then claim that the accuser has committed a corresponding infringement. Until recently, opposition and litigious activities have tended to be low in these industries. One participant of the industry attributed this to the fact that it was less expensive and easier to file for new and more patents then to oppose or to challenge a competitor's patents.[20]

Thus, the proliferation of patents creates rearmament of patents until the parties have reached a 'mutual assured destruction' (MAD) capability.[21] In other words, the increasing number of patents in one industry actually encourages more patents to be taken out in the industry, and not the opposite.

Research into the patenting activities before the European Patent Office in Munich (EPO) shows, first, that strategic patenting activities are conducted and, secondly, that it is more prevalent in certain industries and with certain firms.[22] Thirdly, so-called complex patents are increasing,[23] while the quality, generally, of the patents granted by the EPO is falling.

Certain industries stand out more than others when it comes to implementing strategic patenting strategies. For example, the telecommunications, IT and the electric device industries are plagued with firms conducting strategic patenting practices. They have a strategy of patent

---

[19] The notion of patent flooding is normally connected with the biotech industry. Dietmar Harhoff et al., 'The Strategic Use of Patents and its Implications for Enterprise and Competition Policies', in final report to the Commission in Tender for NO ENTR/05/82, (8 July 2007), 175.

[20] B.H. Hall et al, A Study of Patent Thickets (UK Intellectual Property Office 2013), 8.

[21] Cf. Richard Gilbert and David Newberry, 'Preemptive Patenting and the Persistence of Monopoly', (1982) 72 *The American Economic Review*, 514, discussing the ability of large firms to maintain their dominance through pre-emptive patenting.

[22] See, generally, Dietmar Harhoff et al., 'The Strategic Use of Patents and its Implications for Enterprise and Competition Policies', in final report to the Commission in Tender for NO ENTR/05/82, (8 July 2007), with many references.

[23] The EU development seems to mirror the US development: cf. J. R. Allison and M. A. Lemley, 'The Growing Complexity of the United States Patent System', (2002) 82 *Boston University Law Review*, 77.

portfolio maximization.[24] Historically, the strategy of patent portfolio maximation or the MAD strategy seems to have been initiated by one firm breaking the gentleman's agreement not to start filing for patents during the standardization process.[25]

In the industries where MAD capability seems to be needed to enable firms to enter and to maintain a presence on the relevant markets, the patents are of lower quality with respect to the patent law requirements of 'obviousness' and 'an inventive step'.[26] Actually, the research shows that the few firms trying to enter markets where there is clear evidence of strategic patenting try extra hard to reach MAD capability quickly. This is necessary since, without MAD capability, the firm would face infringements suits from the incumbent firms that have already reached such a capability. In the effort to reach MAD capability, the firm trying to enter will apply for many dispersed patents of a low quality. Several of the patents applied for do not genuinely reflect the firms current core R&D activities. These firms apply for a diverse set of patents just to build a reputation for MAD capability. Moreover, when the firms eventually reach MAD capability, they seem to file for fewer patents but these patents have a higher quality and may reflect the core R&D activity of the firm.[27] Notwithstanding this, the share of the four most frequent patent applicants are still higher in industries where MAD capability is needed to be able to enter the market, such as in audiovisual technology, telecommunications, and optics, than in other industries.[28]

In addition, strategic patenting may cause firms in the negotiations to define the relevant technology to be standardized in the SSOs so as to apply for 'divisionals' of already submitted patent applications. This also happens in technical committees in more formal SDOs. Firms file for patent protection with certain patent claims and descriptions of a

---

[24] Dietmar Harhoff et al., 'The Strategic Use of Patents and its Implications for Enterprise and Competition Policies', in final report to the Commission in Tender for NO ENTR/05/82, (8 July 2007), 11 and 146 et seq.

[25] Claudia Tapia, *Industrial Property Rights, Technical Standards and Lincesing Practices (FRAND) in the Telecommunications Industry* (Carl Heymanns Verlag – eine Marke von Wolters Kluwer Deutschland GmbH 2010), 10 et seq., referring to a memo written by Jörn Hoff in 1992, then CEO of Ericsson, explaining how Ericsson had not played its cards right in the face of Motorola's strategy of obtaining SEPs early on in the standardization process.

[26] Dietmar Harhoff et al., 'The Strategic Use of Patents and its Implications for Enterprise and Competition Policies', in final report to the Commission in Tender for NO ENTR/05/82, (8 July 2007), 200 et seq.

[27] Ibid. 207 et seq.

[28] Ibid. 147.

technology just before the first meeting in the technical committee of the SDO, and while the negotiations in the technical committee of the relevant SDO develop in one direction or another, the firm essentially applies to divide the patent application by adding patent claims and new descriptions so as to trail the negotiations in the technical committee.[29]

Today, a new product standard will, in general, be created within one year of the first meeting of the technical committee, while there is an 18 months delay in publishing patent applications.[30] Thus, by the time the standard has been established, it may still be some months before patents emerge within the standard.[31] By this means, the patentee creates not only more patents but also standard essential patents that will appear after the standard has been launched.[32] As long as the firm apply for the patent before the first meeting in the technical committee, brings its applications to the attention of the chairman of the technical committee and informs the chairman that they may become standard essential patents and the discussion of the technology for the standard in the technical committee should be considered confidential, this conduct will not be perceived as a patent ambush. Empirical research shows that

---

[29] Cf. Claudia Tapia, *Industrial Property Rights, Technical Standards and Lincesing Practices (FRAND) in the Telecommunications Industry* (Carl Heymanns Verlag – eine Marke von Wolters Kluwer Deutschland GmbH 2010), 90 et seq. and 231 et seq. Industry-wide standards used to take on average five years to complete.; German Institute for Standardization e. V (DIN), *Economic Benefits of Standardization: Summary of Results* (DIN, Beuth Verlag, 2000), 16.

[30] Ibid.

[31] The larger SDOs, e.g. ETSI, have entered into collaboration agreements with EPO so to collaborate about what might be regarded as 'prior art' before EPO. If the information in the technical committee is considered public, it should constitute prior art. See e.g. http://www.etsi.org/news-events/news/310-news-release-24th-november-2009. Accessed 27 February 2014.

[32] Cf. Dietmar Harhoff et al., 'The Strategic Use of Patents and its Implications for Enterprise and Competition Policies', in final report to the Commission in Tender for NO ENTR/05/82, (8 July 2007), at 128, 166, noting that the share of divisionals is growing and interpreting that as a sign that firms are using the patent system strategically; see also M. A. Lemley and K. A. Moore, 'Ending Abuse of Patent Continuations', (2004) 84 *Boston University Law Review*, 63, 69 et seq., noting that whole original patent applications took 1.96 years on average to issue in the US, while patents with at least one divisional took 4.16 years to issue. OECD, *Competition, Patents and Innovation II*, DAF/COMP (2009), 22 . Rambus was accused of such conduct, In re Rambus, Inc. No. 9302 F.T.C. July 31, 2006), 67 et seq. However, the D.C Circuit did not take this into consideration: Rambus Inc. v FTC, 522 F.3d 456 (D.C. Cir 2007), cert. denied 123 S Ct 1318 (2009).

divisionals are common in the information technology, telecommunications (information and communication technology (ICT)),[33] and audio-visual sectors. They are even more common in the chemical, pharmaceutical/biotech and medical engineering industries.[34]

A different form of strategic patenting is to create infringement situations. Under this strategy, the firm keeps its application pending and unpublished until a competitor has developed its own related technology. Then, the first company modifies its own pending patents through additional divisionals to make them cover the rival's technology.[35] To prevent this, the patentee (i.e. the second firm) may file applications for additional patents that will surround the first patent so to protect it from strategic patenting but also to prevent designing around the first patent.[36] These strategies seem to be more common in the chemical/pharmaceutical and biotech industries, where firms are also more prone to launch opposition procedures against the patent office than firms are, for example, in the telecommunications industry.[37]

Firms' conduct of defensive patenting, with a MAD goal and strategic patenting, seems to lead to oligopolistic markets where, primarily, vertically integrated firms hold several very similar patents and implicitly or explicitly cross-license these patents to each other (or multilaterally refrain from asserting their patents among each other). There has historically been little patent litigation between such firms in these markets. Some researchers, as well as businessmen in these businesses, claim or seem to imply that new entrants are often singled out and attacked with patent infringement litigation or opposition claims with the relevant patent offices. They are singled out since they have not reached

---

[33] The ICT sector has been defined as 'a combination of manufacturing and services industries that capture, transmit and display data and information electronically'. OECD Report, *Measuring the Information Economy Available* (2002), 19.

[34] Dietmar Harhoff et al., 'The Strategic Use of Patents and its Implications for Enterprise and Competition Policies', in final report to the Commission in Tender for NO ENTR/05/82, (8 July 2007), 175.

[35] M. A. Lemley and K. A. Moore, 'Ending Abuse of Patent Continuations', (2004) 84 *Boston University Law Review*, 63 66.

[36] Ibid.

[37] Dietmar Harhoff et al., 'The Strategic Use of Patents and its Implications for Enterprise and Competition Policies', in final report to the Commission in Tender for NO ENTR/05/82, (8 July 2007), 11. There is, however, evidence that in the general pharma industry there are few oppositions and the high number of oppositions found by Harhoff and his team may be attributed to the cosmetic industry rather than the pharma industry.

MAD capability and are safe targets for the incumbent firms.[38] There seems even to be economic research that suggests collusion on the behalf of the incumbent firms, i.e. some kind of truce agreement between the incumbent firms with a general understanding they will try to prevent new entrants.[39] In practice, there are also cases regarding 'privateering', joint litigation agreements and even the accusations of the creation of joint patent trolls that aim to stop and hold-up competitors. Privateering is when a firm outsources its patents to a PAE for it to attack competitors. The strategy prevents the defending party from countersuing the (original) patentee for infringement because the PAE is not producing under the standard.[40] For example, a respondent in the Microsoft/Nokia transaction claimed that Nokia had sold or transferred SEPs on 17 times since 2007 to PAEs.[41]

There seems even to be evidence that there has historically been a correspondence between the major patent holders of the GSM technology to the effect that FRAND commitments under ETSI would not be applicable outside the jurisdiction of ETSI.[42] The effect of that would, of course, be that the incumbent firms who are in agreement may prevent

---

[38] Mario Calderini and Guiseppe Scellato, 'Intellectual Property Rights as Strategic Assets: the Case of European Patent Oppostition in the Telecommunication Industry', *KITes Working Paper* (2004) 158, Centre for Knowledge, Internationalization and Technology Studies, Universita' Bocconi. See also, John Barton, 'Antitrust Treatment of Oligopolies with Mutual Blocking Patent Portfolios', (2002) 69 *Antitrust Law Journal*, 851, 854.

[39] Generally, Mario Calderini and Guiseppe Scellato, 'Intellectual Property Rights as Strategic Assets: the Case of European Patent Opposition in the Telecommunication Industry', (2004) *KITes Working Paper* (2004) 158, Centre for Knowledge, Internationalization and Technology Studies, Universita' Bocconi.

[40] Tom Ewing, 'Indirect Exploitation of Intellectual Property Rights By Corporations and Investors', (2011) 3 *Hastings Sci & Tech Law Journal* 1 and Thomas L. Ewing, 'Practical Considerations In the Indirect Deployment of Intellectual Property Rights by Corporations and Investors', (2011) 4 *Hastings Sci & Tech Law Journal* 109, for a good analysis of privateering.

[41] Commission decision, 4 December 2013, Case No COMP/M.7047 – Microsoft/Nokia, 38.

[42] Claudia Tapia, *Industrial Property Rights, Technical Standards and Licensing Practices (FRAND) in the Telecommunications Industry* (Carl Heymanns Verlag – eine Marke von Wolters Kluwer Deutschland GmbH 2010), 47 making reference to evidence provided under discovery in a court case: letter from Chief Executive Director of Motorola, George M.C. Fischer to Chief Executive Officer Dr. Lars Ramquist, 5 December 1991 in Ericsson Inc. v. Harris corp (District Court 2001), ERA 095019, Plaintiff's exhibit 146.

entry to the GSM technology, or at least claim supra FRAND royalty rates outside the 'jurisdiction' of ETSI.

However, the behaviour of singling out new entrants by bringing infringement claims and objections before the patent offices may reflect a unilateral logical conduct by the incumbent firms. They do not need to enter into an agreement to this effect. Going after infringing firms that do not have the capacity to counter sue is rather a reflection of the general MAD patent strategy. Thus, markets with a MAD requirement are plagued with high barriers to entry, barriers built of patents and aggressive litigations by the incumbent firms vis-a-vis new entrants.

Notwithstanding the above, the historically calm situation in markets with MAD requirements is not true anymore for the telecommunication industry and the IT sector. This is because these two industries are actually merging under the smart phone technology concept. This is why we see so many patents wars at this moment. Two industry 'galaxies' or 'clusters' of several different standards, i.e. literally thousands of patents and technology copyrights, and business cultures are colliding under the smart phone concept.[43]

The problem with defensive and strategic patenting is that it does not generally reflect a genuine innovation effort, but rather an effort on the behalf of the firms' IP legal departments to file patents.[44] More patents are taken out on research portfolios that have already been invented than on new genuine research. As discussed *infra* under the next heading, global investment in R&D has, when taking into consideration the overall growth of the economy and inflation, actually been fairly constant from 1959 until today, while the number of patents has exploded.[45]

---

[43] In reference to culture differences, it seems clear the FRAND royalties for SEP-licences were customary practice in the telecommunication sector, while, in the information technology sector, the general consensus seem to have been for no or zero royalty rates. Cf. Marcus Glader, 'Open Standards: Public Policy Aspects and Competition Law Requirements', (December 2010) 6 *European Competition Journal*, 611, 644.

[44] John Barton, 'Antitrust Treatment of Oligopolies with Mutual Blocking Patent Portfolios', (2002) 69 *Antitrust Law Journal*, 851, 852 et seq.

[45] It has fluctuated between 1–1.5 per cent to 2.5 per cent of global GNP. It was lower in the 1970s compared to the 1980s. Cf. US Bureau for Economic Analysis, *2006 Research and Development Satellite Account Preliminary Estimates of R&D for 1959-2002: Effect on GDP and Other Measures* (BEA 2006), 17. See, generally, for EU/US comparison where the numbers are pretty constant, Eurostat statistic: http://epp.eurostat.ec.europa.eu/tgm/table.do?tab=table&init=1&language=en&pcode=tsc00001&plugin=1, accessed 3 April 2009.

A third reason for the proliferation of patents and overlapping patents in industries is that certain industries are more and more transparent. R&D is in many cases technology-standards driven or, at least, incrementally driven.[46] Technology avenues and R&D goals are presented and agreed upon by system leaders in the pre-standardization phase in the technical committees under SSOs.[47] Standard-setting is a collective effort to create a collective innovation.[48] There is also clearly a proliferation of industrial or technology standards, and the standards are decided in some industries earlier and earlier in the life cycle of the technology.[49] Indeed, it may be so that successful standards create a proliferation of patents, even patent thickets. It could be suspected that standards are not the solution to the bargaining problems of the patent thickets, but in some way their cause because they act as agreements between competitors on under what technology to apply for patents, i.e. where to conduct R&D and file for patents.[50]

Some new research seem even to suggest that in those sectors where productivity of R&D is high, sectors with large technical opportunity, the patent rate is low, while when productivity of R&D is low, the competition for patents is higher and, hence, this intensifies effort to apply for patents.[51] In other words, patent thicket may reflect low productivity in R&D, while the firms instead focus on applying for patents based on their current patent and know-how portfolio.

---

[46] Cf. Maurits Dolmans, 'Standards For Standards', (2002) 26 *Fordham International Law Journal*, 163, 171 et seq., especially 172.

[47] Ibid.

[48] Josef Drexl, 'Anti-competitive Stumbling Stones on the Way to a Cleaner World: Protecting Competition in Innovation Without a Market', (2012) 8 *Journal of Competition Law & Economics*, 507.

[49] Carl Cargill, 'Intellectual Property Rights and Standard Setting Organizations: An Overview of Failed Evolution', (2002) 27 March FTC/DOJ Hearings on Competition and Intellectual Property Law and Policy in the Knowledge-Based Economy, 1, 2 et seq.

[50] This seems to have been the experience when the GSM technology and standard were developed. The GSM standard created an incentive to conduct R&D and to obtain SEPs under the technology, while it was only covered by few patents when implemmented. Discussed infra Chapters 2.5.1, 2.9 and 4. Compare Carl Shapiro, 'Navigating the Patent Thicket: Cross Licenses, Patent Pools and Standard Setting ', in Adam Jaffe et al. (eds), *Innovation Policy and the Economy* (MIT Press 2001), indicating that standards would be the solution of the patent thickets rather then a facilitating factor.

[51] B.H. Hall et al, A Study of Patent Thickets (UK Intellectual Property Office 2013), 22, with references.

The proliferation of industrial or technology standards is due to a number of reasons. First, the de-regulation, especially under EU law, of technical specific requirements and public technical specifications and standards. Under the New Approach implemented in the EU during the 1980s and 90s, technology standards are not generally the result of a legislative process in Brussels and/or the Member States but, instead, the result of negotiations primarily between private parties in SDOs.[52] Secondly, the need for product interoperability makes technical standards focused on interoperability more and more important. Firms are required to collaborate to create interoperability standards. That interoperability is needed in network industries such as the ICT sector is clear. Thirdly, globalization implies that there is tendency for one global standard rather than several regional or national standards. The end result is that patents cluster under the *de facto* and *de jure* defined standard technologies. It is clear that early, possibly successful, technology standards attract more R&D and so more patents are created under the relevant standard than around other solutions.

Finally, empirical research shows that the proliferation of patents and patent applications is specifically prevalent in industries in which strategic patenting seems to be a general business practice, e.g. in the telecommunication industry.[53]

The proliferation of patents creates in the end a patent thicket, thus, a layer of fragmented patents, sometimes complementary and sometimes blocking, which subsequent (i.e. follow-on) inventors or producers need to penetrate in order to be able to either conduct research or manufacture products based on the protected technology. Individual firms holding essential patents may be able to 'hold up', or ambush the efficient exploitation of a technology on the product markets. So-called 'patent ambush', where a firm deliberately yet confidentially tries to get a technology standard to correspond to its patents or patent application, is a concern.[54] By not revealing essential patents or patent applications during

---

[52] Harm Schepel, The Constitution of Private Governance – Product Standards in the Regulation of Integrating Markets (Hart, 2005), 63 et seq.

[53] Dietmar Harhoff et al., 'The Strategic Use of Patents and its Implications for Enterprise and Competition Policies', in final report to the Commission in Tender for NO ENTR/05/82, (8 July 2007), 179 et seq. and 249 et seq.

[54] Several cases in the patent war concern patent ambush and FRAND ambush. These involve some of the largest firms in the world. Nonetheless, one of the first 'patent ambush' case seems to have been In re Dell, 121 F.T.C. 616, 616-18 (1996) (resolved by consent order.). For later cases, see e.g., The FTC challenges In re Rambus, No. 9302 (F.T.C. 2002); In re Rambus, Inc. No. 9302

the drafting of a technology standard, which become 'submarine' patents, a patentee may reap supra-competitive royalties when firms have adopted and invested in a technology standard. Moreover, 'FRAND ambush' is frequent. This is where a firm acknowledges holding SEPs and commit to FRAND terms but, after the standard is adopted, requests supra competitive royalties, often linked to a threat to initiate injunction suits otherwise. Interestingly, the patent war between firms in the ICT sector is also a reflection of two industry-wide 'clusters': the cluster for telecommunications and the cluster for information technology where, respectively, many standards and probably thousands of patents are merging. From having produced separate products, i.e. computers and mobile phones, the relevant product for these industries is becoming the same, i.e. the smart phone, smartphones being both mobiles phones and computers.

This may, of course, potentially create enormous hold-ups, where the system's leaders in both industries can hold up each other, without being involved in conduct that might be considered patent or FRAND ambush. Actually, one effect of this collision is the contradictory problem, often referred to as a 'reverse FRAND hold-up', where large firms that have previously not been accustomed to pay for intellectual property rights, refuse to pay any royalties for SEPs.

2.3 PATENT THICKETS

According to Carl Shapiro, in several key industries, including semiconductors, biotechnology, computer software, and the internet, our patent system is creating a patent thicket: an overlapping set of patent rights requiring those seeking to commercialize new technology to obtain

---

F.T.C. July 31, 2006) and In re Rambus, Inc. No. 9302 (F.T.C. Feb 2, 2007); In re Union Oil Co. of Cal., No. 9305 (F.T.C. Mar. 4 2003) (Resolved by consent order) and Rambus Inc. v. Infineon Technologies AG, 318 F.3d 1081 (Fed. Cir. 2003). Infineon defended the infringement action by stating that the Rambus suit was fraudulently based on the 'patent ambush' concept. However, see Rambus Inc. v FTC, 522 F.3d 456 (D.C. Cir 2007), cert. denied 123 S Ct 1318 (2009). In Europe, the first cases could have concerned Philips. Philips lost an infringement suit when a Dutch court agreed Philips had omitted to declare it had an essential patent even though it was a member of the SDO and involved in drafting the standard. See LG Electronics v. Koninklijke Philips Electronics N.V., The District Court of The Hague, rolnummer 287026 / KG ZA 07-528, 11 June 2007. See also the German case LG Dusseldorf, WuW 13.12.2007, heft 12, Seite 1278-1288, DE-R 2120-2130.

licences from multiple patentees.[55] Often, these patents may be of poor quality and cover trivial features or technologies.[56] Over the last ten years or so, there has been a growing policy concern about so-called 'patent thickets'.[57] This policy development was mainly based on anecdotal evidence supporting the possibility that patent thickets actually exist and that they have proliferated in recent history.

Following Shapiro's definition, at least two requirements for establishing a patent thicket seem to be needed: (i) several patents covering a defined technology or standard, i.e. essential patents; and (ii) these patents being held by several different patentees.

As discussed above, the underlying assumption is that the recent (perceived) proliferation of thickets comes largely from an excessively lenient application by the PTOs in applying traditional patentability criteria. In particular, it is felt that many patents that are actually granted do not reflect a sufficient 'inventive step' or obviousness in the eyes of the industry or could even be considered as not fulfilling the requirement of novelty. If patents are easily obtained on 'small bits' of knowledge, then it is more likely that the 'bits' that are necessary to produce anything useful will fall into a large variety of hands.[58] In addition, we now know that patent thickets are connected to the patent strategies developed in certain industries. Notwithstanding this, it should also be acknowledged that in certain industries the complexity and specialization in R&D have increased to a point where patent thickets can evolve 'naturally', since incumbent firms cannot develop 'whole technologies', but only different fragments of the same.

In recent years, economists have started to create and establish tests for identifying and measuring patent thickets. Economists have come up with several different theoretical and empirical approaches to establish and

---

[55] Carl Shapiro, 'Navigating the Patent Thicket: Cross Licenses, Patent Pools and Standard Setting ', in Adam Jaffe et al. (eds), *Innovation Policy and the Economy* (MIT Press 2001), 119.

[56] Cf. Mark Lemley, 'Ignoring Patents', (2008) *Michigan State Law Review* 19, 27.

[57] Pierre Regibeau and Katharine Rockett, 'Assessment of Potential Anti-competitive Conduct in the Field of Intellectual Property Rights and Assessment of the Interplay Between Competition Policy and IPR Protection', in COMP/2010/16 (ed), (European Union, 2011), 12 et seq. http://ec.europa.eu/competition/consultations/2012_technology_transfer/study_ipr_en.pdf. Accessed 21 September 2012.

[58] Ibid. 16 et seq. B.H. Hall et al, A Study of Patent Thickets (UK Intellectual Property Office 2013), 38.

measure the thicket.[59] They are generally built on a notion of whether, and to what extent, patents and firms, within one identified technology, are cited or should be cited in the patent applications as prior art.[60] Based on this they try to identify whether there are blocking and even mutually blocking patents. Finally, pictures of these citations may be drawn to depict the patent thicket.

The establishment of a patent thicket, as for example, a 'barrier to entry', is not a legal requirement under antitrust law. To get lenient treatment under antitrust law, the parties do not need to establish the existence of a patent thicket. For example, establishing a patent pool under Art 101 TFEU, or for defending/demanding access under Art 102 TFEU to a SEP, the parties, or the defendant/plaintiff, do not need to show that there was a patent thicket in the first place. Nonetheless, the notion of a patent thicket has been the intellectual excuse to allow several collaborative ventures under antitrust law, and to a certain extent to allow access to SEPs. Since patent thickets lie at the heart of why a more lenient antitrust treatment should be implemented, be it in reference to patent pools or patent policies with SSOs, or for that matter as a source for perceiving patent and FRAND ambush as an anti-competitive conduct, perhaps the intellectual alleged patent thicket needs to be addressed and established also under antitrust law.[61]

The proliferation of patents is not necessarily a problem if it is possible to gain access to markets by licensing the intellectual property rights. More problematic are situations where patent 'thickets' occur in network industries or in industries governed by interoperability technology standards.[62]

---

[59] Pierre Regibeau and Katharine Rockett, 'Assessment of Potential Anti-competitive Conduct in the Field of Intellectual Property Rights and Assessment of the Interplay Between Competition Policy and IPR Protection', in COMP/2010/16 (ed), (European Union, 2011), 12 et seq. http://ec.europa.eu/competition/consultations/2012_technology_transfer/study_ipr_en.pdf. Accessed 21 September 2012.

[60] B.H. Hall et al, A Study of Patent Thickets (UK Intellectual Property Office 2013), 39.

[61] This is especially true under circumstances where the relevant industry could harbor several design or product standards because the relevant markets are not plagued by network effects or tipping. For these markets, an all industry-wide patent pool should be exempted under antitrust law if the parties are able to show that there is a patent thicket. Discussed infra in Chapter 7.2.

[62] For definitions of network industries and tipping, see Michael Katz and Carl Shapiro, 'Systems Competition and Network Effects', (1994) 8 *Journal of Economic Perspective*, 93, 105 et seq.; Mark Lemley and David McGowan,

Similar effects appear when the market participants agree on a technology in a technology standard. *Ex ante*, several technology alternatives may exist while *ex post* when the standard is agreed upon, only one technology will presumably prevail ('winner takes all' scenario).[63]

Some scholars have even gone so far as to say that the patent thicket may create the problem of so-called 'anticommons'.[64] The problem of anticommons may be described as the result of several persons holding rights to one valuable source of income, which may exclude each of them from that source: the source will not be used to its full extent. It is clear that in certain industries, such as in the ICT industry, this has happened.[65] Firms holding essential patents demand supra-competitive royalties for each of their essential patents, creating a stack of royalties which, in total, are too much for the product markets to bear.[66] Certain technology-only firms, or as they are called today, patent assertion entities (PAEs), have additionally been accused of stalling the implementation of new technologies by demanding excessive royalty rates for SEPs under these scenarios.[67]

'Legal Implications of Network Economic Effects', (1998) 86 *California Law Review* 479, 500 et seq.; and Mark Lemley, 'Intellectual Property Rights and Standard-Setting Organizations', (2002) 90 *California Law Review*, 1889, 1896 et seq.

63 Mark Lemley, 'Antitrust and the Internet Standardization Problem', (1996) 28 *Connecticut Law Review*, 1041, 1059 et seq.

64 See Michael Heller, 'The Tragedy of the Anticommons: Property in the Transition from Marx to Markets', (1998) 111 *Harvard Law Review*, 621; Michael Heller and Rebecca Eisenberg, 'Can Patents Deter Innovation? The Anticommons in Biomedical Research', (1998) 280 *Science*, 698, 698 et seq. According to some disputed research, the problem of anticommons do not exist, cf. John Walsh et al, 'Research Tool Patenting and Licensing and Biomedical Innovation', in Cohen and Merrill (ed), Patents in Knowledge-Based Economy 2002), 285 et seq. The Walsh study has been criticized by, inter alia, Professor Paul David as unfounded. Cf. Michael Mireles, 'An Examination of Patents, Licensing, Research Tools, and the Tragedy of the Anticommons in Biotechnology Innovation', (2004, Fall) *University of Michigan Journal of Law Reform*, 141, 185 et seq., with references.

65 See Rudi Bekkers et al., 'Case studies on the interface between research and standardisation, and case studies on patent pools as a coordination mechanism', in (INTEREST consortium Priority 8 No. Contract 503 594, EU 6th Specific Targeted Research Project, 2006), 105 et seq. [The document is on file with the author.]

66 Ibid. 56.

67 In essence, Qualcomm was accused of being a 'patent troll' in the telecommunication industry: ibid. 116, et seq. See also EU Commission's

In turn, this creates a need for some kind of mechanism to grant access to the essential patents on fair and non-discriminatory terms so that downstream product manufacturers enjoy efficient access to input intellectual property, and so that the firms that have conducted relevant research are able to collect royalties.[68] It is clear that pre-standardization consortia are often created when there is a patent thicket.[69] Indeed, some kind of tool was needed to penetrate the patent thicket.[70] The state-suggested mechanisms for gaining such order and access are again collaborations, such as cross-licensing, patent pools or standard agreements with IP policies, or arrangements with *de jure* or *de facto* requirements to license on fair, reasonable, and non discriminatory (FRAND) terms under industrial or technology standards.[71]

Memo/Press Release, MEMO/07/389, dated 1st October 2007 'Commission Initiate Formal Proceedings against Qualcomm'. On the joint complaint of Nokia, Ericsson, Texas Instruments, Broadcom, NEC and Panasonic, the EU Commission started an investigation into whether Qualcomm was abusing its dominance based on patent rights included in the 3G system, since it did not license these rights on Fair, Reasonable, and Non-Discriminatory (FRAND) terms. In the biotechnology industry there is a practice of using so-called 'reach-through' licences, in other words royalty clauses that are based on the success of the products invented by the inventor using the technology protected by the upstream patent. Cf. Michael Heller and Rebecca Eisenberg, 'Can Patents Deter Innovation? The Anticommons in Biomedical Research', (1998) 280 *Science*, 698, 698 et seq.

68 Barton claims that at the end of the twentieth century intellectual property law got the upper hand on US antitrust law, giving licensors greater freedom to use various devices in their distribution arrangements to increase their monopoly rent. Cf. John Barton, 'Antitrust Treatment of Oligopolies with Mutual Blocking Patent Portfolios', (2002) 69 *Antitrust Law Journal*, 851, 851.

69 Justus Baron and Tim Pohlmann, 'Who Cooperates in Standard Consortia – Rivals or Complementors' (2013) 9 *Journal of Competition Law & Economics*, 905, 912.

70 For the mosaic description, see Hanns Ullrich, 'Patent Pools: Approaching a Patent Law Problem via Competition Policy', in Claus-Dieter Ehlermann & Isabela Atanasiu (eds), *European Competition Law Annual 2005: The Interaction Between Competition Law and Intellectual Property Law* (Hart Publishing, 2007), 322. Regarding patent thickets, see Carl Shapiro, 'Navigating the Patent Thicket: Cross Licenses, Patent Pools and Standard Setting', in Adam Jaffe et al. (eds), *Innovation Policy and the Economy* (MIT Press, 2001), 119 et seq.

71 See the Standards Development Organization Advancement Act of 2004, discussed, infra, in Chapter 4.1. See also Business Review Letters from Thomas O. Barnett to Robert Skitol and Michael A. Lindsay, regarding the VITA and EEEI SDOs, respectively, dated 30 October, and 30 April, 2007, addressing the issue of negotiation of the terms of IP licensing under a contemplated technology

2.4 THE RISE OF AGREEMENTS ON TECHNOLOGY

2.4.1 Standards, What Are They?

As stated above, products today need to interoperate with their 'eco-system' to a much greater degree than before. In fact, a product's degree of compatibility is of significant importance when the general consumer makes his or her decision whether to purchase that product or not. To achieve compatibility firms need agree on the interfaces between products so that the essential parts of a product may interoperate with its surrounding. Several definitions of standards are given in the literature, by standard-setting organizations and political institutions. The European Commission defines standards as a 'technical specification' relating to a product or an operation, which is recognized by a large number of manufactures and users.[72] 'Technical specification' on the other hand is defined in Directive 98/34/EC Art. 1 para. 2 as a specification contained in a document, which lays down the characteristics required of a product, such as the levels of quality, performance, safety or dimensions, including the requirements applicable to the product as regards the name under which the product is sold, terminology, symbols testing and test methods, packaging, marking or labelling and conformity assessment procedures. The Horizontal Guidelines stipulates:

> Standardization agreements have as their primary objective the definition of technical or quality requirements with which current or future products, production processes, services or methods may comply. Standardization agreements can cover various issues, such as standardization of different grades or sizes of a particular product or technical specifications in product or services markets where compatibility and interoperability with other products

---

standard. Both may be found on http://www.usdoj.gov/atr/public/busreview/letters.htm#08, accessed 3 April 2011. For a European legal point of view, see generally, Gil Ohana et al., 'Disclosure and Negotiation of Licensing Terms Prior to Adoptation of Industry Standards: Preventing another Patent Ambush', (2003) 24 *E.C.L.R*, 644 and Maurits Dolmans, 'Standards For Standards', (2002) 26 *Fordham International Law Journal*, 163, with references and cases. For an empirical overview of the telecom industry, see generally, Rudi Bekkers et al., 'Case studies on the interface between research and standardisation, and case studies on patent pools as a coordination mechanism', in (INTEREST consortium Priority 8 No. Contract 503 594, EU 6th Specific Targeted Research Project, 2006), 53 et seq., 116 et seq., 149 et seq. [The document is on file with the author.]

[72] See European Commission, 'Communication on Intellectual Property Rights and Standardization', COM (92) 445, published on 27 October 1992.

> or systems is essential. The terms of access to a particular quality mark or for approval by a regulatory body can also be regarded as a standard. Agreements setting out standards on the environmental performance of products or production processes are also covered by this chapter.[73]

ISO/IEC Guide 2:1996, definition 3.2 defines a standard as:

> A document established by consensus and approved by a recognized body that provides for common and repeated use, rules, guidelines or characteristics for activities or their results, aimed at the achievement of the optimum degree of order in a given context.

Given the above, the definition of a standard is wide, including not only interoperability standards, but also, for example, product, service, safety and environmental standards. It seems actually that a standard at its widest definition could plainly be described as *a structure for a solution to a demand*. Naturally, standards may be divided into different groups. They are given different names depending who is discussing standards. The ISO classification of standards may be divided into eight groups:[74]

(i) Basic standard has a broad ranging effect in a particular field. (These standards could be called and regarded as infrastructure standards.)
(ii) Terminology standards define words permitting representatives of an industry to understand and communicate.
(iii) Testing standards define the test methods to be used to assess the performance or other characteristics of a product.
(iv) Product standards establish qualities or requirements for a product (or related group of products) to assure that it will serve its purpose effectively.
(v) Process standards specify requirements to be met by a process, such as an assembly line's operation, in order to function effectively.
(vi) Service standards, such as for servicing or repairing a car, establish requirements to be set in order to achieve the designated purpose effectively.
(vii) Interface/interoperability standards, such as the point of connection between a telephone and a computer terminal, are concerned with the compatibility of products.

---

[73] Horizontal Guidelines, para. 257

[74] See Liguo Zhang, *Standardization and Patent Licensing in the European Union* (Oy Nord Print Ab 2012), 26, with references.

(viii) Standard on data. The last type provides a listing of characteristics for value of data specifying a product, service, etc.

In addition to the above, product and service standards, but also other forms of standard such as interoperability standards, may be divided into performance (also called general uniformity or non-product standard) and design standards (also called prescriptive or product standards). A performance standard implies that the standard only stipulates certain performance that the product or service should meet to fulfil the standard, while a product or design standard stipulates specific requirements for the goods.

From a competition law perspective, it is of fundamental importance to grasp what sort of standard is up for scrutiny. Under antitrust law, several types of standards should be acknowledged as well as their different implications for markets and competition. Interoperability or interface standards, which guarantee that products made by different firms can interoperate, should be distinguished from general uniformity standards (sometimes called performance or non-product standards). Similarly, general uniformity standards (performance standards), which set minimum requirements for all products on a market, should be distinguished from design standards.[75]

Performance standards/general uniformity standards are often set by SDOs connected to trade organizations, while interoperability or design standards are more specific and may, in combination with relevant intellectual property rights, restrict competition and product diversity. Actually, a design or prescriptive or, in other words, technical requirement standard regarding the parts, content or form of a product or technical solution, such as cement, tyres or even technologies for storing music or film (e.g. Memory stick, VHS, CD-ROM or DVD technology) is a fundamentally different standard from a interoperability standard, which, in turn, *de facto* may reflect an infrastructure standard. Design or product standards may reflect a standard for one solution on a market that may efficinelty harbour several different such standards or technologies.

Basic or infrastructure standards may have significant implications for an industry. They constitute the fundaments for where trade will take place and several of the interoperability standards developed today are the infrastructure of the present and the future. Presumably, examples of

---

[75] For a somewhat similar division, cf. Gregory Tassey, 'Standardization in Technology-Based Markets', (2000) 29 *Res. Pol'y* 587, 589 et seq.

such standards are the different generations of telecommunications network technologies.

Likewise, a design standard is, from a competition law perspective, different from a general uniformity or performance standard, where the standard only stipulates certain requirements for the product to fulfil to be able to meet the standard. A general performance standard, for example certain environmental or safety standards, may represent a competition law problem less often since it seldom implies that certain products or firms will be excluded from the relevant market or technology. Such standards only stipulate certain requirements for the performance of the product, e.g. what kind of heat a product should withstand or what degree of emission a product may give off, and, thus, give the manufactures the liberty to compete through innovation over how to fulfil these requirements.

It seems that the notion of interoperability is also used now for standards that were previously considered infrastructure standards. For example, standards for the railway system (e.g. for the gauge, couplings, brakes, and signalling), and standards for public safety (e.g. fire fighting material), or for the armed forces, are today considered to be interoperability standards, while previously they were considered basic infrastructure standards.

Clearly interoperability standards refer to the ability of different (technical) units to combine, but it may today also be used in reference to organizations. Nonetheless, internet or Telecom interoperability, the technology of the internet or the telecom technology of UNMTS or 3G must be treated differently in reference to interoperability and/or infrastructure standards from prescriptive or design standards.[76] Prescriptive design standards may very well reflect a new product in an existing market with other competitive solutions, while interoperability standards, through for

---

[76] Furthermore, interoperability means different things also within IT and telecoms. According to ISO/IEC 2382-01, Information Technology Vocabulary, Fundamental Terms, interoperability is defined as follows: 'The capability to communicate, execute programs, or transfer data among various functional units in a manner that requires the user to have little or no knowledge of the unique characteristics of those units'. Under telecoms, interoperability is under said ISO standard defined differently: 'The ability of systems, units, or forces to provide services to and accept services from other systems, units or forces and to use the services exchanged to enable them to operate effectively together. The definition can be extended to the condition achieved among communications-electronics systems or items of communications-electronics equipment when information or services can be exchanged directly and satisfactorily between them and/or their users'.

example network (tipping) effects on the market, may very well develop or represent *de facto* virtual infrastructure. The market and industry will only, efficiently, be able to facilitate one such standard, and, while there may be dynamic competition over what it should be in the pre-standardization phase, when the technology is fixed, it will be the infrastructure for other markets to develop under.

Notwithstanding these fundamental differences (which will be highlighted throughout this book), the standards discussed in this book are mainly *interoperability* network-driven standards for the telecom sector or ICT sector, while other more 'product-oriented' standards, such as standards for tyres, cement or for different data/music storage solutions also will be discussed. There are standards that are in-between, such as AVC/H.264 video code for the internet, and they will also be discussed, while general uninformative or performance standards will not be analysed because they, as stated, seldom represent competition law problems.

In other words, one could identify standards and/or technologies, and collaborations connected to them, and divide them loosely into four categories, depending on their potential anti-competitive effects. This is difficult because standards are in many ways overlapping. Especially, there is an overlap between the notion of infrastructure and interoperability standards. Nonetheless, from a competition law perspective the division helps when analysing their different potential anti-competitive effects

A.	B.	C.	D.
Basic/ Infrastructure technologies	Interface/ Interoperability Network technologies	Patent thicket plagued Products/ technologies	Design/ product standards

This devision will be used to explain, classify and discuss standards and their potential anti-competitive effects in this book. The division is interlinked to a division between 'failed' markets where only competition by imitation can be upheld, and markets where competition by substitute may exist. The A, B and C standards may be the solution (and cause) to create competition by imitation on markets that may only harbour one standard, while D standards should not be drafted and enacted so to limit competition by substitute.

2.4.2 What are the Sources of Standards?

There are numerous fora for the development of technology standards. The traditional (European) approach is that standards are developed through fora for voluntary consensus, including formal standard development organizations such as the European Telecommunications Standards Institute (ETSI) or the US Institute of Electrical and Electronics Engineers (IEEE). These are formal or semi-formal organizations, with several of them being accredited as European standard-setting organizations or with the American National Standard Institute (ANSI). These organizations decide on standards that reflect today's often virtual infrastructure, while they also decide on prescriptive standards that only reflect the ingredients of a product, e.g. the five different ways to develop cement under the Portland cement technology.[77]

Nonetheless, there is also a robust ecosystem for informal standard development, and a clear interaction between the traditional way of developing standards and the informal consortia-driven way of developing standards.[78] The EU Commission has even recognized that the standardization landscape has changed dramatically over the last decade. 'Alongside the traditional standard setting organisations, specialised and mostly global fora and consortia have become more active and several

---

[77] Compare the telecom standards developed by ETSI (e.g. 3G) with the EN 197-1 Standard ('the Standard') that was adopted in April 2000 by the 19 national standards bodies that were members of CEN at that time. It was developed by a CEN technical committee, CEN/TC 51 'Cement and building limes' and Cembureau, a trade organization, under a mandate M/114, which was granted by the Commission and the European Free Trade Association (EFTA) pursuant to Directive 89/106. That mandate defined the scope of application of the Standard, set out the list of products that had to be taken into consideration and stated that the Standard would be expressed, as far as practicable, in product performance terms, having regard to the interpretative documents. The Standard defined each of the 27 common cement products, that is to say, the common cements described by the various national standards bodies within CEN as traditional and well tried. Those products are further grouped into five main cement types (CEM I to CEM V) according to the proportions in which the main constituents were to be combined to produce those distinct products in a range of six 'strength classes'. Each main cement type was composed of a certain percentage of Portland cement clinker combined with varying levels of constituents. That definition included requirements which the constituents have to satisfy, and mechanical, physical, chemical and durability requirements for the 27 common cement products and 'strength classes'.

[78] Stacy Baird, 'The Government at the Standard Bazaar', (2007) 18 *Stanford Law & Policy Review*, 35, 42 et seq.

have emerged as world-leading ICT standards development bodies, such as those responsible for the standards covering the internet and the world wide web'.[79] The Commission even states that without decisive action 'the EU risks becoming irrelevant in ICT standard setting which will take place almost entirely outside Europe, and without regard for European needs'.[80] The risk of becoming irrelevant would arise if the EU were to fail to master the information society.[81]

The consortia way of developing standards often implies that fewer firms with greater commonality of interest, but also competing interests, join together to agree on a technology path, often to promote a technical solution. These consortia may often meet up early in the development of a technology.

It is clear that joint R&D, technology standards and technology pools can appear separately from each other. Nonetheless, when analysing several of the high profile patent pools, it is obvious that the defined technology in the patent pool was derived from an agreement on standard:[82] Standards are also derived from consortia and standards produced by consortia are often adopted by formal SDOs. The Justice Department has also, in two Business Review Letters, specifically allowed for this interaction between standard-setting consortia and patent pools.[83] There are, in fact, several examples of standards derived from consortia (even joint R&D) that have developed into patent pools or at least joint licence schemes. An example is the Moving Picture Experts Group (MPEG) digital audio and video compression specification standards, including MPEG-2, MPEG-4, Thompson's MPEG-1, and Leyer-III (MP3).[84]

---

[79] Commission White Paper 'Modernising ICT Standardisation in the EU – The Way Forward', COM(2009) 324 final, 2 et seq.

[80] Ibid.

[81] Ibid.

[82] Stacy Baird, 'The Government at the Standard Bazaar', (2007) 18 *Stanford Law & Policy Review*, 35, 50 et seq.

[83] Compare the VITA Business Review Letter from Thomas O. Barnett to Robert A. Skitol, dated 30 October 2006; and IEEE Business Review Letter from Thomas O. Barnett to Michael A. Lindsay, dated 30 April 2007, with the RFID Business Review Letter from Thomas O. Barnett to William F. Doland and Geoffrey Oliver, dated 21 October 2008. The letters can be found on http://www.justice.gov/atr/public/busreview/letters.html#page=page-1. Accessed 9 April 2014.

[84] Stacy Baird, 'The Government at the Standard Bazaar', (2007) 18 *Stanford Law & Policy Review*, 35, 52 et seq.

Other examples of consortia-created standards are the joint ITU-ISO/IEC specification AVC/H.264 video codec (included in both Blu-Ray and HD DVD),[85] Small Computer System Interface (SCSI), USB and USB2, AT Attachment (ATA), and several more standards.[86] Some of these standards represent technologies for interoperability, while others more represent a competing technical solution in a present or future relevant market, where there will be room also for other solutions.

Notwithstanding the above, Stacy Baird has provided several examples of standards created through consortia: Bell Laboratories C Programming language, NSO CAT-5 cable (and other such cable specifications developed by the Telecommunication Industry Association, a trade association and ANSI–accredited standard developing organization) and hundreds of IT standards (many designated as ISO and ANSI standards) developed by the International Committee for Information Technology Standards (INCITS, an ANSI-accredited standards development organization supported by the Information Technology Industry Council (ITI), a trade association); Adobe's PDF format (various parts of which have been submitted to ISO for adoption as an open standard).[87]

The US market for standard consortia has always been flourishing. However, Knut Blind and Stephan Gauch have found that in Europe, as well, consortia-produced standards are rising quickly in numbers.[88] In fact, over 200 consortia are now registered with the European Committee for standardization (CEN). An interesting observation made by Blind *et al* is that the number of consortia reflects the stage of development of the technology and also the general economic up- and down-turns. In a

---

[85] For an interesting historical development of the H.264 standard, see United States District Court Western District of Washington at Seattle, Microsoft v. Motorola, Case no. C10-1823 JLR, Findings of Fact and Conclusion in Law, 25 April 2013., paras 126 et seq. There is a patent pool connected to the H.264 standard, the MPEH H.264 pool. See paras. 467 et seq.

[86] Stacy Baird, 'The Government at the Standard Bazaar', (2007) 18 *Stanford Law & Policy Review*, 35, 52 et seq.

[87] Stacy Baird, 'The Government at the Standard Bazaar', (2007) 18 *Stanford Law & Policy Review*, 35, 50 et seq Stating that Video standards such as the VGA and SXGA analog computer display standards (VESA); digital transmission standards such as digital subscriber line or DSL (DSLForum), Internet related developer standards such as HTML (W#C), XML, SOAP and OpenCable Application Platform (OCAP) are all derived from consortia. See also Marcus Glader, 'Open Standards: Public Policy Aspects and Competition Law Requirements', (2010) 6 *European Competition Journal*, 611, 623 et seq.

[88] Knut Blind et al., 'How Stakeholders View the Impacts of International ICT Standards', (2010) 34 *Telecommunications Policy*, 162, 163, 165.

down-turn of the economy, fewer consortia are formed and some consortia are dismantled, while in an up-turn the number of consortia increases.[89] The number of new standards reflects a similar sensitivity to the general economic situation. In an up-turn of the economy more standards are created while, in a down-turn of the economy, fewer standards are produced. But the number of new standards developed and the number of consortia also reflects the technical development in a market or industry.[90]

A technology will, after a while, be fully covered by standards, and the consortia will have to focus on other technical areas. For example, in the mid 1990s, the area of ISDN and a telecommunications network were being developed and therefore needed much standardization work, while these areas were covered by standards by the beginning of 2000. The effort then shifted to fibre-optics communications and audio, video and audiovisual engineering and electromagnetic compatibility.[91] The fall in consortia that were focused on standards for ISDN and telecommunications also led to a reduction in technical committees being formed with the relevant SDOs in these areas, according to Blind *et al.*[92]

Blind *et al* also found that while there are generally more standards in the telecommunication sector, there are more consortia in the IT sector.[93] This would point to the fact that there is a substitute relationship between consortia and formal SDOs. However, Knut Blind *et al* argue to the contrary. At least for the IT sector, increased collaboration in consortia leads to an increased number of technical committees being formed in formal SDOs.[94] They conclude that it is known that several formal standards have a predecessor in the consortia world.[95]

The implication of their empirical research is that firms like to create standards both in consortia and in formal SDOs. Consortia are preferred, or make commercial sense, when the consortium focuses on something which is close to the company's own R&D core activity, while the formal

---

[89] Cf. Knut Blind and Stephan Gauch, 'Trends in ICT standards: The Relationship between European Standardisation Bodies and Standard Consortia', (2008) 32 *Telecommunications Policy*, 503.

[90] Knut Blind and Stephan Gauch, 'Trends in ICT standards: The Relationship between European Standardisation Bodies and Standard Consortia', (2008) 32 *Telecommunications Policy*, 503.

[91] Ibid., 507.

[92] Ibid., 509.

[93] Ibid., 511.

[94] Ibid., 511.

[95] Ibid., 511.

SDOs are to be preferred when the technology decided upon (in a consortium) needs to be implemented with the downstream customers and/or upstream suppliers. The customers need to be convinced to adopt the new technology, and the suppliers need to adapt their content, products or services.[96] Thus, SDOs involve all stakeholders, while consortia represent competitors collaborating.

Indeed, joint R&D and consortia may be important for the creation of technology standards.[97] The standardization process may start with a pre-standardization phase where often firms in small groups prepare standards *en petit comité* by entering joint R&D agreements or consortia joint ventures, so as to present a joint solution for adoption as a standard.[98] These joint R&D ventures may be encompassed by antitrust safe harbours such as the NCRPA or the R&D block exemption and are often rather exclusive groups.[99] The results of the joint R&D are either presented directly to an SDO or, first, an SSO is created and then the consortia or SSO tries to obtain approval for itself and the technology standard it governs from ISO, IEC or ANSA (or, in certain industries, a technology standard may not have been created, merely 'open specifications').[100] These consortia can be made up of so-called 'system leaders', i.e. the technology leaders of certain markets. Given the market power of system leaders, and their head start in the pre-standardization phase, they can steer the relevant SDOs to adopt their technology or get their relevant SSO to become an SDO. In fact, they may represent the vast majority of the voting rights in the relevant technical committee of the SDO. This is, of course, more troublesome if the standard is a product or design standard, where the standard can be directed towards certain patents. A product standard may prevent other products apart from the matching product from being developed under the standard.

However, as in other forms of standards, it is very important that an early lead in R&D in, for example, nanotechnology can be translated into

---

[96] Ibid., 512.

[97] Marcus Glader, 'Open Standards: Public Policy Aspects and Competition Law Requirements', (2010) 6 *European Competition Journal*, 611, 623 et seq.

[98] Maurits Dolmans, 'Standards For Standards', (2002) 26 *Fordham International Law Journal*, 163, 171 et seq.

[99] Ibid.

[100] See generally Cargill on the evolution of the standardization process over the years, Carl Cargill, 'Intellectual Property Rights and Standard Setting Organizations. An Overview of Failed Evolution', (2002) 27 March FTC/DOJ Hearings on Competition and Intellectual Property Law and Policy in the Knowledge-Based Economy, 1, 2 et seq. [The document is on file with the author.]

a leading position in the international standardization effort. Otherwise, the early starting position in the lead in R&D will probably have been in vain.[101]

Markets governed by technology standards derived from official SDOs, where the standard has not been provided by a tight consortium or joint R&D, e.g. the major standards within telecom, seem to risk being plagued by hold-up problems. There are several examples of successful standards derived from consortia, for example the Bell Laboratories C Programming language and the NSO CAT-5 cable standards, discussed supra, but also the well known CD and DVD consortia/pools that have not faced any hold-up problems after they were implemented.[102] The competition in these cases has been more for the markets, i.e. what technology should be adopted in the first place (e.g. the Blu-Ray v. HD DVD standard war), but when implemented has created efficiencies. Where the technology market is not governed by a tight network of one or several joint R&D venture and consortia, it seems that individual patentees, often technology-only firms (PAEs), are more likely to exist and to try to secure supra-competitive profits from royalty streams based on holding a single or a few essential patents that have slipped under the standard.[103]

Thus, there are many sources for standards. Foremost among the source of standards, as well as patents, is R&D, but clearly standards are derived from collaborations. In fact, some argue that standard setting can be understood as a particular form of collective innovation.[104] There

---

[101] Cf. Knut Blind and Stephan Gauch, 'Research and Standardisation in Nanotechnology: Evidence from Germany', (2009) 34 *Journal Technology Transfer*, 320 for an excellent discussion of German R&D development and its failed effort in the standardization arena.

[102] This is the general picture, which grows out of analysing case law regarding the telecommunication industry and the consumer electronics industry. However, joint R&D ventures in the consumer electronic industry between, for example, Sony and Philips seem less plagued by hold-up problems than the telecommunications industry.

[103] For a good analysis of the telecommunication industry and the problems with the 3G patent licensing platforms, see Rudi Bekkers et al., 'Case studies on the interface between research and standardisation, and case studies on patent pools as a coordination mechanism', in (INTEREST consortium Priority 8 No. Contract 503 594, EU 6th Specific Targeted Research Project, 2006), 116 et seq. [The document is on file with the author.]

[104] Josef Drexl, 'Anti-competitive Stumbling Stones on the Way to a Cleaner World: Protecting Competition in Innovation without a Market', (2012) 8 *Journal of Competition Law & Economics*, 507.

seems to be a general consensus that it is almost impossible for a company to get 'its technology' standardized with an SDO without being part of the standardization process and negotiating with its peers.[105] In addition, the investment needed to get 'its technology' standardized in the process seems to be increasing. Thus, a serious contender for having 'its technology' being accepted as part of an important standard for the industry needs to have several representatives holding many votes on the technical committee of the relevant SDO, all 'lobbying' on behalf of the contender.[106] Moreover, standards are today not only derived from formal SDOs, but, more often, from consortia or actually from the interface between consortia and more formal SDOs. Nonetheless, the SDOs play an important part in the standard-setting process, and it is the interface between the work of private undertakings in the technical committees and the ultimate adoption of a standard that has received most interest from the academic community.

Finally, we also have open source as a source for standards. Open standards rely on several groups including representatives from vendors, academicians and others holding a stake in the development of a new standard. The group, much like a regular standard setting group or technical committee, discusses and debates the technical and economic merits of different technical ideas, with the aim of coming up with a common protocol that everyone can endorse. The standard is released to the public for everyone to use freely and to no cost, i.e. Zero-FRAND.[107]

2.4.3 Consortia and Coopetition

The patent strategy model that seems to be detectable from these collaborations, including joint R&D, patent pools and technology

---

[105] Cf. Mark MacCarthy, 'Open Standards, Competition and Patent Policies', (unpublished manuscript, Georgetown University, 2009), http://explore.georgetown.edu/publications/index.cfm?Action=View&DocumentID=43082. Accessed 10 August 2012.).

[106] Claudia Tapia, Industrial Property Rights, *Technical Standards and Licensing Practices (FRAND) in the Telecommunications Industry* (Carl Heymanns Verlag – eine Marke von Wolters Kluwer Deutschland GmbH, 2010), 90 et seq. and 231 et seq.

[107] For an interesting analysis of open standard, see Marcus Glader, 'Open Standards: Public Policy Aspects and Competition Law Requirements', (2010) 6 *European Competition Journal*, 611.

standardization agreements, describes, to some extent, the phenomenon that has become known in the academy as 'coopetition'.[108]

Unlike the binary notions of pure competition versus true collaboration, 'coopetition' recognizes that firms need to collaborate closely *and* compete intensely at the same time with a changing set of actors. For example, firms that conduct joint R&D and agree on a standard compete under different brands when selling products to consumers in the end-product markets. Moreover, some firms may be active only on the innovation and technology markets and have, thus, abandoned selling end products to firms or consumers altogether. However, although coopetition scholars acknowledge that coopetition is highly contextual – that different competition strategies are more or less suited to different industries, different locations, and at different periods of evolution – there has been little, if any, research on how antitrust affects the evolution of specific coopetition systems.

Consortia and coopetition are on the rise. It is interesting quantatively to compare R&D consortia to R&D as such. In relation to percentage of GNP and adjusted for inflation, investment in R&D in the US in 2006 did not materially trump R&D investments in 1996 or for that matter investments made in 1984 or 1959.[109] Thus, when taking into consideration the overall growth of the economy and inflation, investment in R&D has actually been fairly constant from 1959 until today.[110] Likewise, the investments made by private firms in relation to public spending

---

[108] Hanns Ullrich, 'Expansionist Intellectual Property Protection and Reductionist Competition Rules: A TRIPS Perspective', (2004) 7 *Journal of International Economic Law*, 401, 420.

[109] See generally, US Bureau for Economic Analysis, *2006 Research and Development Satellite Account Preliminary Estimates of R&D for 1959-2002: Effect on GDP and Other Measures* (BEA 2006),). See http://www.bea.gov/scb/pdf/2006/12december/1206_rd_article.pdf, accessed 5 April 2014. For Europe see, e.g., Eurostate website with similar statistics: http://epp.eurostat.ec.europa.eu/tgm/table.do?tab=table&init=1&language=en&pcode=tsc00007&plugin=1, accessed 18 April 2009, indicating a constant amount spent on R&D by the public sector in Europe and the US during the years 1997 to 2007.

[110] It has fluctuated between 1–1.5 per cent to 2.5 percent. It was lower in the 1970s compared to 1980s. Cf. US Bureau for Economic Analysis, *2006 Research and Development Satellite Account Preliminary Estimates of R&D for 1959-2002: Effect on GDP and Other Measures* (BEA 2006), 17. See, generally, for EU/US comparison where the numbers are pretty constant, Eurostat statistic: http://epp.eurostat.ec.europa.eu/tgm/table.do?tab=table&init=1&language=en&pcode=tsc00001&plugin=1, accessed 18 August 2009.

have globally been constant over the last ten years.[111] Private businesses invest more into R&D than the government in the United States.[112] However, private business investment in R&D has lately been decreasing in the United States. Actually, it is dropping to such an extent that overall R&D investment in the United States decreased yearly between 2000–2006.[113] In the United States, business R&D intensity reached 1.84 per cent of GDP in 2006, down from 2.05 per cent in 2000, whereas in Japan it reached a new high of 2.62 percent in 2006. In 2007, the EU reached R&D investment of 1.85 percent of GDP, with Sweden delivering 3.6 percent; Germany 2.54; France 2.08 and the UK 1.79 percent. Interestingly, public-private R&D consortia are increasing both in number and in size.

This is also reflected when measuring patent output. While the United States continues to account for the largest share of triadic patent families (patents filed in the United States, Japan and the EU to protect the same invention), its share has diminished, as has that of the EU25. At the same time, the share of patent families from Asia has risen.[114] During 2010, in

---

[111] See, e.g., Eurostat statistic for the last ten years: http://epp.eurostat.ec.europa.eu/tgm/refreshTableAction.do?tab=table&plugin=1&init=1&pcode=tsc00001&language=en, accessed 18 August 2009. Regarding patent pools and standards, it seems that public money has been used to conduct research to create some of the large standard technologies in, e.g., the telecommunications industry. This aspect seems to be neglected under EU competition law, cf. Rudi Bekkers et al., 'Case studies on the interface between research and standardisation, and case studies on patent pools as a coordination mechanism', in (INTEREST consortium Priority 8 No. Contract 503 594, EU 6th Specific Targeted Research Project, 2006), 123 et seq. regarding UNMTS telecommunication technology and R&D. [The document is on file with the author.]

[112] US Bureau for Economic Analysis, *2006 Research and Development Satellite Account Preliminary Estimates of R&D for 1959–2002: Effect on GDP and Other Measures* (BEA 2006), 17. See http://www.bea.gov/scb/pdf/2006/12december/1206_rd_article.pdf, accessed 18 August 2008.

[113] See US Bureau for Economic Analysis, *2006 Research and Development Satellite Account Preliminary Estimates of R&D for 1959–2002: Effect on GDP and Other Measures* (BEA 2006), 16 et seq. See http://www.bea.gov/scb/pdf/2006/12december/1206_rd_article.pdf, accessed 18 August 2008. See also Eurostat statistic for the last ten years: http://epp.eurostat.ec.europa.eu/tgm/refreshTableAction.do?tab=table&plugin=1&init=1&pcode=tsc00001&language=en, accessed 8 May 2009; *OECD, OECD Science, Technology and Industry Outlook 2008: Highlights, (2008)*, http://www.oecd.org/dataoecd/18/32/41551978.pdf, accessed 20090507.

[114] See Eurostat statistics for the number of patents granted by the USPTO for the period 1992 to 2003: http://epp.eurostat.ec.europa.eu/tgm/table.do?tab=

Europe, US firms accounted for 26 per cent of all patent applications, Japanese firms for 18 per cent and China 5 per cent. Siemens, Philips and BASF applied for most European patents in 2010.[115] In 2012, the Asian countries had increased their share of the patent applications.[116]

Thus, in contrast to the general opinion, the amount of investment in R&D has globally been constant for some time. However, coopetition and networks, e.g., strategic joint R&D ventures and alliances are increasing in number and in 'value'.[117] Both the number of collaborations

---

table&init=1&language=en&pcode=tsiir070&plugin=1, accessed 2 April 2009. See also OECD, OECD report 2008, at http://www.oecd.org/dataoecd/18/32/41551978.pdf, accessed 7 May 2009.

[115] European Inventor Award 2011, Press information [the document is held by the author].

[116] Cf. EPO Annual report for 2012, http://www.epo.org/about-us/annual-reports-statistics/annual-report/2012.html. Accessed 24 February 2014.

[117] Two data sources frequently used in economic literature, when discussing collaboration schemes, are the MERIT-CATI database and the Thomson Financial database on strategic alliances. Analysis of the MERIT-CATI data source reveals that strategic technology 'partnering' has increased by around 170 per cent between 1980 and 1998. This is a higher growth rate than the increase in (or rather the constant level of) R&D investments. See Pernilla Lundin et al., 'International Collaboration in R&D Structure and Dynamics of Private Sector Actors', in *Internationalisation of R&D – Implications to science and technology policy*, ProACT programme (interim Report 1, Gaia Group, Oy & RAND Europé, 2004), 17 et seq. http://proact.ktm.fi/index.phtml?menu_id=155&lang=3. Accessed 9 September 2009, with references to Rajneesh Narula, 'Globalisation and Trends In International R&D Alliances', in *Research Memoranda, Nr. 001* (MERIT, Maastricht Economic Research Institute on Innovation and Technology in its series Research Memoranda, Nr 001., 2003). Cf. Rajneesh Narula and James Hagedoorn, 'Innovating through Strategic Alliances: Moving towards International Partnerships and Contractual Agreements', (1998) 19 *Technovation*, 283 and Daniele Archibugi and Simona Iammarino, 'The Globalization of Technological Innovation: Definition and Evidence', (2002) 9 *Review of International Political Economy*, 98. This seems to indicate a positive trend for R&D collaboration and a shift from in-house R&D towards collaborations. Cf. Pernilla Lundin et al., 'International Collaboration in R&D Structure and Dynamics of Private Sector Actors', See Pernilla Lundin et al., 'International Collaboration in R&D Structure and Dynamics of Private Sector Actors', in *Internationalisation of R&D – Implications to science and technology policy*, ProACT programme (interim Report 1, Gaia Group, Oy & RAND Europe), 17 et seq. http://proact.ktm.fi/index.phtml?menu_id=155&lang=3. Accessed 9 September 2009, with references to Rajneesh Narula, 'Globalisation and Trends In International R&D Alliances', in *Research Memoranda, Nr. 001* (MERIT, Maastricht Economic Research Institute on Innovation and Technology in its series Research Memoranda, Nr 001, 2003). Other scholars have indicated the development

and the size of the investments put into these joint efforts have been increasing globally since the 1980s by as much as 170 per cent over 18 years according to some studies.[118]

When taking into consideration the finding that investment in R&D is constant, or even decreasing, a conclusion to be drawn is that joint R&D is actually increasing in relation to overall investment in R&D.[119] Thus, unilateral R&D is presumably sacrificed for collaborative R&D.[120] In addition, public-private partnerships where the public often provide the researchers and the investment in basic R&D are more and more fashionable.

The start of the proliferation of joint R&D in the United States has been indentified as when Congress decided to enact the US antitrust exemption, the National Collaboration Research Act (NCRA).[121] The basic reason for enacting the NCRA was to increase the competitiveness of US industry in the face of Japanese competition consisting of collaborative industrial groups rather individual firms.[122] Even though it

---

towards a greater interest in joint R&D, see Rajneesh Narula and James Dunning, 'Explaining International R&D Alliances and the Role of Governments', (1998) 7 *International Business Review*, 377, 379 et seq. and 382 et seq., with references.

118 Ibid.

119 Cf. Pernilla Lundin et al., 'International Collaboration in R&D Structure and Dynamics of Private Sector Actors', in *Internationalisation of R&D – Implications to science and technology policy*, ProACT programme (interim Report 1, Gaia Group, Oy & RAND Europé, 2004), 17 et seq. Rajneesh Narula and James Dunning, 'Explaining International R&D Alliances and the Role of Governments', (1998) 7 *International Business Review*, 377, 379 et seq.

120 Research into R&D collaborations notified under the US NCRPA shows that the majority of the scrutinized collaborations were entered into by competitors jointly outsourcing R&D to a third, possibly R&D only, firm. See Suzanne E. Majewski, 'How Do Consortia Organize Collaborative R&D? Evidence from the National Cooperative Research Act' (SSRN 2004), 12 et seq. See discussion. infra Chapter 4.3.

121 In his research, Donald Siegel observed a dramatic increase in the number of research partnerships during the last two decades, and he specifically relates this to, inter alia, the 'relaxation of antitrust enforcement related to collaborative research'. Cf. Donald Siegel, 'Data Requirements for Assessing the Private and Social Returns of Strategic Research Partnerships. Analysis and Recommendations', (2003) 15 Tech. *Analysis & Strategic MGMT*, 207, 207.

122 See discussion, infra, in Chapter 4.1.

is clear that technology standards are derived from joint R&D,[123] economists' and jurists' research into joint R&D (both prior to the enactment of the NCRA and thereafter) has focused almost exclusively on the combination of different parts of R&D, rather than the result.[124] In fact, the research has been accused of being disconnected from reality.[125]

An underlying current is also, according to anecdotal evidence at least, that private R&D investments are more focused on applied science (development) than basic science (research).[126] Anecdotal evidence suggests that even the largest of firms are abandoning research into basic science, while continuing to conduct incremental research.[127] It is perceived as too expensive and risky to conduct basic or 'new' research. Instead, universities and other publicly-funded institutions are conducting basic R&D. The rise of public/private R&D collaborations should be viewed in this light. The outcome of a development in which basic research is conducted by vertically integrated firms with decreasing frequency is difficult to predict. Logically, more development and less basic research creates shorter life cycles for products. Presumably, technologies are in their nature cumulative and the proliferation of patents around certain successful technologies will increase.

Furthermore, research into joint R&D ventures notified under the NCRPA suggests that, often, competing firms agree on a technology and then jointly outsource the basic and even applied R&D to an R&D only firm, which is often closely connected to a university. The R&D only firm is obliged to transfer any resulting intellectual property rights back

---

[123] Cf. Hanns Ullrich, 'Patent Pools – Policy and Problems', in Josef Drexl (ed), *Research Handbook on Intellectual Property and Competition Law* (Edward Elgar, 2008), 160.

[124] See generally Stephen Martin, 'The Evaluation of Strategic Research Partnerships', (2003) 15 *Tech. Analysis & Strategic MGMT*, 159, 159.

[125] Regarding the theoretical economical research of joint R&D ventures, Stephen Martin declared that the 'theoretical research … is a largely self-contained activity, firmly insulated from vagaries of evidence about the subjects it analyses', ibid., with references.

[126] See e.g., the *Economist* 3–9 March 2007, 'The Rise and Fall of Corporate R&D', 69, with references. See http://www.ebusinessforum.com/index.asp?layout=rich_story&channelid=5&categoryid=15&title=The+rise+and+fall+of+corporate+ R%26D&doc_id=10225, accessed 1 May 2009.

[127] The specialized R&D departments inhabited by men in white robes conducting research disconnected from everyday commercial conduct do, generally, not exist anymore. Ibid.

to the principals.[128] By jointly outsourcing R&D, the parents prevent overlapping research and save costs but they can also be fairly certain that their competitor will not pursue any other technical solutions.

Patent pools are also increasing in number. Patent pools as global commercial enterprises were, according to some authors, nonexistent between the 1960s and 1990s.[129] Scholars in the 1960s declared with great enthusiasm that large global patent pools had disappeared due to diligent antitrust enforcement by the US Justice Department and that only 'patent puddles' continued to exist.[130] Patent pools did exist before the 1960s in the assembly industries and the system technologies, where they served to combine independent inventions created in different countries for the establishment of emerging global markets.[131] Patent pools had a

---

[128] From data consisting of 142 Joint R&D agreements, Suzanne Majewski concludes that it seems that most joint R&D agreements are entered into by product market competitors. These competing firms tend in their agreements to outsource their collaborative R&D to third parties. By outsourcing they benefit from shared costs and reduction in duplicative efforts. They also avoid spillover effects and opportunistic problems of having researchers from the firms interacting. However, it also shows that there is a new sort of firm emerging that only conducts R&D. These R&D-exclusive firms tend to cater to product market competitors but conduct their work exclusively in the innovation and technology markets. Cf. Suzanne E. Majewski, *How Do Consortia Organize Collaborative R&D? Evidence from the National Cooperative Research Act* (SSRN 2004), 12 et seq. Cf. also Suzanne E. Majewski and Dean V. Williamson, *Endogenous Spillovers, Strategic Blocking, and the Design of Contracts in Collaborative R&D: Evidence from NCRA filings of R&D Joint Ventures* (SSRN 2002)., 20 et seq.

[129] Cf. Rudi Bekkers et al., 'Case studies on the interface between research and standardisation, and case studies on patent pools as a coordination mechanism' (INTEREST consortium Priority 8 No. Contract 503 594, EU 6th Specific Targeted Research Project, 2006), 91. [The document is on file with the author.] It states that no new patent pools were established approximately between the 1920 and 1990s.

[130] Joseph Iandiorio, 'Patent Pools and the Antitrust Laws', (1964) *The Patent Office Society*, 712, 713.

[131] Cf. Hanns Ullrich, 'Patent Pools – Policy and Problems', in Josef Drexl (ed), *Research Handbook on Intellectual Property and Competition Law* (Edward Elgar, 2008), 140 et seq. There are several authors who have listed known patent pools that have existed during the twentieth century. See, e.g., Rudi Bekkers et al., 'Case studies on the interface between research and standardisation, and case studies on patent pools as a coordination mechanism', in, (INTEREST consortium Priority 8 No. Contract 503 594, EU 6th Specific Targeted Research Project, 2006), 161 et seq. [The document is on file with the author.] See also, David Serafino, 'Survey of Patent Pools Demonstrates Variety of Purposes and

revival in the case law in the 1990s, when the Justice Department and the EU Commission accepted these collaborations and agreed on the governance rules for the establishment of patent pools. Thereafter, patent pools, as commercial consortia, have increased in numbers while they are not common in case law. The structure and the rules governing these collaborations are now set.

There has been a proliferation of global SSOs and global technology standards. In the fifteen years between 1985 and 2000, both in the telecommunication sector and the IT sector, the industry went from having technology standardized largely in the formal SDOs to using a multitude of organizations, ranging from SDOs to open source.[132] Consortia are especially involved in the standard setting in the IT industry. In 2007, 60 per cent of the standards originated from consortia and fora in the ICT sector. The most widely implemented standards, such as HTTP, HTML, Wifi and XML, are the result of informal standardization organizations.[133] The culture of standards created by consortia have existed in the USA for a long time, but now the number of consortia is increasing in Europe as well as the USA. Moreover, international markets for technology standards are clearly emerging, with consortia originating in different parts of the world competing.[134] The increase in SSOs might be connected to the opinion that the competitive stake with respect to which technology is selected is growing in importance. Technologies are today selected globally rather than on a national level. Furthermore, in some industries, technology standards are created much

---

Management Structures', in *Knowledge Ecology Int'l* (KEI Research Note 2007:6, 2007), http://www.keionline.org/misc-docs/ds-patentpools.pdf. Accessed 9 September 2009.

[132] Carl Cargill, 'Intellectual Property Rights and Standard Setting Organizations: An Overview of Failed Evolution', (2002) 27 March FTC/DOJ Hearings on Competition and Intellectual Property Law and Policy in the Knowledge-Based Economy, 1, 2. See also generally Knut Blind and Stephan Gauch, 'Trends in ICT standards: The Relationship between European Standardisation Bodies and Standard Consortia', (2008) 32 *Telecommunications Policy*, 503 and Stacy Baird, 'The Government at the Standard Bazaar', (2007) 18 *Stanford Law & Policy Review*, 35.

[133] Marcus Glader, 'Open Standards: Public Policy Aspects and Competition Law Requirements', (2010) 6 *European Competition Journal*, 611, 617 with references.

[134] Carl Cargill, 'Intellectual Property Rights and Standard Setting Organizations: An Overview of Failed Evolution', (2002) 27 March FTC/DOJ Hearings on Competition and Intellectual Property Law and Policy in the Knowledge-Based Economy, 1.

earlier in the lifecycle of a technology than before and technology standards pre-empt the actual development of the technology; hence, the development of competition for the best technology.[135] The technology market is agreed upon before the technology exists. Also, the purpose, notion and concept of technology standards and technology standard organizations have changed over the years.[136] Previously, technical committees in SSOs were inhabited by engineers and the focus seems to have been on very technical specific issues, while, today, competitive concerns are taken into consideration.

In light of the above, not only is joint R&D increasing at the expense of unilateral R&D, but, possibly, standardization agreements are proliferating at the expense of product competition to establish the superior technology. Finally, patent pools seem to have become normal business practice, while a unilateral licence under standards is even in some cases considered to be anti-competitive because it may cause hold-up problems.

Whether these collaborations were created to meet the need for interoperability, or to overcome patent thicket and anticommons problems, or whether they reflect other priorities, is difficult to say. For example, the incumbent firms holding large patent portfolios or having MAD capability will engage in a strategy to extract revenues by deciding on the dominant technology. Nonetheless, it is clear that even though there is a proliferation of collaborations, the problems of anticommons, hold-ups and patent thickets are increasing, rather than decreasing. Thus, these problems seem to be connected to the increasing number of standards. Consequently, standardization agreements do not seem to be the cure for the anti-competitive conduct animating network markets, rather they represent an additional strategy for some firms. That said, standardization agreements can still be a better solution than competition, especially for industries with network effects. Competition without standardization agreements may allow single firms to gain monopoly power. In fact, it seems that certain industries, i.e. the industries that are plagued by different patent strategies, are identifiable. It seems to be markets where the participants in collaboration govern the definition of the solution to a problem, and where different patent strategies are

---

135 Ibid.

136 Cf. Carl Cargill, 'Intellectual Property Rights and Standard Setting Organizations: An Overview of Failed Evolution', (2002) 27 March FTC/DOJ Hearings on Competition and Intellectual Property Law and Policy in the Knowledge-Based Economy, 1, 2 et seq. [The document is on file with the author.]

proliferating. Some of the most striking industries will be analysed in more detail below.

2.5 CONSUMER ELECTRONICS, TELECOMMUNICATION, INFORMATION TECHNOLOGY AND TO A LESSER EXTENT PHARMA AND BIOTECH

2.5.1 The ICT Industry

The information and communications technology (ICT) sector has been defined as a combination of manufacturers and service providers that capture, transmit and display data and information electronically.[137] It concerns, mainly, the IT and the Telecom industries, but the consumer electronic, telecommunications and IT sectors are growing more and more together. The new products, such as smart phones and smart TV sets, are in fact evidence of these industries merging. Interestingly, this implies that different cultures in technology standard creation are also forced to merge.

As stated above, generally the standards in IT sector are created by consortia.[138] Video standards such as the VGA and SXGA analog computer display standards (VESA), digital transmission standards such as digital subscriber line or DSL (DSLForum), internet-related developer standards such as HTML (W3C), XML, SOAP and Synchronized Multimedia Integration Language (SMIL, W3C), and the OpenCable Application Platform (OCAP) are all derived from consortia.[139] Furthermore,

---

[137] OECD Report, *Measuring the Information Economy Available* (2002), 19.

[138] Commission White Paper, 'Modernizing ICT Standardistion in the EU – The Way Forward', COM(2009) 324 final, 2.

[139] Stacy Baird, 'The Government at the Standard Bazaar', (2007) 18 *Stanford Law & Policy Review*, 35, 50 et seq., stating that video standards such as the VGA and SXGA analog computer display standards (VESA), digital transmission standards such as digital subscriber line or DSL (DSLForum), internet related developer standards such as HTML (W#C), XML, SOAP and the OpenCable Application Platform (OCAP) are all derived from consortia. See also Marcus Glader, 'Open Standards: Public Policy Aspects and Competition Law Requirements', (2010) 6 *European Competition Journal*, 611, 623 et seq.

in the IT and software industry, standards have often implemented royalty-free policies.[140]

Generally, these collaborations are often hailed in the US for the efficient way they operate and because the end result benefits the market and end-consumers. There are, however, exceptions to the rule. For example, DeLacey, Herman, Kiron and Lener, at Harvard Business School, have empirically studied the WIFI-standard and their finding shows that the standard-setting procedure descended into horse-trading or impasses between competing intellectual property owners. Finally the standard actually included two competing technologies.[141] There are also other examples of failed standard setting procedures:

> The OCAP was the name of a set of standards to facilitate the interactive video interoperability for set-top boxes, consumer electronic devices, game devices, digital video recorders, PC etc. It was the result of the joint work by a consortium CableLabs. OPAC used patented software that was licensed to users of the standard developed by CableLabs.[142] In fact, CableLabs developed into a patent pool closely connected to these standards.[143] According to Baird, there were many concerns for the standards governed by OCAP and designed by the consortium CableLabs.[144] CableLabs was created by the US cable companies. Initially, it worked with consumer electronics companies but excluded companies from the computer and the software industries. There was, according to Baird, consternation that CableLabs was developing standards that implicated industries other than cable and consumer electronics without allowing for the input from these other industries. In 2003, the Federal Communications Commission (FCC), an independent agency of the United States government, agreed with the commentators and issued an order requiring CableLabs to consider input from these industries. FCC also created the possibility to appeal CableLabs decision on standards, where CableLabs

140 Marcus Glader, 'Open Standards: Public Policy Aspects and Competition Law Requirements', (2010) 6 *European Competition Journal*, 611, 621. See also Commission White Paper 'Modernising ICT Standardisation in the EU – The Way Forward', COM(2009) 324 final, 9.

141 Brian DeLacey et al., 'Strategic Behavior in Standard-Setting Oganizations', in *Harvard University Working Paper* (SSRN, 2006).

142 Stacy Baird, 'The Government at the Standard Bazaar', (2007) 18 *Stanford Law & Policy Review*, 35, 43, fn 14.

143 Tim Simcoe, 'Open Standards and Intellectual Property Rights', in *Open Innovation: Researching New Paradigm* (Oxford University Press, 2006), 173.

144 Stacy Baird, 'The Government at the Standard Bazaar', (2007) 18 *Stanford Law & Policy Review*, 35, 43, fn 14.

had the burden to prove their objectivity in denying technical recommendations made by these industries.[145] In the end, it seems that the consumer electronic industry, with the support from the computer and software industry, filed a proposal that FCC should withdraw its support and authorization of OCAP altogether.[146]

The consumer electronic industry, even though based on general governmental infrastructural standards for TV and radio, is often based on *de facto* or consortia-driven product standards. The CD, DVD and Blu-ray standards are well known examples, as is the twisted nematic crystal LCD standard/technology, and collaborations connected to it. The consortia in consumer electronics product standards seem often to develop into patent pools.[147]

IT standards derived from consortia have developed into patent pools, in fact the ISO-adopted Moving Picture Experts Group (MPEG) run several of these patent pools. MPEG governs some digital audio and video compression specification standards, including the MPEG-2, MPEG-4, Thompson's MPEG-1, and Leyer-III (MP3).[148]

The telecommunication industry is a prime example of a network industry in which coopetition is necessary. In particular, the mobile telecommunication industry has established several technology interoperability (infrastructural) standards, of which the latest is the 4G technology (the IMT-Advanced standard) now being launched in several countries. Before that. it was the 3G mobile network technology or the UMTS standard and previously it was the GSM telecommunication standard.[149] These mobile infrastructure technology standards have, like

---

145 Stacy Baird, 'The Government at the Standard Bazaar', (2007) 18 *Stanford Law & Policy Review*, 35, 43, fn 14.

146 Ibid. 43, fn 14. with references, and 66.

147 For a discussion of the CD and DVD patent pools, cf. infra. The LCD technology has been plagued by a cartel and several competition authorities have delivered decisions and fines against companies participating in the cartel. See, for example, the EU Commission decision of the 8 December 2010, Comp 29.309. LCD.

148 Stacy Baird, 'The Government at the Standard Bazaar', (2007) 18 *Stanford Law & Policy Review*, 35, 52 et seq.

149 Rudi Bekkers et al., 'Case studies on the interface between research and standardisation, and case studies on patent pools as a coordination mechanism' (INTEREST consortium Priority 8 No. Contract 503 594, EU 6th Specific Targeted Research Project, 2006), 121 et seq. [The document is on file with the author.]

clockwork, been implemented at ten years intervals.[150] Nonetheless, these infrastructural telecommunications standards have been negotiated and produced within more formal standard development organizations, that is, the European Telecommunications Standardization Institute ('ETSI') and its predecessors, rather than by consortia. Even though implementing infrastructural standards normally ensures a smooth enactment of technology standards, the mobile telecommunication industry has evidently been plagued by hold-up problems. Certain firms have been accused of trying to exclude competition by not granting access to essential patents and to have consequently caused the hold-up of the development of the technology. At first, some firms were singled out as patent trolls for this conduct, but recently the patent war has also been played out between the largest firms.[151]

As stated above, the current patent war is clearly evidence that the IT and telecommunication industries are merging. Such a merger implies that two enormous industries or ecosystems of patents and technical copyrights, the IT sector and the Telecom sector, or as a matter of fact, the IT and the telecom patent thickets, are colliding.

Clearly, there has also been an unrivalled attempt to get patents declared essential under the ETSI standards. No technology standard has ever claimed to harness more essential patents.[152] In ETSI's database for

---

[150] For a short description of the history, see also Liguo Zhang, 'How IPR Policies of Telecommunication Standard-Setting Organizations can Effectively Address the Patent Ambush', (2010) 41 *IIC*, 380, 380 et seq.

[151] See the current investigations by the EU Commission into the conduct of Motorola, Samsung, Microsoft, Nokia and, to some extent, Honeywell: http://ec.europa.eu/competition/sectors/telecommunications/news.html. Accessed 14 September 2009. See also Case No. IV/35.06 – ETSI IPR Policy [1995] O.J. C76/5. Cf. Gil Ohana et al., 'Disclosure and Negotiation of Licensing Terms Prior to Adoptation of Industry Standards: Preventing another Patent Ambush', (2003) 24 E.C.L.R, 644, 648 et seq.; Maurits Dolmans, 'Standards For Standards', (2002) 26 *Fordham International Law Journal*, 163, 181; and Rudi Bekkers et al., 'Case studies on the interface between research and standardisation, and case studies on patent pools as a coordination mechanism' (INTEREST consortium Priority 8 No. Contract 503 594, EU 6th Specific Targeted Research Project, 2006), 121. [The document is on file with the author.]

[152] Cf., generally, Rudi Bekkers, 'Patent Drag and Stacking IPR fees – Are the IPR Policies of Standard Bodies Failing or Should we Better Address Excessive Technology Inclusion?', (2007), position paper for high level workshop on standardization, IP licensing and antitrust, (2007) [The document is on file with the author].

the UMTS 3G standard, 8,666 IPRs have been declared essential.[153] The standard before that, GMS, had 140 essential patents in 1998.[154] In March of 2010, the number had increased and, in the US alone, there were 25 firms that had declared 699 U.S. patents to be essential for the GSM standard.[155] The telecommunication industry is therefore an interesting industry for analysing the interface between joint R&D and technology standards.

The early history of implementing a European infrastructure standard for telecommunications – first the NMT[156] and later the GSM – involves joint R&D ventures and negotiations in the pre-standardization phase of the technical committee. For the GSM, high-level political negotiations had to resolve the differences. At least, some evidence suggests a blocking strategy by the incumbent holders of essential patents for the GSM technology vis-à-vis third party licensees, and the existence of strategic technical alliances by the incumbent firms with covenants regarding the exclusive licence of SEPs and/or agreement on the joint development of the technology.[157]

GSM technologies as a standard (or standards) were finally decided in 1987 by an organization that primarily represented the European telephone operators, CEPT. The establishment of the basic standards in switching, speech coding, encryption, and radio transmission, making up the GSM, followed a dispute between two technologies, of which one was a joint effort by French and German undertakings. The GSM technologies were presented and represented by Ericsson, which took the lead and had, without taking out any patents on the technologies, lobbied

---

[153] Liguo Zhang, 'How IPR Policies of Telecommunication Standard-Setting Organizations can Effectively Address the Patent Ambush', (2010) 41 *IIC*, 380, 380, 384.

[154] According to Bekkers, there were 380 listed essential patents for the GSM with ETSI but, when comparing with the Rspacenet database, the number can be reduced by double counts to 140 SEPs: Rudi Bekkers et al., 'Intellectual Property and Standardization: The case of GSM', (2002) 26 *Telecommunication Policy* 171, 175 et seq. Around 1999, Ericsson and Nokia seem to have applied for several patents of low quality. See B.H. Hall et al, A Study of Patent Thickets (UK Intellectual Property Office 2013), 23.

[155] Liguo Zhang, *Standardization and Patent Licensing in the European Union* (Oy Nord Print Ab, 2012), 70 et seq.

[156] For a very interesting historical exposé of the early mobile telephone history, see Liguo Zhang, *Standardization and Patent Licensing in the European Union* (Oy Nord Print Ab 2012), 70

[157] For example, Rudi Bekkers et al., 'Intellectual Property and Standardization: The Case of GSM', (2002) 26 *Telecommunication Policy* 171, 175 et seq.

various companies to disseminate the GSM technologies and make GSM the preferred choice of as many manufacturers and operators as possible. The representatives for France and Germany only finally agreed to the establishment of GSM, after it was decided it should include technology (i.e. essential patents) also held by firms from these Member States.[158]

Some researchers claim that Ericsson's efforts in disseminating GSM also led Motorola, in particular, to picking up technical knowledge and information and also filing for patents based on the knowledge and information provided in the technical committees mostly by Ericsson. Ericsson, on the other hand, had not realized the potential market power inherent in essential patents and believed that there still existed something of a gentleman's agreement during the pre-standardization phase between the manufacturers in the technical committees to share knowledge but not to file for patents based on that knowledge.[159]

Interestingly, when the GSM was established, Motorola held most of the SEPs and used that platform to enter into exclusive technology transfer agreements with the other incumbent SEP holders or prominent players. In fact these five firms, Motorola, Ericsson, Siemens, Nokia and Alcatel, simply by entering exclusive technology transfer agreements, closed the market to several other firms, both European and Asian. It would take five years before these firms finally got access to these SEPs.[160] The firms that did not succeed in gaining access to all the SEPs were prevented from entering the downstream GSM standard product markets.[161]

The subsequent openness of the GSM was not only a curse, it was also a blessing. Since the GSM was open, with relatively few and narrow patents in the beginning compared to the US equivalent CDMA where Qualcomm held broad patents, it was an invitation for R&D intensive firms to enter the technology. As Zhang describes, several firms joined the GSM R&D race shortly after the standard was agreed upon.

---

[158] Rudi Bekkers et al., 'Intellectual Property and Standardization: The Case of GSM', (2002) 26 *Telecommunication Policy* 171, 175 et seq.

[159] Ibid. See also, Ove Granstrand, *The Economics and Management of Intellectual Property* (Edward Elgar, 1999), 204.

[160] Rudi Bekkers, et al., 'Intellectual Property and Standardization: The Case of GSM', (2002) 26 *Telecommunication Policy* 171, 175 et seq

[161] According to a researcher into one of the firms, Dancall, it did not get access to the necessary licence and filed a complaint with the EU Commission. Cf. Rudi Bekkers et al., 'Intellectual Property Rights, Strategic Technology Agreements and Market Structure. The Case of GSM', in *MERIT Working Paper* (2000), 11, fn. 9. Several East Asian firms were also prevented for at least five years from getting access to all the necessary licences.

Although, from the outset, the CDMA provided higher capacity from a technical aspect and was more easily upgraded, the R&D surge started in the GSM technology. Also, Ericsson and Nokia seem to have applied for several patents of low quality in the GSM R&D race.[162] Early on, the SIM card was developed for the GSM, which provided that consumers could easily change hand-set, while retaining their number and billing from a third provider. The CDMA also had some early technical problems, which Qualcomm could not solve efficiently.[163] Thus, the GSM standard was a relative open standard with few SEPs and this spurred on its competitiveness and also caused many firms to invest in R&D under the standard. This is one major reason why all the SEPs are under the GSM standard.

In addition to the exclusive strategic technology transfer agreements, that in fact set the tone for the early development of the GSM technology, several other strategic alliances were entered into between firms to conduct joint R&D or product development. Bekkers *et al* clearly show that the increase and number of SEPs closely followed the increase and number of strategic alliances.[164] Thus, the clear increase during the early 1990s of SEPs was closely coherent with these collaborations.

The ETSI, which from the late 1980s set the telecommunications standards in Europe, tried as early as 1993 to make SEPs available to all manufacturers and to prevent hold-ups. It put forward a proposition to its general assembly, which was approved, that members of an SDO should be obliged to license their current and future intellectual property rights under the contemplated technology standards, or, otherwise, clearly state what intellectual property rights it would not make available under the standard (licence-by-default).[165] The members were also, inter alia, obliged to notify the maximum royalty rate that would apply for its

---

[162] See B.H. Hall et al, A Study of Patent Thicket (UK Intellectual Property Office 2013), 23.

[163] Liguo Zhang, *Standardization and Patent Licensing in the European Union* (Oy Nord Print Ab 2012), 109 et seq., making reference to Graham Lynch, 'How GSM Beat CDMA', (2001) 105 *American Network*, 45.

[164] For a general overview of early European standardization history regarding telecommunications, see Rudi Bekkers and Isabella Liotard, 'European Standards for Mobile Communication: The Tense Relationship Between Standards and Intellectual Property Rights', (1999) 21 *European Intellectual Property Review*, 110, specifically 121 et seq.

[165] Apparently the initial position of the EU Commission was that the licence-by-default deprived the patentees of the freedom to license and removed the incentive to develop new technologies. Cf. Maurits Dolmans, 'Standards For Standards', (2002) 26 *Fordham International Law Journal*, 163, 181.

essential patents.[166] The penalty for not adhering to the rules was that the patentee would 'lose' their licences from the other patentees under the standard.[167] Thus, the rules were harsher than the current rules in force.

ETSI was forced to withdraw the rules since the EU Commission was unwilling to provide negative clearance or an individual exemption under then Art. 85(3) of the EC Treaty.[168] The Commission objected to the licence-by-default mechanism. The US government also lobbied to have the ETSI IPR-policy annulled, and a US trade body (CMEMA) filed a complaint with the EU Commission.[169] The ETSI instead, as discussed above, enacted a milder version stating that the members were obliged to disclose essential intellectual property rights *ex ante* (however not requiring members to conduct IPR searches) and would be requested to license essential intellectual property rights on FRAND terms. The rules are still relevant to the current IPR policy.[170]

---

166 Case No. IV./35.06 – ETSI IPR Policy [1995] O.J. C76/5, para. 8.

167 Mark Lemley, 'Intellectual Property Rights and Standard-Setting Organizations', (2002) 90 *California Law Review*, 1889, 1917. This is an example of probably one of few possibilities to contractually force a patentee to adhere to FRAND requirements.

168 Case No. IV/35.06 – ETSI IPR Policy [1995] O.J. C76/5, para. 1. See also Maurits Dolmans, 'Standards for Standards', (2002) 26 *Fordham International Law Journal*, 163, 181, indicating what the Commission stated in its preliminary position.

169 Rudi Bekkers et al., 'Case studies on the interface between research and standardisation, and case studies on patent pools as a coordination mechanism', (INTEREST consortium Priority 8 No. Contract 503 594, EU 6th Specific Targeted Research Project, 2006).121. [The document is on file with the author.]

170 ETSI IPR policy, see http://www.etsi.org/WebSite/document/Legal/ETSI_IPR-Policy.pdf. Accessed 7 April 2009. Interestingly, the development seems to indicate that SDOs may treat holders of essential intellectual property rights more strictly under both US and EU antitrust laws and possibly the licence-by-default may have a renaissance both in Europe and the US. See e.g., the SDO Business Review Letters published by the US Justice Department in 2006 and 2007, where the SDOs require members to declare the maximum royalty rates discussed supra in Chapter 4.1.5 and, to some extent, the 3G Comfort letter/Business Review Letters where a licence-by-default was allowed both by the EU Commission and the US Justice Department within the realms of patent pools discussed infra. See also Philip Nelson, 'Patent Pools: An Economic Assessment of Current Law and Policy', (2007) 38 *Rutgers Law Journal*, 539, 562 et seq. Lemley claims that SSOs may not prohibit members from owing or licencing intellectual property rights under standards. See Mark Lemley, 'Intellectual Property Rights and Standard-Setting Organizations', (2002) 90 *California Law Review*, 1889, 1944 et seq. For an equivalent view on EU Competition law, see Maurits Dolmans, 'Standards for Standards', (2002) 26 *Fordham International*

Interestingly, the VITA Business Letter of 2006 displayed a very similar licence-by-default rule, which was accepted by the Justice Department, while the ETSI IPR policy introduced in 1993 was considered anti-competitive.[171] In addition, the EU Commission clearly reconsidered its standpoint on licence-by-default and IP policies generally during the ETSI and Sun antitrust investigation conducted from 2000 to 2005. Sun was investigated for declaring it had essential patents after the standard had been agreed, published and promulgated. Following DG Competition intervention, no reference was made to Sun patents under the standard. In 2005, in connection with the Sun investigation, the EU Commission decided to investigate whether ETSI's rules made it possible for Sun and others to implement 'patent ambush' strategies.[172] In the course of the Sun investigation DG Competition took the preliminary view that ETSI's rules about intellectual property rights did not provide sufficient protection against the risk of a patent ambush during the standard-setting procedure.[173] In response to the accusation of facilitating patent ambush, ETSI decided to examine whether to change its rules and allow for *ex ante* licensing.[174] The EU Commission therefore decided to drop the investigation, indicating that it found *ex ante* licensing, i.e. where royalties were set or discussed before a standard was agreed, to be possibly pro-competitive.[175] In the light of the Commission's disapproval of the 1995 ETSI licence-by-default rules, the Commission in its Sun investigation certainly made a U-turn and changed its standpoint. It would now allow SDOs to place more pressure on holders of essential patents to state whether they would license their SEPs and on what terms, and, presumably, also to implement licence-by-default rules.[176]

Law Journal, 163, 182 et seq. Dolmans claims it might be considered a boycott to demand royalty-free licences.

[171] VITA Business Review Letter from Thomas O. Barnett to Robert A. Skitol, dated 30 October 2006, and IEEE Business Review Letter from Thomas O. Barnett to Michael A. Lindsay, dated 30 April 2007. See also RFID Business Review Letter from Thomas O. Barnett to William F. Dolan and Geoffrey Oliver dated 21 October 2008, 8.

[172] See Commission press release IP/05/1565, 12 December 2005.

[173] Ruben Schellingerhout, 'Standard-setting from a Competition Law Perspective', (2011) 1 *Competition Policy Newsletter*, 3, 5.

[174] Ibid.

[175] Ibid. See also TT Guidelines, para. 225.

[176] It should be noted that the EU Commission's standpoint corresponds to the ex ante licensing and disclosure rules that the US Justice Department supported under two recent Business Review Letters. Business Review Letters from Thomas O. Barnett to Robert Skitol and Michael A. Lindsay, regarding the

The UMTS standard set by ETSI is the standard for the third generation mobile telecommunications technology, that is, for the generation after GSM.[177] Part of the UMTS technology or standard originates from research activities funded by the EU under the so-called RACE-1 programme which ran from 1988 to 1992. After 1992, under RACE-2, two mobile projects were included: one focusing on the technology called CDMA and the other concerning an advanced form of TDMA. Behind both programmes were certain firms that had also represented different joint R&D ventures in what earlier had become the GSM standard. In 1995, the UMTS was about to be defined. Again, the CDMA (supported by Ericsson and Nokia among others) and the TDMA (supported, inter alia, by Siemens and Alcatel) systems were studied. It was however difficult to create a standard when the two joint R&D groups were so evenly matched in reference to market and political influence.[178]

After competitive pressure, primarily from Japan – a 3G mobile technology standard was about to be or had been launched there – the two R&D groups agreed on a joint standard, UMTS, under the ETSI.[179] It developed into the 3GPP, which was also adopted in Japan, and 3G patent platforms. In parallel to this development, the 3GPP2 standard was being developed in the USA. This standard also generally used the CDMA technology and the US firm Qualcomm held several essential patents in the United States. A problem with the UMTS standard, which

---

VITA and EEEI standards, respectively, dated 30 October and 30 April 2007. The letters address the issue of negotiations of the term of licensing under an agreed upon industrial standard. For the letters, see http://www.usdoj.gov/atr/public/busreview/letters.htm, accessed 4 April 2009.

177 For an interesting historical overview of the second and third generation, see Rudi Bekkers et al., 'Patent pools and non assertion agreements: Coordination mechanisms for multi-party IRP holders in standardisation', in EASST 2006 Conference, 2006), 25 et seq. [The document is on file with the author.] Cf. also Rudi Bekkers et al., 'Case studies on the interface between research and standardisation, and case studies on patent pools as a coordination mechanism' (INTEREST consortium Priority 8 No. Contract 503 594, EU 6th Specific Targeted Research Project, 2006). 153 et seq. [The document is on file with the author.]

178 Ibid.

179 Rudi Bekkers et al., 'Case studies on the interface between research and standardisation, and case studies on patent pools as a coordination mechanism' (INTEREST consortium Priority 8 No Contract 503 594, EU 6th Specific Targeted Research Project, 2006), Appendix 2, 156. [The document is on file with the author.]

was based to a great extent on the CDMA technology, was that Qualcomm claimed to hold several essential patents also for this telecommunications standard in Europe, and did not agree to license the essential patents on fair, reasonable and non-discriminatory terms and conditions (FRAND) as stipulated in the ETSI IP policy. According to the ETSI Rules of Procedure and its IP policy, a holder of essential patents to a standard needs to agree to these terms otherwise the standard will be abandoned (see discussion supra). Thus, the UMNTS standard should then have been disbanded.[180]

The deadlock over the UMTS standards was thought to have been solved by an agreement and transfer between Ericsson and Qualcomm where, inter alia, Qualcomm agreed to license its essential patent on FRAND terms.[181] However, the problems continued and in 2005 Nokia, Ericsson and Panasonic among others complained to the EU Commission that Qualcomm had abused its dominant position by not adhering to the FRAND terms. Qualcomm was accused of refusing to license some firms, especially potential chip set manufacturers, and by charging excessive and discriminating fees for its essential UMTS patents compared to its US 3GPP2 patents.[182] In 2007, the EU Commission decided to open an investigation into the matter of Qualcomm, although when the parties settled, the Commission ended its investigation.[183] Before that, Qualcomm and Nokia had battled in various court rooms in the US (California, Texas, Wisconsin, and Delaware, before the ITC) and in Europe (UK, Germany and the Netherlands). The feud between Qualcomm and Nokia started when Nokia refused to pay the increased royalty rates Qualcomm was demanding for alleged telecom essential patents in 2007. It ended with a settlement agreement in 2008 after Nokia won a decisive victory in the UK, where the High Court ruled that one of

180 Ibid. 126.

181 Ibid. 127.

182 Ibid. 128.

183 See, EU Commission's Memo/Press Release, MEMO/07/389, dated 1st October 2007 'Commission Initiates Formal Proceedings against Qualcomm'. On the joint complaint of Nokia, Ericsson, Texas Instruments, Broadcom, NEC and Panasonic, the EU Commission started an investigation whether Qualcomm was abusing its dominance based on patent rights included in the 3G system since it did not license these rights on Fair, Reasonable, and Non-Discriminatory (FRAND) terms. In the middle of 2008, Qualcomm and Nokia reached a settlement and all cases were dropped. Cf. Matt Richtel, 'In Settlement, Nokia Will Pay Royalties to Qualcomm', in *New York Times* 24 July 2008, http://www.nytimes.com/2008/07/24/technology/24qualcomm.html?_r=1&scp=1&sq=nokia%20qualcomm&st=cse, accessed 7 April 2009.

Qualcomm's patents was invalid and Nokia did not infringe the rest of Qualcomm's patents. Furthermore, the administrative judge in the ITC case found that Nokia did not infringe Qualcomm's patents.[184]

It should, of course, be acknowledge that several firms have conducted R&D in these areas of telecommunications and, thus, hold narrow patents. In the end, several firms have declared essential intellectual property rights under the UMTS and the GSM standards (the ETSI database contains around 4,500 declared essential rights under the GSM, while more than 8,500 patents are declared essential under UMTS[185]).

Moreover, it should be clear that the fusion between the telecom sector and the information technology sector as a result of products such as smart phones was the starting point for the larger patent wars we see today.[186]

2.5.2 Patent Wars

The interface between the telecom and the computer industries, i.e. the smartphone industry today, is characterized by thickets of patents and wars based on those patents. It seems that every day brings a new lawsuit, or a development in a lawsuit already launched between Apple, HTC, Microsoft, Motorola Mobility ('MMI'), Nokia, and Samsung. The lawsuits span numerous courts and several continents. They often pit Apple or Microsoft on one side and manufacturers of Google's Android operating system – HTC, MMI, and Samsung – on the other.[187]

In the past year, it has become increasingly difficult to keep track of the numerous lawsuits and court decisions regarding smartphone patents. Looking across the landscape of decisions in various jurisdictions, one primary distinction involves that between SEPs and non-SEPs. Generally, courts have tended to deny injunctions when patentees have sought to

---

[184] Nokia also assigned several essential patents for 2G and 3G under the settlement agreement to Qualcomm. For a comprehensive description concerning the litigation between Nokia and Qualcomm see Liguo Zhang, *Standardization and Patent Licensing in the European Union* (Oy Nord Print Ab 2012), 80 et seq.

[185] Liguo Zhang, *Standardization and Patent Licensing in the European Union* (Oy Nord Print Ab 2012), discusses this, 15 et seq.

[186] Clive-Steven Curran et al., 'Patent Indicators for Monitoring Convergence – Examples from NFF and ICT', (2011) 78 *Technological Forecasting and Social Change* 256, 256, 256 et seq.

[187] Michael A. Carrier, 'A Roadmap to the Smartphone Patent Wars and FRAND Licensing', (2012) April *CPI Antitrust Chronicle*, 1.

block competitors from using SEPs while being more likely to grant them when seeking injunctive relief for non-SEPs.[188]

The patent wars are mainly connected to injunctions or FRAND suits, but there are two developments. First, there are still a few suits where holders of SEPs refuse access to the SEPs altogether or demands exorbitant licensing fees. These are the PAEs lawsuits. And, after the *eBay* case in the US and the European developments under the EU Commission's settlement procedure, these lawsuits seem to become fewer and fewer. Secondly, instead the patent war is actually played out between the large incumbent firms in the telecommunications industry and the IT industry, respectively.

In Europe, the cases originate mainly from German courts but the Hague court has also been utilized. In the USA, there have been cases mainly in several jurisdictions but the most noteworthy cases are between Apple and Samsung in northern California and cases between Motorola and Apple before, among others, Judge Posner in Chicago, Illinois. Several injunction cases, possibly including several if not all of the firms involved in the smartphone industry, are being litigated under the International Trade Commission (ITC). In addition, the *Broadcom v. Qualcomm* cases are very interesting.[189]

The patent war in the ICT has its origin in the merger between two galaxies or clusters of standards and patents under the new 'standard', i.e. under the creation of the smart phone. The smartphone concept implied a collision between the information technology sector patent mosaic and the telecom sector mosaic and this is the source of the current patent wars. The clash is also between two different cultures about whether to accept royalty payments or not. The IT industry has traditionally shunned royalties, even fair toyalties under FRAND and aimed for standards to be royalty free. For example, the important standard-setting organization IETS that established the internet protocols, and the W3C that produced, inter alia, the web accessibility guidelines, have pushed for royalty free standards and technology. Often this has been supported, or even driven, by the open source community. In fact, there has even been discussion whether the strategy in the IT sector not to accept FRAND may amount to an antitrust violation consisting of a monopsony agreement to force

---

188 Ibid.

189 Cf discussion, infra, in Chapter 6.

low royalties, or even that it could amount to a group boycott to exclude technology that is protected under patents.[190]

These wars will probably soon end in settlements, and agreements to use FRAND at a level which both the Telecom and the IT sector can accept, but for now they rage on.

2.5.3 Standards and Outsourcing

Generally, we have also seen clear signs of specialization. Large firms have outsourced part of their R&D, for example Nokia Solution Networks seem to have transferred its R&D capacity in 2010.[191] Some firms have abandoned the product market altogether, and focus mainly or only on R&D (for example Qualcomm). Other firms seem clearly to be focusing on network and network services (Ericsson), while others are focusing on design (Apple) and purchase at least the telecom parts from other firms. Yet others focus on becoming pure production companies. The latest step in this development is the transfer in 2013 of the mobile devices production from Nokia to Microsoft, where the production of phones, smartphones and tablets were transferred with a ten years portfolio license to Micrsoft. Micrsoft received a portfolio license, while Nokia retained the patent portfolio.[192] Few firms, if any, seem today to be truly vertically integrated within the ICT industry.

The above is no real news, but the latest step in that development is interesting. Large firms that previously were considered to be R&D driven seem today rather to be purchasing patents or innovation through extensive R&D strategic alliances, while in-house they rather cultivate the patent portfolio.[193]

---

[190] Marcus Glader, 'Open Standards: Public Policy Aspects and Competition Law Requirements', (2010) 6 *European Competition Journal*, 611, 645 et seq., arguing that lobbying and implementing a royalty free standard would not amount to an antitrust violation.

[191] See for example Nokia 'outsourcing', i.e. transferring several of its R&D personnel from several global R&D centres to Renesas Electronics, http://www.hannessnellman.com/news-seminars/news/hannes-snellman-advises-renesas-electronics-acquisition-nokia-s-wireless-modem-bu., accessed 21 January 2013.

[192] Commission decision 4 December 2013, Case No COMP/M.7047 – Microsoft/Nokia, 34 et seq.

[193] Ibid. Nokia transferred several of its R&D personal from several global R&D centres to the Japanese firm Renesas Electronics, http://www.hanness nell man.com/news-seminars/news/hannes-snellman-advises-renesas-electronics-acquisition-nokia-s-wireless-modem-bu., accessed 21 January 2013.

The next generation, the 4G mobile systems, were initiated in 2007 and are a collection of wireless standards. They are being deployed on a large-scale commercial scale; already around a 1,000 patents have been declared essential.[194]

There is a similar development in other innovation-driven industries. The biotech sector has seen a development of the creation of several R&D only firms often connected to universities, while large pharmaceutical firms purchase R&D results and focus, rather, on the service of getting pharmaceuticals tested and finally approved under the national and regional approval process.[195] These are often called public-private partnerships and they are on the increase.

Moreover, in the consumer electronics sector it seems clear that firms are purchasing more and more R&D services from R&D intensive firms, often connected to universities, while restructuring their own R&D departments. In the consumer electronics industries, the production of products has long been the prerogative of some firms in South East Asia.

When analysing the background of some of the high-profile patent pools scrutinized in Business Review Letters from the end of the 1990s, for example the DVD pool collaboration between Koninklijke Philips Electronics N.V. (Philips), Sony Corporation of Japan (Sony) and Pioneer Electronic Cooperation of Japan (Pioneer), it becomes apparent that the participants jointly researched and developed the technology before setting up the patent pool.[196] Accordingly, Philips and Sony have been jointly engaging in research under the supervision of the Japanese Government for a long period of time, coming up with technologies such as the VCR Video, CD, Minidisc and DVD. These product or technology requirement standards, including their accompanying patent pools, were first considered benign under both US and EU antitrust law, but were later questioned in several jurisdictions. Apparently, at least as regards the CD-ROM technology, the parties later had to dissolve the relevant technology pool.[197] The main complaint by the licensees was that the

---

194 Liguo Zhang, *Standardization and Patent Licensing in the European Union* (Oy Nord Print Ab 2012), 77.

195 Irina Haracoglou, *Competition Law and Patents* (Edward Elgar, 2008), 3 et seq. with several references.

196 See the 3DVD pool Business Review Letter from Joel Klein to Gerrard Beeney dated 16 December 1998. See http://www.usdoj.gov/atr/public/bus review/2121.htm, accessed 1 April 2009.

197 See EU Commission press release IP/03/1152; 07/08/2003, 'Commission Clears Philips/Sony CD Licensing Programme' and EU Commission press release IP/06/139, 09/02/2006 'Commission Closes Investigation Following

patent pools contained patents that were not necessary or essential to produce products under the technology, and that the royalty fees amounted to more than 40 per cent of the end-product price. This made it allegedly impossible for licensees to produce products profitably. There was no competing technology and firms that had the relevant know-how and assets to develop a competing technology were already included in the pool as licensors.

It is evident that global standards are derived from joint R&D ventures performed by very large firms. Undoubtedly, the VCR technology and CD technology have been beneficial to consumers. However, from a dynamic competition perspective, parties perhaps ought to research independently, and purchasers in the relevant market should indicate, under the pressure of competition, that a certain technology is preferred. However, this depends on what sort of standard is supposed to be implemented. There is a difference between interoperability and product standards. When implementing a new sort or infrastructure or interoperability, perhaps society is better off having firms negotiate and agree on a standard *ex ante*, while if the technologies represent products on a relevant market, it is better that the firms compete with their technologies for the establishment of a standard *ex post*. Furthermore, issues such as efficiencies and transaction costs clearly play a role, while the existence of a patent thicket becomes important.

The telecommunications industry has also witnessed a struggle between firms that conduct R&D and profit from the licensing of the result of that R&D, and the firms that both conduct R&D and produce

---

Changes to Philips CD-Recordable Disc Patent Licensing'. For the famous Chinese Taipei case see OECD, 'Roundtable Discussions Regarding Intellectual Property in 2004', 21 January 2005, 117 et seq., http://www.oecd.org/dataoecd/61/48/34306055.pdf. The Chinese Taipei case resulted in very interesting litigation concerning patent rights and misuse of patent rights, see the ITC case, 'Notice of Commission on Determination of No Violation of Section 337, In the Matter of Certain Recordable Compact Discs and Rewritable Compact Discs', Investigation No. 337-TA-474. See also United States Court of Appeals for the Federal Circuit U.S. Philips Corp. v. International Trade Commission, 424 F.3d 1179 (Fed. Cir. 2005). For an even earlier case concerning Philips and Sony cooperation over VCR video technology, see Commission Decision Videocassette Recorders, OJ 1977 L 47/42. Cf. Maurits Dolmans, 'Standards for Standards', (2002) 26 *Fordham International Law Journal*, 163, 175. The US FTC also did an early analysis of the licensing agreements for the CD-ROM pool in the 1980s. See Carl Shapiro, 'Navigating the Patent Thicket: Cross Licenses, Patent Pools and Standard Setting', in Adam Jaffe et al. (eds), *Innovation Policy and the Economy* MIT Press, 2001), 20.

products such as mobile telephones. The intense competition in this market has caused the standards process to develop slowly. Patent pools have not been formed, mainly because firms cannot agree on royalty levels. Instead, hold-up problems have prevailed and slowed down the development of technology standards. Otherwise, the telecommunications industry would be an example of patent pools created due to the patent thicket or anticommons. In the telecommunication industry there have been different R&D poles, and, hence, according to the theories of the anticommons and patent thicket, market participants would later start to collaborate in patent pools. Such a development cannot be identified. Patent pools are not created due to the fact that some of the most important technology-only firms – the firms making only profit on royalty rates and not producing mobile handsets – are not willing to reduce royalty rates to the level at which the firms conducting both R&D and producing handsets are comfortable.[198]

Interestingly, in the pharmaceutical industry, the opposite situation prevails. In the pharmaceutical industry, R&D firms are relatively small in comparison to the larger pharmaceutical firms, which are focused on distribution and obtaining the approval of the different FDA authorities globally. From a business strategy point of view, there are similarities between the ICT sector and the testing and approval procedure for pharmaceuticals. The standard-setting procedure in the ICT sector, without being legally binding, seems to have become the means to get technologies approved for the market, similarly to the testing and approval procedure for pharmaceuticals under national FDAs. While

---

[198] For a good analysis of the telecommunication industry, see generally Rudi Bekkers et al., 'Case studies on the interface between research and standardisation, and case studies on patent pools as a coordination mechanism' (INTEREST consortium Priority 8 No. Contract 503 594, EU 6th Specific Targeted Research Project, 2006). Appendix 2. [The document is on file with the author.] Regarding the cases between Qualcomm and Nokia see somewhat outdated list of mostly the European legal actions: http://www.reuters.com/article/companyNewsAndPR/idUSL1722345120070817, accessed 19 August 2007. These cases have been dropped after Nokia and Qualcomm reached a settlement in the middle of 2008. See Matt Richtel, 'In Settlement, Nokia Will Pay Royalties to Qualcomm', in *New York Times*, 24 July 2008, http://www.nytimes.com/2008/07/24/technology/24qualcomm.html?_r=1&scp=1&sq=nokia%20qualcomm&st=cse, accessed 7 April 2009. In October 2007 the EU Commission initiated formal proceedings against Qualcomm. See http://ec.europa.eu/competition/antitrust/cases/decisions/39247/proceedings.pdf. See also Qualcomm Inc. v. Nokia Corp. 466 F.3d 1366 (Fed. Cir. 2006). Broadcom v. Qualcomm Inc. 501 F.3d. 297 (3d Cir. 2007).

certain firms today focus on the standard-setting procedure, purchasing R&D and outsourcing production in the ICT sector, pharmaceutical companies seem to have focused on different core activities of either (i) R&D (often smaller firms), (ii) the regulatory procedure and the approval process or (iii) the actual production of pharmaceuticals. Within the approval process, several services are purchased (outsourced), such as the different testing procedures (e.g. clinical trial: phase I, II and III). The larger multinational firms seem to focus on step (ii), where future drugs are being selected.

There is anecdotal evidence that large pharmaceutical firms shelve new innovations by entering joint R&D agreements with exclusive joint exploitation covenants.[199] Interestingly, the EU Commission is currently investigating a case where Servier is considered to have violated both Article 101 and 102 TFEU. The Commission stated that it had objections to specific sets of practices by Servier, which appears to be dominant in the market for Perindopril. The first practice being that Servier purportedly acquired and shelved scarce competing technologies to produce Perindopril, rendering generic market entry more difficult or delayed. This behaviour (and the purported settlement agreements with other generic manufacturers), if established, infringes EU Antitrust rules that prohibit restrictive business practices and the abuse of a dominant market position (respectively Articles 101 and 102 of the Treaty on the functioning of the European Union – TFEU).[200]

That exclusion of competitors by the acquisition of competing technologies may be a violation of Articles 101 or 102 TFEU, and is of great interest also in the world of standard essential patents, which have seen several large acquisitions of portfolios of SEPs, and where shelving competing innovation could be prevalent.

Moreover, the groundbreaking *AstraZeneca* case must be mentioned. The CJEU confirmed the Commission finding that misuses of regulatory procedures can in certain circumstances constitute abuses of a dominant position within the meaning of EU antitrust rules (Article 102 TFEU). The judgment also confirms the Commission's method in defining the relevant product market and the existence of a dominant position in an

---

[199] See Saami Zain, 'Suppression of Innovation or Collaborative Efficiencies? An Antitrust Analysis of a Research & Development Collaboration that Led to the Shelving of a Promising Drug', (2006) 5 J. *Marshall Rev. Intell. Prop. L*, 347, 350 et seq. with references. See also Davis Hamilton, 'Silent Treatment: How Genetech, Novartis Stifled a Promising Drug', (2005) *Wall. St. J.*, A1.

[200] See EU Commission press release: http://europa.eu/rapid/press-release_IP-12-835_en.htm, accessed 21 January 2012.

intellectual property rights industry, i.e. the pharmaceutical sector, where AstraZeneca was found to have abused and misused the regulator procedure.

Misusing the standardization process, or, for that matter, the regulator procedure for obtaining patents, by utilizing the standardization process, e.g. information obtained in connection with a technical committee meeting, could, in light of the *AstraZeneca* ruling, be at risk of infringing Article 102 TFEU.

The same or a similar development as has played out in the pharmaceutical sector may also play out in the telecommunications and consumer electronic markets. R&D will be conducted by small specific R&D firms, often connected to a university, and at least partially funded by public means (the so-called Public-Private Partnership). The larger firms will instead employ and instruct these smaller exclusively R&D firms in joint R&D ventures, while they provide the standard-setting and marketing and licensing of well-known trade marks, and profiting from licensing SEPs.[201] Manufacturing-only firms produce actual products under joint production ventures or on an assignment basis from the larger firms. They enter licensing agreements under IP arrangements or technology pools. The manufacturing-only firms also need to license trademarks from the larger firms focused on standard-setting. Thus, the powerful firms in these businesses are the firms that control the standard-setting and, in addition, have the strong trademarks and the large marketing resources.

2.6 BUSINESS PATENT STRATEGY MODELS

The R&D-only firms do not necessarily need to immerse themselves as licensees or PAEs in the technology market, because they can sell their services and assign or licence patents, rather than have a business strategy for extracting (high) royalties from manufacturing-only or vertically integrated firms. Instead, R&D-only (including biotech) firms proliferate more as pure R&D firms, to which larger firms unilaterally or

---

[201] A difference between SDOs and SSOs is that SSOs often employ a 'pay to play' rule. Even though SDOs are inexpensive in comparison, SSOs are clearly in some industries winning in the competition against SDOs. Cf. Carl Cargill, 'Intellectual Property Rights and Standard Setting Organizations: An Overview of Failed Evolution', (2002) 27 March FTC/DOJ Hearings on Competition and Intellectual Property Law and Policy in the Knowledge-Based Economy, 1, 6.

collectively outsource their research.[202] Thus, the aggressive 'patent trolls' or PAEs active in the technology market soliciting patents and seeking out firms using the relevant technology to enter licensing agreements and extract royalty rates, are in the minority, and probably less prevalent then the pure R&D firms innovating diligently for one or a few vertically integrated firms to create new technologies, solutions and products. This would especially hold true for the R&D firms that larger leading technology firms engage under public-private partnerships, where the R&D on many occasions is publicly funded. The larger leading technology firms are engaged in the standard-setting process and negotiating the new technology path and standard, while engaging R&D-only firms to conduct R&D that matches the negotiations. The R&D result is then fed back in the standard-setting effort conducted in the technical committees. In these circumstances, the standard-setting process must be understood as a form of collective innovation, and also collective competition, where the end result is a standard that meets the demands of society as a whole.[203]

Generally, R&D firms conduct research on assignment from large vertically integrated multinational firms. Generally, the vertically integrated firms are holders of large patent portfolios. They give access to background patents and outsource or assign the R&D to the specialized firms. They still conduct in-house reasearch, but the general trend is towards purchasing this service.

In the biotech area, the large pharma firms provide the service of testing and getting the few successful drugs through the approval process. In transactions with the R&D-only firms, they gain the patents and other intellectual property rights that are the results of the research. Often, the R&D firms develop the drugs up to and including Phase I clinical trials before licencing it to larger pharma companies. In the consumer electronic and other industries, two or more competing vertically integrated

---

202 Researchers at the Justice Department analysed R&D agreements that had been filed under the NCRPA so as to enable the participants to gain access from the safe harbour. Cf. Suzanne E. Majewski, *How Do Consortia Organize Collaborative R&D? Evidence from the National Cooperative Research Act* (SSRN 2004), 12 et seq., 13 and cf. Suzanne E. Majewski and Dean V. Williamson, *Endogenous Spillovers, Strategic Blocking, and the Design of Contracts in Collaborative R&D: Evidence from NCRA filings of R&D Joint Ventures* (SSRN 2002), 1 et seq.

203 Josef Drexl, 'Anti-competitive Stumbling Stones on the Way to a Cleaner World: Protecting Competition in Innovation without a Market', (2012) 8 *Journal of Competition Law & Economics*, 507, 534.

firms often collectively outsource their R&D to an R&D intensive firm.[204] The definition of the assigned or outsourced R&D may correspond to a loosely predetermined technology standard agreed upon the vertically integrated firms in the pre-standardization phase.[205]

To the business strategy model presented in the first chapter therefore, a new layer should be added consisting of small specialized R&D intensive firms (see Figure 2.1).

A plausible scenario is that multinational firms, 'system leaders' and 'collectors' of intellectual property rights in their industry,[206] i.e. the IP Banks, often acquire the relevant intellectual property rights by licensing or purchasing such property from smaller R&D-only firms. Intellectual property is acquired through joint R&D ventures, where competing system leaders often jointly assign the R&D-only firm to conduct specific R&D focused on a contemplated technology standard. The R&D-only firm can be independent or connected to a university, however, that does not ensure that the invented technology is ground-breaking. Industries plagued by network effects and defensive patenting, or where network

---

[204] From data consisting of 142 Joint R&D agreements, Dr. Suzanne Majewski concludes that it seems that most joint R&D agreements are entered into by product market competitors, i.e. vertically integrated firms. These competing firms tend in their agreements collectively to outsource their R&D to third parties. By outsourcing they benefit from shared costs and a reduction in duplicative efforts. They also avoid spillover effects and the opportunistic problems of having researchers from the firms interacting. However, by not interacting, the supposedly welfare enhancing exchange of ideas (spillover) is minimized. Synergy effects are lost if the parties do not conduct the research jointly. This was also supported by the fact that in only 14 per cent of the analysed R&D joint ventures were the scientists allowed to rotate between the participating firms. However, it also shows that there is a new sort of firm emerging – firms that only conduct R&D. These exclusively R&D firms tend to cater for product market competitors but conduct their work exclusively in the innovation and technology markets. Cf. Suzanne E. Majewski, *How Do Consortia Organize Collaborative R&D? Evidence from the National Cooperative Research Act* (SSRN 2004), 13. See, supra, Chapter 2.2.3.

[205] Cf. Maurits Dolmans, 'Standards For Standards', (2002) 26 *Fordham International Law Journal*, 163, 171 et seq. regarding joint R&D during the pre-standardization phase.

[206] For discussion of 'system leaders' cf. Hanns Ullrich, 'The Interaction between Competition Law and Intellectual Property Law – An Overview', in Claus Dieter Ehlermann & Isabela Atanasiu (eds), *European Competition Law Annual 2005: The Interaction between Competition Law and Intellectual Property Law* (Hart Publishing, 2007), xlviii.

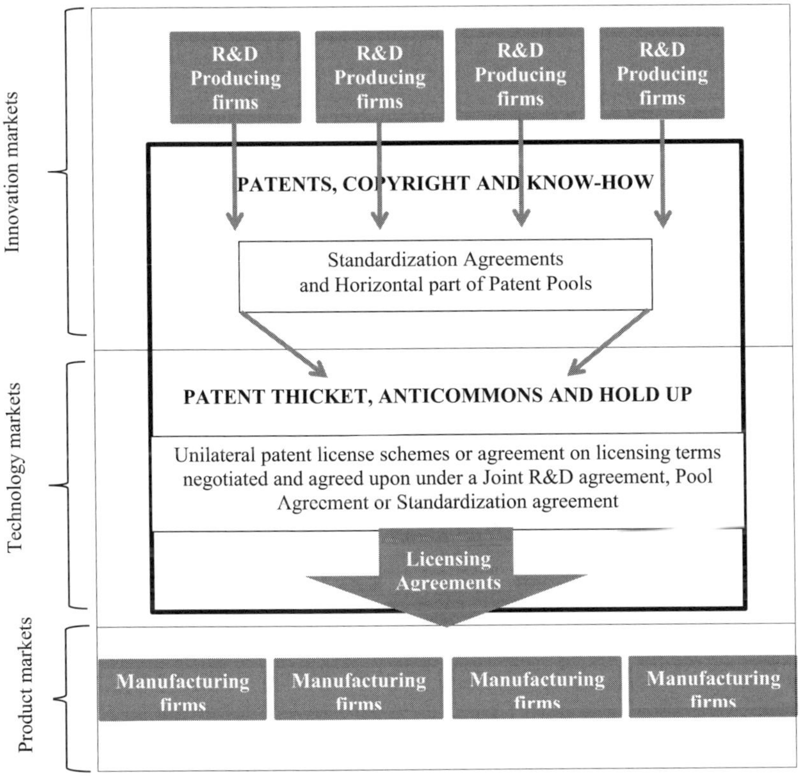

Figure 2.1 Business patent strategy model

effects are created through technology standard-setting,[207] often implement technologies that are not the 'high-key' technologies of the industry, but rather are compromises based on already invented portfolios of innovations.[208] Thus, the system leaders want to make use of their old

---

[207] It seems clear that the system of agreeing and implementing standards inherently creates network effects, instant tipping or 'winners (being several) takes all' outcomes. Cf. Michael Schallop, 'The IPR Paradox: Leveraging Intellectual Property Rights to Encourage Interoperability in the Network Computing Age', (2000) 28 *AIPLY Quarterly Journal*, 195, 235.

[208] Cf., generally, regarding the practice of taking out patents on a portfolio of already invented products and systems: John Barton, 'Antitrust Treatment of Oligopolies with Mutual Blocking Patent Portfolios', (2002) 69 *Antitrust Law Journal*, 851, 853 et seq, and 856 et seq. Regarding how SSOs may implement low-key technologies, cf. Michael Schallop, 'The IPR Paradox: Leveraging

patents. The effect of this conduct is that 'low-key' technology can gain industry wide recognition by 'tipping' the industry under a technology standardization agreement.[209] The system leaders, by agreeing on technology under a consortium or the joint R&D agreement, also negotiate so that the resulting intellectual property rights fit the relevant technology standards, or perhaps the other way around.[210] This is a reason why technology standards may become too broad and deep.[211]

On the other side of the spectrum, there are other firms focusing on the manufacturing of products and, perhaps, so-called second-generation innovations. These manufacturing-only firms are mostly clustered in Asia. Vertically integrated firms outsource production to these manufacturing-only firms. However, that does not prevent the manufacturing-only firms from engaging in their own follow-on development or manufacturing. In fact, these firms need to be controlled by grant-back, grant-back FRAND, field-of-use and most-favoured-nation covenants under the licensing agreement so not to develop the technology in a direction not envisioned by the original licensors.

The model shows the paramount importance of being able to influence relevant joint R&D/standard-setting consortia and licence agreements, i.e.

Intellectual Property Rights to Encourage Interoperability in the Network Computing Age', (2000) 28 *AIPLY Quarterly Journal*, 195, 235; Hanns Ullrich, 'The Interaction between Competition Law and Intellectual Property Law – An Overview', in Claus Dieter Ehlermann and Isabela Atanasiu (eds), *European Competition Law Annual 2005: The Interaction between Competition Law and Intellectual Property Law* (Hart Publishing, 2007), xvii, 1 fn. 155; and Neil Gandal, 'Compatibility, Standardization, and Network Effects: Some Policy Implications', (2002) 18 *Oxford Review of Economic Policy*, 80, 88.

[209] Cf. Hanns Ullrich, 'The Interaction between Competition Law and Intellectual Property Law – An Overview', in Claus Dieter Ehlermann and Isabela Atanasiu (eds), *European Competition Law Annual 2005: The Interaction between Competition Law and Intellectual Property Law* (Hart Publishing, 2007), l, fn 155. For definition of 'tipping' see Michael Katz and Carl Shapiro, 'Systems Competition and Network Effects', (1994) 8 *Journal of Economic Perspective*, 93, 105 et seq.

[210] Daniel A. Crane, 'Patent Pools, RAND Commitments, and the Problematics of Price Discrimination', (2008) *Cardozo School of Law Working Paper* (2008) no. 232, 7 and 9, has noticed the same possibility for strategic use of patents.

[211] Rudi Bekkers et al., 'Case studies on the interface between research and standardisation, and case studies on patent pools as a coordination mechanism'(INTEREST consortium Priority 8 No. Contract 503 594, EU 6th Specific Targeted Research Project, 2006), 53. [The document is on file with the author.]

the value chain from the joint innovation/standard-setting procedure under the SSO to the patent pool. It seems that it is firms with large patent portfolios that enter into pre-standardization consortia, and that firms with similar R&D and business models often are members of these collaborations.[212] Here, R&D avenues may be plotted and also that membership in a related consortium increases the capacity of a firm to influence the voting behavior of other companies in the SDO.[213] In a different conception, a consortium is an alliance of firms joining forces in order to leverage their voting power in the SDO.[214] Thus, 'vertically integrated' firms within the black square in the business model above hold market power. They act as gatekeepers or as centralized organs for accepting inventions, technology and products. They master the interface between joint R&D, technology standard setting and IP policies or patent pools and make that into a business in itself. However, to be able to master the interface, and actually provide that service to the value chain from invention to end-products, demands investment in time and recourses in SSOs and SDOs and, foremost, a large portfolio of patents and other intellectual property rights.[215] Firms, such as Qualcomm and now Nokia could be considered mastering the interface in the telecom industry and are now more of 'IP Banks' then 'regular' vertical integrated multinationals.

Interestingly, the effect of all-industry inclusive standardization agreements is that stable oligopolies are created. This set-up prevents network effects with the result that short-lived monopolies are no longer created. Instead large firms divide the markets between themselves. However, they do this by using network effects in their joint interest, since it is

---

212 Justus Baron and Tim Pohlmann, 'Who Cooperates in Standard Consortia – Rivals or Complementors' (2013) 9 *Journal of Competition Law & Economics*, 905, 921, 928.

213 Aija E. Leiponen, 'Competing Through Cooperation: The Organization of Standard Setting in Wireless Telecomminucations', (2008) 54 *MGMT. SCI.*, 1904.

214 Justus Baron and Tim Pohlmann, 'Who Cooperates in Standard Consortia – Rivals or Complementors' (2013) 9 *Journal of Competition Law & Economics*, 905, 908.

215 Interviews with representatives from the telecommunication industry indicate the amount of time and resources that are spent on joint R&D and industrial standard setting activities. Rudi Bekkers et al., 'Case studies on the interface between research and standardisation, and case studies on patent pools as a coordination mechanism' (INTEREST consortium Priority 8 No. Contract 503 594, EU 6th Specific Targeted Research Project, 2006), 53 et seq. [The document is on file with the author.]

difficult, to the point of being impossible, to establish a stand-alone competing technology. There will be no demand for that technology. Thus, the need for consensus under SDOs creates oligopolies also within the 'new economy', as well as oligopolies thrived in the old economy based on economies of scale.

In addition to deciding on standards and assigning R&D to R&D-intensive firms, these IP Banks also invest in marketing and in their trade marks. All leading firms in the industries discussed in this book, i.e. telecommunications, consumer electronics, IT, and, to no less an extent, the pharma industry invest heavily in marketing and the branding of products. This is essential to be able to control the value chain from developing new products to manufacturing these products when the IP Banks *de facto* neither innovate nor produce in-house.

In essence, they are above all 'IP Banks', i.e. holders of business assets, with the ability to overlook development and with the business idea of exclusion rather than innovation or production. They represent MAD capability as a revenue-creating source of income. Indeed, the incentive would be to increase royalty levels and streams.[216] Interestingly, this implies that they do not really need to employ that many people, nor are they tied to any physical location on the globe.

It is clear that the R&D, technology and manufacturing-only firms benefit from the IP Banks in the short run and, thus, coopetition in this way is beneficial to welfare and innovation. Specialized R&D firms or manufacturing-only firms would not exist without coopetition or networks. However, it is also clear that these smaller firms may be obliged to enter into R&D collaborative and licensing agreements that might substantially restrict their growth. Indeed, restrictions on non-competitors under the collaborations analysed in this book are generally, under competition law, legal, per se. Restricting R&D-only firms vertically is allowed. Thus, prohibition from unilaterally entering segments vertically, other than the segment in which the firm is currently active is an example of a benign covenant. For example, it might be a contract violation for an

---

[216] Compare the concern put forward by respondents in the Microsoft Nokia merger, that Nokia post merger would become a gigant PAEs and increase royalty levels, the respons by Nokia. Commission decision 4 December 2013, Case No COMP/M.7047 – Microsoft/Nokia, 34 et seq. EU Competition Commissioner Joaquin Almunia also warned Nokia of becoming a patent troll. In my view Nokia will not become a patent troll, rather a IP Bank. See Don Reisinger, 9 December 2013, 'EU to Nokia: Don't become a 'patent troll'', http://news.cnet.com/8301-1035_3-57614945-94/eu-to-nokia-dont-be-a-patent-troll/. Accessed 27 February 2014.

R&D firm, which has a long-standing R&D collaboration with multinational firms, directly to approach a manufacturing firm or another multinational firm. Such behaviour might violate the field-of-use restriction or the exclusivity covenant in the R&D or licence agreement. Such covenants are benign under competition law. Indeed, R&D specialized firms are less protected than any other forms of firm under antitrust law on either side of the Atlantic. By restricting R&D-only firms and manufacturing-only firms to growing vertically, system leaders may prevent the emergence of horizontal competitors. This limits the participators in the black square in the business model above and the interaction between R&D-only and manufacturing-only firms.

Moreover, when the manufacturing-only firms and other follow-on innovators start to catch up through their subsequent, follow-on research, they are obliged to grant back these patents to the holders of the original SEPs under the license agreements.

Depending on the royalty stream mechanism in relevant patent pool agreements, new SEPs will dilute the royalty stream so that the original licensors receive ever fewer royalties.[217] In turn, this creates the incentive for the original licensors to set up a new technology standard and a new pool. The new standard or pool should still be backwards compatible with the former technology but include so much new technology that a new standard or pool can technically be created.[218] In other words, these pools are often legal creations based on a new use of old general original patents, but excluding some follow-on innovations.[219] The result is that the new pools lack the follow-on innovations produced by manufacturing-only firms; however, they might still need, and allow, the original licensors to include their old broad patents in the new pool. Examples of new 'generations' of standards, patent pools based on similar technical solutions are DVD to Blu-Ray and 3G to 4G telecom standards.

---

[217] See, e.g., the MPEG-2 pool where the mechanism was triggered by the number of patents contributed to the pool. See the MPEG-2 Pool Business Review Letter to Gerrard Beeney dated 26 June 1997, 6. See http://www.usdoj.gov/atr/public/busreview/215742.htm, accessed 3 May 2009.

[218] For further discussion regarding so-called planned obsolescence, which I am not able to discuss in detail in this book, cf. Jeremy Bulow, 'An Economic Theory of Planned Obsolescence', (1986) 101 *The Quarterly Journal of Economics*, 729, and Michael Waldman, 'A New Perspective on Planned Obsolescence', (1993) 108 *The Quarterly Journal of Economics*, 273.

[219] See, generally, regarding defensive patenting and giving the example of the semiconductor industry, John Barton, 'Antitrust Treatment of Oligopolies with Mutual Blocking Patent Portfolios', (2002) 69 *Antitrust Law Journal*, 851, 853 et seq.

The PAEs are the mavericks of the technology markets and might be regarded as misusing the standard-setting process if conducting patent ambush and similar acts.[220] There was almost a general consensus that patent trolls were abusing the standard-setting system. But now the lines between PAE and IP Banks are not so clear anymore. Moreover, it seems obvious that PAE and IP Banks are collaborating. Privateering, where a large system leader (IP Bank) outsources its patents to a PAE for it to attack competitors of the IP Bank, seems to be increasing.[221] Microsoft and Nokia have been accused of setting up their own PAE/patent pool/troll, Mosaid.[222] Likewise, Philips has been accused in different blogs of outsourcing patents to a PAE (Sisvel).[223] In addition, creatures such as the private equity fund, Intellectual Ventures, which seem to act as an insurance solution on the technology markets, have appeared. Intellectual Ventures utilize intellectual property both offensively and defensively. For example, they purchase patents so that firms sued for infringement can make use of them to counter-sue. In fact, even though they seem to be joint defence agreements, these forms of collaboration fit within the dotted area and are very difficult to address as anti-competitive collaborations.

However, the material difference when analysing the whole picture, including joint R&D ventures, standardization agreements and technology pools, compared to scrutinizing each collaboration separately, is that the firms engaged in all these collaborations, i.e. the IP Banks, under the classical definition of competitor within both US antitrust law and the EU competition rules, do not have, generally, any competitors. Generally, the agreements they enter are vertical. The IP Banks hold such large patent portfolios that they always have some patents that are blocking. Furthermore, they conduct neither R&D nor do they manufacture or sell products and, ironically, on the technology markets, it seems that as the number of patents a firm holds increases, the number of horizontal

---

220 Edward Wyatt, 'F.T.C. Turns a Lens on Abuse of Patent System', *New Yotk Times,* 16 July 2013 ,

221 Tom Ewing, 'Indirect Exploitation of Intellectual Property Rights by Corporations and Investors', (2011) 3 *Hastings Sci & Tech Law Journal* 1 and Thomas L. Ewing, 'Practical Considerations In the Indirect Deployment of Intellectual Property Rights by Corporations and Investors', (2011) 4 *Hastings Sci & Tech Law Journal* 109, for a good analysis of privateering.

222 Ibid. According to news articles, Google has submitted a complaint regarding the creation of Mosaid to the EU Commission. See e.g. Suzanne Tindal, 'Nokia, Microsoft support patent trolls: Google', *ZDnet,* 1 June 2012 .

223 Together with several other firms, cf. www.sisvel.com/index.php/history, accessed 10 July 2013.

agreements or competitors that firm faces decreases. The firms with the largest patent portfolios might formally have the fewest competitors, even though, logically, it should be the other way around. The firms that hold many patents should generally be active in more markets than firms holding fewer patents, and therefore have more competitors, but that is not the case under antitrust law anymore. *De lege lata*, the opposite is true and that is an antitrust paradox. In fact, the large IP Banks are promoted at the expense of the small R&D intensive firms. The question is whether competition law prevents or promotes this development. Does competition law try to detect and disseminate the market power inherent in the IP Banks and their collaborations? Or, is it the other way around: does competition law in fact promote the establishment and the prolongation of IP Banks? Before that analysis is conducted, the basic theories of intellectual property and competition law will be revisited.

2.7 TECHNOLOGY CONSORTIUM

Several economists have theorized about the 'technology consortia' and network industries. William Baumol, for example, stated that members of a technology consortium acquire an enormous competitive advantage over non-members. Particularly if the arrangements last for a considerable time, so that the exchanges constitute a much-repeated game, the consortium members will be able to offer their final-product customers all the new products at the lower cost resulting from the R&D activities of their fellow members as well as their own. A rival who goes it alone will have access only to its own innovations. In an industry with, say, ten firms similar in output and investment in R&D, each member of a nine-firm technology consortium can expect to obtain immediate access to nine times the number of innovations that the remaining firm can anticipate, on average.[224] This saves transaction costs but will presumably

[224] William Baumol, 'Horizontal Collusion and Innovation', (1992) 102 The Economic Journal, 129, 134. Regarding technology sharing consortia see also William Baumol, Entrepreneurship, Management and the Structure of Payoffs (MIT Press 1993)., 193 et seq. See also Maria Luise Petit & Boleslaw Tolwinski, 'Technology Sharing Cartels and Industrial Structure', (1996) 15 *International Journal of Industrial Organisation*, 77 and Claudio Ciborra, 'Alliances as Learning Experiments: Cooperation, Competition and Change in Hightech Industries', in Lynn Mytelka (ed), *Strategic Partnerships and the World Economy* (Pinter Publishers, 1991), 53, with references.

lessen consumer choice and prevent the competitive innovative trial and error process.

Moreover, if nine firms in an industry conduct R&D in collaboration, or at least decide on a technology path during the standard-process, they will also be able to create a technology standard. As empirical research has shown, standards can facilitate information exchange between members of technical committees and thus reduce risk and spending in R&D.[225] It may avoid duplicate investment in R&D. Joint R&D, in combination with a technology standard and a patent pool, creates the possibility of creating strategic alliances.[226] This may help the parties to these alliances to reduce cost and risk, while increasing profit. However, it increases the risk of the creation of close cooperations that might lead to monopolistic structures.[227] Some even assert that it may carry the risk that the consortia deciding to have 'low-key' technology become the dominant and successful standard.[228] Thus, a nine-firm cartel, as Baumol was contemplating, with majority voting power in the relevant SSO, in the innovation 'market' implies that they, in theory, do not have to invest in great leaps of innovation. Rather, they would satisfy all the members patent portfolios, and be better off, by agreeing on an inexpensive technology that fits their strategic purpose, i.e. a solution that they control through intellectual property rights.

Notwithstanding the above, a collaboration including several, if not all, of the interested stakeholders in an industry, would be able to conduct research much more efficiently. One compatible solution would emerge out of the standardization-process, created as a joint effort with the minimum of transaction costs and with reduced search costs. Of course, these benefits must be weighed against the drawbacks of such a structural procedure in the creation of innovations. Competition and innovation as a process of rivalry is lost, while transaction costs are saved.

Thus, a joint R&D and standard-consortium can obtain market power to an extent that competition would diminish. The anti-competitive aspect is, however, not the merger of assets but that 'technology cartels' are able

---

[225] DIN, German Institute for Standardization e. V (DIN), *Economic Benefits of Standardization: Summary of Results* (DIN, Beuth Verlag, 2000), 15 et seq.

[226] Ibid. 14 et seq.

[227] Ibid.

[228] Hanns Ullrich, 'The Interaction between Competition Law and Intellectual Property Law – An Overview', in Claus Dieter Ehlermann & Isabela Atanasiu (eds), *European Competition Law Annual 2005: The Interaction between Competition Law and Intellectual Property Law* (Hart Publishing, 2007), 1, fn. 155.

to control the development of the technology by colluding, not on price and output, but on what constitutes the winning technology. The technology will match the members' patent portfolios.[229] Technology competition or innovative competition may be lost when firms, under a joint R&D and standardization agreement, can decide which technology wins.

Therefore, all industrial inclusive standard-setting procedures should be collaborative, where firms engage in discussion and negotiation regarding standard setting, while the R&D under such collaborations shall preferably be conducted unilateral. Thereby, SSOs or SDOs will have a choice of technology when selecting the standard.

An innovation 'market' which contains three to four joint ventures in research including most of the prominent firms, will discourage new entrants. This will be enforced, if the firms are also collaborating in an SSO and have agreed on a technology standard, a research focus, and which patents are essential for the standard. Practitioners indicate that R&D collaborations among large firms in the phase leading up to an agreement on a technology standard are common practice.[230] From research into 142 joint consortium agreements notified under the NCRPA, Suzanne Majewski concludes that it seems like most joint R&D agreements are entered into by product market competitors. These competing firms tend in their agreements to jointly outsource their collaborative R&D to third parties.[231]

These instruments allow the incumbent firms to control an industry in a way not possible with a price cartel. By controlling the standard, they are actually controlling what technology constitutes the winning innovation. By setting up a matching patent pool, they may either prevent new entrants or, at least, be able to collect profit from new entrants into the product market through royalties. These royalties might be set at a level of perfect monopolistic royalties.[232] The licensing agreement from the pool might contain grant-back clauses with rights to sub-lease, which

[229] Daniel A. Crane, 'Patent Pools, RAND Commitments, and the Problematics of Price Discrimination', *Cardozo School of Law Working Paper* (2008) no. 232, 238 et seq.

[230] Generally, Maurits Dolmans, 'Standards For Standards', (2002) 26 *Fordham International Law Journal*, 163, 171 et seq., especially 172. Ibid.

[231] Cf. Suzanne E. Majewski, *How Do Consortia Organize Collaborative R&D? Evidence from the National Cooperative Research Act* (SSRN 2004), 13.

[232] Stephen Maurer and Suzanne Scotchmer, 'Profit Neutrality in Licensing: The Boundary Between Antitrust Law and Patent Law', (2006) 8 *American Law and Economics Review*, 476476, 484 et seq. Cf. also Susanne Scotchmer, *Innovation and Incentives* (MIT Press, 2004), 113 et seq.

effectively – at least in theory – limit follow-on innovations. Moreover, by controlling the technology standard, resources do not need to be invested in new research. The outcome is that the R&D markets and the technology markets will be collectively or jointly monopolized and the innovation rate deteriorates.

In light of the above, it is quite evident that 'technology consortia' might be anti-competitive. Evidently, these collaborations may reduce R&D, and exclude competitors from markets. For example, to remain outside a 'technology consortium', as Baumol today prefers to call it, may be very risky.[233] Anyone not joining may be eliminated by not gaining access to either technology or rights. Thus, the incentive to innovate or even to stay in the market is lost by the firms that do not enter the consortium from the beginning. Moreover, if, using the notions of game theory, the game is repeated, i.e. as the industry evolves through cumulative innovations, cheating by members of the consortium may be minimized. Firms within the consortium would not dare to limit access to their innovations since being ejected from the consortium implies great losses. Members will adhere to the rules of the consortium since the risk of being ejected from the consortium constitutes a powerful deterrent.

Comparing the above description with the conventional wisdom on cartels is quite interesting. A price cartel and/or output cartel is often, at least in theory, plagued with cheating since each member of the cartel has a strong incentive to secretly sell more than agreed. The goal of the cartel is to reap supra-competitive profits and, since selling at supra-competitive prices implies limiting output, the members must agree to cut output. This in itself creates an incentive to make secret sales, since such sales would amount to incremental profits. Thus, for a price cartel to work properly, powerful and often costly, monitoring and punishment mechanisms must be implemented.[234]

All this is well known, but some consequences bear repetition. Above all, a successful price cartel may, for the reasons given above, only be implemented in certain industries whose products are few and whose rate

---

[233] Baumol called these phenomena 'technology cartels' in his article of 1992, however he changed the notion to 'technological consortium' in his books from 1993 and 2002, respectively, see William Baumol, 'Horizontal Collusion and Innovation', (1992) 102 *The Economic Journal*, 129, 135 et seq., William Baumol, *Entrepreneurship, Management and the Structure of Payoffs* (MIT Press 1993), 193 et seq. and William Baumol, *The Free-Market Innovation Machine* (Princeton University Press 2002), 73 et seq.

[234] Massimo Motta, *Competition Policy* (Cambridge University Press 2004), 150, 343 and 420.

of innovation is low.[235] Interestingly, it must also be stressed that the dangers of price cartels are two. First, the price will evidently increase, which in the end will misallocate resources. Second, cartels also facilitate survival of the weak, inefficient and unlucky. Cartels create a safe harbour or subsidize those competitors who would, in the case of fierce competition, perish since their costs exceed the competitive price.

However, these effects are similarly true for technology consortia. It is quite evident that these consortia facilitate protection for inefficient innovators, since they obtain access to their competitors' technology through the standard-setting process. Likewise, this increases the breadth of standards. In order to facilitate agreement between the possible losers in the technology competition or collaboration in the pre-standardization phase on the technology standard, some of their patents often need to be included in the standard.[236]

Regarding price, if the intellectual property were already exclusive due to intellectual property protection, and the technology within the pool were complementary, why would proprietors even need to decide on the price for the downstream products in a consortium? The price of the products would in theory already be supra-competitive since each proprietor would charge as close to perfect monopoly royalties for its patent as possible.[237] Nonetheless, patent pools can become a vehicle for competitors both to agree on price and also to squeeze out competitors on the downstream products markets. If the royalties charged are high enough,

---

235 William Baumol, 'Horizontal Collusion and Innovation', (1992) 102 *The Economic Journal*, 129, 130 et seq.

236 Cf. Rudi Bekkers, 'Patent Drag and Stacking IPR Fees – Are the IPR policies of Standard Bodies Failing or should we better Address Excessive Technology Inclusion?', (2007) Position Paper for High Level Workshop on Standardization, IP Licensing and Antitrust, and Douglas Melamed, 'Patents and Standard: The Unimportance of Being Essential' (unpublished work, 2006). [The documents are on file with the author.] Regarding an example where an SDO has used monopsony power to select a low key above a high key technology, see Maurits Dolmans, 'Standards for Standards', (2002) 26 *Fordham International Law Journal*, 163, 180 et seq.

237 Probably, there is even more profit to be gained from pooling rights. Thus, an even higher price may be extracted from the market than could be done based exclusively on a single, or a few, intellectual property rights. Cf. George Priest, 'Cartels and Patent Licensing Arrangements', (1977) 20 *Journal of Law and Economics*, 309, 314 et seq. Also, in practice, the joint litigation force implicit in the patent pool would increase the royalty rate. The proprietors are more confident that they can actually collect their royalties under a patent pool or IP arrangement, and can thus charge more royalties.

licensees will not be able to survive in the product markets, while patentees receive subsidies from the pool. Stating this, it seems clear that patent pool participants generally receive less royalty than the PAE in the ICT sector that utilizes SEPs under a standard, who stay away from becoming a member of the patent pool.[238] That is however a sign that there is a patent thicket or mosaic. An agreement on FRAND under a standard may also leave room for hard negotiations regarding what should constitute FRAND in the bilateral relationship. This is especially true when the firms are both patentees and licensees.[239] Thus, to create a collusive effect, the standard must be connected to a patent pool where the parties have agreed on a price.

Finally, there is less incentive to cheat in consortium since, first, cheating can be punished severely if the standard-setting procedure is a repeated game, and, secondly, there is no clear correlation between gaining extra profits by secretly investing in a *competing* technology for a firm within the consortium, since the members of the technology consortium still control the incumbent or prevailing technology standard.

There is a possibility of cheating by creating SEPs and not letting the consortium know about it, i.e. patent ambushing. As stated above, in network industries standard setting is pro-competitive and to have members of the consortium cheating may endanger the system as a whole, and prevent pro-competitive standard-setting collaborations. Therefore, to protect the standard-setting process, patent ambush must be considered a violation of competition law.

In other words, price and output cartels are strongly connected to static competition and are the prime anti-competitive tool used in markets where the innovation rate is low. For example, in the market for selling asphalt, it is evident that a cartel's control of the price or output is the prominent tool for inflating the price of the products and eliminating competition. However, in high-tech markets or other markets where the rate of innovation is much higher, and where the average life span of a product is perhaps six to twelve months, an agreement regarding price does not amount to the anti-competitive objective of entering an agreement with competitors. Hence, a more fruitful cooperation, in pursuit of anti-competitive aims, would be an agreement on the features of the future products, i.e. the technology. By knowing what will become the next product, the competitors will be able to reduce R&D investment,

---

[238] See the discussion in Judge Robart case between Microsoft v. Motorola discussed, infra Chapter 6.

[239] Doug Lichtman, 'Understanding the RAND Commitment', (2010) 47 *Houston Law Review*, 1023, 1045.

create barriers for entry, and thus dismantle competition. Hence, in 'high-tech' markets, a cartel regarding price has no real use, but a cartel deciding on which innovation will be the successful innovation would be the anti-competitive agreement of choice.

Notwithstanding the above, the collaborative work conducted in the technical committees in SDOs is necessary. To create the virtual infrastructure or interoperability, the standard-setting procedure needs to be an open venture where firms negotiate and collaborate on technology, while conducting unilateral R&D.[240] Such a procedure creates an agreement on technology, but other forms of procedure for creating the 'best' technology (such as competition) may create suboptimal results. Then a *de facto* technology will, due to network effects, be implemented. Such technology may often be attributed to one firm's first mover advantage and gain its monopoly position due to network effect. Such monopolies should, according to theory, be short-lived, but that is a risk that few legislators and competition authorities are willing to take.

On the other side of the spectrum, there may also be great benefits in all-industry inclusive collaborations for industries and markets that are network driven, and where society today is developing virtual infrastructures such as the World Wide Web or the different generation of telecommunication networks. Where it is clearly proven that the market and consumers will not agree to engage in a 'trial and error' pursuit of developing the product or technology, there must be ways to jointly develop a solution that is beneficial in creating markets. Here a 'trial and error' development implies that a *de facto* standard will develop to reflect the first mover's technology, and may be substandard compared to the standard that would evolve from a joint standard-setting procedure.

2.8 THE FUNCTIONS OF PATENTS

Today, a growing body of literature suggests that we would be far better off with less patent and copyright protection in terms of both duration and scope.[241] Perhaps the intellectual property systems we have are worse than not having any protection at all. According to Hovenkamp,

[240] Josef Drexl, 'Anti-competitive Stumbling Stones on the Way to a Cleaner World: Protecting Competition in Innovation without a Market', (2012) 8 *Journal of Competition Law & Economics*, 507, 534.

[241] Cf. Adam Jaffe and Josh Lerner, Innovation and its Discontents (Princeton University Press, 2004), and Susanne Scotchmer, *Innovation and Incentives* (MIT Press, 2004), 74 et seq.

this poor fit would rebut any presumption that competition policy should yield to intellectual property policy: 'We know pretty well what competition is and that it should be protected. However, we hardly know what intellectual property is and if it should be protected'.[242] Nevertheless, many legal scholars agree that the general problem of imperfections in the IP system is not an antitrust concern. The purpose of antitrust law is not to correct, *ex post*, flawed political process or to repair defective intellectual property right statutes.[243] In principle, according to these researchers, the intellectual property law system should create its own balance between the notion of property and competition for the creation of rights, while the expression or conduct of these rights may be judged under competition law. Others claim that intellectual property is not about property but about incentive to innovate.[244] Intellectual property should, thus, only be protected so far so that innovations are created.

It is clear that the political system has not been able to fix the intellectual property system. The recent *Orange-Book-Standard* case[245] in Germany and, most recently the US FTC *Google* settlement[246] mirror a development where 'fair competition' clearly trumps intellectual property rights. An infringer of an SEP may continue to infringe the SEP without having a contract with the patentee, if the requirements in these cases are fulfilled. That said, the *eBay* case[247] still shows that competition policy issues may be solved within intellectual property law, while taking fairness into consideration to an extent seldom seen in competition law cases.

---

[242] Herbert Hovenkamp, 'Signposts of Anti-competitive Exclusion: Restraints on Innovation and Economies of Scale', in Barry E. Hawk (ed), *International Antitrust Law & Policy 2006* (Juris Publ., Fordham Competition Law Institute, 2007), 413 et seq.

[243] Herbert Hovenkamp, 'Signposts of Anti-competitive Exclusion: Restraints on Innovation and Economies of Scale', in Barry E. Hawk (ed), *International Antitrust Law & Policy 2006* (Juris Publ., Fordham Competition Law Institute, 2007), 413 et seq.

[244] Rudolph J.R. Peritz, 'Competition within Intellectual Property Regimes – The Instance of Patent Rights', in Steven Anderman and Ariel Ezrahi (eds), *Forthcomming in Intellectual Property and Competition Law: New Frontiers* (Oxford University Press, 2013).

[245] See discussion, infra, Chapter 6.7.

[246] See discussion, infra, Chapter 6.7.3.

[247] See discussion, infra, Chapter 6.7.2.

Patents and competition are not inconsistent notions: they are complementary. Patents are the very foundation of competition.[248] Competition is based on the basic concept of a market where trade is taking place. Patents create markets by limiting information (knowledge) and by commercializing it, hence, giving the inventor certain specific rights to this information.[249] This enables trade to happen because it generates rivalry by limiting the free supply of some specific knowledge for the purpose of commercial use.[250] This creates incentives to innovate. The intellectual property system, by turning knowledge or information into a product, constitutes the framework for markets.[251]

Patents, and other intellectual property, as property, should not be dealt with differently from any other property.[252] Hence, intellectual property rights create a 'new' layer or dimension to competition. Competition will take place on the level of intellectual property rights.[253] Nevertheless, this

---

248 Hanns Ullrich, 'Legal Protection of Innovative Technologies: Property or Policy?', in Owe Granstrand (ed), *Economics, Law and Intellectual Property* (Springer Science+Business Media Dordrecht, 2003), 447 et seq.

249 According to some scholars, Kenneth Arrow was the first to conclude that patents and other intellectual property rights concern the markets for information. Cf. Kenneth Arrow, 'Economic Welfare and the Allocation of Resources for Invention', in R. Nelson (ed), *The Rate and Direction of Inventive Activity: Economic and Social Factors* (National Bureau of Economic Research, 1962), 609 et seq. The rights included within a patent are, e.g., a distribution right (including a rental right), a manufacturing right and a user right.

250 Hanns Ullrich, 'Legal Protection of Innovative Technologies: Property or Policy?', in Owe Granstrand (ed), *Economics, Law and Intellectual Property* (Springer Science+Business Media Dordrecht, 2003), 448 et seq. Participants to the FTC hearing regarding the interaction between competition law and intellectual property law support the proposal that granting a patent actually marks the beginning of commerce. When the US Supreme Court in Diamond v. Chakrabarty 447 U.S. 303 (1980) granted a patent for a live, human-made microorganism, it did create the fundamentals for the genetic engineering industry as such. See FTC, *To Promote Innovation: The Proper Balance of Competition and Patent Law and Policy* (FTC 2003), 21, with references.

251 Hanns Ullrich, 'Legal Protection of Innovative Technologies: Property or Policy?', in Owe Granstrand (ed), *Economics, Law and Intellectual Property* (Springer Science+Business Media Dordrecht, 2003), 450.

252 Ibid. 448 et seq.; See also the Department of Justice and the Federal Trade Commission, *Antitrust Guidelines For the Licensing of Intellectual Property* (1995), Appendix D, regard IP as basically similar to other property.

253 Cf. Hanns Ullrich, 'Intellectual Property, Access to Information, and Antitrust: Harmony, Disharmony, and International Harmonization', in Rochelle Dreyfuss et al. (eds), *Expanding Boundaries of Intellectual Property* Springer (Science+Business Media Dordrecht, 2001), 368 et seq.

does not imply that it should not be possible to eliminate or limit invalid or overly broad patents within the context of competition law, interpreted in the light of intellectual property law.[254] Art. 102 TFEU and, on the US side, doctrines under intellectual property law (cf. the injunction doctrine under the *eBay* case) should also be available in limited form to grant access to intellectual property rights based on, for example, the refusal to supply/access doctrines. Furthermore, it does not imply that competition law should be discouraged from protecting open standards or free knowledge as such, if that would enhance competition. Competition and intellectual property law even seem to be able to directly or indirectly limit the return of standard essential patents, even though, at least under US antitrust law, excessive pricing is not considered an antitrust violation. However, there still is a clear divide between the US and the EU application of competition law to intellectual property rights. As Peritz develops, the US Supreme Court in *Verizon*[255] has in effect gutted the essential facility doctrine as a basis for antitrust liability. Patent rights trump US antitrust policy, in fact, making it impossible to gain access to patents under competition law, while, also, the US courts seem indisposed to grant compulsory licenses under intellectual property law (however, the *effect* of the *eBay* precedent is similar to a compulsory licence scheme).[256]

The notion of an exclusive area for intellectual property not being accessible to competition law has been abandoned and should not be resurrected.[257] Intellectual property should be regarded as any other property, with the special or non-special limits and restrictions attached

---

[254] See C-457/10 AstraZeneca v. Commission, 6 December 2012, not yet published. For a US case regarding the validity of patents and competition law see FTC v. Actavis, Inc. 570 U.S. June 17, 2013. See also Schering-Plough Corp. v. Federal Trade Commission, 402 F.3d 1056 (11th Circ. 2005) stating that it is impossible to measure a patent settlement's effect on competition without deciding on the issue of the validity of the relevant patent.

[255] Verizon Communication Inc. v. The Law Offices of Curtis v. Trinko LLP, 124 S. Ct. 872 (2004).

[256] Rudolph J.R. Peritz, 'Competition within Intellectual Property Regimes – The Instance of Patent Rights', in Steven Anderman and Ariel Ezrahi (eds), in *Intellectual Property and Competition Law: New Frontiers* (Oxford University Press, 2013), 42.

[257] Cf. Hanns Ullrich, 'The Interaction between Competition Law and Intellectual Property Law – An Overview', in Claus Dieter Ehlermann and Isabela Atanasiu (eds), *European Competition Law Annual 2005: The Interaction between Competition Law and Intellectual Property Law* (Hart Publishing, 2007), xviii et seq. with references (see especially fn 2.)

to property. Competition law is one of these restrictions that limits intellectual property law. It may trump even core notions and rights within the bundle of rights making up, for example, a patent.

To some extent, the competition authorities on both sides of the Atlantic have adopted the notion that intellectual property is similar to physical products. For example, the US Licensing Guidelines stipulate this as a guiding principle.[258] Nevertheless, they do not enforce it. *Ebay,* and now the FTC's decision in *Google,* clearly represent a finding that the holder of intellectual property may not be able in certain cases to permanently stop an infringer. Similarly, under the *Orange-Book-Standard* case, the *Google* merger case, and probably soon under the *Google* settlement, the same rules will apply in Europe: permanent injunctions for SEPs are, in most cases, no longer available. This means that the SEPs are liabilities, mirroring fair 'taxes', but they do not resemble property because the right to exclude is missing.

In light of the above, the notion of making property out of knowledge as a way to promote innovation seems difficult to pin down. It is somewhat of a moving target. In some cases, the doctrine is upheld vigorously, while in other cases it is not. To create property rights out of innovations is different from other types of incentives for creating innovations. Normally three forms of system for creating incentives to innovate are discussed in the academy:[259] first, a system where the inventor is rewarded or granted funds either through public funds or private investment to invent; secondly, a liability system where the inventor is given a fair return for his invention but may not prevent the dissemination of knowledge;[260] thirdly, a property system, such as the

[258] US Department of Justice and the Federal Trade Commission, *Antitrust Guidelines for the Licensing of Intellectual Property*, 6 April 1995, http://www.justice.gov/atr/public/guidelines/0558.htm. Accessed 12 May 2013 (hereinafter *The IP Guidelines*, 2.

[259] See e.g., Paul David, 'Intellectual Property Institutions and the Panda's Thumb: Copyrights, and Trade Secrets in Economic Theory and History', in National Research Council (ed), *Global Dimensions of Intellectual Property Rights* (1993), 29 et seq. with references.

[260] Cf. Pamela Samuelson et al., 'A Manifesto Concerning the Legal Protection of Computer Programs', (1994) 94 *Columbia Law Review*, 2308; Hanns Ullrich, 'Legal Protection of Innovative Technologies: Property or Policy?', in Owe Granstrand (ed), *Economics, Law and Intellectual Property* (Springer Science+Business Media Dordrecht, 2003), 463; and Robert Merges, 'Institutions for Intellectual Property Transactions: The Case of Patent Pools', in Rochelle Dreyfuss et al. (eds), *Expanding Boundaries of Intellectual Property*, (2001), 128 et seq, 131 et seq. with reference to his own article: Robert Merges, 'Contracting

patent system, where the inventor is able, with some exemptions, to claim an exclusive right to the knowledge that is protected.

The advantages of the patent system compared to the other systems are several. Primarily, a patent system leaves the consumers or customers to value the invention. Thus, the reward for the knowledge created is given *ex post* based on its utility in competition. Innovation that does not facilitate utility will not be rewarded, and costs the inventor or investor. This might seem harsh but it constitutes a pre-eminent part of the innovation process, since scarce resources are thereby allocated most efficiently.[261]

Notwithstanding the above, the system also implies that the inventor may refuse access to the patented knowledge. Thus, it can make the knowledge scarce and therefore more costly. In comparison, the ability to price and, furthermore, to decide at all what to do with the patent is circumscribed in a liability system where the patentee may not refuse to issue licences.[262]

However, these essential principles, which underlie the basic idea that intellectual property law creates property, are not really applicable where there is a patent thicket, and then there is clear evidence of the problem of the anticommons. It is quite clear, for example, that if several patentees hold SEPs under a standard in the telecommunications industry, several of these SEPs do not represent 'inventive steps', but only tokens for bargaining when entering cross-licence agreements. Being essential, these rights may have stand-alone relevant markets, but these are actually active on hypothetical markets, which have been created by the decision to adopt a standard. Thus, the use of SEPs that do not represent an 'inventive step' should be limited under intellectual property law. The EU Commission may perhaps have taken a smart and bold step by stating that each SEP is a market in itself in the Google/Motorola merger case. Some technical issues may arise, such as how the relevant market for a patent pool filled with SEPs should be established when each SEP is a relevant technical market. How will this rule interface with excessive pricing and the refusal to license doctrines? Perhaps, the FTC struck a better balance when deciding that the acts complained of were unfair competition, not monopolization, in the Google FTC settlement. Under

---

into Liability Rules: Intellectual Property Rights and Collective Rights Organizations', (1996) 84 *California Law Review*, 1293.

261 Regarding the competitive process, see supra, under Chapter 5.

262 Cf. Hanns Ullrich, 'Legal Protection of Innovative Technologies: Property or Policy?', in Owe Granstrand (ed), *Economics, Law and Intellectual Property* (Springer Science+Business Media Dordrecht, 2003), 464.

the EU system, an unfairness doctrine would have implied that the Member States' patent laws would have facilitated the exemption based on fairness, and it would not have been placed under EU competition law. At the same time, competition law should be able to restrict patent law in any case where it can be shown that competition law has been violated.

We still have a problem with the SEPs that truly represent an inventive step. What about the situation where an R&D-only driven firm has conducted truly ground-breaking research under a standard, or come up with an innovation which will be the basis of a standard? What should be done in these situations, when it might be fair for the innovator to receive a return on its innovation that actually corresponds to the market penetration of the standard? Some commentators argue that these situations are so rare that we do not need to ponder this question. This is perhaps true, but should the incentive for innovators, be it large or small firms, really be entirely limited to FRAND in standard settled markets? Is that good competition and intellectual property law policy? If the patent system is a lottery system, there must be room for (a few) firms to win the grand prize. The illusion must be kept alive for the future inventors.

However, if the SEP represents a truly innovative step, and the patent in question represents value greater than FRAND, presumably the patentee may obtain the surplus my starting production and entering the relevant product market downstream. If the SEP really represents valuable knowledge, then that will materialize in the form of profits and market share on the product market. So the incentive with the recent development under the FRAND rules is actually to force firms to vertically develop.

Furthermore, from an intellectual property law perspective, collaborative R&D, technology standard setting and patent pools do not match the legal system of property creation. First, under these collaborations, firms may contractually convert their properties into liabilities, or rights to fair returns. Under the IP arrangements, technology-only firms may be forced to license on fair terms. Secondly, the consumers are not the masters of selecting successful innovations. Standards are provided for them with only a slight possibility of selection.

Patent law in both civil law and in common law countries seems to contain as a basic presumption that the inventor is a single person or entity and competes to attain patents.[263] Only under such a presumption may individual rivalry be introduced into the patent system. Two or more firms compete to obtain a patent right; when one of them succeeds, the others are correspondingly informed of that fact through the patent and then understand what they have to discover to obtain a separate patent, which further develops the product.

Nevertheless, it is evident that firms collaborate to create innovations and standards.[264] The interaction between joint R&D and intellectual property law is different from the interaction between individual R&D and intellectual property rights. Thus, the incentives within the patent system may be distorted if all or many firms are allowed to cooperate. If the research effort is a joint effort, the intellectual property rights only become a means for the parties within the joint R&D to distance them from the outside. Individual rivalry between the participants in the joint R&D is lost. Moreover, the rights only become a means for dividing ownership between the parties, transferring them into liability rules because they may not refuse the exploitation of the right by the other party.[265] So, it is of vital importance that joint R&D ventures do not become over-inclusive. This logic, taken to its conclusion, also indicates that the result of all-inclusive joint R&D should be exempted from the protection of intellectual property rights or that the return for the R&D collaborators should at least be limited to FRAND. In other words, there should be a remuneration formula akin to the result of the current legal regime under the large SDOs and their IP policies, which take into consideration whether the patents granted have been based on the collective effort of the consortium, or whether a firm has unilaterally achieved a breakthrough through innovation. In the former case the royalty should be limited to FRAND, in the later not.

---

[263] Under Swedish law there even seems to be confusion about the interaction between joint ownership of inventions/innovations and joint proprietors to patents, see Peter Adamsson et al., Lagarna inom Immaterialrätten (Norstedts Juridik, 2008), 209, compared to Malin Bronthron and Peter Danowsky, (ibid.), 20, who have different opinions whether the Act of Joint Ownership of 1904 is applicable to patents or not.

[264] Cf. Hanns Ullrich, 'Patent Pools: Approaching a Patent Law Problem via Competition Policy', in Claus-Dieter Ehlermann and Isabela Atanasiu (eds), *European Competition Law Annual 2005: The Interaction Between Competition Law and Intellectual Property Law* (Hart Publishing, 2007), 316 et seq.

[265] See Art 3 of the R&D block exemption. Notice also the extended exemption, i.e., no threshold for market power, seven years for joint exploitation of the result of the joint research if a new market is created.

2.9 FOLLOW-ON INNOVATION

> Overprotecting intellectual property is as harmful as under-protecting it. Creativity is impossible without a rich public domain. Nothing today, likely nothing since we tamed fire, is genuinely new: culture, like science and technology, grows by accretion ... Overprotection stifles the very creative force it's suppose to nurture.[266]

New innovations lean heavily on previous innovations.[267] If the 'old' innovations are public knowledge, the firm will access them without problems. However, if intellectual property rights protect the knowledge, the firm will need to enter a licensing contract allowing it access to the protected knowledge and the surrounding know-how.

Evidently, so-called follow-on innovations are very important for the general welfare.[268] Generally, breakthrough inventions do not generate wealth for the wider society to the extent that follow-on innovations do. Follow-on, incremental, innovations normally adapt the breakthrough invention to fit societal needs. Thus, they sell better and create more job opportunities and wealth. However, for follow-on innovations to appear, their creators need access to the knowledge embedded in breakthrough innovations and other innovations. For breakthrough innovations to occur, the theory is that the inventors must be able to prevent, or at least profit from, the follow-on innovations. Otherwise, the first inventor will not invest the needed capital and time to develop the inventions.

Amongst academics, there seems to be a general consensus that dissemination of knowledge, in order, among other things, to create

---

[266] Judge Kozinski in his dissent in White v. Samsung Electronics America Inc., 989 F2.d 1512, 1513 (9th Cir. 1993).

[267] This is especially true in the biotechnology industry, where broad innovations are more or less tools for finding new innovations. However, the same is true for computer software. If copyright protection extends to the reverse engineering of computer programmes or to interfaces, the copyright protection can effectively limit or stop a variety of related or follow-on technologies, similar to the case of patented research tools in the biotech industry. For example, could a copyright-protected spreadsheet programme clog the entire spreadsheet market?

[268] Cf. John Barton, 'Patent and Antitrust: A Rethinking in Light of Patent Breadth and Sequential Innovation', (1997) *Antitrust Law Journal* 449, 453. Cf. William Baumol, *The Free-Market Innovation Machine* (Princeton University Press, 2002), 120 et seq. There are several research findings on the economics of incremental and sequential innovation. Cf. e.g., Susanne Scotchmer, 'Standing on the Shoulders of Giants: Cumulative Research and the Patent Law', (1991) 5 *Journal of Economic Perspective*, 29.

follow-on innovations, is welfare enhancing. However, there is a difference in opinion regarding the extent to which the first inventors should be able to benefit from, and control, follow-on or imitative innovations, i.e. to control dissemination. Should other firms be able to use this information when, for example, conducting research without the direct permission of the first inventor? Intellectual property rights imply that society tries to limit 'spillover effects', i.e. the unintentional dissemination of knowledge, to enhance contractual transfer of technology. This limits the amount of free knowledge. It also limits competition, since only predetermined licensees gain access to knowledge and may contractually be controlled by the licensor. However, on the other hand, free access to inventions may, of course, limit the incentive and, in the end, create too few inventions.[269]

As discussed above, the openness of the GSM was not only a curse, it was also a blessing. The GSM was 'open', with relative few, and narrow, patents, compared to the US equivalent, CDMA, where Qualcomm held broad patents. This was an invitation for R&D intensive firms to enter the GSM technology. As Zhang describes, several firms joined the GSM R&D race. However, from the outset, the CDMA, from a technical aspect, was superior.[270]

Theoretically at least, under SSOs' IP Policies, under the extensive cross-license schemes regarding SEPs and non-SEPs and under patent pools, it is evident that holders of SEPs may force licensees to sublicense their technology, through outright or implied cross-license demands and grant-back clauses.[271] It should furthermore be noticed that it is almost impossible to invent something within the standardised technology (or a technology encompassed by a patent pool) without first being a licensee of the relevant SEPs.[272] The experimental or research exemptions stipulated under European and US patent laws are too narrow in scope to make it possible to research without a license. At least in the US, it only

---

269 Cf. Stephen Martin and John T. Scott, 'The Nature of Innovation Market Failure and the Design of Public Support for Private Innovation', (1999) 29 *Research Policy*, 437, 439 et seq. for a discussion regarding the appropriate level of public support for innovation.

270 Liguo Zhang, *Standardization and Patent Licensing in the European Union* (Oy Nord Print Ab 2012), 109 et seq. making reference to Graham Lynch, 'How GSM Beat CDMA', (2001) 105 *American Network*, 45.

271 Regarding the grant-back clause in the MPEG-2 pool, see, infra, Chapter 5.4.2.

272 RFID Business Review Letter dated 21 October 2008, http://www.usdoj.gov/atr/public/busreview/238429.htm, accessed 4 April 2007.

applies in non-profit situations.[273] In light of the fact that the great majority of all standardized technology today include US patents, and normally only global licenses are provided, any research must obey the US rules in this area.[274]

Grant back clauses prevent or at least limits the effect of follow-on innovations. These innovations are through the grant back clauses actually dispersed to all patentees holding SEPs under a standardised technology, if all SEP holders stipulate grant-back covenants in each other's license agreements. This implies that new innovations do not change the market share for the innovator in the product market since all its competitors get access to the same innovation.[275] Thus, a follow-on innovator would make a profit of grant back-licensing, but that profit is often secondary to the profit it makes on the product market. More dramatically, the inventor/licensee would not alter its market share on the product market in comparison to other licensees since any innovation would be made available to all competitors almost simultaneously. An innovator could not expand its market share at the expense of other licensees. Instead, it must grant them equal access to the innovation.[276] This, of course, limits the incentive to innovate a technology and makes it more difficult for manufacturing-only firms to increase their market share.

Traditionally, follow-on innovations have been seen primarily as an issue of intellectual property law, while covenant issues, for example, grant-back clauses, are competition law issues. Nonetheless, the recent decisions and rulings under EU competition law regarding access to SEPs and standard essential copyright (e.g. *IMS Health*) indicate that competition law may also govern the issue of follow on innovation. At least under EU competition law, under the *IMS Health* and *Magill* line of case law, suppressing progress in the development of technology and new products seems to be an independent harm to competition. Accessing

---

[273] Madey v. Duke University, 307 F.3d 1351 (Fed. Cir. 2002).

[274] Patent pools stipulating grant back clauses therefore constantly attract new patents, and can survive far beyond the statutory limitations of the original essential patents.

[275] There are several scholarly works on the economics of incremental and sequential innovation, however this synergy effect between grant-back clauses, patent pools and the interaction between technology and product markets seems to have been forgotten. Cf. William Tom and Joshua Newberg, 'Antitrust and Intellectual Property: From Separate Spheres to Unified Field', (1997) *Antitrust Law Journal*, 167, 183, fn. 87.

[276] United States v. General Electric et al 82 F. Supp. 753, 856 (1949).

SEPs to develop the technology may be a value to be protected under competition law.

2.10 INCENTIVE TO INNOVATE AND THE DISCOVERY PROCESS

It should be emphasized that the patent system to some extent works like a lottery.[277] The patent system actually infuses the invention process with rivalry and facilitates the introduction of the competition process by promising exclusivity.

Competition is a process of creating and selling new products and services, rather than a static situation focusing on efficiencies. Competition is therefore, on a grander scale, not for price or output, but for innovation. Joseph Schumpeter stated that the essential point to grasp is that, in dealing with capitalism, we are dealing with an evolutionary process of creative destruction. Capitalism is, by nature, a form or method of economic change and is never and can never be stationary.[278] The important part of capitalism is not how efficiently current structures are administrated, whereas the relevant issue for prosperous capitalism is to keep markets competitive by preserving the faculty of destroying old structures to create new ones. On the contrary, a system that at every point in time fully utilizes its possibilities to the best advantage may yet in the long run be inferior to a system that does so at no given point of time, because the latter's failure to do so may be a condition for the level or speed of long-run performance.[279]

The salient feature of the competition process is its unpredictability. No one knows everything. It is impossible to know the outcome of the process before it is completed. In other words, it is not feasible to know which goods are scarce, or even which things are goods, before they are exposed to competition, i.e. to presumptive consumers. According to Friedrich Hayek, were another system put in place, i.e. a system in which

---

[277] Fredric Scherer, 'The Innovation Lottery', in Rochelle Dreyfuss et al. (eds), *Expanding the Boundaries of Intellectual Property* (Oxford University Press, 2000), 4 et seq. Cf. Hanns Ullrich, 'Legal Protection of Innovative Technologies: Property or Policy?', in Owe Granstrand (ed), *Economics, Law and Intellectual Property* (Springer Science+Business Media Dordrecht, 2003), 463 et seq.

[278] Joseph Schumpeter, *Capitalism, Socialism and Democracy* (George Allen & Unwin, 1976 (first published in 1943)), 82.

[279] Ibid. 83 et seq.

some authority, or for that matter a cartel, decided which things were goods and their scarcity (price), it is quite evident that they would not reach, for society, as good a decision as a decentralized process of competition, which is based, in fact, on the will of the consumers themselves. Competition generally allocates resources better than authorities. Regarding price, this notion is commonly accepted. Neither a public authority nor a cartel should decide the price of a product. However, the same logic also works for what constitutes a product. Thus, should an authority or a cartel decide what constitutes an innovation, there will be products and services which will not be exposed to competition. Consequently, there will be material and human capital which will not be discovered and utilized in an efficient way.[280]

Accordingly, when viewing competition as a discovery process of creative destruction, the focus should not be on 'high' prices, profits or output. The prospect of supra-competitive profits is instead the incentive for the entrepreneur to push the process forward. What is important is that nothing impairs the entrepreneur from gaining access to the possibility of supra-competitive profit other than the result of other entrepreneurs trying to gain the same profit. Thus, the importance of competition in innovation is that access to markets is available. Exclusion seems to far exceed price collusion as creating anti-competitive harm.[281]

If firms were allowed to hamper the discovery process by excluding firms from markets and thereby making it, perhaps, in the short run, more transparent, and predictable, and hence enable the incumbent firms to become more efficient, progress may be reduced. For example, the members of a standard consortium may, in light of profit maximization incentives, be compelled to spend less in total on research compared to the situation in which the market was governed by competition. They are able jointly to guide the technology progress, calculate and predict the R&D of their competitors and they will adapt their individual decisions

---

[280] Cf. Friedrich A. Hayek, *New Studies in Philosophy, Politics, Economics, and the History* of Ideas (Routledge and K. Paul, 1978), 185 et seq. See also as a matter of fact, Communication from the Commission – Notice – Guidelines on the Application of Article 81(3) of the Treaty Official Journal C 101, 27.04.2004, 97-118 (hereinafter 81(3) Guidelines), para. 15, stating that collusion which falls within Art 81 (now Art. 101) includes agreements or concerted practices which eliminate or substantially reduce uncertainty between parties.

[281] For a different notion of efficiency, see Dominick Armentano, 'Competition Theory and the Market Economy', in Jack High and Wayne Gable (eds), *A Century of The Sherman Act: American Economic Opinion, 1890–1990* (George Mason University Press, 1992), 217 et seq.

accordingly.[282] A similar development will be detectable regarding production. Knowing the likely future output of your competitors, and what kind of research they do, may mean that no 'over-bidding' in either future output or research will take place.[283] This might be efficient in the short run, but would lessen innovation in the long run since it eliminates rivalry between the firms.

Depending on the size and the importance of the joint venture, investments outside the venture will also be adjusted. Contrary to theory, firms would seldom be set up, in-house or through a third party, a competing research effort to the joint venture because such an effort would cannibalize their own efforts and spending within the venture.[284]

Of course, the research done within the joint venture would in theory be efficient. No firms would have overlapping research findings, which would be the case if the firms did their research on their own. Knowing what the other firms invest in research, the firms could also prevent 'over-bidding' for innovations. No dual cost would be incurred and failures might be minimized. However, obviously, society would be robbed of new innovations and competition for new products would be eliminated by the cooperation, which in fact is an agreement to dismantle creative destruction or competition in innovation.

When comparing different concepts of competition it becomes evident that they differ in the very basic definition of the notion. The model of perfect competition, or industrial organization as a whole, is based on a notion that any agreement, conduct or unilateral act must have a detrimental effect on equilibrium in order to be anti-competitive. Thus, only agreements or conducts that reduce output or increase prices are detrimental to competition. On the contrary, the notion of competition as a discovery process is based on a definition of competition as trial and error, the repeated game or effort of two or more parties acting independently to secure the business of third parties by offering the most

---

[282] Cf. John T. Scott, 'Diversification versus Cooperation in R&D Investment', (1988) 9 *Managerial Decision Economics*, 173, 180 et seq. Regarding technology cartels or consortia, cf. William Baumol, *The Free-Market Innovation Machine* (Princeton University Press, 2002), 86 et seq.

[283] John T. Scott, 'Diversification versus Cooperation in R&D Investment', (1988) 9 *Managerial Decision Economics*, 173, 182 et seq.

[284] See, e.g., United States v. Penn-Olin Chemicals Co. 378 U.S. 158, 169 (1964). This seems somewhat in line with Arrow's discussion about what disincentives a monopolist may have to create new innovations: Kenneth Arrow, 'Economic Welfare and the Allocation of Resources for Invention', in R. Nelson (ed), *The Rate and Direction of Inventive Activity: Economic and Social Factors* (National Bureau of Economic Research, 1962), 620 et seq.

favourable terms.[285] Thus, if these parties agree to act dependently, for example, because they have decided on the technology, competition, in theory, is lost even though this could imply that output actually increases or prices fall.

2.11 DYNAMIC V. STATIC COMPETITION

As discussed above, establishing a basic or an interoperability standard is not a rigorous, scientific process driven by identifying the 'best' technology in a particular field. Rather, technology is included in a standard through a collaborative process, the standard-setting procedure.[286] It draws heavily on prior standards, and may involve evaluation of, or selection, or even compromise between competing technical approaches.[287]

Nonetheless, inclusion of competing technologies within a standard, as well as exclusion of competing technologies in the standard, may have anti-competitive effects. However, we have a problem with these effects. Shapiro stated that the conception of the standard-setting process when patents are involved is 'ex ante competition among different holders of intellectual property rights to get their property into the standard'.[288] It has been elegantly argued that 'competition' in economic analysis consists of two components.[289] Emphasized by Adam Smith, and typical of the dominant strain of economic thought of Hayek and Schumpeter, and during the eighteenth and nineteenth centuries, is 'an independent striving for patronage'.[290] The second component, characteristic of the semi-modern approach of the Chicago economic school, is the market

[285] Cf. Dominick Armentano, 'Competition Theory and the Market Economy', in Jack High and Wayne Gable (eds), *A Century of The Sherman Act: American Economic Opinion, 1890–1990* (George Mason University Press, 1992), 202 with references.

[286] Josef Drexl, 'Anti-competitive Stumbling Stones on the Way to a Cleaner World: Protecting Competition in Innovation without a Market', (2012) 8 *Journal of Competition Law & Economics*, 507, 534.

[287] Carl Shapiro, 'Navigating the Patent thicket: Cross Licenses, Patent Pools and Standard Setting', in Adam Jaffe, et al. (eds), Innovation Policy and the Economy 2001)., 142.

[288] Jonathan J Rubin, 'Patents, Antitrust, and Rivalry in Standard-Setting', (2007) 38 Rutgers Law Journal, 509, 520.

[289] Ibid.

[290] F.M. Scherer & David Ross, Industrial Market Structure and Economic Performance (Houghton Mifflin Company 1990), 15.

process by which resources are allocated toward supply or demand.[291] Under the Chicago school, the 'perfect competition model' is the framework for establishing anti-competitive conduct and effects based on the idea that efficiencies prevail over rivalry. Thus, from an economic perspective, the process of standard setting fails to fulfil this second technical definition of competition.[292] Standard-setting participants are not involved in a market where resources are allocated and there is no mechanism for finding the equilibrium of supply and demand, or any determination of the price of exchange.[293] Therefore, a standard-setting process involving the pre-standardization phase of the selection of patented (or non-patented) alternatives is more akin to a beauty contest for engineers, where a more precise term for the relationship between the contestants is 'rivalry'.[294] As a general rule, according to Scherer *et al*, the allocation of resources occurs elsewhere, outside the voluntary consensus process that characterizes standard-setting. In fact standard-setting disaggregates the two principal components of competition: rivalry and resource allocation.[295]

The issue is then whether competition law can still regulate rivalry without the existence of trade or a relevant market. Should all conduct before there is a relevant market be exempted under antitrust law, or may we still find conduct that we agree is not 'competition on the merits'? Both under US antitrust law and EU competition rules, regulating *ex ante* competition, as Shapiro terms it, is done through good governance rules. SSOs must be transparent, have open memberships etc. so as to take advantage of the safe harbours. Nonetheless, there are prohibited 'black' clauses still applicable in the regulation of R&D and SSO under US antitrust law and EU competition rules. These will be discussed infra in chapter 4. In next section the ideas of Arrow, Hayek and Schumpeter will be revisited, regarding whether anything they say should matter under competition law when regulating standard-setting, or whether the lack of relevant markets to evaluate or judge standard-setting and other conduct should exempt the same under antitrust law.

---

291 Ibid.

292 Jonathan J Rubin, 'Patents, Antitrust, and Rivalry in Standard-Setting', (2007) 38 Rutgers Law Journal, 509, 520.

293 Ibid.

294 Ibid. referring to F.M. Scherer & David Ross, Industrial Market Structure and Economic Performance (Houghton Mifflin Company 1990), 16.

295 Ibid.

2.12 MONOPOLY V. COMPETITION

There seems to be a consensus between the economists of today and the philosophers of yesterday that the greatest prosperity is not acquired by daily competition for the production and sale of the cheapest products, but instead by the daily development of new and improved products and services. Unfettered innovation far exceeds the potential gain from making markets more competitive by driving prices closer to marginal costs.[296] Thus, the creation and development of new products, for example computers or mobile phones, creates more wealth for both firms and societies than perfect price competition. An important consequence of this proposition is, from an antitrust policy perspective, that agreements restraining innovation can be significantly more harmful than even naked price-fixing cartels.

Notwithstanding these arguments, the US and EU policies in the field of joint R&D, standard setting and patent pooling may provocatively be claimed to exempt these from scrutiny or, at least, to be an experiment in Schumpeterian theory that monopolies or oligopolies create more innovations than systems governed by rivalry.[297]

In *The Theory of Economic Development* in 1934, Schumpeter envisioned technological development as the consequence of a never-ending cycle of entry by innovative firms, commercial application of new products or processes, the displacement of incumbent firms, to be followed by entry of a new generation of innovative firms. This model of innovative activity suggests that ease of entry will promote innovation and that small- and medium-sized enterprizes will most often be the vehicles of technological advance. The early Schumpeter did not rule out innovation by established firms, but he thought it an exceptional phenomenon:[298]

> The same is true if a new enterprise is started by a producer in the same industry and is connected with his previous production. This is by no means

---

[296] Phillip Areeda and Herbert Hovenkamp, *Antitrust Law – An Analysis of Antitrust Principles and Their Application* (Aspen Publishers, 2005), 113 with many references. See also Monopolkommission, *Huaptgutachten: Wettbewerbspolitik vor neuen Herausforderungen* (Nomos Baden-Baden, 1990), 342 et seq.

[297] Schumpeter did not express himself in such simple terms, cf. Joseph Schumpeter, Capitalism, Socialism and Democracy (George Allen & Unwin, 1976 (first published in 1943)), 82 et seq.

[298] Cf. Stephen Martin and John T. Scott, 'The Nature of Innovation Market Failure and the Design of Public Support for Private Innovation', (1999) 29 *Research Policy*, 437, 438.

> the rule; new enterprises are mostly founded by new men and the old businesses sink into insignificance.[299]

It is the later Schumpeter, displayed in *Capitalism, Socialism, and Democracy*, who maintains a higher profile in policy discussions and is frequently quoted. Here Schumpeter conceived technological progress as emanating from the industrial research laboratories of large firms that enjoyed positions of static market power. He argued that such firms would use their economic profits to finance risky, large-scale R&D activity that would simultaneously leave society better off, in a dynamic sense, and allow the firms to maintain positions of static product-market dominance:[300]

> As soon as we go into details and inquire into the individual items in which progress was most conspicuous, the trail leads not to the doors of those firms that work under conditions of comparatively free competition but precisely to the doors of the large concerns … and a shocking suspicion dawns upon us that big business may have had more to do with creating that standard of life than with keeping it down.[301]

Even though Schumpeter, in this section of his book, discussed the downfall of capitalism as an intermediate step to a wholly exclusive society for entrepreneurs where freedom is lost, he argues that large firms are able to innovate more efficiently than smaller firms. Such firms would be more capable of financing investment in innovation and could take advantage of such economies of scale as might exist in the R&D process. Because they typically produce a diversified range of products, they would be more likely to find commercially viable applications for new technological developments. He also viewed risk as an inherent aspect of research, development, and commercialization, and saw market power as a way of providing 'insurance' against such risk.[302] This second view suggests that the rate of technological advance will be greater where a few large firms dominate product markets.

---

[299] Cf. Joseph Schumpeter, *The Theory of Economic Development* (Harvard Univ. Press, 1934, reprinted 1961), 162.

[300] Stephen Martin and John T. Scott, 'The Nature of Innovation Market Failure and the Design of Public Support for Private Innovation', (1999) 29 *Research Policy* 437, 437 et seq.

[301] Joseph Schumpeter, *Capitalism, Socialism and Democracy* (George Allen & Unwin 1976 (first published in 1943)), 82.

[302] Cf. Stephen Martin and John T. Scott, 'The Nature of Innovation Market Failure and the Design of Public Support for Private Innovation', (1999) 29 *Research Policy*, 437, 437 et seq.

Today, the opposing view to Schumpeter is normally attributed to Kenneth Arrow. Arrow famously argued that a monopolist's incentive to innovate is less than that of a competing firm, due to the monopolist's disincentive to cannibalize his pre-existing monopoly. An *e contrario* interpretation of Arrow's viewpoint would be that firms not holding market power would have a greater incentive to innovate; thus, competition spurs innovation.[303]

Arrow does not take into consideration an evolutionary approach to competition or innovation: that, even though the new innovation is not in competition with the old innovation, innovation and competition can still be restricted since few large firms would possibly come up with fewer innovations than a multitude of firms.[304] A strict use of Hayek's notion of market competition and evolutionary economics would imply that monopolies are not pro-innovation even though their new hypothetical innovation would not cannibalize on old sales.[305] Since competitive markets logically hold more firms that monopolistic markets, and competition spurs development, there are more sources for innovations on competitive markets then on monopolistic markets.

In the end, it almost seems, generally stated, as if theories of industrial organization typically predict that innovation will decline with competition, while empirical work finds that it increases.[306] The early stages of the modern economic literature on R&D were largely devoted to sorting out the implications of these two divergent positions. The debate remains a lively one.[307] Some researchers argue the existence of an inverted-U between competition and innovation.[308] In the contemporary

---

303 Kenneth Arrow, 'Economic Welfare and the Allocation of Resources for Invention', in R. Nelson (ed), *The Rate and Direction of Inventive Activity: Economic and Social Factors* (National Bureau of Economic Research, 1962), 620 et seq.

304 Wolfgang Kerber, 'Competition, Innovation and Maintaining Diversity through Competition Law', in Josef Drexl, Wolfang Kerber, and R. Podszum (eds), *Economic Approaches to Competition Law: Foundation and Limitations* (Edward Elgar, 2010).

305 Ibid.

306 Philippe Aghion et al., 'Competition and Innovation: An Inverted-U relationship', (2005, May) *The Quarterly Journal of Economics* 701, 701, with many reference.

307 Stephen Martin and John T. Scott, 'The Nature of Innovation Market Failure and the Design of Public Support for Private Innovation', (1999) 29 *Research Policy*, 437, 437 et seq.

308 Philippe Aghion, et al., 'Competition and Innovation: An Inverted-U relationship', (2005, May) *The Quarterly Journal of Economics* 701.

debate, the concept of network effects has also been added. Some economists argue that monopoly power is desirable. They accept the drawbacks of monopoly power: that a proprietary standard is entailed and could be offset by the economic gains derived from large networks. Having a single standard results in a large network and is a desirable outcome. It is argued that the substantial investment that the development and promotion of standards require will only be undertaken if firms have the prospect of (true) monopoly profits.[309]

Carl Shapiro has recently dissected the innovation literature in detail. Interestingly, Shapiro points to the fact that competition is often not defined as rivalry in economic organization theory. Instead, it is defined as, for example, 'less product differentiation' in the theoretical research undertaken by many industrial economists. According to Shapiro, these models were never designed to study rivalry in developing new and improved products and processes, and they may help to understand why we have many brands of toothpaste, but not so much innovation in line with the definition preferred by Shapiro.[310] Shapiro also rejects a definition of competition as 'more imitation', and then, specifically, the work based on the existence of an inverted-U relationship between 'competition' and innovation. Shapiro argues that increased imitation implies reduced appropriability for the inventor. Likewise, 'less product differentiation' implies less appropriability. He concludes that if imitation is allowed under a judicial system, it reduces the incentive to innovate. That is no surprise. But that is not equivalent to the statement that increased competition would reduce innovation. The result of the research of Aghion *et al,* which Shapiro criticizes, in fact argues for implementing intellectual property protection, while it does not 'hit the bulls eye', according to Shapiro, when it comes to creating a competition policy that will increase innovation.[311]

Shapiro continues and reviews what the empirical evidence really tells us. He states that the inverted-U shaped relationship between market concentration and innovation has not held up well under empirical

---

[309] Susanne Scotchmer, *Innovation and Incentives* (MIT Press, 2004), 296 et seq., 289 et seq. See also Kamiel J. Koelman, 'An Exceptio Standardis: Do We Need an IP Exemption for Standards', (2006) 7 IIC, 823, 239 et seq., making reference to Scotchmer.

[310] Carl Shapiro, 'Competition and Innnovation: Did Arrow Hit the Bull's Eye?', in Josh Lerner and Scott Stern (eds), *The Rate & Direction of Economic Activity Revisited* (University of Chicago Press 2012), 371.

[311] Ibid. 373 et seq.

scrutiny, especially after correcting for industry differences in technological opportunity and for endogeneity of product market structure.[312] He, furthermore, refers to studies that show that there is a significant difference between 'more competition' and 'more imitation', while referring to several empirical researches and studies that support the general idea that competitive pressure spurs firms to innovate to get ahead of their rivals[313].

Shapiro is not alone in his critique of the theoretical research into the interface between innovation and competition.

Several economists have theorized about whether innovation is promoted or restricted by collaborative research, and about when collaborators are dominant enough to find that the diminishing competitive pressure reduces their incentive to innovate.[314] Some argue that, as long as the technical development is fast moving, joint R&D promotes social welfare irrespective of market power.[315] Others are more careful.[316] Industrial organization models often examine the interaction between

---

[312] Ibid. 380.

[313] Ibid. 381 et seq.

[314] Cf, e.g., Josh Lerner and Robert Merges, 'The Control of Technology Alliances: An Empirical Analysis of the Biotechnology Industry', (1998) 46 *Journal of Industrial Economics*, 125; Michael Katz, 'An Analysis of Cooperative Research and Development', (1986) 17 *Rand Journal of Economics*, 527; Thomas Jorde and David Teece, 'Innovation and Cooperation: Implications for Competition and Antitrust', (1990) 4 *Journal of Economic Perspectives*, 75; Thomas Jorde and David Teece, 'Rule of Reason Analysis of Horizontal Arrangements: Agreements Designed to Advance Innovation and Commercialize Technology', (1993) *Winter Antitrust Law Journal*, 579; Thomas Jorde and David Teece, 'Acceptable Cooperation among Competitors in the Face of Growing International Competition', (1989) *Antitrust Law Journal*, 529; and, generally, Gene Grossman and Carl Shapiro, 'Research Joint Ventures: An Antitrust Analysis', (1986) 2 *J. L. Econ. & Org.*, 315.

[315] See, e.g., Thomas Jorde and David Teece, 'Innovation and Cooperation: Implications for Competition and Antitrust', (1990) 4 *Journal of Economic Perspectives*, 75, 85 et seq.; Thomas Jorde and David Teece, 'Rule of Reason Analysis of Horizontal Arrangements: Agreements Designed to Advance Innovation and Commercialize Technology', (1993, Winter) *Antitrust Law Journal*, 579, 600 et seq. Thomas Jorde and David Teece, 'Acceptable Cooperation among Competitors in the Face of Growing International Competition', (1989) *Antitrust Law Journal*, 529, 543 et seq.

[316] See e.g., Josh Lerner and Robert Merges, 'The Control of Technology Alliances: An Empirical Analysis of the Biotechnology Industry', (1998) 46 *Journal of Industrial Economics*, 125, 132 et seq.; Michael Katz, 'An Analysis of Cooperative Research and Development', (1986) 17 *Rand Journal of Economics*, 527, 537 et seq.

product market competition, defined as imitation, and joint R&D. These models examine cost-reducing R&D and associated spill over, and the result varies depending on the amount of spill over. The amount of spill over indicates the amount of knowledge transferred between the two collaborators or to the general public, which does not necessarily concern the joint R&D venture but is beneficial for overall development. Part of this research indicates that collaborations among product market competitors are beneficial when the degree of product market competition is low, when there is R&D spillover in the absence of cooperation, when a high degree of sharing is technologically feasible, and when the agreement concerns basic research rather than development activities.[317]

Several scholars, however, have recently criticized these results and the modelling used by the theorists in this area. According to this criticism, the specialization within this area of economic research has become so great that it is difficult to see its usefulness. One economist analysing the economic research into joint R&D specifically concluded that, 'theoretical research … is largely self-contained activity, firmly insulated from vagaries of evidence about the subjects it analyses'.[318]

There is, however, empirical research into joint R&D collaboration agreements (and, thus, standard consortia) that have been notified under the NCRPA.[319] These studies suggest that there has been a dramatic increase in the number of partnerships during the last two decades. Donald Sigel assumes that the relaxation of antitrust enforcement caused this increase.[320] The research conducted identifies the industries in which joint collaboration regarding research and/or consortia-created standards is conducted and the possible market power of the participants. From these facts, academic research tries to conclude whether these joint ventures are pro-innovation or not. Interestingly, many observers conclude that it is difficult to find a clear answer from these empirical studies as to whether joint agreements on technology are welfare enhancing. The main issue is whether the welfare-enhancing spill over

---

[317] Michael Katz, 'An Analysis of Cooperative Research and Development', (1986) 17 *Rand Journal of Economics*, 527, 527, 542 et seq.

[318] Stephen Martin, 'The Evaluation of Strategic Research Partnerships', (2003) 15 *Tech. Analysis & Strategic MGMT*, 159, 159.

[319] For a review of the empirical research, see, generally, Donald Siegel, 'Data Requirements for Assessing the Private and Social returns of Strategic Research Partnerships: Analysis and Recommendations', (2003) *15 Tech. Analysis & Strategic MGMT*, 207.

[320] Ibid.

effects are substantial, something which is difficult to quantify and measure.[321]

2.13 WHY THE THEORIES OF DYNAMIC COMPETITION CANNOT BE APPLIED TO SOME STANDARD-SETTING PROCEDURES

It seems that there are clear arguments for why neither Schumpeter's theories of dynamic competition, nor Hayek's concept of competition as a discovery procedure, may apply for certain standard-setting processes.

It seems that their ideas of rivalry and competition are based on two assumptions. First, as Drexl states 'the functioning of Schumpeterean competition relies on particular assumptions that correspond to the economic assumptions of traditional patent law. In particular, it is assumed that each product competing in a relevant market is protected by a single, discrete patent. In this 'ideal world of Schumpeterean competition', patent-holding manufacturers only compete in product markets and use their patents as instruments for protecting investment in better products against imitation for free.[322] Second, both Schumpeter and Hayek assume that the market in question is a functioning market where different products/technologies may compete for the benefit of customers. In todays new economy neither of these assumptions will always hold true. Firstly, there is patent mosaic in certain markets where the relevant market is covered by several patents held by several firms, and, second, there are markets that may not in the long run bear competition between different solutions for a demand. Markets plagued by network effects will likely develop an omnipresent standard, while they may furthermore be considered natural monopolies or otherwise 'failed' markets where competition by substitute need to be sacrificed for benefits of competition by imitation.

---

[321] Cf. Suzanne E. Majewski, *How Do Consortia Organize Collaborative R&D? Evidence from the National Cooperative Research Act* (SSRN 2004), 3 et seq., 8 et seq. and 12 et seq., and, generally, Suzanne E. Majewski and Dean V. Williamson, *Endogenous Spillovers, Strategic Blocking, and the Design of Contracts in Collaborative R&D: Evidence from NCRA filings of R&D Joint Ventures* (SSRN 2002).

[322] Josef Drexl, 'Intellectual property in competition: How to promote dynamic competition as a goal' in Josef Drexl et al (eds), *More Common Ground For International Competition Law?* (Edward Elgar, 2011), 211 et seq.

As stated above, standards today reflect fundamentally different market solutions. Some standards represent infrastructure, others interoperability solutions, which will *de facto* create not only new downstream markets but possibly are the new 'structures' for these markets, while other standards reflect the joint effort of firms to sell products in existing relevant markets.

However, implementing an infrastructure standard implies selecting one solution for an industry or market. Such infrastructure standards are not developed through a 'trial and error' method in which the consumers are exposed to different solutions. Infrastructure standards are rather developed through a standard-setting process where the relevant parties negotiate and agree on the infrastructure while conducting R&D during the period the standard is developed. These standards should, therefore, not be considered the same kind of goods and services which Hayek, and for that matter, Schumpeter were discussing. In many ways, these authors discuss, even though in the abstract and theoretically, goods and services over which consumers and society *de facto* have a choice; where the market has not failed.[323] In other words, where the consumer may select a good, consume it or try it out, and purchase another good if the first good did not meet their satisfaction. Thus, where there is no market failure and the fundamental principles of Hayek, Schumpeter and Arrow work (i.e. that there is a choice), the innovation or competition process through 'trial and error' may be applied. However, in today's 'high-tech' industries, certain technologies, which are currently being standardized, are more akin to infrastructure than to goods. The reason for this is that these industries are often plagued by network effects and customers/consumers are locked in when the technology is selected. As Drexl states, '[m]arkets characterized by network effects will unavoidably migrate towards technological standards. The market position gained by the person controlling the standard based on IPRs is therefore to be considered a natural monopoly, which is economically superior to forced competition.'[324] Thus, society needs to agree, *de jure*, on, or accept, *de*

[323] See Drexl for a discussion regarding external market failure and competition law. Josef Drexl, 'Abuse of Dominance in Licensing and Refusal to License: A More Economic Approach to Competition by Imitation and to Competition by Substitution', in Claus-Dieter Ehlermann and Isabela Atanasiu (eds), *European Competition Law Annual 2005: The Interaction Between Competition Law and Intellectual Property Law* (Hart Publishing, 2007), 652 et seq.

[324] Josef Drexl, 'Intellectual property in competition: How to promote dynamic competition as a goal' in Josef Drexl et al (eds), *More Common Ground For International Competition Law?* (Edward Elgar, 2011), 212 et seq.

facto, a standard, and it is unlikely that the parties to these standards, including suppliers, content providers and consumers, will be able to back-track when the technology or standard is selected. They are, even though sometimes short-lived, still infrastructure or even natural monopolies. For these standards, competition as a process, unfortunately, does not suffice as a theoretical groundwork to select the best technology for society. First, a 'trial and error' method could be a very costly method for selecting infrastructure. Secondly, if these standards are not agreed upon, *de facto* standards due to network effects will soon emerge. However, *de facto* standards created through network effects and 'tipping' could very well be inferior to a *de jure* (i.a. agreed upon) standard. Due to the network effects and tipping, a 'trial and error' method would imply that a less good solution would possibly become the *de facto* standard. Instead, the parties must be allowed, under dynamic competition, to not only choose between available technologies, but also discuss the pros and cons of different technical solutions, while individually continuing to conduct R&D efforts. In these circumstances, the standard-setting process must be understood as a form of collective innovation and also collective competition, where the end result is a standard that meets the demands of society as a whole.[325] Under such standards there will, however, in certain circumstances only be room for competition by imitation, while competition by substitution will not suffice due the inherent market failure of creating one omnipresent standard.[326]

On the other hand, where there is room in the market for consumers to choose between different solutions to a problem, firms must have the ability to compete for the demand. Therefore, standards which represent products on a given technology market should be developed through a 'trial and error' method, i.e. exposed to consumers. In these markets, different forms of consortia may compete with different standards.

Thus, a standard such as the one reflecting 3G telecommunications technology should be dealt with differently under competition law, than 'product standards' such as a standard for cement, tyres, or a pump. Under competition law, we must tolerate more collaboration between

---

[325] Josef Drexl, 'Anti-competitive Stumbling Stones on the Way to a Cleaner World: Protecting Competition in Innovation without a Market', (2012) 8 *Journal of Competition Law & Economics*, 507, 534.

[326] Josef Drexl, 'Abuse of Dominance in Licensing and Refusal to License: A More Economic Approach to Competition by Imitation and to Competition by Substitution', in Claus-Dieter Ehlermann and Isabela Atanasiu (eds), *European Competition Law Annual 2005: The Interaction Between Competition Law and Intellectual Property Law* (Hart Publishing, 2007), 651 et seq.

competitors when creating *de jure* or *de facto* standards reflecting infrastructure or interoperability, e.g. the 3G standards, while opposing firms that try to inhibit or hold up such standards from being implemented properly. Thus, competition by imitation under such standards should be promoted, while competition by substitution will not be present.

On the other hand, a product standard on a market without network effects that reflects one technology, e.g. one sort of cement, out of several technologies in a market can create anti-competitive effects if that standard *de jure* or *de facto* excludes competition, inter alia by locking all participants into that standard. Where there are competing technologies on a relevant technology market, or where there are several future possible competing products, the collusive character of a consortium deciding on one standard should be the less tolerated if that were to imply that competition by substitution had been eliminated.

However, firms trying to 'hold up' technical solutions in such markets should be treated with more tolerance. Such 'hold-up' strategies may reflect competition on the merits, i.e. normal conduct in the dynamic competitive process. Thus, for these product standards, collaborations that decide what technology will be implemented in markets and society, without *de facto* protecting substitute competition in the downstream markets where different firms may present their different technology alternatives to consumers, should be scrutinized more carefully.[327] If technologies which represent different competing solutions/supplies for a given demand may coexist in a relevant market, the standardization agreement would benefit from a heightened antitrust scrutiny. Such a standardization agreement should in the best of worlds be a performance standard, and only stipulate that a technology should be the omnipresent product standard if considerable efficiencies can be attributed to such a decision.

That said, an additional problem is the patent thicket and the notion of anticommons. This may also create market failures. Certain product standards, especially in the IT sector, but also in parts of the telecom sector and the consumer electronics sector, are plagued with patent thicket problems. These technologies are still not to be considered infrastructure, or even technologies for interoperability, but they cannot be effectively utilized without the ability to access standard essential patents. Thus, certain markets and products will not emerge without

---

[327] For the notion of contestable markets, see Carl Shapiro, 'Competition and Innnovation: Did Arrow Hit the Bull's Eye?', in Josh Lerner & Scott Stern (eds), *The Rate & Direction of Economic Activity Revisted* (University of Chicago Press, 2012).

collective action under standards and patent pools to counteract the patent thicket. Standardization plays here a significant role in codifying fragmented technologies.[328] For these markets, IP arrangements under standard agreements and patent pools are necessary in order to create effective markets and competition in downstream markets.

The opposite holds true when discussing the standards and the markets connected thereto, which are not plagued by a patent thicket, i.e. product, and not performance, standards for, for example, cement and tyres. Such product standard collaborations, such as joint R&D in the pre-standardization phase, which create a common standard and IP arrangements under standards and patent pools, should be scrutinized more carefully to establish whether they exclude competition. If there is no network effect on the relevant market, an all-industry inclusive standard should benefit from a higher antitrust scrutiny.

In other words, as stated above, one could divide the anti-competitive effects of standards and their connected collaborations into four categories.

A.	B.	C.	D.
Basic/ Infrastructure technologies	Network/ Interoperability technologies	Patent thicket plagued Products/ technologies	Product standards

Collaborations and unilateral conduct under these four categories of technology deserve different antitrust treatments. An A standard is often derived from a completely open inclusive standard-setting process, where the organizations inherent collusive character must be tolerated, while access to membership and results are often granted and protected under competition law, since such standards create markets and competition. B network/interoperability standards should receive similar treatment but there should be a requirement that the network and tipping effects of the technology and standard are demand-driven rather that created by the suppliers of the standard (this issue is discussed infra in connection with the discussion of DVD technology and the HD-DVD v. Blu-Ray war).

On the other hand, under a D standard, an all-industry inclusive standard-setting effort would diminish competition. Design or product standards (D) are those standards that mirror a product, e.g. cement or a

[328] Liguo Zhang, *Standardization and Patent Licensing in the European Union* (Oy Nord Print Ab, 2012), 104 et seq.

specific tyre, which in fact is only a product among others on an existing or soon to emerge relevant market. Standards that identify one product as 'the standard' on such markets may cause exclusionary anti-competitive harm to competing solutions. The object behind such a standard can be collusion, to limit the number of products so to enable a price cartel. Exclusion of competing products or technologies might occur, or even be the aim of such a standard.[329]

For C standards, a decision on a standard may still be efficient. If there is a patent thicket that prevents relevant downstream product markets from materializing, or from working efficiently, a standard with connected IP arrangements or patent pools may very well be the tool that enables firms to penetrate the patent thicket. Thus, these forms of product or design standard could, under certain circumstances, be exempted from competition law.

2.14 CONCLUSION: DYNAMIC COMPETITION AND THE NEED FOR A MARKET?

In this chapter, the background economic theories to the notion of competition in innovations have been presented and discussed. The magnitude of the economic research and the theories regarding competition in innovations are immense, and the effort in this chapter is only to provide a platform for further analysis. Nonetheless, some interesting conclusions can be drawn. First, new virtual infrastructure, such as the internet and the telecommunications technologies are created by private firms and also *de facto* regulated under SDOs by private firms. Competition through 'trial and error' does not seem to be the best way to develop these technologies, since there can through 'infrastructure network effects' only be one solution. Here collective innovation must prevail. To create competition, access in downstream markets is important. It is in the downstream market that competition will, hopefully, flourish.

Secondly, private standard setting under official SDOs in network/interoperative-driven industries seems not to cause markets to be

---

[329] Several price cartels that have been analysed by the EU Commission and Justice Department have a standard-setting side by which the members of the cartel reduce the number of product choices on a market so as to enable the price cartel. See e.g. Joined cases 96 to 102, 104, 105, 108 and 110/82 IAZ and others v. Commission [1983] ECR 3369 and Commission Decision in Case IV/35.691, Pre-insulated Pipes, OJ L 24, 30.1.1999, p. 1.

monopolized by single firms but leads instead to oligopolies. This is quite significant. It implies that standard setting under SDOs may avoid or lessen the demand-driven network effects, even in the IT sector. Thus, these industries will no longer have short-lived temporary monopolies,[330] which could be the effect of *de facto* standard setting, i.e. network effects. Instead, large firms will negotiate and agree on the technology in technical committees under SDOs and, thus, create oligopolies. These oligopolies may survive longer, while still updating the standard regularly. Collusive effects from these collaborations may surface, while access is also important to prevent anti-competitive effects.

Thirdly, from a competition law perspective, patent thickets play a part for those products or technologies that are not active on markets with network effects. Fourthly, we do still have markets which do not display network effects or, for that matter, are not dampened by patent thickets, i.e. the regular markets of industrial economics. These markets may appear also in the ICT sector. Presumably, as this sector matures, and the innovation rate declines, these markets will start to proliferate. Therefore, standard setting in these markets must be analysed differently from the competition law perspective, and should benefit from a heightened competition law scrutiny. Actually, standard setting in this sort of industry has long been scrutinized under antitrust law for the anti-competitive effects created by these collaborations. This is due to the fact that anti-competitive effects are more easily detectable for this form of standard.

Schumpeter's, Hayek's and Arrow's theories on the innovation and competition process are relevant to a different degree depending on which technologies and markets are under scrutiny. However, competition law should not refrain from finding certain conduct to be a violation of 'competition on the merits', irrespectively of finding anti-competitive effects under the model of perfect competition, if the judge can conclude that the conduct would restrict or limit innovation. This antitrust tool should of course be handled with care, but to exempt all conduct undertaken before there is a relevant market would exempt too much potentially anti-competitive conduct especially in the 'new economy'.

---

[330] Carl Shapiro and Hal R. Varian, *Information Rules* (Harvard Business School Press, 1999), 173 et seq.

3. The governance and institutional structure of SSOs

3.1 INTRODUCTION

As Schepel has said, the widespread scholarly neglect of the phenomenon of standard development organizations (SDOs) and product standards in modern market regulation seems striking in the light of the preoccupation of scholars with a whole series of processes that standardization seems to exemplify. 'Against the backdrop of the process of globalisation and differentiation, the national state generally loses its centrality in the activity of government, and in this general landscape, SDOs, neither public nor private, nationally based but structurally locked into global frameworks, mediating between market demands and legal requirements, seem to flourish.'[1]

To take the regional SDO, *European Committee for Standardization* (CEN) as an example, it governs more than 14,000 standards, has 299 committees and 1,411 working groups, engaging more than 60,000 technical experts. Almost exclusively, these committees and working groups are staffed by representatives of undertakings even though the national standardization organizations in CEN, e.g. the Danish SDO DIS and the Swedish SDO SIS, formally have the ultimate voting power.[2]

Standardization bodies take on greater prominence at both the international and domestic level of government, not because of a general decision to cede power to the private sector, but rather because of a number of independent factors such as, presumably, markets, and because private actors can approach problems without the arbitrary territorial boundaries. Self-regulatory private or semi-private agencies can also normally command a higher degree of expertize and technical knowledge

[1] Harm Schepel, *The Constitution of Private Governance – Product Standards in the Regulation of Integrating Markets* (Hart, 2005), 11.

[2] CEN website: http://www.cen.eu/cen/AboutUs/Pages/default.aspx, accessed 6 May 2011.

of practice and innovatory possibilities than independent agencies, hence monitoring and enforcement costs are reduced.[3]

While private standards are on the rise, public standards are on the decline. Less formalized, faster, and more efficient than public institutions, members of SSOs are also less accountable for any wrongdoing. Private standards are, presumably, immune to the reach of e.g. Article 34 TFEU, or, for that matter, the US dormant commerce clause, while public standards, in cases like *Dassonville*[4] and *Keck,*[5] have been under attack for preventing the possibility of accessing markets.[6] Similar case law, may be found in the US under the dormant commerce clause: see *Minnesota v. Clover Leaf Creamary Co.*[7] and *Bibb v. Navajo Freight Lines*[8], but also with reference to private parties' handling of patents, under the patent misuse doctrine.

This chapter will initially discuss the *de jure* structure and governance rules of SDOs, generally: their by-laws, IP and antitrust policies or rules, and rules of engagement and participation. What internal and external rules exist to regulate these organizations, and what kind of regulations should govern the SSOs? As a background to that discussion, the deregulation of drafting public technical specifications to SSOs is discussed. The so-called New Approach, under which, the EU de-regulated technical specifications to SSOs is analysed. The conclusion is that while standards today originate from firms' reaction to the need for, for example, standards for interoperability (a bottom up approach), infrastructure standards, at least under the EU system, have originated historically from public efforts to regulate society.

Moreover, I will discuss the *de facto* structure and work of SDOs and standardization process. This is to show that there are business customs and norms which are not covered by the by-laws but still restrict and 'regulate' the stakeholders. The by-laws and IP policies are in fact rather

---

3 Harm Schepel, *The Constitution of Private Governance – Product Standards in the Regulation of Integrating Markets (*Hart, 2005), 11 et seq.

4 Case 8/74 Dassonville [1974] ECR 837.

5 Joined cases C-267 and 268/91 Keck and Mithourd [1993] ECR I-6097.

6 It should be mentioned that in an isolated obiter dictum in *Dansk Supermarked*, the ECJ held in 1981 that 'it is impossible in any circumstances for agreements between individuals to derogate from the mandatory provisions of the Treaty on the free movement of goods.' Case 58/80 Dansk Supermarked v. Imerco [1980] ECR 181, para 17. Even though the ECJ thereafter ignored this statement, it gives support for a general principle under free trade rules also to apply them to standard agreements.

7 Minnesota v. Clover Leaf Creamary Co, 449 U.S. 456 (1981).

8 Bibb v. Navajo Freight Lines, 359 U.S. 520 (1959).

rudimentary legal systems and must be ‘fleshed out’ with the often strong business culture that has been developed in certain industries and under certain SSOs to protect and regulate the integrity of the standard-setting procedure. It should also be remembered that pre-standardization consortia is common in industries or technologies where there are patent thickets and where patent rights are held by several different firms. These consortia are important and it is clear that SDOs would like to collaborate with them. The global ISO, for example, explicitly states that its goal is to increase and deepen its cooperation with informal consortia, if it adds value or increases the efficiency of developing standards.[9] Thus, the consortia must also be taken into consideration when analysing the regulation of standard-setting procedure.

3.2 THE *DE JURE* INSTITUTIONAL STRUCTURE OF SDOS

3.2.1 The Guiding Principles of WTO

The guiding principles for standard setting stipulated in connection with the Agreement on Technical Barriers to Trade have had an important influence on not only the international standard-setting organizations but also on the European and US standard-setting organizations.[10] The principles are

---

[9] ISO Strategic Plan 2011-2015: Solutions to Global Changes, 8. http://www.iso.org/iso/iso_strategic_plan_2011-2015.pdf. Accessed 24 February 2014. Discussed in Justus Baron and Tim Pohlmann, ‘Who Cooperates in Standard Consortia – Rivals or Complementors’ (2013) 9 *Journal of Competition Law & Economics*, 905, 907.

[10] See Articles 2, 5 and Annexes III to the WTO/TBT Agreement and thereto connected decisions. Annex III of the TBT Agreement is the Code of Good Practice for the Preparation, Adoption and Application of Standards, which is known as the WTO Code of Good Practice. In accepting the TBT Agreement, WTO Members agree to ensure that their central government standardizing bodies accept and comply with this Code of Good Practice and agree also to take reasonable measures to ensure that local government, non-governmental and regional standardizing bodies do the same. The Code is therefore open to acceptance by all such bodies. In addition, the TBT Agreement is reviewed annually and triennially and the reviews become important interpretations of the document. Under the TBT, decisions and recommendations setting out criteria defining the principles of an international standards developing organization have been issued. These decisions/principles came out of the Second Triennial Review (23 May 2002) and specifie to the WTO-TBT criteria for an ‘international standards developing organization’ are: transparency; openness; impartiality;

developed in quite some detail but are divided into: (i) transparency; (ii) openness; (iii) impartiality and consensus; (iv) effectiveness and relevance; (v) coherence; (vi) development dimension.

The WTO principles have guided both US and EU regulation of standards. Under EU law, the recently enacted (October 2012) Regulation on European Standardization uses these principles when stipulating requirements for the indentification of consortia-derived standards to be used for ICT technical specification which may be referred to in public procurement procedures.[11] The regulation under US law, e.g. the National Technology Transfer and Advancement Act of 1995 (NTTAA), does not stipulate similar requirements for consortia-created standards. Instead, it states that federal agencies, with respect to their use of, and participation in, the development of voluntary consensus standards, should adopt them wherever possible, in lieu of creating proprietary, non-consensus standards.

Volentary standards in the USA are developed by standard-setting bodies accredited by the American National Standard Institute (ANSI).

ANSI does not write standards. Instead, the Institute accredits standards developers that will establish consensus standards among interested parties. In 1998, ANSI entered into a memorandum of understanding with NIST (National Institute of Standard and Technology). In it ANSI pledged to publish American national standards of interest and consensus, and to meet the principles of openness, due process, balance of interests and consensus, and to meet the obligations of the WTO Code of Good Practice.[12]

Also, the more official European standard-setting organizations follow the WTO principles. While the EU Regulation on European Standardization is the first EU law that accredits consortia-created standards, the European system had up until then mainly been driven by the European

effectiveness; relevance; consensus; performance-based; coherence; due process and technical assistance. See WTO, Decisions and Recommendations adopted by the WTO Committee on Technical Barriers to Trade since 1 January 1995, G7TBT/1/Rev.10, 46. See http://ec.europa.eu/enterprise/tbt/index.cfm?fuseaction=library.viewLibrary&section_id=6&dspLang=EN Accessed 6 September 2012.

[11] Regulation (EU) No 1025/2012 of the European Parliament and of the Council of the 25 October 2012 on European standardisation, OJ L 316 of 14 November 2012., Art 13 and Annex II.

[12] See ISO website http://www.iso.org/iso/ru/home/about/iso_members/iso_member_body.htm?member_id=2188. Accessed 4 february 2014.

Standard Setting Organizations (ESOs): European Standardization Committee (CEN); the European Committee for Electrotechnical Standardization (CENELEC); and European Telecommunications Standards Institute (ETSI), and they will be discussed below.

3.2.2 The European System

The difference between standard-setting organizations is significant. Not only is there a difference between the hierarchical structure of the European SSOs compared to their US counterparts, but also the organizational structure of the SSOs varies within Europe and the US. Some standard-setting bodies are government organizations, while others are private. In some Member States, the standard-setting is centralized to one official institution, while other Member States have sector-specific standard organizations.

The general perception, as reflected in the discussion above, is that, in the US, the standard-setting organization are mostly private sector specific organizations, while in Europe the general model consisted of, and to some extent still consists of, centralized national private non-profit associations enjoying public recognition and (monopoly) power, elaborating and promulgating standards according to a rather homogeneous and harmonized procedure.[13]

BOX 3.1

The European Standardization Committee (CEN) is in a somewhat central position in the landscape of European standard-setting. The CEN was established in 1961 by several national standards bodies and acts as an umbrella organization. CEN's national members are the National Standards Organizations (NSOs) of the 28 European Union countries and the three countries of the European Free Trade Association (Iceland, Norway and Switzerland). There is one member per country. The European Commission is a counsellor to CEN and there are also a number of associated members, i.e. representatives of

[13] Harm Schepel, *The Constitution of Private Governance – Product Standards in the Regulation of Integrating Markets* (Hart, 2005), 101.

organizations at European level, e.g. the European Environmental Citizens Organization for Standardization (ECOS).[14]

CEN national members have exclusive voting rights in the general assembly and on the administrative board of CEN, and they provide delegations to the technical board of CEN. It is the responsibility of the CEN national members to implement European standards as national standards. The NSOs distribute the implemented European standard and have to resolve any conflicting national standards.[15] Thus, there is a harmonization effort of standards under the CEN and under the semi-private/public regulatory scheme, since under the so-called New Approach, CEN standards have not only precedence and primacy over national standards, they are also recognized in the EU as European standards.[16]

The New Approach is a regulatory technique and strategy that was first laid down by the Council Resolution of 1985 on the New Approach to technical harmonization and standardization.[17] It was the starting point of a de-regulation and 'outsourcing' for creating product requirements to SDOs. There has been a lively and extended debate about the democratic deficit created by the New Approach. Consumer organizations and SMEs have historically, for example, not been engaged to a satisfactory level.[18] This will possibly change in the future because the Regulation on European standardization implements a system where consumer groups will get union financing to take part in standard-setting activities.

The New Approach established the following principles: (i) legislative harmonization in the EU is limited to essential requirements that products and services placed on the Community market must meet, if they are to benefit from free movement within the Community; (ii) the technical specifications of products meeting the essential requirements set out in the directives are laid down in harmonized standards drafted and

---

14 For further details see CEN website: http://www.cen.eu/cen/pages/faq.aspx, accessed 9 May 2009.

15 CEN/CENELEC Internal Regulation part 1 et seq.

16 Ibid.

17 Council Resolution (85/C 136/01) – OJ C 136 of 4 June 1985.

18 Bent Ole Gram Mortensen, *Standardisering og certifiering som instrument på miljøområdet* (JØF 1999), 82 et seq.

produced by organizations competent in standard-setting. Application of harmonized or other standards remains voluntary, and the manufacturer may always apply other technical specifications to meet the requirements; and (iii) products manufactured in compliance with harmonized standards benefit from a presumption of conformity with the corresponding essential requirements.[19]

Harmonized standards are a specific category amongst standards. They ensure that products meet the essential requirements of harmonized EU legislation. The terminology used in New Approach directives is a legal qualification of technical specifications existing as 'European standards', but to which a special meaning has been given to harmonized standards by the relevant directives.[20] The number of European standards that are harmonized has increased in two decades from 3.55 percent to 20 percent in 2009. The other European standards are adopted outside EU legislation on the initiative of undertakings or other stakeholders.[21] The New Approach was updated in 2008 with a number of regulations, but without altering these basic premises.[22]

The Commission formally requests the European standards organizations (e.g. CEN) to present European standards by issuing a mandate.[23] The European Standards Organizations (ESOs) will formally take a position on a mandate from the

[19] EU Commission, 'Guide to the Implementation of Directives based on the New Approach and the Global Approach 2000' p. 27 et seq.: http://ec.europa.eu/enterprise/policies/single-market-goods/files/blue-guide/guidepublic_en.pdf [accessed 2 August 2011.] In addition, it should also be mentioned that public procurement often requires or stipulates that the bidders adhere to the European standard applicable. See also Directive 98/34/EC.

[20] Ibid.

[21] Commission Staff Working Paper, 'Executive Summery of the Impact Assessment', SEC(2011) 672 final, 1 et seq.

[22] Regulation 764/2008 of 9 July 2008 'Laying down Procedures Relating to the Application of Certain National Technical Rules to Products Lawfully Marketed in Another Member State' OJ L 218, 13 August 2013, 21 et seq.; Regulation No 765/2008 of 9 July 2008 setting out the requirements for accreditation and market surveillance relating to the marketing of products, OJ L 218, 13 August 2008, 30 et seq. and Decision 768/2008 of 9 July 2008 on a 'Common Framework for the Marketing of Products' OJ L 218, 13 August 2008, 82 et seq.

[23] Prior to this the Commission consults the committee established under Directive 98/34/EC, and, in some cases, the sectoral committee set up under the

Commission in conformity with their internal regulations. Acceptance of the mandate and the subsequent work programme of these organizations initiates the stand-still period as provided for in their internal regulations and in Directive 98/34/EC and Regulation 1025/2013.[24] The stand-still period was implemented due to the 'standard war' about colour TV in the 1960s.[25] Thus, formally, the Commission may initiate the process, but creating a European standard is an SDO matter and the initiative comes normally from the industry.

CEN is one of the three European Standards Organizations (ESOs) with the primary objective of removing trade barriers within the EU. However, in order to promote European standards in a globalized world, CEN cooperates more and more with CENELEC, the European Committee for Electrotechnical Standardization, and ETSI. CENELEC and is responsible for standardization in the electrotechnical engineering field. It was created in 1973 as a result of the merger of two previous European organizations: CENELCOM and CENEL.[26]

CENELEC's set-up is similar to that of CEN and they share the same internal regulations for governance and for drafting and implementing standards.[27] CEN and CENELEC are recognized under Directive 98/34/EC (see Article 1(7) and annex I of this Directive) as standard-setting bodies, e.g. ESOs.

The standard-setting process in the EU is governed by the new Regulation on European Standardization. It stipulates the rules for the standard-setting process for the ESOs. It focuses on (i) transparency of the work programme; (ii) transparency of the standards; (iii) stakeholders' participation, with specific focus on SMEs, consumer groups and public authorities; and (iv) consensus. There are also specific rules

---

directive in question. Reaching consensus within the committee under directive 98/34/EC implies wide consultation of sectoral authorities at national level. Thus, the mandate provides a strong indication of the expectations of public authorities.

[24] Ibid.

[25] Marc T. Austin and Helen V. Milner, 'Strategies of European Standardization', (2001) 8 *Journal of European Public Policy*, 411, 423.

[26] CENELEL website. http://www.cenelec.eu/aboutcenelec/whoweare/index.html, accessed 9 May 2009.

[27] CEN/CENELEC, Internal Regulation part 1 et seq.

concerning harmonized standards, which may be objected to, rescrutinized and revised.

Nonetheless, in comparison with the requirements for indentifying ICT technical specifications, i.e. standards derived from consortia in the ICT sector (cf. Annex II Regulation of 1025/2013), the rules governing ESOs are more limited. Moreover, these rules seem somewhat restrictive in comparison to the WTO principles for standardization. In fact, the EU seems to lean on the fact that ESOs have developed by-laws reflecting these principles and rules.

The Regulation on European Standardization stipulates a pathway to establish consortia-developed standards in the ICT sector. Such standards may be indentified for use (referred to) in public procurement procedures under Art 13 of the Regulation. The requirements for indentifying of ICT technical specifications in Annex II of the EU Regulation of European Standardization for public procurement procedures may be summarized as follows:

Process:

> *Openness*: The standardisation development process occurs within a non-profit making organisation on the basis of open decision making accessible to all interested parties. The open standardisation process is driven by the relevant stakeholder categories and reflects user requirements.
>
> *Consensus*: The standardisation process is collaborative and consensus based. The process does not favour any particular stakeholder.
>
> *Balance*: The standardisation process is accessible at any stage of development and decision making to relevant stakeholders. Participation of all interested categories of stakeholders is sought with a view to achieving balance.
>
> *Transparency*: The standardisation process is accessible to all interested parties and all information concerning technical discussions and decision making is archived and identified. Information on (new) standardisation activities is widely announced through suitable and accessible means. Consideration and response is given to comments by interested parties.[28]

---

[28] Commission White Paper 'Modernising ICT Standardisation in the EU – The Way Forward', COM(2009) 324 final, 9.

Standards:

> *Maintenance*: Ongoing support and maintenance of published standards, including swift adaptation to new developments which prove their necessity, efficiency and interoperability, is guaranteed over a long period.
>
> *Availability*: Resulting standards are publicly available for implementation and use at reasonable terms (including for a reasonable fee or free of charge).
>
> *Intellectual property rights*: IP essential to the implementation of standards is licensed to applicants on a (fair) reasonable and non-discriminatory basis ((F)RAND), which includes, at the discretion of the IPR holder, licensing essential IP without compensation.
>
> *Relevance*: The standard is effective and relevant. Standards need to respond to market needs and regulatory requirements, especially when those requirements are expressed in standardisation mandates.
>
> *Neutrality and stability*: Standards should whenever possible be performance oriented rather than based on design or descriptive characteristics. They should not distort the (global) market and should maintain the capacity for implementers to develop competition and innovation based upon them. Additionally, and in order to enhance their stability, standards should be based on advanced scientific and technological developments.
>
> *Quality*: The quality and level of detail are sufficient to permit the development of a variety of competing implementations of interoperable products and services. Standardised interfaces are not hidden or controlled by anyone other than standard setting organisations.

These requirements or principles are difficult to interpret and research shows that the notion of 'openness' for example may be interpreted very differently by SSOs and SDOs alike. Some organizations welcome everyone: inter alia, SSOs such as W3C and IETF, while having a more closed final voting process. Other organizations perhaps only allow official national SDOs to be members, while have a formal open voting procedure.[29]

European standards are, inside the SDOs, developed by technical committees. These technical committees are interesting from the point of view of competition law. They receive and come up with proposals, and decide whether to pursue a standard. Its members – the national standard-setting organizations (NSOs) of the EU and EFTA countries, among others – operate the technical committees that draw up the

[29] Marcus Glader, 'Open Standards: Public Policy Aspects and Competition Law Requirements', (2010) 6 *European Competition Journal*, 611, 622 et seq.

standards. The CEN-CENELEC Management Centre (CCMC) in Brussels manages and coordinates this system for the CEN-CENELEC technical committees. Meetings of CEN or CENELEC technical committees are attended by delegations from those NSOs that are interested in the subject matter being discussed. The national delegations comprise experts who may come from a wide range of technical backgrounds. However, mostly these persons are from the relevant or concerned industry. In other words, even though the make-up of the delegations is decided by each NSO, representatives of the relevant industry are often on the delegations and, thus, the active *de facto* members of the technical committees.[30]

The working groups, which are responsible to the technical committees for the actual drafting of the work, are often comprised even more of experts from the industry in the field of standardization under consideration.[31] These groups are often formed by private undertakings and staffed by technical experts.

Thus, the members of the CEN are not undertakings but NSOs. However, the standards are developed by technical committees and, more specifically, by working groups comprising of representatives of volunteers from the industry. These delegations and working groups comprise representatives of the undertakings interested in the standardization, but they are officially appointed by the NSOs.[32]

In principle, anyone can propose a standard to an NSO, or directly to a technical committee. It is the relevant technical committee that makes the decision to adopt a proposal and initiate drafting work in a working group.[33] The work in the technical committees is overseen by a chairman appointed by the technical board and the chairman must maintain strict impartiality and divest him- or herself of a national point of view. The chairman must do anything possible to obtain a unanimously decision, or at least consensus among the members in the technical committee, regarding the proposed technical standard.

---

[30] Ibid.

[31] Ibid.

[32] CEN/CENELEC Internal Regulation part 2, para. 3.4.2. Members of an associated organization also may be appointed to working groups.

[33] If the proposal is for a new field of standardization activity, a decision is made by the CEN Technical Board first. The participants in the Technical Board include all National Standards Bodies and all standardization partners such as consumers, trade unions, European industry and the counselors, namely the European Commission (EC) and European Free Trade Association Secretariat (EFTA). See CEN/CENELEC Internal Regulation part 1 et seq.

CEN adheres to the ISO definition of consensus as general agreement characterized by the absence of sustained opposition to substantial issues by an important part of the interests concerned and by a process that involves seeking to take into account the views of all the parties concerned and to reconcile any conflicting arguments.[34] In the end there should be a right to appeal the decisions. Once the draft of a European standard is prepared, it is released for public comment, a process known as the 'CEN Enquiry'. During this stage, everyone who has an interest (e.g. manufacturers, public authorities, consumers) may comment on the draft. Taking into account the comments resulting from the CEN Enquiry, a final version is drafted which is then submitted to the members for a weighted formal vote. Acceptance by at least 71 per cent is needed for the adoption of a European standard. The standard can thereafter be adopted by the EU under the New Approach.

In ETSI, on the other hand, undertakings can also become official members and vote directly on the proposed standard. Moreover, depending on global turnover, the voting power is weighted in ETSI, where the largest undertakings' votes may have up to 45 times more weight than a vote from the smallest members (e.g. SMEs, consumer organisations or universities). Hence, ETSI consists of large firms in the ICT (Information and Communications Technologies) sector. Amongst ETSI's present members are the largest undertakings in the ICT sector as well as many government and regulatory bodies. ETSI has more than 700 members drawn from 62 countries and has been closely connected to the development of mobile telecommunication networks in Europe, e.g. GSM, 3G and now 4G mobile telephone networks.[35]

Like most standards organizations, much of ETSI's work is carried out in committees and working groups composed of technical experts drawn from ETSI's member companies and organizations. In the ETSI terminology, these committees are referred to as technical bodies. For certain urgent items of work, ETSI may also convene a Specialist Task Force (STF). STFs are small groups of technical experts, usually seconded from ETSI members, which work intensively over a period of time, typically a few months, to accelerate the drafting work. Each STF reports to an ETSI technical body.[36]

---

34 CEN/CENELEC Internal Regulation part 2, part 3.2.3.3, and part 6 et seq.

35 Cf. ETSI website: http://www.etsi.org/about, accessed 11 July 2011.

36 ETSI, 'How We Work, see http://www.etsi.org/WebSite/AboutETSI/HowWeWork/Howwework.aspx, accessed 20 October 2011.

3.2.3 The European Member States SDOs

The Europeanization of standardization has had significant effects on national standard bodies and the way standards are created and defined. The New Approach strengthened the position of the European standard-setting bodies, such as CEN, but it also strengthened the selected national standard-setting bodies (NSOs) connected to CEN in relation to other standardizing bodies.

The system effectively gives the CEN, CENELEC and ETSI network somewhat of a monopoly on creating European standards that has procedure and primacy over national measurers. Also, for private parties, these bodies become the focal point for their effort to affect the development of the technology agreed upon.

In almost every member state there is an equivalent national organization to CEN, which not only incorporates standards on the national level, but also acts as an entrance for private parties wishing to take part in the standard-setting procedure within the relevant ESO. These private parties gain access to become representatives for the national standard-setting organizations and to be part of the delegation to the CEN, CENELEC or ETSI.

Thus, there are now, in several Member States, national organizations equivalent to CEN, CENELEC and ETSI.

On the other hand, CEN, CENELEC and ETSI are the regional mirror bodies to their international counterparts, i.e. ISO (the International Organization for Standardization), IEC (the International Electrotechnical Commission) and ITU-T and ITU-R (the International Telecommunication Union, telecommunication standardization sector and radio-communication sector), respectively. These organizations have entered into cooperation agreements with each other.[37] These agreements seem primarily to imply that the ESOs will adopt international standards when applicable.[38] According to the Vienna agreement, CEN needs to consider existing ISO standards or working drafts and, if no such standard is

[37] The Vienna agreement between CEN and ISO; the Dresden agreement between CENELEC and IEC; and the MoU Telecommunication sector and Radio-communication sector agreements between ETSI and ITU-T and ITU-R, respectively.

[38] It seems that EU Member States started to develop mirror organizations to CEN, CENELEC and ETSI, even though the differences are considerable between the different Member States. For further information see Harm Schepel, *The Constitution of Private Governance – Product Standards in the Regulation of Integrating Markets* (Hart, 2005), p. 111 et seq.

available, needs to offer to conduct work to develop the standard to ISO, i.e. to develop a standard that is mutually acceptable.[39]

3.2.4 The International Standard-Setting Organizations

Like CEN, CENELEC and ETSI, ISO and IEC and ITU-T are organized as semi-public/semi-private organizations. ISO, CEN's mirror organization, is the world's largest developer of international standards and is (also) a network of the national standards institutes of 160 countries, one member per country, with its head-quarters, which coordinates the system, in Geneva, Switzerland. Thus, the general national standard institutes are members of the ISO: SFS, SIS ANSI, etc. CEN is not a member of ISO but, as noted above, CEN and ISO collaborate under the Vienna agreement of 1991.[40] CEN has no voting power, and, formally, merely implements an adopted ISO standard.

ISO standards are likewise developed by technical committees, subcommittees or project committees comprising experts from the industrial, technical and business sectors, which have asked for the standards, and which will subsequently put them to use.[41] These experts may be joined by representatives of government agencies, testing laboratories, consumer associations, non-governmental organizations and even members from academic circles.[42] These technical committees, subcommittees or project committees can themselves initiate and draft a new proposal for a standard. If there is no relevant committee, the need for a standard, usually put forward by an industry sector, often means that a national member body proposes a new work item to ISO. Once the need for a standard has been recognized and formally agreed, the first phase involves the definition of the technical scope of the future standard, and

---

[39] The effect of these collaborations is that the ESO standards correspond to the international standards to a large extent. According to Schepel, roughly 40 per cent of CEN standards correspond to ISO standards and 70 per cent of the CENELEC standards correspond to IEC standards. The US SDOs are far less successful in implementing their standards in the international arena. Less than 10 per cent of ANSI standards correspond to ISO standards. Cf. Harm Schepel, *The Constitution of Private Governance – Product Standards in the Regulation of Integrating Markets* (Hart, 2005), p 191.

[40] Several organizations are in liaison with ISO.

[41] For how ISO develops standards, see http://www.iso.org/iso/home/standards_development.htm, accessed 24 January 2014.

[42] Ibid.

the setting up of a new committee or group comprising representatives from the industry and from countries interested in the subject matter.[43]

ISO standards need to be based on a 'consensus' of international expert opinion. Consensus, which requires the resolution of substantial objections, is essentially a procedural principle. Although it is necessary for the technical work to progress speedily, sufficient time is required before the approval stage for the discussion, negotiation and resolution of significant technical disagreements. The definition notes: 'consensus need not imply unanimity'.[44]

In practice, the national delegations of experts on a committee meet to discuss, debate and argue until they reach consensus on a draft international standard (DIS). The 'organizations in liaison' also take part in this work, e.g. CEN. In some cases, advanced work within these organizations means that substantial technical development and debate has already occurred, leading to some international recognition. In this case, a document may be submitted for 'fast-track' processing.[45]

In any case, the resulting document is circulated as a DIS to all ISO's member bodies for voting and comments over a period of five months. It is approved for submission as a final draft international standard (FDIS) if a two-thirds majority of the members of the relevant committee are in favour and not more than one-quarter of the total number of votes cast are negative.[46]

The FDIS is circulated to all ISO member bodies for a final vote within two months and the text is approved as an international standard if a two-thirds majority of the members of the relevant technical committee or subcommittee is in favour and not more than a quarter of the total number of votes (of all ISO members) cast are negative. If these approval criteria are not met, the standard is referred back to the originating technical committee, subcommittee or project committee for reconsideration in light of the technical reasons submitted in support of the negative votes received.[47]

CEN / CENELEC, and IEC generally have similar procedures as ISO for adopting standards. The ITU-T, on the other hand, is organized in a somewhat similar manner to ETSI. Membership of ITU is open to

---

43 Ibid.

44 This is followed by all regional bodies too. Ibid.

45 Stages of the development of international standards: http://www.iso.org/iso/standards_development/processes_and_procedures/stages_description.htm, accessed 20 October 2011. Discussed infra.

46 Ibid.

47 Ibid.

governments, which may join as Member States, as well as to private organizations such as equipment manufacturers, research and development firms and international and regional telecommunication companies. They can join ITU as sector members. However, in the standard-setting specific sectors of ITU, ITU-T and ITU-R, the actual drafting work is conducted by representatives from interested undertakings in working parties subordinated to study groups, i.e. by the so-called 'rapporteurs'.[48]

Study groups conduct their work primarily in the form of 'study questions'. Each of these addresses technical studies in a particular area of telecommunication standardization. They have a chairman and a number of vice-chairmen appointed by the World Telecommunication Standardization Assembly (WTSA).[49] To assist in the organization of the work, the study group may break down into a number of working parties. The working party is the next organizational unit down stream from the study group, while the latter coordinates a number of study questions on a related theme.[50]

The team of experts working on a specific question is known as the rapporteur-group within the working group. Their meetings are chaired by the relevant rapporteur. Having considered the text of the question and guidance from the study group, the participants determine what standards are required and develop text for these standards, taking all relevant inputs into account and consulting other relevant parts of ITU-T.[51]

---

[48] ITU website: http://www.itu.int/net/about/membership.aspx, accessed 20 October 2011.

[49] ITU website: http://www.itu.int/ITU-T/studygroups/, accessed 20 October 2011.

[50] ITU website: http://www.itu.int/net/ITU-T/info/development.aspx, accessed 20 October 2011.

[51] The area of study of the project within ITU-T is defined by the text of the question, and this is generally approved by the study group itself. For a new question to be established, it is necessary that a number of members commit to support the work. Questions address technical studies in a particular area of telecommunication standardization, and are driven by contributions. A question is normally terminated once the defined work has been completed, or the task is revised in the light of developments, which can be technical, market-oriented, network or service driven. The text for each of the questions assigned to a study group can be found on its web page, http://www.itu.int/net/ITU-T/info/development.aspx., accessed 20 October 2011.

BOX 3.2

There are two procedures for adopting standards, the traditional model and the fast-track alternative adoption model (AAP). AAP is a fast approval procedure that was developed to allow groups to speed up the process of adopting standards.[52] The AAP approval procedure was implemented in 2001 and is estimated to have cut the time involved in this critical aspect of the standardization process by 80 to 90 per cent. This means that an average standard which took around four years to approve and publish until the mid nineties, and two years until 1997, can now be approved in an average of two months, or as little as five weeks. The vast majority of standards originating in the ITU are approved in this way. Only those that have regulatory implications are not: they use what is called the traditional approval process (TAP). The introduction of AAP also formalizes public/private partnership in the approval process by providing opportunities for both sector members and member states in the approval of technical standards.[53]

Thus, the ITU and ISO fast-track procedure for creating technical standards is the adoption of rules through, essentially, default. Approval is given by members being passive, rather than actively approving the standard in question. Such a procedure increases the influence of the rapporteurs when introducing standards.

3.2.5 The US Standard-Setting Organizations

The US model for adopting standards is considered to be different from that of the European (and the international) model, although it is still based on the work of technical committees employed by the important SDOs to develop and produce the standards. The US system is perceived as more of a decentralized, 'bottom-up' 'private' approach, while the

[52] ITU website: http://www.itu.int/en/ITU-T/aap/Pages/default.aspx, accessed 8 May 2011.

[53] ITU website: http://www.itu.int/net/ITU-T/info/approval.aspx, accessed 20 October 2011.

European approach is often accused of being centralized and governmental in character. It is estimated that in the US today there are hundreds of 'traditional' standards developing organizations – with the 20 largest SDOs producing 90 per cent of the standards – and hundreds more 'non-traditional' standards development bodies, such as the so-called consortia set up by a few firms to promote their technology or product. It is further estimated that there are 49,000 private standards in place in the United States, developed by over 600 trade associations, professional societies and other organizations.[54] Some of these standards and standard bodies are in outright competition with each other.

At the top of the US pyramid (if it can be viewed as a pyramid), is the American National Standards Institute (ANSI), which accredits standard developers.

BOX 3.3

ANSI does not write standards; rather, the Institute accredits standards developers that will establish consensus among interested parties.[55] ANSI publishes American national standards that meet the principles of openness, due process, balance of interests and consensus according to the WTO Code of Good Practice. The ANSI procedures are followed by 220 entities currently accredited to develop and maintain nearly 10,000 American National Standards (ANS). ANSI is thus somewhat equivalent to CEN in the European system. ANSI's membership comprises a broad range of businesses and industrial organizations, standard-setting and conformity assessment bodies, trade associations, labour unions, professional societies, consumer groups, academia, and government organizations, divided into three main categories: (i) company members; (ii) government members; and (iii) organizational members. Though all ANS are developed as voluntary documents, U.S. federal, state,

[54] Knut Blind and Stephan Gauch, 'Trends in ICT Standards: The Relationship between European Standardisation Bodies and Standard Consortia', (2008) 32 *Telecommunications Policy*, 503, 145, with references.

[55] Much of the facts about ANSI provided in this box stems from ANSI's website: http://www.ansi.org/about_ansi/introduction/history.aspx?menuid=1. Accessed 1 February 2012. See also ISO's website: http://www.iso.org/iso/about/iso_members/iso_member_body.htm?member_id=2188. Accessed 1 February 2012.

or local bodies are increasingly referring to ANS for regulatory or procurement purposes. Many ANS are also national adoptions of globally relevant international standards.[56]

ANSI has been described as an abandoned child whom the US government generally regards as an excuse for its own inactivity, and a mask for business's preference for non-regulation. However, the introduction of ANSs implicitly implied power to regulate in the hands of ANSI.[57]

The 220 accredited standard developing entities fall into three categories: (i) organizations that develop and maintain standards according to ANSI's procedures for 'canvassing' (canvassing is a formalized public review system, often conducted contemporaneously with the process and after the standard has been developed by a consortium[58]); (ii) fully accredited organizations, following their own operating methods and procedures as approved by ANSI (in this category, all the well-known standard bodies from IEEE to ASME International are included); and (iii) committees of several organizations usually reflecting the needs of a whole industrial sector.

An example of a fully ANSI accredited SDO is the ASME International (formally American Society of Mechanical Engineers). It was established in 1880, has over 125,000 members, and has published over 600 codes and standards. It has worked hard to establish itself as an international standard organization and even objected to ISO and CEN being qualified as consensus standard organizations under US Federal legislation.[59] Also the IEEE, VITA and TIA (telecommunication) are ANSI accredited SDOs.[60] In comparison to Europe, there are not (52) state SDOs: rather, there are large industry /broad technology SDOs.

---

[56] ANSI website: http://www.ansi.org/news_publications/other_documents/halo_effect.aspx? menuid=7, accessed 24 January 2014.

[57] Samuel Kirslow, *Nations Choose Product Standards and Standards Change Nations* (University of Pittsburgh Press, 1997), 114.

[58] See ISO's website http://www.iso.org/iso/about/iso_members/iso_member_body.htm?member_id=2188. Accessed 1 February 2012. Harm Schepel, *The Constitution of Private Governance – Product Standards in the Regulation of Integrating Markets* (Hart, 2005), 147.

[59] Harm Schepel, *The Constitution of Private Governance – Product Standards in the Regulation of Integrating Markets* (Hart, 2005), 150 et seq.

[60] For description of the IEEE and VITA SDOs, see supra.

Committees and other organizations may adopt ANSI's model procedures or develop their own, as long as they are consistent with ANSI's basic requirements.[61] ANSI's basic requirements are based on the WTO Code of Good Practice, which several large US SDOs, e.g. ASTM International, follow directly. There are nine requirements, which are quite similar to the requirements of CEN (and ISO and IEC and ITU-T): (i) the standardization process needs to be open to all and anyone effected by the activity; (ii) there shall be a balance of interests among the participants of the SDO; (iii) single entities or groups of participants with similar interests must not be dominant; (iv) efforts in good faith shall be made to resolve potential conflicts between and among existing ANSs; (v) the notification of a standard must be done through a suitable media for facilitating participation; (vi) written views and opinions shall be taken into consideration; (vii) standards shall be adopted by consensus; (viii) the opportunity for appeal must be available; and (ix) procedure shall be in writing.[62]

An example of the criteria for consensus includes a requirement that a majority of the relevant body cast a vote (counting abstentions) and at least two-thirds of those voting approve (not counting abstentions). The developer may submit for approval an alternative methodology for determining consensus.

By comparison, the rules and principles stipulated at (ii) and (iii) above are rather absent in the by-laws of the European and the International SDOs. Instead, national standardization organizations (NSOs) and the members of the relevant committees are supposed to be neutral and not favour any stakeholder. Whether this can be presumed seems somewhat unrealistic. Given the fact that, in some organizations, standards are enacted by default rather than through the active participation of the majority of the members, the requirement that the working group should represent all interests in a standard seem to be well motivated but somewhat utopian. As mentioned above, there has also been a concern regarding the democratic deficit of SSOs.

Furthermore, and more importantly, these requirements are not rules in the sense that the SSO would be reprimanded or punished for failing to meet them. The legislator here allows competition law to play that role.

---

[61] Harm Schepel, *The Constitution of Private Governance – Product Standards in the Regulation of Integrating Markets* (Hart, 2005), 145 et seq.

[62] ANSI, *Essential Requirements*, (New York, ANSI, 2014), Chapter 1 et seq., http://publicaa.ansi.org/sites/apdl/Documents/Standards%20Activities/American%20National%20Standards/Procedures,%20Guides,%20and%20Forms/2014_ANSI_Essential_Requirements.pdf, accessed 24 January 2014.

In many ways, it seems that there is a connection between these basic governance requirements for SSOs and the rules for when immunity from competition becomes applicable under, on the one hand, the NCRPA and, on the other, the EU competition law system of block exemption and the 'safe harbour' stipulation of the Horizontal Guidelines.

3.3 IP POLICIES

The latest development within the sphere of standardization is the requirement for SDOs to have intellectual property policies (IP or patent policies). In the EU Horizontal Guidelines, having an IP policy is even a requirement for taking advantage of the 'safe harbour' under EU antitrust rules.[63]

The introduction of IP policies was a major turning point for several SDOs and SSOs. Even though intellectual property issues had been discussed and been an issue, the aim of the SDOs and the SSOs before the introduction of IP policies had been to get the, from an engineering point of view, superior technology standardized. Intellectual property rights issues were, before the introduction of IP policies, a concern but the overriding issue was the quality of the standard; so the SDOs did not deal with IPRs. When implementing IP policies, SDOs faced not only the intellectual property issues, such as hold-up, but also the issue of the cost of a standard as such. Should the members of the technical committees base their decision on the superiority of a technology or on an analysis of price v. technology? That would be something new and became, as it still is, an issue for several SDOs. Moreover, if price were now part of the standardization process, could SDOs become vehicles for collusion? To prevent the risk of cartel litigation, the EU Commission and the US antitrust agencies, plus the US Congress, were quick to exempt SDOs from the ambit of cartel regulation.

Many regional and national standard-setting organizations have implemented IP or patent policies. The joint ITU, ISO and IEC patent policy is a 'code of practice' for patents, covering, to varying degrees, the subject matter of the international standard. The code has inspired other SDOs when drafting IP policies, but is somewhat of a 'bottom line' approach.

The rules of the 'code of practice' are simple and straightforward. According to the drafters, the patent policy is non-binding. Nonetheless, a patent embodied fully or partly in a standard must be accessible to

---

[63] See discussion, infra, Chapter 4.2.

everybody 'without undue constraints'. To meet this requirement in general is the sole objective of the code of practice. The detailed arrangements arising from patents (licensing, royalties, etc.) are left to the parties concerned, as these arrangements might differ on a case-by-case basis.[64]

BOX 3.4

The code of practice of many SDOs may be summarized as follows[65]:

(i) Any party participating in the work of a technical committee should, from the outset, draw the attention of the committee to any known patent or to any known pending patent application, either their own or of other organizations.

(II) If a standard is developed and such information as referred to in paragraph (i) has been disclosed, three different situations may arise:

- (a) The patent holder is willing to negotiate licences free of charge with other parties on a non-discriminatory basis on reasonable terms and conditions. Such negotiations are left to the parties concerned and are performed outside the SDO.
- (b) The patent holder is willing to negotiate licences with other parties on a non discriminatory basis on (fair) reasonable terms and conditions ((F)RAND). Such negotiations are left to the parties concerned and are performed outside the SDO.
- (c) The patent holder is not willing to comply with the provisions of either paragraph (a) or paragraph (b); in such case, the standard shall not include provisions depending on the patent.[66]

---

[64] See the Common Patent Policy, e.g. http://www.iec.ch/members_experts/tools/patents/patent_policy.htm. Accessed 21 October 2011.

[65] Ibid.

[66] Ibid.

In reference to the above, the patent policy includes two parts: a disclosure rule and a licensing commitment requirement. Under the disclosure rule, any member should disclose any known patent or pending patent application. This is an ongoing obligation throughout the life of the standard concerned. Once the patent is disclosed, the holder is requested to make a choice between (a)–(c) above. If the holder chooses (c) the standard will normally be redesigned.[67] How effective this non-requirement is in practice is doubtful.[68] That said, it should be emphasized that there is no requirement for members to conduct a patent search.[69]

Some regional SDOs have somewhat different policies. ETSI requires each member to inform it about its own and others' essential IPRs, especially when a member has submitted a technical proposal. The members are not obliged to conduct a patent search. The owner of the essential IPR is obliged to grant an irrevocable licence based on FRAND. If an IPR owner is not willing to grant a licence that has been requested, an alternative technology can be selected. If no alternative exists, ETSI will again contact the owner to request it to reconsider. Similarly, if, after the standard has been published, an IP owner does not grant a FRAND licence, the owner will be requested to do so and if the owner does not adhere, the General Assembly will vote whether to refer the standard to a technical committee for redrafting. If a vote to refer does not succeed, the General Assembly will contact ETSI's counsel, or specific members, to

---

[67] It is very hard to say whether the ITU patent policy has been successful. Researchers have analysed patent holders' activities both under the ITU patent policy and in relation to patent pools. Their research has shown that the ITU patent policy has rarely been complied with and that the patent pools have had had far more success in attracting potential essential patent holders. Cf. Huaiwen He, 'A Self-Defeating Framework: How Far Could ITU Policy Go', (2009) 31 *E.I.P.R.*, 343, 343 et seq.

[68] See discussion, supra Chapter 2, section 2.5.1.

[69] In a perfect world, SDOs would mandate all participants to make an exhaustive search of their patent portfolios and then disclose all patents and pending applications that cover the standard or related technologies. The SDO would then enforce contract provisions providing for penalties, such as withholding royalties, if any member violated the disclosure rules. However, mandatory search provisions would discourage participation in the SDO due to fear of liability, both contractually and under US/EU antitrust laws. See Joel M. Wallace, 'Rambus v. F.T.C. in the Context of Standard-Setting Organizations, Antitrust, and the Patent Hold-Up Problem', (2009) 24 *Berkley Technology Law Journal*, 661, Chapter A. and Joseph Farrell et al., 'Standard Setting, Patents, and Hold-up', (2007) 74 *Antitrust Law Journal*, 603, 625 et seq., 646.

find a solution. Lastly, if the standard has been implemented and, post-implementation, an essential patent that has emerged, the EU Commission may be contacted to see what actions it might take, including non-recognition of the European standard in question under the New Approach.[70]

However, ETSI has developed its IP policy even further. ETSI's policy includes recommendations regarding *ex ante* disclosure of licensing terms. *Ex ante* disclosure is a mechanism for committing to licensing terms before the protected technology has been selected as part of a standard. In other words, it is a mechanism for submitting anticipated licensing terms for a particular draft standard before the contribution is locked in as a standard. A recommendation for *ex ante* disclosure of licensing terms should not be confused with a disclosure or a licensing commitment requirement, since it actually goes beyond such requirements and stipulates that the patentee should commit to a specific standard licensing agreement (or term sheet).[71]

Interestingly, ETSI's US competitor, TIA, has a more flexible IPR policy that does not require disclosure of essential patents.[72] The UN connected organization, ITU, has an IPR policy that more closely resembles ETSI's IPR policy.

3.4 THE *DE FACTO* WORK IN SSOs AND SDOs

Empirical work by Harvard Business School has given a rare glimpse into the work of standard-setting in SSOs and SDOs under the US consortia-driven standard-setting procedure.[73] Academics conducted a case study of, inter alia, the WiFi standard and how it was developed over 16 years from 1990 to 2006. WiFi is the technology that allows consumers to use their laptops, pads, and smart phones to access wireless the internet at airports, universities, coffee shops and at home. WiFi is the technology that enables information to be transferred between computers, televisions, video games and other electronic devices without the physical connection. WiFi devices transmit and receive signals on specific

[70] Cf. *ETSI Guide to IPRs* (2008), http://www.etsi.org/WebSite/document/Legal/ETSI_Guide_on_IPRs.pdf., accessed 21 October 2011.

[71] Ibid.

[72] Liguo Zhang, *Standardization and Patent Licensing in the European Union* (Oy Nord Print Ab, 2012), 205 et seq.

[73] Brian DeLacey et al., 'Strategic Behavior in Standard-Setting Oganizations', in a *Harvard University Working Paper* (SSRN, 2006).

radio frequencies, and at an effective range of 100 metres. The WiFi connection has been considered slower than broadband but faster than connection over the 3G telecommunication networks.[74]

BOX 3.5

The first standard regarding WiFi, the original 802.11 was ratified in 1997. Many consider the industry-wide commitment to the 802.11 standard was instrumental in the development of the WiFi market as a whole. It was developed within the US-based IEEE, a US and global SDO.[75]

Inside the IEEE, competing firms and engineers worked with and against each other on 802.11 technical committees to approve technologies to be incorporated in the standard. IEEE makes use of an open consensus-driven process. Consensus implies 75 per cent approval of the balloting groups (which were producers, users and general interest, no interest category should be able to comprise of over half of a balloting group). Large companies, with complimentary individual memberships may nonetheless send a block of people and pack a group. According to DeLacey *et al*, a senior executive stated that it should be noted that IEEE is a 'very political body, and often what happens when they can't get a resolution between option A or option B is that they approve both, which can be the worst answer of all'.[76] In addition, the standards are written specifications and in need of interpretation when implemented. 'Often there is a 800lb gorilla in the market, like Intel, which interprets the standard its own way, and the rest of the industry falls in line with that interpretation'. But with the 802.11 there wasn't any 800lb gorilla for everyone to follow, so there were multiple interpretations of the standard, which resulted in incompatibility.'[77]

In the beginning, two WiFi standards were enacted – 802.11a and 802.11b – but they were soon superseded by the 802.11g. However, unlike the previous standards, the enactment of

[74] Ibid 4 et seq.

[75] Ibid.

[76] Brian DeLacey et al., 'Strategic Behavior in Standard-Setting Oganizations', in *Harvard University Working Paper* (SSRN, 2006), 9 with references.

[77] Ibid, 9 with references.

802.11g was an extended political battle, primarily between Intersil and Texas Instruments. They had both developed competing technologies that they each wanted to become the 11g. The two substitute technologies were very different and in a heated meeting in May 2001, none of the solutions reached the 75 per cent consensus threshold. Being so different, it was difficult to find a common ground, so no mutually acceptable compromise position was indentified.[78] This created an impasse. The industry saw the potential of WiFi and product manufacturers started to produce devices that claimed to meet the standard, although the standard was not yet agreed upon. In the end, Intersil and Texas Instruments agreed to compromise and a new 802.11g, which included not more than four substitute technologies or standards, gained the consensus vote.[79]

Developing the next generation, 802.11n was even a harder battle. It was predicted that the market would explode with a new WiFi standard for speeds up to and beyond 100Mbs. 'The size and breadth of this potential market has made the battle over 802.11n a fight over more than just a standard.'[80] All agreed that the stakes were very high: 'This is really about creating an ecosystem that will allow the unification of the digital home', an analyst said. 'So getting this out to consumers, rather than waiting for the IEEE, is the priority.'[81] Forty technologies were presented to IEEE, and while two technologies or groups quickly became the main contenders, the process of deciding how the different solutions should be presented to the technical committee took a year in itself. According to DeLacey *et al*, the IP arrangements of the two different contenders here played a role. The first group implemented a RAND-Zero policy, implying that the 'responsible' royalty was zero. This group included both the previous combatants over the 802.11g standard, Intersil and Texas Instruments. These firms had seen their market shares slip with the 802.11g and wanted a new standard to gain market presence. The other group, more R&D heavy and including Intel, Sony, Toshiba and Atheros, had difficulty in embracing the zero royalty arrangement. The two groups were asked to come up with a compromise solution, but failed. The large semiconductor

78 Ibid, 9 with references.
79 Ibid, 9 with references.
80 Ibid, 9 with references.
81 Ibid, 9 with references.

firms formed a third group, outside IEEE, which pushed forward a *de facto* standard. This group included 90 per cent of the latest WiFi technology. This was an unusual step. The group was accused of hijacking the standard-setting process and, thus, excluding groups from the standard setting by taking the standard outside the IEEE. Others accused certain members of the technical committee in IEEE of stalling the process of implementing the new 802.11n standard, since implementing that standard would lead to lower sales under the 802.11g and, consequently, loss of revenue for these firms. Some claimed that IP companies (PAEs) had tried to stop the new standard since their SEPs fitted the old but not the new standard.[82]

The breakout group did develop its proposal, and then, finally, caved in and submitted the proposal to the relevant technical committee within the IEEE where it gained the required majority of 75 per cent.[83]

Even though the authors indicated that the development of the 802.11n was political, in the sense that the result was finally developed outside the SDO, the development of 802.11n is not unique. There are examples of similar cases.[84] Interestingly, it also shows that deciding on a standard does not imply that one stringent technology solution is being implemented. Rather, it seems that several substituting technologies may be included under one standard.[85] The process is by no means a scientific procedure, rather a process where private interests are pitted against each other in the hope that the outcome will benefit not only the private interests but also the public interest.

[82] Ibid, 16 et seq.

[83] Ibid.

[84] Ibid. 17.

[85] A patent pool was developed under the original 802.11 standard under Via Licensing. See United States District Court Western District of Washington at Seattle, Microsoft v. Motorola, Case no. C10-1823 JLR, Findings of Fact and Conclusion in Law, 25 April 2013, paras. 548 et seq.

3.5 THE PATENT GAME IN THE TECHNICAL COMMITTEES

In general, a new regular standard will be created within a year of the first meeting of the technical committee.[86] By then, the technical committee will have developed and agreed on a technology to standardize and the formal decision to adopt the standard will have been made. This should be compared to the 18 months delay in publishing patent application under patent law. This is quite a crucial time difference according to the research of Claudia Tapia.[87] From her interviews with public officials at the patent offices, officers of SDOs, and employees of large firms engaged standard-setting, it seems that it was common practice in certain industries for firms to either file a patent application just before the first meeting of the technical committee, or even file it based on information obtained as a member of the technical committee. Alternatively, firms file for patent protection, with some patent claims and a description of a technology, just before the first meeting of the technical committee of the SDO. While the negotiations in the technical committee of the relevant SDO develop in one direction or another, the firm essentially applies for divisions, i.e. dividing the patent application by adding patent claims and new descriptions so as to trail the negotiations in the technical committee.[88] Possibly the information included in the first application was actually obtained in the e-mails sent around among the participants of the technical committee before the first meeting.[89]

Thus, by the time the standard is established after 12 months, it may still take some months before patents 'pop up' right within the standard. The SDO or the concerned parties may not be informed by the relevant patent office that there may soon be standard essential patents. By this

---

86 Several standards have taken much longer to be implemented. See Brian DeLacey et al., 'Strategic Behavior in Standard-Setting Oganizations', in *Harvard University Working Paper* (SSRN, 2006), 30 et seq. giving the example of 14 years for ADSL and VDSL technologies.

87 Claudia Tapia, *Industrial Property Rights, Technical Standards and Licensing Practices (FRAND) in the Telecommunications Industry* (Carl Heymanns Verlag – eine Marke von Wolters Kluwer Deutschland GmbH 2010), 90 et seq. and 231 et seq.

88 Cf. Claudia Tapia, *Industrial Property Rights, Technical Standards and Licensing Practices (FRAND) in the Telecommunications Industry* (Carl Heymanns Verlag – eine Marke von Wolters Kluwer Deutschland GmbH 2010), 90 et seq. and 231 et seq.

89 Ibid.

means, the patentee creates not only more patents but also standard essential patents that will appear after the standard has been launched.[90] Empirical research shows that divisionals are common in both the information technology, telecommunications (ICT) and the audiovisual sectors, and even more common in the chemical, pharmaceutical biotech, and medical engineering sectors.[91] Thus, this conduct is present both in sectors with many standards and in industries which are patent prone and R&D driven.

As discussed below in chapter 4, the above scenario might be in violation of the IP policy of the SDO, if the member does not disclose the patent application, and amount to the abuse of 'patent ambush' under competition law. If the firm discloses the patent application and agree to FRAND, then the above business strategy should be benign from a competition law perspective. It should be mentioned that the European Patent Office has entered into memorandum of understanding with large SDOs that promote the idea that the information discussed in the technical committees should be considered 'prior art' if not specifically indicated as confidential.[92] This would of course restrict the possibility to file for patents based on information obtained or discussed in the technical committees. In fact, should this be implemented in a successful way then a standard decided by these SDO may act as a clear limitation of the creation of patent thickets. It could effectively immunize the technology standardised from patents. Whether this in practise will happen remains however to be seen.

---

[90] Cf. Dietmar Harhoff et al., 'The Strategic Use of Patents and its Implications for Enterprise and Competition Policies', in final report to the Commission in Tender for NO ENTR/05/82, (July 8, 2007), at 128, 166, noting that the share of divisionals is growing and interpreting that as a sign that firms are using the patent system strategically; see also M. A. Lemley and K. A. Moore, 'Ending Abuse of Patent Continuations', (2004) 84 *Boston University Law Review*, 63, at 69 et seq., noting that whole original patent applications took 1.96 years on average to issue in the US, but patents with at least one divisional took 4.16 years to issue. OECD, 'Competition, Patents and Innovation II', DAF/COMP (2009) 22 . Rambus was accused of such conduct. In re Rambus, Inc. No. 9302 F.T.C. July 31, 2006) 67 et seq. However, the D.C Circuit did not take this into consideration: Rambus Inc. v FTC, 522 F.3d 456 (D.C. Cir 2007), cert. denied 123 S Ct 1318 (2009).

[91] Dietmar Harhoff et al., 'The Strategic Use of Patents and its Implications for Enterprise and Competition Policies', in final report to the Commission in Tender for NO ENTR/05/82, (July 8, 2007), 175.

[92] See for example MOU between EPO and ETSI, http://www.etsi.org/news-events/news/310-news-release-24th-november-2009, accessed 2 February 2013.

The scenario also shows a correlation well between, on the one hand, the governance rules of SDOs and, on the other, competition law. In fact, at least in the US, SDOs were pushed to adopt IP policies to prevent or limit patent ambush incidents. They were thereby to some extent given the task of regulating and governing the antitrust issues of patent ambush.

3.6 GENERAL COMMENTS AND CONCLUDING REMARKS

Interestingly, an analysis of the by-laws and the IP rules of SDOs reveals that they are similar, and quite under-developed. It reveals the nature and origin of standard-setting as an engineer-driven practice. The standard-setting procedure depends on a collaborative process where the members of the SDOs consult each other, conduct R&D, and negotiate about the standard. The general rules are crude and not specific with regard to upholding transparency, balance of interest and due process, in the sense that everyone, including consumer groups, should be heard and have a say in the standard-setting process. The rules reflect that these organizations are result driven rather than created to protect various 'minority' and societal interests, such as consumer protection. These organizations aim to create standards, not to uphold competition or minimize problems such as patent ambush, or, for that matter, protect other public policy goals. The IP rules, as described above, are a very short minimum list, enacted to satisfy the critique that patent ambush is becoming a problem. On the contrary, Claudia Tapia's research shows that 'patent ambush' or something very close to it was rather a common practice in technical committees. Tapia also raises the interesting issue of how and why the collaborators under a standard, where the engineers have consulted each other during the procedure, should get patent protection for their innovations in the first place.[93] The innovations are known to everyone in the industry, is the 'news requirement' under patent law really fulfilled? Or should the information made available in the technical committees be considered prior art? This issue does not seem to have been resolved by the CJEU or the US Supreme Court but the EPO has entered into agreements with several of the larger SDOs to the effect that information

---

[93] Claudia Tapia, *Industrial Property Rights, Technical Standards and Licensing Practices (FRAND) in the Telecommunications Industry* (Carl Heymanns Verlag – eine Marke von Wolters Kluwer Deutschland GmbH 2010), 90 et seq. and 231 et seq.

discussed in the technical committees should, generally, be considered 'prior art'.[94]

What is not reflected in the rather crude by-laws and the IP policies of the SSOs are the clear indications that the standard-setting process in the technical committees is still surrounded by business practices or industrial custom. The firms and their representatives know very well how to interact, and what is customary and what is not customary behaviour in the technical committees. In fact, the crude by-laws and IP policies should, for example when analysing whether an infringement of competition law should be dependent on breach of these by-laws, be interpreted in the light of the customary rules and mores that actually do exist and are used by the firms and their representatives when meeting and discussing the standard and the technology in the technical committees. In addition, there is, in certain industries, often an exchange of cross-licence agreements between the largest contributors of technologies under a standard (for example under the telecom standards), where these firms cross-license their entire relevant patent portfolios, often with the minimum of clauses and covenants, and without specifying individual SEPs in the cross-licence agreements. Such cross-licence agreements can be a crucial part in agreeing on standards.

If 'misuse of the standard-setting process' is a threshold of anti-competitive conduct or harm, then by that test we should, possibly, also include fundamental customary rules and norms that have been developed in the SDOs, including possibly even the rules stipulated in the industry-wide accepted licence agreements, and not only the crude by-laws and IP policies.

SDOs were created to enact technologies that all members of the technical committees can agree upon, and that is a substantial task in itself. This is also reflected in the fact that, even though the SDOs are fundamentally different with regard to what markets or industries they govern, their rules and procedures are very similar. As stated in the conclusion to the last chapter, from an antitrust perspective, the likely anti-competitive or pro-competitive effects of the standard-setting process is very much dependent on the industry and market being governed. For example, if the SDO in question normally enacts product standards (D-standards, see supra) for markets with low innovation rates and generic goods, the SDO should possibly have more elaborate rules regarding what standards can be enacted and what information may be exchanged in the technical committees. Presumably, the standard enacted should be a performance standard rather

94 See for example MOU between EPO and ETSI, http://www.etsi.org/news-events/news/310-news-release-24th-november-2009, accessed 2 February 2013.

than a design/product standard. By this means, competition between different kinds of technical solution is upheld. Moreover, should the by-laws of the SDO stipulate that only narrow product standards may be enacted? If they enact a broad product standard that includes all members of the technical committee's technologies, while the market do not show signs of network effect and would be able to contain several competing technologies, should that be a violation of the by-laws, the good governance rules and, hence a competition law violation? Should the members of a technical committee for a standard like this, i.e. where there are no sunk costs or lock-in effects of the standard, be allowed to mention, discuss and agree on royalty rates for SEPs under the proposed standard? Possibly, should the standard fail, the enactment of a new standard in a market with a low innovation rate is not so burdensome, so that the parties should not be allowed to discuss royalty rates in the pre-standardization phase. Should the SDO regulate whether the members of a technical committee, as described above, should be allowed to set up a patent pool? In fact, we are here discussing the boundaries of collusive behaviour, where perhaps the standing-setting context should not exempt the collaboration.

By contrast, a technical committee under ETSI, trying to agree a new infrastructural and interoperability standard for a new development in the ICT industry, which would cause the users of such a standard to invest heavily in the technology selected, should be allowed to discuss and elaborate more under the relevant by-laws. Here, there are good reasons for the members of the technical committee to agree on a technology, and to develop it through R&D, while negotiating the standard. These standards are more fundamental in character and there is therefore more need for a collaborate alternative. Hence, more concern should be taken that transparency and equal voting rights, etc. are present while all industry collaboration is pro-competitive. Moreover, for the technical committee to identify whether there is a patent thicket, or whether there are SEPs, under the negotiated technology, and the applicable royalty rate, makes common sense. The development of the 802.11g and 802.11n WiFi standards are good examples of the horse-trading going on in the technical committees, and while some of the agreements on technology in these groups *de facto* reflected substitute technologies, the antitrust risk and harm in these groups is rather that the standard-setting procedure is held up by firms invested in the old standards. Firms holding market share of relevant product markets connected to the standard, and also PAEs holding SEPs under the old standard, may try to hold-up the development of new standards. Notwithstanding the above, if a standard *de facto* includes substitute or even competing technologies, there could be substantial antitrust harm if all holders of SEPs were able to create one patent pool or IP arrangement.

In light of the above, it is clear that the SDO's mission is to create standards, while governments' strategy of delegating the responsibility for creating or upholding competition or the rate of innovation on markets to these organizations is not, and will not be, successful. These concerns must instead, primarily, be met under intellectual and competition law and the relevant market must be analysed in detail under competition law to find anti-competitive effects and remedies.

So, finally, we will discuss the competition law perspective. In the next chapter, agreement on technology in standardization agreements, pre-standardization agreements, joint R&D with the focus on creating standards, and SDOs' IP policies are scrutinized in light of competition law. Thus, the collusive character of these agreements will be analysed, while unilateral conduct will be discussed in Chapter 6.

The United States regulation of the National Collaborative Research and Production Act (NCRPA) will be analysed. The NCRPA encompasses, and exempts from US Antitrust law, after its latest amendments, not only joint R&D, but also the conduct of Standard Development Organizations (SDOs), and 'standard-setting activities'. Standard-setting activities encompass IP arrangements under SDOs' IP policies. The NCRPA still makes reference to the 'innovation market', and this concept will be explored.

The equivalent EU competition law regulations will be discussed. The rules governing the exemption under EU competition law of standardization agreements are analysed. The R&D block exemption and the latest Horizontal Guidelines mirror the latest development under US antitrust law of including SDOs with IP policies, while, to some extent, being even slightly more lenient then its US counterpart. Furthermore, the scant case law in Europe and the USA will be analysed.

In the end, it is argued that, from a competition law perspective, standards should be divided into four groups depending on whether they allow for competition in between solutions/standards, i.e. 'competition by substitution', and why that is the case or not. Some standards are infrastructure standards and then, perhaps, competition is not the best 'tool' to select them. Such standards reflect natural monopoly more than the result of 'trial and error'. Other markets are plagued by patent thickets, and a standard with a patent pool is needed to penetrate the thicket. What standard is under scrutiny has a major impact on how competition law should be applied both in reference to the collusive character of a standardization agreement but also with reference to unilateral conduct under standards. Finally, it should also influence the application of competition law to patent pools.

4. The regulation of standardization agreements and adjoining collaborations

4.1 THE US ANTITRUST LAW REGARDING STANDARD-SETTING COLLABORATIONS

4.1.1 The NCRPA

In 1984, Congress enacted the National Cooperative Research Act (the NCRA).[1] The NCRA was the first antitrust statute to address joint research cooperation. The Act was amended in 1993 to also include joint production ventures and the word 'Production' was added to the name, i.e. National Cooperative Research and Production Act (the NCRPA). The Act clarified that courts had to measure joint R&D ventures against the standard of the rule of reason, regardless of whether the joint research was attacked under Federal or State antitrust laws. It introduced the stipulation that a plaintiff needed to prove anti-competitive restraints on an R&D market.[2] Moreover, the Act stipulated, *inter alia*, that if the Attorney General or the FTC were notified about the joint venture, the parties were not obliged to pay treble damages should the joint venture eventually be regarded as anti-competitive in a court of law. Instead, they would be liable for the actual damages caused by the anti-competitive

---

[1] For an analysis of the Act, see Hanns Ullrich, *Kooperative Forschung und Kartellrecht* (Verlag Recht und Wirtschaft, 1988), 91 et seq. See also Andreas Fuchs, *Kartellrechtliche Grenzen der Forschungskooperation* (Nomos Verlaggesellschaft, 1989), 92 et seq.

[2] The relevant legal text stated, '... such conduct shall be judged on the basis of its reasonableness, taking account of all relevant factors affecting competition, including, but not limited to, effects on competition in properly defined, relevant R&D markets'. See Sec. 3 NCRA. The text seems to imply that an R&D market always needs to be identified where at least some anti-competitive conduct is manifest. The text was later altered in the NCRPA, see discussion infra.

harm that was created by the collaboration.[3] Finally, the NCRA included provisions obliging the losing party to pay the attorneys' fees of the prevailing party.

These changes had rather profound effects. It was not only a clear theoretical break with the previous application of antitrust law to R&D collaborations under the Justice Department Antitrust Guide Concerning Research Joint Ventures from 1980 (the Guide). Private antitrust enforcement in the area of R&D collaboration was also severely limited. From the very beginning, it should have been clear to Congress that the Act eliminated the incentive for private plaintiffs, and limited the incentives for the antitrust enforcement agencies, to launch any suits based on antitrust law in the field of R&D. Congress created a 'safe harbour' for R&D collaboration.

In addition, it should be mentioned that the NCRA and later the NCRPA is applicable to all 'antitrust laws', both Federal and State, and, thus, also under, for example, Sec. 2 of the Sherman Act. This section is perhaps not so often applicable to R&D but, in the latest amendment, Standard Development Organizations were included under the NCRPA. For such organizations, the non-application of the NCRPA under Sec. 2 of the Sherman Act and its equivalent is of interest.[4]

(i) Exempted SDOs

In 2004, the NCRPA was amended by the Standards Development Organization Advancement Act, in order to extend the protection from the antitrust laws to specified activities of Standards Development Organizations (SDOs). If an SDO discloses the scope and nature of its activities to the Department of Justice, it may take advantage of the NCRPA.[5] Formally, the NCRPA stipulates three different results of its applicability: (a) the per se rule under antitrust law is not applicable;

---

[3] An amendment provided that a plaintiff could still obtain treble damages in circumstances in which a joint venture violated not only the antitrust laws but also violated a court or FTC order concerning the conduct of the joint venture. See Thomas W. Queen, 'Recent Development in Federal Antitrust Legislation', (1984-1985) 53 *Antitrust Law Journal*, 443, 448.

[4] It seems that the NCRPA is applicable under the Sherman Act and the Clayton Act, but not the FTC Act, see 15 U.S.C.A § 4301, making reference to 15 U.S.C.A § 12.

[5] For a background to the amendment and a scholarly argument in support of its implementations, see generally Mark Lemley, 'Intellectual Property Rights and Standard-Setting Organizations', (2002) 90 *California Law Review*, 1889 and specifically 1970.

(b) 'loser pays principle', i.e. plaintiffs have to reimburse the defendant should the plaintiff not be successful in an antitrust suit; and (c) no trebling of damages. *De facto,* these three limitations imply that any collaboration or conduct is exempted at least from private suits.

The term 'Standard Development Organization' (SDO) has a specific meaning when discussing standardization under the NCRPA. An SDO is a Standard Setting Organization that has been accredited with the International Standardization Organization (ISO) or the International Electronic Commission (IEC). An SSO is therefore a larger term including not only SDOs but also, for example, private consortia of firms joining together to advance a technical solution to an issue.

In practice, SSOs were using the NCRPA before the 2004 amendment.[6] According to practitioners, it was customary for consortia to be notified under the NCRPA, given the wide definition of 'research' stipulated therein. Consortia activities could, thus, fall under the definition of 'research', make use of the NCRPA, and thereby limit their antitrust exposure.[7]

However, the SSOs do not need to claim to be R&D joint ventures after the 2004 amendment. The parties to a joint research venture can set up an SDO as long as it fulfils the requirements of the NCRPA of, inter alia, openness, balance of interest, and due process.[8] Neither the NCRPA,

---

[6] See Carl Cargill, 'Intellectual Property Rights and Standard Setting Organizations: An Overview of Failed Evolution', (2002) 27 March FTC/DOJ Hearings on Competition and Intellectual Property Law and Policy in the Knowledge-Based Economy, 1, 1 fn. 1. [The document is on file with the author.]

[7] Cf. Carl Cargill, 'Intellectual Property Rights and Standard Setting Organizations: An Overview of Failed Evolution', (2002) 27 March FTC/DOJ Hearings on Competition and Intellectual Property Law and Policy in the Knowledge-Based Economy, 1, 3 et seq. [The document is on file with the author.] Cf. also, Jack Brown, 'Technology Joint Ventures to set Standards or Define Interfaces', (1992–1993) 61 *Antitrust Law Journal*, 921, 933.

[8] According to 15 U.S.C.A § 4301(a)(8) the term 'Standards Development Organization' indicates a domestic or international organization that plans, develops, establishes, or coordinates voluntary consensus standards, and uses procedures that incorporate the attributes of openness, balance of interests, due process, an appeals process, and consensus in a manner consistent with the Office of Management and Budget Circular Number A-119, as revised Feb. 10, 1998. Accordingly the said circular ,which is produced by the executive body of the US government, provides for: 'consensus, which is defined as general agreement, but not necessarily unanimity, and includes a process for attempting to resolve objections by interested parties, as long as all comments have been fairly considered, each objector is advised of the disposition of his or her

nor the Budget Circular referred to in the NCRPA, makes reference to the rules or the accrediting of the ISO, IEC or the American National Standard Institute (ANSI), even though their rules have been the source of inspiration when implementing the definition of SDOs in the NCRPA.[9] This would imply that not only official SDOs are encompassed by the new amendment, but private consortia may also benefit from the new amendment if they fulfil the requirements, which mirror the model rules for what should be included in the by-laws of an SSO to be accredited under ANSI.[10]

According to the NCRPA, 'standard development activities' conducted by an SDO may include any action for the purpose of creating, developing or maintaining a consensus standard.[11] This is a wide definition. Any decision on what technology to use, or not use, and, implicitly, on the aims of the technology falls within the definition.[12] Indeed, one purpose of the Standards Development Organization Advancement Act was that the NCRPA should cover the handling of the members' intellectual property rights by the SDOs.[13] At least unilateral public announcements of royalty rates by patentees and SDO members

---

objection(s) and the reasons why, and the consensus body members are given an opportunity to change their votes after reviewing the comments', see http://www.whitehouse.gov/omb/circulars/a119/a119.html#4, accessed 7 April 2009.

[9] ANSI is the sole US organization under the International Organization for Standardization (ISO) and International Electronic Commission (IEC) that can accredit Standard Development Organizations (SDOs). However, the NCRPA is open to the possibility that SSOs could also benefit from the act. For a definition of different forms of standard-setting organization, see Carl Cargill, 'Intellectual Property Rights and Standard Setting Organizations: An Overview of Failed Evolution', (2002) 27 March FTC/DOJ Hearings on Competition and Intellectual Property Law and Policy in the Knowledge-Based Economy, 1, 3 et seq. [The document is on file with the author.]

[10] Whether the Standards Development Organization Advancement Act encompasses both SDOs and SSOs is not an important practical issue since SSOs before the 2004 amendment were often notified under the NCRPA.

[11] 15 U.S.C.A § 4301(c).

[12] The Supreme Court stated in Allied Tube that, 'agreement on a product standard is, after all, implicitly an agreement not to manufacture, distribute or purchase certain types of products. Accordingly, private standard-setting organizations have traditionally been objects of antitrust scrutiny'. Allied Tube and Conduit Corp. v. Indian Head, Inc. 486 U.S. 492, 500 (1988).

[13] See H.R. REP. 108-125, reprinted 2004 U.S.C.C.A.N. 609, 610 et seq. It should be noted that Congress was (to a lesser extent) concerned with so-called 'patent ambush', i.e., firms which do not admit having filed patents and try to steer the standard in order to create the highest impact for them.

are encompassed by the Act.[14] Interestingly, what can be included as 'standard development activities' according to the NCRPA is, inter alia, standardization agreements, IP policies or IP rules.[15] Thus, in essence the NCRPA creates immunity for SDOs with respect to the agreement among the licensors regarding the technology and the licensing of intellectual property rights under the industrial or technology standard. One interpretation would be that an agreement on royalty rates can be included under the Act and still exempt the SDO (but perhaps not its members).[16] It is the SDOs that need to stipulate the framework and implement it. Indeed, the NCRPA delegates the responsibility for creating and upholding competition to SDOs.

(ii) Innovation market under the NCRPA

The relevant section of the NCRPA states:

> In any action under the antitrust laws, or under any State law similar to the antitrust laws, the conduct of any person in making or performing a contract to carry out a [R&D] joint venture or a standard development organization while engaging in a standard development activity shall not be deemed illegal *per se*; such conduct shall be judged on the basis of its reasonableness, taking in to account all relevant factors affecting competition, including, but not limited to, effects on competition in properly defined, relevant *research, development, product, process, and service markets*. For the purpose of determining a properly defined, relevant market, *worldwide capacity* shall be considered to the extent that it may be appropriate in the circumstances (*emphasis added*).[17]

---

[14] According to the amendment, the term 'standards development activity' does not only mean any action taken by a standards development organization for the purpose of developing, promulgating, revising, amending, reissuing, interpreting, or otherwise maintaining a voluntary consensus standard, or using such standard in conformity assessment activities, but also actions relating to the intellectual property policies of the standards development organization. See 15 U.S.C.A § 4301. (c). It should be noted that allocation of markets is not within the notion of standard-setting activities nor is any agreement on price for any product or service. Though deciding price for the licensing of intellectual property rights does seem to be included under the term 'standard development activity', see 15 U.S.C.A § 4301(c).

[15] It corresponds, inter alia, to the horizontal part of patent pool agreements.

[16] Cf. discussion infra.

[17] See 15 U.S.C.A § 4302.

The predecessor to the NCRPA, the NCRA, stipulated that an R&D joint venture should be judged in the relevant R&D market.[18] The rule of reason, as such, under the NCRPA, is similar to the rule of reason invented in the *Chicago Board of Trade* case.[19]

When introduced in the NCRA, the concept of the R&D market attracted some, but only a little, attention.[20] In 1993–1995, after its (re-)introduction in the NCRPA and the IP Guidelines, the concept of 'innovation markets' became the subject of heated discussion.[21]

The concept of 'innovation market' brought with it a new, or, at least, a greater focus on specific anti-competitive harm. Firms that are able to reduce spending on R&D due to the fact that the innovation market becomes too concentrated through their joint R&D collaboration are possibly entering into an anti-competitive agreement. Thus, decreased spending on R&D may be an anti-competitive harm.

The definition of an 'innovation market' is a market consisting of R&D, directed at particular new and improved goods or processes, and at the close substitutes for that R&D. Close substitutes are R&D efforts, technologies, and goods that significantly constrain the exercise of market power with respect to the scrutinized R&D. For example, research limiting the ability and incentive of a hypothetical monopolist to slow down the pace of its own R&D.[22] When introduced, the theory was that

---

[18] IP Guidelines, 12 et seq. Example 4 is an illustration of the contemporary application of US Antitrust Law to R&D joint ventures (note, e.g., that there is no analysis of whether the participants in the joint R&D could have conducted the research independently).

[19] Ibid.

[20] Jorde and Teece made some contribution to the R&D market concept, which probably partly caused the adjustment of the R&D market concept in the 1993 amendment. See Thomas Jorde and David Teece, 'Innovation, Cooperation and Antitrust', (1989) 4 *High Tech Law Journal*, 1, 65 et seq., with references.

[21] Two Deputy Assistant Attorneys initiated the discussion in an article, outlining the 'innovation market' concept, see Richard Gilbert and Steven Sunshine, 'Incorporating Dynamic Efficiency Concerns in Merger Analysis: the Use of Innovation Markets ', (1995) 63 *Antitrust Law Journal*, 569, 574 et seq. Several commentators have commented on and criticized their views. See, e.g., Robert Hoerner, 'Innovation Markets: New Wine in Old Bottles?', (1995–1996) 64 *Antitrust Law Journal*, 49; George Hay, 'Innovations in Antitrust Enforcement', (1995-1996) 64 *Antitrust Law Journal*, 7; and Richard Rapp, 'The Misapplication of Innovation Market Approach to Merger Analysis', (1995–1996) 64 *Antitrust Law Journal*, 19. See also Gilbert's and Sunshine's reply: 'The Use of Innovation Markets: A Reply to Hay, Rapp, and Hoerner', (1995–1996) 64 *Antitrust Law Journal*.

[22] IP Guidelines, 11.

an innovation market was identified through an analysis of the set of R&D activities that a monopolist would profitably be able to reduce by a small yet significant reduction in R&D spending.[23] Thus, a monopolist was defined as a firm able profitably to reduce R&D spending on an innovation market. If there were no other R&D efforts to compete with and force the monopolist to invest in research, logically, a firm could reduce its R&D spending. The test, as introduced by the economists at the Justice Department, Richard Sunshine and Steven Gilbert, focused on whether a firm was able to reduce R&D investment by a small but significant amount without losing market share. If the firm were able to do so by, for example, 5–10 per cent, without losing any market share, it should be considered to be holding monopoly, or market, power.[24]

Sunshine's and Gilbert's definition of an innovation market, relying on the logic of the significant non-transitory increase in relative price (SSNIP) test,[25] thus acknowledged actual market power in real product markets. According to Sunshine and Gilbert, the conduct would have to be considered anti-competitive only if the parties could limit the output effect of a reduction in innovation in classic goods or service markets.[26] Thus, the parties would be dominant in the research market, if they were able to limit R&D investment and continue to defend their market share in the relevant end markets.

According to the IP Guidelines, market shares in related product markets are of great interest when establishing market power in an innovation market.[27] The definition of the innovation market, relying on a reversed SSNIP-test for R&D investment, made use of the actual market power in real product markets and whether it would be lessened. According to Sunshine and Gilbert, only if the parties can prevent the transmission of the reduction in innovation into an output effect in

---

23 Thus, appealing to similarities with the SSNIP test, see Richard Gilbert and Steven Sunshine, 'Incorporating Dynamic Efficiency Concerns in Merger Analysis: the Use of Innovation Markets', (1995) 63 *Antitrust Law Journal*, 569, 594.

24 Cf. Richard Gilbert and Steven Sunshine, 'Incorporating Dynamic Efficiency Concerns in Merger Analysis: the Use of Innovation Markets', (1995) 63 *Antitrust Law Journal*, 569, 594 et seq.

25 See, generally, 'Commission Notice on the Definition of the Relevant Market for the Purposes of Community Competition Law', OJ C372, 9.12.1997, 5 et seq.

26 Richard Gilbert and Steven Sunshine, 'The Use of Innovation Markets: A Reply to Hay, Rapp, and Hoerner', (1995–1996) 64 *Antitrust Law Journal*, 79.

27 IP Guidelines, 10 et seq.

'classic' goods or service markets should their conduct be considered anti-competitive.[28]

Notwithstanding the above, today the concepts of a 'research market' under the NCRPA and of an innovation market are similar, dormant doctrines. Thus, as discussed below, the concept of an innovation market seems out of date since several conceptual faults have been identified within the doctrine. Nonetheless, *de lege lata*, the NCRPA still stipulates that an innovation market can and, presumably, should be identified.

Interestingly, the notion of an innovation market when introduced was mostly criticized for the fact that such markets were not real markets where a purchaser and a seller transferred products or services at market value,[29] that the doctrine of 'potential competition' could also encompass innovation markets,[30] and that the Justice Department would use the new innovation market as a way to attack conglomerate mergers.[31] However, the early critique appears to have been somewhat oblivious of the most striking feature of the concept. In almost all cases, firms' market influence or dominance diminishes on the larger innovation markets. By increasing the size of the relevant market in all respects, i.e. the number of technologies or products to be encompassed, the geographic scope and also the period of (future) time to be analysed, very few firms can be regarded as holding market power. Innovation markets may diminish the effect of the conduct of large firms in the innovation race. Indeed, for large firms, system leaders, and competitors on product markets, the concept opens up an opportunity to collaborate over, for example, R&D or standard setting while claiming to have no market power on the innovation market. Their innovation markets may contain several more firms not active on their product markets, and, hence, diminish the importance of their dominant position in connected product markets.

---

[28] Richard Gilbert & Steven Sunshine, 'The Use of Innovation Markets: A Reply to Hay, Rapp, and Hoerner', (1995–1996) 64 *Antitrust Law Journal*, 79.

[29] See, e.g., John Temple Lang, 'European Community Antitrust Law: Innovation Markets and High Technology Industries', in Barry E. Hawk, *International Antitrust Law & Policy* (Bender, 1996), 557 et seq. Lang also claims that there is a right to a compulsory licence under Art 81 EC Treaty, see ibid., 570. See also Robert Hoerner, 'Innovation Markets: New Wine in Old Bottles?' (1995–1996) 64 *Antitrust Law Journal*, 49, 53.

[30] George Hay, 'Innovations in Antitrust Enforcement', (1995–1996) *64 Antitrust Law Journal*, 7, 9 et seq. Richard Rapp, 'The Misapplication of Innovation Market Approach to Merger Analysis', (1995–1996) 64 *Antitrust Law Journal*, 19, 21.

[31] Robert Hoerner, 'Innovation Markets: New Wine in Old Bottles?', (1995–1996) 64 *Antitrust Law Journal*, 49, 55 et seq.

(iii) Standard-setting activities on innovation markets

One of few cases where the courts come quite close to recognizing an innovation market (without using the term 'innovation market') and, more importantly, declaring a reduction in innovation and R&D spending as anti-competitive harms, was *Automobile Manufacturing's Association*.[32] In that case, a major US car manufacturer was alleged to have collusively conspired to implement a substandard technical solution and to not conduct R&D in order to slow down technical advances in the area of environmental-friendly exhaust technology. Connected to the selected technology was also a joint and free cross-licence (patent pool) scheme between the collaborators. The consent decree prohibited certain exchanges of technical information and the royalty-free patent licence scheme between the defendants.

The IP Guidelines comment on the *Automobile Manufacturing's Association* case by noting that the anti-competitive effect of pooling arrangements may occur if the arrangement deters or discourages participants from engaging in research and development, thus holding back innovation. The IP Guidelines continues:

> [f]or example, a pooling arrangement that requires members to grant licenses to each other for current and future technology at minimal cost may reduce the incentives of its members to engage in research and development because members of the pool have to share their successful research and development and each of the members can free ride on the accomplishments of other pool members. However, such an arrangement can have pro-competitive benefits, for example, by exploiting economies of scale and integrating complementary capabilities of the pool members, (including the clearing of blocking positions), and is likely to cause competitive problems only when the arrangement includes a large fraction of the potential research and development in an innovation market.[33]

Apart from the *Automobile Manufacturing's Association* case, there is little case law regarding pure R&D ventures, and the interface between joint R&D and standards.[34]

---

[32] 307 F. Supp. 617 (C.D. Cal. 1969), appeal dismissed, 397 U.S. 248 (1970).

[33] See generally United States v. Mfrs. Aircraft Ass'n, Inc., 1976 1 Trade Cas. (CCH) ¶ 60,810 (S.D.N.Y. 1975); United States v. Automobile Mfrs. Ass'n, 307 F. Supp. 617 (C.D. Cal 1969), appeal dismissed sub nom. City of New York v. United States, 397 U.S. 248 (1970), modified sub nom. United States v. Motor Vehicle Mfrs. Ass'n, 1982-83 Trade Cas. (CCH) ¶ 65,088 (C.D. Cal. 1982).

[34] See also the Open Software Foundation Inc et al. v. United States Fidelity and Guaranty, 307 F.3d 11 (1st Cir. 2002).

The concept of an innovation market seems recently to have had somewhat of a revival. The criticism of the innovation market doctrine, raised by European scholars, and the reason for the non-use of the doctrine under EU competition law, is based on the argument that an innovation market cannot be a market at all. Innovations are not traded in the way that technology, products or services are, and without purchasers that define the demand, it is impossible to define a market. As Drexl put it, the term 'innovation market' is theoretically misguided.[35] From a practical perspective, the concept of innovation market seems to receive far more attention than it reserves.

Even in the latest US Horizontal Merger Guidelines, the US agencies have abstained from using the innovation market doctrine and use the concept 'innovation competition' to indentify anti-competitive conduct which may restrict innovation.[36] Nonetheless, the NCRPA still stipulates that standard-setting activities may be anti-competitive, and exempted, on a relevant research market. Whether the innovation market concept has any relevance still remains to be seen. It is clear that in the few cases there are, which also make up the background to why the Standard Development Organization Advancement Act was enacted in 2004, market effect, i.e. effect under the rule of reason, is proven by showing that the anti-competitive standard has been adopted by state or local-level governments.[37] By this means, the plaintiff is able to prove effect on the relevant product market, and does not need to be dragged into the very difficult job of proving effect on a relevant innovation market.

4.1.2 Background to the Standards Development Organization Advancement Act

According to the legislative history, there were three cases that triggered the new amendment concerning liability for SDOs, in which members of the SDOs interfered with the standard-setting process to their advantage.[38] These cases were directly overturned by the 2003 amendment.

---

[35] Josef Drexl, 'Anti-competitive Stumbling Stones on the way to a Cleaner World: Protecting Competition in Innovation without a Market', (2012) 8 *Journal of Competition Law & Economics*, 507, 516 et seq.

[36] US Horizontal Merger Guidelines, para 6.4.

[37] Allied Tube and Conduit Corp. v. Indian Head, Inc. 486 U.S. 492, 502 et seq. (1988).

[38] See also Harm Schepel, *The Constitution of Private Governance – Product Standards in the Regulation of Integrating Markets* (Hart, 2005), 285 et seq.

Interestingly, these cases focus on the application of Sec. 2 Sherman Act rather than Sec. 1 Sherman Act. However, the immunity for SDOs under the Standards Development Organization Advancement Act affects the application of Sec. 1 Sherman Act as well.

(i) ASME

BOX 4.1

In the ASME v. Hydrolevel case, ASME set standards for a variety of mechanical devices. A divided Supreme Court held ASME liable under the treble damages provisions of the Sherman Antitrust Act.[39] Hydrolevel, a water boiler manufacturer, alleged that the Chair and Vice Chair of the Subcommittee, overseeing a section of ASME's Boiler and Pressure Vessel Code Committee, manipulated an interpretation of ASME's Code in furtherance of a conspiracy in restraint of trade. Hydrolevel contended that this interpretation prevented it from achieving market penetration with a technologically superior low-water-cut-off device. The interpretation was solicited by McDonnell and Miller, long the dominant manufacturer of low-water-cut-off devices used on heating boilers. This interpretation was then composed by the Subcommittee Vice Chair, who was also a McDonnell and Miller employee, and subsequently transmitted over the signature of his employer before being approved by the Subcommittee Chair. Approval by the Subcommittee Chair and Vice Chair allegedly occurred after a meeting between these two individuals and representatives from McDonnell and Miller. This seemingly innocuous interpretation of ASME's Code addressed the use of a time delay feature which was similar to that being offered by Hydrolevel. It was then aggressively used by McDonnell and Miller's sales force to assert that Hydrolevel's device did not meet Boiler Code requirements. Hydrolevel alleged this thwarted an anticipated market breakthrough by Hydrolevel's supposedly superior device. Hydrolevel's low-water cut-off device was met with stiff market resistance because of the perception that its device did not comply with ASME's Boiler

[39] American Society of Mechanical Engineers (ASME) v. Hydrolevel, 456 U.S. 556 (1982).

Code, which had been adopted as a regulatory requirement and given the force of law by most states. As a result, Hydrolevel was subsequently forced out of the market.[40]

The initial target of Hydrolevel's antitrust suit was McDonnell and Miller, the purported beneficiary of the alleged conspiracy. ASME was perceived as a relevant, but not necessary, defendant. However, before trial, McDonnell and Miller settled with Hydrolevel, leaving ASME as the sole defendant. The trial judge instructed the jury that ASME could be found liable only if it had ratified or adopted the actions of its Subcommittee officers in order to advance ASME's market interests. Notwithstanding these instructions, the jury returned a verdict against ASME for $3.3 million, prior to trebling. The appeals court supported ASME's liability under the antitrust laws by concluding that liability could attach if ASME's agents had acted within the scope of their 'apparent authority'. On appeal, a divided Supreme Court affirmed and amplified this view.[41]

In a dissent joined by Justices Rehnquist and White, Justice Powell stated: 'The Court today adopts an unprecedented theory of antitrust liability, one applied specifically to a non-profit standard-setting association but a theory that could encompass a broad spectrum of our country's non-profit associations. The theory, based on the agency concept of 'apparent authority,' would impose the potentially crippling burden of treble damages. In this case, the Court specifically holds that standard-setting organizations may be held liable for the acts of their agents even though the organization never ratified, authorized, or derived any benefit whatsoever from the fraudulent activity of the agency. [S]uch an expansive rule of strict liability, at least as applied to non-profit organizations, is inconsistent with the weight of precedent and the intent of Congress, unsupported by the rules of agency law that the Court purports to apply, and irrelevant to the achievement of the antitrust laws.'[42]

---

40 The facts in this box are derived from H.R. REP. 108-125, reprinted 2004 U.S.C.C.A.N. 609, 612 et seq.

41 Ibid.

42 American Society of Mechanical Engineers (ASME) v. Hydrolevel, 456 U.S. 556, 579 (1982).

(ii) ASTM

> **BOX 4.2**
>
> The ASTM litigation, initiated by an ASTM member against ASTM and other members, arose after consensus standards were developed in a process initiated upon the request of the Environmental Protection Agency ('EPA'). In particular, the EPA requested that ASTM develop alternative assessment standards to supplement its own internal inspection process for assessing underground storage tanks ('USTs'). This request was issued to help implement an EPA regulation mandating that all USTs be upgraded, replaced, or eliminated by 1998. Following transparent voluntary standards development procedures, ASTM produced a document which incorporated alternative methods of assessment. This process was vigorously opposed by proponents of the existing method, the tank inspectors, and tank liners. ASTM subsequently approved a standard – which received the full backing of the EPA – that enhanced competition by expanding the number of EPA-approved UST assessment methods from one to four. After six years of participation in the ASTM process, opponents of the standards filed an antitrust suit naming Corporate Companies, WRA/Rogers, and ASTM as defendants.[43]

While all parties to this suit agreed to a sealed settlement early in 2002, proponents of the amendment to the NCRPA pointed to the chilling effect of this litigation on standard-setting activities by SDOs.

(iii) Allied Tube

> **BOX 4.3**
>
> The National Fire Protection Association (NFPA) – private SSO – had permitted electrical conduit made of steel under a fire

[43] H.R. REP. 108-125, reprinted 2004 U.S.C.C.A.N. 609, 612 et seq..

hazard standard.[44] NFPA sets and publishes fire protection standards through a member voting process. Standards approved by a majority of NFPA members are generally adopted as state law and codified in the National Electric Code. In 1980, this Code permitted the use of steel, but not plastic electrical conduits. The defendant was the nation's largest steel conduit manufacturer and an NFPA member. Allied Tube, a plastic electrical conduit manufacturer, had proposed the inclusion of plastic electrical conduits in the 1981 Code and received preliminary approval by an NFPA panel. Prior to the 1980 meeting at which the final NFPA vote occurred, however, the defendant and other steel industry and NFPA members agreed to 'pack' the NFPA with new members in order to defeat the proposal. The proposal was rejected by a membership that included 230 such 'new' members.[45]

Allied Tube successfully sued in the federal district court, alleging unreasonable restraints on trade in violation of the Sherman Act. After that decision was overturned on appeal, the Supreme Court held for Allied Tube, rejecting defendant's argument that it was immune from the antitrust laws under what is commonly referred to as the Noerr-Pennington doctrine (which effectively, makes 'concerted efforts to restrain or monopolize trade by petitioning government officials' immune from the antitrust laws). In doing so, the Court held that while standards development activities, by their nature, may provide an opportunity for anti-competitive behaviours, 'private standard-setting programmes can be pro-competitive when they are based on the merits of objective expert judgments and through procedures that prevent the standard-setting process from being biased by members with economic interests in stifling competition.'[46] Responding to the defendant's asserted defence, the Court held that the statutory adoption of a private standard does not determine whether that private entity's conduct is immune from the antitrust laws. Rather, the scope of protection afforded by

---

[44] The facts in this box is derived from H.R. REP. 108-125, reprinted 2004 U.S.C.C.A.N. 609, 612 et seq.

[45] Ibid.

[46] Allied Tube and Conduit Corp. v. Indian Head, Inc. 486 U.S. 492, 500, 509 (1988).

Noerr-Pennington 'depends on the source, context, and nature of the anti-competitive restraint at issue'.[47]

These cases indicate, according to the legislative history, first, that it was not certain that standard-setting activities would be judged under the rule of reason, and, secondly, that the antitrust risk for SDOs, in general, needed to be reduced.[48] SDOs could, according to Congress, be included and entangled in suits that in reality were addressed to members of that organization. This was one reason why SDOs were to be encompassed under the NCRPA.

There were cases around this time in which the SDO was not found to have violated competition law. In *Adamaxx v. Open Software Foundation*[49], a case concerning the software industry and several standards in this industry, the District Court found that under the rule of reason there was a genuine issue on the facts whether the OSF UNIX standard excluded competition and mirrored the creation of a monopsony (buyer cartel). The Open Software Foundation (OSF) was a standard-setting organization, but had on its enactment in 1988 been registered as a joint R&D venture under the NCRA, the precursor to NCRPA. It had, as a one objective, the development of an alternative UNIX operating system (OFT-1), as a competitor to the UNIX systems being developed by, inter alia, AT&T. OFT decided to include certain security software in the operating system OFT-1 and therefore contacted two security software developers, of which Adamaxx was one, with a request for technology. Adamaxx software was not selected and while OFT-1 did not seem to have been a success, Adamaxx sued OFT and two founders for, inter alia,

---

47 Ibid. 511. For an older case see also Radiant Burners, Inc. v. Peoples Gas Light & Coke Co., 364 U.S. 656, 659 et seq. (1961) where per se violation of Sec. 1 Sherman Act was found. See also H.R. REP. 108-125, reprinted 2004 U.S.C.C.A.N. 609, 613.

48 For a discussion whether SDOs were exposed to a per se or rule of reason application of US antitrust law prior to the 2004 amendment, cf. Jack Brown, 'Technology Joint Ventures to Set Standards or Define Interfaces', (1992–1993) 61 *Antitrust Law Journal*, 921, 925 et seq., especially 929 et seq. and Mark Lemley, 'Antitrust and the Internet Standardization Problem', (1996) 28 *Connecticut Law Review*, 1041, 1079 et seq.

49 See the U.S. District Court case, Addamaxx Corp. v. Open Software Foundation Inc. et al., 888 F. Supp. 274 (D.Mass. 1995); Addamaxx Corp. v Open Software Foundation Inc 152 F.3d 48 (1st Cir 1998), and also Open Software Foundation Inc et al. v. United States Fidelity and Guaranty, 307 F.3d 11 (1st Cir. 2002).

exclusionary boycott. The District Court, and later the Circuit Court, found, under the rule of reason and on the facts, that Adamaxx's loss was not materially caused by the defendant's conduct – its security software was too expensive, too complex, etc. for the standard.[50]

Interestingly, all these cases concern product standards and not standards for interoperability. In fact, they concern, first, the members of a standard-setting organization, and, secondly, a standard-setting organization itself, deciding to promote one substitute or competing solution above others on a relevant market (by selecting it as the standard), and thereby excluding a competing technology. These cases tell us that this may be in violation of US antitrust laws. It is therefore difficult, to say the least, to draw any form of antitrust law conclusion from these cases when scrutinizing infrastructural or interoperability standards. Nonetheless, they show that members of a SDO may, by abusing 'the governance rules' or the standard-setting process, be considered to be in violation of US antitrust law under *Allied Tube*.

In addition to the above cases, so-called 'patent ambush' incidents were increasing both in the US and Europe in 2004.[51] The 'patent ambush' incidents, or, more generally, the patent hold-up cases, emerged in the US and concern unilateral conduct by a patentee and a member of an SDO. As discussed above, patent ambush arises when an SDO negotiates to implement a standard and a member omits to disclose that it has a patent, or that it has applied for a patent, that will correspond to the contemplated standard. Access to the patent becomes necessary or essential for firms wishing to adhere to the technology standard. After the technology standard has been implemented, and firms in the industry have invested accordingly, the member reveals its patent, which has now

---

[50] Addamaxx Corp. v. Open Software Foundation Inc 152 F.3d 48 (1st Cir 1998).

[51] Recently, see, e.g., Rambus, Inc. v. F.T.C. 522 F.3d 456 (D.C. Cir 2008), cert denied. History: the FTC challenges In re Rambus, No. 9302 (F.T.C. 2002); In re Rambus, Inc. No. 9302 F.T.C. July 31, 2006) and In re Rambus, Inc. No. 9302 (F.T.C. Feb 2, 2007); In re Dell, 121 F.T.C. 616(1996) (Resolved by consent order.); In re Union Oil Co. of Cal., No. 9305 (F.T.C. Nov. 25 2003) (Resolved by consent order.); Rambus Inc. v. Infineon Technologies AG, 318 F.3d 1081 (Fed. Cir. 2003). The SDO was not charged with fraud. Recently, in Europe, Philips lost an infringement suit when the Dutch Court agreed it omitted to declare it had a patent even though a member of the SDO and involved in drafting the standard. See LG Electronics v. Koninklijke Philips Electronics N.V., The District Court of The Hague, roll number 287026 / KG ZA 07-528, 11 June 2007. See also the German case LG Dusseldorf, WuW 13.12.2007, helft 12, Seite 1278-1288, DE-R 2120-2130.

become essential. The patentee demands a royalty for accessing the patent that reflects not only the innovative step inherent in the intellectual property right, but, mainly, the exclusive effect created by the standardization agreement. In other words, the royalty rates reflect a monopoly position.

To prevent these patent ambush incidents, several voices were raised contending that SDOs should be able to adopt technology standards that take into consideration the existence and cost of presumably essential intellectual property rights. Thus, the SDOs should be able to demand that members reveal, for example, their patents and the rate at which they are willing to grant access to these patents. However, SDOs have generally shunned this responsibility by stating that they might violate the antitrust law prohibitions on requiring their members to discuss intellectual property rights and, especially, royalty rates. In essence, they argue that this was not the responsibility of SSOs. Nonetheless, the NCRPA clearly marked a turning point when SSOs had to take on this responsibility. Hence, the second reason for encompassing SDOs under the NCRPA was to create a safe haven for SDOs to discuss IP issues and, even, royalty rates. Thus, it exempted the IP policies discussed above from antitrust controls.

In these hold-up or patent ambush cases, it would, after the amendment, be rather futile to initiate an antitrust suit against the SDO for either taking steps to prevent a patent ambush scenario or even against an SDO that is an accomplice to creating a royalty cartel. The SDO could have recourse to the NCRPA, irrespective of whether the case were launched under Sec. 2 Sherman Act or Sec. 1 of the Sherman Act.

Moreover, the 2004 amendment introduces an additional leverage or protection for SDOs. While it exempts SDOs from the risk imposed by the patent ambush cases, it also exempts the actions taken by the SDOs to prevent patent ambush and hold-up situations.

Under the NCRPA, patentees holding essential patents for a contemplated technology standard can be made to agree on, or at least publically disclose, the terms on which they would license their essential patents if the contemplated technology standard were to encompass them. Indeed, not only are the SDOs protected from antitrust liability risk in reference to the patent ambush cases, but they may also take active steps to prevent hold-up situations. In essence, the NCRPA facilitates SDOs in forcing patentees of essential patents to license and to agree to certain terms for such licenses, and still avoid antitrust action under the antitrust laws. Thus, the NCRPA not only exempts SDOs' actions under antitrust law, but also delegates the responsibility to them for creating, regulating and upholding competition in the markets standardized by the SDOs. The weapon the SDOs are allowed to use, and for which they are exempted from the prohibitions under antitrust law, is thus the threat of excluding patentees who do not want to license on FRAND terms alone. This is quite revolutionary.

4.1.3 Members of the SDOs under the NCRPA

As mentioned above, the Standards Development Organization Advancement Act 'only' exempted the SDOs, not the members of the SDOs. The question is whether it is possible to make this distinction and also whether *de facto* members of SDOs are encompassed by the 2004 amendment. In theory, since members of the SDO are not covered by the NCRPA, a member and patentee could face the risk of a regular antitrust suit even in the event that the SDO were exempted under the NCRPA.[52] This seem somewhat odd, and if the SDOs are allowed to make a decision to this effect under the NCRPA, the members voting to support such a decision must also logically often be exempted.

Moreover, the question is whether either of the two doctrines below, which aim to protect the political system as such, would enable the members of an SDO not to fall foul of US Antitrust law.

The state action exemption under US antitrust law, first established in *Parker*[53] immunizes the federal and state government and agencies, and the doctrine of petitioning immunity, established in *Noerr*,[54] protects citizens' involvement in politics. This division works fine in theory: the state action doctrine protects public regulation, however anti-competitive,

---

[52] One problem with this logic is, of course, that these members can be either R&D joint ventures or SSOs, and hence, already covered by the NCRPA. Compare Cargill, Melamed and Dolmans who discuss the issue that SSOs and SDOs may be influenced by the parties having the largest stake in the downstream product markets controlled by the standardized technology, and the business strategy of conducting joint R&D in the pre-standardization phase. See Carl Cargill, 'Intellectual Property Rights and Standard Setting Organizations: An Overview of Failed Evolution', (2002) 27 March FTC/DOJ Hearings on Competition and Intellectual Property Law and Policy in the Knowledge-Based Economy, 1. [The document is on file with the author.]; Douglas Melamed, 'Patents and Standard: The Unimportance of Being Essential', unpublished, 2006). [The document is on file with the author.]; and Maurits Dolmans, 'Standards For Standards', (2002) 26 *Fordham International Law Journal*, 163, 178 et seq.

[53] Parker v. Brown 317 US 341 (1943).

[54] Eastern Railroad Presidents Conference v. Noerr Motor Freights 365 US 127 (1961).

based on the theory that the actions of the Government should have prerogative powers to identify what is in the public interest and what shall be prioritized. The *Noerr* doctrine, on the other hand, immunizes private parties in their efforts to lobby the government even though the purpose of the lobbying effort is anti-competitive.[55]

This division may work fine in theory but what should be done about private parties exercising regulatory functions or trying to influence private SDOs to regulate certain sectors? The Parker doctrine seems to only be applicable to state actions acting as sovereign according to *Goldfarb*.[56] The policy and restraint of competition must be a product of a conscious political choice and furthermore supervized by the public. That said, generally, in later cases, the private parties seem also to be immunized.[57] Furthermore, the *Noerr* immunity, i.e. that the petitioners that provide input in a decision-making process should also be immune, seems attractive for members of SDOs.

Nonetheless, it is obvious that the Supreme Court in *Allied Tube* rejected the notion that SDOs were in effect 'governmental agencies' and therefore should benefit from the state action doctrine.[58] Hence, the *Noerr* doctrine should not be applicable to SDOs and their members. However, paradoxically, there is US case law which seems to suggest that SDOs, and their members, may possibly benefit from less intrusive review due to the inherent problem of judging whether the result of the process actually is pro- or anti-competitive. Hence, lower US courts focus on whether the procedure reflects good governance, and whether the procedural rules have been violated; if so, the antitrust laws will not have been triggered. Although this seems to be in violation of *Allied Tube*, it still seems to be the way the district courts are going.[59]

Thus, it seems to be a real possibility that members of an SDO may also avoid antitrust liability, under either the NCRPA or the *Noerr* doctrine, if they can prove that the rule of governance, i.e. the procedural 'good governance' rules of the SDO, have not been violated. However, since *Allied Tube* and the other cases have not been overruled, it must

---

55 Harm Schepel, *The Constitution of Private Governance – Product Standards in the Regulation of Integrating Markets* (Hart, 2005), 300 et seq.

56 Goldfarb v. Virginia State Bar 421 US 773, 791, 789 (1975)

57 Southern Motor Carriers Rate conference v. US 471 US 48, 57 (1985).

58 Allied Tube and Conduit Corp. v. Indian Head, Inc. 486 U.S. 492, 501. Compare the ECM case below, Chapter 4.2, where CJEU seemed to accept that SDOs can be lobbied.

59 Harm Schepel, *The Constitution of Private Governance – Product Standards in the Regulation of Integrating Markets* (Hart, 2005), 304, with references.

still be clear that abusing or misusing the standard-setting process, e.g. violating or undermining the good governance rules of the SDOs, may constitute a breach of the US antitrust laws. A course of discrimination, exclusion, or an unduly restrictive procedure, or standard, may be considered antitrust harm in these circumstances. So the issue is, when can an SDO and its members still be found to violate US antitrust laws?

4.1.4 What is Anti-competitive in the Standard-Setting Process under US Antitrust Laws?

(i) The SDOs

The NCRPA places very few restraints on the SDOs. Excluded from the notion of standard development activities under the Act are: (i) agreements on allocation of markets between competitors; (ii) agreements or conspiracies that would restrain the price of goods and services; and (iii) covenants on the exchange of any competitively strategic information regarding, for example, costs or profitability.[60] Thus, in this case, a per se rule may still apply to the conduct of the SDO.

It should be noted that the NCRPA does not exclude decisions on royalty rates under the concept of 'standard development activities'.[61] Indeed, an agreement between patentees on what should be the total royalty rate, how the royalty stream should be divided, and other terms for licensing can be a 'standard development activity' for the SDO (hereinafter an agreement to this regard is defined as 'IP arrangement').

Moreover, it should also be noted that the NCRPA does not require that the SDOs' 'handling of the intellectual property rights', i.e. IP policies, is only available to holders of essential patents. As a matter of fact, the IP policies can be applicable to all holders of patents under the standard in question. In other words, IP policies are also applicable to holders of competing patents as long as they fit within the standard. An IP policy that includes public announcements by holders of patents that

---

[60] 15 U.S.C.A. § 4301(c).

[61] 'The Act seeks to encourage owners of intellectual property to disclose relevant intellectual property rights and proposed licensing terms.' 'It further encourages discussion among intellectual property owners and other interested standards participants regarding the terms under which relevant intellectual property should be made available for use in conjunction with the standard or proposed standard.' See H.R. REP. 108–125, reprinted 2004 U.S.C.C.A.N. 609, 617.

are, or might be, competing would still not exclude the SDO from the application of the NCRPA.[62]

It seems that the amendment in 2004 did not take into consideration the horizontal effects of these collaborations. Instead, the viewpoint was that of PAEs abusing the system. It should be noted that the theoretical monopolistic 'patent ambush' cases are rare compared to cooperative conduct by holders of competing patents, allowed for under the latest amendment to the NCRPA.

More importantly, the seller (patentee) v. purchasers (SDO) relationship, which is the logic behind the IP policy amendment to the NCRPA, and for that matter the approach taken by the Justice Department, is perhaps not the most common situation or scenario in which a technology standard is set.[63] Rather, the normal procedure is that firms in a collegiate collaboration develop, define and implement the technology as members of the SDOs. As happened in the standard setting of 802.11, they can disagree and be forced to compromise and include substitute technologies under the same standard. Should they then be allowed to discuss royalty rates under the SDO?

---

[62] The strict requirements for setting up a patent pool as stipulated in the now famous Patent Pool Business Review Letters from the end of the 1990s are not utilized under the NCRPA. For example, the restriction on including competing patents is not a requirement under the NCRPA when engaging in *ex ante* IP disclosure, IP arrangements or agreements. Indeed, the participants in the IP arrangement may still make use of the NCRPA, e.g., the rule of reason provision, even though including all or mostly competing patents. Cf. the MPEG-2 Pool Business Review Letter from Joel Klein to Gerrard Beeney dated June 26, 1997, 6, the 3DVD Pool Business Review Letter from Joel Klein to Gerrard Beeney dated Dec. 16, 1998, 5 et seq. and the 6DVD Pool Business Review Letter from Joel Klein to Carey Ramos dated June 10, 1999. All can be found at http://www.justice.gov/atr/public/busreview/letters.html#page=page-1. Accessed 19 March 2012. In other words, the per se prohibition on setting up a patent pool with competing patents, as stated in e.g., Standard Oil, Standard Oil Co. v. United States 283 U.S. 163, 176 (1931), has been overruled if the IP arrangement is carried out under the supervision of an SDO. That said, it should be acknowledged that the Justice Department has not stated its view on IP arrangements between competitors and it is likely that the Department under the rule of reason would find these arrangements anti-competitive. Cf. also Richard Gilbert, 'Antitrust for Patent Pools: A Century of Policy Evolution', (2004) *April Stanford Technology Law Review*, 3, 8.

[63] U.S Dep't of Justice & Fed. Trade Comm'n, 'Antitrust Enforcement and Intellectual Property Rights: Promoting Innovation and Competition', (DOJ/FTC, 2007), 33 et seq., especially 50 et seq. (Hereinafter IP 2 Report).

It should be stressed that demanding *ex ante* disclosure of licensing terms, or even *ex ante* negotiations among the patentees, is a way to diminish hold-up situations.[64] Neither reasonable and non-discriminatory (RAND) requirements nor other non-structural requirements have proven effective at preventing hold-ups or patent ambushes, so perhaps *ex ante* disclosure or negotiations may be more efficient.[65] However, depending on who is the patentee and who has most influence in the SDO, the standard, in theory, can become a vehicle for collusion or exclusion.

It is therefore clear that a plaintiff who perceives him or herself to have been hindered commercially by a standard may feel inclined to attack the SDO in the hope of having the court declare the standard 'void'. Under *Allied Tube*, even within the limits set by Congress through the NCRPA, this should still be possible. As long as the plaintiff meets the requirement under the rule of reason, and is prepared to face the other limitations stipulated by the NCRPA (pay attorney fees, etc.) joining the SDO in a suit vis-a-vis the members of the SDO may be fruitful. Under *Hydrolevel*, the Supreme Court held that the SDO may be liable under the rule of reason when its members misuse the standard-setting process to anti-competitive ends.[66]

Notwithstanding the above, the rules on what conduct falls within the NCRPA and, thus, what is exempted under US antitrust law, are detailed and set clear boundaries to the conduct of SDOs and their members. It is clear that members of SDOs can be found to be violating US antitrust laws.

(ii) The members of the SSOs

A. Collusion There are several cases concerning members of SSOs, both in reference to collusive and to joint exclusionary conduct. Historically, as we will discuss under 'Patent Pools' in Chapter 5, the US antitrust case-law books were (and still are) fairly filled with cartels, thinly

---

64 Ibid. 37. See also Gerald Masoudi, 'Efficiency in Analysis of Antitrust, Standard Setting, and Intellectual Property', paper given at High-Level Workshop on Standardization, IP Licensing, and Antitrust 2007, TILEC, University of Tilburg. See http://www.usdoj.gov/atr/public/speeches/220972.htm, accessed 21 April 2012.

65 Scott Peterson, 'Consideration of Patents During the Setting of Standards', in FTC/DOJ (ed), FTC/DOJ Hearings on Competition and Intellectual Property Law and Policy in the Knowledge-Based Economy 2002), 6. [The document is on file with the author.]

66 See also Radiant Burners v. People's Gas light & Coke Co. 364 U.S. 656 (1961).

disguised as standard-setting organizations or patent pools. For example, the *Standard Sanitary* case[67] concerned a cartel where the ring-leader licensed the finishing process to other cartel members. Products (sanitary enameled ironware, such as bath tubs, wash bowls, drinking fountains, sinks, closets etc) treated to the licensed process were sold at agreed prices in the US, while the products that did not meet the standard needed to be sold outside the US. The effect of the collaboration was to set prices, but the standard also facilitated the cartel by decreasing product variety. Products that did not meet the standard could not be sold in the US, presumably because they would have been sold at a lower price. Interestingly, many of these old cartels and patent pool cases have a technology standard angle to them too and concern markets where there are no network effects.[68]

---

[67] Standard Sanitary Mfg. Co. v. United States, 226 U.S. 20 (1912).

[68] Even Standard Oil concerned a standard: Standard Oil is a complicated and contradictory case concerning several issues. The history of the Standard Oil patent pool may be briefly stated. For about half a century before 1910, gasoline had been manufactured from crude oil exclusively by distillation and condensation at atmospheric pressure. When the demand for gasoline grew rapidly with the widespread use of the automobile, methods for increasing the yield of gasoline from the available crude oil were sought. It had long been known that from a given quantity of crude, additional oils of high volatility could be produced through so-called 'cracking', i.e. a technology and *de facto* standard by applying heat and pressure to the residuum after ordinary distillation. But a commercially profitable cracking method and apparatus for manufacturing additional gasoline had not yet been developed. The first such process was perfected by the Indiana Company in 1913; and for more than seven years this was the only one practised in the USA. During that period the Indiana Company not only manufactured cracked gasoline on a large scale, but also licensed the technology to fifteen independent firms to use that process. Meanwhile, since the phenomenon of cracking was not controlled by any fundamental patent, other firms had been working independently to develop commercial processes of their own. Most prominent among these were the three other primary defendants, the Texas Company, the New Jersey Company, and the Gasoline Products Company. Each of these firms secured numerous patents covering their respectively cracking processes. Beginning in 1920, conflict developed between the four companies concerning the validity, scope, and ownership of patents that had been issued. The primary defendants asserted that it was these difficulties which led to their executing the three principal agreements making up a patent pool, which the Justice Department had attacked; and that their sole object was to avoid the litigation and losses incident to conflicting patents (Standard Oil Co. v. United States 283 U.S. 163 (1931)). See also E. Bement v. Nat'l Harrow Co., 186 U.S. 70 (1902); Carpet Seaming Tape Licensing Corp. v. Best Seam Inc., 616 F. 2d 1133 (9th Cir. 1980); Kobe, Inc. v. Dempsey Pump Co., 198 F.2d 416 (10th Cir.

There are also cases from the 1960s and 70s concerning product standards rather than interoperability standards and concern antitrust harm theories such as collusive conduct in the form of buyer and seller cartels. There is, for example, the famous *Macaroni* case[69] where the defendants responded to a temporary shortage of durum semolina wheat by setting a product standard for pasta that only required 50 per cent durum semolina and 50 per cent of inferior wheat. Hovenkamp argued that, by changing the standard, the defendants intended to suppress the price of durum semolina wheat input, and, of course, the defendants' costs.

The *C-O Two* decision[70] and the *Household Radiators* case[71] revolved around the issue that by creating a narrow product standard, product differentiation was either completely lost or at least reduced to the extent that prices (and costs) among the members became aligned to the point that the court found the collaborations to be seller cartels. There are several similar cases from the 60s and 70s, and Hovenkamp agrees that, while one or two of them were too far reaching, most probably still reflect accurate antitrust law and policy. They carry an important message according to Hovenkamp: that product differentiation is still an important antitrust value, and, thus, 'standards that do no more than reduce product differentiation in order to facilitate price matching do not provide a social benefit'.[72]

In the early patent ambush cases, where the notion of 'patent trolls' originated, there was a discussion, specifically when Qualcomm became the defendant in several cases, that the PAEs were actually the victims of buyer cartels, monopsonies, where mainly vertically integrated (telecommunications) firms collectively tried to reduce the royalty rate by

---

1952); Baker-Cammack Hosiery Mills, Inc. v. Davis Co., 181 F.2d 550 (4th Cir. 1950); Cutter Labs., Inc. v. Lyophile-Cryochem Corp., 179 F.2d 80 (9th Cir. 1949); King v. Anthony Pools, Inc., 202 F. Supp. 426 (S.D. Cal. 1962); United States v. Singer Mfg. Co., 374 U.S. 174 (1963); United States v. New Wrinkle, Inc., 342 U.S. 371 (1952); United States v. Line Material Co., 333 U.S. 287 (1948); United States v. U.S. Gypsum Co., 333 U.S. 364 (1948); Hartford-Empire Co. v. United States, 323 U.S. 386 (1945).

[69] Nat. Macaroni Mfrs. Ass'n., 65 FTC 583 (1964), enforced, 345 F.2d 421 (7th Cir. 1965).

[70] C-O-Two Fire Equip. Co. v. United States 197 F2d 489 (9th Circ), cert. denied, 344 U.S. 892 (1952).

[71] United States v. Am Radiator and Standard Sanitary Corp. 433 F2d 174, 185 (3rd Cir 1970), cert denied, 401 U.S. 948 (1971).

[72] Herbert Hovenkamp, 'Standard and Ownership Policy', (2007) 48 *Boston College Law Review*, 87, 95.

colluding over the calculation of FRAND and what FRAND might be when it came to royalty rates. The difference between this situation and the cases above is the infrastructure character of the relevant telecom standards. GSM and UMTS (3G) standards are both interoperability and infrastructure standards which need to be accessible by product manufacturers, while, for example, *Standard Sanitary* and *Macaroni* involved standards which *de facto* limited choice in an effort to increase or reduce prices on markets which were able to hold different products. The argument that PAEs were exposed to anti-competitive monopsonies in the telecom sector was mainly put forward in Europe, and had no, or very limited, success. The cases with Qualcomm were settled.[73]

The successful cases concerning collusion under SSO concern either buyer and seller cartels, but the cartels are present and the effect of the cartels are on product markets. The standards facilitate the product markets cartels.

B. Group boycott, including exclusionary standards Most cases concerning standards and standard setting outside the field of intellectual property law (e.g. cases where a technology was not selected because of the number and cost of SEPs, or patent ambush, or other cases based on unilateral actions by patentees), concern firms whose technology or services were rejected as the standard or part of the standard.[74] These cases border on a collective refusal to deal, and many of them concern membership on or acceptance by various accreditation boards. However, the concern is mainly about an SSO selecting a product standard that *de facto* excludes competing or substitute technologies.

The *Allied Tube* line of case law fits within this category. In these cases, the plaintiffs were able to show that the standard-setting procedure had been abused with the result that competition had been excluded. See also *Hydrolevel,* where the Supreme Court found that an officer of the SSO acted almost fraudulently to exclude a competitor's or potential competitor's technology. The leading case regarding an exclusionary

[73] Mainly Geradin seem to have had this point of view. See Damien Geradin, 'Standardization and Technological Innovation: Some Reflections on Ex-ante Licensing, FRAND, and the Proper Means to Reward Innovators', (2006) 29 *World Competition*, 511; Damien Geradin et al., *Elves or Trolls? The Role of Non Practicing Patent Owners in the Innovation Economy* (SSRN 2008). Geradin seems to have acted as an attorney on the behalf of Qualcomm before the EU Commission.

[74] Hertbert Hovenkamp et al., *IP and Antitrust: An Analysis of Antitrust Principles Applied to Intellectual Property Law* (Aspen Publishers, 2010), § 35.4.

standard is, however, the *Radiant Burners,*[75] where the Supreme Court seems to indicate that the intent of the defendants, i.e. the members of the group boycott, will determine whether there might be antitrust exclusion. A purpose of unlawful combination and conspiracy by the members of a SSO by not certifying a specific burner, and by not providing gas for the same, constituted an antitrust offence in *Radiant Burner,* where anti-competitive harm and effect was proven.

There are also cases at a District Court level using a similar line of thinking when it comes to interoperability or network standards. In the *Golden Bridge* cases,[76] a plaintiff asserted that some members of one of the 3G standards/platforms (3GPP) had restricting the standard to such extent that the plaintiff's technology ceased to be included and it, thus, lost revenues from this exclusion due to the delisting of its patents as essential under the standard. The plaintiff provided the court with some evidence of conversations between members of the SDO, which had taken place outside the technical committee, which the plaintiff said showed a purpose of narrowing the standard ('clean it up') and, hence, of lessening the number of technologies under the standard. The District Court did not, in the end, find any evidence of illegal antitrust conspiracy. However, it seems that the District Court allowed a discovery procedure on a per se standard based on the possible establishment of a group boycott under Sec 1 Sherman Act. The Fifth Circuit affirmed this decision without commenting on the use of the per se rule.[77]

The case is somewhat different from the cases above, *C-O Two*[78] and *Household Radiators,* and also from the *Allied Tube* line of case law. *Golden Bridge* reflects the fact that there are many patents which are claimed to be essential under the 3G standard, and also that the 3G standard was too wide, i.e. it included too many technologies. Thus, the defendants had a good explanation for their conduct, and the claim of conspiracy therefore fell flat. Furthermore, in this case, the plaintiff

---

[75] Radiant Burners, Inc v. People's Gas and Coke Comp. et al 364 U.S. 656, 81 S, Ct. 365 (1961).

[76] Golden Bridge Technology Inc. v. Nokia Inc. 416 F.Supp.2d 525. See also Golden Bridge Technology Inc. v Nokia, Inc. 527 F.3d 1318, 87 U.S.PQ.2d 1049 (Fed. Cir 2008) and Golden Bridge Technology Inc. v (Motorola, Inc. 547 F.3d 266 (Fed. Cir 2008). For a similar case dismissed for lack of stating claim see Trueposition, Inc. v. LM Ericsson Telephone Company 2012 WL 33075 (N.D. Cal. May 14, 2012).

[77] Golden Bridge Technology Inc. v Motorola, Inc. 547 F.3d 266 (Fed. Cir 2008).

[78] C-O-Two Fire Equip. Co. v. United States 197 F2d 489 (9th Circ), cert. denied, 344 U.S. 892 (1952).

demanded that its technology should be included in the standard; thus, that its technology should be considered essential and within the group of patents that downstream manufacturers must license. The plaintiff could still market its technology, while it would not be considered an SEP. *Allied Tube* and the other cases concerned plaintiffs who wanted to get their substitute competing technologies certified so as to be able to *de facto* compete in the downstream markets. However, without certification they were excluded from the market.

Thus, it seems, ordinarily, when launching an antitrust claim for abuse of the standard-setting process, it will only be possible to demonstrate an effect on competition when the market can sustain several standards or technologies (no network effects) and the SSO and its members have *de facto* excluded a competing technology, derived from a competing firm.[79] In addition, as discussed above, the standard must have exclusionary effect, which is most often proven by the fact that the standard is adopted as a regulation by state or local governments[80], or at least is *de facto* implemented on the market with the same effect as a regulation. The markets in *Allied Tube*, *Hydrolevel* and *Radiant Burners* could all accommodate different standards or products. In other words, in *Golden Bridge* the outcome would perhaps have been different had the plaintiff been able to show that his technology was a substitute and that, had it been recognized under the relevant standard, it would have increased competition on the downstream market.

Given the cases above, a successful plaintiff needs to show that two basic requirements have been fulfilled: (i) the market that is being standardized can sustain several standards and (ii) deciding on one standard *de facto* excludes a competitor or competing standard/ technology from the market.

The courts also seem to set up two more requirements for a successful antitrust case. *Radiant Burners*[81] seems to indicate that a plaintiff needs to identify anti-competitive intent on the part of at least some competitors in the SSO. *Radiant Burners* concerned a plaintiff who developed

---

[79] Hertbert Hovenkamp et al., *IP and Antitrust: An Analysis of Antitrust Principles Applied to Intellectual Property Law* (Aspen Publishers, 2010), 35.4, 35-31.

[80] Cf. the National Technology Transfer and Advancement Act of 1995, stating that Federal Agencies should make use of private sector standards as far as possible.

[81] Radiant Burners, Inc v. People's Gas and Coke Comp. et al 364 U.S. 656, 81 S, Ct. 365 (1961).

ceramic gas burners and the complaint alleged that the relevant standard-setting organization, due to undue pressure by its members, had arbitrary denied approval of the plaintiff's burner. Without an approval, the gas companies (which were members of the SSO) refused to provide gas for the plaintiff's burners. *Consolidated Metal Pro,*[82] was a case concerning the standardization and approval of rods in the oil industry and alleged delay of certifications for such rods by a trade association. The Fifth Circuit indicated that unlawful purpose (i.e. conspiracy and concerted attempt) or anti-competitive effect is needed for the court to find a violation under the rule of reason. The other successful cases, *Allied Tube* and *Hydrolevel* also discussed misuse or abuse of the standard-setting process to the point where there was fraudulent conduct on the behalf of certain members of the SDO. It seems therefore, according to Hovenkamp, that under US antitrust law, a successful plaintiff needs to show some form of anti-competitive intent, at least where there is no clear anti-competitive effect. As Hovenkamp discusses, showing intent with reference to an association is difficult, while perhaps the intent of individual competitors and members, who have used the SSO to exclude a competitor, may be shown more easily.[83] Intent helps to distinguish the intention to restrict competition from, rightly or wrongly, technical decisions to reject a technology.[84] However, perhaps intent should be reserved for the few cases where the technology not selected for the standard is not present on the market and is only a substitute technology (i.e. no direct anticompetitive effects), and where there has been a misuse of the standard-setting process which does not amount to a violation of the SDO's by-laws, only to the customary rules and mores of the SDOs and the industry. Only in these rare cases should the court start analysing the intent of the parties involved.

Finally, when the plaintiff has shown all the above, i.e. exclusionary effect and anti-competitive intent, the defendants may exculpate themselves, according to Hovenkamp, by showing the superiority of the

---

[82] Consolidated Metal Prod. v. American Petroleum Inst. 846 F.2d 284, 293 et seq, (5th Circ 1988).

[83] See Moore v Boating Industry Assn. where the court found that the members of the boat trailer association were not competitors of the tail light company that alleged that their standard excluded its product. Hence, the court found that there was no motive to exclude. 819 F.2d 693 (7th Cir. 1987).

[84] Hertbert Hovenkamp,et al., *IP and Antitrust: An Analysis of Antitrust Principles Applied to Intellectual Property Law* (Aspen Publishers, 2010), §35.4, 35-34. A difficult issue is how to attribute the anti-competitive intent of a few members to other members or to the organization.

standardized technology. According to Hovenkamp, the courts should be very reluctant to embroil themselves in evaluating complex technical concepts, but there are times when the courts are forced to do so. Where an antitrust plaintiff has shown that one standard was chosen over others, that prima facie, the other technologies were rejected for anti-competitive purposes, and that that has had relevant economic effects on the market by making the market less competitive, it is likely that the standard was not selected on technical merits. However, the defendants should be able to argue as a defence that the selected technology is still superior and was selected on its merits. The burden of proof is on the defendant.[85] The defendants should therefore be allowed to put forward objective justifications for the choice of technology.

The test described above should also, with some alteration, be put to use regarding membership in the standard-setting organization, and then presumably also regarding membership in the relevant technical committee. Possibly, if the standard-setting process under an industry-wide SDO aims to develop an infrastructure standard which will deny a competitor membership, based on an anti-competitive motive, it could be considered antitrust violation. That said, it should still be remembered that a group boycott intended to exclude a competitor from an association does not seem to be regarded as a per se violation under Sec. 1 Sherman Act (cf. *Northwest Wholesalers*). The rule of reason should be applied in standard-setting scenarios. The essential facility doctrine seems, after *Verizon,* not to be applicable in the US antitrust system under Sec. 1 Sherman Act. Nonetheless, perhaps access to the result of the standard-setting process should be litigated under IP law. Regarding SEPs, and access to such patents as held by members of an SSO under a dominant or monopoly standard, the *eBay* rule under US intellectual property law could be utilized by a licensee/defendant. The question is whether US antitrust law has any tools available to a licensee in these situations. It depends how the recent decision by FTC in the *Google* case is interpreted.

Thus, in conclusion, it seems that conduct that might fall outside the NCRPA exemption should not be presumed to be anti-competitive. Likewise, conduct that might fall inside the NCRPA may still, without too much imagination, be thought to cause anti-competitive harm. This might give an indication that the objective of the NCRPA is not to

---

[85] Hertbert Hovenkam et al., *IP and Antitrust: An Analysis of Antitrust Principles Applied to Intellectual Property Law* (Aspen Publishers, 2010), § 35.4, 35-35.

identify anti-competitive harm, but instead to promote the regulation certain business activities by SDOs. Clearly, the members of SDOs can still be addressed with anti-competitive suits. The test discussed above seems difficult to apply, but it is still a valid test for indentifying anti-competitive conduct in the standard-setting process.

It is interesting to analyse the cases according to whether they concern product standards or other forms of standards, i.e. network-driven interoperability or infrastructure standards. Under the rule of reason, US courts seem to have been able to distinguish these standards, since plaintiffs will have a difficult time proving an anti-competitive effect if the market can only hold one standard. In these cases it is very difficult to prove that the natural exclusive effect of selecting a standard is anti-competitive.

The cases above seem to point to a test that includes the following criteria. A plaintiff needs to show:

1. that the market can sustain several standards or technologies (effectively excluding all cases derived from the network-driven industry, i.e. interoperability or infrastructure standards);
2. that the decision on a product standard *de facto* excludes a competitor or potential competitor by excluding a competing or substitute standard or technology from the market. Thus, there is an anti-competitive or potentially anti-competitive effect;
3. that there has been misuse of the standard-setting process by either violation of the by-law and IP policy of the SSO or of the customary business practice under the SDO; or a conspiracy on the part of the members of the SSO, inter alia, through an anti-competitive intent to exclude.

The allegation can be defeated by an objective justification by the members showing that the selected technology is superior. The existence of a patent thicket would also be a defence. In fact, the discussion about the superiority of the technology could be included under (3) where the plaintiff needs to show anti-competitive intent. This test still seems to remain intact, even after the implementation of the Standard Development Organization Advancement Act under the NCRPA.

4.1.5 The Business Review Letters on SDOs

(i) Introduction

Interestingly, the Business Review Letter procedure is applicable if the parties to a joint R&D or SDO are not sure whether they are inside the safe harbour of the NCRPA.

Under the Business Review Letter procedure, which is separate from the NCRPA, parties can informally ask the Justice Department how it would view a proposed arrangement from an antitrust perspective. The Justice Department is not bound to make a decision and, if it does, it is not legally bound to follow it in the future. However, the procedure is an efficient and informal way to have *ex ante* control of a proposed joint venture before the parties committed to the standard through investments. They can still also make use of the NCRPA, even if they apply for a Business Review Letter.

A positive Business Review Letter does not formally eliminate the risk that the Justice Department will later charge the collaborators with breaching the antitrust laws. However, in practice, the risk is minimal.[86] Therefore, the combination of the NCRPA and the Business Review system enables the collaboration to be immune against both private and public suits. The elegance of this system is impressive especially with reference to an antitrust jurisprudence which often is not very clear-cut. However, the elegance is somewhat tarnished by two elements: first, the R&D market or innovation market concept is vague. It is difficult to distinguish whether a joint effort is conducting R&D within an innovation market that contains other competitors. For an adequate analysis, the Justice Department would need more information than will be provided under the NCRPA or under the Business Review Letter procedure. R&D is often conducted under strict confidence.

In some recent Business Review Letters, the Justice Department has indicated where it stands with reference to SDOs, IP arrangements under SDOs, and the interaction between SDOs, patent pools and members of the same.[87] The Justice Department does not go as far as the NCRPA in

---

86 To the author's knowledge, no collaboration approved under a Business Review Letter has later been challenged by the Justice Department.

87 VITA Business Review Letter from Thomas O. Barnett to Robert A. Skitol, dated 30 October 2006, and IEEE Business Review Letter from Thomas O. Barnett to Michael A. Lindsay, dated 30 April 2007. See also RFID Business Review Letter from Thomas O. Barnett to William F. Dolan and Geoffrey Oliver dated 21 October 2008, 8. For an interesting, latter, Business Review Letter, see American Welding Society Business Review Letter from Charles James to

the Business Review Letters. In other words, the immunity under the NCRPA for private plaintiffs or in-between parties is wider than what the Justice Department seems willing to accept. The NCRPA covers joint R&D ventures, SDOs and, to some extent, pools and with the Business Review Letters analysed below, the Justice Department makes a similar but narrower 'soft' exemption available for members of SDOs.

The background to the letters is formed by the heated discussion regarding the interpretation of RAND terms, the definition of patent ambush and, more generally, the belief that the SDO working groups drafting technology standards should have access to the prices and other terms for which technologies are available before they make a selection of a technology path.[88]

The Justice Department states in the letters, under the rule of reason, that SDOs' IP policies may contain requirements for members who are working on drafting a new standard to reveal essential patents, and patent applications that might become essential patents, under the new standard. Moreover, the IP policies may require the members to reveal the maximum royalty rates and the other most restrictive non-price related licensing terms in reference to these patents or patent applications. In addition, the VITA business letter states that if a member fails to disclose draft non-licensing terms, the member company must accept certain covenants in its standard licensing agreement. VITA only allows for specific limited grant-back clauses or reciprocal licence requirements, non-assert requirements, not-to-sue limitations and defensive suspension provisions in these circumstances. If a working group member fails to disclose a known essential patent and/or fails to declare the most restrictive licensing terms, the proposed VITA IP policy states that the essential patent needs to be licensed royalty-free.

Douglas Mcdonald, dated 7 October 2002, where the Justice Department stated that it does not consider whether one standard is better than the other, only whether the process of standard setting has been abused. The letters can be found on http://www.justice.gov/atr/public/busreview/letters.html#page=page-1, accessed 19 March 2012. The American Welding Society letter is discussed in Peter Plompen, 'The New Technology Transfer Guidelines (TTG) as Applied to Patent Pools and Patent Pool Licensing: Some Observations Regarding the Concept of 'Essential Technologies', in Claus Dieter Ehlermann and Isabela Atanasin (eds), *European Competition Law Annual 2005: The Interaction between Competition Law and Intellectual Property Law* (Hart Publishing, 2005), 300 fn. 11.

[88] Ibid. Historically, many SDOs required holders of essential patents to make them available royalty-free on reasonable and non-discriminatory terms.

The VITA letter goes far in allowing SDOs to demand that SEP holders abide by stringent licensing requirements.

It should also be noted that in the IEEE letter, the Justice Department agrees that the SDO may set up systems which would also enable non-members to claim that the terms a patentee publicly discloses to a SDO should apply to them.[89] However, it should be clear that neither system, with reference to specific licensees, contractually binds patentees actually to license the patents on the terms disclosed to the SDO in question.[90] Nonetheless, there are legal doctrines that may be available to enforce such terms.[91]

The Justice Department states that unless the standard-setting process is used as a sham to cloak naked price-fixing or bid-rigging, action or conduct under the standard-setting process will be judged under the rule of reason.[92] However, in a footnote to the IEEE letter, the Department indicates that it would typically apply a rule-of-reason analysis to joint negotiations of licensing terms in the standard-setting context.[93]

Whether the Justice Department allows for SDOs' IP disclosure rules only with reference to essential patents or more broadly is not clear. The letters state that the SDOs and SSOs may oblige the patentees to disclose publicly the terms within the licensing agreements. This is however not limited only to essential patents under the contemplated standard. The members may than take the licensing costs into consideration when establishing the technology standard.

---

[89] See IEEE Business Review Letter from Thomas O. Barnett to Michael A. Lindsay, dated 30 April 2007, http://www.usdoj.gov/atr/public/busreview/222978.htm. Accessed 23 May 2012.

[90] This is, of course, dependent on the national law under which the individual case is tried. See Mark Lemley, 'Intellectual Property Rights and Standard-Setting Organizations', (2002) 90 *California Law Review*, 1889, 1909 et seq., especially 1914 et seq. Lemley seems to indicate that generally under US contract law there might be ways to bind patentees contractually to what they have disclosed to the SDOs.

[91] See the Qualcomm and Broadcom saga, discussed infra Chapter 6.

[92] An often repeated phrase at the beginning of Business Review Letters. See the VITA Business Review Letter from Thomas O. Barnett to Robert A. Skitol, dated 30 October 2006; and IEEE Business Review Letter from Thomas O. Barnett to Michael A. Lindsay, dated April 30, 2007. The letters can be found on http://www.justice.gov/atr/public/busreview/letters.html#page=page-1. Accessed 19 March 2012.

[93] See the IEEE Business Review Letter from Thomas O. Barnett to Michael A. Lindsay, dated 30 April 2007, fn. 47. http://www.usdoj.gov/atr/public/bus review/222978.htm., accessed 24 May 2012.

Moreover, the Justice Department has not taken a stand on IP arrangements or agreements entered into *ex ante* agreement of the technology standard. At least the Justice Department has decided not to give its view on joint negotiations or discussion of the licensing terms among the working group members or with third parties *ex ante* the technology standardization agreement entered into.[94] It is clear that parties are allowed to set up a patent pool after the implementation of a technology standard.[95]

None of the SDOs' IP policies notified under the Business Review Letter scheme allowed for straight *ex ante* negotiations regarding terms, so that the Justice Department did not have to address the issue. The antitrust enforcement agencies are however not against *ex ante* IP negotiations, so long as they are not sham agreements to cover price cartels in product markets.[96] Therefore, IP arrangements or agreements will likely be judged under the rule of reason should they be addressed under the Business Review Letter scheme.[97] However, one reason for caution is that the SDOs discussed above deal mainly with high-tech network-driven industries. The question is whether the Justice Department would be as generous to an SDO creating standards for regular 'old economy' products, when the relevant market may be open for several products/standards to compete.

In conclusion, still according to the Justice Department, patentees may not set prices for the products to be produced in the downstream market through an IP arrangement; however, agreement on royalty rates should

---

[94] See the IEEE Business Review Letter from Thomas O. Barnett to Michael A. Lindsay, dated 30 April 2007, fn. 47, http://www.usdoj.gov/atr/public/busreview/222978.htm., accessed 24 May 2012.

[95] Compare the VITA Business Review Letter from Thomas O. Barnett to Robert A. Skitol, dated 30 October 2006, and the IEEE Business Review Letter from Thomas O. Barnett to Michael A. Lindsay, dated 30 April 2007, with the RFID Business Review Letter from Thomas O. Barnett to William F. Doland and Geoffrey Oliver, dated 21 October 2008. The letters can be found on http://www.justice.gov/atr/public/busreview/letters.html#page=page-1. Accessed 19 March 2012.

[96] See IP 2 Report, 37. See also IEEE Business Review Letter from Thomas O. Barnett to Michael A. Lindsay, dated 30 April 2007 where the Justice Department deliberately states that it is not offering a view of joint negotiations during the standard-setting process. See http://www.usdoj.gov/atr/public/busreview/222978.htm, accessed 19 March 2013.

[97] See the IEEE Business Review Letter from Thomas O. Barnett to Michael A. Lindsay, dated 30 April 2007, fn. 47. http://www.usdoj.gov/atr/public/busreview/222978.htm. Accessed 19 March 2012.

be judged under the rule of reason according to the NCRPA.[98] Thus, 'price maintenance clauses' or price-fixing for the product markets would be judged under the per se rule.[99]

4.1.6 Conclusion

The 2004 amendment to include SDOs under the NCRPA seems to have had the expected effect. Formally, the NCRPA stipulates three different consequences as a result of its applicability: (i) the per se rule under antitrust law is not applicable; (ii) the 'loser pays principle', i.e. plaintiffs have to reimburse the defendant should the plaintiff not be successful in an antitrust suit; and (iii) no trebling of damages. *De facto*, these three limitations imply that several kinds of collaboration or conduct are exempted under US Antitrust law, at least from private suits.[100]

Nonetheless, the case law regarding standard setting indicates that there still is a way to deal with members of SDOs for both collusive and exclusionary conduct. Nonetheless, the rule of reason test implemented by the Supreme Court and lower courts stipulates a high threshold.

---

[98] See VITA Business Review Letter from Thomas O. Barnett to Robert A. Skitol, dated 30 October 2006 and IEEE Business Review Letter from Thomas O. Barnett to Michael A. Lindsay, dated 30 April 2007. The letters can be found on http://www.justice.gov/atr/public/busreview/letters.html#page=page-1. Accessed 19 March 2012.

[99] See VITA Business Review Letter from Thomas O. Barnett to Robert A. Skitol, dated 30 October. 2006, 7. An agreement the price at which licensees should market goods is perhaps not infringing US antitrust law, see generally U.S. v. General Electric Company et al., 272 U.S. 476, 477 (1926). It is questionable whether this precedent still reflects applicable law, see Lawrence Sullivan and Warren Grimes, *The Law of Antitrust: An Integrated Handbook* (Thomson/West, 2006), 910 et seq. However, by overruling Dr. Miles in Leegin Creative Leather Products, Inc. v. PSKS, Inc. et al., 127 S. Ct. 2705, U.S., June 28, 2007, perhaps the Supreme Court is telling us to view General Electric in a new way. Cf. also, William Tom and Joshua Newberg, 'Antitrust and Intellectual Property: From Separate Spheres to Unified Field', (1997) *Antitrust Law Journal*, 167, 176 et seq., especially 178. They seem to imply that Price Maintenance Clauses in patent pool agreements are not per se illegal.

[100] The legal history clearly reflects Congress's opinion that the NCRPA stipulates immunity under the antitrust laws. See H.R. REP. 108–125, reprinted 2004 U.S.C.C.A.N. 609, 612 et seq.

4.2 STANDARDIZATION AGREEMENTS UNDER EU COMPETITION RULES

4.2.1 Introduction

Where participation in the standard-setting procedure is unrestricted and the process for adopting the standard in question is transparent, standardization agreements which contain no obligation to comply with the standard and provide access to the standard on fair, reasonable and non-discriminatory terms will normally not restrict competition within the meaning of Article 101(1) TFEU.[101] This safe harbour was introduced in 2010 with the new Horizontal Guidelines.[102] The Horizontal Guidelines stress that a high market share held by the parties in the markets affected by the standard will not necessarily be a concern in the canalysis of a standardization agreement.[103] Thus, the agreement establishing the standard is legitimate even though entered into by parties who jointly or separately hold a dominant position on the product market, as long as the standard is free for other (competitors) to adopt and influence.

In this section I will discuss standardization agreements under EU competition law. First, immunity under EU competition law for SDOs will be discussed. That immunity is built on two pillars: (i) the definition of 'undertaking' and to some extent 'agreement' in EU competition law; and (ii) the block exemption for R&D agreements and the safe harbour in the Horizontal Guidelines. Thereafter, the scant case law and the Horizontal Guidelines will be analysed to see whether there is a prevailing test under EU competition law for when standardization agreements may be violating competition law. Before the comparative analysis, the interface between joint R&D and standardization agreements will be eliminated.

4.2.2 Undertaking and the Connection between Competition Law and the Free Trade Rules

While private standards, as discussed above, are on the rise, public standards are on the decline. Less formalized, faster, and more efficient than public institutions, there is also less accountability for SSOs and

---

[101] Horizontal Guidelines, para. 280.

[102] Also, the EU Commission states that this is a safe harbour, see Commission Press Release 'Competition: the Commission Adopts Revised Competition Rules on Horizontal Co-operation Agreements', IP 10/1702.

[103] Horizontal Guidelines, para. 296.

their members. Private standards have also, presumably, been considered immune to the reach of e.g. Article 34 TFEU, or for that matter the US dormant commerce clause, while public technical regulations, in cases like *Dassonville*[104] and *Keck,*[105] have been under attack for preventing access to markets.[106] As discussed above, similar case law regarding public technical regulations may be found in the USA under the dormant commerce clause, see *Minnesota v. Clover Leaf Creamary Co.*[107] and *Bibb v. Navajo Freight Lines*[108].

While the dichotomy between public regulations and private standards is still relevant, the recent *SELEX*[109], *Fr.bo*[110] and *OTOC*[111] cases have, at least, opened up a small opportunity to use Art 34 TFEU in connection to privately produced standards and SSOs also.

(i) SELEX case

> **BOX 4.4**
>
> In the *SELEX* case,[112] first the General Court and then the CJEU shed some light on the standard-setting process and the interaction between research and development and standards. The Courts had to scrutinize an international standard-setting body, the European Organization for the Safety of Air Navigation

---

[104] Case 8/74 Dassonville [1974] ECR 837.

[105] Joined cases C-267 and 268/91, Keck and Mithourd [1993] ECR I-6097.

[106] It should be mentioned that in an isolated obiter dictum in Dansk Supermarked, the ECJ held in 1981 that 'it is impossible in any circumstances for agreements between individuals to derogate from the mandatory provisions of the Treaty on the free movement of goods', case 58/80 Dansk Supermarked v. Imerco [1980] ECR 181, para 17. Even though the ECJ has thereafter ignored this statement, it gives support to a general principle under free trade rules to apply them also to standard agreements.

[107] Minnesota v. Clover Leaf Creamary Co, 449 U.S. 456 (1981).

[108] Bibb v. Navajo Freight Lines, 359 U.S. 520 (1959).

[109] C-113/07 P – Selex Sistemi Integrati v Commission [2009] ECR I-02207 and T-155/04 – SELEX Sistemi Integrati v Commission [2006] ECR II-04797.

[110] Case C-171/11 Fr.bo SpA v. DVGW, not reported yet.

[111] C-1/12 OTOC v. Autoridade da Concorrencia, not reported yet.

[112] C-113/07 P – Selex Sistemi Integrati v Commission [2009] ECR I-02207 and T-155/04 – SELEX Sistemi Integrati v Commission [2006] ECR II-04797.

(Eurocontrol),[113] which primarily set standards in the area for air navigation to enable the participating states to create a uniform system for Air Traffic Management (ATM). Eurocontrol was set up by contracting States, and the CJEU describes its role as being akin to that of a minister, who, at national level, prepares legislation or regulatory matters which are then adopted by the government. The second area of activity was its research and development tasks. The research activity consisted of spearheading joint studies of new technologies in the ATM sector. It acquires and develops prototypes of ATM equipment and systems, for example radar systems, with a view to using that equipment and knowledge to validate and define new standards and technical specifications. Under its research activity, Eurocontrol created a regime of intellectual property rights in relation to the prototypes purchased under research contracts from undertakings. Access to these rights becomes important for competing undertakings should the prototype lead to enactment of a standard. Access to these rights was however dependent on whether Eurocontol or the developer of the prototype held the necessary rights in question. The applicant, SELEX, accused the Commission of not taking action against Eurocontrol and its regime of intellectual property rights developed under its research of prototypes. Eurocontrol's research created, according to SELEX, factual monopolies in the systems that eventually became standards and the firms that provided the prototypes were therefore in a particularly advantageous position compared to their competitors. This situation was all the more serious because Eurocontrol did not use a transparent, open and non-discriminatory system for the acquisition of the prototypes and, thus, for establishing the standards.

The case regarding the non-action of the Commission was based on the applicability of Article 102 TFEU and not Article 101 TFEU. Nevertheless, some interesting conclusions may be drawn. Firstly, the General Court concluded that Eurocontrol's standardization activities could not be regarded as economic activities and the EU competition rules were therefore not applicable.[114] The General Court carefully distinguished between

[113] Not the first time. See also C-364/92 – SAT Fluggesellschaft v. Eurocontrol [1994] ECR I-00043.

[114] See C-113/07 P – Selex Sistemi Integrati v. Commission [2009] ECR I-, paras 59 et seq.

researching, developing and adopting standards and, initially, scrutinized each activity individually. According to the General Court there was no market for a technical standardization service in the sector of ATM equipment. Thus, Eurocontrol could not be regarded as offering a service. Secondly, the General Court stated that nor could the research and development activities be regarded as economic activities, since the acquisitions did not involve the offering of goods or services on a given market. This was further supported by the fact that the intellectual property rights developed under the research were made available to anyone concerned at no cost. Only some confidential information held by the firm which sold the prototype to Eurocontrol was not available to competitors. The intellectual property rights pool was also to be considered ancillary to the 'non-economic' research and development activity.[115] The Court continued that even if it were established that Eurocontrol did not have a system in place for distinguishing between rights and technologies, e.g. source codes, developed under the research contracts and background software, it did not make the intellectual property rights regime economic in nature.

The CJEU went beyond the findings of the General Court and struck down the General Courts dichotomy between different conducts of Eurocontrol. According to CJEU the adoption of standards could not be separated from the production of the same, and that preparation and production of standards could not be separated from the public task (or the expression of public power) vested in Eurocontrol of managing air space and developing air safety.[116] Therefore, Eurocontrol was not to be considered an undertaking.

The question is whether this case relieves all forms of standard development body, such as CEN, CENELEC and even ETSI, and also their handling of intellectual property rights and R&D, from the ambit of EU

[115] The Court also distinguishes Eurocontrol from collective societies since they, according to the Court, collect fees for their members and therefore do conduct an economic activity. See point 78.

[116] C-113/07 P – Selex Sistemi Integrati v. Commission [2009] ECR I-02207, paras 89 et seq.

competition law.[117] Clearly, the case opens up an avenue for arguing that SDOs with the public task of producing standards may not be undertakings. Somewhat alarming is the way CJEU did not stop with such a conclusion, but, instead, disregarded the General Court's division of conducts in preparation, production and adoption of standards. CJEU's method or test for tying the conducts together, and finding them all fall under the 'public power and thereto connected conduct' exemption, not only seems to be redefining the boundaries between an undertaking and the exercise of public power set out in earlier case law,[118] it makes it also more difficult to argue that members of technical committees of SDOs may violate EU competition law when creating a standard that may possibly try to restrict competitors or exclude competing technical solutions. It should be acknowledged that ETSI accepts that its members are undertakings and it is an association of undertakings under EU competition law. Nonetheless, the *SELEX* case seems to establish an exemption under EU law that resembles the 2004 amendments under the US NCRPA, which effectively exempts all SDOs and their handling of technologies and of intellectual property rights.

(ii) Fr.bo case[119]

BOX 4.5

In the recent *Fr.bo* case the CJEU takes a new but expected step in the direction established in the *SELEX* judgement and actually finds that an SSO, and standards, can be scrutinized under Art 34 TFEU.

---

[117] According to the Horizontal Guidelines, the European standardization bodies recognized under Directive 98/34/EC of the European Parliament and of the Council of 22 June 1998 laying down a procedure for the provision of information in the field of technical standards and regulations and on rules on Information Society services (2) are subject to competition law to the extent that they can be considered to be an undertaking or an association of undertakings within the meaning of Articles 101 and 102 (3). Horizontal Guidelines, para. 258.

[118] See case 246/86, Belasco v. Commission [1989] ECR 2117, para 49, making reference to Commission decision 86/399 /EEC (1986) OJ L 232 /15, para. 73.

[119] Case C-171/11 Fr.bo SpA v. DVGW, not reported yet.

The background of the case is the following. According to a German Regulation on general conditions of Water Supply copper parts of water pipes must comply with recognised rules (standards) for the supply of water. Copper components labelled with the German review and standard body DVGW brand were assumed to fulfil the rules.

DVGW is an SSO, a private non-profit organization made up of members which may be utility, gas-and-water sector companies, public institutions and individuals focusing on the promotion of the gas and water sector without being a defendant of the interest of the manufacturers of those sectors. Fra.bo, on the other hand, was an Italian company which produced and sold copper parts. In 2000 Fra.bo [was] granted the right to label their products with DVGW mark for a period of five years. Following a complaint from a third party, DVGW reconsidered and revaluated its decision to grant Fr.bo the right to use the brand. DVGW performed new tests on the copper parts. The copper parts could not pass some of the tests and Fra.bo was given three months to submit a report showing that the copper parts managed the technical requirements stipulated. Fra.bo submitted a report from an Italian laboratory, but this was not adopted because the laboratory was not an 'approved' laboratory according to DVGW. In the meantime, DVGW introduced new tests under the standard for copper parts. Manufacturers of certified copper parts were given three months to submit reports whether their products met the new standards. In 2005, DVGW withdrew the certificate it had issued for Fr.bo in 2000, as Fra.bo had not submitted a report regarding the new tests. Fra.bo appealed DVGW decision to Cologne Regional Court, arguing that the decision on revocation of the certificate presented an obstacle to the free movement of goods under Article 34 TFEU or a violation of Article 101 TFEU. The court dismissed the complaint. The ruling was appealed to the Oberlandesgericht Düsseldorf in 2011 requested a preliminary ruling by the CJEU.

The CJEU considered several factors when analysing whether to use Art 34 or 101 TFEU. The main thrust of the analysis focused on DVGW's special position: it being mentioned in the German Regulation, being *de facto* the only body able to certify copper fittings, and, thus, being able to restrict the marketing and market of products which are not certified by the body. CJEU concluded therefore that Article 34 TFEU was applicable and breached. The CJEU therefore did not need to establish whether Art 101 TFEU was applicable, or not.

The Fr.bo case is an interesting development. In line with case law development in the other areas of free movement (e.g. the *Laval* case[120]), it also provides an opening to judge standards not only in the light of the objectives and aims acknowledged under competition law, but possibly also under other public policy objectives recognized and easily applicable under the Free Trade rules. Clearly, European SDOs risk violating Art 34 TFEU under the *Fr.bo* case.

(iii) OTOC case[121]

BOX 4.6

In a recent case, the CJEU touched upon these issues again. Now in reference to an association for Chartered Accountants in Portugal; Ordem does Técnicos Oficiais de Contas (the OTOC). The OTOC had set up a system of compulsory training for chartered accountants. It seemed clear to the CJEU that even though allowing competing training bodies to provide compulsory training, the OTOC claimed certain courses exclusively.

The CJEU had an interesting discussion and it established that OTOC was regulated under public law and held a public service mission. However, this was immaterial, given its wide discretion vis-a-vis the State in setting up this training. It only held a non-exclusive right to provide training under the law, and the OTOC *de facto* was acting in a relevant market for the professional training of chartered accountants. The relevant rules under OTOC by-laws were found in the end to have violated Art 101 TFEU, since it reflected an exclusionary agreement among its members to exclude competing course providers.

In many ways this case follows the older case law concerning exclusionary certifications. However, it seems clear that SSOs connected to trade

120 C-341/05 – Laval un Partneri [2007] ECR I-11767.

121 C-1/12 OTOC v. Autoridade da Concorrencia not reported yet.

associations, i.e. consortia and fora, would be considered associations of undertakings according to Art 101 TFEU under *OTOC*.[122] The evaluation includes a test with respect to the freedom to decide what to decide about, and whether SSOs act in a standard-setting market. However, the outstanding issue, even after *OTOC*, is still whether collusion within technical committees in the more official SDOs may be addressed under EU competition law.

It seems clear that the SDOs themselves may be exempted under the *SELEX* doctrine. Furthermore, under *Fr.bo* these SDOs may be scrutinized under Art 34 TFEU. The *EMC* case, discussed infra, sheds some more light on the issue whether to use Art 34 TFEU or 101 TFEU, and against what entities. According to the Commission in *EMC*, CEN is a recognized standard body under Directive 98/34/EC and therefore a body entrusted with the general economic interest. This would not totally exclude the possibility of the EU competition law being applied to CEN, while Art. 106 TFEU would possibly need to be applied were the members of CEN proven to consist of 'undertakings'. However, neither the EU Courts nor the EU Commission have yet made a final decision about whether the members of the technical committees may be scrutinized under Art 101 TFEU. Moreover, a plaintiff should be able to utilize the Regulation on European Standardization[123] horizontally vis-a-vis ESOs that are not, for example, transparent. Also, governments making use of ICT corsortia-derived standards that do not live up to the requirements in Annex II of the Regulation on public procurement procedures may be challenged.[124] Thus, a plaintiff that would like to bring an action against CEN does better to use both Art 34, including the Regulation of European Standardisation, and Art 101/102 TFEU.

4.2.3 Cases Concerning Assessment under Art. 101 TFEU

The EU Courts have, in the few early cases where they have addressed standards, found that they either (i) reflected agreements between the members or parties to standardization agreements, or (ii) were decisions

[122] See for example joined cases T-213/95 and T-18/96 SCK and FNK v. Commission [1997] ECR II-1739.

[123] Discussed supra chapter 3.2.2.

[124] Whether a government making use of a harmonized standard that does not live up to the requirements in Annex II may also be sued under the EU law generally and the Regulation specifically is presumably a matter for the CJEU to decide.

by associations of undertakings. In the *IAZ* case[125], the EU Commission was confronted with collusion similar to the collaborations scrutinized in the US *Radiant Burners* case and the *Fr.bo* case. The Belgian trade association, CEG, and other Belgian trade associations of manufacturers and sole importers of dishwashers and washing machines concluded an agreement with the National Association of Water Suppliers (ANSEAU) to monitor compliance with Belgian regulations on water quality. The legislation stipulated that only devices complying with Belgian standards were to be connected to the water supply system. To that end, CEG issued a label of conformity and ANSEAU ensured that only machines bearing the label would be connected. ANSEAU also drew the attention to dealers and consumers to the possible consequences of failure to comply with the standard and the regulation. The Court found that this was a private attempt to re-establish the internal market by restricting parallel trade[126]. Regarding intent to restrict competition, the Commission declared that it did not need a show of intent but that the parties had clearly declared in their correspondence their intention to use the standard as a weapon against parallel traders.[127] The effect on trade and competition was proven, since the restriction under the standard constrained parallel traders, at least potentially.[128]

In a similar case, the General Court addressed a Dutch certification body, Stichting Certificatie Kraanverhuurbedrijf (SCK), set up by Dutch firms hiring out mobile cranes. The SCK was a certification institution recognized by the Certification Council which complied with the European standards, but that did not prevent the Commission and later the Court from applying Art. 101 TFEU. SCK certified companies were obliged to comply with several statutory requirements but the agreements/rules stipulated that any certified firm should not sub-contract

---

[125] Joined cases 96 to 102, 104, 105, 108 and 110/82 IAZ and others v. Commission [1983] ECR 3369.

[126] For a comprehensive analysis, see Harm Schepel, *The Constitution of Private Governance – Product Standards in the Regulation of Integrating Markets* (Hart, 2005), 290.

[127] Joined cases 96 to 102, 104, 105, 108 and 110/82 IAZ and others v. Commission [1983] ECR 3369, 3391.

[128] Harm Schepel, *The Constitution of Private Governance – Product Standards in the Regulation of Integrating Markets* (Hart, 2005), 289 et seq., 311 et seq.

non-certified firms. This found this to impede parallel trade and create a barrier against entry to the relevant Dutch market.[129]

In a decision from 1986 in *Belasco*[130], the Commission and the Court were faced for the first time with a heavily regulated SDO closely connected to the Belgian state. Belasco was an association of Belgian roofing manufacturers. The Commission had an issue with a blatant price cartel agreement connected to the association's conduct of drafting of technical specifications. The Commission thereby tried to stay clear of the standard-setting part of Belasco, where it implemented IBN standards. Belasco appealed specifically on this point, stating that implementing IBN standards would make it immune to Art 101 TFEU but the Court agreed with the Commission.[131]

Finally, in the *EMC* case[132], the Commission and later the Courts found that a standard developed within the Europeans standard system under CEN at least could be addressed under Art. 101 TFEU. The Commission, and the Courts, left unanswered whether the work of a technical committee under an SDO can be regarded as an agreement between undertakings.[133] However, the Commission acknowledged that not only are the members of the technical committees experts representing undertakings, but also the national representations to CEN are staffed with members who originate from the relevant industry. It seems that they, in their capacity as members of the technical committees, still conduct an 'economic activity', and do not lose their standing as 'undertakings' under EU competition law. The Commission made an analysis of all the requirements of Art. 101 TFEU and, since the safe harbour was applicable to CEN and the technical committee and the adjoining standard-setting trade association, it did not address the difficult issue of whether the conduct of a technical committee can be considered an agreement under Art. 101 TFEU.

In light of the above, a plaintiff must under the EU system make use of two lines of arguments which may prove very contradictory if it wishes to bring an action against a standard, an SDO or the members (of the

---

129 Joined cases T-213/95 and T-18/96 SCK and FNK v Commission [1997] ECR II-1739.

130 Case 246/86 Belasco v. Commission [1986] ECR 2117.

131 Harm Schepel, *The Constitution of Private Governance – Product Standards in the Regulation of Integrating Markets* (Hart, 2005), 289 et seq., 311 et seq.

132 Case COMP/F-2/38.401 EN 197 1 Standard- EMC/European Cement.

133 Case COMP/F-2/38.401 EN 197-1 Standard- EMC/European Cement, para. 75.

technical committee) of an SDO under EU law. Perhaps, Art 34 TFEU could best be utilized (if applicable) vis-a-vis the SDO, while Art 101 TFEU should be applied to the members of the SDO. This seems to be the distinction that the Commission and the Courts have tried to carve out. The question is whether this would lead to the same result. Art 34 and 36 TFEU seem to offer greater opportunities to use public policy arguments both for a plaintiff and a defendant, while the anti-competitive effect under Art 101 TFEU might be difficult for a plaintiff to prove. Furthermore, as will be discussed below, there is a block exemption and a safe harbour that may be applicable under Art. 101 TFEU, which is not applicable under Art. 34 TFEU.

Finally, it is interesting to see that the early cases coming from the Commission and the Court, where the defendants have been found in breach of EU competition law, concern, like the US line of cases, design/product or descriptive standards and standard-setting, which have been abused by the members to exclude competition originating from firms situated in other Member States. None of the cases concern interoperability standards.

4.2.4 The Application of the R&D Block Exemption to Standard-setting Activities

The De Minimis Notice can be utilized so that joint standard-setting activities escape Art. 101(1) TFEU. The De Minimis Notice may become available more often for standard-setting activities, rather than for other activities, given that the former are often developing rules for new products and markets,[134] where no-one yet holds market power. As with joint R&D efforts, standard-setting activities enjoy an indirect exemption under EU competition law because competition over innovation is only acknowledged to a limited extent. The market share ceiling in the De Minimis Notice is thus only interesting in reference to the technology and products market(s) defined or created by the standardization agreement.

There is no block exemption for standard-setting activities under EU competition law.[135] Neither the R&D nor the other block exemptions are

---

[134] Maurits Dolmans, 'Standards For Standards', (2002) 26 *Fordham International Law Journal*, 163, 172.

[135] Under the enabling regulation, Council Regulation (EEC). No. 2821/71 of 20 December 1971 on the application of Art. 85(3) of the Treaty to certain categories of agreements, decisions and concerted practices, OJ L 285 29.12.1971, p. 46: Vol II, App C.2, Art 1(l)(a), the Commission has the power to

directly concerned with standard-setting activities in the way that the NCRPA has become after the latest amendment. Nonetheless, SSOs have made use of the broad definition of research under the R&D block exemption for pre-standardization activities and standard-setting activities as well.[136] Moreover, the Commission has addressed standard-setting activities in some (old) individual decisions about the R&D exemptions.[137]

Small groups of firms may prepare standards *en petit comité* by entering into joint R&D agreements in the pre-standardization phase, so as to present a joint solution for adapting a standard.[138] The R&D block exemption may be applicable if the collaboration meets the conditions stipulated therein.[139]

The parties are treated more leniently under the block exemption if they are not considered competitors.[140] Then it does not matter whether

---

grant block exemptions to agreements which have as their object 'the application of standards or type', but that power has not been exercised in a broader sense.

[136] However, it is not as wide as the definition of research in the previous block exemption. The 2000 R&D block exemption Art 2(4) stated, 'research and development means the acquisition of know-how relating to products or processes and the carrying out of theoretical analysis, systematic study or experimentation, including experimental production, technical testing of products or processes, the establishment of the necessary facilities and the obtaining of intellectual property rights for the results'.

[137] For example, the Corning saga of cases. See Commission decision, Optical Fibres, OJ 1986 L 236/30.

[138] Maurits Dolmans, 'Standards For Standards', (2002) 26 *Fordham International Law Journal*, 163, 172.

[139] The De Minimis Notice should presumably apply. The interaction between the De Minimis Notice and the R&D block exemption is not clear, given the fact that the R&D block exemption specifically addresses the issue of R&D agreements between non-competitors. The black list contained in the R&D block exemption should presumably be applicable also to agreements which could fall under the De Minimis Notice. Contra, Maurits Dolmans, 'Standards For Standards', (2002) 26 *Fordham International Law Journal*, 163, 172.

[140] A difference compared to the old Regulation 418/85 and the 2000 R&D block exemption is that competing undertakings are defined in more detail in the current R&D block exemption. First, an 'actual competitor' is defined as an undertaking active on either the same product or technology market as the outcome of the R&D will be engaged with. Secondly, 'potential competitor' means an undertaking that, in the absence of the R&D agreement, would, on realistic grounds, and not just as a mere theoretical possibility, in the event of a small but permanent increase in relative prices, be likely to undertake, within not more than three years, the necessary additional investments or other necessary switching costs to supply a product, technology or process capable of being

one of the participants has more than a 25 per cent market share in the relevant market, which is the threshold for the application of the block exemption.[141] Parties are, moreover, as discussed above, not considered competitors if they carry out joint research they are not able to do on their own, or if the result of their joint R&D will create a completely new market.[142] For that reason, there exists perhaps an incentive to claim broad and far-reaching aims for the research so as to be able to maintain that the parties are not competitors. In certain standard-setting consortia this might prove useful. If the collaborators are not competitors, the block exemption stipulates a seven-year immunity. The exclusivity period is, with some exceptions, seven years for each developed product or technology, but that does not mean the R&D cooperation has to be confined to seven years. As long as the research develops into new products, the parties are, under the block exemption, free to cooperate beyond the seven years stipulated in it.[143] This could, for example, enable the standard-setting parties to agree explicitly not to admit outsiders.

The R&D block exemption may therefore be applicable during the standard-setting process when members discuss the pros and cons of different technical solutions, whilst individual members continue their semi-individual R&D efforts.[144]

---

improved, substituted or replaced by the contract product or contract technology on the relevant geographic market. See Art. 1 R&D block exemption. See also Horizontal Guidelines, para. 10, fn. 3. In the 2000 R&D block exemption 'competing undertaking' was defined as 'competing undertaking means an undertaking that is supplying a product capable of being improved or replaced by the contracted products (an actual competitor) or an undertaking that would, on realistic grounds, undertake the necessary additional investments or other necessary switching costs so that it could supply such a product in response to a small and permanent increase in relative prices (a potential competitor)'. Regarding the definition of innovation markets, see supra and cf. Richard Gilbert and Steven Sunshine, 'Incorporating Dynamic Efficiency Concerns in Merger Analysis: the Use of Innovation Markets', (1995) 63 *Antitrust Law Journal*, 569.

[141] R&D Block Exemption Art 4.

[142] See TT Guidelines, para. 4, and Horizontal Guidelines, para. 130.

[143] Confusingly, Art 4(1) of the R&D block exemption states that the exclusivity period is seven years from the time the contracted product or technology is first put on the market. However, if the research continues with the aim of creating another product, the parties seem to be free to continue cooperating. Unfortunately, there is no definition of a new product.

[144] Josef Drexl, 'Anti-competitive Stumbling Stones on the Way to a Cleaner World: Protecting Competition in Innovation Without a Market', (2012) 8 *Journal of Competition Law & Economics*, 507, 534.

Standard-setting activities may also be exempted under Art. 101(3) TFEU if they may be motivated by reasons of efficiencies, even though, for example, the competition or rivalry may be limited to a few firms.[145] The Commission has, moreover, taken a broad initiative and the guidelines on the application of Art 101 of the TFEU to horizontal cooperation agreements (hereinafter Horizontal Guidelines) states that some agreements are *possibly* lawful, i.e. not falling within the ambit of Art. 101(1),[146] even though shutting out third parties, namely: (i) co-operation between non-competitors; (ii) co-operation between competing companies that cannot independently carry out the project or activity covered by the cooperation; and (iii) cooperation concerning an activity which does not influence the 'relevant parameters' of competition.

4.2.5 The Horizontal Guidelines

The main focal point in the Horizontal Guidelines published on 14 January 2011 was technology standards in information technology markets. The main idea seems to have been to establish a safe harbour for standard-setting activities similar to the immunity created by the US 2004 Standard Development Organization Advancement Act. With that aim, the chapter concerning standardization agreements starts with exempting technical standards that stem from the execution of public power.

The European standardization bodies are recognized under Regulation 1025/2012 and Directive 98/34/EC of the European Parliament and of the Council of 22 June 1998 laying down a procedure for the provision of information in the field of technical standards and regulations.[147] They are rules subject to competition law to the extent that they can be considered to be an 'undertaking' or an association of undertakings within the meaning of Articles 101 and 102.[148] As discussed above, under *SELEX,* that might happen seldom.

[145] See e.g., Commission decision, Open Group, OJ 1987 L 35/36, where the Commission agreed to a limitation on the number of participants in a joint R&D and standard-setting joint venture.

[146] Guidelines on the application of Art 81 of the EC Treaty to horizontal cooperation agreements, OJ C 3, 06/01/2001, 2 (the 2001 Horizontal Guidelines), para. 24. See, now, Guidelines on the application of Art 101 on the functioning of the European Union to horizontal co-operation agreements, OJ C 11, 14/01/2011, 1 (previously defined as Horizontal Guidelines), paras. 129 et seq.

[147] Horizontal Guidelines para. 258.

[148] See Case C-41/90 Höfner v. Macroton [1991] ECR I-1979, but also Case C-113/07, SELEX, [2009] ECR I-2207,

The guidelines thereafter define standardization agreements in a broad sense.[149] This was probably a mistake by the Commission, given that there are many standards that are not problematic, and thus, even pro-competitive. Perhaps, the Commission should instead have focused more narrowly on those standard agreements that might be problematic from a competition law perspective. These standards, being voluntary technical standards, which have been defined either individually by undertakings or jointly in private SSOs or collectively under SDOs cannot be applied without access to certain essential patents.[150] Had the Commission followed such a line of reasoning, focusing on these collaborations only, then the guidelines could have been firmer and 'crisper'.

As respects standard-setting agreements, the Horizontal Guidelines do not recognize an innovation market; only innovation competition. Instead, standardization agreements may produce their effects on four possible markets according to the Horizontal Guidelines: 'First, standard setting may have an impact on the product or service market or markets to which the standard or standards relates. Second, where the standard setting involves the selection of technology and where the rights to intellectual property are marketed separately from the products to which they relate, the standard can have effects on the relevant technology market. Third, the market for standard setting may be affected if different standard-setting bodies or agreements exist. Fourth, where relevant, a distinct market for testing and certification may be affected by standard setting.'[151]

The initial assumption in the Horizontal Guidelines is that standard-setting agreements are pro-competitive. Only in specific circumstances may these agreements give rise to restrictive effects on competition. This can occur through three main channels, namely reduction in price competition, hindering of innovative technologies, and exclusion of, or

---

[149] Horizontal Guidelines, para. 252.

[150] For a similar line of reasoning, see Hanns Ullrich, 'Patents and Standards – a Comment on the German Federal Supreme Court Decision Orange Book Standard', (2011) 41 *IIC*, 337, 337; and Joseph Drexl et al., 'Comments of the Max Planck Institute for IP, Competition and Tax Law on the Draft Commission Block Exemption Regulation on R&D Agreements and the Draft Guidelines on Horizontal Cooperation Agreements' (2010), *Competition & Tax Law Research Paper* No. 10-12 (Max Planck Institute for IP), paras. 40 et seq.

[151] Horizontal Guidelines, para. 261.

discrimination against, certain companies by preventing their effective access to the standard.[152]

The Horizontal Guidelines actually divide up the value chain of creating products under standards. First, according to the Horizontal Guidelines, there are upstream-only companies that solely develop and market technologies. These R&D-only firms' only source of income is licensing revenue and their incentive is to maximize their royalties. Secondly, the Horizontal Guidelines continues, there are manufacturing-only companies that solely manufacture products or offer services based on technologies developed by others and which do not hold relevant IPR. Royalties represent a cost for them, and not a source of revenue, and their incentive is to reduce or avoid royalties. Finally, there are vertically integrated companies that both develop technology and sell products. They have mixed incentives. On the one hand, they can draw licensing revenue from their IPR. On the other hand, they may have to pay royalties to other companies holding IPR essential to the standard. They may therefore cross-license their own essential IPR in exchange for essential IPR held by other companies.[153]

The Horizontal Guidelines states that 'fraud' standardization agreements, i.e. disguised price cartels will be considered to be restricting competition by object, irrespective of whether the fixed prices appear on a product or technology market. Interestingly, in a footnote, the Commission restricts this rule by stating it 'should not prevent unilateral *ex ante* disclosures of most restrictive licensing terms ...'[154] Also, according to the Commission, it does not prevent patent pools created in accordance with the principles set out in the TT Guidelines, or a decision to license IPR on royalty-free terms that is essential to a standard.

With those limitations, it is fair to say that it is, at least, difficult for a plaintiff to make out what would be considered objectively anti-competitive, and even harder to show it. How does a plaintiff show that the standardization agreement is a cover-up for a price cartel when it is benign to disclose royalty rates *ex ante* and jointly set royalty rates under a patent pool *ex post* the standard? It seems that the plaintiff cannot only show actual conduct, which would be normal under the 'anti-competitive by object' rule, but must instead actually show anti-competitive intent, i.e. intent to enter the joint price scheme to create a price cartel, rather than the intent being to enter a benign standard-setting agreement with a

---

152 Horizontal Guideliens, paras. 262 et seq.

153 Horizontal Guidelines, para 267.

154 Horizontal Guidelines, para. 274, fn. 1.

patent pool connected to it that also includes a joint royalty agreement. Given the amount of evidence a plaintiff needs to bring to court, it is doubtful an offense could still be classified as 'anti-competitive by object'. In fact, the Commission is here trying to find a dichotomy between the cases where it previously had found cartels, e.g. the *IAZ*, *Belasco* and *SCK* cases, and the standard-setting procedure for telecommunication and other interoperability technologies and industries. Here the Commission should have been much helped by presenting different standards and different markets, and thus different antitrust policies, depending on what standard and what market was under scrutiny. Possibly, the Commission is here addressing the cases it has handed down regarding product standards where different solutions or standards may prevail on the relevant market. While cartels can be identified here, the need to find anti-competitive intent implies that the test is not the regular objective test, but, rather, a test perhaps mirroring the US test where anti-competitive intent may be part of showing that the standardization agreement in fact represents collusion with anti-competitive effect.

Thereafter, the Guidelines define the safe harbour. Where participation in standard-setting is unrestricted and the procedure for adopting the standard in question is transparent, standardization agreements which contain no obligation to comply with the standard and provide access to the standard on fair, reasonable and non-discriminatory terms will normally not restrict competition within the meaning of Article 101(1).[155]

Transparency implies that the standard-setting organization must be open and *de facto* inform all stakeholders of upcoming rule making. In case the standard involves IPR, the standard-setting organization needs to have a clear and balanced IPR policy adapted to the particular industry at hand, including FRAND and good faith disclosure requirements. The EU Commission refers to the *X/Open Group* case[156] and states that if the SSO is closed to competitors and stakeholders in the market affected, and, hence, only certain firms are allowed to become members, then the safe harbour will not apply and Art 101(1) TFEU may be breached. The

---

[155] Horizontal Guidelines, para 280. See also the certification case, joined cases T-213/95 and T-18/96 SCK and FNK v. Commission [1997] ECR II-1739, an action against Commission decision IV/34.179 – SCK and FNK, (1995) OJ L 312 / 79.

[156] The X/Open Group case dealt with a joint standard-setting effort between the largest EU-based firms to develop the Unix system and, thus, to create their own operating system. It did not materialize. See Commission decision Open Group, OJ 1987 L 35/36.

EU Commission makes a connection between effect and the likely market impact of the standard and its potential wider field of application. The *Open Group* case involved a collaboration between very large EU-based firms that did want to limit the number of members when developing a operating system. The collaboration was exempted under Art. 101(3) because the members agreed to give access to the result. They also wanted to have a closed group to prevent members trying to stall the development of the standard.

As long as the standard-setting organizations follow these basic rules regarding transparency and accountability, they are safe within the harbour.[157] The *EMC* case shows this quite well.

(i) The EMC case[158]

> **BOX 4.7**
>
> In the *EMC* case, EMC Development AB (EMC) challenged the Commission's decision to reject the complaint against European Portland cement producers, the European Cement Association

[157] The Commission discusses FRAND terms in the Horizontal Guidelines without adopting any decisive method of establishing FRAND terms. In case of a dispute, the assessment of whether fees charged for access to IPR in the standard-setting context are unfair or unreasonable should be based, according to the Commission, on whether the fees bear a reasonable relationship to the economic value of the IPR. According to the Commission, there are various methods available to make this assessment. In principle, cost-based methods are not well adapted to this context because of the difficulty in assessing the costs attributable to the development of a particular patent or group of patents. Instead, it may be possible to compare the licensing fees charged by the company in question for the relevant patents in a competitive environment before the industry has been locked into the standard (*ex ante*) with those charged after the industry has been locked in (*ex post*). Another method according to the Commission could be to obtain an independent expert assessment of the objective centrality and essentiality to the standard at issue of the relevant IPR portfolio. In an appropriate case, it may also be possible to refer to *ex ante* disclosures of licensing terms in the context of a specific standard-setting process. This also assumes that the comparison can be made in a consistent and reliable manner. The royalty rates charged for the same IPR in other comparable standards may also provide an indication for FRAND royalty rates. Finally the Commission states that it does not seek to provide an exhaustive list of appropriate methods to assess whether the royalty fees are excessive.

[158] Case T-432/05 EMC Development AB [2010] ECR II-01629.

(Cembureau) and the European Committee for Standardization (CEN) for creating a cartel in the European cement market. The allegation was that these bodies had collusively agreed to create barriers to entry to the European cement market by means of an industrial standard.

According to CJEU, the EN 197-1 Standard ('the Standard') was adopted in April 2000 by the 19 national standards bodies that were members of CEN at that time. It was developed by a CEN technical committee, CEN/TC 51 'Cement and Building Limes' ('CEN/TC 51'), under mandate M/114 which was granted by the Commission and the European Free Trade Association (EFTA) pursuant to Directive 06.[159] That mandate defined the scope of application of the Standard, set out the list of products that had to be taken into consideration and stated that the Standard would be expressed, as far as practicable, in product performance terms, having regard to the interpretative documents.[160]

The Standard defined each of the 27 common cement products, that is to say, the common cements described by the various national standards bodies within CEN as traditional and well tried. Those products were grouped into five main cement types (CEM I to CEM V), according to the proportions in which the main constituents were to be combined to produce those distinct products in a range of five 'strength classes'. Each main cement type was composed of a certain percentage of Portland cement clinker combined with varying levels of constituents. That definition included requirements which the constituents have to satisfy, and mechanical, physical, chemical and durability requirements of the 27 common cement products and 'strength classes'. According to the applicant and Cembureau, 'real' Portland cement corresponded to products of the main cement type CEM I, as defined by the Standard. Blended cements

[159] This standard has been considered one of the major failures of the New Approach. See Harm Schepel, *The Constitution of Private Governance – Product Standards in the Regulation of Integrating Markets* (Hart, 2005). CEN has previously been found not to be an undertaking, or at least to be an international organization entrusted with tasks in the public interest. Case T-4/92 Evangelos Vardakas v. Commission [1993] ECR II-357, para. 47.

[160] Case T-432/05 EMC Development AB [2010] ECR II-01629.

corresponded to cement of the four other main types, CEM II to CEM V.[161]

The cement produced by EMC, on the other hand, was energetically modified cement, a technology which was developed by, inter alia, EMC in the early 1990s. This cement was produced by high intensity grinding/activation of Portland cement with different materials such as fly ash, blast furnace slag or fine quartz sand, and, thus, did not fit the Standard. EMC therefore claimed that the standard effectively excluded EMC from the market.[162]

Interestingly, even though, EMC claimed that the Standard reflected the result of a cartel, and thus was the result of collusion in some form, neither the Commission nor the General Court actually analysed whether there was a cartel behind the Standard. The Commission and the Courts stated that EMC had not provided any evidence supporting its claims. Instead, the Commission and the Courts rejected EMC claims with an analysis of whether the standardization agreement met the requirements for a safe harbour in the Horizontal Guidelines.[163] EMC claimed that the procedure for adopting the Standard was discriminatory since it was designed, thanks to the close cooperation between Cembureau and CEN/TC 51, to favour existing major cement producers in the market. According to EMC, although the Commission did not deny that Cembureau influenced the procedure, which was in fact controlled by Cembureau and the chairman of CEN/TC 51, it nevertheless concluded that the activities of Cembureau had not exceeded the limits of normal lobbying activity. The EMC continued and claimed that the procedure was neither transparent nor open. Finally, that the standard was *de facto* binding. According to EMC, it was binding for two reasons. First, because the products covered by the Standard dominated the market, hence the Standard dominated the market, and secondly, because cement was often purchased under public procurement procedures and they often were obliged to rely on standards.[164]

161 Ibid.
162 Ibid.
163 Ibid.
164 Ibid.

The General Court dismissed EMC's claims one by one (correctly, since EMC lacked necessary evidence). The Commission seems also to have done an investigation, while it did not conduct a dawn raid. The interesting feature of the case is not whether the safe harbour was applicable or not but the fact that neither the Commission nor the Court analysed the Standard from the outset as to whether there was a cartel in the first place, e.g. misuse of the standard-setting procedure creating an agreement to shut out competitors. They did not recognize the possibly inherent anti-competitive features of the standard-setting process as such. Instead, they established that the safe harbour in the Horizontal Guidelines was applicable. Thus, the Court (and the Commission) only found the procedural rules fulfilled and did not analyse the *effect* or the result of the standard-setting process or the alleged collaboration. That was, presumably, up to the SDO to control. As a matter of fact, neither the Court nor the Commission even took the claim that the standard should have been a performance standard rather than a descriptive product standard into serious consideration. They seem to have backed away in the face of a regulatory process, and to have decided that the result of such a process must be accepted.

It is difficult to make out what evidence there was, but the EMC case seems to be somewhat of a change from early standard-setting cases, where the Commission did analyse whether the standard agreed upon was a sham, i.e. whether there were reasons to believe that the standard was intended to restrict members freedom to differentiate their products.[165]

Thus, the regulation of the safe harbour for standards and standard-setting organizations under EU competition law reflects the use of rules for establishing per se legal conduct under Art 101(1) TFEU. If the rules for the safe harbour are obeyed it does not matter that the conduct *de facto* has such an effect that Art 101(1) would normally be triggered. It should, for example, be noted that EMC argued that a performance standard would have been enough and that the design product standard went too far in that they excluded competition when that was not indispensible for setting up the standard. In fact, this could have been a successful line of argument to object a use of Art. 101(3) TFEU, but the case had not reached that point. EMC was not able to pull CEN or Cembureau out of the safe harbour under Art. 101(1) TFEU.

Nonetheless, it seems that neither the Commission nor the Court found CEN or Cembureau to be undertakings, while still acknowledging

---

[165] Commission decision 86/399/EEC (1986) OJ L 232/15, para. 73. See also case 246/86, Belasco v. Commission [1989] ECR 2117, para 49.

Cembureau's right to lobby CEN politically. Thus, under *EMC* it seems that at least undertakings taking part in the drafting of standards and the lobbying of SDOs could be scrutinized under Art 101 TFEU, while the court would still take into consideration the right of undertakings to lobby the SDO.

4.2.6 What is Anti-competitive under EU Competition Law with Reference to Standard-setting?

(i) Article 101(3) TFEU

In the Horizontal Guidelines, the Commission continues to lay down rules for how firms should behave outside the safe harbour so not to violate Art. 101. Thus, the Commission states rules for collaboration that fall outside the safe harbour but still should not be addressed under Art. 101. From this one can deduct that, if competition exists, firms may depart from the rules for setting up the safe harbour mainly by way of denying the standard to outside firms. In other words, the safe harbour stipulates the harshest rules for transparency, openness and even to some extent accountability, while a less 'democratic' order may suffice if there is competition on the relevant market, e.g. between different standard-setting organizations, technology providers or product manufacturers.[166] Thus, if the market can only hold one standard due to network effects or because the standard reflects a technology so basic it, *de facto*, represents a natural monopoly, the standard-setting procedure should be as open and as transparent as possible. On the other hand, when there is room for competition, the Horizontal Guidelines state that the standard-setting procedures may uphold competition by limiting transparency and access to membership. The Commission here actually also implies that the market share of the technology or product covered by such a standard should be evaluated so to establish the competitive effect of the contemplated standard. Here in fact, the Commission makes a very important point. Where the markets can bear competition, such competition should be promoted and protected.

In addition, the 'objective' rule discussed above should be judged in light of the scant case law where, in fact, the Commission has found cartels being facilitated by standards on product standard markets, e.g. *IAZ*. Here, clearly, the Commission was dealing with a misuse of the standard-setting procedure in a market which was able to accommodate several standards.

---

[166] Horizontal Guidelines, paras. 295 et seq.

Finally, the Commission defines the application of Art 101 (3) and stipulates that the exemption may very well be applicable if neither the safe harbour nor the effect-based test will save the collaborators. The Commission states[167]:

> [u]nion wide standards may facilitate market integration and allow companies to market their goods and services in all Member States, leading to increased consumer choice and decreasing prices. Standards which establish technical interoperability and compatibility often encourage competition on the merits between technologies from different companies and help prevent lock-in to one particular supplier. Furthermore, standards may reduce transaction costs for sellers and buyers. Standards on, for instance, quality, safety and environmental aspects of a product may also facilitate consumer choice and can lead to increased product quality. Standards also play an important role for innovation. They can reduce the time it takes to bring a new technology to the market and facilitate innovation by allowing companies to build on top of agreed solutions.

Given such a wish list, it is not difficult to come up with a reason why a standard should be exempted under Art. 101(3).

(ii) IGR/Salora[168]

The first Commission case regarding a standard under Art 101 TFEU was the *Salora v. IGR Stereo Television*. German colour TV manufacturers of television transmission and receiving equipment had agreed on a technology and pooled their patents under the company, IGR. IGR granted licences to these manufacturers, but decided to license non-members only after a certain date, and for a limited number of sets. IGR refused to license Salora, a small Finnish company, and then used its patent rights to prevent Salora from supplying stereo TV sets to two large mail order firms in Germany. Salora was therefore being prevented from supplying and complained to the Commission. Salora requested interim measures, which the Commission has power to order in appropriate cases. IGR agreed to grant licences immediately and free of restrictions as to quantity.[169] The case was therefore dropped.

---

[167] Horizontal Guidelines, para. 308.

[168] See IGR in Commission Report on Competition 1984, p. 94 and IGR Stereo Television in Commission Report on Competition 1981, p. 92. See also Concast/Mannesmann in the Commission Report on Competition 1981, p. 93. See also the 90/446/EEC Commission decision of 27 July 1990 Konsortium ECR 900. OJ L 228 22.08.1990, p. 31 et seq.

[169] John Temple Lang, 'The Application of the Essential Facility Doctrine to IP rights under European Competition Law', in Francois Lévêque and Howard

(iii) Restricting product diversification

The Commission has seldom found standardization agreements to be restrictive agreements on their own. An agreement on standards must, however, according to the Commission, not reduce product diversity. Licensees should be able to develop products outside the technology standardized under the agreement. For instance, Sony and Philips entered into a patent pool/cross-licensing agreement with other VCR producers on the uniform application of technical standards for the VCR system, which the Commission found to be anti-competitive.[170] Under the agreement, the parties were not allowed to implement other systems or standards or develop the Philips system without the consent of the other parties. The Commission refused an exemption on the ground that implementation of the agreement would lead to exclusion of other, perhaps better, systems or standards.[171] In other words, the parties must be free to develop the technology and use competing technologies.

The case indicates that the Commission did believe that there was room for competition between standards or competition by substitution. The VCR technology was not an omnipresent basic or interoperability standard. Only if there were room for competition by substitution could Sony's and Philips' covenant in their standard/patent pool /cross-licence agreement have an anti-competitive effect.

The Commission has also held that several cartel agreements, which had adjoining standard agreements, restricted product diversification. Apart from the cases discussed above, *IAZ*, *SCK* and *Belasco*, the Commission stated in the well-known decision, *Pre-insulated Pipes*

Shelanski (eds) *Antitrust, Patents and Copyright EU and US Perspectives* (Edward Elgar, 2005), 56 et seq. Cf. also John Temple Lang speech in 1996 http://ec.europa.eu/competition/speeches/text/sp1996_0541_en.html. Accessed 3 September 2012.

[170] The Philips and Sony VCR cross-licensing agreement, which was found to have negative effects upon competition within the European Community since the system shut out perhaps better systems, was not granted exemption under the third paragraph. Commission decision Videocassette recorders, OJ 1977 L 47/42. The US FTC also did an early analysis of Philips and the Sony's licensing agreements for CDs in the 1980s. See Carl Shapiro, 'Navigating the Patent Thicket: Cross Licenses, Patent Pools and Standard Setting', in Adam Jaffe et al. (eds), *Innovation Policy and the Economy* (MIT Press, 2001), 20.

[171] For comment on the Videocassette case, see Maurits Dolmans, 'Restriction on Innovation: An EU Antitrust Approach', (1997–1998) 66 *Antitrust Law Journal*, 455, 480 et seq.

cartel,[172] 'ABB's internal documentation confirms that compliance with standards was being used as a means of keeping up price levels. Recalling that EuHP standard was set up with the purpose of excluding 'new foreign competitors especially in Eastern Europe', a senior ABB official warned in July 1993 'that a relaxation of technical norms under the standard would lead to an opening of the market'. The Commission concluded that using norms and standards in order to prevent or delay the introduction of new technology that would result in price reductions is an antitrust violation.[173]

(iv) Buyer cartels, collective obligation to supply and monopsonies

The ETSI, which sets the telecommunications standards in Europe, tried in 1993 to prevent hold-ups.[174] It put forward a proposition to its general assembly, which was approved, that members of the SDO should be obliged to license their current and future intellectual property rights under contemplated technology standards or otherwise clearly state what intellectual property rights it would not make available under the standard (licence-by-default).[175] The members were also, inter alia, obliged to notify the maximum royalty rate that would apply for their essential patents.[176] The remedy for not adhering to the rules was that the patentee would lose the licences from the other patentees under the standard (pool).[177] These proposed rules were harsher than the current rules in force under the ETSI IP policy.

---

[172] Commission Decision in Case IV/35.691, Pre-insulated Pipes, OJ L 24, 30.1.1999, p. 1.

[173] Furthermore supported by the fact that this case is referred to under the Horizontal Guidelines as an example of a standardization agreement which is anti-competitive by object. Cf. Horizontal Guidelines, para. 273.

[174] For a general overview of early European standardization history regarding telecommunications, see Rudi Bekkers and Isabella Liotard, 'European Standards for Mobile Communication: The Tense Relationship Between Standards and Intellectual Property Rights', (1999) 21 *European Intellectual Property Review*, 110, specifically 121 et seq.

[175] Apparently, in a preliminary position, the EU Commission regarded the licence-by-default as depriving them of freedom to license and the incentive to develop new technologies. Cf. Maurits Dolmans, 'Standards For Standards', (2002) 26 *Fordham International Law Journal*, 163, 181.

[176] Case No. IV./35.06 – ETSI IPR Policy [1995] O.J. C76/5, para. 8.

[177] Mark Lemley, 'Intellectual Property Rights and Standard-Setting Organizations', (2002) 90 *California Law Review*, 1889, 1917. This is probably one of few measures to contractually force a patentee to adhere to FRAND requirements, for example.

ETSI was forced to withdraw the rules since the EU Commission was hesitant to provide negative clearance or an individual exemption under the then Art. 85(3) EC Treaty.[178] The US government also lobbied to have the ETSI IPR policy annulled and a US trade body (CMEMA) filed a complaint with the EU Commission.[179] The ETSI instead, as discussed above, enacted a milder version stating that the members were obliged to disclose essential intellectual property rights *ex ante* (however not requiring members to conduct IPR searches) and would be requested to license essential intellectual property rights on FRAND terms. The rules are still relevant for the current IPR policy.[180]

Interestingly, the VITA Business Letter from 2006 displayed a very similar licence-by-default rule, which was accepted by the Justice Department, but the ETSI IPR policy introduced in 1993 was considered anti-competitive.[181]

---

[178] Case No. IV./35.06 – ETSI IPR Policy [1995] O.J. C76/5, para. 1. See also Maurits Dolmans, 'Standards For Standards', (2002) 26 *Fordham International Law Journal*, 163, 181, indicating what the Commission stated in its preliminary position.

[179] Rudi Bekkers et al., 'Case studies on the interface between research and standardisation, and case studies on patent pools as a coordination mechanism', (INTEREST consortium Priority 8 No. Contract 503 594, EU 6th Specific Targeted Research Project, 2006). 121. [The document is on file with the author].

[180] ETSI IPR policy, see http://www.etsi.org/WebSite/document/Legal/ETSI_IPR-Policy.pdf. Accessed 7 April 2012. Interestingly, the development seems to indicate that SDOs may treat holders of essential intellectual property rights more strictly under both US and EU antitrust laws and possibly the licence-by-default may have a renaissance both in Europe and the US. See e.g., the SDO Business Review Letters published by the US Justice Department in 2006 and 2007, where the SDOs require members to declare maximum royalty rates, and to some extent the 3G Comfort letter/Business Review Letters where a licence-by-default was allowed both by the EC Commission and the US Justice Department within the field of patent pools. See also Philip Nelson, 'Patent Pools: An Economic Assessment of Current Law and Policy', (2007) 38 *Rutgers Law Journal*, 539, 562 et seq. Lemley claims that SSOs may not prohibit members from owning or licensing intellectual property rights under standards. See Mark Lemley, 'Intellectual Property Rights and Standard-Setting Organizations', (2002) 90 *California Law Review*, 1889, 1944 et seq. For an equivalent view on EC Competition law, see Maurits Dolmans, 'Standards For Standards', (2002) 26 *Fordham International Law Journal*, 163, 182 et seq. Dolmans claims it might be considered a buyer's cartel to demand royalty-free licences.

[181] VITA Business Review Letter from Thomas O. Barnett to Robert A. Skitol, dated 30 October 2006, and IEEE Business Review Letter from Thomas O. Barnett to Michael A. Lindsay, dated 30 April 2007. See also RFID Business

In addition, The EU Commission clearly reconsidered its standpoint on IP policies during the ETSI and Sun antitrust investigation, conducted during 2000–2005. Sun was investigated for declaring that it had essential patents after the standard had been agreed, published and promulgated. Following DG Competition intervention, no reference was made to Sun patents under the standard. In 2005, the EU Commission also decided to investigate whether ETSI's rules made it possible to conduct patent ambush.[182] In the course of the Sun investigation, DG Competition took the preliminary view that ETSI's rules about intellectual property rights did not provide sufficient protection against the risk of a patent ambush during the standard-setting procedure.[183] In response to the accusation of facilitating patent ambush, ETSI decided to examine whether to change its rules and allow for *ex ante* licensing.[184] The EU Commission therefore decided to drop the investigation indicating that it found *ex ante* licensing, i.e. where royalties are set or discussed before a standard is agreed, as possibly pro-competitive.[185]

In the light of the Commission's disapproval of the 1995 ETSI licence-by-default rules, the Commission in its Sun investigation certainly made a U-turn and changed its standpoint. It would now allow SDOs to place more pressure on holders of essential patents.[186] The Commission has not initiated an investigation into the VITA IP Policies, implying that the EU Commission agrees with the Justice Department's conclusions. In fact, to have a very stringent IP policy is now even a requirement for making use of the safe harbour in the Horizontal Guidelines. The Commission even states in the Horizontal Guidelines:

Review Letter from Thomas O. Barnett to William F. Dolan and Geoffrey Oliver dated 21 October 2008, 8.

[182] See Commission press release IP/05/1565, 12 December 2005.

[183] Ruben Schellingerhout, 'Standard-setting from a Competition Law Perspective', (2011) 1 *Competition Policy Newsletter*, 3, 5.

[184] Ibid.

[185] Ibid. See also TT Guidelines para. 225.

[186] It should be noted that the EC Commission's standpoint corresponds to such ex ante licensing and disclosure rules which the US Justice Department supported under two recent Business Review Letters. Business Review Letters from Thomas O. Barnett to Robert Skitol and Michael A. Lindsay, regarding the VITA and EEEI standards, respectively, dated Oct. 30, and April 30, 2007. The letters address the issue of negotiations of the term of licensing under a conceived industrial standard. For the letters, see http://www.usdoj.gov/atr/public/busreview/letters.htm, accessed 4 April 2009.

> standard-setting agreements providing for *ex ante* disclosure of the most restrictive licensing terms, will not, in principle, restrict competition within the meaning of Article 101(1). In that regard, it is important that parties involved in the selection of a standard be fully informed not only as to the available technical options and the associated IPR, but also as to the likely cost of that IPR. Therefore, should a standard-setting organization's IPR policy choose to provide for IPR holders to individually disclose their most restrictive licensing terms, including the maximum royalty rates they would charge, prior to the adoption of the standard, this will normally not lead to a restriction of competition within the meaning of Article 101(1). Such unilateral *ex ante* disclosures of most restrictive licensing terms would be one way to enable the standard-setting organization to take an informed decision based on the disadvantages and advantages of different alternative technologies, not only from a technical perspective but also from a pricing perspective.

In other words, the EU Commission and the Justice Department have, from 1995 until today, gone from establishing that IP policies obliging individual SEP holders to license by default, or under FRAND, are monopsonies or buyer cartels, to being so pro-competitive that it is a requirement under the safe harbour. This is a change indeed! In fact, the rule must be more nuanced than the Commission and the Justice Department seem to imply. Of course, IP policies that force SEP holders to license but, in fact, never make injunctions available as a weapon for the patentees, is taking the rule too far. First, as this book argues, if competition can prevail on the market, through competing standards or 'by competition by substitution', the IP policies cannot be so stringent that every SEP holder must grant access to its patent. That would limit dynamic competition. Secondly, injunctions must also possibly be available, under strict conditions, when we are discussing SEPs for interoperability standards. Otherwise, genuine inventors will not be reimbursed for their inventions and the equilibrium between patentees and licensees may actually render a result that the patentees receive not even royalties on FRAND-levels.[187]

(v) Joint exploitation of the regulatory standard system

The EU Commission opened antitrust proceedings in 2011 concerning agreements between Honeywell and DuPont for the development of a new refrigerant for air-conditioning systems in cars.[188] According to the Commission, a new refrigerant known as '1234yf' was announced as a

---

[187] See discussion infra in Chapters 6 and 7.

[188] See EU Commission press release: http://europa.eu/rapid/press-release_IP-11-1560_en.htm?locale=en. Accessed 1 May 2013.

suitable global replacement for the previous refrigerant R134a, which did not meet the new EU standards as regards its global warming potential. The selection of 1234yf was the result of a process conducted under the auspices of the Society of Automotive Engineers, which represents the interests of all groups involved in the automotive sector.[189]

The Commission is investigating whether Honeywell and DuPont have entered into anti-competitive arrangements as regards the development of the new generation of refrigerants. Specifically, the Commission will investigate whether 'joint development, licensing and production arrangements' entered into between the two companies in relation to these refrigerants restrict competition on the markets.[190] Such behaviour may infringe Article 101 TFEU according to the Commission.

The Commission is also examining whether Honeywell engaged in deceptive conduct during the evaluation in the standard-setting body of 1234yf between 2007 and 2009. The complainants that Honeywell did not disclose its patents and patent applications while the refrigerant was being assessed and then failed to grant licences on fair and reasonable (so called 'FRAND') terms.[191]

This case seems to be the first to focus on joint anti-competitive conduct leading to the establishment of a standard, and it seems to be innovative in two ways. First, it is focused on the conduct leading up to the establishment of the standard, and, secondly, the Commission is dealing with two firms, i.e. some form of alleged collusion, rather than unilateral conduct. The case is not resolved yet, but it could be a new development in this field of competition law.

Conclusion

It seems that the EU Commission in light of rather scant case law and the Horizontal Guidelines is still carving out a test for standard-setting procedure. As discussed above, the Commission seems clear that if the industry and the market can hold several standards (no network effects), competition should be promoted. Then, firms may limit access to the SSO, depending on the market power of the standard under the Horizontal Guidelines. However, more importantly it is in these circumstances that the Commission has found violations of Art. 101 TFEU. All the successful cases above, *IAZ*, *SCK*, *Belasco*, and the *Pre-insulated Pipes* concerns markets where the standard *de facto* excluded competing

[189] Ibid.
[190] Ibid.
[191] Ibid.

standards or 'competition by substitution', while simultaneously having collusive price increasing effects. In these cases, the Horizontal Guidelines imply that the objective test should apply, although the test is probably more intricate and a successful plaintiff needs to show misuse of the standard-setting procedure or even anti-competitive intent. There are two concerns: the safe harbour is too big and it should be more nuanced, depending on whether there is a competing solution and the market is able to bear competing standards or competition by substitution. The guidelines should also emphasize the great difference different standards may cause. Product or design standards should be treated differently from performance standards, while the safe harbour should cater almost exclusively to basic or interoperability standards. The fact that neither the Commission nor the Court indentified these differences in the *EMC* case was a lost opportunity.

Lastly, there is a clear connection between market integration and European-wide standard setting. Private or semi-private organizations, such as the ETSI, regulate trade on the internal market in a way that makes not only the EU competition law rules potentially applicable, but could also infringe the free trade and free movement rules. Interestingly, the right to free movement and to access markets is a horizontal right under the TFEU according to *Fr.bo*, i.e. horizontal in the sense that these rules also govern the conduct of private individuals and firms *vis-a-vis* each other.[192] This would imply that it may also be possible to scrutinize privately-drafted, industry-wide standards under the free goods provisions. Clearly, constitutionally, private organizations may also be scrutinized under, for example, free movement of goods, services or the right of free establishment, even though they lack any official power or connection to a Member State or the ability to produce official public law.[193] The standard, as such, could, thus, be attacked under Art 34 TFEU, while exempted under Art 36 TFEU. It is outside the ambit of this book to suggest what such an analysis or test under the free movement of goods should look like. However, the facts of *Fr.bo* are similar to, on the one hand, *IAZ* and, on the other, the US case *Radiant Burners*. It is not therefore far reaching to suggest that these cases should be dealt with in a similar fashion. Thus, the test should be similar irrespective if the

---

192 See generally Case C 415/93 Union royal belge des societes de football association ASBL et al v. Jean-Marc Bosman [1995] ECR I-4921, where private regulations of UEFA and FIFA were scrutinized under the rules of free movement.

193 See e.g., the Case C 415/93 Union Royal Belge des Societes de Football Association ASBL et al v. Jean-Marc Bosman [1995] ECR I-4921, para. 83.

standard should be analysed under Art 34 or Art 101 TFEU. The test tries to pin-point design or product standards where the standard-setting organization may be abused or used for excluding competitors. To have these cases scrutinized under Arts 34 and 36 TFEU and related doctrines could possibly be a development that would imply that economic effect need not be shown, or at least taken for granted, when the connection between national legislation and the standard is demonstrated. Art 34 TFEU is applicable *per se* to a greater degree than Art 101 TFEU in standard-setting circumstances. However, the conduct of the members of the technical committees must presumably be analysed under Art 101 (or 102) TFEU, rather than Art 34 TFEU.

The US equivalent to *Fr.bo* would be the *Parker* case. There, the SSO claimed exemption from antitrust law because it was a public organ conducting a public task. From the US perspective, this is far reaching, almost inconceivable. SSOs are, according to *Parker*, private collaborations in the US system.

4.2.7 EU Commission Case Law on the Interface between Joint R&D and Standard Setting

(i) Introduction

Apart from the pure standard-setting cases, there are several joint R&D cases, which the EU Commission has scrutinized in older case law under the scrapped exemption procedure under former Art 85 (3) TFEU. These, *de facto,* should be defined as standard-setting consortia, or at least joint R&D ventures with the aim of agreeing a global technology and *de facto* standard. In fact, the standard perspective of these collaborations seemed to have been lost in the contemporary analysis, but they are quite interesting to analyse here. They are also interesting to analyse with reference to the issue whether competition law should take innovative competition (or conduct on the innovation market) into consideration. It should also be remembered that all the technologies discussed in the R&D cases below, to the best of the author's knowledge eventually wound up as formal standards approved by SDOs.

(ii) Optical Fibres

The Optical Fibres case concerned Corning Ltd, a US firm, which invented and developed optical fibres in the 1970s for transferring data and other broadband communication.[194] Corning held several patents to

---

[194] See Commission decision Optical Fibres, OJ 1986 L 236/30.

the technology but there were also competitors and other competing technologies, such as the 'incumbent technology' consisting of old telephone lines made by copper threads. Corning had entered into several joint development agreements including either licensing agreements, or joint venture agreements, or both, with the major cable manufacturers and telecom firms in the largest EU Member States. Subsequently, Corning exclusively licensed the optical fibre technology under its patents in the Member States to the respective joint venture or, in some cases, directly to the major national cable manufacturer.[195] The Commission stated that at the time of signing these agreements the parties were neither competitors nor potential competitors in the optical fibres technology (market) because of the legal restrictions implied in the patents held by Corning. Corning could exclude any firm from the optical fibres technology with its European patents.

Given that the parents of the joint ventures were not under EU competition law competitors, the Commission was mostly concerned about the competition between the different joint ventures in each member state. The joint ventures were, according to the agreements, able, both actively and passively, to sell into each other's territories. However, the licensing agreements stipulated restrictions based on national intellectual property rights that limited this possibility. It was, moreover, alluded to in the decision that Corning, as a major shareholder of the joint ventures, could limit each venture's output in order to limit cross-border sales within the EU, preventing the joint ventures in the different member states from entering each other's territories and competing.

The Commission granted the Corning system of joint ventures and licensing agreements an exemption under paragraph 3 only after the parties minimized some of the restrictive restraints of the agreements. Corning was given lesser managerial power, and the exclusive territorial restrictions were dismantled.[196]

The *Optical Fibres* case is interesting from many perspectives. The case concerned a defendant who systematically entered into R&D agreements with, arguably, the most potent potential competitors in each national market within the EU. This enabled the defendant to control the evolution of the research and keep the new products within the desired field of technology.[197] Thus, in many ways, Corning Ltd., by entering these joint R&D agreements, contractually established the *de facto*

[195] Ibid.

[196] Ibid.

[197] See Commission decision Optical Fibres, OJ 1986 L 236/30.

standard for the broadband technology. The broadband service became – rightly or wrongly – connected to optical fibre technology.

In the *Optical Fibres* case, the Commission eventually approved a network of inter-related joint ventures all featuring, on the one hand, Corning, the major producer and patent holder of optical fibres under the relevant standards[198] and, on the other, large cable manufacturers in each large Member State of the EU.[199] Independently, all the joint ventures were legitimate, since, according to the Commission, the partners in each of the joint ventures were neither competitors nor potential competitors.[200] However, the Commission found that the network of joint ventures was anti-competitive since competition between the joint ventures was limited.[201] Given the exclusive licensing agreements, both active and passive sales were prevented. The optical fibres and cable markets were, according to the Commission, highly oligopolistic in that it had high entry barriers consisting of patent rights. Also, the ultimate purchasers of cables were often national authorities favouring local suppliers.

The mere existence of the joint ventures between Corning and the cable manufacturers made other cable manufacturers aware of the fact that all the large cable manufacturers in Europe had chosen to use optical fibres. Hence, should the manufacturer also choose optical fibres, it would not be likely choose the wrong technology for the new service market rapidly developing under the name of 'broadband'.

The ventures were collaboration in the development of an established technology rather than research ventures. They were to develop the cabling technology necessary for cable optical fibres in the respective Member States. Corning withheld access to developing the optical fibre technology from the joint ventures. It was only the cable technology that was to be developed.

Irrespective of calling them R&D agreements, the overall picture underscores the fact that the agreements with each national incumbent

---

[198] Optical fibres are governed by a number of standards published by the ITU, including the ITU-T D.651 and ITU-T D.652 for the fibres themeselves. There are also performance standards for the fibres, transmitters and receivers, e.g. 100 gigabit Ethernet, 10 gigabit Ethernet, HIPPI etc.

[199] Compagnie Générale d'Electricité (CGE) in France, Industrie Pirelli S.p.A in Italy, Siemens AG in Germany and N.V. Philips Gloeilampenfabrieken in the Netherlands and in Belgium. See Commission decision Optical Fibres, OJ 1986 L 236/30.

[200] See Commission decision Optical Fibres, OJ 1986 L 236/30.

[201] Ibid.

were *de facto* agreements that in Europe the standard technology should be optical fibres for the broadband service or for fast telecommunications in general.

Indeed, the system was a standardization agreement connected with vertical licensing agreements and R&D joint ventures for follow-on R&D.

The research by joint ventures into optical fibres technology was effectively prevented by the fact that each joint venture had to grant back to Corning, on a non-exclusive basis, any improvements, developments, inventions, changes and innovations, to ensure a uniform technology development. Thus, knowing that any improvements would be distributed through the network to all joint ventures, each individual joint venture (or cable manufacturer) lacked an incentive to do any research regarding optical fibres. The result of the joint R&D ventures would wind up, through Corning, with both its competitors or potential competitors and any potential customer of the improvement.[202] Furthermore, Corning had the right to select a technical manager in each joint venture. The system – being almost all-industry inclusive – effectively eliminated competition for the development of better fibres or cables within the EU.

The Corning system had the potential for damping the innovation rate by contractually discouraging the larger potential competitors from developing alternative technology to optical fibres, or from developing the optical fibres technology further. The joint ventures were effectively discouraged from developing future generations of optical fibres by the grant-back covenants and by the appointment of technical managers in each joint venture.

Interestingly, the grant-back clauses also alerted Corning of any new invention that might threaten its home market (US) from potential EU competition. Moreover, the joint ventures prevented the market since they implied that the largest producers of cables in several of the largest EU

---

[202] Where the proprietor of a patent controls a whole technology, grant-back clauses can be pro-competitive, since, first, the licensor implicitly accepts that the licensee conducts research within the area of the patent claims. This may otherwise be an infringement under some jurisdictions. Secondly, if a follow-on innovation is perceived, the licensor (proprietor) will not object to the licensee licensing the possibly blocked patent. This line of reasoning makes sense when there are potential customers for the follow-on innovation. However, it seems that in the Optical Fibers case possibly all follow on innovation would be distributed through Corning to all possible customers, without the inventing licensee being able to gain any supra-competitive profit. See Commission decision Optical Fibres, OJ 1986 L 236/30. For a more economic discussion see Susanne Scotchmer, *Innovation and Incentives* (MIT Press, 2004), 137 et seq.

Member States would most likely purchase, or support the purchase of, optical fibres or optical cables from the ventures over other sorts of fibres. Thus, the Corning system of joint ventures may be regarded as not only a *de facto* agreement on a technology standard, but also an agreement on the joint control and exchange of future follow-on innovation and intellectual property rights.

Actually, the Corning case should be regarded as a failure to protect competition in innovation and competition as whole on the fibre cable or broadband market. The industry-wide system of joint ventures with grant-back clauses locked in all the major potential competitors and purchasers of competing technologies. The system created a *de facto* standard under an IP arrangement which belonged to only one firm. Corning was thereby able contractually to gain an EU-wide monopoly position regarding what technology to be utilized. It did not need to fear that any competing technology would threaten its position.

BOX 4.8

The German Bundeskartellamt also analysed part of the Corning joint venture scheme and eventually disapproved of it. Apparently in Germany, Corning and Siemens (through a joint-owned subsidiary), Philips, AEG, Standard Elektrik Lorenz und Kabelmetal electro established a joint venture for the production of optical fibres cables for cable TV. This joint venture was supposed to produce the optical fibres cables and sell these to the parent companies.

The Bundeskartellamt reached a diametrically different conclusion to the EU Commission regarding whether the participants were competitors, potential competitors or neither. It saw the crucial questions from a competition law perspective as being, first, whether the potential competition between copper cable and optical fibres cable producers was limited by the joint venture. The Bundeskartellamt saw the second crucial question as being whether the joint production of optical fibre cables eliminated competition in the input market for optical fibres.

The Bundeskartelamt answered both these questions in the affirmative, and concluded that the technical or innovative competition between the participants was limited by the collaboration.[203] According to the German authority, the joint monopsony created by the joint venture eliminated the possibility of other producers of fibres entering the market, since all potential buyers were integrated into the joint effort and would presumably only buy fibres from Corning or the joint venture.[204]

It is very interesting to see how different outcomes depend on whether one would argue that the market for the development of optical fibres was shut down by Corning. The Commission evidently found that the fiber standards were the only standards. There was no room for competition or competition by substitute. The market was even shut down to the extent that the parents (the large European telecom firms) would not enter it independently. Hence, they were non-competitors. However, the Bundeskartellamt went further and argued that the market for optical fibres could hold other technologies and firms than Corning and that such firms should get access to purchasers and the downstream markets. It included copper cables in the market, which in hindsight was, probably, a more accurate analysis. First, there was a huge breakthrough (innovation) in the development of fast broadband via the old copper cables during the 1990s and beginning of 2000s (under the DSL standards).[205] Secondly, consumers, even before this innovation, did consider the two technologies as interchangeable.[206] It actually took some time

[203] Monopolkommission, *Huaptgutachten: Wettbewerbspolitik vor neuen Herausforderungen* (Nomos Baden-Baden, 1990), 357. See also WuW/E BkartA 2143 'Glasfaserkabel'.

[204] The EC Commission did not raise this question since the parties changed the licensing agreement from an exclusive manufacturing right for the joint ventures to a non-exclusive right. See Commission decision Optical Fibres, OJ 1986 L 236/30, 41.

[205] For the interesting story about how that innovation became a standard, see Brian DeLacey et al., 'Strategic Behavior in Standard-Setting Oganizations', in *Harvard University Working Paper* (SSRN, 2006).

[206] Studies show that consumers made little of differences between, e.g., the two forms of broadband connection. See also the national (Swedish) TeliaSonera case, which deals with this issue when establishing the relevant market. Furthermore, it is clear that copper cables have had a remarkable development spurt in the past decade. See Konkurrensverket, *The Swedish Annual Competition Report, 2006*, 186 et seq.

before consumers realized that fiber broadband was faster than DSL broadband, but by then the DSL standards had developed very rapidly to become much faster.

Another interesting case regarding the interaction between R&D agreements and their later exploitation by means of a market dominant standard and IP arrangement is the *Continental/Michelin* case.[207] The notified R&D effort aimed at creating tyres that could be used even after they had been damaged and normally would be considered 'flat'. Michelin was the second largest producer of tyres in the world at this time and Continental was the fourth largest. Their combined world market share was estimated at 22 per cent, of which they held a 46 per cent share in the EU. The parties proposed to give up their individual research effort in selected areas of the technology for a combined but divided effort to exchange information regarding the mounting systems, architecture and geometry for the new tyres. Each party would hold the intellectual property rights that reflected its innovations, but a common entity was to be set up for granting a worldwide, non-exclusive licence under the technology for anyone interested. The parties would also provide mutual assistance in actions against patent infringements, with the common entity paying for the expenses incurred.[208]

Goodyear and Firestone submitted comments raising a concern that the new technology standard would not be made available to them, or would be made available to them in a belated fashion, and that this would seriously affect their ability to compete.[209]

The Commission found that the parties would objectively be able to develop the technology independently. Both were at a very late stage of developing it. Elimination of this possibility by the agreement and the prohibition on independently granting licences for the technology rendered the cooperation anti-competitive in the light of Art. 101(1). Nonetheless, the research cooperation was exempted under Art. 101(3) for a period of ten years following the first introduction of the new tyre. The joint entity for the exploitation of the intellectual property rights was, however, exempted for 20 years from the time when the 'contracted products' were supposed to be distributed. Thus, the Commission viewed the technology standard body with the connected IP arrangement much

207 Commission decision Continental/Michelin, OJ 1988 L 305/33.
208 Ibid.
209 Ibid.

more leniently than it viewed the actual research cooperation.[210] The creation of an IP arrangement or a patent pool under a perhaps world-dominant standard was supported even though it would most likely extract supra-competitive profits. Under the pool, the parties would be able to set royalty rates at a level which could imply not only a cartel price for the technology but also collusion regarding the price of the tyres. From the decision, it may also be concluded that the patents in the IP arrangement vehicle would actually be competing. Or, at least, the Commission failed to address that issue.

(iv) Asahi/St Gobain

The *Asahi/St Gobain*[211] venture revolved around a joint R&D arrangement between the two largest producers at that time of automobile glass in the world. When applying for exemption under the prevailing individual exemption procedure they stated: 'Any development of a new technology at first requires the selection of a specific R&D track, depending on the existing level of knowledge as well as an assessment of the probability of success of the various lines which are theoretically possible'. The parties therefore agreed on a joint R&D track in the agreement. However, both parties essentially continued to work separately and unilaterally in R&D but they agreed on a framework of a programme defining annual goals for their independent R&D. This allowed each partner to be kept informed of any development made by the other, and permitted joint decisions in relation to investment in R&D. The parties would also license the technology under the joint venture to each other and third parties when the objective of the agreement was reached and the technology was finally developed. The joint venture would act as a 'medium' through which the selected technology would be decided and licensed. The set-up seems to include pre-standardization collaboration, joint R&D, agreement on standard, and a joint licence scheme, i.e. a patent pool.

The parties in all honesty said that they wanted to decide in what direction the technology development in the market should go. Asahi and St Gobain would thereby secure not only their own existence in the market by the cooperation but also be able to control their competitors' existence and possibly extract licensing fees from them as well by securing the intellectual property rights to the technology. It is difficult to

---

210 Ibid. para. 34 et seq.

211 Commission decision Asahi/Saint-Gobain, OJ 1994 L 354/87.

see why they would fail in their pursuit since they were the two leading firms in the market.

The Commission stated that in the case of final product joint ventures, the commonality of costs and the proximity of the parents' cooperation in the final product market are such that appreciable spillover effects are very likely to occur (for example alignment of sales prices), in particular where the parties have an important market share or operate in an oligopolistic market. However, the *Asahi/St Gobain* joint venture was, according to the Commission, not a final product joint venture.

The indispensability requirement in paragraph 3 has often caused problems for parties wanting to limit each other beyond what might be considered indispensable to the joint venture. The Commission also limited the *Asahi/St Gobain* joint venture into automotive safety glass to ten years instead of the proposed 30 years. The Commission concluded that bearing in mind the parties combined market share of more than 50 per cent, the 30 years time period was not indispensable to creating the innovation.[212]

As stated above, the Commission granted exemptions in these cases to show that, because of overall economic advantages, it was prepared to consider certain joint ventures favourably even though they did not fulfil the conditions set out in the block exemptions and they involved competitors with market shares exceeding the thresholds laid down in these regulations.[213] The economic advantages referred to by the Commission were all based on the notion of perfect competition or classical price theory, i.e. they accomplished cost savings. Even though not expressed explicitly the enactment of the NCRPA in the 1993 (not having an upper market share ceiling) could have influenced the Commission to make these decisions.

---

212 The issue of whether the joint R&D was indispensible might be raised since the parties seemed able to conduct the joint R&D independently. Viewed from this perspective, the case clearly indicates how far the Commission was prepared to go to accept joint R&D.

213 Commission, *Report on Competition Policy 1994*, 105 et seq. However, it must be stated that the Commission had previously granted exemptions to joint ventures which created combinations with high market shares. See the case ten years previously, Commission decision Bayer/Gist-Brocades OJ 1976 L 30/13, which bears many resemblances to the Pasteur Mérieux-Merck case (among others the market shares). See Commission decision Pasteur Mérieux-Merck, OJ 1994 L 309/1.

4.2.8 Conclusion

Initially, it should be acknowledged that even though this area of competition law went through large changes during the period from 1968 until today, and the Commission was indicating that it had a new more lenient approach, the Commission was also inclined to grant exemptions before 1993, even for all industry-inclusive R&D ventures that aimed to create global technology standards. It is therefore questionable whether in the end fewer situations are caught and prohibited by Art. 101 TFEU today than before the more economic approach. Even before 'the turning point' to a more economic approach in 1993[214], the Commission was not enforcing a stringent policy. It has been a restructuring of the method for applying Art. 101 rather than an implementation of a more lenient economic approach. However, that is not to say that the changes indicated a start to a shift towards a new effect-based approach. The more effect-based Chicago school-oriented approach actually began with these changes in 1993.

It is evident that several of the agreements, scrutinized by the Commission under the now scrapped individual exemption procedures were captioned R&D agreements, revolved less around creating a technical solution and more around establishing a standard or a pool for the promotion of the technology, innovation or product in question.[215] Thus, the cooperation consisted of two stages, namely (i) a joint R&D and standard-setting stage and (ii) joint industrial exploitation of the results of the joint venture through a pool, where the necessary intellectual property rights are placed for the (sub-) licensing to anyone interested. It is also

---

[214] See the Commission, *Report on Competition Policy 1993*, 130 et seq. and the Commission, *Report on Competition Policy 1994*, 105 et seq. An example of the exempted cases was the 1993 Philips-Thomson-Sagem joint venture into development, design, and manufacture of matrix liquid crystal displays (LCD). The exemption was granted, by the Commission, in light of Japanese competition. Apart from the Pasteur Mérieux-Merck joint venture into development and sales (the manufacturing was performed separately by the parents), all other cases in 1994 essentially involved joint R&D, with joint production but separate distribution of the final product. See Philips/Osram, Asahi/St Gobain and Fujitsu/AMD. Exxon/Shell concerned a final product joint venture. See the Commission, *Report on Competition Policy 1994*, 105.

[215] See, e.g., Commission decision Asahi/Saint-Gobain, OJ 1994 L 354/87 and Commission decision Open Group, OJ 1987 L 35/36.

clear that the R&D block exemption is used also in standard-setting activities.[216]

Regarding innovation competition, it also seem that firm can rather use it as an excuse to collaborate. They may point to all other R&D centres available globally and that other firms at least have the facilities to create similar innovation and therefore they should be allowed to collaborate.

4.3 REGULATION OF STANDARDS UNDER COMPETITION LAW, *DE LEGE FERENDE*

The courts seem, from the scant case law available under Art 101 TFEU and Sec. 1 Sherman Act to focus on exclusionary conduct of design or product standards rather than collusive behaviour. The safe harbours for collaborations stipulated in the Horizontal Guidelines and the NCRPA are broad and imply that the SSOs have been delegated the responsibility to regulate and uphold competition within the collaboration, and try to eliminate collusion.

What is missing from the case law, and also from the guidelines produced by the antitrust agencies, is an analysis of different standards and their inherent anti-competitive effects.

In other words, as described above, one could divide the anti-competitive effects of standards and related collaborations into four categories and from such a division in more detail regulate the potential anti-competitive conduct of each sort of standard collaboration:

A.	B.	C.	D.
Basic/ Infrastructure technologies	Interface/ Interoperability/ Network technologies	Patent thicket plagued Products/ technologies	Design standards

[216] The general rules stipulated for standard-setting activities under the Horizontal Guidelines are seldom seen in practice: '[a]s a general rule there should be a clear distinction between the setting of a standard and, where necessary, the related R&D, and the commercial exploitation of that standard. Agreements on standards should cover no more than what is necessary to ensure their aims, whether this is technical compatibility or a certain level of quality.' See Horizontal Guidelines para. 173.

Collaborations and unilateral conduct under these four categories of technology deserve different antitrust treatments. In fact, antitrust agencies should only focus on those standards that might constitute an antitrust problem.[217]

An A standard should preferably be derived from an all inclusive standard-setting process, where the organization's inherently collusive character must be tolerated, while access to membership and results must be protected under competition law, since such standards create markets and competition. Examples of standards under the A category would be the world-wide-web and the telecommunication network technologies. Thus, technologies which, in one way or another, represent natural monopolies and where access to the standard and also the standard-setting process becomes more important than competition for the technology or competition by substitution for the standard as such.

Under these technologies, which are our virtual infrastructure, collaboration so as to create a joint solution is a better outcome than competition. The reason for this is that these markets are plagued by network effects and tipping and, without a standard-setting effort, these technologies can easily be hijacked by the first mover or for that matter the firm with the most developed strategic alliances. To get the 'best' standard possible implemented, the SDO should employ a competitive all-inclusive standard-setting process. The organization creating an A standard should thus be open, unrestricted and the procedure for adopting the standard in question should be transparent, fair and access to the result should be granted on fair, reasonable and non-discriminatory terms which will normally not restrict competition within the meaning of Article 101(1).[218]

On the other hand, under a D standard for design, an all-industry inclusive standard-setting effort, would diminish competition. Here the standard effort represents a joint venture between firms to create a product, and, of course, there is an incentive for these members to claim that the product being developed actually is the only standard/product the

---

[217] Joseph Drexl et al., 'Comments of the Max Planck Institute for IP, Competition and Tax Law on the Draft Commission Block Exemption Regulation on R&D Agreements and the Draft Guidelines on Horizontal Cooperation Agreements', *Competition & Tax Law Research Paper* No 10–12 (Max Planck Institute for IP, 2010).

[218] Horizontal Guidelines, para 280. See also the certification case Joined Cases T-213/95 and T-18/96 SCK and FNK v. Commission [1997] ECR II-1739, an action against Commission decision IV/34.179 – SCK and FNK, (1995) OJ L 312 / 79.

market would be able to engage with. That would not only lead to great royalty profits but also at least a first mover advantage on the downstream product markets.

Several of the cases in which the courts have been involved revolve around design standards and attempts by members of the SSO to create a monopoly technology. The US cases like *Allied Tube* and *Radiant Burners*, on the one side, and *IAZ*, *EMC* and also *Fr.bo*, on the EU side, represent this line of case law quite well regarding collective exclusion or boycott. The test seems to include the following steps: (i) the market will sustain several standards (competition by substitution); (ii) deciding on one or more standard with its related terms of use *de facto* excludes a competitor or competing standard/technology from the market if, for example, the standard is elevated into a regulation; (iii) a plaintiff needs to identify a potential anti-competitive effect on competition and/or parallel trade either by showing misuse of the standard-setting process, or, in rare circumstances, an anti-competitive intent in the setting up of the standard on behalf of at least some competitors in the SSO; and, finally, (iv) when the plaintiff has shown the above (i.e. exclusionary effect and anti-competitive intent), the defendants may exculpate themselves, according to Hovenkamp, by demonstrating the superiority of the standardized technology. As Hovenkamp develops the argument, the courts should be very reluctant to become embroiled in evaluating complex technical concepts, but there are times when the courts are forced to do so.

Design standards should often instead be drafted as performance standards. For these forms of design or product standards, the way the standard is described can furthermore create anti-competitive effects: (i) 'overstandardization', i.e. the breadth and depth of the technology standard excludes new and competing technologies;[219] (ii) 'understandardization', i.e. the technology is still regulated under the standard but the breadth or depth of the standard is too narrow and grants an exclusive field-of-use to certain intellectual property holders within the technology.[220]

Examples of design/product standard setting and joint R&D are also the tyre technology in *Michelin/Goodyear* and the glass in *Asahi/St*

---

[219] Cf. Dolmans regarding standardization depth, i.e., what freedom is left for firms to develop future improvements under a technology standard. Maurits Dolmans, 'Standards For Standards', (2002) 26 *Fordham International Law Journal*, 163, 172 et seq. See also Marcus Glader, 'Open Standards: Public Policy Aspects and Competition Law Requirements', (2010) 6 *European Competition Journal*, 611, 615 et seq.

[220] For a similar but different list, cf. the headings of Maurits Dolmans, 'Standards For Standards', (2002) 26 *Fordham International Law Journal*, 163.

Gobain. Here, the EU Commission should possibly have tried to uphold competition in a more adequate manner. These markets may allow competition by substitution and, by allowing these joint R&D/standard-setting consortia, the Commission agreed to too much market power being combined, both with reference to the relevant markets and innovation competition.

The B standards are different, and here the courts need to hesitate and conduct an analysis of the relevant markets and innovation competition. Interface or interoperability standards are very close to infrastructural standards. They represent markets where network effects can be very strong and may only hold one technology or product. If there is a *pure* interface standard, such standard-setting processes ought possibly to be treated in the same manner as an infrastructure standard. However, it is a very difficult analysis to conduct for the courts. Several of the technologies that we today see as just one competing technology on a larger relevant technical market, were considered to be both interface technology and the only solution for a demand, when the pioneer technology was launched.

The web browser market was identified by several commentators as only holding one software product, without any room for competition by substitute. Thus, only one 'product' could survive the competitive process, and it also represented the interface between the operating system (even the PCs as such) and the internet.[221] In hindsight, we now know that that was not true. There exist several web browsers today used by consumers. However, somewhere in the development of this market, it went from being a unilateral to multilateral technology solution market.

The CD technology when launched may perhaps be considered as interoperability technologies, where the relevant market may be interpreted as being plagued by network effects. Several standards on the internet relating to the transfer of meta-data are about interoperability. But, what about the DVD and the Blu-Ray technologies? Here the alleged network effects seem actually to have been produced by the content and the technology providers. It seems that the different DVD and Blu-Ray technologies represented different collaborations, between different providers of content or technology. Legally, these partner collaborations (consortia) were made up of exclusive cross licence agreements. The exclusivity of these agreements could have constituted a

---

[221] The Microsoft case displays the antitrust application to a *de facto* interoperable standard. United States v. Microsoft Corp., 253 F.3d 34 (D.C. Cir. 2001) (en banc).

competition law issue, while the technologies seem both to be able to be present on the relevant market should these exclusive agreements be void.

In fact, the network effect seems to have been an effect of exclusive agreements between content providers and technology providers in the DVD and Blu-ray wars. If these exclusive arrangements had been eliminated these two technologies could have competed.

Possibly, today the DVD and Blu-Ray collaborations would actually be considered collusions to create dominant D standards and should benefit from a heightened antitrust scrutiny. These forms of technologies for holding content (music and film) are no different from sticks, MP3, the technology supporting Netflix, or for that matter the technology supporting the website, *Pirate Bay.com*! Perhaps, if the competition authorities had tried to uphold competition between these two different technologies and joint ventures on the relevant technology and product markets, so that content providers could have launched on both systems, problems, such as are represented by *Pirate Bay,* would not have materialized. The price of the technologies in question would in any case possibly have been a lot less than they became.

In fact the B standards seem, generally, to be derived from standard consortia/joint R&D ventures between competitors. When the technology is acquired, in an attempt to get suppliers (content providers) and consumers to accept these standards, they are presented with an SDO. Often they represent an inventive leap but they are not basic infrastructural standards. Thus, these standards may easily fool us into believing that they represent the only solution, although these markets would often benefit from several standards competing.

C standards are product standards but where the standard agreement is entered into to create a relevant market and a product out of a patent thicket. In other words, a joint effort where the standard is drafted so as to enable trade and competition by creating a collaboration between all essential patentees. These should even be allowed to become industry-wide collaborations, as long as the SSO and the members are able to prove that there is a patent thicket problem. Examples of standards for this are the Moving Picture Experts Group (MPEG) digital audio and video compression specification standards including MPEG-2, MPEG-4, Thompson's MPEG-1, and Leyer-III (MP3). It should be noted that in the DVD Business Review Letters, the parties claimed that there was a patent thicket in the technology, while this seems less certain in hindsight. These C standards are in fact horizontal agreements for the creation of patent pools.

5. Patent pools

5.1 INTRODUCTION

When the US Justice Department decided to focus on patent pools at the end of the 1990s, it signalled the start of the latest peak of interest in them.[1] Now, more than a decade later, the interest in patent pools, or, more broadly, collaborative schemes for licensing intellectual property rights, is strong and developing.

The EU Commission has monitored and followed the US development of patent pools. Perhaps more accurately, the Commission has not shown its standpoint with reference to the antitrust treatment of patent pools as publicly as the US antitrust agencies; or, at least, it has avoided revealing its own standpoint until the US antitrust agencies have published their opinion.

Notwithstanding this, the development of the European telecommunications industry and its need for workable Europe-wide and global standards and intellectual property rights management has motivated the EU Commission to take an in-depth look at patent pools and the interaction between patent pools and standardization agreements. In addition, in comparison to the US antitrust agencies, the EU Commission is, perhaps, taking a different standpoint on some issues. It considers, for example, in contrast to the US standard, that IP arrangements and patent pools are similar collaborative creatures.[2]

How patent pools are regulated under antitrust law in the United States and in the European Union is the topic of this chapter. The level and threshold of legal scrutiny, i.e. the regulation, of patent pools under US and EU antitrust laws will be analysed. A comparison with the more leniently regulated IP arrangements under SSOs will be undertaken. Patent pools benefit from a higher level of scrutiny than these SSO

[1] Of course, patent pools were the topic of US antitrust law also in 'olden times'. In fact several of the seminal cases under US antitrust law from the 1940s and 50s relate to patent pools.

[2] See TT Guidelines para. 225.

arrangements. A further issue analysed in this chapter is whether society could benefit from a more intense antitrust scrutiny of patent pools.

The chapter is divided into five parts: (i) this introduction; (ii) an analysis of the structure of patent pools and their alleged pro- and anti-competitive effects. Thereafter, (iii) US and (iv) EU antitrust policies are analysed separately, before concluding with (v) a comparative analysis, where the standard-derived patent pools are discussed.

5.2 THE STRUCTURE OF TECHNOLOGY POOLS AND SOME ALLEGED PRO- AND ANTI-COMPETITIVE EFFECTS

5.2.1 Structure

Patent pools are complex contracts that explicitly or implicitly imply four agreements. First, there is the clear pool agreement, where the contributors of patents agree on (i) the definition of the technology (i.e. often identical to the technology defined under a technology standardization agreement), and (ii) the terms (e.g. royalty rates) on which downstream product manufacturers should get access to the essential intellectual properties. Secondly, the patent pools include standard licensing agreements from the pool to third party licensees. Thirdly, implicitly or explicitly, there is also an agreement to exchange licences between the patent providers (pool builders) that are also active in the downstream product markets. Thus, there is a horizontal aspect between the firms that both contribute patents and take out licences from the pools compared to the otherwise vertical set-up of patent pools. Fourthly, implicitly, pooling may include an agreement on where to develop the technology further through grant-back clauses or cross-licensing covenants for future innovations and patents.

All these agreements are to a different degree vertical or horizontal, depending on what parties are analysed and from what market perspective the pool is perceived. For example, *de lege ferenda,* a licence from the pool to a licensee may have horizontal effects if the licensee and the relevant patent contributor to the pool are competitors in the product market, even though they are not competitors in the technology market. Correspondingly, contributors to the pool can be competitors either dynamically, i.e. competing in developing new innovations, or in downstream products markets, even though they possibly hold blocking or complementary patents.

When it comes to the structure of technology pools, and SSOs in general, the parties to the pool agreement may be placed in the following categories: (i) 'technology-only' firms, i.e. pure innovators or patent collectors (PAEs) that conduct R&D or purchase patents and generally do not manufacture products; (ii) 'Manufacturing-only' firms, i.e. firms that manufacture products and do not conduct 'break-through' inventions but sometimes conduct follow-on R&D; and (iii) vertically integrated firms, i.e. the 'original' multinational firms that conduct both R&D and produce products under the invented technology.

Depending on which parties make up the licensor and the licensing community of a patent pool, the pool may have more or less horizontal competitive features. Apart from having a different competitive relationship within a patent pool, these firms do have different incentives. The 'technology-only' firms' incentive is to have as high royalty rates as possible, while 'manufacture only' firms and the vertically integrated firms normally try to either reduce the royalty rate or, as for vertically integrated firms, keep them at least at modest levels. The vertically integrated firms still make the bulk of their revenues by manufacturing products under the relevant technology rather than revenues gained from royalties.[3] Hence, those firms are often more interested in the exchange of licences within the patent pools, and in being able to produce products for downstream markets without infringing the relevant intellectual property rights.

As many commentators have discussed, the different incentives explain, for example, the tense debate regarding the telecommunication standards set by the European Technology Standard Institute (ETSI)[4].

[3] Rudi Bekkers, et al., 'Case studies on the interface between research and standardisation, and case studies on patent pools as a coordination mechanism' (INTEREST consortium Priority 8 No. Contract 503 594, EU 6th Specific Targeted Research Project, 2006), 53 et seq. [The document is on file with the author.]

[4] For the European discussion, see generally Hanns Ullrich, 'Patente, Wettbewerb, under technische Normen: Recht- und ordnungspolitische Fragestellungen', 10 *GRUR* 2007, 817; Gil Ohana et al., 'Disclosure and Negotiation of Licensing Terms Prior to Adoptation of Industry Standards: Preventing another Patent Ambush', (2003) 24 *E.C.L.R*, 644; and several articles by Damien Geradin: see e.g., Damien Geradin, 'Standardization and Technological Innovation: Some Reflections on Ex-ante Licensing, FRAND, and the Proper Means to Reward Innovators', (2006) 29 *World Competition*, 511; Damien Geradin et al., *Elves or Trolls? The Role of Non-Practicing Patent Owners in the Innovation Economy* (SSRN 2008), 5 et seq. For comments on the US developments, see generally Joseph Farrell et al., 'Standard Setting, Patents, and Hold-up', (2007)

They are also the underlying issue in the European cases concerning the interpretation of fair, reasonable and non-discriminatory (FRAND) terms.[5] Patent pools did not work in the telecom sector due to the different business models for the firms involved.

However, as Ullrich has argued, the difference in incentives between vertically integrated firms and firms only involved in one segment of the industry also affects aspects of patent pools other than the level of the royalty rates.[6] Pooling involves not only a decision on the level of royalties to charge but also on the selection of patents to pool.

The decision on what patents to pool is actually the interface between technology standard-setting and pool agreements. The breadth of the technology under a technology standardization agreement, and thus, what patents to include in the pool, is adjusted given the competitive position of the pool builders or SSO members, on the downstream product markets.[7] Whenever one or more of the members is present on product markets, pool building is a tactical exercise serving their strategic

---

74 *Antitrust Law Journal*, 603, 604 et seq.; Daniel Swanson and William Baumol, 'Reasonable and Nondiscriminatory (RAND) Royalties, Standards Selection, and Control of Market Power', (2005) 73 *Antitrust Law Journal*, 1; Anne Layne-Farrar et al., 'Pricing Patents for Licensing in Standard-Setting Organizations: Making Sense of FRAND Commitments', (2007) 74 *Antitrust Law Journal*, 671; Mark Lemley and Carl Shapiro, 'Patent Holdup and Royalty Stacking', (2007) 85 *Texas Law Review*, 1991.

[5] See particularly EC Commission's Memo/Press Release, MEMO/07/389, dated 1 October 2007 'Commission Initiates Formal Proceedings against Qualcomm'. On the joint complaint of Nokia, Ericsson, Texas Instruments, Broadcom, NEC and Panasonic, the EU Commission started an investigation into whether Qualcomm was abusing its dominance based on patent rights included in the 3G system since it did not license these rights on Fair, Reasonable, and Non-Discriminatory (FRAND) terms. The contractual agreements at issue relate to the standard-setting procedures of the European Telecommunications Standardization Institute ('ETSI') regarding the licensing of essential patents. Nokia and Qualcomm reached a settlement in the middle of 2008. See Matt Richtel, 'In Settlement, Nokia Will Pay Royalties to Qualcomm', in the *New York Times,* 24 July 2008), http://www.nytimes.com/2008/07/24/technology/24qualcomm.html?_r=1&scp=1&sq=nokia%20qualcomm&st=cse, accessed 7 April 2009.

[6] Cf. Hanns Ullrich, 'Patent Pools – Policy and Problems', in Josef Drexl (ed), *Research Handbook on Intellectual Property and Competition Law* (Edward Elgar, 2008), 146 et seq. discussing how members in a patent pool will act according to their competitive position in the market including whether they are active on the product markets. See also Daniel A. Crane, 'Patent Pools, RAND Commitments, and the Problematics of Price Discrimination', *Cardozo School of Law Working Paper* (2008) no. 232, discussed infra.

[7] Ibid.

interests in these markets.[8] In that sense, cross-licensing and pooling are complementary exercises. The former, i.e. the agreement in each individual case on whom to include and to exchange licenses with, determines the technology defined under the pool agreement and in the technology standardization agreement under the SSO. It is exactly this decision or agreement that has, with the latest amendment, been encompassed under the NCRPA in the United States and thus benefits from the NCRPA's more lenient treatment.

Of course, it is clear that if the definition of the technology under a technology standard is too wide, royalties will reflect a bundle of too many patents for the actual needs of the manufacturing firms producing products under the pooled technology.[9] There are some indications that the definition under technology standardization agreements and pools may in some cases be too wide.[10] This will increase royalty rates. However, even though the issue of the breadth of the pooled technology concerns the royalty rates, it more directly concerns dynamic competition: what technology will win; who will have exclusivity in certain areas of the product markets under a standardized technology; what technologies have been standardized in the first place and, more importantly, which technologies will not become successful.

If the technology standard is narrow – in the sense that the patentees and pool builders saved some field of technology use for themselves which was outside the pool by limiting the breadth of the standard – other forms of anti-competitive effect may arise. First, such a set-up may create exclusive patches in the technology where the licensee must go outside the pool to obtain licences directly from patentees. The royalty rates for these patches may be substantial, or the patentees may possibly reserve these areas of the technology for themselves.[11]

---

[8] Ibid.

[9] Cf., e.g., generally Douglas Melamed, 'Patents and Standard: The Unimportance of Being Essential' (unpublished, 2006). [The document is on file with the author.]; Rudi Bekkers, 'Patent Drag and Stacking IPR fees – Are the IPR Policies of Standard Bodies Failing or Should we Better Address Excessive Technology Inclusion?' (2007), position paper for High Level Workshop on Standardization, IP Licensing and Antitrust. [The documents are on file with the author.]

[10] Ibid. See also the discussion regarding standard 802.11, discussed supra.

[11] Possibly, in the latest Business Review Letter, the Justice Department allows for differentiated royalty rates depending on different fields of use under a patent pool. See RFID Business Review Letter from Thomas O. Barnett to William Dolan and Geoffrey Oliver, dated 21 October 2008, http://www.usdoj.gov/atr/public/busreview/238429.htm. Accessed 4 April 2007.

The technology-only firms are not as interested in the connection between product markets and the breadth of the technology standard, or the 'exchange of licences' aspect of patent pools as the vertically integrated firms. Instead, they are interested in high royalty levels. That does not, however, imply that they would totally disregard the breadth of a technology standard. The development of the technology as such may affect technology-only firms' R&D and joint R&D tactics, which may even cause them to take an interest in licensing certain patents under the pool.

Manufacturing-only firms are, of course, interested in low royalty rates but also in the technology standard actually correlating with the customers' and eventually the consumers' demand. The technology should be neither too wide nor too narrow and the patents in the pool should be essential not only in light of the definition of the technology standard but also in light of customer and consumer demand for the technology.

5.3 THE MODERN APPROACH TO PATENT POOLS UNDER US ANTITRUST LAW

5.3.1 The Early Business Review Letters

(i) Introduction

The current US jurisprudence regarding patent pools is interesting from two perspectives: first, in its own right and secondly as a benchmark for analysing IP arrangements under the IP policies of SSOs. Patent pools are generally regulated by three Business Review Letters from the end of the 1990s,[12] the writings of the IP Guidelines and other guiding documents from the antitrust authorities,[13] and lately a new Business Review Letter regarding the interface between technology standard setting, IP arrangements and patent pool building.[14]

---

[12] Business Review Letters from the end of the 1990s, i.e., Business Review Letter for the MPEG-2 Pool, Business Review Letter from Joel Klein to Gerrard Beeney dated 26 June 1997, 6, the 3DVD pool Business Review Letter from Joel Klein to Gerrard Beeney dated 16 December 1998, 5 et seq. and 6DVD Business Review Letter from Joel Klein to Carey Ramos dated 10 June 1999. See http://www.usdoj.gov/atr/public/busreview/letters.htm, accessed 4 April 2009.

[13] For example, the IP 2 Report.

[14] See latest RFID Business Review Letter from Thomas O. Barnett to William Dolan and Geoffrey Oliver, dated 21 October 2008. See also VITA Business Review Letter from Thomas O. Barnett to Robert A. Skitol, dated 30

The early Business Review Letters from the end of the 1990s, which initiated the current interest in patent pools, became so important when setting them up that even representatives of the Justice Department have found them too dominant.[15] They were regarded as carving out an exemption, safe harbour or per se legal area for technology pools, and many feared that straying too far outside the set-up defined in the letters would cause the pool to to be in breach of the antitrust law. However, that is not to say that patent pools have not been under scrutiny before under the Business Review Letter scheme, or that pools are not continuously analysed by the antitrust authorities.[16] In some speeches, representatives from the Justice Department have hinted that they might be inclined to lower or at least re-evaluate the requirements stipulated in the Business Review Letters from the end of the 1990s.[17] These speeches indicate that the rules stipulated in the letters are not a 'white list' of exempted

---

October 2006. and IEEE Business Review Letter from Thomas O. Barnett to Michael A. Lindsay, dated 30 April 2007. All can be found on http://www.justice.gov/atr/public/busreview/letters.html#page=page-1. Accessed 4 April 2009.

[15] Gerald Masoudi, 'Antitrust Enforcement and Standard Setting: the VITA and IEEE Letters and the IP2 Report', paper to the Spring Meeting of the American Intellectual Property Law Association, 2007; Gerald Masoudi, 'Efficiency in Analysis of Antitrust, Standard Setting, and Intellectual Property', speech to High Level Workshop on Standardization, IP Licensing, and Antitrust, 2007, TILEC, University of Tilburg. See http://www.usdoj.gov/atr/public/speeches/speech_2007.htm, accessed 1 May 2009.

[16] According to some commentators, earlier pools, e.g. the CD-rom pool, were analysed by the Justice Department at the beginning of the 1980s. See Carl Shapiro, 'Navigating the Patent Thicket: Cross Licenses, Patent Pools and Standard Setting ', in Adam Jaffe et al. (eds), *Innovation Policy and the Economy* 2001), 137.

[17] This would imply, e.g., that patent pools would be able to encompass wider grant-back clauses and field-of-use stipulations making it possible to discriminate in price between different licensees active on different product markets, or even prevent exhaustion of the Intellectual property rights in certain markets. Such covenants might also be the effect of the IP negotiations that can take place under the NCRPA. Gerald Masoudi, 'Antitrust Enforcement and Standard Setting: the VITA and IEEE Letters and the IP2 Report', paper to the Spring Meeting of the American Intellectual Property Law Association 2007; Gerald Masoudi, 'Efficiency in Analysis of Antitrust, Standard Setting, and Intellectual Property', speech to High-Level Workshop on Standardization, IP Licensing, and Antitrust, 2007, TILEC, University of Tilburg, see http://www.usdoj.gov/atr/public/speeches/speeches.htm. Accessed 11 April 2009.

covenants in a sea of otherwise anti-competitive and illegal covenants. Instead, there is room for new or different restrictions.[18]

(ii) MPEG-2

The MPEG-2 pool was the first to be scrutinized under the Business Review Letter procedure and in many aspects it represents a 'model citizen' and an example of when patent pools should be used due to a prevailing 'patent thicket'.[19] When it was approved by the US Department of Justice in 1997, through Assistant Attorney General Joel Klein, it initially contained 27 essential patents originating in nine firms.[20] The technology built on the Motion Picture Exert Group standard implemented by ISO, IEC and ITU in 1995. An independent expert scrutinized more than 8,000 US patents granted to more than 100 patentees or assignees to establish whether they were essential, or not, in light of the MPEG-2 protocol, i.e. the MPEG-2 technology standard. Indeed, the 27 patents were technically essential or necessary. They did not have substitutes nor could they be 'invented around'.

The MPEG-2 pool made it possible to have only one licence and is thus a 'one stop shop', for at least a great majority of the whole technology. The company administrating the protocol and the pool is a limited liability company based in Colorado, USA named MPEG LA, which also grants the licences.[21]

---

[18] The possibility of employing more elaborated field-of-use restrictions and related differentiated royalty rates seems to be a change to the patent pool jurisprudence sought by the business community, cf. Robert Skitol, (2002) DOJ/FTC Hearings on Competition and Intellectual Property Law and Policy in the Knowledge-Based Economy [The document is on file with the author.]

[19] MPEG-2 pool Business Review Letter from Joel Klein to Gerrard Beeney dated 26 June 1997. See http://www.usdoj.gov/atr/public/busreview/215742.htm. Accessed 7 April 2009.

[20] Ibid. Also, the EC Commission has on a number of occasions had the opportunity to analyse MPEG LA for pooling patents and know-how. The members of the pools have notified the EC Commission when new pools have been established: see e.g., 'Case Notification of Agreement COMP 3/C-3-38143, OJ C 174/07, 19.6.2001, 6. It should be noted that among the founding members are Philips and Sony, since the MPEG-2 technology, as the technology for CDs and DVDs, originated in their combined research efforts. See Rajneesh Narula, *Globalization and Technology* (Polity Press, 2003), 115.

[21] MPEG LA administrates several different patent pools, e.g., the MPEG-4 pool contains the right to the MPEG protocol for transmitting audio and video over the internet.

According to the MPEG Business Review Letter, the administration (pool) agreement requires the pool to be open to new comers, i.e. anyone wishing to become a licensee should be able to do so. The term of the licences has, since 1 June 1994, been from the date of entering into the agreement to 31 December 2010, and the term may thereafter be extended for successive five-year periods.[22] When renewed in 2010, the royalty may not increase by more than 25 per cent, with a few exceptions. Each patent in the pool was valued equally. There is no difference in the remuneration based on the actual use of the individual patents by the licensees.[23] Each licensor receives the same return based on the number of patents it holds in the pool. This implies that, whenever a new patent is added, the royalty return for the existing licensors is diluted.[24]

The portfolio licences also included a 'most favoured nation' clause. The licensing agreement contains a standard grant-back clause, obligating licensees to offer their technology to either a licensor or another licensee should their technology be *necessary* for complying with the MPEG-2 standard.[25] Whether this is an expansion of the technical definition of essentiality, which was set out in the Business Review Letter to also include necessity from a practical viewpoint, is difficult to discern from MPEG LA's website. According to the licensing agreements, the remuneration should be 'fair and reasonable' for a licence 'granted back'.

The pool had grown and included, in 2010, more than 700 patents (134 patent families and worldwide counterparts) contributed by at least 24 companies from Europe, Japan and USA.

MPEG LA administers the MPEG-2 pool and offers package licences to all essential patents for the MPEG-2 protocol, solicits licensees and enforces the licensing agreements.[26] It also offers additional non-essential licences. These licences were not mentioned in the Business Review

---

[22] MPEG-2 pool Business Review Letter from Joel Klein to Gerrard Beeney dated 26 June 1997. See http://www.usdoj.gov/atr/public/busreview/215742.htm. Accessed 7 April 2009.

[23] Steven Carlson, 'Patent Pools and the Antitrust Dilemma', (1999) 16 *Yale Journal of Regulation*, 359, 371.

[24] Josh Lerner et al., *The Structure and Performance of Patent Pools: Emperical Evidence,* (Harvard University and NBER, 2003) 33.

[25] Ibid. Cf. Steven Carlson, 'Patent Pools and the Antitrust Dilemma', (1999) 16 *Yale Journal of Regulation*, 359, 371. MPEG-2 pool Business Review Letter from Joel Klein to Gerrard Beeney dated 26 June 1997, 7 et seq. See http://www.usdoj.gov/atr/public/busreview/215742.htm. Accessed 7 April 2009.

[26] See abbreviation of the standard license agreement at MPEG LA website: http://www.mpegla.com/m2/m2-agreement.cfm, accessed 4 April 2006.

Letter but they are possibly licences derived from so-called 'related patents'. 'Related patents' were given a very broad definition in the pool agreement encompassing all those patents that have a claim covering products utilizing the MPEG-2 technology. The Justice Department in its Business Review Letter did state that in practice the notion of related patents cannot be used so broadly, but it has been interpreted quite broadly, enabling several connected patents to flow into MPEG LA.[27]

The technology defined in the patent pool agreement of the MPEG-2 pool was not analysed by the Justice Department. The Department was satisfied that the technology had been approved as an international standard by the International Organization of Standards (ISO), the International Electrotechnical Commission (IEC) and by International Telecommunication Union Telecommunication Standardization (ITU-I).[28] The technical requirement of essentiality in combination with the independent expert as an arbiter of the patents' continuous status as essential was to the satisfaction of the Department. The Justice Department concluded that licensing a combination of complementary intellectual property rights, especially rights that block the application for which they are jointly licensed, can be an efficient and pro-competitive method of disseminating rights to would-be users.[29] The Department, thus, found that the main purpose of the patent pool was benign from an anti-competitive perspective.

The restrictive covenants allowed by the Justice Department deserve some comment. Whether 'most favoured nation' clauses should be regarded as pro-competitive, as the Justice Department maintains, may be disputed.[30] They communicate the message that licensees should not try to renegotiate the licensing agreement. If they do, they do it on behalf of all licensees. The licensee may not obtain any specific competitive advantages by negotiating. If the licensee is able to renegotiate, many

---

27 MPEG-2 pool Business Review Letter from Joel Klein to Gerrard Beeney dated June 26, 1997, 12 et seq. n. 33. See http://www.usdoj.gov/atr/public/busreview/215742.htm, accessed 4 April 2009.

28 For an interesting Business Review Letter of somewhat later date, see American Welding Society Business Review Letter from Charles James to Douglas McDonald, dated 7. Oct. 2002, where the Justice Department stated that it is not concerned whether one standard is better than the other, only whether the process of standard setting has been abused. See http://www.usdoj.gov/atr/public/busreview/200310.htm. Accessed 19 March 2009.

29 Ibid. 5 et seq.

30 Also called 'English clauses', See MPEG-2 pool Business Review Letter from Joel Klein to Gerrard Beeney dated 26 June 1997, 4 et seq. n. 23. See http://www.usdoj.gov/atr/public/busreview/215742.htm, accessed 4 April 2009.

others, possibly competitors, will piggyback on that negotiation. A 'most favoured nation' clause therefore risks creating a stagnant market with high prices where the licensees do not have the incentive to even negotiate the royalty rates in the beginning of the business relationship.

'Most favoured nation' clauses can also be anti-competitive for other reasons. They may easily, *de facto,* slip into obligations on the *licensees* to report if they obtain the technology less expensively elsewhere. The licensor(s) then agree(s) to match those prices. Does that imply that the licensees are obliged to a licence from the licensors? If that is the case, 'most favoured nation' clauses could be regarded as exclusivity or 'single brand' clauses, or even 'tie-out' clauses.[31] The licensees are not allowed to use other technology than the technology provided for in the pool. Of course, standardization agreements connected to dominant pools are *de facto* tie-out agreements.[32]

Moreover, in addition to the 'normal' grant-back clause, the licensing agreement included a right for licensors, in certain instances, to order the removal of individual patents from the scope of licences granted to a specific licensee.[33] A licensee who brought a lawsuit against a licensor for infringement of either an essential or a 'related' patent, and refused to license the patent on which the infringement suit was based to the licensor, could lose the right to license the licensors patent.[34] 'Related patents' are actually any technology remotely related to the defined

---

[31] Also called 'English clauses'. Given the fact that pools today are allowed to contain some non-essential patents, it is also difficult to interpret what the pool actually agrees to do. Will the total royalty rate of the pool be matched against single competitive patents outside the pool? If that is the case, the incentive to invent outside the pool but under the standardized technology is practically non-existent.

[32] However, the latest report published by the Agencies does not comment on tie-outs, cf. IP 2 Report.

[33] This could possibly extend to the litigant being refused access to any patent in the pool. See MPEG-2 pool Business Review Letter from Joel Klein to Gerrard Beeney dated 26 June 1997, 9 et seq. See http://www.usdoj.gov/atr/public/busreview/215742.htm. Accessed 4 April 2009.

[34] MPEG-2 pool Business Review Letter from Joel Klein to Gerrard Beeney dated 26 June 1997, 8 et seq. See http://www.usdoj.gov/atr/public/busreview/215742.htm. Accessed 4 April 2009. See abbreviation of the standard licence agreement at MPEG LA website: http://www.mpegla.com/m2/m2-agreement.cfm, accessed 4 April 2006.

technology.[35] Thus, it is an extended 'non-challenge clause', which extends to a right for the licensor either not to be challenged over his conduct, or to be granted access to the patent which the licensor is itself allegedly violating.[36] Generally the licensees' essential and related patents must be either disregarded in relation to, or granted back to, the original licensors.[37] The Justice Department discussed this termination and grant-back clause in depth and concluded that it should not be regarded as anti-competitive, mainly due to its bilateral rather than multilateral approach. Interestingly, similar termination or non-challenge clauses have now caused the EU Commission to find the Google FRAND licence agreement to possibly be anti-competitive.[38]

However, the letter misses one crucial point. As with essential patents granted back through the normal grant-back clause, the licensor, receiving the related patent, based on this covenant, will probably place it (or them) in the pool too. The patents are not essential, but can be placed in the pools as related patents and licensed separately. Thus, related patents or technologies will be accessible to all firms connected to the pool, or at least to the licensor(s).

From the viewpoint of the licensee that invented the non-essential but 'related' patent, this might be a disaster. It implies that all competitors, or at least the most important competitors (the licensors), will get access to the innovation almost at the same time as the inventor. The inventor cannot then use the innovation to gain market shares on the product

---

35 MPEG-2 pool Business Review Letter from Joel Klein to Gerrard Beeney dated 26 June 1997. See http://www.usdoj.gov/atr/public/busreview/215742.htm, accessed 4 April 2009, 12 et seq., n. 33.

36 The question is to what extent this sort of right may be regarded as a breach of antitrust law. Compare Intel Corp. v. Intergraph Corp., 195 F.3d 1346 (Fed. Cir. 1999) (Intellectual property owner was free to terminate licence of licensee who sued it for infringement of licensee's own intellectual property) with In re Intel Corp., Dock. NO. 288 (F.T.C. 1999) (where Intel agreed in a settlement with the FTC not to withhold product or technical information for reasons relating to an intellectual property dispute). According to Pitofsky, there were significant legal and factual differences between these cases (even though originating in the same procedure), see Robert Pitofsky, 'Antitrust and Intellectual Property: Unsolved Issues at the Heart of the New Economy', (2001) 16 *Berkeley Technology Law Journal*, 535, 549 et seq. fn 45, with references.

37 The agencies seem to be aware of this; see IP 2 Report, 69.

38 See discussion, infra, in Chapter 7.

market at the expense of its competitors. Logically, this reduces incentives to innovate.[39] The Business Review Letter also lays down something of a FRAND requirement for follow-on innovators. Accordingly, they should make licences available on 'fair and reasonable' terms. Hence, follow-on inventors are deprived of any remuneration higher than 'fair and reasonable'. 'Fair and reasonable' creates a ceiling to the amount a follow-on inventor can invest in R&D under the MPEG-2 technology.

The regular grant-back covenant, together with the extended termination clause, implies that the inventors may not block the technology nor anything related to the technology. These requirements create an efficient patent pool, but are they pro-innovation? Why should follow-on innovators only obtain fair returns while the original royalty rate for the first essential patents possibly could be more than fair and reasonable?[40] On top of that, why should follow-on innovators be prevented from exclusively creating competing technologies and winning customers on the product markets? The termination/non-challenge clause connected to the related patents might prevent this.

---

[39] Cf the Phoebus cartel described in United States v. General Electric et al 82 F. Supp. 753, 856 (1949).

[40] However, why would follow-on inventors need a licence in the first place? First, the fact is that licensees are most likely to develop a technology or to innovate under a technology. Secondly, even though they may be a 'greenfield' innovator without any prior activities in the technology, the innovator might need a licence from the pool. In light of the prevailing US patent jurisprudence under the Duke case, Madey v. Duke University, 307 F.3d 1351 (Fed. Cir. 2002), a commercial inventor, in most cases, needs a licence to conduct research. See also RFID Business Review Letter from Thomas O. Barnett to William F. Dolan and Geoffrey Oliver, dated 21 October 2008 supporting this view. See http://www.usdoj.gov/atr/public/busreview/238429.htm, accessed 3 May 2009. There is only a limited experimental use exception under US patent law jurisprudence. Thus, from a US perspective, an inventor needs to take out a licence. Otherwise, the researcher is already in breach of the patents in the pool when conducting research into how he can invent around the pool. However, as with many pools, the MPEG LA licences are limited to certain fields of research. In the MPEG-2 case, it seems that the licensees may manufacture, sell and in most cases use the technology. Possibly use implies R&D, otherwise it actually seems that any firm wanting to conduct research in the field of the MPEG 2 needs to obtain individual licences from each member of the pool. See, generally, MPEG-2 pool Business Review Letter from Joel Klein to Gerrard Beeney dated 26 June 1997. See http://www.usdoj.gov/atr/public/busreview/215742.htm, accessed 4 April 2009.

According to the Justice Department, the MPEG-2 pool overall creates benefits for society. MPEG LA and the MPEG-2 pool were able to disseminate and give access to the technology in a way that single proprietors could not.[41] Undoubtedly, the arrangement accelerated dissemination and cut through the patent thicket. Moreover, it has eliminated the cost of firms having to scan the whole market for prospective patents that they would risk infringing should they enter the MPEG-2 business.

The MPEG-2 Business Review Letter was the initial step in creating a check-list of approximately nine to 11 requirements for setting up a patent pool, including: (i) only essential patents are to be included in the pool; (ii) pool members should be allowed to grant individual licences; (iii) the pool must be open if representing market power; (iv) the grant-back clauses, applicable to all licensees, must be limited to essential patents; (v) the technology in the pool must be licensed on (F)RAND terms; moreover, (vi) 'most favoured nation' clauses are pro-competitive; (vii) pool members should take out licences from the pool; (viii) the parties to the pool should be free to conduct R&D; and (ix) the licensors should erect firewalls to protect competitively sensitive information from reaching each other and to keep it confidential.[42]

In hindsight, this is an important and impressive list. It carves out a middle way between the extremes that have been the antitrust jurisprudence vis-a-vis patent pools during history. Nonetheless, the Justice Department failed to discuss some relevant issues.

By 2010, the patents contained in the MPEG-2 pool had increased from 24 to 700. According to the Business Review Letter, the expiry of a licensor's last portfolio patent, or a final adjudication of invalidity or unenforceability for its last remaining patent, terminates the licensor's participation in the patent pool and the agreement among the licensors. The Department assumed that, when an essential patent expired, it would be deleted from the pool.[43] One can thereby imagine that the Department

---

[41] It should however be remembered that this pool does derive a lot of technology from joint R&D made by Philips and Sony. According to Narula, Philips and Sony developed the DVD technology together with the AC-3 technology: see Rajneesh Narula, *Globalization and Technology* (Polity Press, 2003), 115.

[42] For a very clear and similar list see Commission, *Report on Competition Policy 2002*, 194.

[43] MPEG-2 pool Business Review Letter from Joel Klein to Gerrard Beeney dated 26 June 1997, 6. See http://www.usdoj.gov/atr/public/busreview/215742.htm, accessed 4 April 2009.

probably took it for granted that the pool would eventually dissolve when the last of the essential patents had expired. Especially since the original patents were, according to the Department, technically essential, i.e. not possible to invent around. However, it is not certain that the pool will dissolve. As noted above, the pool in 2010 contained 700 patents while it initially held 24. The participating firms have however only increased by 15. One might therefore draw the conclusion that the founding members hold most or at least some of the patents that were added after the pool was set up. Since they are able to find new essential technologies to patent within the sphere of the MPEG-2 protocol, the pool will continue to be active.[44] *De lege ferenda*, what is missing is an end date or an analysis of when the patent pool will have lost it purpose, even though still containing one or a few essential patents. When the collusive effects become greater than the collaborative justification based on efficiency, the pool should be dissolved. The Department failed to recognize this fact. Unfortunately, this seem to be happening with all successful standards and patent pools. They offer an incentive for firms to take out essential patents under the technology and *ex post* insert them in the standard or pool agreement. The telecom sector displays a similar pattern. The 3G and the UMTS standards/pools saw an increase in essential patents that were created after the standards/pools had been agreed upon. The paradox is that these collaborations, which were created, at least partially, to give efficient access to SEPs, now act as incentives for firms' (legal departments) to take out more SEPs on technologies that have clearly already been invented, and even standardized.

Interestingly, from the MPEG website, it is evident that the licensors of the essential patents under the MPEG LA will collectively bring a lawsuit against any producer that tries to develop and produce hardware or software that might infringe the essential patents of the pool. The press releases on the website reveal that the proprietors of the essential patents

---

[44] This is also supported by the fact that pools multiply and develop. The DVD and Blu-ray pools probably developed out of the early CD-ROM pool and probably contain similar, and even the same, essential patents. Thus, in reality there is a strong possibility that the pool will not come to an end until a new leap of innovation creates a whole new solution to that particular customer demand. In other words, the pool will – as other pools – probably last for the life cycle of the MPEG-2 or AC-3 technology rather than the fixed statutory limit for the patents. The antitrust enforcement agencies are today well aware of the fact that successful patent pools will last until the technology is obsolete. See IP 2 Report, 64, with references.

joined forces when, for example, a DVD disc manufacturer did not take out a licence from MPEG LA before starting production. As I understand it, all these lawsuits have been settled before going to trial by the manufacturers taking out licences.[45] Such joint defence agreements were considered anti-competitive under the old jurisprudence: see, for example, the *Singer* case or *Krasnov* case.[46] It prevented weak patents from being litigated since they were hidden in the joint onslaught on both good and weak patents.

(iii) The DVD Business Review Letters[47]

The Justice Department delivered two Business Review Letters regarding a technology closely related to the MPEG-2 shortly after the MPEG-2 letter. The subsequent cases that dealt with DVD technology and the interaction between the two DVD pools, and also the MPEG-2 pool, are not entirely clear from reading these letters.[48] Generally, the Justice Department stuck to the list of requirements for setting up a pool and

---

[45] See press releases MPEG, http://www.mpegla.com/news.cfm, accessed 16 April 2006. All cases have been settled.

[46] United States v. The Singer Manufacturing Comp. 374 U.S. 174 (1963); United States v. Krasnov, 143 F. Supp 184 (E.D. Pa 1956) aff'd. 355 U.S. 5 (1957). Cf. Richard Gilbert, 'Antitrust for Patent Pools: A Century of Policy Evolution', (2004) April *Stanford Technology Law Review*, 3, 33, noting that joint patent defence might be a sign of substitute patents.

[47] For the EU equivalent, see Commission, Report on Competition Policy 2000, Part 2, Chapter I.A.2.1.2 and Commission, Report on Competition Policy 2002, 194.

[48] The background seems to be as follows: 'Sony and Philips worked together in the late 1970s to develop the audio CD. Philip's work on LaserDisc and Sony's digital error correction encoding resulted in a huge leap forward for consumer audio that delivered high quality sound on a durable medium with instant playback. In the early 1990s, the two companies began collaborating on an inexpensive new video version, called the MultiMedia Compact Disc. At the same time, a group led by Toshiba, and including Pioneer and JVC, introduced the SuperDensity Disc. For a year and a half, the companies tried without much luck to interest consumers in the two formats. In 1995, the groups united to form the DVD Consortium, later called the DVD Forum. That cooperation helped the single new DVD format to be adopted rapidly. DVDs use ISO standard MPEG-2 video compression and digital audio, typically delivered as Dolby Digital AC-3 or DTS surround sound. Using standard, interoperable formats based on patent pools from established technical leaders meant that DVDs could be delivered by any hardware manufacturer under reasonable and non-discriminatory licensing'. See http://www.roughlydrafted.com/2007/08/29/origins-of-the-blu-ray-vs-hd-dvd-war/. Accessed 8 February 2008. Thus, a DVD manufacturer needs to take out licences from the MPEG-2 pool and the DVD pools.

thereby established it as a 'white list' that could gain an exemption under antitrust law. However, some legally significant, and some minor, differences in comparison to the MPEG-2 case may be detected from reading these letters.

Initially, the background technology standard was not an ISO standard but it was based on a technology standardization agreement between two groups of firms for two similar technologies that connected and interacted with a more generally agreed technology standard.[49] Secondly, the pools described in the DVD letters have fewer licensors and a wider definition of essentiality in comparison to the MPEG-2 letter.[50] Not only technically essential patents are allowed into the pools, but also those for which existing alternatives are economically unfeasible.[51] Thus, in theory, although not financially feasible, a firm could invent around the patents included in the pool and still adhere to the defined technology. Whether there would have been even fewer licensors had the technically-oriented definition of essentiality in the MPEG-2 case been utilized is not certain. However, it is likely that the reason for implementing a wider definition would be to encompass not only more patents but also more patentees. The 3C DVD pool included 210 patents, mostly from two firms. The 3C DVD technology, as well as the CD technology to a large extent, was derived from two companies' joint R&D venture.[52] Thus, while the MPEG-2 pool was a tool to overcome the patent thicket, the 3C DVD pool was mainly derived from a joint R&D venture.[53] The third

---

[49] See Rudi Bekkers, et al., 'Case studies on the interface between research and standardisation, and case studies on patent pools as a coordination mechanism' (INTEREST consortium Priority 8 No. Contract 503 594, EU 6th Specific Targeted Research Project, 2006), 105 et seq., for the fascinating story behind the DVD standards. [The document is on file with the author.] See also International Norcent Technology v. Koninklijke Philips Electronics N.V., not reported, in F. Supp.2d, 2007 WL 4976364, C.D. Cal., 2007. Oct 29, 2007 for a competitor's view of the DVD patent pools.

[50] Today, there seem to be several licensors for patents connected to the DVD technology. Or, at least there are several licensors of patents under the AC-3 technology developed by Dolby Inc., which created several innovative technologies within the sphere of the DVD technology.

[51] See e.g., 3DVD Pool Business Review Letter from Joel Klein to Gerrard Beeney dated 16 December 1998, fn. 8.

[52] That would imply that the 3C DVD pool was or could have been judged under the NCRPA.

[53] The IP 2 Report, 69.

firm (Pioneer) was mostly a large manufacturer indicating to the market that there was manufacturing capacity under the 3C DVD pool.[54]

Secondly, the fee mechanism in the DVD letters compared to the MPEG-2 letter was more advanced. An initial entrance fee was deducted and, in addition, there was a running fee based on production per unit, tagged to the actual use of the individual patents that were taken out. The running fees had a lower floor set in US dollars. The allocation of royalties among the licensors was not a function of the number of patents contributed to the pool, but actual use by the licensees. This is connected to an obligation to make available production data and books to the patentees. For litigation, each licensor was obliged to notify the others of possible infringers and there seemed to be a stipulation of sharing joint infringement expenses.

A general difference between the MPEG-2 pool and the DVD pools was that the MPEG-2 or AC-3 technology was a technology rather than a business network or business model. The DVD pools were in reality business networks based on two different standards but the two different consortia included collaborators representing production capacities, content, trademarks, etc. They both proposed to provide consumers with a new technical solution, including content. They were ecosystems rather than standards.

(iv) Analysis

It is interesting to analyse these three letters in light of the fact that patent pools are complex agreements. The legal structure of the pools that is described in the letters is an effort to prevent collusion by implementing the legal requirement that patent pools may only contain essential patents; no substitute or competing patents are in principle included. This in turn prevents, in theory, collusion on the technological market. This was the main horizontal requirement for the pool agreement. If fulfilled, the main purpose of the agreement would be benign from an antitrust

---

[54] Rudi Bekkers, et al., 'Case studies on the interface between research and standardisation, and case studies on patent pools as a coordination mechanism' (INTEREST consortium Priority 8 No. Contract 503 594, EU 6th Specific Targeted Research Project, 2006), 105 et seq. [The document is on file with the author.]

perspective according to the Justice Department. Formally, the technology pool then becomes a vertical creation due to the legal requirements of essentiality and complementary patents.[55]

There are no requirements from the Justice Department regarding the definition of the technology under the standard, whether it is too wide or too narrow, but the Justice Department found it to be beneficial that the technology were also a standard enacted by official standard-setting organs, including SDOs.

The Justice Department did not discuss the implied exchange of licences between the patentees and its effect on dynamic competition and royalty rates in the letters. A common argument for not analysing the quality, breadth or depth of the pooled technology is that the standard-setting process is 'democratic' and ensures a fair outcome. It should be noted that the DVD letters concerned, at least initially, are private technology standardization agreements rather than ISO official standards. Indeed, private standards are allowed to create the basis for a patent pool without the Justice Department scrutinizing, for example, the breadth or depth of the technology encompassed by the standard. Neither DVD standard was analysed in relation to whether it reflected a demand from customers; the DVD standards were only analysed in relation to whether the patents were essential in light of a definition of technology agreed upon by the firms themselves. The DVD firms in the two competing groups had also been picked to represent either technology (i.e. patents or content such as films or software to put on the DVDs) or pure manufacturing capacity. One would therefore imagine that the line had been carefully drawn for each standard between what should be inside and what outside the technology to serve the interests of the firms, the overall business model, or the networks' strategic position in the markets. This strategic line-drawing also reflects the exchange of licences that inherently takes place under a patent pool. This 'cross-licence feature' of pools was however disregarded by the Justice Department. It would have been interesting for the Justice Department not only to scrutinize the licence mechanism in the pool agreement but also the larger business model, including the content and the manufacturing (product and service) markets. The DVD pool agreements actually concerned not only horizontal agreements, but also vertical agreements, in the sense that content and manufacturing firms also agreed on the technology, as well as the

[55] William Tom and Joshua Newberg, 'Antitrust and Intellectual Property: From Separate Spheres to Unified Field', (1997) *Antitrust Law Journal*, 167, 216 et seq.

patentees. It should also be noted that even though some pools employ an independent expert for analysing their essentiality, the validity of patents is not scrutinized. Moreover, the fact that the R&D to some extent was jointly conducted and agreed upon in the DVD technology was also met with silence.

The Justice Department clearly allowed for a number of covenants that restrict follow-on innovations. The 'grant-back' or rather cross-licensing clauses in the licensing agreements were substantially more elaborate than would have been allowed under the old regime of patent pools.[56] They relate to all current and future patents held by the licensee, which are essential to the technology in question.[57] The grant-back clauses have in practice evolved to become, and are labelled, cross-licensing agreements rather than grant-back obligations. Thus, in consideration of the grant given by the pool proprietors, the licensee agrees to license all current and future patents. Whether this implies that the licensee must license the pool royalty free if it invents under the standard is not certain.[58]

The Business Review Letters discuss invalid patents but there is actually no requirement that the pool should include only valid intellectual property rights, or that the independent expert scrutinize the alleged essential patents for validity. Patent pools can prevent licensees or licensors from challenging arguably invalid patents. Invalid patents block access to knowledge that should be free from an intellectual property law

---

[56] Grant-back clauses were one of the Nine No-Nos. The then Deputy Assistant Attorney General Bruce B. Wilson toured the country and presented the Nine No-Nos' for the State Bar Antitrust sections, see e.g., ABA, The Federal Antitrust Guidelines For Licensing of Intellectual Property Origins and Applications (American Bar Association, Section of Antitrust Law 2002), referring to the presentation before the Michigan State Bar Sept. 21, 1972.

[57] Whether such a clause would survive the termination of the agreement is not certain. Often licensing agreements do contain a clause that all provisions of the agreement are intended to survive (whether express or implied) the expiry or termination of the said agreement. Grant-back clauses may therefore actually survive the expiry of the licence agreement, creating the obligation to grant-back innovation after the relationship has ended. Cf. Roger Andewelt, 'Analysis of Patent Pools under Antitrust Laws', (1985) 53 *Antitrust Law Journal*, 611, 617, regarding the anti-competitive effects of pools for existing and future patents.

[58] Cf. Garrard Beeney, 'Pro-Competitive Effects of Intellectual Property Pools: A Proposal for Safe Harbor Provisions', in *Patent Pools and Cross-Licensing: When Do They Promote or Harm Competition? under the Antitrust Enforcement and Intellectual Property Rights: Promoting Innovation and Competition Hearings* (US Department of Justice and Federal. Trade Commission, 2002), n. 12, 16, discussing this, for licensees, rather urgent issue.

perspective. From a patent law perspective, patent litigations regarding the validity of patents are important since many Patent Offices do not control patent applications in depth.[59] Nonetheless, some scholars have argued that one advantage with patent pools is that they prevent patent litigation.[60] They seem to imply that pools may scrutinize patents to see if they are valid or not by employing an independent expert.[61]

It is also quite plausible that when the pool is created, few dare to enter that market without extracting a licence and even fewer would actually initiate litigation against a pool for invalidation of patents. It is evident that the original licensors approach an alleged infringer jointly.[62] If all the licensors collectively approach a non-licensee, the sheer weight of all those patents, may, of course, discourage even the most stout hearted from litigation. It is sufficient for only one of the patents to be regarded as valid for the non-licensee to lose in the litigation.

However, would these patent pools that were scrutinized in the Business Review Letters actually be considered anti-competitive under the early case law? Indeed, the Justice Department implied that it was carving out a safe harbour for contemporary patent pools out of the previous case law.[63] For practitioners, they became a useful tool for setting up joint licensing schemes.

A closer analysis of the early case law shows that the actual pooling of essential (or complementary) patents would be judged under the rule of reason. However, the Justice Department under the 1990s Business

---

[59] For example there is no valid patent control in France, and in the USA, the PTO has been accused of opening the floodgates so to enlarge the number of US Patents. Cf. Adam Jaffe and Josh Lerner, *Innovation and its Discontents* (Princeton University Press, 2004), 25 et seq, 75 et seq.

[60] Even in the very early court decisions, where patent pools were considered per se legal, non-prohibition was justified in part by the fact that the pool provided the basis for settling infringement litigations. See E. Bement v. Nat'l Harrow Co., 186 U.S. 70 (1902), 93. Cf. Joshua Newberg, 'Antitrust, Patent Pools, and the Management of Uncertainty', (2000) 3 *Atlantic Law Journal*, 1, 8.

[61] See the IP 2 Report, 65, with references.

[62] Joint strategies of blocking or holding competitors out of markets with the help of patents may be anti-competitive under American antitrust law, see United States v. The Singer Manufacturing Comp. 374 U.S. 174 (1963). Whether the court was utilizing a per se rule or a rule of reason in this case is somewhat difficult to establish given the fact that Singer held approx. 50 percent of the US market for sawing machines. There are other cases which state that joint defence funds are per se antitrust violations. See e.g., United States v. Krasnov, 143 F Supp 184 (E.D. Pa 1956) aff'd., 355 U.S. 5 (1957).

[63] The early case law was disregarded as not reflecting contemporary economic thinking. See the IP 2 Report, 66 n. 49.

Review Letters went further than that and actually allowed industry-wide market power to build up. The covenants that were accepted in the Business Review Letters but would possibly not have passed the test set in the early case law. Given that some of the patents in, for example, the DVD pool were possibly not blocking, only complementary, the covenants accepted by the Justice Department in the letters are beyond that which would have been accepted by, for example, the Roosevelt or White Supreme Courts.

Actually, the Business Review Letters mirror the somewhat awkward *Standard Oil* case by disregarding the market power created in the technology market. Indeed, the letters represent a step beyond the *Standard Oil* case, since covenants accepted under the letters would probably not have passed the White Supreme Court as they create, in combination, an onerous collusive royalty scheme. The licensors must also still be careful not to infringe the per se rule against joint enforcement actions stipulated in, for example, the *Singer* or *Krasnov* cases.[64] However, it is difficult to say whether these cases still reflect good antitrust law.

If these pools could have been set up under the early case law, and the letters only acknowledge that complementary patents may be pooled and that the Justice Department will look more favourably upon restrictive covenants in licensing agreements from pools holding dominant positions on the technology market, how did the Business Review Letters from the end of the 1990s dissolve the patent thicket and anticommons problem? The remedy does not address this problem. Maybe, by making pools more attractive to PAEs tempted to hold up the technology, the patent thicket would shrink because some of them accepted membership in technology pools. However, that was not one of the arguments put forward when the letters were published.

---

[64] United States v. The Singer Manufacturing Comp. 374 U.S. 174 (1963); United States v. Krasnov, 143 F. Supp 184 (E.D. Pa 1956) aff'd. 355 U.S. 5 (1957). Cf. Richard Gilbert, 'Antitrust for Patent Pools: A Century of Policy Evolution', (2004 April) *Stanford Technology Law Review*, 3, 33, stating that joint patent defence might be a sign of substitute patents.

5.3.2 The *US Philips I* Case[65]

The *US Philips I* case does not concern antitrust law directly. Instead, it was decided under the patent misuse doctrine.[66] Nonetheless, the case does shed some light on the application of the antitrust laws to patent pools. The case concerns CD-ROM technology jointly researched and developed by Philips and Sony and had its origin in Chinese Taipei where certain manufacturing-only firms alleged they had been victims of antitrust violations under the CD-ROM pool. Several CD-R manufacturers had filed a complaint with the Taiwanese Federal Trade Commission (TFTC), alleging that in 1996, Philips, Sony and Taiyo-Yuden jointly formed a patent pool to monopolize the CD-R technology market, granting a package licence to downstream manufacturers for a royalty, which indicated a misuse of market power.[67]

After an investigation, the TFTC found in 2002 that Philips, Sony and Taiyo-Yuden were horizontal competitors in the CD-R manufacturing technology market through their ownership of technologies and patents related to that activity.[68] By the joint decision on the royalty rate and the joint licensing of patents, the companies acquired, according to the TFTC, a monopolistic position in the CD-R technology licence market in Chinese Taipei, where they unduly maintained abusive royalty rates. The TFTC also found that the pool participants bundled rights since the pool included non-essential patents and that the licensees were not given any alternative other than to license the entire package of patents. Thus, the only available alternative was a package including licences to all patents worldwide. Furthermore, the licensees were prohibited from objecting to the validity of the patents in the pool. The pool was therefore declared void by the TFTC due to abusive conduct, and the Taipei firms did not have to pay the high royalty fees.

US Philips 'contested' the decision by complaining to the US International Trade Commission (ITC) that the CD discs produced in Chinese

---

[65] See generally US Philips Corp. v. International Trade Commission 424 F3d 1179 (Fed. Cir. 2005) cert. denied sub nom. Princo Corp. v. U.S. Philips Corp., 126 S. Ct 2899 (2006).

[66] George Gordon and Robert Hoerner, 'Overview and Historical Development of the Misuse Doctrine', in ABA Section of Antitrust Law (ed), *Intellectual Property Misuse Licensing and Litigation* (ABA, 2000).

[67] OECD roundtable discussions regarding Intellectual Property in 2004, Jan. 21 2005, 117 et seq., see http://www.oecd.org/dataoecd/61/48/34306055.pdf Accessed 1 May 2009.

[68] Ibid.

Taipei and exported to the USA after the decision by the TFTC, infringed the patent rights held by Philips in the US.[69] They should therefore not be imported into the USA.

An administrative judge, on behalf of the ITC, investigated the complaint.[70] The judge concluded that Philips and Sony, together with other third parties, had set up different patent pools for the different CD-ROM technologies. The pools and the essentiality of the patents included in the pools were judged according to the technical requirements of different CD-ROM technology standards that were published in the so-called 'Orange Book'. The original CD-ROM standard licensing agreements provided a package of licences for some 45 patents. This system had, after a while, been changed to a system which involved a series of essential and non-essential packages, where the licensees were obliged to take out and pay for the essential licenses but did have a choice whether to take out licenses for the non-essential patents. If they chose to do so, they acquired these licences royalty-free. For the essential patents, the licensees had to pay a single fee of three per cent of net sales or a minimum of 10 yen per disc. This fee was not a heavy burden for the manufacturers at the beginning of the CD-ROM technology boom, when the price per disc amounted to USD 7. However, the minimum fee of 10 yen (approximately US 8 cent) became a burden when the prices for discs dropped to US 50 cent.[71]

---

[69] See Notice of Commission on Determination of No Violation of section 337, In the matter of Certain Recordable Compact Discs and Rewritable Compact Discs, Investigation No. 337-TA-474. It also seems as if Philips complained to the EC Commission since the EC Commission conducted anti-dumping proceeding concerning imports of CD-Rs originating from Taiwan. At the conclusion of the investigation in late 2001, the EC determined that CD-R discs manufactured in Taiwan had been 'dumped' in the common market. See generally ITC, the Administrative Law Judge final initial determination (ID) of Oct. 24, 2003.

[70] See generally ITC, the Administrative Law Judge final initial determination (ID) of Oct. 24, 2003. In the matter of Certain Recordable Compact Discs and Rewritable Compact Discs, Investigation No. 337-TA-474. [The document is on file with the author.]

[71] Ibid. paras. 139 et seq. The minimum royalty rate ranged from four and a half cents to eight cents depending which programme was implemented. Furthermore, Philips employed compliance programmes where the rates were lower because Philips required the licensee to submit yearly a list of equipment used for producing CD-ROMs and verify that the equipment used came from a Philips licensee. See ibid. para. 174. The judge also made some remarkable general findings concerning the business of licensing. In 2003, when he rendered his final initial determination, approximately 65 per cent of the discs produced

In response to the complaint made by Philips, the Taiwanese manufacturers raised the defence of 'patent misuse'. Philips patents were non-enforceable since they, as part of the pools, placed an imposition on the respondents that violated US antitrust law or otherwise unreasonably restrained trade.

The administrative judge concurred with the respondents and found that the patents had been misused since the pools were considered to have market power both in the product and the licensing markets for the relevant CD-Rs in the US.[72] Philips, together with its licensor colleagues, had misused its patent rights both under a per se standard and a rule of reason standard.

The misuses consisted of, first, price-fixing, since the pools were deemed to constitute horizontal agreements among competitors to control and enact high (abusive) royalty rates. Apparently, the judge implied cartel royalties were extracted from the market by comparing the 'normal' return of royalties, e.g., IBM's return of approximately 1 per cent of the sales price of a product, with the 20 per cent royalty of the CD pool.[73] The rates constituted a major part of the price of the discs. Secondly, US Philips was also considered to have per se misused its patent since it employed a price discrimination scheme, differentiating between different licensees. US Philips demanded the same or higher royalties from individual bilateral licences as in the pool licensing agreements.[74] Within the pool, the same royalty also had to be paid

worldwide were produced under a licensing agreement from the pool. However, the main licensors, Philips and Sony, held a combined market share of the product market of 10 to 13 per cent. Philip made EUR 500 million in 2002 from licensing royalties. However, several of the major technology companies, including IBM, Ericsson, Qualcomm, InterDigital and Rambus, garnered an ever larger part of their revenues from licensing their intellectual property rights compared to their revenues from end-products, see ibid. paras. 199 et seq.

[72] The US was considered the geographic market since US patents and all other patents are inherently connected to the state issuing them: see the Administrative Law Judge final ID of Oct. 24, 2003, paras. 167 et seq.

[73] The evaluation regarding essentiality under the pool seems in practice to be very difficult and subjective. The analysis by the judge in his final ID is proof of that: see the Administrative Law Judge final ID of Oct. 24, 2003, paras. 408 et seq. Interestingly, the judge's evaluation and the later appeals court decision do not seem to logically work together.

[74] Interestingly, one could argue that the 'most favoured nation' or 'most favourable conditions' clause, often contained in licensing agreements from pool to licensees, eliminated the possibility of the licensor setting lower royalties in individual licensing agreements outside the pool. Thus, the very mechanism to

irrespective of whether the licensee needed just one of several of the patents in the pool for its production. Thirdly, US Philips was also considered to be misusing its patents by tying licences for essential patents to licences for non-essential patents.[75] The judge finally concluded that the royalty rate mechanism of the patent pooling arrangements was an unreasonable restraint of trade.[76]

After the finding of the administrative judge, the ITC issued a determination that the US patents asserted by US Philips were unenforceable for patent misuse, and did not therefore find any violation by the Taiwanese manufacturers of the US Tariffs Act of 1930. The patents were found to be unenforceable due to patent misuse in accordance with both per se and rule of reason standards since the mandatory package licensing constituted a tying arrangement between licences for essential patents and licenses for non-essential patents.

The ITC took no position on the finding of the judge that the licensing programme constituted per se and rule of reason price-fixing and price discrimination, or that the price mechanism constituted an unreasonable restraint of trade.[77] By choosing not to pursue the price-fixing (and to a lesser degree price discrimination) charges, the ITC implicitly also refocused the analyses of the patent pool from Sec. 1 Sherman Act to Sec. 2.

By electing only to pursue a tying offence, the ITC limited the case to questions regarding the availability of a per se misuse defence for tying as such and for tying of patent rights specifically. Also, the question whether the patents were essential or non-essential, as the administrative

---

create non-discrimination between pool licensees may create price discrimination between pool licensees and non-pool licensees. See the Administrative Law Judge final ID of Oct. 24, 2003, paras. 114 et seq. See discussion, supra, regarding the Matsushita Electric case regarding how price discrimination may be handled.

[75] The Administrative Law Judge final ID of 24 October 2003, paras. 167 et seq.

[76] The judge also discussed the fact that the pool licensing agreement had contained much wider grant-back clauses. However, the licensors had changed them in newer agreements so as to correspond to the later Business Review Letters. See Administrative Law Judge final ID of Oct. 24, 2003, para. 120. Apparently, the pool had not utilized any independent expert when establishing whether the patents were essential from the start, but later did employ one. Ibid. paras. 174 et seq.

[77] See Notice of Commission on Determination of No Violation of section 337, In the matter of Certain Recordable Compact Discs and Rewritable Compact Discs, Investigation No. 337-TA-474, 51.

judge had found, became a major dispute when establishing the tying defence as the case went on.

The case was appealed by US Philips to the US Court of Appeals for the Federal Circuit and the Federal Circuit took a different stand compared to the ITC and the Administrative Judge.[78] It concluded that Philips had not misused its patents.

First, the Federal Circuit found that there was a difference between the tying of one product to another product or a right to a product, and, by contrast, tying a right to another right. According to the Court, non-exclusive licences work as insurance against being sued. Thus, tying an essential patent to a non-essential (even though purportedly essential) patent does not imply that the licensee is obliged to use the non-essential technology. The licensor only certifies that it will refrain from suing the licensee for infringement.

The Court also concluded that the ITC had not showed that the royalty would have fallen should the pool have contained only essential licenses. Thus, the Court implied that the licensees were not coerced into using the non-essential technology.

The Court went on to state that tying an essential right to a non-essential one is no more anti-competitive than surrendering the non-essential right as such to the public. The package licensing arrangement cannot, therefore, be considered to be exploiting market power in one market to gain competitive advantages in another. Hence, Philips was not broadening the scope of the patents.[79] The activities of Philips could thereby not be considered as constituting a per se violation of the patent misuse doctrine.

The Court also overruled the ITC on the facts. According to the Court, there was no economically viable alternative to the non-essential patents. According to the Court there was no proof that commercially viable alternatives existed and, even if such technologies existed, the ITC had not shown that there was a demand for these technologies from the licensees, which went unmet. Since there was no proof which supported a finding of non-essentiality, the ITC's finding of a rule of reason violation was overruled. Unfortunately, overruling the ITC on the facts resulted in the exclusionary effects of the tying practice not being

---

[78] United States Court of Appeals for the Federal Circuit U.S. Philips Corp v. International Trade Commission, 424 F.3d 1179 (Fed. Cir. 2005).

[79] The EU Court of Justice appears to have an equivalent line of reasoning in the case 65/86 Bayer and Hennecke v. Süllhöfer (1990) 4 CMLR 182.

scrutinized.[80] Perhaps, had the Court analysed the effects of this for competitors in the tied technology market, Philips' practice could have been considered as obstructing new technology. However, since the Court concluded that there was no new technology, no exclusion could be established.

The Court, furthermore, found several instances of the pro-competitive effects of the pools. According to the Court, the pool reduced uncertainty, since the investor (licensees) could be sure that they were not going to be accused of infringement when taking out a licence from the pool. It was also much easier to value the patents in the pool when it encompassed the technology of a whole range of products. Furthermore, the manufacturers did not have to approach all proprietors in the technology market to obtain licences; instead, they needed only to approach the pool. Thus, the Court found several cost efficiency reasons why Philips' and Sony's patent pool should be regarded as pro-competitive.

From the *US Philips I* case it is quite evident that contemporary, legally-schooled professionals are not in agreement about how to judge these cooperative phenomena. What may be considered extensively anti-competitive to one appears to be even pro-competitive to others. In the end, the case revolved around the tying offence or defence under the patent misuse doctrine. The ITC indivertibly limited the case to deal with the patent misuse doctrine.[81] However, the basic conduct in this case

---

[80] The Court of Appeals limited, in this case, the per se tying of patent misuse offences to an antitrust offence. Thus, if the licensee had to pay for something it did not want, i.e., was forced to use it, then there was a per se violation, otherwise not. To my mind, this is to diminish the effect of the per se patent misuse doctrine. The per se violation was instituted to allow the court to avoid the complexity of an economic enquiry into the precise harm caused by a specific practice and the excuse business gave for its use. Thus, tying is a violation of the patent misuse doctrine; end of story. There is no need to analyse the reasons behind the tying. For the per se violation see Senza-Gel v. Seiffhart 803 F.2d 661 (Fed. Cir. 1986), which states that the misuse offence does not require an anti-competitive effect. See also Northern Pacific R. Co. v. United States, 356 U.S. 1, 5 (1958) which stated that, because of their pernicious effect on competition and lack of any redeeming virtue, viz. their anti-competitive effect and improbable pro-competitive benefits, certain practices are deemed unlawful per se.

[81] For a rare recent case concerning antitrust law and one of the DVD pools, see Matsushita Elec. Indus. Co. v Cinram Int'l, Inc., 299 F. Supp. 2d 370 (Del 2004).

could instead have been judged under the antitrust laws if the defendants had instead sued US Philips for antitrust violations.[82]

Why the administrative judge, compared to the Federal Circuit, came to such different conclusions is of great interest. Obviously, both courts are battling the somewhat difficult notion of tying on the technical market. The concepts of essential and non-essential patents become difficult to handle within the barriers of one technology. However, the starting point that Philips and Sony held a 65 per cent combined market share on the technical market but only perhaps 13 per cent on the global product market, indicates that, presumably, they held a joint dominant position on the technical market but not on the product market.

(i) Essentiality under the *US Philips I* case

Essentiality is not only an issue when setting up a pool. In time, the essentiality evaluation might prove wrong. The issue then is whether there are commercially feasible alternatives to the patent included in the pool in the (technology) market. This would imply that if there is a patent outside the pool which is a feasible alternative to a patent in the pool, the patent within the pool – according to the above – needs to exit it.[83] However, the proprietor can prevent the patent from exiting the pool by

---

[82] One argument under such an antitrust suit for not utilizing the per se rule would then be that the NCRPA obliges courts to use the rule of reason if a patent pool is derived from joint R&D. In this case, several of US Philips' patents were derived from joint R&D with Sony. Possibly the NCRPA might have been applicable had the case been decided under the antitrust laws. It is somewhat illogical that a per se rule should apply when a patentee tries to protect its intellectual property from infringement, but a rule of reason should apply if the same patentee is sued for the same conduct under the antitrust laws. This may create bizarre incentives for patentees and alleged antitrust victims. Neither the ITC nor the Federal Circuit discusses the NCRPA, even though the Federal Circuit does derive many principles from antitrust tying cases. It should further be noted that had the NCRPA been applicable, Philips probably should not have been considered dominant in the innovation market. The NCRPA stipulates at least a presumption that innovation markets shall be utilized and, possibly, any exclusionary effects of new innovation have to be determined in such a market. However, there were several other technologies and possible technologies conceived and hence applicable to the defendants in this case instead of the technology held by US Philips. Thus, the defendants could not – successfully – make the argument that US Philips or the CD pool prevented them from conducting research, or innovating.

[83] Interestingly, the joint decision to exclude a non-essential patent may be viewed as a boycott. Cf. Philip Nelson, 'Patent Pools: An Economic Assessment of Current Law and Policy', (2007) 38 *Rutgers Law Journal*, 539, 559.

giving access to it for free. Then the convenience argument or transaction cost argument still prevails according to the Federal Circuit in the *US Philips* case.[84]

Depending on the interpretation of the *US Philips* case, the Federal court states that a licensor can retain the non-essential patent in the pool if access is given to it for 'free'.[85] But, what constitutes 'free'? Should the patents have been added to the public domain? Whether this means that the proprietor would also not be allowed to pursue firms infringing the patent which are not licensees of the pool is somewhat unclear. Possibly the licensor might be able to attack non-licensees and not be forced to abandon the patent to the public domain, only licensing it for free to patent pool licensees.[86]

Irrespective of the above questions, the Federal court in the *US Philips* case dismissed the essential test and applied a tying test to whether the pool was anti-competitive or not. Tying non-essential patents to essential patents is not a violation under the patent misuse doctrine according to the *US Philips* case, as long as a separate demand for the non-essential patents does not exist.[87] The Federal Circuit reversed the ITC's finding that Philips and other members of the CD-RW pool had misused their patents by alleged tying essential and non-essential patents. The Federal Circuit found that there was no tie in an economically feasible sense since there was no separate demand. Interestingly, the court stated that it would conduct the evaluation under the rule of reason rather than under a per se rule. This might be in line with the *Microsoft* case,[88] but it is somewhat inconsistent with *Jefferson Parish*.[89] In *Jefferson Parish*, the Supreme Court reaffirmed that tying is a per se violation. In other words, proof of whether the tying creates competition injury or effect is not necessary. *Jefferson Parish* requires the plaintiff to show that there are

---

[84] US Philips Corp. v. International Trade commission 424 F3d 1179 (Fed. Cir. 2005) cert. denied sub nom. Princo Corp. v. U.S. Philips Corp., 126 S. Ct 2899 (2006).

[85] Ibid.

[86] See U.S. Philips Corp. v. ITC,424 F.3d 1179, 1190 (Fed. Circ. 2005) cert. denied sub nom. Princo Corp. v. U.S. Philips Corp., 126 S. Ct. 2899 (2006).

[87] Se generally US Philips Corp. v. International Trade commission 424 F.3d 1179 (Fed. Cir. 2005) cert. denied sub nom. Princo Corp. v. U.S. Philips Corp., 126 S. Ct. 2899 (2006).

[88] United States v. Microsoft Corp., 253 F.3d 34 (D.C. Cir. 2001) (en banc). The Microsoft case raised the issue of a technology tie between one software to another software.

[89] Jefferson Parish Hospital No. 2 v. Hyde, 466 U.S. 2 (1984).

two separate products which are tied, i.e. the separate demand test, and that the alleged monopolist holds market power in the tying product market.[90]

One might argue with the Federal Circuit as to whether there was no tie in an economically feasible sense, i.e. that the tie actually did create inefficiencies. If licensors can keep a patent in the pool when there has emerged a competing patent outside, the pool could shut out the technological market for that emerging patent. The potential customers for the patent would likely already be licensees to the pool and would rather use the inclusive technology than pay for an outside patent, even though that patent would be compatible with the prevailing standard. The incentive to innovate and to create the alternative patent would be lost if the inventor knew he would not get any remuneration for his patent or innovation.

From the viewpoint of the licensor in the pool there would – of course – be no cost involved in giving access to the now non-essential patent. There is no – or very little – marginal cost for licensing intellectual property.[91] As long as the patentees still hold the remaining essential patents, the total royalty obtainable under the pool would be the same. The pool is still the 'gatekeeper' for accessing the downstream product markets as long as the pool contains at least one essential patent in relation to the standard defining the product or technology. Actually, as long as there is a single essential patent in the pool for accessing the product market(s), as defined by the standard, the licensor(s) can extract supra-competitive profits through the pool.

However, if the non-essential patent is forced out of the pool, the royalty for the remaining pool may need to be reduced. Or, at least, if the pool continues to charge the same royalty and there exist two complementary patents outside the pool, the pool member with essential patents

---

90 Jefferson Parish Hospital No. 2 v. Hyde, 466 U.S. 2 (1984), 22. See also the International Manufacturing Co. v. Landon 336 F.2d 723 (9th Cir. 1964) and American Security Co. v. Shatterproof Glass Corp. 268 F.2d 769 (3rd Cir. 1959). If the so-called per se rule for tying were eliminated, a plaintiff would need to show market power also in the market for the tied product. See e.g., Jefferson Parish Hospital No. 2 v. Hyde, 466 U.S. 2 (1984), at 34 (O'Connors, concurring).

91 See Gilbert and Tom stating that the difference between the new and the old technology is that the model of perfect competition does not fit high-tech markets. The marginal costs are possibly non-existent for distributing one more software, while the initial R&D cost can be very high. Richard Gilbert and William Tom, 'Is Innovation King at the Antitrust Agencies? The Intellectual Property Guidelines Five Years Later', (2001) 69 *Antitrust Law Journal*, 43, 45 et seq.

inside the pool and one non-essential patent outside the pool may find it more profitable to charge also for the outside patent. This would be the case if the pool royalty is set exactly so as to extract as much supra-competitive profit as possible from the technology market and the downstream product markets. If the pool before the emergence of the competing patent has created a perfect monopoly, charging a little extra would imply a fall in quantity, to the extent that total royalties would decrease. However, such a scheme implies a very intricate pricing mechanism in the pool agreement. For the individual licensor it may be profitable to charge for the now non-essential patent outside the pool, even though his part of the pool royalty stream would fall a bit. Due to the perfect monopoly pricing being interrupted, licensees would exit in response to higher total royalties (pool royalty and extra royalty for the exited technology). If that is the case, then keeping the non-essential patent within the pool would only be pursued by the pool in order to create disincentives to innovate under the standard.[92]

The Federal Circuit's findings in the *US Philips* case, which dealt with patent misuse doctrine rather than antitrust law, suggests that patent pools that contain some non-essential patents will not be analysed under the per se standard.[93] The case also demonstrates the mismatch between the

[92] From a legal point of view, this would imply that perhaps the Federal Circuit should not have analysed whether there was a separate demand for the non-essential patent in question in the US Philips case. Instead, the court should have asked whether, from the viewpoint of the holder of the purported non-essential patent, would the holder have been better off having the patent outside the pool than inside, 'but for' the market power of the pool. Is the only reason the patentee wanted to have the patent still in the pool that the outside competing patent would be eliminated and the pool could thereafter extract supra-competitive prices? Could the patentee extract any extra royalties from the non-essential patent outside the pool? Would the patentee from a short-term profit maximising perspective have been better off with the patent outside the pool? If that were the case, than the only reason to keep it inside the pool is to minimize the possibility of outside parties inventing under the standard. *De lege ferenda*, a 'but for' rule, derived from Sec. 2 the Sherman Act theory, is possibly the better alternative for analysing whether a patent should be inside the pool or outside, rather than the technically driven essentiality concept. Cf. A. Douglas Melamed, 'Exclusive Dealing Agreements and Other Forms of Exclusionary Conduct – Are There Unifying Principles?' (2006) 73 *Antitrust Law Journal,* 375, 389 et seq. and his 'no economic sense test'.

[93] Philip Nelson, 'Patent Pools: An Economic Assessment of Current Law and Policy', (2007) 38 *Rutgers Law Journal*, 539, 558.

technical terms used by the Justice Department (essential, non-essential, etc.), which do not correspond to a classical antitrust notion, such as tying.[94]

Under EU competition law the plaintiff needs to show non-essential technologies under the pool to be able to prove tying. However, with the difference form US law, this may be done by engineers showing that technologies inside the pool are substitute with technologies outside the pool. Thus, under EU law, there is no need to identify competiting technologies or, thus, a relevant market for the tied technology.[95]

The above indicate that the courts in the US will demand a showing of anti-competitive effect both under alleged anti-competitive harm of collusion and exclusion. This includes showing of separate demand (i.e. that the market holds room for separate technologies and there are

---

[94] Possibly, the tying offence is not the best argument in practice when dealing with potential anti-competitive patent pools. Instead, the Court should perhaps consider why the pool still gives away licences for free to non-essential patents. If a competing patent or technology emerges and, in line with antitrust pool theory, the now non-essential patent has to leave the pool, it should be more profitable for the patentee to actually remove that patent from the pool. Then the patentee may still gain some royalty from licensing it. The pool may not charge any fee for it. The pool, still holding the remaining essential patents, may still charge the same royalty since it is the gatekeeper to the technology. On the whole, the patentee of the non-essential patent must therefore make more profit, from a short-term profit maximizing viewpoint, removing the non-essential patent than if he retains the patent in the pool but gives access to it for free. Actually, the only reason for keeping the now non-essential patent in the pool must be to protect the dominance of the pool, i.e., to send a message that inventors should not try to invent under the pooled technology. The pool will protect its future dominance, sending the message that it is futile to develop a competing technology under an established and prevailing patent pool. However, disregarding the dominance of the pool, a patentee should exit the pool so as to obtain some royalty for the non-essential patent. The above reasoning is of course not novel, it echoes the monopolization argumentation made by the Justice Department in some interesting cases under Sec. 2 Sherman Act. See, e.g., the United States v. AMR Corp., 335 F.3d 1109 (10th Cir 2003), United States v. AMR Corp., 140 F. Supp. 2d 1141, 2001, which is the benchmark for abusive monopolization presented by some commentators. Douglas Melamed seems to be the foremost creator of the 'but for' benchmark under Sec. 2. Sherman Act. Cf. A. Douglas Melamed, 'Exclusive Dealing Agreements and Other Forms of Exclusionary Conduct – Are There Unifying Principles?' (2006) 73 *Antitrust Law Journal*, 375, 389 et seq. For a critique, see, e.g., Steven C. Salop, 'Exclusionary Conduct, Effect on Consumers, and The Flawed Profit-Sacrifice Standard', (2006) 73 *Antitrust Law Journal*, 311, 318 et seq.

[95] New TT Guidelines paras. 236 and 245.

alternatives), dominance on the part of the standardised technology and showing of exclusion or collusion.

5.3.3 The Latest Business Review Letters

In 2008, a new Business Review Letter regarding a patent pool was released by the Justice Department. The pool concerned ten of the essential patents for the Gen-2 standard, which had been decided and issued by the private SSO EPCglobal, Inc.[96] The patents were provided by seven different patentees and the 10 patents did not consist of all of the essential patents for the standard.[97] The set-up was very similar to the early patent pool letters from the end of the 1990s, but there were some differences.

First, the standard licensing agreements from the pool to the licensees contained separate royalty rates for different types of devices to be produced.[98] In the Business Review Letters from the end of the 1990s, the royalty rate was similar irrespective of the use of the portfolio licence. In the 2008 letter, the Justice Department allowed for separate royalty rates for different fields of use (possibly different product markets). This would enable the patent pool to extract more royalties and to set the royalty rates at or close to perfect monopoly level for each product market.

Secondly, the anticommons or patent thicket argument for creating patent pools has been abandoned for the 'hold-up', 'hold-out' and the 'patent ambush' arguments.[99] Patent pools, according to the Justice Department, warrant lesser royalty rates, not increased royalty rates (i.e. contrary to what is claimed in the Patent Pool Business Review Letters from the 1990s).[100]

Thirdly, a new and interesting argument for the benefits of patent pools is forwarded. Maverick players that intend to develop the technology in a

---

[96] The standard had been ISO certified. See RFID Business Review Letter from Thomas O. Barnett to William F. Dolan and Geoffrey Oliver, dated 21 October 2008, 1. See http://www.usdoj.gov/atr/public/busreview/238429.htm, accessed 3 May 2009. The RFID pool did only contain essential patents. Whether that commitment is of any value when the firms also control the definition of the technology could be discussed.

[97] There was no clear consensus among industry participants as to how many other essential patents existed. Ibid. 3.

[98] Ibid, 5.

[99] Ibid, 7.

[100] The Patent Pool Business Review Letters are discussed supra chapter 5.4.2.

new direction will gain access to the relevant patents and the patentees cannot object to it. Patent pools must be open to anyone seeking a licence and should be open so that inventors can get access to patents in order to conduct R&D. This argument certainly shows that according to the Justice Department R&D-only or technology-only firms that want to conduct R&D under the technology should presumably also have a licence.

Fourthly, there is no requirement for the patentees to market individual licences outside the pool structure. They should be allowed to license, but there is no obligation.[101]

Finally, and most interestingly, the parties to the pool admit to having concluded prior licence commitments for their UHF RFID patents while participating in the standard-setting process or because of bilateral licensing agreements.[102] The Justice Department acknowledges that it has been informed and that the standard-setting consortium has a mechanism for accommodating any such commitments.

This implies that the parties have made use of the 2004 amendment to the NCRPA. The SDO, and presumably the agreement that in the patent pools from the late 1990s would have be considered the 'patent pool agreements', were in this case encompassed by the NCRPA. From the letter we do not know whether the 10 patents originate from joint R&D or unilateral R&D or whether the SDO in this case is also a joint R&D venture. However, the SSO and, possibly, the parties in this case are insulated from private litigation due to the applicability of the NCRPA. Indeed, the agreement on technology and, by making the licence commitments under the SSO, the SSO with the commitments, is exempted under the NCRPA. By being granted a favourable Business Review Letter they do not need to fear the Justice Department either. Thus, their agreements and the arrangement are *ex ante* exempted under US antitrust law.

5.3.4 Future Patent Pools or Joint Defence Solutions?

It should be added that the Justice Department, through a Business Review Letter, recently analysed an Intellectual Property Exchange[103], which seems to be an independent and open SSO/patent pool for any

101 Ibid, 4.

102 Ibid.

103 See IPXI Business Review Letter from William J. Baer to Garrad R. Beeny, dated March, 26, 2013. See http://www.usdoj.gov/atr/public/busreview/, accessed 3 May 2013.

patentee to apply to. In fact it stipulates that it is an exchange for intellectual property rights, and especially essential patents. I guess it implies that purchaser and sellers may meet on the exchange to purchase or sell intellectual property licenses. The Justice Department refused to give it clearance in the Business Review Letter, since the exchange seem to have as an idea to bundle patents in reference to a technology (standards) and sell access to it over this exchange. The Justice Department found both collusive problems with the idea (bundling competing patents) and that exchange of confidential information may take place when setting up such bundles.

Likewise there are articles[104] and comments in reference to the entity, Intellectual Ventures, and its collaboration with both larger patentees and smaller R&D intensive firms. What the business idea of Intellectual Ventures actually is may be difficult to define. It has been perceived as a private equity firm setting up funds focusing on intellectual property. Presumably, it has a defence mechanism and insurance scheme for its investors.[105] A collaboration in which Intellectual Ventures (or its funds) purchases patents, which can be utilized by investors in Intellectual Ventures should they need them. For example, an investor may use patents held by Intellectual Ventures when it has been sued for patent infringement. Then an investor may utilize such patents to counter-sue or settle the case in a beneficial way. However, lately Intellectual Ventures have been accused of privateering on behalf of their investors.

These two entities may be both antitrust solutions and antitrust problems. They are collaborations mainly on the technology markets, but future will tell how they should be viewed.

5.3.5 Conclusion

The antitrust policy vis-à-vis patent pools have gone from extreme to extreme. The Business Review Letters from the beginning of the 1990s were clearly an attempt by the Justice Department to present a possible set-up for these collaborations. The requirements reflect a genuine attempt to weigh pro- and anti-competitive effects. The dichotomy between, on the one hand, essential and non-essential, and, on the other, between complementary and competing patents was presented. However,

[104] For example, Robin Feldman & Tom Ewing, 'The Gigants Among US', (2012) 1 Stanford Technology Law Review, 1.

[105] Thomas L. Ewing, 'Practical Considerations In the Indirect Deployment of Intellectual Property Rights by Corporatiosn and Investors', (2011) 4 *Hastings Sci & Tech Law Journal* 109.

when the step had been taken, it was clear that the law vis-à-vis patent pools would grow more lenient. This is especially true in the area of essentiality of patents, where the Justice Department initially demanded that the patents were technically essential to the technology, but soon accepted economic essentiality. In fact, the Federal Circuit in *Philips I* completely rejects this dichotomy and instead utilized the test for tying, and a strict test of showing anti-competitive effect. Tying is a exclusionary abuse, and, as will be discussed below under *Philips II*, the Federal Circuit has also dismissed the essential test when dealing with collusion, i.e. that the patent pool by including substitute patents actually represents a cartel, and a plaintiff must show anti-competitive effect.

Whether the Federal Circuit thereby made the antitrust agencies back track and state in the IP 2 Report that product market collusion and restriction of R&D investment are the *only* two antitrust harms that that a patent pool can cause is not certain. Whether this statement is true or not remains to be seen. If it is then the 'refinement' of the current antitrust policy may be discussed or even rebuffed.

5.4 THE EU ANTITRUST APPROACH TO PATENT POOLS

5.4.1 Structure

As stated previously, patent pools are complex contracts that explicitly or implicitly imply four agreements: first, there is an agreement to exchange licences or joint R&D in the pre-standardization phase by the patent and technology providers (pool builders) that are also active on the downstream product markets. Secondly, there is the clear pool agreement, where the contributors of patents agree on (i) the definition of the technology (i.e. often identical to, or the same thing as, a technology standardization agreement identified already in the pre-standardization phase), and (ii) terms (e.g. royalty rates) on which downstream product manufacturers will get access to the essential intellectual properties. Thirdly, the patent pools include standard licensing agreements from the pool to third party licensees. Fourthly, implicitly pooling may also include an agreement on how to develop the technology further through grant-back clauses or cross-licensing agreements for future innovations and patents.

As also described above, the parties to the pool may be divided into the following categories: (i) 'technology-only' firms, i.e. pure innovators or patent collectors, which conduct R&D or purchase patents and generally do not manufacture products; (ii) 'manufacturing-only' firms, i.e. firms than manufacture products and do not pursue 'break-through' inventions but sometimes conduct follow-on R&D; and, finally, (iii) vertically integrated firms, i.e. the 'original' multinational firms that conduct both R&D and produce products under the invented technology.

This sub-section will deal with the EU antitrust approach to the above structure. First, the patent pools which have been scrutinized by both the US Justice Department under the Business Review Letter procedure, and by the EU Commission will be *briefly* analysed. Secondly, the structure of patent pools is discussed, and how the structure is addressed under EU competition law. The difference between the patent pool rules in the TT Guidelines and the regulation of cross-licensing agreements in the block exemption for technology transfer (TTBER) will be commented on.[106] Thirdly, the telecommunication industry and its special problems regarding the interface between standard setting and patent pools will be scrutinized. Regarding the 3G telecommunication standard, the US Justice Department's comments in a Business Review Letter will be discussed in a comparative fashion.

5.4.2 The Famous Patent Pools

The early antitrust history concerning patent pools was played out in American courtrooms. The patent pools of the 'trust bust era' were not, generally, illegal under the European jurisdictions. Even after the introduction of general competition law in the TFEU, the EU Commission was less interested than the Justice Department in patent pools. In the early 1980s, the Commission addressed some pool agreements and, even though not declaring them objectively anti-competitive, stated that they must seek exemption under the third paragraph and inter alia that they must be open for new members.[107]

---

[106] The different regulation of cross-licensing agreements and patent pools under EC competition law creates disharmony in the EC's regulation of patent pools. The cross-licence aspect of patent pools is disregarded by the EC Commission. See Commission regulation (EC) No. 772/2004 on the application of Art 81(3) of the Treaty to categories of technology transfer agreements [2004] OJ L 123/11 (defined earlier as TTBER). In comparison, under US antitrust law, cross-licence agreements and patent pools are treated under the same standard. See IP Guidelines, 28 et seq. See IP 2 Report, 59 et seq.

[107] See IGR Stereo Television in Commission, Report on Competition Policy 1984, 94 and IGR Stereo Television in Commission, Report on Competition Policy 1981, 92. See also Concast/Mannesmann in the Commission, Report on

The US Justice Department's resurgent interest in patent pools at the end of the 1990s and the development of the consumer technology and telecommunication industries, with their need for workable standards and intellectual property rights management, forced the EU Commission to take a more active role.

Under the EU comfort letter procedure (and its predecessor), the Commission has analysed several of the patent pools that were analysed by the Justice Department under the Business Review Letter scheme.[108] It must be noted that the EU Commission agreed with the US Justice Department on how to analyse these collaborations and on what level of scrutiny the pools should be exposed to. Thus, generally there was no difference in the application of EU competition law to these collaborations from the approach of the US Justice Department. The basic structure of what to analyse and identify stems from the US decisions.

For example, the DVD 6C pool was analysed on two occasions: first in 2000, and then in 2002, when it was amended.[109] In the re-examination in 2002, the Commission, interestingly enough, stated that 'it examined the possible anti-competitive effects of the patent pool and came to the conclusion that the anti-competitive effects were unlikely in any of the three of the markets affected, namely a technology market for DVD, a *general market for innovation* and several vertically related markets covering video and audio products as well as the mass replication of optical discs' [authors italic].[110] The statement is interesting for a number of reasons.

First, this is one of very few occasions on which the Commission has acknowledged that an innovation market exists. Secondly, patent pools, according to the Commission, should be analysed in all the markets they effect.

Competition Policy 1981, 93. See also Commission decision Konsortium ECR 900, OJ 1990 L 228/31.

[108] For the MPEG-2 pools see press release reference number: IP/98/1155, dated 1998.12.18. It was cleared under Art 85(3) with a comfort letter. The DVD 6C pool, press release reference number IP/00/1135, dated 09.10.2000 was also cleared under the third paragraph. See also the Commission, *Report on Competition Policy 2000*, 147 et seq. and Commission, *Report on Competition Policy 2002*, 194 et seq. with reference to the 3C DVD pool.

[109] See Commission, *Report on Competition Policy 2000*, 147 et seq. and *Commission, Report on Competition Policy 2002*, 194 et seq. See also evidence that the 6DVD patent pool was notified to the EC Commission, OJ C 242 27.08.1999, 5 et seq.

[110] Commission, *Report on Competition Policy 2002*, 194.

It must be stated that patent pools not only interact with technology standards but also with joint R&D. Joint R&D results in patents, which in turn lead to an agreement on technology standards and patent pools. Patent pools, on the other hand, may result in joint follow-on R&D as the *Optical Fibres* case adequately showed.[111] The Commission disregards these interfaces, however. Implicitly it bases its application of EU Competition Law to patent pools as if patent pools normally stem from the combination of unilateral and independent technologies under a technology standard, while they often stem instead from joint R&D. The horizontal and the vertical aspects of patent pools will be discussed in more detail below.

In the DVD 6C pool, the Commission clarified what would become the usual criteria under the TT Guidelines for exempting patent pools under Art. 101(3) TFEU and, even though it was the US Justice Department that first addressed patent pools under the Business Review Letter procedure, the Commission was first making concrete these clear rules: (i) only essential patents were to be included in the pool; (ii) pool members should be allowed to grant individual licences, which extended to products irrespective of their conformity with the DVD standard specifications; (iii) the pool must be open to third parties that have acquired additional essential patents; (iv) the grant-back clauses, applicable to all licensees, must be limited to essential patents; (v) the technology under the pool must be licensed under fair terms; (vi) most favoured nation clauses impeded discrimination between pool members (defined as licensors) and third parties, as well as among third parties; (vii) pool members should take out licences from the pool; (viii) the royalties did not represent a very significant part of the final prices of the end-product (in this case the DVD products); (ix) licensors should have erected firewalls to protect competitively sensitive information from reaching each other and to keep it confidential;[112] and, finally, (x) the Commission got the licensors to agree to offer licensees a side letter limiting the scope of the licence to a specific category of products.

The Commission generally follows this ten-step outline when scrutinizing patent pools. The steps are drafted in the TT Guidelines (an additional requirement is that any R&D should be free for the collaborators to pursue). They have been somewhat rewritten in the new (draft)

[111] See Commission decision Optical Fibres, OJ 1986 L 236/30. See discussion supra in Chapter 4.2.8.

[112] See Commission, *Report on Competition Policy 2002*, 194.

TT Guidelines[113], where the Commission seems to have left this ten-step outline for a more indepth analysis of both the horizontal and the vertical effects of patent pools. Nonetheless, the Commission stipulates a list of requirements for the pool to fall outside Art. 101(1): (a) participation in the standard and pool creation process is open to all interested parties; (b) sufficient safeguards are adopted to ensure that only essential technologies (which therefore by necessity are also complements) are pooled; (c) sufficient safeguards are adopted to ensure that exchange of sensitive information is restricted to what is necessary for the creation and operation of the pool; (d) the pooled technologies are licensed into the pool on a non-exclusive basis; (e) the pooled technologies are licensed out to all potential licensees on FRAND terms; (f) the parties contributing technology to the pool and the licensees are free to challenge the validity and the essentiality of the pooled technologies, and; (g) the parties contributing technology to the pool and the licensee remain free to develop competing products and technology. Indeed, the patent pools are per se legal if the above criteria are followed.

5.4.3 The EU Pool Structure

(i) General overview

Interestingly, in order to exempt technology pools, under the EU competition law system, they needed to be distinguished from cross-licensing agreements, standardization agreements and from regular bilateral licensing agreements.

Bilateral and cross-licensing agreements between (two) competitors licensing competing technologies for the production of 'contracted products' are addressed in the TTBER under the concepts of licensing agreement and reciprocal licensing agreements respectively. The TTBER is not, however, directly applicable to the pool agreements, or, as stated in the TT Guidelines: '[a]greements establishing technology pools and setting out the terms and conditions for their operation are not – irrespective of the number of parties – covered by the block exemption'.[114] The reason for this was two-fold: first, a regrettable distinction

113 The current TTBER and TT Guidelines will expire on 30 April 2014 and the Commission has launched a public consultation of draft TTBER and TT Guidelines. Cf. the Commission website for public consultations: http://ec.europa.eu/competition/consultations/2012_technology_transfer/index_en.html. Accessed 9 January 2013. (Hereinafter new TT Guidelines).

114 TT Guidelines, para. 212.

between bilateral and multilateral agreements in Regulation 19/65;[115] and secondly, the pool agreements have also been distinguished from licensing agreements on the basis of not involving consent to exploit the licensed technology.[116] Pool agreements are instead accords among licensors regarding whether and on what terms to grant (sub-)licences.

Patent pools implicitly entail interplay between horizontal and vertical competitive relationships, and between bilateral and multilateral agreements. The TT Guidelines did not take correct notice of the licensing exchange under a technology pool.[117] The later horizontal relationships were however, as under US antitrust law, not discussed by the EU Commission. The licensing agreements under a patent pool were instead considered vertical by the Commission, irrespective whether the licensee also contributed patents to the pool. According to the Commission, the patentees vertically license the pool vehicle, if such a vehicle exists, which in turn vertically licenses the patents in a bundle to licensees.[118] In the new TT Guidelines, the horizontal effect is acknowledged and there is a clear dichotomy between horizontal and vertical effects.

The dichotomy between a horizontal pool agreement and vertical licensing agreements is legally 'technical' in nature. A court may very well 'pierce the veil' of the Commission's construction and declare that there are horizontal agreements or licence exchanges under the pool between the licensors which should, at least by analogy, be judged according to the rules in the TTBER for reciprocal agreements.

The non-recognition of the horizontal aspect disregards the fact that the decision on the definition of the technology will be influenced by what patents are available. This is especially the case if there are vertically integrated firms involved in the pool building that want free and clear access to product markets.[119]

---

[115] However, the TT Guidelines state that it is the particular issues to which a pooling arrangement gives rise that make them inapplicable for the block exemption, see TT Guidelines, para. 212.

[116] TTBER Recital 7 and TT Guidelines, para. 41.

[117] Hanns Ullrich, 'Patent Pools: Approaching a Patent Law Problem via Competition Policy', in Claus-Dieter Ehlermann and Isabela Atanasiu (eds), *European Competition Law Annual 2005: The Interaction Between Competition Law and Intellectual Property Law* (Hart, Publishing, 2007), 307 et seq.; and Hanns Ullrich, 'Patent Pools – Policy and Problems', in Josef Drexl (ed), *Research Handbook on Intellectual Property and Competition Law* (Edward Elgar, 2008), 145.

[118] For further discussion regarding the exchange or cross licence aspects to patent pool, see ibid.

[119] Ibid. 146 et seq.

There are several reasons why the horizontal aspects of patents pools have been neglected under EU competition law. The US antitrust enforcement agencies do not address the horizontal aspect of patents pools either. However, US antitrust law presumably treats cross-licensing agreements and technology pools according to the same standard.[120] There is no block exemption for cross-licensing agreements under US antitrust law. The discrepancy is smaller there than under EU competition law, where cross-licensing (or reciprocal licensing agreements) should be judged according to the TTBER, while pool agreements should be judged according to the TT Guidelines.

The absence of regulation addressing the issue of whether the horizontal licence exchange should be regulated by the TTBER may also be caused by the fact that pools, especially pools supporting technology standards, inherently have as their objective to 'monopolize' markets. Pools supporting technology standards represent an exception under antitrust since they are allowed to gain market power.[121] Patent pools therefore fit badly with the block exemption for technology transfer, which stipulates market share ceilings of 20 per cent and 30 per cent for its application, depending, on whether the parties are, respectively, competitors, or not. Thus, had the old structure of block exemption been retained, (bilateral) patent pools could also have been addressed in the block exemption.[122]

---

[120] The reality is not that clear. The US Justice Department tries to distance itself from the early patent pool case law in the IP2 Report by stating that several of the 'patent pools' that were struck down by the courts were in fact were cross-licence agreements, and the case-law should therefore implicitly be disregarded. This would indicate that there is a difference under US antitrust law between cross-licence agreements and patent pools. See the IP 2 Report, 66 n. 49

[121] When addressing patent pools, the Guidelines seldom refer to pools as being dominant, only that they can have a significant position on the market. Of course, the pool must avoid being regarded as a vehicle for collective dominance under Art 102. See e.g., the Dyestuff case, Case 48-69 ICI v. Commission [1972] ECR 619; or the Airtours case, 342/99, Airtours v. Commission [2002] ECR II-02585.

[122] Even more fundamentally, the TTBER is still based on the notion that allocation of scarce resources is most efficiently done through stand-alone competition, which does not perhaps correspond to the cooperative thinking behind pool agreements. Pool agreements and standardization agreements – which can be the same creatures – aim at market dominance through collective strategic conduct. Hanns Ullrich seems to have reached a comparable conclusion. Cf. Hanns Ullrich, 'Patent Pools – Policy and Problems', in Josef Drexl (ed), *Research Handbook on Intellectual Property and Competition Law* (Edward

Oddly enough, as will be discussed below, the TT Guidelines and officials from the Commission stated that licensing agreements from the pool to third parties (licensees) may be exempted under the TTBER. In the new TT Guidelines, the EU Commission has realized this oddity and now claims that the licence agreements between a pool and third parties in principle fall outside the TTBER. Likewise, the standardization agreement is regulated in the Horizontal Guidelines, which stipulates, in many respects, different rules compared to how pool agreements are regulated in the TT Guidelines.

5.5 COMPARATIVE ANALYSIS OF PATENT POOLS IN THE LIGHT OF STANDARD SETTING

5.5.1 Introduction

In this sub-section, the application of antitrust law to patent pools will be discussed comparatively. The difference in application between US and EU antitrust law will be analysed. The few cases there are from the US, i.e. the Federal Circuits decisions regarding the Philips and the CD-rom pools, indicate a clear difference between how the Justice Department and the Federal Circuit viewed patent pools and the sort of test that should be applied to them. The Justice Department's application of competition law in the Business Review Letters applied a test for the safe harbour that is based on the dichotomy between essential and non-essential patents, while the Federal Circuit used the regular tests for tying and cartels. The EU Commission has stuck with the Justice Department and use a test based on the essentiality of the patents.

Moreover, the interface between joint R&D, standard setting and patent pools in the telecoms sector and DVD/Blu-Ray techology will be discussed. How the technology was developed and agreed upon is of importance to the likelihood of establishing a successful patent pool, while may it also influence its regulation under competition law.

Elgar, 2008), 154 et seq. Cf. also Hanns Ullrich, 'Patente, Wettbewerb, under technische Normen: Recht- und ordnungspolitische Fragestellungen', (2007) 10 *GRUR* 2007, 817, 819 et seq.

5.5.2 Telecommunications and the Problem of Developing Patent Pools

Telecommunications can be seen as a prime example of an industry in which interoperability is at stake, and where a virtual infrastructure has been created by essential private firms. Telecommunications is a broad industry and most patent-related academic studies have concerned the mobile telecommunications sector. It is also the scene currently most exposed to network effects and patent-related problems.[123] When the current mobile standard for transmitting data, 3G or UMTS, was about to be launched, the European Telecommunications Standardization Institute ('ETSI') tried to set up a patent pool or patent platform organization for the market. Each of the five platform companies controlled a separate technology for transmitting data with sufficient speed and volume to be regarded as 3G technology. There were only technical essential patents in each platform company or firm. However, that does preclude the possibility of a licensee in individual cases being obliged to license from licensor-members of separate platform cooperations.

Regarding the 3G platforms (also called 3G3P for a while), the Commission approved the division of the 3G technologies into five platforms or pools (e.g., UMTS, cdma2000, EDGE) instead of one, so that each pool only contained essential patents for each technology platform,[124] implying that none of the platforms supervised competing patents.

The then usual requirements for patent pools (cf. requirements (i) to (vi) and (i) to (iv) in Chapter 5.4.2 above) applied, as did the prohibition

[123] Cf. Rudi Bekkers et al., 'Case studies on the interface between research and standardisation, and case studies on patent pools as a coordination mechanism' (INTEREST consortium Priority 8 No. Contract 503 594, EU 6th Specific Targeted Research Project, 2006),131 et seq. [The document is on file with the author.]

[124] Dolman claims that the EU Commission demanded five different alternative technologies under the standard. Cf. Maurits Dolmans, 'Standards For Standards', (2002) 26 *Fordham International Law Journal*, 163, 176. By contrast, the Justice Department seemed less than happy about that idea. See 3G Business Review Letter from Charles James to Ky P. Ewing dated 12 November 2002, addressing the 3G patent platforms for the third generation mobile communication systems. See http://www.usdoj.gov/atr/public/busreview/200455.htm, accessed 3 May 2009. Another explanation could also be that the division into five pools stem from the International Telecommunications Union ITU. The relevant parties could not reach consensus on a single global air interface standard and instead adopted a family of five standards.

on including covenants against R&D.[125] The difference between a regular patent pool and the 3G concept was that individual licences under respective platforms were to be negotiated between the patentee and the potential licensee but there was always a default licence on which the licensee could fall back. It stipulated accordingly a price cap of 5 per cent for royalties. It facilitated the possibility of negotiation between the licensors and potential licensees with the twist that during the process of negotiating, a default standard licensing agreement governed their relationship. Such an agreement facilitated licensee activity in respect of the technology while negotiating. The aim of the system was that a patentee should be able neither to block the 3G technology nor charge excessive royalties. The individual licensor and licensee would try to reach an understating under the prevailing rule that the terms should be 'fair and reasonable' (FRAND). If they did not reach an understanding, the 3G platform provided an arbitration mechanism to decide what would be 'fair and reasonable' in the individual case. The system thus did not in reality provide a one-stop-shop for the 3G system, or even a patent pool, but rather a mechanism for distributing competition to the product markets rather than have a standard and patent war with blocking patents and IP litigation.[126] The default agreement was in fact a contractually stipulated compulsory licence scheme.

The US Justice Department also criticized the EU Commission for not setting up the most efficient system in this regard.[127] The Justice Department pointed to the fact that if the system had bundled all the

---

[125] See press release 'Antitrust Clearance for Licensing of Patents for Third Generation Mobile Services' reference number IP/02/1651, dated 12.11.2002, and Dessy Choumelova, 'Competition Law Analysis of Patent Licensing arrangements – the Particular Case of 3G3P', (2003) 1 *EU Commission, Competition Policy Newsletter*, 1, 41 et seq.

[126] See generally regarding the 3G platforms, Dessy Choumelova, 'Competition Law Analysis of Patent Licensing arrangements – the Particular Case of 3G3P', (2003) 1 *EU Commission, Competition Policy Newsletter*, 141 et seq.

[127] The EU Commission, the US Justice Department and the Japanese competition authority all published their findings regarding the platform construction the same day, 12 November 2002. See 3G Business Review Letter to Charles James to Ky P. Ewing, dated 12 November 2002, addressing the 3G patent platforms for the third generation mobile communication systems. See http://www.usdoj.gov/atr/public/busreview/200455.htm, accessed 1 May 2009. Cf. also Rudi Bekkers, et al., 'Case studies on the interface between research and standardisation, and case studies on patent pools as a coordination mechanism' (INTEREST consortium Priority 8 No. Contract 503 594, EU 6th Specific Targeted Research Project, 2006), 133. [The document is on file with the author.]

rights together and put a price on the bundle, such an arrangement would have been more efficient. Nonetheless, competing patents would then have been licensed together. Five platforms would ensure competition between different technologies, according to the EU Commission. Possibly, the Commission created so many gatekeepers to such an essential technology because it was not ready to accept competing patents in one patent pool.

Interestingly, in hindsight, it is also evident that the system of patent platforms failed. Only one platform actually came into use. In 2004, a W-CDMA patent licensing programme was established for UMTS patents, including 7 licensors, but only concerning a fraction of the claimed essential patents.[128] Some have claimed that a reserve fund was even developed to help with antitrust issues and clearance in connection with the platform. However, the largest holders of essential patents to the 3G never agreed to become members of the licensing program, and in 2011 the W-CDMA patent licensing programme was dismantled when the limited company W-CDMA was dissolved.[129]

There are several reasons for why the 3G platforms failed. There were a large amount of standard essential patentees. In fact, there were so many patentees that the share magnitude made the negotiation cost insupportable. However, more damaging for creating an old fashion patent pool, were the different business strategies of the patentees. Some were vertically integrated and mainly sought profit from downstream product markets, while other firms were R&D intensive and only sought profit from royalty streams. The strategies of these two firms are difficult to reconcile under a patent pool. An additional factor for the failure of patent pools in the area of infrastructure standards is that many of the patents may be of a very low quality. Just to weed these out may be very expensive and also represent a possible antitrust risk.[130]

The 3G platforms tried to reconcile this with a price mechanism that made it possible to still be on the platform but negotiate separate licence agreements. In fact, this solution mirrors much of the IP arrangements under current SDOs, where the notion of FRAND being capable of being independent and treating each licence as different is accepted.

Recently, large licensees and licensors have engaged in litigation in both the US courts and European courts, and complained to the EU Commission, since they are not licensed on such 'fair' terms as agreed

---

[128] Ibid.

[129] Liguo Zhang, *Standardization and Patent Licensing in the European Union* (Oy Nord Print Ab 2012), 132 et seq.

[130] Ibid.

under the FRAND covenant under the standard.[131] Furthermore, there is an issue whether firms do have the essential patents, the patent applications and the future patents that they purported to have when the 3G technology was created and the royalty mechanisms were decided.[132]

It should be mentioned that the telecommunications industry has seen several smaller patent pools/standardization consortia. The consortium of the large telecom firms (Ericsson, Nokia, Motorola and Siemens) in 2003

---

[131] Infra Chapter 6. See also EC Commission's Memo/Press Release, MEMO/07/389, dated 1 October 2007 'Commission Initiates Formal Proceedings against Qualcomm'. On the joint complaint of Nokia, Ericsson, Texas Instruments, Broadcom, NEC and Panasonic, the EU Commission started an investigation whether Qualcomm was abusing its dominance based on patent rights included in the 3G system, since it did not license these rights on Fair, Reasonable, and Non-Discriminatory (FRAND) terms. The contractual agreements at issue related to the standard-setting procedures of the European Telecommunications Standardization Institute ('ETSI') regarding the licensing of essential patents. See also Qualcomm's suit against Nokia for patent infringement, Qualcomm Inc. v. Nokia Corp.466 F.3d 1366 (Fed. Cir. 2006). In a case, the plaintiff, Nokia, filed suit in the Court of Chancery of the State of Delaware seeking declaratory relief and specific performance to enforce terms of alleged contracts existing between it and the defendant Qualcomm. See furthermore, Broadcom v. Qualcomm Inc. 501 F.3d. 297 (3rd Cir 2007). For comments on the US development, cf. Joseph Farrell, et al., 'Standard Setting, Patents, and Hold-up', (2007) 74 Antitrust Law Journal, 603, 604 et seq., Daniel Swanson and William Baumol, 'Reasonable and Nondiscriminatory (RAND) Royalties, Standards Selection, and Control of Market Power', (2005) 73 Antitrust Law Journal, 1. See also Anne Layne-Farrar, et al., 'Pricing patents for Licensing in Standard-Setting Organizations: Making Sense of FRAND Commitments', (2007) 74 *Antitrust Law Journal*, 671. For the European discussion, see Hanns Ullrich, 'Patente, Wettbewerb, under technische Normen: Recht- und ordnungspolitische Fragestellungen', (2007) 10 *GRUR* 2007, 817; Gil Ohana et al., 'Disclosure and Negotiation of Licensing Terms Prior to Adoptation of Industry Standards: Preventing another Patent Ambush', (2003) 24 *E.C.L.R*, 644, and several articles by Damien Geradin: e.g., Damien Geradin, 'Standardization and Technological Innovation: Some Reflections on Ex-ante Licensing, FRAND, and the Proper Means to Reward Innovators', (2006) 29 *World Competition*, 511.

[132] Ibid. There is an interesting EU sponsored project on mobile communication for the next generation involving 40 partners, where patents are not taken out for the R&D conducted but where early publishing is the goal of the research. This would then hinder all involved and other firms from getting patents in the research output. Rudi Bekkers, et al., 'Case studies on the interface between research and standardisation, and case studies on patent pools as a coordination mechanism' (INTEREST consortium Priority 8 No. Contract 503 594, EU 6th Specific Targeted Research Project, 2006), 57. [The document is on file with the author.]

was based on joint R&D with the aim of creating and implementing a global telecom standard, the push-to-talk technology, which was considered anti-competitive by many since the firms must jointly have represented more than 25 per cent of the telecom market.[133] This need not to be the case, however, since the push-to-talk technology could be considered a whole new market where these parties did not hold any market power (yet). Thus, under the then R&D block exemption such collaboration should be exempted irrespectively of market shares held on the neighbouring 3G telecommunication network and hand-set markets.

There was also the Bluetooth standard and patent pool, facilitating wireless communication; developed by Ericsson but disseminated through the Bluetooth Special Interest Group (SIG). To my knowledge it has never been accused of being in breach of competition law, even though the consortium must have contained several firms with market power in their respective markets when launched.

5.5.3 The Difference between, on the one hand, the JVC-Betamax, DVD and Blu-Ray Standard Wars and, on the other hand, the Telecommunications Industry

The old, and very much discussed, VHS v. Betamax standard war, seem to have happened so long ago, that it may support any view of standard setting. Often, it is argued that VHS won the war, not due to better technology, but by collecting better strategic partners and thus thereby obtaining content.[134] Possibly, this would seem a way to exclude Betamax from the input content market. Others argue that VHS represented a superior technology, and put forward strong evidence that points in that

[133] Claudia Tapia, *Industrial Property Rights, Technical Standards and Licensing Practices (FRAND) in the Telecommunications Industry* (Carl Heymanns Verlag – eine Marke von Wolters Kluwer Deutschland GmbH, 2010), 84, with reference in fn. 392. It may furthermore be argued that the very early telecom network technologies NMTS and GSM were developed in consortia fashion and that there was some form of standard or technology wars in which different member State governments were also involved to promote the technologies developed by national (champions). Cf. Maurits Dolmans, 'Standards For Standards', (2002) 26 *Fordham International Law Journal*, 163, 181; and Rudi Bekkers, et al., 'Case studies on the interface between research and standardisation, and case studies on patent pools as a coordination mechanism' (INTEREST consortium Priority 8 No. Contract 503 594, EU 6th Specific Targeted Research Project, 2006), 121.

[134] For example Liguo Zhang, *Standardization and Patent Licensing in the European Union* (Oy Nord Print Ab 2012), 140 et seq.

direction.[135] Nonetheless, the VHS v. Betamax war and the outcome should not be considered the rule, rather as the exception, to a standard war. Clearly, there have been other standard wars, and even oligopoly equilibriums in standard wars. For example, the game console standard war is continuing without any side gaining the upper hand and creating one omnipresent technology.

Several of the patent pools scrutinized by the competition authorities in both the US and Europe stem, to a greater or a lesser degree, from standards and joint R&D. Certainly, the MPEG-2 pool was created out of a mission to unite a technology under a patent thicket, where there was no technological unity before. However, the DVD technology was generally created by joint R&D ventures. When analysing the background of the DVD pool collaboration between Koninklijke Philips Electronics N.V. (Philips), Sony Corporation of Japan (Sony) and Pioneer Electronic Cooperation of Japan (Pioneer), it becomes apparent that the participants went so far as to research and develop the technology together before setting up the patent pool.[136] Accordingly, Philips and Sony have been jointly engaging in research under the supervision of the Japanese government for a long time, coming up with standard-setting technologies such as the VCR video, CDs, Mini-discs and the DVD. These standards, and the related patent pools, were first allowed under both US and EU law, but the set-up was called into question in several jurisdictions and, at least as concerns the CD-rom technology, the parties later had to dissolve the pool.[137] The background seems to be as follows:

---

[135] Julian Christ and André Slowak, 'Why Blue-Ray v. HD-DVD is not VHS v. BETAMAX: The Co-evolution of Standard Setting Consortia', (2009) *FZID Discussion Papers*, Universität Hohenheim,, 4 et seq. with references.

[136] See the 3DVD Pool Business Review Letter from Joel Klein to Gerrard Beeney dated 16 December 1998 5 et seq. See http://www.usdoj.gov/atr/public/busreview/2121.htm, accessed 3 May 2009.

[137] See EC Commission press release IP/03/1152; 07/08/2003, 'Commission Clears Philips/Sony CD Licensing Program' and EC Commission press release IP/06/139, 09/02/2006 'Commission Closes Investigation following Changes to Philips CD-Recordable Disc Patent Licensing'. For the famous Chinese Taipei case see the OECD roundtable discussions regarding intellectual property in 2004, 21 January 2005, 117 et seq., http://www.oecd.org/dataoecd/61/48/34306055.pdf, accessed 3 May 2009. The Chinese Taipei case resulted in very interesting litigation concerning patent rights and misuse of patent rights, see the ITC case Notice of Commission on Determination of No Violation of section 337, In the matter of Certain Recordable Compact Discs and Rewritable Compact Discs, Investigation No. 337-TA-474. See also U.S. Philips Corp. v. International Trade Commission, 424 F.3d 1179 (Fed. Cir. 2005). For an even

'Sony and Philips worked together in the late 1970s to develop the audio CD. Philip's work on LaserDisc and Sony's digital error correction encoding resulted in a huge leap forward for consumer audio that delivered high quality sound on a durable medium with instant playback. In the early 1990s, the two companies began collaborating on an inexpensive new video version, called the MultiMedia Compact Disc. At the same time, a group led by Toshiba including Pioneer and JVC introduced the SuperDensity Disc. For a year and a half, the groups tried without much luck to promote interest among consumers in the two formats. In 1995, the groups united to form the DVD Consortium, later called the DVD Forum. That cooperation helped the single new DVD format to be adopted rapidly. DVDs use ISO standard MPEG-2 video compression and digital audio, typically delivered as Dolby Digital AC-3 or DTS surround sound. Using standard, interoperability formats based on patent pools from established technical leaders meant that DVDs could be delivered by any hardware manufacturer under reasonable and non-discriminatory licensing'.[138]

The standard wars of VHS v. Betamax and, to some extent, the pool wars 3C DVD v. 6C DVD and also Blu-ray v. HD DVD seem somewhat artificial. In light of the above, these technologies and standards/patent pools represent different products in relevant technology markets; or, at least, they are in competition with each other and other technical formats during the period of the development of the technology. These are close-knit collaborations trying to implement their technology as the standard in competition with other consortia.

Patent pools created out of a patent thicket or a need to solve the anticommons problem are therefore perhaps not as common as one would think. Instead, patent pools arise out of joint R&D ventures that also create the standard and the IP rights. They are consortia, where the participants may both have competed and collaborated. From a technology point of view the result of their joint effort may often be a technology or design rather than an infrastructure or interoperability.

---

earlier case concerning Philips and Sony cooperation in VCR video technology see discussion infra and Commission decision, Videocassette Recorders, OJ 1977 L 47/42. The US FTC also did an early analysis of Philips and Sony's licensing agreements for CDs in the 1980s: see Carl Shapiro, 'Navigating the Patent Thicket: Cross Licenses, Patent Pools and Standard Setting', in Adam Jaffe et al. (eds), *Innovation Policy and the Economy* (MIT Press, 2001), 20.

[138] See http://www.roughlydrafted.com/2007/08/29/origins-of-the-blu-ray-vs-hd-dvd-war/, accessed 8 February 2008. Thus, a DVD manufacturer needs to take out licences from the MPEG-2 pool and the DVD pools.

Sometimes the result of their effort is considered the only plausible solution on a market, although perhaps on a closer look that might prove wrong.

Give that contemporary competition over standards takes place between consortia and not between single firms, the outcome of these wars does not need to be decided by technology supremacy, which would lead to a fast adoption rate by consumers, but rather by supply side conduct. Thus, the network effects and tipping effects in certain markets are not, as Shapiro *et al* discussed, driven by demand, but instead are supply driven.[139] For example, according to research conducted by Christ and Slowak, the Blu-Ray v. HD DVD standard war differs from well-established literature on network effects and standard wars because, contrary to VHS v. Betamax, the HD patent pool war, it was not decided by the demand side (consumers), nor was it a case of obvious technological supremacy for one technology over the other.[140] Instead, Christ and Slowak concluded that the exclusive backing of various content providers, as well as exclusive agreements with various movie rental chains, created the needed 'tipping effect' that made Blu-Ray the omnipresent and winning technology.

These consortia construct technologies that imply joint efforts to create a technology for a market that only holds one solution to a demand, i.e. a network or interface technology. But, in fact, the network effects are more contractual then inherent effects of the market. They are created because of the exclusive content agreements, forcing the consumer to select certain technology. While these consortia may perhaps be regarded as promoting one product, i.e. a system including content, a court may find that content and technology actually have separate demand curves and that consumers would not select content and technology in a bundle if they could. In other words, these technologies, and the consortia efforts to get corresponding standards, are disguised efforts to create network-driven standards, with patent pools originating from joint R&D ventures/consortia in order to create essential patents to chaperone the technology. They should perhaps instead be regarded as regular design standards.

This is not different from a standard regarding tyres, where the producers or standard setters of the tyres have been able to obtain exclusive arrangements with both car manufacturers and re-sellers of

---

[139] Carl Shapiro and Hal R. Varian, *Information Rules* (Harvard Business School Press, 1999), 173 et seq.

[140] Julian Christ and André Slowak, 'Why Blue-Ray v. HD-DVD is not VHS v. BETAMAX: The Co-evolution of Standard Setting Consortia', (2009) *FZID Discussion Papers*, Universität Hohenheim.

tires. This would also create 'tipping effects' on the tyres market. If this were the case with the DVD and Blu-Ray standards, they should be regarded as representing products on a bigger consumer market for storing and privately watching films. They should consequently receive a higher antitrust scrutiny as design or product standards.

Notwithstanding the above, if the parties can prove either that the market was plagued by a patent thicket or that the tipping effect actually is demand driven, then the antitrust burden would lessen and collusive or exclusionary conduct could be exempted.[141] It is clear that market failure can appear in the evolution of the market, while it may also be caused by the parties in the market, and if the market has evolved and accepted one solution as the *de facto* standard, then courts and competition authorities need to accept this.

The telecommunications standards are different. They represent interoperability infrastructure standards, which, in the case of GSM and 3G, have been developed in a competitive R&D and standard-setting fashion. As a matter of fact, they represent new markets with new demand. The failure of the 3G platforms is only an indication of this. When a new infrastructure is created, the parties to the standard and the actors in the downstream market will have business strategies that are too dispersed to be able to create one patent pool. These standards truly represent infrastructure developed by private parties with different business strategies, and, therefore, it is almost impossible to create a comprehensive patent pool to govern the standard.

5.5.4 When is a Standard Derived Patent Pool an Anti-competitive Cartel?

After the above general outline of what standards and patent pools should be considered suspicious from an anti-competition perspective, and what collaborations should be considered pro-competitive from the outset, the issue has come down to what requirements courts should set up to establish antitrust harm in the form of collusion or exclusion.

First, it should be acknowledged that were the EU Commission or the US antitrust agencies to find an agreement, at least on a market that holds several different products, which is an actual hardcore horizontal agreement to blatantly restrict product diversification and/or to not conduct or limit R&D, this may very well be regarded as anti-competitive by object

[141] Under the Business Review Letter for the DVD patent pools, the applicants argued that there was a patent thicket on the market and not that the market had natural tipping effects, see supra Chapter 5.4.2.

under EU competition rules, or per se violation of US antitrust law.[142] Thus, there is still room for per se violations.[143]

Under both the US and EU technology pool jurisprudence, the rules or criteria that were originally stipulated in the Business Review Letters from the end of the 1990s had the appearance of being per se to be followed; If not, the pool would be condemned under, at least, a truncated (quick look) rule of reason. These rules were procedural as regards the decision making and transparency of the collaboration in question, as well as focused on specific licence terms. Thus, several of the rules only protected competition indirectly by being good governance rules.

However, violating the requirements which are included in the list of covenants for setting up a patent pool within a safe harbour under the current antitrust rules would not cause a per se violation. Thus, even if there are price collaborations between competitors, antitrust effect needs to be proven. According to the Business Review Letters from the end of the 1990s, technology pools were not allowed to contain competing patents since that would imply a price cartel on the technology market.[144] That is not the case anymore. Pools may contain some substitute patents and still make use of the safe harbour. Furthermore, if members of an SDO under an IP arrangement agree on a joint royalty rate under a technology standard that includes competing patents, that agreement should, at least, not be a per se violation under the NCRPA nor the new

[142] See EU Pre-insulated Tube Cartel case, or the US Automobile Association case. Both are discussed supra Chapters 4.2.6 and 4.1.1.

[143] In re Summit Tech. Inc., 127 F.T.C. 208 (1998), In re VIXS Inc., 127 F.T.C. 136 (1999). The FTC negotiated a consent decree that was premised on the allegation that the formation of a patent pool had stopped competition between two firms. Specifically, Summit and VISX had competing claims to the exclusive rights to technology for photorefractive keratectomy ('PRK') vision-correcting eye surgery that was the subject of litigation. They settled the litigation by forming a patent pool in which the parties shared the revenues derived from licensing fees to the combined technology. The FTC alleged that, but for the patent pool, the parties 'could have and would have competed with one another in the sale or lease of PRK equipment by using their respective patents, licensing them, or both.' This matter was settled by consent agreements that required royalty free cross-licensing to support competition between the two firms.

[144] See e.g., Hartford-Emprise et al. v. United States, 46 F. Supp. 541 (1942), modified 323 U.S. 386 (1945).

TT Guidelines.[145] Indeed, it would be judged under the regular rule of reason standard.[146]

BOX 5.1

In light of the few restraints stipulated for SDOs, the SDO or the connected joint R&D ventures can oblige licensees of the essential patents to accept a number of obligations and still take advantage of the NCRPA. For example, the patentees can decide on grant-back or cross-licensing obligations, which are wider than the grant-back clauses normally allowed under patent pools, e.g., covenants for exclusive transfer of rights to the licensor.[147] The covenants can even include sub-licensing rights for the licensors. The SDO or the joint ventures can decide on a lump royalty for access to essential patents in connection with the running royalties.[148] Up-front lump sum royalties may easily discourage smaller firms from entering the market. Moreover, the connected joint ventures, but not the SDOs, can stipulate field-of-use restrictions and still make use of the NCRPA. The relevant patentee can hence retain an input market for itself.

---

145 See US. Department of Justice and Federal Trade Commission, *Antitrust Enforcement and Intellectual property Rights: Promoting Innovation and Competition* (2007), 7 et seq., www.ftc.gov/reports/index.shtm. Accessed 3 May 2009.

146 In the latest IP 2 Report, the antitrust enforcement agencies declared that patent pools including some substitute patents should not be presumed to be anti-competitive and should be judged under a rule of reason. See US. Department of Justice and Federal Trade Commission, *Antitrust Enforcement and Intellectual property Rights: Promoting Innovation and Competition* (2007), 7 and 9.

147 Regarding the possibility of negotiating grant-back clauses *ex ante* or under a FRAND requirement in connection to an SDO or SSO, cf. Mark Lemley, 'Intellectual Property Rights and Standard-Setting Organizations', (2002) 90 *California Law Review*, 1889, 1966. Cf. Scott Peterson, 'Patent and Standard Setting Process', in FTC/DOJ (ed), FTC/DOJ Hearings on Competition and Intellectual Property Law and Policy in the Knowledge-Based Economy (FTC, 2002). [The document is on file with the author.]

148 Such an arrangement can, if carefully adjusted, enable proprietors to create a perfect monopolistic price structure. Cf. Susanne Scotchmer, *Innovation and Incentives* (MIT Press, 2004), 137 et seq.

The latest Business Review Letters indicate that an SDO can apparently even decide on reciprocal licensing obligations, non-assertion clauses, non-challenge covenants and defensive suspension provisions.[149]

Overall, it is difficult to draw precise boundaries for what members of joint ventures with a joint SDO may not decide upon and still make use of the NCRPA.

Under US antitrust law, IP arrangements in connection to a standard are treated more leniently than a patent pool, at least when following the statements by the Justice Department. Under EU law, a discrepancy between IP arrangements under IP guides and patent pools has not emerged. Rather the opposite: under the TT Guidelines, the Commission welcomes *ex ante* negotiations and agreements on licence terms before the technology is decided upon. At least, it is in the technology pool chapter in the TT Guidelines where *ex ante* negotiations are discussed.[150] Moreover, as mentioned above, the new TT Guidelines clearly indicate that the Commission believes that IP arrangements under SDOs and patent pools are more or less the same thing. At least, potential patent pool licensors may discuss royalty rates in the pre-standardization phase, even though such discussion would include the rate of at least some competing patents.

There is support in the academy for treating SSOs' IP arrangements and technology pools differently.[151] Lemley admits that SSOs behave like patent pools in certain respects. Nonetheless, Lemley argues that SSOs with IP arrangements and patent pools should be treated differently for three main reasons: first, SSOs are more concerned with the technical outcome of the collaboration than patent pools; secondly, while SSOs' IP arrangements are set *ex ante* the implementation of the technical standard, patent pools are set *ex post*; thirdly, SSOs with IP arrangements are concentrated in network industries, while patent pools are distributed randomly across industries.

The question is whether these three reasons are sufficient to make IP arrangements under SSOs, or SDOs in practice, per se legal under US

---

[149] The VITA Business Review Letter from Thomas O. Barnett to Robert A. Skitol, dated 30 October 2006, 7. See http://www.usdoj.gov/atr/public/busreview/219380.htm. Accessed 23 May 2009.

[150] TT Guidelines, para. 225.

[151] Mark Lemley, 'Intellectual Property Rights and Standard-Setting Organizations', (2002) 90 *California Law Review*, 1889, 1951 et seq.

antitrust law. I would argue to the contrary. Patent pools, as well as IP arrangements, are more common in network industries than in other industries. The horizontal aspect of technology pools is very similar to, or as a matter of fact, often the result of the technology standardization agreements. In sum, there is no convincing reason for treating IP arrangements differently and they should therefore be treated similarly to patent pools under antitrust law.

However, IP arrangements and patent pools should instead be treated differently depending on whether the relevant technology markets may hold different substitute technologies. If that is the case, a patent pool or an IP arrangement under a SDO may very well be a disguised cartel if it contains competing technologies. As discussed above with the 802.11g WiFi standard, there is a clear risk that SDOs, when not reaching a result reflecting one technology, either decide on multiple standards or on one large standard encompassing several technologies. If this is the case, then creating an *ex ante* IP arrangement including also substitute technologies, or *ex post* creating a patent pool that *de facto* corresponds to a standard that covers more than one technology, could have collusive effects on the technology market.

There are also quite recent cases under both US antitrust law and EU competition rules regarding collusion under patent pools where the cartel is in the downstream product markets, which is facilitated by a patent pool. Apart from *Belasco*[152], the *C-O Two* decision[153] and the *Household Radiators* case[154] also revolved around the issue that, by creating a narrow product standard, product differentiation was either completely diminished, or, at least, reduced to the extent that prices (and costs) among the members aligned sufficiently for the court to find that the collaborations were a cartel in the product markets. Hovenkamp also concluded that product differentiation is still an important antitrust value, and, thus, 'standards that do no more than reduce product differentiation in order to facilitate price matching do not provide a social benefit'.[155]

As Crane discusses, when private parties are able both to control the technology to be standardized and create related patent pools, there is a risk that they will select the technology to be standardized that fits their

---

152 Case 246/86 Belasco v. Commission [1986] ECR 2117.

153 C-O-Two Fire Equip. Co. v. United States 197 F2d 489 (9th Circ), cert. denied, 344 U.S. 892 (1952).

154 United States v. Am Radiator and Standard Sanitary Corp. 433 F2d 174, 185 (3rd Cir 1970), cert denied, 401 U.S. 948 (1971).

155 Herbert Hovenkamp, 'Standard and Ownership Policy', (2007) 48 *Boston College Law Review*, 87, 95.

patent portfolios.[156] By controlling the standard they also control what should be regarded as complements and substitutes, and, thus, of course, what are essential IPRs under the standard and patent pool. The *U.S. Philips II* case deals with this scenario.

(i) U.S. Philips II case[157]

There are two U.S. Philips cases originating from US Courts. *U.S Philips I* is discussed supra[158]. As with the *U.S. Philips I*, the *U.S. Philips II* case does not concern antitrust law primarily. It was decided under the patent misuse doctrine.[159] However, the Federal Circuit when exonerating U.S. Philips yet again discussed at length, not only antitrust law and the interface between antitrust law and the patent misuse doctrine, but also the interface between R&D, standardization and patent pooling.

U.S. Philips II was decided by the Federal circuit in 2010.[160] The Supreme Court failed to grant certiorari. The case again concerned the CD-ROM technology (CD-R and CD-RWs) and the Recordable CD technology standard researched and developed by Philips and Sony, and whether Princo, manufacturer of products under the standard, had infringed on one of Philips' patents that was included in the CD-rom patent pool, the Raaymaker patent. The short name for the CD technology standard in question is Orange Book, and this standard has been recognized by ISO/IEC, through the work of regional SDOs where, inter alia. representatives of Philips had been taking an active part.[161]

---

156 Daniel A. Crane, 'Patent Pools, RAND Commitments, and the Problematics of Price Discrimination', *Cardozo School of Law Working Paper* (2008) no. 232, 7 and 9.

157 616 F.3d 1318 (Fed. Cir. 2010).

158 Supra Chapter 5.4.4.

159 George Gordon and Robert Hoerner, 'Overview and Historical Development of the Misuse Doctrine', in ABA Section of Antitrust Law (ed), *Intellectual Property Misuse Licensing and Litigation* (ABA, 2000).

160 The *en banc* decision in Philips II capped a trilogy of Federal Ciruit decisions arising under the International Trade Commission patent infringement litigation. See also U.S. Philips Corp. v. Princo. Corp., 173 Fed. Appx. 832 (Fed. Cir. 2006); U.S. Philips Corp. v. Int'l Trade Comm'n 424 F.3d 1179 (Fed. Cir. 2005).

161 It was recognized by ISO/IEC, by ECMA, and by the TC31-optical disks and cartridges committee chaired by a representative of Philips. Cf. Hanns Ullrich, 'Patents and Standards – a Comment on the German Federal Supreme Court Decision Orange Book Standard', (2011) 41 *IIC*, 337, fn. 18. See also http://en.wikipedia.org/wiki/Red_Book_(CD_standard)#cite_note-3. Accessed 20 November 2011.

The Federal Circuit heard the *U.S. Philips II* case *en banc*. The issue at stake was whether Philips had misused its Raaymaker patent in relation to a licensee (Princo), by enclosing an, at least, substitute technology in the pool. This was the Lagadec patent and technology, developed by Sony exclusively in the CD-ROM patent pool, i.e. the Orange Book patent pool, even though Philip's alleged substitute Raaymaker patent was already included. The Lagadec technology did not fit the Orange Book standard and Philips claimed in the proceedings that the Lagadec was a blocking patent in reference to the Raaymaker patent and therefore included in the pool.[162] The package licence agreement stipulated a field-of-use requirement that the licences could only be used in such a way as to adhere to the Orange Book standard. Thus, the issue was whether an alleged anti-competitive horizontal agreement not to develop or market Lagadec as a competing or, at least, as a separate substitute technology to Raaymaker could be a patent misuse?

The majority held that the alleged agreement restricting the availability of the Lagadec technology was not a misuse of the Philips patents, in particular, the Raaymaker patent. Such conduct did not fit the majority's notion of the patent misuse doctrine. The court determined that the doctrine of patent misuse was based on the notion of 'leveraging',[163] that is, for example, contractually leveraging more power from the rights making up a patent under US law. The pool agreement between two patentees to include both Raaymaker and Lagadec, even though purportedly anti-competitive and in violation of US antitrust law, did not fit that definition of the doctrine. According to the majority, there was no link between the putative misconduct and the Raaymaker patents.[164] Philips was therefore acquitted.

Notwithstanding the above, was there an antitrust violation? The Federal Circuit developed this point. While the existence of such horizontal agreement was never determined by the ITC (i.e. the lower 'court'), the majority in the Federal Circuit case found that such collaboration would nonetheless not have an anti-competitive effect since the Lagadec patent/technology was not a viable alternative to the Raaymaker technology.[165]

---

162 616 F.3d 1318, 1324 compare to 1344, fn 5. (Fed. Cir. 2010).

163 Ibid, 1331 et seq.

164 Ibid, 1332.

165 The concurrent judge did not agree with the majority in reference to the width of the patent misuse doctrine, but agreed that Princo had failed to show anti-competitive effect. The concurrent also reserved judgment on the precise boundaries of the patent misuse doctrine.

The majority also found the Philips-Sony agreement to be irrelevant to the patent misuse analysis, since the patent misuse issue concerned the package licence between the pool and the licensee, not the horizontal agreement between Philips and Sony. A licensee of a package of patents cannot rely on an agreement between the R&D collaborators or licensors to suppress a competing technology even though this technology is also provided in the package.

The majority actually made several innovative statements: they dissected the horizontal agreement under the R&D agreement/patent pool agreement, or the standard agreement, from the perspective of the vertical relationship between the pool and the package licensee. Even though the horizontal agreement between Sony and Philips might infringe antitrust law, that does not, according to the majority, affect the package licence agreement, and whether that agreement was infringing the doctrine of patent misuse.

The dissenting judge found the two agreements to be part and parcel of the same course of conduct. In fact, what the dissent identifies is that Philips' and Sony's actions are part of one grander conduct or collaboration. According to the dissenting judge, the issue at stake was whether the agreement between Philips and Sony to jointly license the Raaymaker patents together with the Lagadec patent implied that the alternative technology embodied in the Lagadec patent will not be marketed separately and in competition with the Raaymaker technology. Furthermore, the issue concerned the effect of the field-of-use requirement, which barred the licensees from developing the Lagadec technology. The dissidenting judge, moreover, pointed to the fact that the effect of the horizontal and vertical covenants was not only that Sony would not develop the Lagadec technology, but neither would anyone else among the package licensees do so due to the field-of-use covenant. The dissenting judge furthermore implied that Philips was actually buying off Sony not to develop the Lagadec technology, since Sony received high returns from the patent pool while only contributing few, if any, essential patents.[166] Thus, it was somewhat of a 'pay for delay' or even 'pay for never entering a market' agreement.

The majority, even though not admitting that there was an anti-competitive agreement, stated that Princo nonetheless failed to show that the alleged agreement had any anti-competitive effect in the relevant market.[167] Princo had failed to show that the Lagadec technology had

---

166 Ibid., 1343 et seq.

167 616 F.3d 1318, 1340.

technical and commercial prospects which could enable it to compete with the Raaymaker technology. The dissenting judge instead placed this burden of proof on Philips.

Some commentators have argued that that requires the plaintiff in these cases to show anti-competitive effect, although alleging that two competitors in a horizontal agreement are suppressing nascent or developing technology may be impossible since the actual anti-competitive effect is not yet present.[168]

In the end, the Federal Circuit found that the alleged agreement between Sony and Philips not to develop the Lagadec technology neither broadened the physical or temporal scope of patent grant impermissibly, nor, even if proven to exist, could have had anti-competitive effect. Thus, the doctrine of patent misuse was not violated, and neither was US antitrust law.

In conclusion, it may be that the majority reached a correct conclusion on the facts, given the narrow and somewhat unimaginative definition of the doctrine of patent misuse. The majority was furthermore helped by making a firm distinction between the agreements that needed to be scrutinized: horizontal versus vertical; antitrust versus patent misuse. The majority failed to see the whole picture as seen by the dissenting judge: an agreement between two global competitors to suppress the development of one technology, invented by one of them, so as to advance the other competitor's technology, and then divide the profit. It could be viewed as broadening the commercial effect or scope of the jointly supported technology (patent) by a correspondingly anti-competitive effect on the suppressed technology, at least in reference to dynamic or innovative competition.

However, from a competition law perspective, the Federal Circuit clearly demanded the showing of anti-competitive effect under the rule of reason. The Federal Circuit found no anti-competitive effect because the Lagadec patent was not a competitive alternative. The interesting aspect is that the majority fails to see that suppressing nascent technology cannot be detected on any market.

I fail to see that the defendant should be under more of a burden than to show (i) the existence of a patent protected technology where the patent claims seem to correspond with the sought after solutions, i.e. substitute patents, and (ii) that the market would be able to hold two

[168] Daryl Lim, 'Misconduct in Standard Setting: The Case for Patent Misuse', (2011) 51 *IDEA: The Journal of Law and Technology*, 557, 598 et seq. with references.

competing technologies in this regard and that there would be a demand for two separate technologies. This would have been in line with *Philips I*, and perhaps this is actually what the court is telling us in *Philips II,* although the defendant was not able to prove (i) or (ii).

Under EU competition law, there does not seem to be a requirement to show anti-competitive effect to the degree that the substitute patent actually is a competing patent with a share of the relevant market. Under both the TT Guidelines and the Horizontal Guidelines, the EU Commission has stipulated that technical substitution is enough. The Horizontal Guidelines stipulate:

> As a general rule standardization agreements should cover no more than what is necessary to ensure their aims, whether this is technical interoperability and compatibility or a certain level of quality. In cases where having only one technological solution would benefit consumers or the economy at large that standard should, be set on a non-discriminatory basis. Technology neutral standards can, in certain circumstances, lead to larger efficiency gains. Including substitute IPR as essential parts of a standard while at the same time forcing the users of the standard to pay for more IPR than technically necessary would go beyond what is necessary to achieve any identified efficiency gains. In the same vein, including substitute IPR as essential parts of a standard and limiting the use of that technology to that particular standard (that is to say, exclusive use) could limit inter-technology competition and would not be necessary to achieve the efficiencies identified.[169]

The new TT Guidelines equally do not require competing, only substitute, patents.[170] In addition, one point made by the dissenting judge in *U.S. Philips II* is quite striking. What should a private plaintiff do if it thinks that a patent pool contains competing patents? The dissidenting judge in the *U.S. Philips II* case acknowledges that antitrust law does not provide any adequate remedy for suppressing nascent competition. Private enforcement of antitrust law in this context is virtually impossible. First, the *Noerr* doctrine would be applicable, but even if the plaintiff could circumvent this, it would run into trouble. A potential competitor cannot sue for damages based on a nascent technology. An injunctive relief at the request of a competitor is unlikely to take effect. Only the doctrine of patent misuse is available.

---

169 Horizontal Guidelines, para. 317.

170 See for example the new TT Guidelines, paras. 234, 236, and 239.

(ii) Summit/VISX patent pool

The Summit and VISX patent pool[171] is a good example of where the FTC, initially, was able to show collusion. It is also a good case for seeing the similarities and differences between a standard/patent pool and a cartel. The FTC alleged that the formation of a patent pool had stopped competition between two firms. Specifically, Summit and VISX had competing claims to the exclusive rights to technology for photorefractive keratectomy ('PRK') vision-correcting eye surgery, which was the subject of litigation. They settled the litigation by forming a patent pool in which the parties shared the revenues derived from licensing fees for the combined technology.

The FTC argued that, but for the patent pool, the parties could have, and would have, competed with each another in the sale or lease of PRK equipment by using their respective patents, licensing them, or both. The parties claimed that there was a patent thicket created by their patents, whereby they were blocking each other. The settlement to set up the pool was the tool by which both parties could access the market. The matter was settled by the FTC through consent agreements that required royalty free cross-licensing to support competition between the two firms.

The Summit/VISX pool was set up by the time of the MPEG-2 pool. Also, the underlying argument for setting up the MPEG-2 pool was the patent thicket. While the MPEG-2 pool was exempted under a Business Review Letter from the Justice Department, the FTC found that the Summit/VISX patent pool was a cartel. The main reason seems to have been that the FTC was convinced that the market held both technologies and that the technologies were competing. Any patent blocking was due to a patent held by VISX that was not valid according to the FTC. Thus, in the Summit/VISX pool there were only two licensors, while in the MPEG-2 pool there were several licensors detached from the party setting up the pool. The Summit/VISX patent pool had 25 patents (7 for Summit and 18 patents for VISX). The patent that the FTC found to have been invalid was later upheld by the PTO and the FTC then reopened the case and dismissed it.

Interestingly, several researchers have analysed and raised critiques against the FTC for its handling of this case. There have been indications that there actually was a patent thicket in the market. Clarkson, for example, has analysed the patents in the markets, their citations and the

---

[171] In re Summit Tech. Inc., 127 F.T.C. 208 (1998), In re VIXS Inc., 127 F.T.C. 136 (1999).

extent to which they overlap the technology in the pool.[172] Shapiro and Newberg have also discussed this case.[173] It clearly shows that to find a cartel, the FTC or a plaintiff need to show that the market is able to hold several technologies at once, and that these technologies are not blocking.

Patent thicket is used as a basis for a more lenient antitrust treatment of patent pools and other related agreements under *de jure* or *de facto* standards. It would seem important to be able to determine when such thickets are indeed present and how severe they are. Possibly, the existence of only a few blocking patents should suggest to firms that they cross-license these patents and not set up a pool. The economic literature offers a variety of measures that might be used in quantifying and measuring thickets. They are mathematical (Ziedonis 2004, Siebert and Von Graeventz 2008) but there are also, as Clarkson's are, more visual. It should be noticed that these methods have also been discussed under EU competition law.[174]

The Summit/VISX pool is also an example of a pool where the market possibly held several standards (so-called product or design standards), but there was a patent thicket so, possibly, it was actually a C standard.

BOX 5.2

As stated above, there was a debate that revolved around the notion of buyer cartels and collective monopsony dominant firms under SDOs.[175] A single patentee can be exposed to a buyer cartel (monopsony) in the form of collaboration under an

[172] Gavin Clarkson and David DeKorte, 'The Problem of Patent Thicket in Convergent Technologies', (2006) *Ann. N.Y. Acad. Sci.* 1093, 180, 193 et seq; Gavin Clarkson, 'Patent Informatics for Patent Thicket Detection: A Network Analytic Approach for Measuring the Density of Patent Space', (in a working paper presented at New York University, 2005), 24

[173] Carl Shapiro, 'Navigating the Patent Thicket: Cross Licenses, Patent Pools and Standard Setting', in Adam Jaffe et al. (eds), *Innovation Policy and the Economy,* (MIT Press, 2001); Joshua Newberg, 'Antitrust, Patent Pools, and the Management of Uncertainty', (2000) 3 *Atlantic Law Journal*, 1.

[174] Pierre Regibeau and Katharine Rockett, 'Assessment of Potential Anti-competitive Conduct in the Field of Intellectual Property Rights and Assessment of the Interplay Between Competition Policy and IPR Protection', in COMP/2010/16 (European Union, 2011), 12 et seq.

[175] Cf., e.g., Robert A. Skitol, 'Buyer Power and Antitrust: Concerted Buying Power: Its Potential For Addressing the Patent Holdup Problem in Standard Setting', (2005) 72 *Antitrust Law Journal*, 727.

SDO.[176] That a patentee needs to *ex ante* reveal his licensing terms or even agree to some licensing terms under the threat that the SDO will change the technology standard and make his innovation superfluous might, of course, be interpreted as a buyer cartel.[177] It would also diminish innovation incentives for smaller firms.[178] As discussed early on in this book, there was a discussion that PAEs were actually victims of buyer cartels or monopsonies, because mainly vertically integrated (telecommunications) firms collectively tried to reduce the royalty rate by colluding under the provisions of FRAND. This discussion also involved the meaning of FRAND. The difference between the telecom situation that these articles related to and the cases above is the infrastructure character of the relevant telecom standards. GSM and UNMTS (3G) standards are both interoperability and infrastructure standards, which need to be accessible by product manufacturers, while, for example, *Standard Sanitary* and *Macaroni* are standards which *de facto* limited choice in an effort to create cartels in markets which were able to hold different products.[179] However, possibly this line of argument could be used if the standard is a D standard. Thus a design or product standard can be hijacked by certain firms by creating a very broad standard and trying to 'collect' competing technologies under grant-back clauses and get them inside the FRAND jurisdiction by increasing the scope of the standard. This may be considered an antitrust harm if the patentee can show that membership and adherence to FRAND is essential to participate in the relevant market. However, such a line of

[176] Mark Lemley, 'Intellectual Property Rights and Standard-Setting Organizations', (2002) 90 *California Law Review*, 1889, 1900, 1939 et seq.

[177] Several authors argue that SDOs should be allowed to negotiate with holders of essential patents. Cf., e.g., Mark Patterson, 'Inventions, Industry Standards, and Intellectual Property', (2002) 17 *Berkeley Technology Law Journal*, 1043, 1078 et seq.

[178] For a general discussion regarding oligopsony and SDOs, cf. Robert A. Skitol, 'Buyer Power and Antitrust: Concerted Buying Power: Its Potential For Addressing the Patent Holdup Problem in Standard Setting', (2005) 72 *Antitrust Law Journal*, 727, 735 et seq.

[179] Geradin seems to have mainly had this view: see Damien Geradin, 'Standardization and Technological Innovation: Some Reflections on Ex-ante Licensing, FRAND, and the Proper Means to Reward Innovators', (2006) 29 *World Competition*, 511; Damien Geradin et al., Elves or Trolls? The Role of Non-Practicing Patent Owners in the Innovation Economy (SSRN 2008).

argument would probably only work for D. standards and not A, B or C standards.

In conclusion, collusion can materialize both in the technical market and the downstream product markets. Thus, when setting up a standard and a pool, the members need to take into consideration, first, whether the technology they are standardizing is in a market which holds several technologies and, secondly, whether there is a patent thicket.

5.5.5 Price Discrimination and Marginal Squeeze

Collusion and exclusion mainly deal with markets and standardization agreements where more than one technology or product prevails on the market, but discrimination in price and marginal squeeze may suffice also under a patent pool for other forms of standards. The reason for that is that these antitrust harms need two markets, and while the technology market may only hold one solution for the demand, the downstream market may hold different products and thus be competitive. Therefore, price discrimination and marginal squeeze may be tools for excluding competitors in the downstream markets.

The new TT Guidelines mention the interface between the IP Guides or IP arrangements under SDOs and patent pools stipulating that agreement on royalty rates is benign. The Commission come as close as you can to acknowledging the interface between standard setting, patent pools and the agreement on price for the technologies developed.

There is also a discussion regarding FRAND and the price discrimination inherent in a patent pool. It seems clear that a pool may have different royalty rates for different markets. However, to avoid the risk of discriminating on price, licensees active on the same relevant market as a patentee should have the same or similar royalty rates under a pool. This seems to be the consensus notion both under RAND[180] and FRAND[181]. The Commission states in the new TT Guidelines that the treatment of licensees should not depend on whether they are also licensors. The Commission will take account of whether licensors and licensees are subject to the same royalty rates, but that is easier said than done.

---

[180] Daniel A. Crane, 'Patent Pools, RAND Commitments, and the Problematics of Price Discrimination', *Cardozo School of Law Working Paper* (2008) no. 232, 13.

[181] Cf. TT Guidelines, paras. 225 et seq.

Under both US Antitrust law and EU competition law, price discrimination may constitute an antitrust violation. Price discrimination that could even be interpreted as a marginal squeeze under EU competition law. It seems actually that price discrimination under US antitrust law and prize squeeze under EU competition law is similar, as regards the effect the plaintiff needs to show. The EU price discrimination (or selective low pricing) rule under both Art 101 and 102 TFEU may actually go beyond the US equivalent, since it is seems there is a need, under US antitrust law, to show that the pool (or licensors) are competing with the licensee allegedly being discriminated against.[182] Such requirement is not present under, for example, Art 102 (c) TFEU.

The Union Courts and the Commission have interpreted 'competitively disadvantaged' widely, applying Article 102(c) (and presumably also Art 101(d)) TFEU to situations where customers compete (and even where they do not compete). Where customers compete, the effect of favouring one customer over another pricewise, and thereby increasing that particular customer's competitiveness compared to other customers, would eventually lead to the exclusion of non-favoured customers.[183] Where downstream customers do not compete (i.e. because they operate in different markets), the effect of price discrimination is truly exploitative.[184] Thus, it seems that the price discrimination offence under EU Competition law may go further than the US equivalent and also include situations where a pool has different royalties for licensees that are active on the same downstream market, irrespective of whether a patentee is active on that market or not. This would also correspond to the text in the new TT Guidelines that indicates that under FRAND a pool may still charge different royalties for the same patent portfolio, depending on which downstream market the licensees are active on.[185]

---

182 See Amicus Curiae brief of F.M. Scherer in Support of Respondent, 2005 WL 2427642 (Sept. 28, 2005) and Brief of Barry Nalebuff, Ian Ayres & Lawrence Sullivan as Amici Curiae in Support of Respondent, 2005 WL 2427646 (Sept.28, 2005), both briefs submitted in Illinois Tool Works, Inc. v. Independent Ink, Inc., 547 U.S. 28 (2006).

183 See Case C-163/99 Portugal v Commission [2001] ECR. I-2613; [2002] 4 C.M.L.R. 31, 52 et seq, where the underlying argument is the exclusionary effect on the downstream market.

184 E.g, COMP/38.745 BdKEP – restriction of mail preparation, 20 October 2004 [2006] 4 C.M.L.R. 981, 92 et seq.

185 New TT Guidelines, para. 235.

Under the US price discrimination rule, and under the EU marginal squeeze offence, there is a need to show anti-competitive effect, and that the dominant defendant is active also on the downstream market in competition with the alleged victim. It implies that the pool or the dominant patentee is vertically integrated and is trying to squeeze out a competitor on the downstream market. This is similar to what seems to need to be proven today under the US price discrimination rule when applied to licences (the Robinson-Patman Act is only applicable to commodities).[186] Thus, in both jurisdictions, the plaintiff needs to show that the incremental margin for the pool (the dominant entity) between incremental cost and revenues is less than the royalty rate charged to the licensees.[187] Of course, this is very difficult calculation for a plaintiff to prove. In fact, several economists have tried to create a price test.[188] However, as Crane noticed, these mechanisms have flaws, and in practice may be very difficult to apply.[189]

In addition, the notion of each market only having one 'monopoly profit' prevails with the Chicago school of economics. Price discrimination cannot have an anti-competitive effect because there is only one monopoly profit available and, thus, having monopolists vertically integrated does not necessarily imply that prices will increase. Perhaps, the same theory can be used for patent pools: there are perhaps no anti-competitive effects in excluding competitors from downstream markets, or discriminating against them, if the licensor is able to charge such monopoly royalties under the pool . The prices for consumers will stay the same while all profit will wind up with the patentee.

Furthermore, it is difficult to apply the doctrine of the marginal squeeze or price discrimination to a pool since the different licensors perhaps use different techniques for charging licensees and/or their own manufacturing units down the vertical line. Moreover, what about intent? As regards, exclusionary conduct under standards, there seem to be, in the old line of case law, a need for a plaintiff, at least under US law, to

---

[186] Daniel A. Crane, 'Patent Pools, RAND Commitments, and the Problematics of Price Discrimination', *Cardozo School of Law Working Paper* (2008) no. 232, 17, with references.

[187] Ibid.

[188] Daniel Swanson and William Baumol, 'Reasonable and Nondiscriminatory (RAND) Royalties, Standards Selection, and Control of Market Power', (2005) 73 *Antitrust Law Journal*, 1.

[189] Daniel A. Crane, 'Patent Pools, RAND Commitments, and the Problematics of Price Discrimination', *Cardozo School of Law Working Paper* (2008) no. 232, 15.

show bad intent, i.e. conspiracy to exclude.[190] Is that possible in relation to a pool with several patentees?

Thus, irrespective of what the EU Commission states in the new TT Guidelines, patent pools and licensors may very well face allegations of price discrimination and, even, collective price squeeze. However, it may be difficult for a plaintiff to prove price discrimination under US law, or marginal squeeze under EU law in practice. Perhaps, price discrimination under EU law is easier to prove. If two licensees active on the same market receive different royalty rates then, possibly, there may be price discrimination, irrespective of whether one of them is also a patentee, or not.

5.6 CONCLUDING REMARKS

The application of antitrust law by the US and EU is similar vis-a-vis patent pools. Nonetheless, the EU Commission has clearly taken the initiative in the new chapter in the TT Guidelines. The difference between the old chapter and the new is not radical, but there are some differences. It is important to note, which the new TT Guidelines do, that patent pools as well as IP arrangements and IP policies under SDOs, generally, cater for one issue. The whole jurisprudence is soaked in the idea that PAEs must be forced to license their SEPs on FRAND terms, and that injunctions should be prevented as far as possible. In fact, patent pools seem to be very attractive vehicles because they, under certain circumstances, actually provide high prices. But, this is merely the price for PAEs not to enforce their patents.

Patent pools will probably soon fall into obliviousness. Not because they do not harbour collusive effects, but rather because the safe harbours are large. In fact, the safe harbours and the pools that fit them are the price to be paid for failed IP law systems with too many narrow patents of low quality. Above all, the problems of patent hold-up and patent ambush under technology standards, and the terms on which essential patents should be made available, have attracted far more interest from

---

[190] See discussion supra Chapter 4.1.4 and Hovenkamp's analysis regarding intent under standardization agreements.

the courts and the agencies.[191] These cases and investigations concern mainly Sec. 2 of the Sherman Act, Art. 5 of the FTC Act and Art. 102 TFEU and will be discussed below.

[191] There are of course exceptions: cf. Rudi Bekkers et al., 'Patent pools and non assertion agreements: Coordination mechanisms for multi-partty IRP holders in standardisation', in, EASST 2006 Conference 2006). [The document is on file with the author.]; Rudi Bekkers, et al., 'Case studies on the interface between research and standardisation, and case studies on patent pools as a coordination mechanism', (INTEREST consortium Priority 8 No. Contract 503 594, EU 6th Specific Targeted Research Project, 2006), 1 et seq. [The document is on file with the author]; Gil Ohana et al., 'Disclosure and Negotiation of Licensing Terms Prior to Adoptation of Industry Standards: Preventing another Patent Ambush', (2003) 24 *E.C.L.R,* 644; Michael Schallop, 'The IPR Paradox: Leveraging Intellectual Property Rights to Encourage Interoperability in the Network Computing Age', (2000) 28 *AIPLY Quarterly Journal*, 195; Nari Lee, 'Patented Standards and the Tragedy of Anti-commons', (2006) *Teollisoikeudellisia Kirjoituksia* VII, 1 et seq.; Hanns Ullrich, 'Patente, Wettbewerb, under technische Normen: Recht- und ordnungspolitische Fragestellungen', (2007) 10 *GRUR* 2007, 817; John Barton, 'Antitrust Treatment of Oligopolies with Mutual Blocking Patent Portfolios', (2002) 69 *Antitrust Law Journal*, 851; Maurits Dolmans, 'Standards For Standards', (2002) 26 *Fordham International Law Journal*, 163; Mark Lemley, 'Intellectual Property Rights and Standard-Setting Organizations', (2002) 90 *California Law Review*, 1889. Carl Shapiro, 'Setting Compatibility Standards: Cooperation or Collusion?', in Rochelle Dreyfuss et al. (eds), *Expanding The Boundaries of Intellectual Property* (Oxford University Press, 2001), 119 et seq.; and also, generally, Hanns Ullrich, 'Patent Pools – Policy and Problems', in Josef Drexl (ed), *Research Handbook on Intellectual Property and Competition Law* (Edward Elgar, 2008), 139 et seq.

6. Unilateral conduct under standards

6.1 THE EARLY PATENT AMBUSH INCIDENTS

One of the first 'patent ambush' incidents that came to the authorities' attention with reference to the 'new economy' seems to have been *In re Dell.*[1] The FTC action against Dell Computers arose out of Dell's membership of the Video Electronics Standards Association (VESA), an SSO comprising computer hardware and software manufacturers. Dell, together with the other members of the SSO, approved a new technology standard for computers (VL-Bus), certifying that the standard did not infringe any of its intellectual property rights. The bus carries information between the computer's central processing unit and the computer's peripheral devices such as a hard-disk drive, a video-display terminal, or a modem. Once the new standard was successfully incorporated and implemented, Dell informed certain VESA members that, by manufacturing computers under the standard, they violated certain patent rights held by Dell. Hence, they needed to enter into a licence agreement with Dell or face the risk of an injunction from the courts. The FTC alleged that Dell's practices constituted unfair competition in violation of Sec. 5 of the FTC Act. Dell entered into a consent order, agreeing not to enforce its patent rights against the standard.[2]

In the following *Re Union Oil Company of California*[3] ('Unocal'), the FTC alleged that in communications with the California Air Resources Board (CARB) and private parties, Unocal failed to disclose that it held pending patent applications that could be relevant to the emission standards and requirements it was promoting for adoption. According to

[1] In re Dell. 121 F.T.C. 616, 616 et seq. (1996) (resolved by consent order.). There are also examples of cases before the in re Dell: Wang Labs, Inc. v. Mitsubishi Elecs. America, Inc. 103 F3d 1571 (Fed. Cir.), cert denied, 522 U.S. 818 (1997).

[2] James B. Kobak, 'Standard Setting, IP and Antitrust', in Practising Law Institute (ed), *Patents, Copyrights, Trademarks, and Literary Property Course Handbook Series; Intellectual Property Antitrust* (2006), 15 et seq.

[3] In re Union Oil Company of California ('Unocal'), Docket No. 9305 (July 7, 2004).

the FTC's complaint, Unocal's misrepresentations induced CARB to adopt standards that Unocal was advocating and the refining industry invested accordingly to comply with the new standard.[4] Once the standards were in place, Unocal announced its patent rights and its intent to enforce them. Several oil companies unsuccessfully attempted to invalidate the patents and were ordered to pay damages to Unocal and take out licences.[5] The FTC charged Unocal with monopolizing, and attempting to monopolize, the production and supply of gasoline under the CARB standard in violation of Sec. 5 of the FTC Act. Unocal contended that because CARB was a state agency, its actions were immunized by the Noerr-Pennington doctrine. The Administrative Law Judge (ALJ) agreed, classifying CARB's rule-making proceedings as legislative and dismissing the complaint. On appeal, the FTC unanimously reinstated the complaint.[6]

According to the FTC, false petitioning, involving misrepresentations in governmental communications, loses the Noerr-Pennington protection when the petitioning occurs outside the political arena, the misrepresentation is deliberate, factually verifiable, and central to the outcome of the proceeding or case, and it is possible to demonstrate and remedy this effect without undermining the integrity of the deceived governmental entity.[7] In the end, the FTC agreed to two linked consent orders, resolving its monopolization claim against Unocal and any antitrust concerns arising from Chevron Corporation's pending acquisition of Unocal. Chevron agreed, upon acquiring Unocal, not to enforce its patents, which could have potentially increased California gas prices by in excess of $500 million per year.[8]

These early cases show the problem of patent ambush quite well. It deals with a member of an SSO that omits to transfer the information to the SSO of an SEP, and when the standard has been adopted, and the

---

[4] Ibid. James B. Kobak, 'Standard Setting, IP and Antitrust', in Practising Law Institute (ed), *Patents, Copyrights, Trademarks, and Literary Property Course Handbook Series; Intellectual Property Antitrust* (2006), 15 et seq.

[5] Ibid.

[6] Ibid.

[7] In re Union Oil Company of California ('Unocal'), Docket No. 9305 (July 7, 2004). Ibid.

[8] Statement of the Federal Trade Commission, In the Matter of Union Oil Company of California, Docket No. 9305, and Chevron/Unocal, File No. 051-0125, available at http://www.ftc.gov/os/adjpro/d9305/050610statement9305.pdf. See James B. Kobak, Jr. and Robert P. Reznick, 'Antitrust Liability for Statements About Intellectual Property: Unocal, Unitherm, and New Uncertainty', *Antitrust* 87 (2004) (discussing possible implications of Unocal decision).

members and other firms have invested in it, the patentee emerges and, knowing the exit cost will be large, charges a royalty rate that reflects both the exit costs and the value of the standard as such, while the patent may only cover a small part of the standardized technology.

The initial issue for the courts to deal with was whether the ambush situation may constitute monopolization or attempt to monopolize under Sec. 2 Sherman Act (or under Sec. 5 FTC Act). However, other issues arose soon after. First, what if a SEP holder, which has committed to FRAND, transfers the relevant patents? Should a transferee or purchaser of the patents also be bound by the FRAND commitments? Secondly, should holders of standard essential patents be allowed to make use of injunctions at all? Thus, even though the SEP holder did not carry out an abuse in the form of a patent ambush, and even committed to FRAND, may it still utilize injunctions based on the SEP to exclude an infringer and thereby eliminate competition? Thirdly, what is 'essential' in reference to a standard? Is it technical essentiality or economic essentiality? Fourthly, how should FRAND be defined and given meaning? What is FRAND on a case-by-case basis? It seems clear that some firms even though committing to FRAND demand royalties that are considered supra-FRAND. Finally, some firms have started to argue that there is a problem of "reverse FRAND ambush" that is taking root in the telecom sector. These issues have intrigued courts and academia for quite some time and are especially topical given the current 'patent war' being played out in courts in several jurisdictions.

It is clear that US and EU law is developing differently in this area in a quite remarkable way. In the USA, the problems described above have been addressed mainly under intellectual property law and by the FTC as unfair competition under Art. 5 of the FTC Act. European courts and the EU Commission have mainly utilized EU competition law to give efficient access to SEPs. In fact, the US courts have avoided taking antitrust action to the point where they have devalued the strength of US intellectual property law to a degree that is hard to imagine in light of the Federal Circuit's push for stronger intellectual property rights in the 1990s. The law is, thus, in a state of flux and the aim of this chapter is to discuss the current state of the law and to make some suggestions about how the law is and should be developing, both in the EU and in the US. As a start, before the four topics above are discussed, the issue of dominance by the patentee will be examined, an issue which also displays a divide between the application of antitrust law in the EU and the US.

6.2 DOMINANCE UNDER US ANTITRUST LAW AND EU COMPETITION RULES

The issue of dominance is much more important under EU competition law than under US antitrust law. Under EU competition law a plaintiff needs to show that the alleged perpetrator of the abuse, i.e. the defendant/undertaking, holds a dominant position on a relevant market. Only after dominance has been established will, normally, the EU courts look into the issue whether there has been an abuse.

Under US antitrust law, a showing of dominant position is not entirely necessary. Sec. 2 of the Sherman Act (and Sec. 5 of the FTC Act) applies to conduct by a single firm to acquire, create or maintain a dangerous probability of creating monopoly power. Even the attempt to monopolize is, under certain circumstances, considered to be an antitrust violation.[9]

The question is whether the added requirement of dominance hinders the effective response of EU competition law to the conduct of patent ambush. Theoretically, it might pose a genuine threshold. A patentee that chooses to utilize a business strategy of patent ambush would conduct R&D mirroring the standard-setting discussion in the technical committee, or might already have a patent that the patentee would like to be included in the standard. The alleged abuse would presumably be that the patentee, first, does not let the chairman of the technical committee know about the patent or the patent application. Secondly, the lobbying to get the committee to agree to a standard that fits the patentees (confidential) patent may be regarded as an abuse in itself. The technical committee and the SDO would thereafter adopt the standard, and, after a period of time, when the industry has accepted it, the patentee would reveal the patent and demand high royalty rates. The quirk here is the issue that the alleged abuse (amongst other things, not telling the chairman of the technical committee of the SEP) took place when the patentee was in all

[9] Spectrum Sports v. McQuillan, 506 U.S. 447, 456 (1993). The notion of dominance with reference to patents has also been an issue under US antitrust law. A patentee has for several decades been presumed to be dominant with reference to the ambit of the patent in certain cases under Sec. 2 of the Sherman Act. This was not formally overruled until *Illinois Tool Works, Inc. v. Independent Ink*, in 2006, where a unanimous Supreme Court overruled the idea of a presumption of dominance on the behalf of the patentee in reference to tying. Nonetheless, in the patent ambush situations described above, proving either dominance or that the patentee, at least, holds enough market power to attempt to monopolize seems fairly straight forward: Illinois Tool Works, Inc. v. Independent Ink, Inc., 547 U.S. 28 (2006).

likelihood not dominant. The patentee's dominance will at the earliest materialize when the standard is adopted. Or, more probable, when a relevant market for the standard can be detected. Under an 'orthodox' application of EU competition law, this is no violation since it is in the reverse order. Abuse happens before dominance and not the other way around.[10]

The EU system has tried to circumvent this problem. First, the Commission started elaborating the notion of dominance in these circumstances. The EU Commission went out on a limb when scrutinizing Google's purchase of Motorola's standard essential patents in 2012.[11] The Commission held that an SEP must be deemed a separate market in itself, as a patentee's competitors have no alternative in complying with the standard but to use the innovation covered by the SEP.[12] It seems that the Commission thereby equates holding an SEP with holding a dominant position. *Ipso facto*, owning an SEP would imply enjoying market power, without the need to actually establish a relevant market in the first place. That the Commission reached this conclusion is not surprising given the earlier press releases and settlement agreements regarding *Rambus* and *IPCom*.[13] Nonetheless, it was interesting to see the Commission making its statement so clearly.

Secondly, the EU Commission can also make use of the exploitative abuse of excessive pricing, or the 'unfair terms' doctrine. In the scenario above, the patentee may, when charging monopoly royalties, be abusing its dominant position by charging excessive prices for the SEPs. While the excessive pricing abuse has not been used for a long time, and was by some considered to be almost extinct, it has had a revival under the patent ambush scenario.[14]

Excessive pricing is however an awkward tool to use. What is the available remedy? Everyone agrees that the anti-competitive harm originated from the patentee not letting the SDO know about the SEP. This is the misuse conducted by the patentee, but that harm cannot be remedied by a finding of excessive pricing. If the technical committee had been granted the knowledge of the SEP, they would perhaps changed the standard so as not to cover the SEP, or demanded FRAND or even zero

---

[10] There are cases in the borderline, cf. Bellamy and Child, *European Union Law of Competition* (Oxford University Press, 2013), 756.

[11] Commission decision Case No COMP/M.6381 Google/Motorola Mobility, 13.02.2012.

[12] Google/Motorola decision, para. 61.

[13] See discussion infra.

[14] Ibid.

royalty, or, in rare circumstances, allowed for the patentee to charge what it might find appropriate. What remedy should the court use? A finding of excessive pricing implies that the patentee needs to lower the royalty rate only enough for it not to be considered excessive. This is often a low threshold and does not really remedy the abuse in the case. Several researchers have discussed the use and limits of the excessive pricing abuse in these circumstances. Can it be used for all kinds of standards, or even, generally, when there is a finding of market failure so that dynamic competition by substitute does not work?[15] Under such circumstances a FRAND commitment may be a 'special responsibility' for the dominant firm, while still the dominant firm may refute such responsibility with a dynamic efficiency defence, i.e. that on balance innovation is promoted on the relevant market without FRAND commitments.

Thirdly, the abuse consisting of refusal to license may become applicable in these circumstances. In *IMS Health* and *Microsoft*, the CJEU indicated that in exceptional circumstances, access to intellectual property rights might be granted under EU competition law. Perhaps, we should define patent ambush as a 'exceptional circumstance' that may cause access to SEPs on FRAND terms.[16] Even though it seems that there are abuses under EU competition law that could cover 'patent ambush', it seems that the EU Commission would like to establish that patent ambush is not beneficial business conduct. Thus, patent ambush as a business strategy is not 'competition on the merits' and is an abuse in itself. Perhaps, the EU Commission like to argue that patent ambush is one of those 'exceptional circumstances' where access to patents may be granted under EU Competition law on fair terms. Patent ambush is a stand-alone abuse but belongs to the same class of abuses (exceptional circumstances) as displayed in *IMS Health* and *Microsoft*.

Nonetheless, under US antitrust law, establishing that patent ambush is an anti-competitive harm and that such conduct which should be addressed under antitrust law is much more important, since neither

---

[15] Cf. Andreas Fuchs, 'Patent ambush strategies and Article 102 TFEU' in Josef Drexl et al (eds), *More Common Ground For International Competition Law?* (Edward Elgar, 2011), 177 et seq. Compare Josef Drexl, 'Intellectual property in competition: How to promote dynamic competition as a goal' in Josef Drexl et al (eds), *More Common Ground For International Competition Law?* (Edward Elgar, 2011), 210 et seq.

[16] In fact, it could be a from of constructive refusal to license, cf. EU Commission Guidance on the Commission's enforcement priorities in applying Article 82 of the EC Treaty to abusive exclusionary conduct by dominant undertakings, OJ C 45, 24/02/2009, 7 para. 79.

refusal to license nor excessive pricing are stand-alone violations of the Sherman Act.

6.3 PATENT AMBUSH

6.3.1 The US *Qualcomm* Cases

In 2007, Qualcomm was counter-sued in a patent infringement case in a District Court in California by Broadcom for misconduct before standard-setting bodies (SDOs), including improperly concealing its patents, reneging on licensing obligations, and exerting dominance through hidden affiliations.[17] The complaint alleged that Qualcomm had engaged in a pattern of misconduct across multiple standard bodies, including ETSI, and especially the bodies responsible for setting mobile cellular, video, and broadband standards globally. Qualcomm had allegedly both not revealed SEPs to SDOs, revealed and agreed to license other SEPs to FRAND, but then refused to license or only licensed the SEPs at royalty rates which allegedly did not match the FRAND commitments. Broadcom claimed that this misconduct constituted fraud, breach of contract, and violation of California's unfair competition statute.[18]

The District Court found in favour of Broadcom and held Qualcomm's patents unenforceable against the world, based on the equitable doctrine of waiver. Qualcomm appealed the ruling to the Court of Appeals for the Federal Circuit; the Federal Circuit limited the District Court's remedy by finding the patents unenforceable except for practising the specific standard (H.264 video compression standard).[19] The Federal Circuit thus held that since Qualcomm knew (i) that the IP policy under the relevant SDO (ETSI) required disclosure of relevant patents, but (ii) acted to shield its relevant patents from disclosure, and (iii) planned to extract royalties from the downstream manufactures of the standard compliant products, its misconduct warranted an application of the equitable doctrine of implied waiver as regards all products manufactured under

---

17 Qualcomm Inc. v. Broadcom Corp. 548 F.3d 1004 (Fed. Cir. 2008).

18 Ibid.

19 Ibid, 1009–10 (Fed. Cir. 2008).

the standard.[20] Thus, Qualcomm was not allowed to demand permanent injunctions based on these SEPs nor charge royalty for the same.

Using similar facts as in the case above, Broadcom also separately brought an action for antitrust violation under Sec. 2 of the Sherman Act in the District of New Jersey.[21] On appeal to the United States Court of Appeals for the Third Circuit, the case presented important questions regarding whether a patent holder's deceptive conduct before a SDO (ETSI) could be condemned under antitrust laws and, if so, what facts had to be pleaded to survive a motion to dismiss. Broadcom alleged that the patent owner, by its intentional deception of private SDOs and its predatory acquisition of a potential rival, monopolized certain markets for cellular telephone technology and components, in violation of the Sherman Act.[22]

The Third Circuit in the end held that (i) in a consensus-oriented private standard-setting environment, (ii) a patent holder's intentionally false promise to license essential proprietary technology on fair, reasonable, and non-discriminatory (FRAND) terms, (iii) coupled with a standards-determining organization's (SDO's) reliance on that promise when including the technology in a standard, (iv) the patent holder's subsequent breach of that promise is actionable anti-competitive conduct and thereafter remanded the case to the District Court where the parties in the end settled.[23]

For the commentators who had argued for the application of antitrust law (and a combination of estoppels and patent misuse doctrine) to patent ambush conduct, this case law development was promising. The US courts seem to see and understand the problems of patent ambush and more generally regard 'standard-setting misuse' as an antitrust violation also in the 'new economy'.[24] However, the *Rambus* saga ended the promising antitrust case law development under US law.[25]

---

[20] Joel M. Wallace, 'Rambus v. F.T.C. in the Context of Standard-Setting Organizations, Antitrust, and the Patent Hold-Up Problem', (2009) 24 *Berkley Technology Law Journal*, 661, chapter 3.

[21] Broadcom Corp. v. Qualcomm Inc., No. 05-3350, 2006 WL 2528545 (D.N.J. Aug. 31, 2006).

[22] Broadcom v. Qualcomm Inc. 501 F.3d. 297 (3d Cir. 2007).

[23] Ibid.

[24] See generally Daryl Lim, 'Misconduct in Standard Setting: The Case for Patent Misuse', (2011) 51 IDEA: The Journal of Law and Technology, 557.

[25] Rambus, Inc. v. F.T.C. 522 F.3d 456 (D.C. Cir 2008), cert denied.

6.3.2 The *Rambus* Case

In *Rambus*, the FTC investigated Rambus for unfair competition and unfair deceptive acts or practices in violation of Sec. 5 FTC Act and Sec. 2 Sherman Act. FTC alleged that Rambus had violated the US antitrust laws by not letting the concerned SDO know about its patents and also by amending patent applications in the accordance with the discussion in the technical committee so as to fit them in with the description of the standard as it was presented to Rambus while it still was a member of the relevant SDO. Rambus' conduct increased its acquisition of monopoly power according to the FTC. The FTC, in the end, found that Rambus should license its essential patents for reasonable royalty rates.[26]

Rambus appealed and the D.C. Circuit found Rambus arguments persuasive and set aside the Commission's order.[27] The Court primarily raised the bar or burden of proof for the plaintiff in patent ambush cases. A plaintiff needs to show that the SDO would have selected another technology because of the nondisclosure or deceptive behaviour of the defendant, but did not. This is a heavy burden. Furthermore, the court, based on the notion that Rambus might possibly have been allowed to hold a lawful monopoly, used the *NYNEX* case[28], regarding deceptive pricing behaviour for exclusion of competitors, rather than the *Microsoft* case regarding deceptive behaviour to gain a monopoly position. By utilizing the *NYNEX* case, the threshold for FTC to show abuse was set higher. The court also stressed that Rambus did not violate the by-laws of the SDO, implicitly making the by-laws the benchmark for when an antitrust violation occurs.[29]

In the end, the D.C. Circuit found that (i) that there was not enough evidence to prove that the SDO would have selected a different technology irrespective of Rambus letting them know about its patent ambition; and (ii) Rambus not abiding by FRAND implied no more than an invitation to enter the market for competitors. Charging excessive

---

[26] The FTC challenges In re Rambus, No. 9302 (F.T.C. 2002); In re Rambus, Inc. No. 9302 F.T.C. July 31, 2006) and In re Rambus, Inc. No. 9302 (F.T.C. Feb 2, 2007); In re Dell, 121 F.T.C. 616 (1996) (Resolved by consent order.).

[27] Rambus, Inc. v. F.T.C. 522 F.3d 456 (D.C. Cir 2008), cert denied.

[28] NYNEX Corp. v. Discon, Inc. 525 U.S. 128 (1998).

[29] Joel M. Wallace, 'Rambus v. F.T.C. in the Context of Standard-Setting Organizations, Antitrust, and the Patent Hold-Up Problem', (2009) 24 Berkley Technology Law Journal, 661. The FTC challenges In re Rambus, No. 9302 (F.T.C. 2002); In re Rambus, Inc. No. 9302 F.T.C. July 31, 2006); and In re Rambus, Inc. No. 9302 (F.T.C. Feb 2, 2007).

prices is, thus, not a violation of US antitrust law. It is an invitation for firms to enter the market and compete.

The Rambus saga also had an EU twist.[30] The EU Commission started investigating Rambus under Article 102 TFEU for patent ambush. The case was settled when Rambus agreed to lower its royalty rates. It should be mentioned that neither in the US cases nor with the Commission did Rambus deny that it held a dominant position. Thus, the EU *Rambus* case seems to have been based on, at least in part, a theory of excessive pricing as anti-competitive harm.

Irrespective of the D.C. Circuit's *Rambus* case, there seem to be, almost, a general consensus among jurists and economists specializing in standards that patent ambush tactics, when patentees and members of SSOs conceal their intellectual property rights before a standard is agreed upon, is not 'competition on the merits', rather a misuse of the standard-setting procedure. Many see a danger in the D.C. Circuit ruling in *Rambus* and the strains it put on SDOs and the standard-setting procedure if the burden of proof is set as high as the D.C. Court now seems to have placed it. It is difficult, to say the least, to show that another technology would have been adopted or enacted 'but for' the confidential essential patents. The danger is that the whole standard-setting system is threatened if the *Rambus* is considered a precedent. Firms will not engage in efficient innovative standard-setting procedures and share new knowledge if there is a risk that other firms will act like Rambus did in the case and engage in patent ambush.

The D.C. Circuit furthermore makes a connection between violating the SDO's by-laws and violating competition law. According to *Allied Tube*, The Supreme Court seems to state that a Court may still identify an antitrust violation even though the by-laws have not been violated, as long as the by-laws have been misused. Given the simplicity and under development of the by-laws discussed in the *Rambus* case, and generally with SDOs, the D.C. Circuit should also have left room for the establishment of violation of antitrust law when members of SDOs do not abide by business or commercial customary norms established in the SDO in question, or perhaps more generally. For example, the notion of patent ambush seems now accepted as a misuse of the standard-setting

---

[30] See press release form 9 December 2009, http://europa.eu/rapid/press-release_IP-09-1897_en.htm, accessed 13 July 2013. The EU commission also during this time went public and stated that it concurred with the DOJ regarding the benefits with IP Policies generally and ex ante unilateral statements of licensing terms. Press Release IP/09/1897, 09.12.2009 and Speech by Neelie Kroes, SPEECH/09/575, date 09.12.2009.

procedures which is not to be tolerated. Such a misuse should be capable of being established under antitrust law if the members of the relevant SDO agreed that patent ambush is not acceptable behaviour, whether or not the text of the by-laws of the SDO in question is 'muddy'. The courts should make independent evaluations under antitrust law to find antitrust harm and conduct, of which patent ambush could be one, irrespective of the stipulations in the by-laws of the SDO.[31] In fact, antitrust courts could even take a further step: an *SDO* not stipulating clear rules regarding patent ambush may conduct an antitrust violation by itself.[32]

6.3.3 The EU *Qualcomm* Case

As an appetizer for the patent war to come, Qualcomm and Nokia in 2007 started litigation in the USA and Europe.[33]

Nokia refused to pay the high royalty rates Qualcomm demanded for its essential patents under the 3G-telecommunication standards. Qualcomm sued Nokia for patent infringement in several jurisdictions. This led to complaints by both Qualcomm and Nokia to the US International Trade Commission (ITC) and by Nokia and five other vendors of telecommunication equipment to the European Commission for Qualcomm abusing its dominant position.[34]

---

[31] Joel M. Wallace, 'Rambus v. F.T.C. in the Context of Standard-Setting Organizations, Antitrust, and the Patent Hold-Up Problem', (2009) 24 *Berkley Technology Law Journal*, 661, Section 4.

[32] Mark Lemley and Carl Shapiro, 'A Simple Approach to Setting Reasonable Royalties for Standard-Essential Patents', (2013) 28 *Berkeley Technology Law Journal*, 1135

[33] Cf. discussion supra, but see also for case law see, e.g., German cases such as LG Dusseldorf, WuW 13.12.2007, helft 12, Seite 1278-1288, DE-R 2120-2130; Dutch cases concerning patent ambush, Vonnis, 11 June 2007 LG Electronics v. Philips, zaaknummer 287026; or English: Sandisk Corp. v. Sisvel et al 2007 EWHC 448.

[34] Regarding Nokia's complaint over Qualcomm to ITC in September 2007, see Press Release http://www.usitc.gov/ext_relations/news_release/2007/er0918ee1.htm. For Qualcomm's complaint over Nokia in July 2006, see http://www.usitc.gov/ext_relations/news_release/2006/er0707dd3.htm. See also EC Commission's Memo/Press Release, MEMO/07/389, dated 1st October 2007 'Commission Initiates Formal Proceedings Against Qualcomm'. On the joint complaint of Nokia, Ericsson, Texas Instruments, Broadcom, NEC and Panasonic, the EU Commission started an investigation into whether Qualcomm was abusing its dominance based on patent rights included in the 3G system since it did not license these rights on Fair, Reasonable, and Non-Discriminatory (FRAND) terms. See also Qualcomm's suit against Nokia for patent infringing,

In 2005, Nokia, Ericsson and Panasonic among others complained to the EU Commission that Qualcomm had abused its dominant position by not adhering to its FRAND commitment under the ETSI IP policy.[35] Qualcomm was accused of refusing to license some firms, especially potential chip set manufacturers, and by charging excessive and discriminating fees for its essential UMTS patents compared to its 3GPP2 patents.[36] In 2007, the EU Commission decided to open an investigation in the matter of Qualcomm.[37]

Nokia and Qualcomm settled their differences during the summer of 2008 and the EU Commission eventually dismantled the investigation into Qualcomm for abuse of dominance, implying that Qualcomm also settled with the other telecommunications firms.[38] Nonetheless, the Nokia and Qualcomm feud was only a taste of what was about to come.

In fact, litigation between SEP holders in the telecom industry and the new firms coming from the IT or software industry, which were starting to produce smart phones, created a demand for purchasing SEPs. The demand was driven by the idea that firms entering the telecom industry needed SEPs or even MAD capability in order to obtain cross-licence agreements with other SEP holders. This raised the issue whether a patentee's FRAND commitment to an SDO was still good when the SEP was transferred to a new owner.

Qualcomm Inc. v. Nokia Corp. 466 F.3d 1366 (Fed. Cir. 2006). See furthermore Broadcom v. Qualcomm Inc. 501 F.3d. 297 (3rd Cir 2007).

[35] Ibid.

[36] Ibid. 128.

[37] See EC Commission's Memo/Press Release, MEMO/07/389, dated 1st October 2007 'Commission initiate formal proceedings against Qualcomm'. On the joint complaint of Nokia, Ericsson, Texas Instruments, Broadcom, NEC and Panasonic, the EU Commission started an investigation whether Qualcomm was abusing its dominance based on patent rights included in the 3G system since it did not license these rights on Fair, Reasonable, and Non-Discriminatory (FRAND) terms.

[38] Regarding the old cases between Qualcomm and Nokia see the somewhat outdated list of mostly the European legal actions: http://www.reuters.com/article/companyNewsAndPR/idUSL1722345120070817. These cases have been dropped after Nokia and Qualcomm reached a settlement in the middle of 2008. See Matt Richtel, 'In Settlement, Nokia Will Pay Royalties to Qualcomm', in, New York Times 24 July 2008). http://www.nytimes.com/2008/07/24/technology/24qualcomm.html?_r=1&scp=1&sq=nokia%20qualcomm&st=cse, accessed 7 April 2009. In October 2007 the EU Commission initiated formal proceedings against Qualcomm. See http://ec.europa.eu/competition/antitrust/cases/decisions/39247/proceedings.pdf. See also Broadcom v. Qualcomm Inc. 501 F.3d. 297 (3d Cir. 2007).

6.4 *IPCOM* AND OTHER CASES CONCERNING THE SALE AND PURCHASE OF SEPS

6.4.1 The Purchasers/Assignees

The issue in the 2009 *IPCom* case[39], which was also to some degree the issue in the *Google/Motorola* case, concerned the purchase of SEPs where the patentee (the assignor) has pledged FRAND to the relevant SDO. This case raised a number of questions: does such a pledge also bind a purchaser of the SEPs under competition law? May a purchaser abide by FRAND and also be required to license under the IP policies of the relevant SDO, when it is not, and was not, a member of the SDO? Furthermore, does an SEP holder need to abide by FRAND vis-à-vis non-SDO members?

In 2007, IPCom acquired the mobile telephony patent portfolio developed by Robert Bosch GmbH (Bosch) between the mid-1980s and 2000, which included patents essential to the GSM and UMTS standards. As a member of the European Telecommunications Standards Institute (ETSI), Bosch took part in the GSM and UMTS (W-CDMA) standard-setting processes. Bosch had declared that it held essential patents in the relevant standards and committed to ETSI 'to grant irrevocable licenses on fair, reasonable and non-discriminatory terms and conditions' for such patents.[40] In 2007, IPCom sued Nokia before the District Court of Mannheim for an amount of EUR 12 billion for infringement. The amount allegedly did not reflect the FRAND promise made by Bosch to ETSI. The case in Mannheim was the start of several cases between these parties, not only in Germany, but also elsewhere.[41]

The EU Commission also got involved and in a press release in 2009, the Commission acknowledged that the transfer of FRAND commitments after the sale of SEPs is important from a competition law perspective. The Commission furthermore 'welcomed' 'the public declaration by German IP licensing company IPCom, following discussions with the

39 See Press release from 10 December 2009, http://europa.eu/rapid/press-release_MEMO-09-549_en.htm., accessed 10 July 2013.

40 Ibid.

41 Nokia seems to have been able to get IPCom to be declared a non-practicing entity and some of its patents to be declared void in the UK. See Bil Ray, 'High Court strikes down IPCom Patents', the *Register*, 19 January 2011. Nokia also seem to have been able to fend off any claims for injunctions in the UK. However, in the end Nokia was considered infringing IPCom's patents in the UK, by a decision in the Court of Appeals 10 May, 2012.

Commission, that it is ready to take over Bosch's previous commitment to grant irrevocable licences on fair, reasonable and non discriminatory (FRAND) terms to patents held by IPCom which are essential for various standards set by the European Telecommunications Standard Institute (ETSI) and Universal Mobile Telecommunications System (UMTS)'.[42] According to the Commission, these are patents that IPCom acquired from Bosch and to which Bosch had previously made such a commitment when the standards in question were developed. The Commission however, publically, refrained from stating that non-compliance with a FRAND commitment made by the assignor/seller would constitute an antitrust violation, or whether Bosch when selling/assigning the SEPs had an antitrust obligation to see to it that the assignee did not charge more than 'the ceiling' imposed by tagging abuse under EU Competition law to the FRAND requirement under the IP Policy. The Commission avoided such a discussion when IPCom committed to licensing on FRAND terms, and the Commission was able to close the investigation.[43]

Around the same time, in 2008, the FTC had the opportunity to analyse a similar case of transferred SEPs a with FRAND commitment, in the *N-Data* case.[44] According to the complaint, Negotiated Data Solutions, LLC (N-Data) had purchased the patents originating with National Semiconductor Corporation (National). National had, however, made a FRAND commitment regarding the patents to IEEE in 1994 that it would offer to license the patents for a onetime fee of USD 1,000. The industry adopted the standard based upon the commitment. National sold the patent to Vertical Networks which began to ask for royalty fees from licensees of the patent exceeding the USD 1,000. Vertical Network then transferred the patent to N-Data. While N-Data purchased the patents knowing about the commitment, it nonetheless demanded royalty fees from the licensees to a level it thought reflected its FRAND. The FTC majority found that this conduct 'could be enormously harmful to standard-setting'. Should N-Data's conduct be accepted business practice,

---

[42] Ibid.

[43] Nonetheless, the close call with the EU Commission did not stop IPCom and Nokia from battling out the notion of FRAND in different courts. At the moment, it seems that the major case in the UK regarding the definition of FRAND royalty is on stay awaiting some cases before the EPO, while Nokia was not granted stay in the case vis-a-vis IPCom to await the ruling of CJEU in the Huawaei v. ZTD case. This case concerns the definition of FRAND, while IPCom was not successful in getting an injunction in the UK, or elsewhere in Europe. Cf. discussion infra Chapter 6.10.

[44] In the Matter of Negotiated Data Solution LLC FTC File No 051 0094.

i.e. purchasers making their own FRAND evaluations, not even the most diligent SSO could rely on the royalty and license commitments made by SEP holders and members.[45]

According to the consent order, N-Data had violated Sec. 5 of the FTC Act by acting unfairly and conducting an unfair method of competition. In other words, the FTC did not find that this violated the Sec. 2 of the Sherman Act, instead N Data's conduct amounted to unfair competition. The FTC thereby opened up Sec. 5 of the FTC Act also to claims outside the more orthodox antitrust doctrine (implying actually that Sec. 5 of the FTC Act goes beyond the Sherman Act).[46] The FTC would later re-establish this dichotomy between the FTC Act and the Sherman Act in the *Google* case. Interestingly, Commissioner Kovacic, dissenting in N-Data, claimed that the reason that the FTC did use Sec. 5 FTC Act in this way was to prevent private suits for treble damage.[47]

Google made a similar FRAND commitment to ETSI and to other SDOs (e.g. IEEE) in 2012 after acquiring Motorola's SEPs portfolio.[48] However, Google's commitment was difficult to interpret. It was not a clean commitment to honour Motorola's pledge to ETSI et al. Nonetheless, the EU Commission viewed it with satisfaction and also stated that Google had in letters to the relevant SDOs agreed to uphold Motorola's FRAND commitment to the SDOs.

The US Justice Department found it less satisfactory.[49] The Justice Department, when scrutinizing the merger, found that Google's possible exercise of its patents in the future remained a significant concern, even though that the acquisition of patents by Google did not substantially lessen competition. In the merger case, both the EU Commission and the Justice Department remained thouroughly vague when it came to the issue of what would happen if Google did not commit to FRAND; would that amount to a violation of competition law?

---

[45] Ibid.

[46] Statement by the majority, In the Matter of Negotiated Data Solution LLC FTC File No 051 0094, 2 referring to FTC v. Ind. Fed'n of Dentists 476 U.S. 477, 454 (1986).

[47] Dissenting Statement by Commissioner William E. Kovacic, In the Matter of Negotiated Data Solution LLC FTC File No 051 0094. For an interesting case also see the Rembrandt case, where the AAI has notified the FTC of a case of different and double FRAND royalties. www.ftc.gov/os/aai.pdf. Accessed 11 July 2013.

[48] Commission decision Case No COMP/M.6381 Google/Motorola Mobility, 13.02.2012.

[49] See statement by the Justice Department from 13 February 2012, http://www.justice.gov/opa/pr/2012/February/12-at-210.html. Accessed 11 July 2013.

The Justice Department was right to be suspicious against Google's FRAND commitment, and soon after the purchase, Google started utilizing the patents in several litigations involving, for example, Microsoft and Apple. The FTC and the EU Commission therefore had to scrutinize the use of FRAND and injunctions again, and specifically Google's FRAND Commitment. The FTC and Google's settlement will be discussed infra, while the EU Commission's investigation into the conduct of Google continues. Notwithstanding this, both antitrust agencies in these investigations seem to take it for granted that Google is bound by a FRAND commitment.

In addition to the above bilateral transactions, there are also transactions where the purchaser is a consortium, with large firms in the ICT sector as members. In 2010, CPT Holding, owned by Microsoft, Oracle, Apple and EMS, acquired a large patent portfolio of Novell. The Justice Department and the German Competition Authority found that the transfer of patents to this consortium could jeopardize the ability of open source software to innovate and compete (e.g. Linux).[50] The transaction was finally cleared after several commitments had been provided. Possibly, the most important being that all patents would be acquired subject to the GNU General Public License (open source licence requirement) and the Open Innovation Network Licence (Linux license requirement).[51]

In a somewhat similar transaction, the consortium Rockstar Bidco (owners of which included Apple, Microsoft, REM, Sony and Ericsson) acquired 6,000 patents from Nortell that were all encompassed by (F)RAND commitments. While the Justice Department did not find that these patents would be used for injunctions or supra-FRAND royalty claims and subsequent cleared the transaction, the Rockstar Consortium (a PAE) was set up based on 2,000 of the patents.[52]

---

[50] This case also shows a gap in the EU Merger Regulation with reference to the transfer of IP.

[51] Justice Department, press release, 20 April 2011 http://www.justice.gov/atr/public/press_releases/2011/270086.htm, accessed 13 October 2011.

[52] Statement of the Department of Justice's Antitrust Division on Its Decision to Close Its Investigations of Google Inc.'s Acquisition of Motorola Mobility Holdings Inc. and the Acquisitions of Certain Patents by Apple Inc., Microsoft Corp. and Research in Motion Ltd. 13 Feburuary 2012, http://www.justice.gov/opa/pr/2012/February/12-at-210.html, accessed 10 June 2012.

6.4.2 The Sellers/Assignors

Few have been scrutinizing, under competition law, the sellers/assignors in reference to transferring SEPs.[53] Clearly, in the *IPCom* case and in the *Motorola/Google* case, the sellers have committed to license the SEPs for FRAND terms. Usually these assignors have entered into cross-license agreements under the successful standards where have they contractually agreed to license their entire relevant patent portfolios on FRAND terms (of, for example, 2 per cent). The firms with MAD capability often combined agreeing to the standard with entering formal cross-licence agreements where their entire portfolios were cross-licensed. However, these agreements did not contain any descriptions of the patents and sometimes did not even identify exactly what patents were enclosed in the cross-license agreements.

If the purchasers/assignees do not abide by the FRAND terms, or even imply that FRAND should be renegotiated in light of their FRAND policy, what can the SDO, a member of the SDO or even a licensee do? May it approach the seller, i.e. the assignor? May transferring SEPs under certain conditions constitute an abuse of dominance/monopolization? What if the assignor knew that the purchaser would engage in litigation so as to obtain monopolistic royalty rates, or even engage in litigation so as to exclude firms from the product market?

Even if the assignor stipulated a 2 per cent royalty rate in its licence agreement, what if the assignor retains some SEPs, still charges 2 per cent and the assignee also claims 2 per cent? Both claim it is FRAND while the licensee went from having a royalty expense of 2 to 4 per cent for the same portfolio. Contractually, perhaps, the licensee may claim any

---

[53] Even though the SDOs relevant IP Policies do indicate the initial declarant obligation when tranferring the SEPs. See for example ETSI IP Guide Art. 61bis stating 'Transfer of ownership of ESSENTIAL IPR FRAND licensing undertakings made pursuant to Clause 6 shall be interpreted as encumbrances that bind all successors-in-interest. Recognizing that this interpretation may not apply in all legal jurisdictions, any Declarant who has submitted a FRAND undertaking according to the POLICY who transfers ownership of ESSENTIAL IPR that is subject to such undertaking shall include appropriate provisions in the relevant transfer documents to ensure that the undertaking is binding on the transferee and that the transferee will similarly include appropriate provisions in the event of future transfers with the goal of binding all successors-in- interest. The undertaking shall be interpreted as binding on successors-in-interest regardless of whether such provisions are included in the relevant transfer documents.'

expenses paid to the assignee from the assignor. However, can the SDO, member of the SDO or even licensees also utilize competition law?[54]

May transferring SEPs with FRAND commitments to a purchaser, knowing that this will increase the costs of the assignor's competitors, be an abuse of dominance? One reason to assign the patents may even be that the purchaser is not a vertically integrated firm, but a PAE, and is not intimidated that the (potential) licensee has reached MAD capability. Thus, if it had been the assignor that initiated the new licence negotiation, the negotiation and possibly the litigation would have come down to both firms claiming injunctions against each other. However, a PAE is not afraid of either injunctions or bad publicity, or of being accused of breaching customary rules and norms of the industry.[55] An assignor may thereby circumvent the cross-licence agreement and the FRAND commitment be transferring the SEPs to litigious third parties, with the aim of increasing costs for, or excluding, competitors. Thus, transferring SEPs to PAEs can be good business not only for the remuneration from the transferred patents, but also to increase costs for competitors.

De lege ferenda, if an assignor transfers SEPs with a FRAND commitment under a basic infrastructure or interoperability standard with the sole purpose of increasing the costs of its competitors, it may be in violation of the cross-licence agreement, but the assignor could also be violating the customary rules inherently included in the FRAND commitment. It may even amount to an antitrust harm and antitrust exclusionary conduct under Sec.2 Sherman Act or Art 102 TFEU. The by-laws of the SSO are not breached, but the spirit and the integrity of the standard-setting procedure, including the members' gentleman's agreement not to pursue litigation against another member, if they have committed to FRAND, are willing potential licensees and engage in the process, seem to be misused.[56]

---

[54] For a similar discussion in reference to PAE and so-called privateering, see Mark Popofsky and Michael Laufert, 'Patent Assertion Entities and Antitrust: Operating Company Patent Transfers', (2013 April) *The Antitrust Source*, 1. See also Tom Ewing, 'Indirect Exploitation of Intellectual Property Rights By Corporations and Investors', (2011) 3 *Hastings Sci & Tech Law Journal* 1 and Thomas L. Ewing, 'Practical Considerations In the Indirect Deployment of Intellectual Property Rights by Corporations and Investors', (2011) 4 *Hastings Sci & Tech Law Journal* 109, for a good analysis of privateering.

[55] Ibid.

[56] The VPC manufacturer in Allied Tube, who enlisted other steel makers in order to block the PVC standard by packing the meeting with new members to vote against the proposal, did not violate any of the by-laws of the organization. The Second Circuit held anyway that the defendant violated the integrity of the

Under certain circumstances, this might constitute a misuse of the rules of the standard-setting procedure.[57] It would, at least, be difficult to argue that this is 'competition on the merits', or for that matter that it does not have anti-competitive effect. The conduct seems to aim intentionally at increasing the costs of a competitor, and indirectly the prices for consumers. Will the assignor create, maintain or strengthen a dominant position? Inherently, by raising a competitors cost, that could be interpreted as an intent to monopolize and perhaps, with the probability of success, especially if the patents are truly SEPs that could be used to force the competitors out of the market. The assignor may objectively justify the transfer by showing that the decision to transfer the patents had a legitimate business purpose, e.g. that the patents do not fit the new business strategy. Otherwise, it may be an abuse.

The test in the *Rambus* case, e.g. that the technology transferred would not have been included in the standard 'but for' a FRAND commitment, is not the accurate test for this scenario.[58] It is actually not the inclusion of the transferred technology in the standard, or stating the FRAND commitment in relation to this technology, which is the conduct under scrutiny, but instead the transfer of said patents from the assignor to the assignee. That transfer may be judged as a misuse of the standard-setting procedure under certain circumstances. The rules or norms related to transfer of SEPs may be regarded as derived under the customary rules of the standard-setting procedure and inherent in connection with the not so developed by-laws.[59] The transfer could furthermore be argued to facilitate litigation as part of a broader monopolistic scheme under an analogy with *Singer*.[60] Presumably, the assignor and the licensee are still competitors on the product market, and perhaps even the assignee is a competitor on a larger technology market of relevant SEPs. The assignee could also

organization's procedure and subverted the organization's standard-setting process for the purpose of achieving an anti-competitive result. Cf. Allied Tube and Conduit Corp. v. Indian Head, Inc. 817 F2.d 938 (2d Cir 1987) aff'd 486 U.S. 492, 500 (1988), 817 F.2d at 947.

[57] Ibid. In Rambus, on the other hand, the Federal Circuit did not venture far from the exact wording of the IP Policy and FRAND commitment. However, it did not discuss whether there are business customary rules which may uphold the integrity of the standard-setting procedure.

[58] For an opposing view see Mark Popofsky and Michael Laufert, 'Patent Assertion Entities and Antitrust: Operating Company Patent Transfers', (2013 April) *The Antitrust Source*, 1, 11 et seq.

[59] Somewhat akin to the rule set forth in AstraZeneca. Cf. COMP/37507 AstraZeneca, 15 June 2005 [2006] 5 CMLR 287, paras 626 et seq.

[60] United States v. The Singer Manufacturing Comp. 374 U.S. 174 (1963).

be regarded as a proxy or an agent for the assignor, i.e. attributing the conduct of the PAE to the assignor. Under US antitrust law, perhaps also Sec. 7 of the Clayton Act could be applicable.

Under EU law, there is the *ITT Promedia* case[61] regarding vexatious litigation[62], where the General Court states that, in principle, bringing an action, which is the expression of a fundamental right of access to the courts, cannot be characterized as an abuse. This is so, unless an undertaking in a dominant position brings an action that cannot reasonably be considered as an attempt to establish its rights and can therefore only serve to harass the opposite party, and is conceived as part of a plan whose goal is to eliminate competition.[63] There is a similar line of case law in the US, i.e. *Handgards*.[64] Both jurisdictions demand to be shown that the rights relied on in the litigation by the plaintiff/dominant firm do not cover the alleged 'infringement' and could not possible yield a successful outcome. They do not really apply to the scenario discussed above, nor generally to so-called 'patent mining'.[65]

The transfer of the SEPs is the conduct under scrutiny. Such transfers may be carried out only if the FRAND terms are transferred to the purchaser/assignee, with the risk that the assignor otherwise may abusing its dominant position, or that the transfer would be considered an anti-competitive agreement under Sec. 1 Sherman Act and Art. 101 TFEU.

---

[61] Case T 111/96 ITT Promedia v. Commission [1999] ECR II-2937, para. 30.

[62] See also Case T-119/09 Protégé International v. Commission [2012] not yet reported.

[63] Case T 111/96 ITT Promedia v. Commission [1999] ECR II-2937, para. 30.

[64] Handgards, Inc. v. Ethicon, Inc. 743 F.2d 1282, 1288 et seq. (1984). Professional Real Estate Investors, Inc. v. Columbia Pictures Industry 508 U.S. 47,113 S.Ct. 1920 (1993).

[65] Patent mining can be defined as trying to get the most out of their patents by asserting them more aggressively than ever against possible infringing firms, even those who are not rivals. See B.H. Hall et al, A Study of Patent Thickets (UK Intellectual Property Office 2013), 22 with references. See also *AstraZeneca*, where the Commission argued that a defence that prolongs a misuse of government procedure may constitute an abuse. COMP/37507 AstraZeneca, 15 June 2005 [2996] CMLR 287, paras 736 et seq.

6.4.3 Conclusion

It seems clear that the integrity of the standard-setting procedure requires that the original owners' FRAND commitments must still encompass SEPs that are assigned to new holders. While this may be difficult to justify, at least in certain jurisdictions, under general contract law, the connection between the by-laws, and generally by whatever rules that uphold the integrity of the standard-setting procedure, and competition law, imply that competition law may become applicable. This line of reasoning is mainly used vis-a-vis the assignee but could also be utilized in reference to the assignor.

It should, however, be mentioned that no court has clearly agreed that, under competition law, the FRAND commitments run with the SEPs when transferred, although the courts still seem to imply that access to SEPs can be granted and that the patentees should only be allowed to obtain fair remuneration for such access.

6.5 ACCESS TO PATENTS, I.E. INJUNCTIONS: A COMPETITION LAW OR IP LAW PROBLEM?

6.5.1 The *Orange-Book-Standard* and Other European Cases

An interesting EU case that possibly shows the difficulties of gaining access to essential patents under a technology standard or a patent pool is the German *Orange-Book-Standard* case.[66,67]

---

[66] Federal Supreme Court (Bundesgerichtshof) May 6, 2009 – Case No. KZR 39/06 *(Orange-Book-Standard)*.

[67] The first case where the German Federal Supreme court encountered the conflict between patent exclusivity and access to a technical standard was the so-called Tight-Head Drum case (cf. infra). In Tight-Head Drum (Standard-Spundfass) an Italian manufacturer of barrels for chemical liquids, was sued for infringing a patent connected to a standard developed by other manufacturers of barrels in conjunction with some major purchasers of barrels. The Italian manufacturer made use of a 'competition law' defence, i.e. counter-sued for damages, arguing that not gaining access to the essential patents under the standard was an abuse of dominance. The patentee was in the end, in practice, obliged to license the essential patent to the entrant under the standard. The case should be not be interpreted as a right to license or even to access a technical standard, but rather a claim not to be hindered in competing, or to be discriminated against because of an undue refusal to deal. Cf. Hanns Ullrich,

In the German *Orange-Book-Standard* case, which concerned the CD-R and CD-RW patent pools, the question was whether a patentee could get injunctive relief following a patent infringement suit, when the infringer had tried to obtain a patent on commercial grounds, but the patentee had refused. Interestingly, the German court, reflecting the EU Commission's Google/Motorola merger decision, started to conclude that licensing an essential patent under a standard is a market in itself and the proprietor is that market's sole supplier, thus a monopolist.[68] The Federal Supreme Court concluded that a defendant may successfully plead that the patentee is abusing its dominant position in the market if the patentee refuses to conclude a patent licence agreement with the defendant on non-discriminatory and non-restrictive terms and conditions.[69] However, the alleged infringer has, under the rules of injunctive relief, the burden of offering evidence that the patentee was given an opportunity to obtain a licence on FRAND terms. It is not the obligation of the patentee to offer such licences, but if it refuses, the patentee may be abusing a dominant position, and the infringer may not face an injunction if it acts like a licensee, e.g. pays royalties to the patentee or into an escrow account and adheres to general licence covenants.[70]

This might be viewed as a very narrow defence. It has therefore been criticized. Is it the licensee that should define the boundaries of what constitutes profit maximization, excessive pricing and refusal to deal under FRAND and under competition law? Can the potential licensee stipulate any conditions precedent, i.e. that the firm will take out a licence under the condition that a court establishes the validity of the patents and/or the FRAND royalty rate? According to the Federal Supreme Court, the potential licensee only has two options: (i) it may offer the patentee a royalty rate that equals the royalty rate customary applied in the industry; or (ii) a royalty rate to be determined by the

---

'Patents and Standards – a Comment on the German Federal Supreme Court Decision Orange Book Standard', (2011) 41 *IIC*, 337, 339 et seq.

[68] Federal Supreme Court (Bundesgerichtshof) May 6, 2009 – Case No. KZR 39/06 *(Orange-Book-Standard).*

[69] The first case where the German Federal Supreme court encountered the conflict between patent exclusivity and access to a technical standard was the so-called Standard Tight-Head Drum case. Case No. KZR 40/02 (*Tight-Head Drum* (Standard-Spundfass) where a patentee who set up a standard together with three other firms was obliged to grant a licence for an essential patent to a foreign entrant under the Standard.

[70] Federal Supreme Court (Bundesgerichtshof) May 6, 2009 – Case No. KZR 39/06 *(Orange-Book-Standard).*

plaintiff, applying the plaintiff's 'reasonable exercised discretion'.[71] On the face of it, it seems that the *Orange-Book-Standard* case does not give any leeway for potential licensees to question either validity or rate. The follow-on cases seem to verify this.

BOX 6.1

Several German cases have followed in the wake of the *Orange-Book-Standard* case. In *Philips v. SonyEricsson*,[72] the District Court of Mannheim dismissed the injunction claim, finding that the defendant had fulfilled the requirements of *Orange-Book-Standard* by offering to license at a fixed rate and depositing the calculated royalties in an escrow account. Some cases exist where the alleged infringers have not been able to meet the stringent requirements in *Orange-Book-Standard*. Motorola/Google for example obtained an injunction against Apple (based on cellular SEP under the GPRS standard, connected to GSM) in December 2011 in the Karlsruhe High Regional Court in Mannheim. The injunction was enforced for a while until suspended for the case to be heard on Appeal in February 2012.[73] The parties then agreed that Apple would take out a licence for a rate to be decided by a court. The Appeal court that heard the *Motorola v. Apple* case found that Apple had to withdraw its motion for nullification of Motorola's patent when Motorola accepted Apple's offer to license. In fact, Apple's licence offer must include a non–challenge termination provision to fulfil the *Orange-Book-Standard* requirements. The courts have even required that a licensee must accept liability for past damages in its licence offer.[74]

[71] Ibid. Lawrence R Gabuzda et al., 'Standard-Essential Patents and Injunctive Relief', (2013), April Jones Day Law Firm Publications, http://www.jonesday.com/standards-essential_patents/, accessed 24 February 2014.

[72] Philips v. SonyEricsson (District Court of Mannheim, May 27, 2011, doc no. 7 O65/10).

[73] Motorola v. Apple (Court of Appeal in Karlsruhe, February 27, 2012, doc. No. 6 U 136/11).

[74] Lawrence R. Gabuzda et al., 'Standard Essential Patents and Injunctive Relief', (2013) April Jones Day Law Firm Publications, http://www.jonesday.com/standards-essential_patents/, accessed 24 February 2014.

These cases have thus resolved some outstanding issues with the *Orange-Book-Standard*. Also, issues such as whether the test applies to both *de jure* and *de facto* standards in now resolved. It applies to both. The courts, furthermore, found that FRAND commitment is a declaration of intent by the patent owner to conclude a binding licence agreement in the future. It fulfils the patentee's obligation under antitrust law, but does not grant a right to use the patent for potential licensees. The potential licensee must still show that it is a 'willing licensee'. The sought after license may be national or global, however if a national licence is asked for then that may be misuse if the licensee continues to infringe the similar patents outside Germany.[75]

The EU Commission is investigating Google for some of the conduct described above. The EU Commission is also, allegedly, investigating Google/Motorola for seeking an injunction against Microsoft. The injunction relief in this case was based on SEPs for the H.264 video code. Microsoft here agreed to pay a royalty rate ten times the MPEG LA pool rate to Motorola and offered furthermore a USD 300 million bond, with room for discussion to increase the amount, as long as an injunction was not enforced during the appeal process. While it seems Google refused and pushed for enforcement against Windows Operating System and the Xbox gaming consoles anyway, it was not successful, since a US District Court and Appeal Court barred the enforcement of the German injunctions. This allegedly made the EU Commission interested. It was actually the District Court in Western District of Washington, Judge Robart that entered into a preliminary relief to extend an earlier temporary restraining order for Motorola. It was now extended to also include the injunction under the Mannheim Regional Court.[76]

In addition to the above, in February 2012 Apple obtained two injunctions against Motorola in the Munich court concerning the

[75] Ibid.

[76] Some of the information in this paragraph was provided by the excellent blog, Foss Patents, written by Florian Mueller. See generally www.fosspatents.com Accessed 11 July 2013; and The Essential Patent Blog, http://essentialpatentblog.com/contact-us/. Accessed 5 July 2013.

slide to unlock feature and for a mobile photo feature.[77] Nokia has been granted injunction against HTC, and Huawei against ZTD.[78]

Excluding Germany, Apple, Samsung, Nokia, HTC, Qualcomm, Intellectual Venture, IPCom and Ericsson are embroiled in several litigations in France, England, the Netherlands (mostly the Hague court) and Japan regarding infringements, FRAND and injunctions. In the Netherlands, there is a similar case law development as *Orange-Book-Standard*, while the Dutch law did not develop under competition law, but instead under intellectual property law. Under Dutch law there are two cases that suggest that when a potential licensee has asked for a licence on FRAND terms, the patentee may not file for an injunction, because of the risk of abusing the good faith requirement to negotiate.[79]

Samsung has not been successful in its litigation and has, also as a response to the investigation by the EU Commission and the EU Commission's subsequent notification of a Statement of Objection, unilaterally stopped all injunction relief cases in the EU and offered commitments to the EU Commission. The EU Commission's investigation into the behaviour of Samsung is related to the use of an injunction against Apple under the ETSI 3G UMTS standard.[80]

The above is only a snapshot of some current litigation. For example, in mid 2012, there were more than 50 or more actions world-wide just between Apple and Samsung

As regards the *Orange-Book-Standard*, there are many claims that, in both the *Google/Motorola* merger case and the *Google* SO, that the EU Commission, if it did not dismiss the *Orange-Book-Standard* rule, did at least display some dissatisfaction with the rule, since it is too difficult to satisfy for the alleged infringers, especially in standard-setting situations.

[77] Michael A. Carrier, 'A Roadmap to the Smartphone Patent Wars and FRAND Licensing', (2012 April) *CPI Antitrust Chronicle*, 1, 3.

[78] Ibid.

[79] Lawrence R. Gabuzda et al., 'Standard-Essential Patents and Injunctive Relief', (2013) April Jones Day Law Firm Publications, http://www.jonesday.com/standards-essential_patents/, accessed 24 February 2014.

[80] Ibid.

Under EU law, the plaintiff may have a case for, in the first place, accessing the standard-setting procedure and the result (inter alia the SEPs), or the patent pool, relying on the EU's 'exceptional circumstances' doctrine under the abuse of dominance rule (Cf. *Magill*, *IMS Health* and *Microsoft*). While these cases lays down a three part test: (i) the product the infringer wants to market must relate to a indispensable input required for the marketing of the (new) product (which the holder of the IPR does not offer), and for which there is a demand; (ii) there is no justification for such a refusal and (iii) the dominant firm has reserved for itself a secondary market. These requirements seem more easily fulfilled than the *Orange-Book-Standard* conditions.[81] Moreover, the Commission may perhaps be purporting that refusing access in standard-setting scenarios not only imply refusal to access but also constitute a misuse of the standard-setting procedure, and, thus, deserve a highten antitrust treatment.

There are furthermore other German standard scenario cases where the requirement for access is not set as high as in *Orange-Book-Standard*. *Tight-Head Drum* is a Germany case of refusal to license SEPs, decided by the Federal Supreme Court five years before *Orange-Book-Standard*.[82] The case arose from of a patent infringement suit in which a German subsidiary of an Italian drum manufacturer successfully pleaded that not to be granted access to a patent, which reflected the collective action of a standard-setting organization, would constitute a violation of German competition law. Even though the case was judged under German competition law, it may give an idea of how a similar standard-setting conduct would be decided under EU competition law.[83]

Leading companies in the German chemical industry, belonging to the Association of the Chemical Industry (VCI), tendered for proposals for a synthetic drum. Four German drum manufacturers presented proposals

---

[81] James Venit, 'Article 82 EC: Exceptional Circumstances – The IP/Antitrust Interface after IMS Health', in Claus-Dieter Ehlermann & Isabela Atanasiu (eds), European Competition Law Annual 2005: The Interaction between Competition Law and Intellectual Property Law (Hart Publishing, 2007)., 7 *et seq*.

[82] See the interesting German case Federal Supreme Court (Bundesgerichtshof) July 13, 2004 – Case No. KZR 40/02 *('Tight-Head Drum' (Standard-Spundfass)* where a patentee who set up a standard together with three other firms was obliged to license a foreign entrant an essential patent under the Standard. For comments in English, see Matthias Leistner, 'Federal Supreme Court (Bundesgerichthof)', (2005) 6 *IIC*, 741. F.

[83] The Federal Court presumably took some notice of TFEU since effect on trade between member states must clearly have been present in the case.

for such a drum in a working group. The plaintiff in *Tight-Head Drum* produced the winning proposal, while the three other German manufacturers in the working group were granted royalty-free licences to the disputed patent. On the facts, the Federal Supreme Court decided that under the standard there was no room for competition by substitution, since the chemical industry in Germany had decided on a general standard for tight-head drums through its self-regulatory body. Therefore, and in the light of the fact that the other three German manufacturers obtained royalty free licenses, infringing the patent could not create an obligation to compensate the plaintiff.

In light of the *Orange-Book-Standard* case's[84] formula for legally infringing standard essential patents, the *Tight-Head Drum* case stipulates a straightforward test based on the notion (or right) of competition by substitution and imitation. Under *Tight-Head Drum,* market dominance has been created through the standard-setting procedure, so that competition by substitution has been eliminated. An infringer may utilize the competition law defence so as to be able to access markets and compete by imitation. The Court also found an element of discrimination between licensees. The German Court did not use the general abuse of dominance rule, but rather a more specific rule against discrimination. Nonetheless, the Court makes it clear that the general rule would have been applicable had the more specific rule against discrimination not been applicable.[85]

The Federal Supreme Court also added two requirements in the *Orange-Book-Standard* to those in *Tight-Head Drum*: (i) offer the patentee an opportunity to obtain a licence on decent (among other things, FRAND) terms; and (ii) act like a licensee, e.g. pay royalties to the patentee or into an escrow account and adhere to the general licence covenants.

Furthermore, it is interesting to see the emphasis that was give to the fact that there was no room for competition by substitution in *Tight-Head Drum*. The court found that there was no room for substitute or

[84] Federal Supreme Court (Bundesgerichtshof) May 6, 2009 – Case No. KZR 39/06 ('Orange-Book-Standard'), http://www.ipeg.eu/blog/wp-content/uploads/EN-Translation-BGH-Orange-Book-Standard-eng.pdf

[85] The *Tight-Head Drum* case is an abuse of dominance case but also concerns the interface between a *collective* development of a new technology, the *joint* adoption of the standard and licensing and the possible existence of an *agreement* of collective refusal to license.

competing technologies. Access to the market /standard therefore become important and, thus, competition by imitation should be supported.[86]

Compared to the EU case law that lays down the 'exceptional circumstances' test in *Magill, IMS Health* and *Microsoft*, the *Tight-Head Drum* case clearly does not stipulate a new product requirement, but instead focuses on whether competition by substitution is available.[87]

From these cases, it seems possible to conclude that a unilateral refusal to license is a violation under EU competition law in the field of standards. However, competition by substitution is not an EU competition law doctrine, rather a German competition law doctrine. Under the *IMS Health* doctrine, access is granted under the doctrine of exceptional circumstances, which in some cases requires that the infringer should provide a 'new product'. However, to some extent the 'new product' requirement was lessened in *IMS Health* compared to the *Magill* case.[88]

Generally, even though the Federal Supreme Court's decision might be interpreted as creating a licence obligation for all patentees holding essential patents under a technology standard, and that such patentees may only license their patents on something similar to FRAND terms, the court make in *Orange-Book-Standard* the defence very difficult to apply. If the potential licensee agrees to license but believes that the court should decide what FRAND is, and still wants to retain the right to challenge the validity of the SEP in a court a law, then an injunction should be granted.[89] Clearly, in comparison with the German *Tight-Head Drum* case, the Federal Supreme Court was more reluctant in *Orange-Book-Standard* to generally accept a competition law defence in patent infringement suits.[90] With reference to US law, the *Orange-Book-Standard* case does not correspond to *Rambus* but does possibly to the *Qualcomm/Broadcom* cases. According to *Rambus* there is no obligation

---

[86] Josef Drexl, 'Abuse of Dominance in Licensing and Refusal to License: A More Economic Approach to Competition by Imitation and to Competition by Substitution', in Claus-Dieter Ehlermann and Isabela Atanasiu (eds), *European Competition Law Annual 2005: The Interaction Between Competition Law and Intellectual Property Law* (Hart Publishing, 2007), 650 et seq.

[87] Ibid.

[88] Ibid.

[89] The EU Commission seems to agree on this point in the Google SO. Discussed infra Chapter 6.5.3.

[90] See generally, Hanns Ullrich, 'Patente under technische Normen: Konflikt under Komplementarität in patent- und wettbewerbsrechtlicher Sicht', in Matthias Leistne (ed), *Europäische Perspektiven des Geistigen Eigentum* (Tübingen, Mohr Siebeck, 2010).

to license under RAND terms, especially if no RAND commitment has been made to an SDO.[91]

Orange-Book-Standard is an interesting ruling and the issue is whether it will be adopted also on the EU level. There are cases, for example the new *Google* and the *Samsung* cases, where the EU Commission will have the opportunity to do so. These cases are not resolved yet. Samsung's proposed commitments to the EU Commission seem to imply that injunction will only be applicable for Samsung after 12 months of negotiation with a potential licensee of the FRAND-terms and, thereto, a possibility for the willing licensee of getting the FRAND rate established through a third party, should the negotiation not render a positive result.[92] Samsung also agreed not to seek any injunctions for a period of five years.[93] More importantly, the CJEU in *Huawei v. ZTD* will have a similar opportunity to discuss both injunctions and the definition of FRAND.

The result of the ruling in *Orange-Book-Standard* should, however, not be underestimated. In essence, it implies that holders of SEPs cannot get permanent injunctions to prevent infringers, if the latter are satisfying the rules of *Orange-Book-Standard,* e.g. paying licence fees and acting as licensees. The effect is that a compulsory licence scheme has been created. Furthermore, more theoretically, it is an exemption from or a restriction on intellectual property. In these situations, intellectual property does not mirror property; instead, competition law transforms intellectual property laws to liability rules.[94]

---

[91] Liguo Zhang, 'How IPR Policies of Telecommunication Standard-Setting Organizations can Effectively Address the Patent Ambush', (2010) 41 *IIC*, 380, 380, 406 et seq.

[92] See EU Commission press releases concerning Samsung and Motorola: http://europa.eu/rapid/press-release_IP-13-971_en.htm and http://europa.eu/rapid/press-release_MEMO-13-910_en.htm and http://europa.eu/rapid/press-release_MEMO-13-403_en.htm. Accessed on 2 January 2014.

[93] Ibid.

[94] Annette Kur and Jens Schovsbo, 'Expropriation or Fair Game for All? The Gradual Dismantling of the IP Exclusivity Paradigm' in Max Planck Institute for Intellectual Property, Competition & Tax Law Research Paper No. 09-14 (2009). Available at SSRN: http://ssrn.com/abstract=1508330 or http://dx.doi.org/10.2139/ssrn.1508330, accessed 4 November 2013.

6.5.2 *eBay* and the ITC Cases that Followed

The *eBay* case[95] is a landmark case where the US Supreme Court decided to sharpen the rules for permanent injunctions under intellectual property law. Prior to the Supreme Court's decision, the Federal Circuit had imposed a mandatory injunction rule that compelled District Courts to issue injunctions once patents had been adjudged valid and infringed.[96]

The background to the case was as follows. Online auction site eBay used a business practice on its online auction site, which a firm named MercExchange purported to have covered in its practice patents. The patents allegedly covered eBay's 'Buy it Now' function, a function which was responsible for over 30 per cent of the company's business. The parties had engaged in negotiations where eBay tried to purchase the patents. However, these negotiations had failed, and MercExchange sued eBay for patent infringement. In 2003, MercExchange was successful and persuaded a jury that eBay had deliberately infringed the firm's patents. MercExchange then tried to obtain a permanent injunction to prevent eBay from infringing its patents, which would effectively have closed down the eBay website. The District Court refused MercExchange the injunction, while the Federal Circuit reversed the District Court conclusion and stated as a 'general rule that courts will issue permanent injunctions against patent infringement absent exceptional circumstances.'[97] eBay appealed to the Supreme Court, and the Court granted certiorari and decided in the favor of eBay. The Court held that:

> The traditional four-factor test applied by courts of equity when considering whether to award permanent injunctive relief to a prevailing plaintiff applies to disputes arising under the Patent Act. That test requires a plaintiff to demonstrate: (1) that it has suffered an irreparable injury; (2) that remedies available at law are inadequate to compensate for that injury; (3) that considering the balance of hardships between the plaintiff and defendant, a remedy in equity is warranted; and (4) that the public interest would not be disserved by a permanent injunction. The decision to grant or deny such reliefs is an act of equitable discretion by the district court, reviewable on appeal for abuse of discretion. These principles apply with equal force to Patent Act disputes.[98]

---

[95] eBay Inc. v. MercExchange, L.L.C., 547 U.S. 388 (2006).

[96] Lawrence R. Gabuzda et al., 'Standard-Essential Patents and Injunctive Relief', (2013) April Jones Day Law Firm Publications, http://www.jonesday.com/standards-essential_patents/, accessed 24 February 2014.

[97] 401 F. 3d 1323, 1339.

[98] eBay Inc. v. MercExchange, L.L.C., 547 U.S. 388 (2006).

The Supreme Court statement must be considered as a departure from the then prevailing general rule, described by the Appeal Court. Given the Supreme Court's comments, it is clear that the Courts need, when deciding on injunctions, to take fairness and equity into account.

However, the Supreme Court struck down the District Court's argument that 'plaintiff's willingness to license its patents' and 'its lack of commercial activity in practising the patents' would be sufficient to establish that the patent holder would not suffer irreparable harm if an injunction did not issue. According to the Supreme Court, traditional equitable principles do not permit such broad classifications, and it continued: 'For example, some patent holders, such as university researchers or self-made inventors, might reasonably prefer to license their patents, rather than undertake efforts to secure the financing necessary to bring their works to market themselves. Such patent holders may be able to satisfy the traditional four-factor test, and we see no basis for categorically denying them the opportunity to do so'.[99]

It seems that the Supreme Court tried to limit the precedent to exactly the entities not mentioned in the text above, i.e. the PAE, or, in other words, the 'patent trolls'. Actually, Kennedy, together with Stevens, Souter and Breyer, in a concurring opinion, develops this point further and states:

> An industry has developed in which firms use patents not as a basis for producing and selling goods but, instead, primarily for obtaining licensing fees. … For these firms, an injunction, and the potentially serious sanctions arising from its violation, can be employed as a bargaining tool to charge exorbitant fees to companies that seek to buy licenses to practice the patent. … When the patented invention is but a small component of the product the companies seek to produce and the threat of an injunction is employed simply for undue leverage in negotiations, legal damages may well be sufficient to compensate for the infringement and an injunction may not serve the public interest.'[100]

Recent research shows that this message has been successfully received and that District Courts generally grant injunctions to universities and self-made inventors, while it denies injunctions to PAEs.[101]

---

99 eBay Inc. v. MercExchange, L.L.C., 547 U.S. 388, 392 (2006).

100 eBay Inc. v. MercExchange, L.L.C., 547 U.S. 388, 400 (2006).

101 Colleen V. Chien and Mark A. Lemley, 'Patent Holdup, the ITC, and the Public Interest', in *Cornell Law Review*; *Stanford Public Law Working Paper* No 2022168 (SSRN, 2012), accessed 7 July 2013.

Notwithstanding the above, due to the raging patent war, the group of firms denied injunctions seems also, today, to include, not only PAEs, but some of the largest telecommunications and IT firms on the planet. Judge Posner, for example, dismissed both Motorola's and Apple's motions for injunctions, and seem to say that an injunction may seldom be available for a patentee holding a SEP as long as there is a possibility of obtaining damages.[102] The original idea in *eBay* was to single out only the PAEs, i.e. not the vertically integrated firms, but now other firms are also denied injunctions (the *Google* consent order will be discussed infra).[103]

BOX 6.2

The story after *eBay* unfolded, not in the Federal Courts but with the International Trade Commission (ITC). Several of the PAEs turned to the ITC to obtain something equivalent to an injunction, a so-called exclusion order or a cease-and-desist order, while the ITC was not bound by *eBay* since the ITC cannot give a ruling for damages (cf. Spansion, Inc. v. ITC, 629 F.3d 1331, 1359 (Fed. Cir.2010)). In the end, a cease-and-desist order is the only remedy the ITC can order. Actually, as the patent war in the telecommunication sector raged on, every major SEP holder in that industry was embroiled in cases under the ITC.[104]

[102] In the United District Court for the Northern District of Illinois Eastern Division, No. 1:11-cv-08540 Apple, Inc. et al. v. Motorola, Inc. and Motorola Mobility, Inc. Opinion and Order June 22, 2012.

[103] Claudia Tapia, *Industrial Property Rights, Technical Standards and Licensing Practices (FRAND) in the Telecommunications Industry* (Carl Heymanns Verlag – eine Marke von Wolters Kluwer Deutschland GmbH, 2010), 69 for an interesting list of clearly *ad absurdum* patent roll cases.

[104] Certain Mobile Devices, Associated Software, and Components Thereof, Inv. No. 337-TA-744 (May 15, 2012) (Final) (Notice of a Commission Final Determination of Violation of Section 337; Issuance of a Limited Exclusion Order; Termination of Investigation; Respondent Motorola Mobility, Inc.); Certain Electronic Devices with Communication Capabilities, Components Thereof, and Related Software, Inv. No. 337-TA-808, 76 Fed. Reg. 60,870 (Sept. 30, 2011) (Preliminary) (Notice of Institution of Investigation; Institution of Investigation Pursuant to 19 U.S.C. 1337; Complainant HTC Corp. and Respondent Apple Inc.); Certain Wireless Devices with 3G Capabilities and Components Thereof, Inv. No. 337-TA-800, 76 Fed. Reg. 54,252, 54253 (Aug. 31, 2011) (Preliminary) (Notice of Institution of Investigation; Respondent Nokia Corp.); Certain Mobile Telephones and Modems, Inv. No. 337-TA-758, 2011 ITC LEXIS

There seem to have been three cases where the ITC called for and obtained written submissions from the parties and the public regarding FRAND: 745 Investigation (Complainant Motorola, Respondent Apple); 752 Investigation (Complainant Motorola, Respondent Microsoft) and 794 (Complainant Samsung, Respondent Apple). All these cases now display a variety of different tactics and accusations of sham licence offers, defences such as Estopple/Unclean Hands, and implied licences. The 745 Investigation is the source of the District Court case, *Motorola v. Apple,* in Wisconsin (discussed infra). The request by the ITC for written submissions from the public has generated many responses from companies, trade groups, agencies and the government. Some of these argue for a per se rule that firms should never be able to obtain exclusive orders. Others, that exclusion orders should be available under certain rare circumstances, while the third group emphasize the special situation and that a case-by-case analysis must be performed: especially when dealing with the IP Policy of ETSI, where the patentees may retain the right to injunctive relief (cf. Qualcomm's submission). The FTC, Justice Department and the USPTO have urged the ITC to use its public policy scrutiny and deny injunctive relief. In fact, these Federal institutions have publically argued to the ITC for the dismantling of the equivalent to injunctive relief in writing and at public hearings before Congress.[105]

1557 (Aug. 11, 2011) (Preliminary) (Order 17; Complainant Sony Corp. and Respondent LG Electronics, Inc.); Certain Electronic Devices, Including Wireless Communication Devices, Portable Music and Data Processing Devices, and Tablet Computers, Inv. No. 337-TA-794, 76 Fed. Reg. 45,860 (Aug. 1, 2011) (Preliminary) (Notice of Institution of Investigation; Institution of Investigation Pursuant to 19 U.S.C. 1337; Complainant Samsung Electronics Co. and Respondent Apple Inc.); Certain Mobile Telephones and Wireless Communication Devices Featuring Digital Cameras, and Components Thereof, at 2, Inv. No. 337-TA-703, 2011 ITC LEXIS 1112 (June 30, 2011) (Final) (Notice of Commission Determination to Affirm in Part and Reverse in Part a Determination of No Violation of Section 337; Remand of the Investigation for Further Proceedings; Respondents Apple Inc. and Research in Motion Ltd.).

[103] Lawrence R. Gabuzda, et al., 'Standard-Essential Patents and Injunctive Relief', (2013) April Jones Day Law Firm Publications, , 8 et seq. http://www.jonesday.com/standards-essential_patents/, accessed 24 February 2014.

One of the latest turns in this saga is the use of a reversed injunction in the District Courts.[106] In the Northern District of California, a federal judge granted under the IEEE 802.11 (WiFi, or WLAN) standard, a preliminary injunction against enforcement of a potential ITC exclusion order based on standard-essential patents (SEPs). The addressee was RealTek Semiconductor; the patent holder was Agere, which was spun off Lucent in 2000 and acquired by Taiwanese integrated circuit designer and supplier LSI, another party to this action, in 2001. The injunction binds LSI and Agere, which (unless they get this injunction lifted) cannot enforce or seek to enforce an exclusion order injunction pending a full FRAND trial, which will result in a rate-setting decision comparable to Judge Robart's recent Microsoft v. Motorola ruling (discussed infra). The ITC itself is free to continue its investigation. But if the ITC found in LSI and Agere's favor and granted 'an exclusion order or injunctive relief' (the latter presumably referring to a cease-and-desist order, which the ITC can grant in addition to an import ban), the preliminary injunction would go into effect and LSI/Agere would face contempt sanctions in California should it actually try to enforce the ITC judgment.[107]

In addition to the above, there have been several notable cases in the courts. Apart from Judge Posner's case in the Northern District of Illinois, Motorola and Apple are battling in courts in Northern California, Wisconsin and in Florida regarding injunctions, FRAND and workarounds. Motorola and Microsoft also had a dispute over the calculation of FRAND before Judge Robart in the Western District of Washington.[108]

There is an international aspect to these cases. US District Courts stopped, by restraining order, injunctions issued in Germany (mainly by the Mannheim Regional Court).[109]

However, the different requirement for obtaining an injunction in the District Court and an order under the ITC has created great concern not only in academia, but also with the general

[106] Cf. http://www.fosspatents.com/2013/05/federal-judge-bars-holder-of-standard.html, accessed 11 July 2013.

[107] Ibid.

[108] Michael A. Carrier, 'A Roadmap to the Smartphone Patent Wars and FRAND Licensing', (2012 April) *CPI Antitrust Chronicle*, 1, 4.

[109] Cf. http://www.fosspatents.com/2013/05/federal-judge-bars-holder-of-standard.html, accessed 10 July 2013.

media and politicians. The FTC tried to change the ITC case law doctrine with amicus briefs in separate cases before the ITC, and generally.[110] Finally, even the executive branch (under President Obama) has now intervened and in the 794 Investigation between Samsung and Apple, the Obama Administration in a letter dated 3 August 2013 disapproved of the ITC's exclusion order and of the ITC's 'cease and desist' order that would otherwise have stopped some Apple products from being imported and sold in the US.

The *eBay* case is very interesting: the Supreme Court has clearly changed the direction of the underlying intellectual property rights policy. The result of the case is that patentees under certain circumstances are prevented from getting injunctions. The political aspects of this are remarkable.[111] Legally, the requirement for the infringer to satisfy is, inter alia, to pay continuing damages mirroring what the patentee could get as a royalty. Technically this is not a compulsory license, but the result is similar.

The result of *eBay* is similar to the result of the *Orange-Book-Standard* case. They both imply that certain patents can be infringed without the patentee being able to go to court and stop the infringement. However, they are based on two different legal systems and two different harms. Under the EU system, there is an EU competition law defence for infringers of patents, while under the US system there is an equity exemption under intellectual property law and injunction doctrine which enable infringers to continue to infringe the said patent under *eBay*. *Orange-Book-Standard* is a refusal to license a case, while *eBay* concerns more a misuse of the injunctive relief instrument.

---

[110] See FTC brief in the matter of certain gaming and entertainment consoles, related softwar, and components thereof Inv. No. 337-TA-752, and FTC, 'The Evolving IP Marketplace: Aligning Patent Notice and Remedies with Competition' (March 2011), 8 et seq., 20 et seq., and 168 et seq. In the later report the FTC also hints that Sec. 5 FTC Act may become applicable in these cases. Richard Epstein et al., 'The FTC, IP, and SSOs: Government Hold-Up Replacing Private Coordination', in a working paper (SSRN, 2011), 4 et seq.

[111] The fundamental idea when the US IP system was remade by Congress in 1982 through the Federal Court Improvement Act was limit the possibilities of escaping injunctions. B.H. Hall et al, A Study of Patent Thicket (UK Intellectual Property Office 2013), 19, with refeerences.

6.5.3 The *Google/Motorola* Cases

(i) Apple v. Motorola

The *Apple v. Motorola* case[112] arose out of a series of counterclaims in the ITC investigation that was initiated by Motorola (745 Investigation). Apple's counterclaim was based on a line of argument that Motorola's pursuit of injunctive relief was a breach of contract in light of its FRAND licensing commitments to the IEEE and ETSI. Judge Crabb at the District Court of Wisconsin concluded that there is no language in either IEEE or ETSI statutes and rules that suggests that Motorola and the SSO intended or agreed to prohibit Motorola from seeking injunctive relief. In fact, both policies are silent on the question of injunctive relief. Such an agreement needs to be clear to deprive a patentee of such a right. Therefore, Motorola cannot commit breach of contract simply by requesting injunctive relief.[113]

Judge Crabb also dismissed Apple's antitrust claims under the Noerr-Pennington doctrine. Motorola benefited from antitrust immunity when petitioning the government (i.e. requesting the ITC) for an exclusion order. Crabb furthermore dismissed Apple's remaining claims and on 5 December 2012 decided in favor of Motorola. The case has been appealed, but it does include a very difficult jurisdictional issue, so which appeal court will eventually deal with these issues is not certain.[114]

(ii) FTC consent order

The FTC investigation into Google's use of the Motorola patents ended in a settlement in January 2013.[115] The Commission's complaint alleged that Google reneged on its FRAND commitments to SSOs (see discussion above) and pursued – or threatened to pursue – injunctions against companies that needed to use the SEPs for producing their devices and were willing to license them on FRAND terms. Specifically, Google

---

[112] Apple, Inc v. Motorola, Inc. No. 1:11-cv-085402012 BL 157789 (N.D. III June 22, 2012).

[113] Lawrence R. Gabuzda et al., 'Standard-Essential Patents and Injunctive relief', (2013) April Jones Day Law Firm Publications, 4 et seq. http://www.jonesday.com/standards-essential_patents/, accessed 24 February 2014.

[114] Ibid.

[115] FTC, Statement in the In the Matter of Google Inc., FTC File No. 121-0120, January 3, 2013. http://www.ftc.gov/os/caselist/1210120/130103googlemotorolastmtofcomm.pdf. Accessed 11 July 2013.

pursued injunctions in the District Court and at the ITC to block competing technology companies from using the standard-essential patents.[116]

The FTC alleged that this type of patent hold-up is what the standard-setting organizations sought to prevent by instituting IP policies with FRAND licensing requirements. According to the FTC, if left unchecked, this type of patent hold-up can lead to higher prices, as companies may pay higher royalties for the use of Google's patents because of the threat of an injunction. They will then pass those higher prices on to consumers[117]. This may cause companies in technology industries to abandon the standard-setting process and limit or forgo investment in new technologies, according to the agency. According to the majority of the Commission, this conduct constitutes an unfair method of competition, as well as unfair acts and practices, in violation of Sec. 5 of the FTC Act. The Google settlement required, according to the press release, Google to withdraw its claim for injunctive relief on FRAND encumbered SEPs around the world, and to offer a FRAND licence to any company that wants to license Google's SEPs.[118]

Clearly, the FTC, in the Google consent order, has agreed that a potential licensee must have the ability to negotiate what may constitute FRAND terms before Google is able to obtain an injunction. Generally, the FTC in the consent order lays down a four-step test on how to establish FRAND between the parties to essential patents (defined in accordance with the ETSI definition of essential, i.e. technical essentiality): (i) the parties need to agree to negotiate for a period of not less than

---

116 Ibid.

117 The FTC refers to Microsoft Corp. v. Motorola, Inc., 696 F.3d 872, 885 (9th Cir. 2012) ('Implicit in such a sweeping promise is, at least arguably, a guarantee that the patent-holder will not take steps to keep would-be users from using the patented material, such as seeking an injunction, but will instead proffer licenses consistent with the commitment made.'); Apple, Inc. v. Motorola, Inc., No. 1:11-cv-08540, 2012 BL 157789 (N.D. Ill. June 22, 2012), at 15 Posner, J., sitting by designation: 'I don't see how, given FRAND, I would be justified in enjoining Apple from infringing the '898 [patent] unless Apple refuses to pay a royalty that meets the FRAND requirement. By committing to license its patents on FRAND terms, Motorola committed to license the '898 to anyone willing to pay a FRAND royalty and thus implicitly acknowledged that a royalty is adequate compensation for a license to use that patent. How could it do otherwise?'

118 Decision and Order. Cf. FTC, Statement In the Matter of Google Inc., FTC File No. 121-0120, January 3, 2013. http://www.ftc.gov/os/caselist/1210120/130103googlemotorolastmtofcomm.pdf. Accessed 11 July 2013.

six months; (ii) after those six months, or on the request of the potential licensee during the six months, Google may deliver the relevant licence agreement; (iii) the potential licensee has thereafter sixty days to either accept the proposed agreement or indicate which covenants it believes do not represent the FRAND commitment made by Google to the relevant SDO, and to what extent and effect these covenants should be altered to fulfill the FRAND commitment; and (iv) thereafter, either a US District Court or arbitration panel, under a somewhat intricate procedure, will determine what rights, obligations and general covenants the licence agreement will include, i.e. the specific FRAND terms for the bilateral collaboration.[119]

Generally, during the procedure described above (or at least during the first six months plus 60 days), Google will not have the right to obtain injunctions vis-à-vis the potential licensee. After this period has elapsed, Google has the right to obtain injunctive relief, but it needs first, generally, to ask the potential licensee whether it agrees to determine the licence agreement, i.e. FRAND, through arbitration. If the licensee accepts that the determination of the licence agreement will be in the hands of the arbitrator, Google will not be able to seek an injunction during the arbitration.[120]

Google will retain the right to obtain injunctive relief directly should the potential licensee (i) in writing refuse to enter into licence agreement, (ii) refuse to enter into a licence agreement on the terms set by a final court ruling or through binding arbitration, or (iii) fail to provide a written confirmation in response to a 'FRAND Terms Letter' from Google, which is a mechanism enabling Google to ensure that the other party will also make its own patents essential to the relevant standards available on FRAND terms (reciprocity). It should furthermore be noted that the consent order only encompasses potential licensees who are inside the jurisdiction of the United States District Courts.

The Google FTC order stipulates a procedure to determine FRAND on a case-by-case basis. Thus, FRAND, according to the order, is not a test or a level, instead it is a *procedure*. These are the cornerstones of the consent order, and while it seems to create a thoughtful procedure to obtain licence agreements based on FRAND, the consent order reflects a settlement agreement that is complicated and there may be situations that are not covered by the order. It seems, for example, that it still provides room for Google to continue the litigation that have already been initiated

---

119 Ibid.

120 Ibid.

(for example vis-à-vis Microsoft and Apple), i.e. when defending itself, Google may still seek and obtain an injunction.[121] Furthermore, Google seemed to claim in court that it may still, after the consent order is issued, *seek* injunctions, just not *obtain* or *enforce* injunctions.[122]

In the statement of the Commission, the majority claims that it is still possible for a patentee to seek and obtain an injunction even if holding a SEP.[123]

Moreover, it must be remembered that the basis on which the FTC and Google settled was the rule regarding unfair competition. According to the statement of the FTC: '[w]e take this action pursuant to the Commission's authority under Section 5 to prohibit unfair methods of competition, which both Congress and the Supreme Court have expressly deemed to extend beyond the Sherman Act'. This implies that Google, according to the FTC majority, is not obliged to give access to the SEPs under antitrust law, but instead under unfair competition law. FTC follows the line of reasoning put forward in its *N-Data* settlement.[124] First, this opens up Sec. 5 of the FTC Act to conduct outside antitrust laws, while, secondly, more disturbing, by indirectly stating that patent ambush is outside the antitrust laws, the FTC disqualifies the courts, the Justice Department and everyone except the FTC to find patent hold-up in violation of competition law. It is actually a decision stating that patent hold-up is not a violation of the antitrust laws. Moreover, this is not the *Rambus* situation, since Google had in this case pledged to abide by FRAND.

When comparing the FTC's Google consent order with, first, its statements to the ITC, and, secondly, its conclusion in the in *re Rosch* merger case, it also seems that Google was able to obtain a consent decree that is open to more interpretation about when injunctions may be regarded as not violating Sec. 5 of the FTC Act. In its correspondence

---

[121] See Commissioner Rosch's separate statement in FTC Google. For example, the case before Judge Posner has evidently continued, and been appealed also by Google. In the United States District Court for the Northern District of Illinois Eastern Division, No. 1:11-cv-08540 Apple, Inc. et al. v. Motorola, Inc. and Motorola Mobility, Inc. Opinion and Order June 22, 2012. Cf. Apple, Inc v. Motorola, Inc. No. 1:11-cv-085402012 BL 157789 (N.D. Ill June 22, 2012).

[122] See Google's appeal against Judge Posner's judgment, ibid.

[123] Statement by the Commission, cf. FTC, Statement In the Matter of Google Inc., FTC File No. 121-0120, January 3, 2013. http://www.ftc.gov/os/caselist/1210120/130103googlemotorolastmtofcomm.pdf. Accessed 10 July 2013. 4, fn 14.

[124] Discussed supra, Chapter 6.4.

with ITC, FTC indicated that injunctive relief was indeed unavailable for the infringement of patents governed by FRAND.[125] In the in *re Bosch* case, the FTC clearly stated that an SEP injunction could on a case-by-case basis be available if: (i) the licensee used the SEP outside the standard; (ii) the potential licensee stated in writing that it would not license on FRAND terms; or (iii) it refused to license its SEPs on FRAND terms.[126] The Google consent order lays down a mechanism under arbitration for establishing FRAND, where an injunction is still the ultimate threat and incentive to enter into licence agreements.[127]

(iii) The EU Commission investigation

The EU Commission has not yet handed down a decision regarding Google and its use of Motorola's SEPs. In April 2012, the EU Commission issued a statement that it was opening proceedings against Motorola (and in another case, but with similar circumstances, against Samsung[128]). The Commission was responding to to complaints by Apple and

---

[125] See Third Party United States Federal Trade Commission's Statement on the Public Interest filed on 6 June 2012 in re Certain Wireless Communication Devices Portable Music & Data Processing Devices, Computers & Components thereof, Inv. No 337-TA-745, www.ftc.gov/os/2012/06/1206ftcwirelesscom-pdf. Accessed 11 July 2013.

[126] In the Matter of Robert Bosch GmbH Docket No. C-4377 File No. 121 0081, Decision and Order, April 24, 2013. Accessed 11 July 2013.

[127] This is clearly in line with what some commentators have argued is the best idea. Thus, FRAND implies a procedure for establishing fair terms of licensing. Cf. Mark Lemley and Carl Shapiro, 'A Simple Approach to Setting Reasonable Royalties for Standard-Essential Patents', (2013) 28 *Berkeley Technology Law Journal* 1135.

[128] See press release regarding Samsung from 31 January 2012, http://europa.eu/rapid/press-release_IP-12-89_en.htm?locale=en, accessed 10 July 2013. There is also a forgotten interesting case regarding Honeywell, where the EU Commission states: 'The Commission is investigating complaints alleging that Honeywell International Inc. and E.I. du Pont de Nemours and Company have entered into anti-competitive arrangements as regards the development of the new generation of refrigerants. Specifically, the Commission will investigate whether joint development, licensing and production arrangements entered into between the two companies in relation to these refrigerants restrict competition on the markets. Such behavior may infringe Article 101 of the Treaty on the Functioning of the EU and Article 53 of the EEA Agreement. The Commission is also examining whether Honeywell engaged in deceptive conduct during the evaluation of 1234yf between 2007 and 2009. It is claimed that Honeywell did not disclose its patents and patent applications while the refrigerant was being assessed and then failed to grant licences on FRAND terms. Such behavior may

Microsoft. The Commission is investigating, in particular, whether by seeking and enforcing injunctions against Apple's and Microsoft's flagship products, such as iPhone, iPad, Windows and Xbox, on the basis of patents it had declared essential for producing standard-compliant products, Motorola had failed to honour its irrevocable commitments to SSOs. In these commitments, Motorola engaged to license those standard-essential patents on FRAND terms. The Commission is examining whether Motorola's behaviour amounts to an abuse of a dominant market position as prohibited by Article 102 TFEU.[129]

In May 2013, the EU Commission took a further step and issued a Statement of Objection against Motorola in reference to its Apple litigation.[130] The Commission's preliminary view was that the acceptance of binding third party determination (for example a court) for the terms of a FRAND licence, in the event that bilateral negotiations do not come to a fruitful conclusion, is still a clear indication that a potential licensee is 'willing' to enter into a FRAND licence. This could be interpreted as not adhering to the *Orange-Book-Standard* test because, in that case, the Federal Supreme Court indicated that the alleged infringer must actually state an amount and stick to that (or accept whatever the patentee says is FRAND and thereafter litigate).[131] There it did not seem to be any room for real negotiations. But the Commission instead states that FRAND is the process by which an adequate remuneration of the SEP-holder is decided. If the infringer commits to the process, seeking or enforcing injunctions is no longer justified.

In addition, in the Commission's preliminary view, the fact that the potential licensee challenges the validity, essentiality or infringement of the SEP does not make it 'unwilling' to license if it otherwise agrees to be bound by the determination of FRAND terms by a third party (e.g.

---

also infringe European competition rules (Article 102 of the Treaty on the Functioning of the EU and Article 54 of the EEA Agreement)'. See EU commission press release regarding Honeywell et al from December 2011, http://europa.eu/rapid/press-release_IP-11-1560_en.htm?locale=en. Accessed 10 July 2013.

[129] See press release by the EU commission regarding Motorola dated 3 April 2012, http://europa.eu/rapid/press-release_IP-12-345_en.htm?locale=en. Accessed 11 July 2013.

[130] 'Antitrust: Commission Sends Statement of Objections to Motorola Mobility on Potential Misuse of Mobile Phone Standard-Essential Patents – Questions and Answers'. Reference: MEMO/13/403 Event Date: 06/05/2013 http://europa.eu/rapid/press-release_MEMO-13-403_en.htm, accessed 11 July 2013.

[131] See discussion, supra.

arbitrator panel).[132] In the case before the Commission, Motorola required non-challenge covenants that prohibited challenges by Apple, even after Apple had agreed to be bound by a third party determination of the FRAND terms. The Commission's preliminary view was that it is in the public interest that licensees should be able to challenge the validity, essentiality or infringement of SEPs. Again, the Commission seems to be more lenient than the German *Orange-Book-Standard* court. The hypothetical licence agreement may thus not include a non-challenge clause and the hypothetical licensee may still try to get a low royalty rate as long as the undertaking commits to a licence and to a process for establishing FRAND.

The Commission also mentioned *Orange-Book-Standard* and stated: 'The [German] Supreme Court's ruling did not specifically relate to SEPs. The Commission's preliminary view is that an interpretation of that ruling whereby a willing licensee is essentially not entitled to challenge the validity and essentiality of the SEPs in question is potentially anti-competitive.'[133] Perhaps, one could conclude that the EU Commission is trying to state that FRAND represents a procedure. If the parties have agreed to FRAND that implies entering into a procedure to establish FRAND, where they will abide by the outcome of the court or arbitration panel proceedings. However, the question is under what rule or doctrine is the EU Commission stating this? It could be that the EU Commission is still working under the doctrine of 'refusal to license' or exceptional circumstances (i.e. *IMS Health* and *Microsft*) and is here focusing on the fair terms for accessing the standard essential or interoperability essential patents. However, it could also be that the EU Commission believes that the terms asked for, i.e. a non-challenge clause, and the burden of defining how a FRAND royalty under *Orange-Book-Standard* applies to the potential licence, are in themselves unfair terms to a degree that amounts to abuse of dominance. Thus, they are unfair trading conditions under Art 102 (a) TFEU. In the TT Guidelines,

---

[132] 'Antitrust: Commission Sends Statement of Objections to Motorola Mobility on Potential Misuse of Mobile Phone Standard-Essential Patents – Questions and Answers'. Reference: MEMO/13/403 Event Date: 06/05/2013 http://europa.eu/rapid/press-release_MEMO-13-403_en.htm., accessed 11 July 2013.

[133] 'Antitrust: Commission Sends Statement of Objections to Motorola Mobility on Potential Misuse of Mobile Phone Standard-Essential Patents – Questions and Answers'. Reference: MEMO/13/403 Event Date: 06/05/2013 http://europa.eu/rapid/press-release_MEMO-13-403_en.htm., accessed 11 july 2013.

non-challenge clauses are treated differently, according to whether they are inside a technology transfer agreement or a settlement agreement.[134] The reason for excluding non-challenge clauses from the scope of the TTBER, according to the Commission, was the fact that licensees are normally in the best position to determine whether or not an intellectual property right is invalid. In the interest of undistorted competition and in conformity with the principles underlying the protection of intellectual property, invalid intellectual property rights should be eliminated. This does not apply to a settlement agreement regarding said rights.

In addition, the CJEU, in the latest development, has recently received a request for a preliminary ruling from a court in Dusseldorf regarding the interface between competition law and intellectual property law with reference to an injunction based on an SEP, where the CJEU is given the opportunity to develop the EU FRAND rules.[135]

6.5.4 The US and EU Doctrines

Interestingly, under US law, the issues of patent ambush and FRAND ambush/hold-up is dealt with under intellectual property law. The *eBay* ruling by the Supreme Court is the cornerstone of the development. Interestingly, the *eBay* ruling is based on the use of words and terms that we seldom hear from the Supreme Court, and, furthermore, nowadays never hear in competition law cases. The Supreme Court's use of 'fairness' and 'equity' in injunction cases, as well as in intellectual property law, seems rather like breaking new ground. It is also a break with the development of tougher and stricter intellectual property laws. The Supreme Court seems to have halted and even reversed the quest by the Federal circuit for stricter intellectual property regulation of infringers.

On the other hand, under antitrust law, neither in *Rambus, the Google* cases, nor now for the *Google* consent order, does any court or the FTC seem bold enough to take the step of stating that a unilateral use of SEPs so to hold up the market is in violation of US antitrust law. The exception is the 3rd Circuit's ruling in *Qualcomm*[136] and the *Apple v. Samsung*[137] case from California regarding patent ambush. Given the fact that the FTC *e contrario* has now stated that patent hold-up is not a violation of US antitrust law, a successful action by a private plaintiff seems

[134] TT Guidelines, paras 111 compared to para. 209.
[135] See C-170/13, Huawei Technologies V. ZTD.
[136] Broadcom v. Qualcomm Inc. 501 F.3d. 297 (3d Cir. 2007).
[137] Apple, Inc. v. Samsung Electronics. Ltd et al, C-11-1846 & C 12-0630.

unrealistic. To summarize the current case law: (i) patent misuse, estoppels, and waiver doctrines, imply that deceiving an SSO may render the SEPs unenforceable (Federal Circuit, *Qualcomm*); (ii) Sec. 2 Sherman Act (attempt to monopolize) may be applicable when a patentee deceives an SSO that it will apply FRAND terms (the 3rd Circuit's ruling in *Qualcomm*); however, (iii), according to *Rambus*, a plaintiff needs to show anti-competitive effect in the form of evidence that the SSO would have selected another technology to standardize had it known about the hidden patents; (iv) charging supra-FRAND royalty is not an antitrust violation, i.e. no benchmark for monopolization; and finally, (v) the use of patent and FRAND hold-up is a violation of Sec. 5 FTC Act as unfair competitive conduct, while it cannot, according to the FTC, be a violation of the antitrust laws.

The conclusion is that US antitrust law plays a minor role in regulating, if not anti-competitive, at least anti-competitor behaviour under standards, and is more patentee friendly than US IP laws and US unfair competition law. The IP law related doctrine under the rules of injunction seems to imply that equity and public policy considerations, above and beyond, the ambit of US antitrust law are applicable, while US antirust law is more limited. US antitrust law is constrained not by a doctrinal idea of the inherency doctrine or the interface between intellectual property law and competition law, but instead because of the impossibility of showing anti-competitive effects with reference to nascent or not yet traded patents or technologies. One of aspect of standards is that they consist of agreements on the establishment of future markets. Such agreements cannot be fitted into the classical notion of anti-competitive harm being conduct on relevant markets, especially when dealing with interoperability standards. Such standards, due to network effects, do not open up for inter technology competition. Therefore, Courts being schooled in the classical Chicago school economics cannot identify the conduct as anti-competitive.

In Europe, it seems that EU competition law is more readily available than the exemptions under Member States' patent laws. This is somewhat odd since these cases are patent infringement cases and an intellectual property law solution could for several reasons be preferable.[138] Possibly, given that, for example German law, unlike US Patent law, does not have

[138] Cf. Marcus Glader, Standards, 'Competition and Intellectual Property Rights – An Overview of Current Controversies', in Hans Henrik Lidgard (ed) *Nordic Perspective on Competition in Innovation Markets*, (Maria Magle Publishing, Lund 2013), 89 et seq, 105 arguing that the EU Commisison should file an amicus curiae brief in specific cases so as to resolve the EU competition law

a public policy exemption under the injunction rules (while there is a public policy exemption under German patent law, as well under most EU Member States' patent laws), the German courts make use of the 'EU defence' in the injunction cases. EU competition law is still applicable, while the public policy exemption is not. In other words, the German court in *Orange-Book-Standard* made use of the 'EU competition law defence' in the patent injunction case, while there is no fairness exemption under the German injunction doctrine. On the contrary, in these situations, the Supreme Court in *eBay* found that the policy requirement was fulfilled by finding an 'exemption' under US patent law, while the US antitrust laws are not applicable according to the FTC in *Google* and the D.C. Circuit in *Rambus*.

The final issue is, then, which jurisdiction is more lenient? The US courts have opened up the possibility of using public policy and equity, which of course have more 'fluffy' boundaries than the rather strict use of EU competition law as an exemption displayed in the German Courts. The Commission now seems to make the EU procedure less harsh. Nonetheless, the US has held the US antitrust law free from any other objectives than the pure 'antitrust value' of efficiency and may therefore develop another doctrine entirely under the *eBay* doctrine, not being tied down by antitrust law doctrines. While this shows that the US Judges have not embraced post-Chicago ideas and still utilize more orthodox neo-conservative pricing tests of perfect competition, it implies that US intellectual property law is developing in a more flexible way and is now more lenient on infringers then US Antitrust law.

In fact, the issue boils down to whether injunctions should be applicable at all in standard setting situations, or whether injunctions should, at least, be applicable when the potential licensee does not even want to license on FRAND terms. Under the European development (under EU competition law) it seems that there is a requirement for a 'willing' licensee, implying that if the potential licensee is an unwilling licensee, i.e. does not even agree to FRAND, then the injunction tool is still available. Under the US development this is not as clear-cut. Judge Posner's decision, which for example, Nokia has attacked in amicus briefs, seem to imply that injunctions should not be applicable in these situations.[139]

issue, while antitrust enforcement in specific cases may not be the most efficient way to provide guidance.

[139] Judge Posners decision in Apple v. Microsoft is discussed in Chapter 6.7. See Apple v. Microsoft, in the United District Court for the Northern District of Illinois Eastern Division, No. 1:11-cv-08540 Apple, Inc. et al. v. Motorola,

6.6 ESSENTIALITY, OVERDECLARING ESSENTIALITY AND WORKAROUNDS

The notion of essentiality under a standard or a patent pool is important. It is the ground of what should constitute SEPs, and also of what patents may be included in a patent pool, if that pool is to come within the safe harbour. There are two different kinds of 'essentiality': technical essential and economic essential. The Business Review Letters chart a development between the MPEG-2 pool and the DVD pools.[140] The pools described in the DVD letters had fewer licensors and a wider definition of essentiality by comparison with the Business Review Letter covering the first modern patent pool, MPEG-2.[141] Technical essentiality implies that these patents cannot be worked around or designed around, if the firm still wants to adhere to the standard or the technology defined in the pool agreement. With regards to the DVD pools, not only were technically essential patents allowed into the pools, but also those for which existing alternatives were economically unfeasible.[142] Thus, in theory, although not technical impossible, a firm could not economically invent around the patents included in the pool and still adhere to the defined technology: such patents were also essential to the pool.

The acceptance of economic essentiality for patent pools was a way of including more patents in the pools. Still, an expert would preferably select the patents for the pool. However, when it comes to the case of a standard, the notion of essentiality becomes somewhat different.

For standard 'essentiality' is a different concept. While the definition under SDOs IP policies often stipulates technical essentiality[143], SDOs

Inc. and Motorola Mobility, Inc. Opinion and Order June 22, 2012, 26 et seq. See also 'Nokia sides with Google against Judge Posner and Apple on FRAND' http://www.fosspatents.com/2013/04/nokia-sides-with-google-against-judge.html. Accessed 11 July 2013.

140 Cf. supra Chapter 5.4.2.

141 Today, there seem to be several licensors for patents connected to the DVD technology. Or, at least there are several licensors of patents under the AC-3 technology developed by Dolby Inc., which created several innovative technologies within the sphere of the DVD technology.

142 See e.g., 3DVD pool Business Review Letter from Joel Klein to Gerrard Beeney dated 16 December 1998, fn. 8.

143 The ETSI IP Guide for example reads: '"ESSENTIAL" as applied to IPR means that it is not possible on technical (but not commercial) grounds, taking into account normal technical practice and the state of the art generally available at the time of standardization, to make, sell, lease, otherwise dispose of, repair, use or operate EQUIPMENT or METHODS which comply with a STANDARD

do not control whether claimed essential patents actually are essential. As a result, firms have claimed that their patents are essential while this is unlikely or even highly unlikely. The incentive for this is to be listed as essential under a standard and thereby receive FRAND royalty payments for firms that utilize the standard.

There is also an incentive for firms to cause patents, which have been claimed to be essential, to become non-essential. In *Nokia v. InterDigital*[144], Nokia argued that a number of patents that were declared essential in the ETSI database for 3G, should be declared non-essential. This was important to Nokia since the parties were to undertake licence negotiations. InterDigital tried to get the case dismissed on the basis that the court did not have jurisdiction. The English court refused InterDigital's motion to dismiss and claimed jurisdiction. According to Tapia, this was the first court ever to do that.[145] The reason for claiming jurisdiction, and for Nokia's well-founded claims, was that the number of essential patents was connected to the size of the royalty rate that needed to be negotiated or litigated. In the end, the court held only one patent covered process to be essential, while InterDigital initially had claimed 29 patents to be essential.[146]

While this was not a competition law case, it still raises the question whether InterDigital was abusing its alleged dominant position. Can 'over-declaring' the number of essential patents under a standard amount to abuse of dominance? Under, for example, the *AstraZaneca* case, misusing the regulatory system for obtaining supplementary protection certificates (SPCs) (i.e. wrongfully gaining five more years of exclusivity for selling a certain drug, Losec) was considered an abuse. Could claiming patents to be essential under a standard, when knowing they are not, be a misuse, amounting to abuse of dominance? The EU commission discussion in the *Google* merger case suggests that InterDigital would

without infringing that IPR. For the avoidance of doubt in exceptional cases where a STANDARD can only be implemented by technical solutions, all of which are infringements of IPRs, all such IPRs shall be considered ESSENTIAL'.

144 Nokia v. InterDigital, English and Wales High Court 802 (Pat), Pumfrey J., 12 April 2006, BL C746.

145 Claudia Tapia, *Industrial Property Rights, Technical Standards and Licensing Practices (FRAND) in the Telecommunications Industry* (Carl Heymanns Verlag – eine Marke von Wolters Kluwer Deutschland GmbH, 2010), 44.

146 Nokia v. InterDigital, English and Wales High Court 802 (Pat), 21 December 2007.

probably be considered dominant even though holding just one essential process claim.

InterDigital claiming more patents to be essential under the standard also raised prices for customers and consumers. Nonetheless, the risk should perhaps still lie with the licensee or potential licensee. Many argue that if a heighten obligation to identify essentiality is set, the standard-setting procedure, as a whole may fail or, at least, not work effectively. Furthermore, it is very difficult to identify technical essentiality. However, given the huge problems with over-declaration, perhaps there should be some disincentives for claiming patents as essential.

On the other hand, with the FTC *Google* settlement decree, the *Orange-Book-Standard* case and the forthcoming EU Commission decision regarding Google's injunction litigation, what patents are essential under a standard, and what patents are not, becomes even more important. Interestingly, the dichotomy between SEPs under a standard and non-SEPs now decides whether an infringer risks being exposed to injunctions or not. If the definition of essential were narrow, i.e. only technical essential, as actually stipulated in, for example, ETSI's definition of essential, then many firms that put their hopes in the FTC *Google* consent decree will be disappointed. For example, should a holder of SEPs be able to claim that injunctions are still available to it because the SEP that has been infringed can be designed around? Google or other firms might claim to ETSI, for example, that their patents are potentially essential but that does not imply that they are essential to that degree that they cannot be worked or designed around.[147] Clearly, there has been an inflation of the term 'essentiality' as regards the patents that a firm can claim are essential to a standard. Some SDOs also allow for potential SEPs to be listed separately. If the *eBay*-rule, FTC *Google* consent decree, and *Orange-Book-Standard* only apply to technical essential patents, then perhaps the problem of injunctive relief will not go away. The fact that the FTC connected its Google order to ETSI's definition of essential is therefore somewhat unsatisfactory. Judge Posner, in his dismissal of both Apple's and Motorola's injunction claims, noted that there might be a difference between notifying a patent as essential for a standard to an SDO, and the conclusion that the patent, upon closer scrutiny, actual was essential. He, thus, acknowledges that firms might have an incentive to notify patents as essential, and he seems to suggest

[147] Judge Posner raised the same issue in Apple v. Microsoft In the United District Court for the Northern District of Illinois Eastern Division, No. 1:11-cv-08540 Apple, Inc. et al. v. Motorola, Inc. and Motorola Mobility, Inc. Opinion and Order June 22, 2012, 15 et seq.

that the patentee claiming the patent as essential will have difficulties in obtaining an injunction under the *eBay* ruling, even though, after more extensive analysis, the patents are found not to be essential.[148]

There is, of course, another side to the discussion about essential patents. Several firms package their essential patents with their non-essential patents, and require licensees to take out a licence for the whole package. Alternatively, holders of SEPs demand that the licensees enter into a cross-licence, including the patentee's whole portfolio, for access to the SEP holders' whole patent portfolio.

Both the FTC and the EU Commission discusse package licences with reference to patent pools, and it seems that the EU Commission may, with respect to patent pools, accept such package licences under Art 101(3) TFEU, even if the patent pool holds a dominant position and a significant number of non-essential patents are included in the pool, if the defendant can show that the package licence is indispensible to the attainment of particular efficiencies.[149] It should, however, be mentioned that the Court in *U.S. Philips I* refused to use the dichotomy produced by ITC regarding essential and non-essential, and instead utilized the test for tying one patent to another. The Court dissmissed, or at least, found it very difficult to find a violation under the rule of reason when analysing tying one patent to another.[150] It seems clear that, at least in the US, the firms licensing essential and non-essential patents as a package may make use of the *U.S. Philips I* case and allege that the non-essential patents are included for 'free'. In addition, they could also probably demand non-essential patents under cross-licence agreements on a voluntary basis. However, under the New TT Guidelines, the EU Commission would find a tie between two patents, outside the sphere of patent pools, and judge that independently, without a similar rule of reason discussion as took place in *U.S. Philips I*.[151] In fact, the burden of proof in these EU situations seem to lie on the defendant to show efficiencies that should exempt the package licences.[152] Under antitrust law, it seems, therefore,

[148] Ibid, 17 et seq.

[149] New TT Guidelines, paras. 163, 245 et seq.

[150] See Chapter 5.3.4.

[151] New TT Guidelines at paras 206 et seq.

[152] The Shenzhen Intermediate People's Court recently issued two decisions in cases filed by Huawei Technologies against InterDigital. One complaint alleged that InterDigital participated in ETSI standards activities but failed to negotiate or offer to license certain SEPs on FRAND terms. The court ruled that InterDigital's offers did not comply with FRAND. In the second case, the court held that InterDigital violated the Anti-Monopoly Law by demanding excessive

that, irrespective of what other commentators claim, binding essential patents to non-essential ones should be judged under a rule of reason, and perhaps will not violate antitrust law. However, an SEP holder demanding non-essential patents under a cross-licence scheme may, perhaps, be regarded as unfair trading conditions under either Art 5 FTC Act, or under Art 102 (a) TFEU. Thus, it does not amount to a FRAND term and does not mirror competition on the merits.

Given the above, the notion of essentiality under SDOs IP arrangements and standards should *de lege ferenda* be economic essential, as the rule is for patent pools, and not technical essential. Furthermore, firms that claim essentiality are at the risk of, in certain grave cases, abusing their dominant position if it becomes clear that the patents are not essential and the holder knowingly deceived the SSO about them. Such a rule would mirror the regulatory misuse doctrine under US antitrust law.

Otherwise, firms may either face injunctions, even though the SEP they are violating is *de facto* not an SEP, or they will try to invent around SEPs under a standard.[153] That might become overly expensive. Under the injunction doctrine, the risk of whether a SEP is a SEP would thus lie with the firm claiming the patent as an SEP, irrespective of what the by-laws or IP policies of the relevant SSO say. In fact, the issue is not whether there is a substitute technology. Instead, it is whether there is a plausible competing technology for the potential licensee.

If there is a viable competing technology (outside or inside the standard) and a firm utilizing the standard violates one of the competing technologies without entering into a licence agreement with the patentee of the SEP, then, possibly, the patentee should still retain the right to seek and obtain injunctions even though the SEP is not essential but only infringed.[154]

Finally, *de lege ferenda*, the issue of tying essential patents to non-essential one, or demanding non-essential patents under cross-licence

---

royalties, tying the licensing of essential patents to non-essential patents, demanding a grant-back of certain patent rights from Huawei, and commencing an action in the U.S. ITC while still in negotiation. See Shylah Alfonso and Kevin Zeck, Tidbits (Report by ABA Intellectual Property Committee), http://www.americanbar.org/content/dam/aba/publications/antitrust_law/at315000_tidbits_20130405.authcheckdam.pdf . Accessed 12 September 2013.

[153] In cases before the ITC, firms have discussed whether an SEP can be designed around to avoid infringing it.

[154] In the United District Court for the Northern District of Illinois Eastern Division, No. 1:11-cv-08540 Apple, Inc. et al. v. Motorola, Inc. and Motorola Mobility, Inc. Opinion and Order June 22, 2012.

agreements should be judged under the specific rules relating to standards. Possibly, such conduct is not 'competition on the merits' and is a violation of the integrity of the standard-setting procedure.[155] However, perhaps this issue will be judged differently should the rules change from technical essentiality to economic essentiality.

6.7 DEFINING FRAND

The definition of FRAND has been a topic of great debate. Several economists have devoted substantial time to working out a test for what might be regarded as FRAND. Swanson and Baumol famously tried to establish a test based on auctioning out standards.[156] Geradin and other commentators have also tried to establish certain tests for establishing FRAND.[157] Furthermore, there has been a big debate whether there is a 25 per cent rule of thumb.[158] Several commentators point to *Unicol v. Microsoft*, and that the 25 per cent rule was dismissed by the Federal Circuit.[159]

---

[155] The EU Commission will be able to comment on this during either its Google/Motorola or Samsung investigation. Furthermore, CJEU may discuss this in Huawei v. ZTD.

[156] Daniel Swanson and William Baumol, 'Reasonable and Nondiscriminatory (RAND) Royalties, Standards Selection, and Control of Market Power', (2005) 73 *Antitrust Law Journal*, 1.

[157] Damien Geradin, 'Standardization and Technological Innovation: Some Reflections on Ex-ante Licensing, FRAND, and the Proper Means to Reward Innovators', (2006) 29 *World Competition*, 511; Doug Lichtman, 'Understanding the RAND Commitment', (2010) 47 *Houston Law Review*, 1023; Anne Layne-Farrar et al., 'Pricing Patents for Licensing in Standard-Setting Organizations: Making Sense of FRAND Commitments', (2007) 74 *Antitrust Law Journal*, 671; Mark Lemley and Carl Shapiro, 'Patent Holdup and Royalty Stacking', (2007) 85 *Texas Law Review*, 1991; Mark Lemley, 'Intellectual Property Rights and Standard-Setting Organizations', (2002) 90 *California Law Review*, 1889; Joseph Farrell et al., 'Standard Setting, Patents, and Hold-up', (2007) 74 *Antitrust Law Journal*, 603, and also to some extent Carl Shapiro, 'Setting Compatibility Standards: Cooperation or Collusion?', in Rochelle Dreyfuss et al. (eds), *Expanding The Boundaries of Intellectual Property* (Oxford University Press, 2001), 81.

[158] For reference and critique, please see Ove Granstrand and Marcus Holgersson, 'The 25% Rule Revisited and a new Investment-based Method for Determining FRAND Licensing Royalties', (2012) 47 *Les Nouvelles*, 3, 188.

[159] Uniloc U.S.A v. Microsoft Corp. 632 F 3.d 1292 (Fed. Cir. 2011).

Furthermore, the level of FRAND is clearly an issue that can trigger almost a debate on ideology. The open source movement has several supporters, and to some extent the IT industry with its inclination to incremental development of several small innovations may be better served with standards that are open and free of charge.[160] In fact, even competition law officers have stated that if there is a non-proprietary alternative to a proprietary technology, selecting the proprietary technology would imply raising costs for the industry as a whole.[161]

There are several cases concerning FRAND. Before Judge Posner in the Northern District of Illinois Eastern Division, Apple and Motorola both sought damages for infringements of SEPs and and asked for related injunctions against each other. Posner dismissed the claims and the case in its entirety, mainly due to the parties' inability to provide evidence for their claims for damages. Nonetheless, he took time to discuss some aspects of the case. Judge Posner made reference to Swanson and Baumol and referred to an *ex ante* as opposed to *ex post* model for establishing damages, where the value of the patent under FRAND would be established from the value of the innovation before it became covered by the standard. Furthermore, Posner discussed several different methods, and also the connection between damages, FRAND, a compulsory licence or 'on-going royalty'.[162] Posner made reference to Kennedy's statement in *eBay*, and stated that the case before him was what Kennedy's statement was all about: the patented invention is but a small component of the product the companies seek to produce and the threat of an injunction is employed simply to obtain undue leverage in negotiations.[163]

Posner then discussed the case-law-based method, the *Georgia-Pacific* factors, regarding what might be considered fair return of a patent.[164]

---

160 Cf. Marcus Glader, 'Standards, Competition and Intellectual Property Rights – An Overview of Current Controversies', in Hans Henrik Lidgard (ed) *Nordic Perspective on Competition in Innovation Markets*, (Maria Magle Publishing, Lund, 2013), 89, 98.

161 See Neelie Kroes, Former European Commissioner for Competition Policy, 'Setting the Standards High', speech before the Harvard Club of Belgium, Brussels, 15 October 2009, accessed 13 October 2011.

162 See Apple v. Microsoft, In the United District Court for the Northern District of Illinois Eastern Division, No. 1:11-cv-08540 Apple, Inc. et al. v. Motorola, Inc. and Motorola Mobility, Inc. Opinion and Order June 22, 2012., 26 et seq.

163 Ibid. eBay Inc. v. MercExchange, L.L.C., 547 U.S. 388, 400. (2006)

164 Referring to a long list of considerations derived from Georgia-Pacific v. United States Plywood Corp. 318 F. Supp. 1116, 1120 (S.D.N.Y 1970).

Posner clearly finds the *Georgia-Pacific* factors too imprecise. Instead, basing his ideas on an *ex ante* versus *ex post* model, where the damages would be based on the value of the patents before they became essential, Posner seems to paint a picture by which such an analysis could also become the basis for the on-going royalty, i.e. *de facto* on-going damages under the *eBay* rule.[165]

Posner's case is under appeal so we do not know the ultimate outcome.[166] Several firms have been critical of Posner's statements. They indicate that Posner implies that injunctions would never be available to SEP holders, whilst there is any possibility of obtaining damages. Nokia has decided to intervene in the Appeal Court case, specifically commenting on the consequences of Posner's discussion. Nokia claims that, according to Posner, injunctive relief will never be applicable to a holder of an SEP.[167] Nokia argues that Posner creates a bright-line rule prohibiting injunctions in standard-essential contexts. According to Nokia, it seems that to Posner injunctions should not be available should a firm refuse to negotiate FRAND licence terms, while it is available only when the firm refuse outright to enter a licence agreement. This would open the way for firms to obstruct the standard-setting process and cause the patentees to have to go the courts on a continual basis. Nokia stresses that Google, in the settlement with FTC, is allowed under certain circumstances to seek and obtain injunctions and that the *eBay* case does not prohibit injunctions, but instead promotes a case-by-case analysis of whether injunctive relief should be available.[168] Thus, Nokia focuses on the definition of a 'willing' potential licensee. The threshold for being

---

165 See Apple v. Microsoft, In the United District Court for the Northern District of Illinois Eastern Division, No. 1:11-cv-08540 Apple, Inc. et al. v. Motorola, Inc. and Motorola Mobility, Inc. Opinion and Order June 22, 2012, 26 et seq.

166 It is possible leaning towards a victory for Apple. Cf. http://www.fosspatents.com/2013/09/apple-winning-posner-appeal-chief-judge.html. Accessed 28 February 2014.

167 'Nokia sides with Google against Judge Posner and Apple on FRAND' http://www.fosspatents.com/2013/04/nokia-sides-with-google-against-judge.html. Accessed 11 July 2013. Ericsson clearly holds the same belief as Nokia. Those injunctive reliefs should be available on a regular basis also for holders of SEPs. Cf. 'New Ericsson Lawsuits against Samsung Indirectly help Apple in Fight against FRAND abuse' http://www.fosspatents.com/2012/11/new-ericsson-lawsuits-against-samsung.html, accessed 11 July 2013.

168 Nokia et al, amicus brief in United States Court of Appeals for the Federal Circuit, case no 12-1548, filed 6 May 2013.

considered a willing licensee, and thereby being protected from injunctions, must be at a level where the potential licensee will not abuse the notion of being 'willing' to enter a licence agreement. There should be a heightened requirement for obtaining the privileged situation that Posner is advancing and it must be clear that the firm is truly willing to enter into a licence on FRAND terms with the SEP holder before being protected from permanent injunction suits.

Nokia has likewise intervened with the similar purpose in the *Apple v. Samsung* case in the Federal Circuit.[169] *Apple v. Samsung* is the high-profile smartphone case originating in Northern California, where Apple at one point was denied a permanent injunction by District Judge Lucy Koh.[170] Nokia's and also Ericsson's concern is that US Courts will eliminate the tool of injunctive relief, while the courts believe that every SEP holder claims excessive royalties. Nokia and Ericsson purportedly do not claim excessive royalties. Instead, they are faced what is called reverse FRAND hold-up: 'unwilling' firms refusing to pay FRAND even though clearly infringing the SEPs. These firms may even have had licence agreements for extended periods but now either refuse to enter new licence agreements or simply refuse to pay the royalties due under the licence agreements.[171] The reason for this behaviour is that the law regarding injunctions and damages for infringement is in a state of flux and these firms try to wait and see whether the US Courts will alter the balance and grant them access under *eBay* and a low 'royalty rate' under the currently developing FRAND case law.

On the other hand, it seems that Microsoft and Apple give more support to the view that injunctions should not be available to SEP holders.[172] Microsoft claims that the standard-setting procedure under SDOs would be a 'blatant antitrust violations' without adherence to FRAND commitments.[173]

---

[169] Nokia files amicus brief supporting Apple's pursuit of a permanent injunction against Samsung, http://www.fosspatents.com/2013/03/nokia-files-amicus-brief-supporting.html, accessed 12 July 2013.

[170] Apple, Inc. v. Samsung Electronics. Ltd et al, C-11-1846 & C 12-0630.

[171] New Ericsson lawsuits against Samsung indirectly help Apple in fight against FRAND abuse, http://www.fosspatents.com/2012/11/new-ericsson-lawsuits-against-samsung.html, accessed 11 July 2013.

[172] Microsoft brief stresses that standard-setting would be a 'blatant antitrust violation' without FRAND, http://www.fosspatents.com/2013/06/microsoft-brief-stresses-that-standard.html, accessed 11 July 2013.

[173] Ibid.

The recent joint statement by the Justice Department and the United States Patent Trademark Office (PTO) to the ITC supports Nokia's view that there cannot be a prohibition on injunctions for holders of SEPs.[174] The statement reads (footnotes omitted):

> An exclusion order may still be an appropriate remedy in some circumstances, such as where the putative licensee is unable or refuses to take an F/RAND license and is acting outside the scope of the patent holder's commitment to license on F/RAND terms. For example, if a putative licensee refuses to pay what has been determined to be a F/RAND royalty, or refuses to engage in a negotiation to determine F/RAND terms, an exclusion order could be appropriate. Such a refusal could take the form of a constructive refusal to negotiate, such as by insisting on terms clearly outside the bounds of what could reasonably be considered to be F/RAND terms in an attempt to evade the putative licensee's obligation to fairly compensate the patent holder. An exclusion order also could be appropriate if a putative licensee is not subject to the jurisdiction of a court that could award damages. This list is not an exhaustive one.'[175]

The agencies seem to leave room for injunctions also when the potential licensee does not engage in licence negotiations, while still not refusing to agree a licence on FRAND terms. Thus, the notion of 'willing licensee' implies an actual engagement to negotiate.

Nokia was also critical of the ideas Posner put forward regarding establishing the damages under a FRAND infringement suit. According to Nokia, Posner puts a cap on the damages by calculating damages base on the smallest saleable component. The damages (royalty rate) must be established taking all the value adding features of the patent into consideration, including the value of the system or products sold by the licensee.[176]

However, there is a US Court that has now tried to establish FRAND. As stated above, Judge Robart tried the *Microsoft v. Motorola* contract case[177]. The main issue of the case was the meaning of RAND. Without a clear understanding of RAND, according to Judge Robart, it would be

---

[174] Justice Department & PTO Policy Statement on Remedies for Standard-Essential Patents Subject to Voluntary F/RAND Commitments, 8 January 2013, http://www.justice.gov/atr/public/guidelines/290994.pdf, accessed 11 July 2013.

[175] Ibid, 7.

[176] Nokia et al, amicus brief in United States Court of Appeals for the Federal Circuit, case no 12-1548, filed 6 May 2013.

[177] United States District Court Western District of Washington at Seattle, Microsoft v. Motorola, Case no. C10-1823 JLR, Findings of Fact and Conclusion in Law, 25 April 2013.

difficult or impossible to figure out if Motorola breached its obligation to license its patents on RAND terms.

The outcome of the case is that a third party may rely on the FRAND statement made by the patentee to the SDO. The courts found that, when a holder of a standards-essential patent makes a commitment to an SDO to license such patents on FRAND terms, it does so for the intended benefit of members of the SDO and third parties implementing the standard. These putative licensees are beneficiaries with rights to sue for breach of that commitment under US contract law.[178]

In the case, Robart delivered a decision where he, by utilizing the Georgia-Pacific factors, establishes the RAND rate. First, Judge Robart stipulated some basic principles[179]:

(i) RAND royalty should be set at a level consistent with the SSO's goal of promoting widespread adoption of its standards.
(ii) The proper methodology should address the risk of royalty-stacking by considering the aggregate royalties that would apply if other SEP holders made royalty demands of the implementer.
(iii) Fundamentally, a RAND commitment should be interpreted to limit a patent holder to a reasonable royalty on the economic value of its patented technology, apart from the value associated with incorporation of the patented technology into the standard. In other words, the *ex ante/ex post* test, and not taking in to consideration any hold-up value for when the patents become SEPs, or the value of the standard as such.
(iv) In the context of a dispute concerning whether or not a given royalty is RAND, a proper methodology used to determine a

[178] See Microsoft Corp. v. Motorola, Inc., 864 F. Supp. 2d 1023, 1030-33 (W.D. Wash. 2012); Microsoft Corp. v. Motorola, Inc.,854 F. Supp. 2d 993, 999-1001 (W.D. Wash. 2012); see also Microsoft Corp. v. Motorola, Inc., 696 F.3d 872, 884 (9th Cir. 2012) (holding that the 'district court's conclusions that Motorola's RAND declarations to the ITU created a contract enforceable by Microsoft as a third-party beneficiary (which Motorola concedes), and that this contract governs in some way what actions Motorola may take to enforce its ITU standard-essential patents (including the patents at issue in the German suit), were not legally erroneous'); Apple, Inc. v. Motorola Mobility, Inc., – F. Supp. 2d – , No. 11-cv-178bbc, 2012 WL 3289835, at *21-22 (W.D. Wis. Aug. 10, 2012); Apple, Inc. v. Motorola Mobility, Inc., No. 11-cv-178bbc, 2011 WL 7324582, at *7-11 (W.D. Wis. June 10, 2011).

[179] United States District Court Western District of Washington at Seattle, Microsoft v. Motorola, Case no. C10-1823 JLR, Findings of Fact and Conclusion in Law, 25 April 2013, 25 et seq, paras 100 et seq.

> RAND royalty should therefore recognize and seek to mitigate the risk of patent hold-up that RAND commitments are intended to avoid. At the same time, a RAND royalty should be set with the understanding that SSOs include technology intended to create valuable standards. To induce the creation of valuable standards, the RAND commitment must guarantee that holders of valuable intellectual property will receive reasonable royalties on that property.[180]

The court thereby adopted a modified version of the Georgia-Pacific factors[181] to recreate a 'hypothetical negotiation between the parties', focusing its analysis on its conclusion that 'the parties in a hypothetical negotiation would set RAND royalty rates by looking at the importance of the SEPs to the standard and the importance of the standard and the SEPs to the products at issue.'[182]

The Georgia-Pacific factors and the Robart court's modified application of the same for (F)RAND are as follows:[183]

(i) Generally, royalties received by the patentee for licensing the patent(s): the royalties considered in the case must, according to Judge Robart, 'be comparable to RAND licensing circumstances', *i.e.*, both 'license agreements where the parties clearly understood the RAND obligation, and … patent pools, will be relevant to a hypothetical negotiation for SEPs'. The court noted that 'as a general matter patent pools tend to produce lower rates than those that could be achieved through bilateral negotiations,' so while 'a pool rate itself does not constitute a RAND royalty rate for an SEP

---

[180] Ibid., para 113.

[181] These have also been discussed in Broadcom v. Qualcomm, 501 F.3d 297, 315 et seq. n. 8 (3rd Cir. 2007).

[182] United States District Court Western District of Washington at Seattle, Microsoft v. Motorola, Case no. C10-1823 JLR, Findings of Fact and Conclusion in Law, 25 April 2013, 25 et seq, paras 113 et seq.

[183] Cf. United States District Court Western District of Washington at Seattle, Microsoft v. Motorola, Case no. C10-1823 JLR, Findings of Fact and Conclusion in Law, 25 April 2013, Paras 100 et seq. See table provided by MCDermott, Will & Emory, 'A First for FRAND: Federal Court in Microsoft v. Motorola Sets FRAND Royalty Rates for Standard Essential Patents', 8 May, 2013, cf. www.mwe.com/A-first-for-FRAND-Federal-Court-in-Microsoft-v-Motorola-sets-FRAND-Royalty-Rates-for-Standard-Essential-Patents-05-08-2013. Accessed 11 July 2013.

holder who is not a member of the pool … under certain circumstances, patent pools can serve as indicators of a royalty rate that falls within the range of royalties consistent with the RAND commitment'.

(ii) Rates paid by the licensee for utilizing comparable patent: Judge Robart considered the MPEG LA H.264 patent pool (similar to the H.264 patents at issue), in which Microsoft is a licensor and licensee.

(iii) The nature and scope of the licence (in terms of exclusivity and territory/customer restrictions): the court seems not to have addressed this factor, but considered the breath of the alleged essential patents.

(iv) The licensor's established policy and marketing programme to maintain its patent monopoly (via selective licensing): the Court found that this factor was inapplicable in the (F)RAND context because the licensor has made a commitment to license on (F)RAND terms and may no longer maintain a patent monopoly by not licensing to others. Thus, according to the court, a (F)RAND commitment implies agreement to license.

(v) The commercial relationship between the licensor and licensee: this factor does not apply in the (F)RAND context, according to the court, because having committed to license on (F)RAND terms, the patentee may no longer discriminate against its competitors, and between licensees, in terms of licensing agreements.

(vi) The effect of selling the patented technology in promoting sales of the licensee's and licensor's other products: it is important to focus the analysis on the value of the patented technology apart from the value associated with incorporation of the patented technology into the standard, along with the contribution of the patent to the technical capabilities of the standard and also the contribution of those relevant technological capabilities to the implementer and the implementer's products. Thus, the value of the patent technology must be separated from the value of the patent in the agreed standard itself.

(vii) The duration of the patent and the term of the licence: the term of the licence will equate to the duration of the patent.

(viii) The established profitability of the product made under the patent: the court seems to have applied the same considerations it applied to factor (vi) above.

(ix) The utility and advantages of the patent property over the old modes or devices: According to Judge Robart, through this factor, the parties to a hypothetical negotiation under a (F)RAND commitment would consider alternatives that could have been written into the standard instead of the patented technology. The focus by the Court is on the period before the standard was adopted and implemented, and the Court seems to suggest a material comparison.

(x) The nature of the patented invention and the character of the commercial embodiment of it as owned and produced by the licensor: according to the court, this factor focuses on the hypothetical negotiation of the contribution of the patent to the technical capabilities of the standard and also the contribution of those relevant technical capabilities to the implementer and the implementer's products. Thus, the importance of the patent for the standard and its implementers.

(xi) The extent to which the infringer has made use of the invention, and the value of that use: the court did not apply this factor nor did it apply the same considerations that it applied to factor (x) above.

(xii) The portion of the profit or of the selling price that may be customary in the particular business, or in comparable businesses, to allow for the use of the invention or analogous inventions. This factor 'must look to customary practices of businesses licensing [F]RAND-committed patents' as opposed to 'non-[F]RAND committed patents'.

(xiii) The portion of the realizable profit that should be credited to the invention itself: according to the court., as with many of the other factors, in the [F)RAND context, it is critical to consider the contribution of the patented technology apart from the value of the patent as the result of its incorporation into the standard (cf. factor (vi)), the latter of which would properly reward the SEP owner for the value of the standard itself.'

(xiv) The opinion and testimony of qualified experts: the court did consider substantial expert testimony.

(xv) The amount that a licensor and a licensee would have agreed upon at the time infringement began if both had been reasonably and voluntarily trying to reach an arm's length agreement: according to Judge Robart, in trying to reach an agreement, the SEP owner would have been obligated to license its SEPs on (F)RAND terms which necessarily must abide by the purpose of the (F)RAND commitment of widespread adoption of the standard through avoidance of hold-up and stacking. The parties would examine a reasonable royalty rate based on the contribution of the patented technology to the capabilities of the standard, and in turn, the contribution of those capabilities of the standard to the implementer and the implementer's products. With respect to stacking concerns, the parties attempting to reach an agreement would consider the overall licensing landscape in existence vis-a-vis the standard and the implementer's products. Finally, reasonable parties in search of a reasonable royalty rate under the (F)RAND commitment would consider the fact that, to induce the creation of valuable standards, the (F)RAND commitment must guarantee that holders of valuable intellectual property will receive reasonable royalties on that property'.[184]

As in the case before Posner, Motorola argued that it was entitled to a royalty rate of 2.25 per cent of the net selling price of Microsoft's product. In this case, it was Windows and Xbox products for both Motorola's H.264 and 802.11 SEP portfolios (i.e., $4.50 for each $200 Xbox). Microsoft argued that the MPEG LA H.264 patent pool (discussed supra) is the best indicator of a FRAND royalty rate for Motorola's H.264 SEPs.[185]

Microsoft received several favourable decisions from the Court. The Court found that several of Motorola's patents provided only a minimal contribution to the standards and had only minor importance in the overall functionality of some of Microsoft's products. Also, Judge Robart concluded that because the characteristics of the MPEG LA H.264 pool of which Microsoft and Google (Motorola's parent) are members 'closely align with all of the purposes of the RAND commitment, the pool rate is a strong indicator of a RAND royalty rate for Motorola's H.264 portfolio.'[186]

Judge Robart favored Microsoft, holding that the FRAND royalty rate for Motorola's H.264 portfolio is 0.555 cents per unit, with the range set at 0.555 to 16.389 cents per unit for Windows and Xbox products, while

---

[184] For a great table see McDermott Will & Emory, 'A First for FRAND: Federal Court in Microsoft v. Motorola Sets FRAND Royalty Rates for Standard Essential Patents', 8 May, 2013, cf. www.mwe.com/A- first-for-FRAND-Federal-Court-in-Microsoft-v-Motorola-sets-FRAND-Royalty-Rates-for-Standard-Essential-Patents-05-08-2013. Accessed 11 July 2013. See also of course Cf. United States District Court Western District of Washington at Seattle, Microsoft v. Motorola, Case no. C10-1823 JLR, Findings of Fact and Conclusion in Law, 25 April 2013, paras 100 et seq.

[185] Ibid. United States District Court Western District of Washington at Seattle, Microsoft v. Motorola, Case no. C10-1823 JLR, Findings of Fact and Conclusion in Law, 25 April 2013, see specificly 514 et seq. and 613 et seq.

[186] Ibid.

for all other Microsoft products, the rate was 0.555 cents per unit. Robart set the FRAND royalty rate for Motorola's 802.11 SEP portfolio at 3.471 cents per unit, with the range set at 0.8 to 19.5 cents per unit for Xbox products. For all other Microsoft products, the royalty rate is 0.8 cents per unit. In total, this is about $560,000 per year above Microsoft's proposal, but about $4 billion below Motorola's demand.[187]

In September 2013, a jury found that Motorola was in breach of contract for making an unreasonable licence offer to Microsoft. Motorola was ordered to pay USD 14.5 million. The jury concluded that Motorola's demand that Microsoft pay 2.25 per cent of the price of its products to license its essential patents was unreasonable and violated Motorola's promise to standard-setting groups to license the patents on (F)RAND terms.[188]

Motorola has appealed, not to the U.S. Court of Appeals for the Ninth Circuit which would normally hear the appeal based on contract law, but because it centres on patent issues, to the U.S. Court of Appeals for the Federal Circuit).[189] It should be noted that Motorola is also trying to get an import ban (exclusionary order) against Microsoft's Xbox gaming consoles, a case that was appealed from the ITC to the Federal Circuit in May of 2013.

Generally, the Robart case concerns the contractual understanding of FRAND (world-wide), going forward, i.e. what is FRAND for the licence agreement to be entered between the parties, while there are also litigations regarding the notion of FRAND (also world-wide) going backward, i.e. under suits for infringement damages, like the Posner judgement from Illinois. However, there is certainly, from a US patent law perspective, a difference between a damages claim based on infringement and a contract case regarding the interpretation of FRAND. Under US Patent law, an infringer normally faces the possibility of paying damages that are in the excess of what the totally royalty rate would have been had the infringer instead become a licensee. Thus, US patent law does not award 'reasonable' royalties, rather the opposite.[190] If it is a

---

[187] Ibid.

[188] Ryan Davis, SEP Owners Face More Contract Suits After Motorola Verdict, Law360, http://www.law360.com/articles/470256/sep-owners-face-more-contract-suits-after motorola-verdict. Accessed 3 February 2014.

[189] United States District Court Western District of Washington at Seattle, Microsoft v. Motorola, Case no. C10-1823 JLR, Findings of Fact and Conclusion in Law, 25 April 2013, see specifically 514 et seq. and 613 et seq.

[190] Doug Lichtman, 'Understanding the RAND Commitment', (2010) 47 *Houston Law Review*, 1023, 1036 et seq.

wilful infringement then the court has the discretion to increase any amount of damages by three. This is, inter alia, to encourage infringers to identify themselves prior to investing in the technology. Also, the ease injunctions were granted before *eBay* constituted one part of a system to encourage infringers to engage in licence agreements.[191] Posner found that the parties could not prove any damages. Nonetheless, it seems that Posner has taken some inspiration from the fact that the FRAND commitment to an SDO creates an implied licence, with the licence rendering moot any claim to triple damages (and injunctions) against a firm that states it will take a FRAND licence, but leaving the court with the power to determine the royalty due.[192]

With reference to the above, it is clear that the incentive for infringers of SEPs to enter into licence agreements with patentees has clearly decreased in the US. Neither the tool 'injunction' nor the tool 'damages' creates an incentive for the licensees to seek out the patentees. In fact, for a potential licensee it is better to wait until a court identifies the royalty. Furthermore, given that an SEP holder has to pay its litigation costs, even if it is successful in the litigation, the potential licensee even has a tool to push the SEP holder to enter a sub-FRAND settlement/licence agreement. In fact, the current trend implies that SEP holders need to venture to the courts increasingly. Perhaps, actually, the trend suggests that SEP holders should increasingly collaborate in patent pools and in joint litigation schemes (defensive funds) to a greater extent than now. That would not be a good development from a competition law perspective.

As regards the definition of FRAND, there are also several cases in Germany. For example, in Mannheim, Apple and Motorola are litigating for a declaratory judgement on FRAND.[193] It seems that the Robart judgement has had some influence with the German judges.[194] Perhaps, Motorola will try a similar case in Germany against Microsoft.[195] In addition to the above, a similar litigation development seems to have developed between Motorola and Apple, Nokia and HTC and Ericsson

---

[191] Ibid. 1039 et seq.

[192] Ibid, 1043; see also Mark Lemley, 'Intellectual Property Rights and Standard-Setting Organizations', (2002) 90 *California Law Review*, 1889, 1924 et seq.

[193] Florian Mueller, 'German Court Unlikely to Approve Google's 2.25% SEP Royalty Demand from Apple as FRAND Rate', http://www.fosspatents.com/2013/06/german-court-unlikely-to-approve.html. Accessed 11 July 2013.

[194] Ibid.

[195] The German courts are considered patentee friendly.

Samsung. Of course, there is also the litigation between Apple and Samsung, as well as other firms.

It is clear that the cases about the definition and level of FRAND originate in the clash over the smartphone concept of two industries and cultures (IT and telecom) when dealing with proprietory isssues in reference to standards. As stated above, the innovation rate in IT is, or, at least, has been, high where innovations have been made without the need for large investments in R&D. On the other hand, to achieve successful innovations in the telecom sector required large investments in R&D, and, thus, also a need for fair returns on these investments. A suspicion also lingers that perhaps in the IT sector, the network effects are so imminent and large that receiving royalties is not necessary. The first mover's advantage in securing a monopoly on the technology is enough for success. The same is not true for the telecom sector, where technologies still need to be included in hardware. It may thus be stated that to be able to uphold the standard-setting system, and defend its integrity, competition law may not be used to require SSOs to implement a system of royalty-free standards. If the legislator has selected the standard-setting system to provide society with products and system requirements, then competition law cannot require that the price of the standard selected is zero. On the contrary, such a requirement could, from a horizontal point of view, be found to violate competition law, whether under a rule of reason or an anti-competitive effect analysis.

6.8 CONCLUDING REMARKS AND A DISCUSSION REGARDING OUTSTANDING ISSUES

There is a clear dichotomy between the US and the EU legal development. The US has decided to use intellectual property law and unfair competition law, while the courts in Europe have decided to use the EU antitrust rules as a tool to access SEPs. By utilizing intellectual property law and unfair competition rules to grant what must be regarded as compulsory licences to infringing firms, the Supreme Court has opened up the possibility of using notions and terms such as 'fairness', 'public interest' and 'excessive' in an attempt to have the courts decide what are reasonable and non-discriminatory royalties under the notion of 'on-going royalties'. This is remarkable in itself, especially giving the fact that few areas are as close to core business conduct as access to standards in the telecom industry. Even more revolutionary is that Judge Posner agreed with Judge Kennedy and embraced this development.

One explanation for this remarkable shift is the US courts' campaign to restrict liability cases in the US in general. Nonetheless, to sacrifice injunctions as the tool for inventors to obtain licence agreements and embrace compulsory licences is such a step that the Supreme Court must also have realized that the development of ever-stronger intellectual property laws and practice needed to be halted. Hence, FTC and the courts have been reluctant accept the possibility of treble liability suits and have only agreed that Sec. 5 of the FTC Act is applicable. Thus, the FTC obtains an exclusive right to initiate cases, and private treble damages suits are off the table.

By demanding that antitrust cases in these situations may only be judged under the rule of reason and demanding a clear showing of anti-competitive effect in the form of exclusionary effect, US antitrust law seem to be effectively limited.

Notwithstanding the above, interestingly there has been no clear decision yet whether failure to honour FRAND commitments by seeking injunctive relief would amount to abuse of dominance or monopolization. Given the above, it seems that this would not be possible in the US. FTC consent orders imply that the FRAND has become a procedure under Sec. 5 of the FTC Act to obtain licence agreements, while access is 'granted' under the Supreme Court's *eBay* decision. Under US antitrust law neither the essential facility doctrine, nor the 'refusal to license' abuse seems to be applicable to SEP users.[196] However, there has been no clear decision in which a US court has refused to use the antitrust laws in this situation.

On the contrary, in similar situations, EU competition law seems to be applicable. The seminal case so far has been *Orange-Book-Standard.* However, EU cases will soon follow. For the development of EU law, the result in *Huawei v. ZTD,* together with the Commission findings in the Google and Samsung investigations, will have a great impact on the issue of whether not honouring FRAND may amount to an abuse of dominance. Moreover, the CJEU and the Commission will have the opportunity to answer several outstanding issues: (i) whether the EU will follow the method applied in *Orange-Book-Standard* or develop its own (less strict) doctrine for when injunctions can or cannot be utilized? (ii) What is a willing licensee? (iii) When, to turn the issue around, will utilizing an injunction by an SEP holder be abuse of dominant position? The

---

[196] See Verizon Commc'ns Inc. v. Law Offices of Curties V. Trinko, LLP, 540 U.S.398, 408. See also Intergraph Corp. v. Intel Corp. 195 F.3d 1346 (Fed.-Circ. 1999) and In re Independent Service Organizations Antitrust Litigation 203 F.3d 1322 (Fed. Cir. 2000).

Orange-Book-Standard can be regarded as awkward and impractical and too patentee friendly, while the use of *IMS Health*, *Microsoft* and the exception circumstances doctrine may very well suffice in the eyes of CJEU.[197]

Hopefully, CJEU will seize the moment and discuss what might be regarded as FRAND under EU competition law. Even though we have not yet seen any decisive decisions from the EU institutions, we should not expect to see them demanding evidence of anti-competitive effect to the degree that, for example, the Federal Circuit demanded in *Rambus*. Possibly, the CJEU will declare that, for example, patent ambush and FRAND ambush are not 'competition on the merits' and, thus, abuses under Art 102 TFEU without the need to show anti-competitive effect. That the conduct is not 'competition on the merits' implies that it does not reflect acceptable business behaviour and it violates the trust needed between firms to conduct a fruitful standard-setting procedure. Perhaps, the protection of the standard-setting procedure is actually what FTC and Posner are striving for when creating the exemption and methods for obtaining 'compulsory licenses' under intellectual property law with the use of ideas like fairness and equity.

Thus, the general development is that US antitrust law is only of slight importance to these issues. However, there are exceptions to this general picture. *Apple v. Samsung* is the high-profile smartphone case originating in Northern California. Apple was denied a permanent injunction by Judge Lucy Koh and the case has an interesting competition law angle.[198] Apple argues that Samsung induced ETSI to select its technology with FRAND commitment but without intending to honour the commitment. The Court agreed with this, stipulating that in a consensus-driven standard-setting environment, a patentee's intentionally false commitment to license on FRAND terms, coupled with the SSO reliance on such a commitment or promise when including the technology in the standard, and the subsequent breach of that promise, is actionable anti-competitive conduct.[199] Judge Lucy Koh's has perhaps here found an antitrust harm and an anti-competitive effect, and thus, a use for US Antitrust law also in these circumstances.

One odd consequence of the courts' development of these patent hold-up cases is that there is a restriction or an exemption, which means that a patentee may not be able to get a successful result when going to

---

197 For a translation of the questions asked see http://www.fosspatents.com/2013/03/german-court-refers-huawei-zte-standard.html Accessed 11 July 2013.

198 Apple, Inc. v. Samsung Electronics. Ltd et al, C-11-1846 & C 12-0630.

199 Apple, Inc. v. Samsung Electronics. Ltd et al, C-11-1846 & C 12-0630.

court to stop someone from infringing its patent. Clearly, under *eBay* and the EU development, there is a restriction in the bundle of rights we call 'ownership' of patents. For example, Posner's judgment is a far-reaching restriction of the notion of property. Does this imply that SEPs are only proprietary rights under intellectual property/competition law? In other words, does a patentee have the right to FRAND terms only, or a right to 'tax' in a fair manner, but not to restrict firms and others from 'trespassing' on its intellectual *property*? What ever these conservative thinkers say, they should agree that this might lessen the incentive to invent, at least for smaller firms and cause other problems we do not know about yet. The Supreme Court's, and even more striking, Posner's, use of such notions and values as 'fairness' and 'public interest' in cases so close to the core of firms' business practices and intellectual property are, thus, not only surprising, but even revolutionary.

7. Comparative analysis and critique

7.1 INTRODUCTION

Standards, and especially standards produced by standard-setting organizations (SSOs), are a growing phenomenon, especially in connection with the 'New Economy'. There are several reasons for this growth. First, we are currently developing the infrastructure of the 'New Economy' and since this is done in cooperation with the relevant stakeholders, rather than unilaterally by public organs, collaboration is essential. Secondly, specialization is also profound among firms in, for example, the ICT sector and therefore agreed and transparent interfaces, decided through standard setting, between products and firms are necessary. Thirdly, globalization demands global joint solutions. In fact, it seems that standard setting is quickly becoming part of the core business practice of several firms with global entrepreneurial aims. Thus, it has become a core part of firms' competitive strategies. Finally, The 'New Economy' is plagued by network effect and markets with network effects migrate towards single standards. Competition law practitioners are quickly realizing this, especially in the light of the current patent war. Nonetheless, it would still be beneficial for standard setting, with adjoining collaboration such as patent pooling and standard-driven joint R&D, to receive more attention from the competition authorities and its importance acknowledged by receiving its own guidelines, where the issues of anti-competitive agreements and monopolization could be addressed.

The aim of this chapter is to provide a general and broad analysis of the US and EU antitrust regulation of standards. It also offers some suggestions for how the standard-setting procedure should be regulated under competition law. More specifically, the US and EU legal doctrines are compared while trying to identify legal tests for the standard-setting procedures.

The starting point is identifying what kind of standards should be addressed under competition law. Clearly, there are standards that do not pose any competitive problem because they do not cause any anti-competitive harm. Furthermore, standards may represent infrastructure, where competition is not the best process for attaining the desired results, implying that competition law is perhaps not the best legal system under which to judge these standards. Indeed, any guidelines or 'tests' should therefore start with indentifying the limits to competition law in this area.

Moreover, with reference to standard setting, the dichotomy between 'undertakings' conducting economic tasks and organs conducting public functions of 'legislation' needs to be analysed. When is competition law applicable to the standard-setting process? When are SDOs exercising public powers and acting as legislators rather than facilitating undertakings in entering standard agreements?

Furthermore, safe harbours must be identified. When are the anti-competitive effects so limited that the standard-setting collaboration falls outside the ambit of US antitrust law or EU competition rules? This is an important issue because standard setting may very well, on the face of it, be regarded as restricting rivalry between firms, even if it is still, generally, precompetitive collaborations and an efficient and effective way to regulate and structure markets. Firms need clear rules and guidance in order to understand what conduct is benign under competition law and exempted.

After discussing these issues, I try to identify the tests for when standard setting causes anti-competitive harm. This should be based on identifying the kinds of standard that need to be under scrutiny, asking whether on a case-by-case basis they have anti-competitive effects. Differences and similarities between the US application of antitrust law and the EU's use of competition rules will be discussed.

In the end, I argue that the 'good governance' rules for SSOs must be developed under competition law. Competition law must be detached from the by-laws of the SSOs, and create its own set of norms on how firms may compete and interact in SSOs. What constitute 'misuse of the standard-setting procedure' under competition law? Conduct, which threatens the 'integrity of the standard-setting process', should be identified as misuse and may be declared as not 'competition on the merits'. Such rules should be firmly based on what *may* cause anti-competitive effects, because the relevant markets have often not yet materialized. Demanding a showing of actual anti-competitive effects is therefore setting the threshold too high. These rules should apply both to the members of the SSOs and to the SSOs themselves when deciding standards for markets where competition between standards can be upheld. In other words, if a member of an SSO misuses or 'games' the good governance rules (including the by-laws) of the SSO, it may to be found in breach of competition law since such conduct may still be a violation of 'competition on the merits'. Similarly, an SSO may, by having lax or vague by-laws, violate competition law, since it *de facto* facilitates anti-competitive collusion or exclusion.

7.2 LIMITS TO COMPETITION POLICY AND LAW

7.2.1 Sometimes No Room for 'Trial and Error'

The theories of static competition, or Hayek's and Schumpeter's concepts of competition as a discovery process, may not apply to certain standard-setting procedures.[1]

Standards today reflect fundamentally different market solutions and should, hence, attract different antitrust responses. For example, performance standards cause little or no anti-competitive effects.

Some standards represent the basic groundwork on which competition thrives. These standards reflect infrastructure or interoperability. For example, the protocols and tools for the virtual infrastructure we call the internet.[2] They stipulate interoperability, which governs the interface between different kinds of product and technology. Such standards may create not only new markets but also competition and wealth on such markets. The demand for basic infrastructure as well as the interoperability technologies is network driven, implying that they tend to migrate towards one solution for the demand.

On the other side of the spectrum, there are product or design standards. They reflect the joint effort or agreement of specialized firms to market a jointly developed product on an existing relevant market. These standards must be judged differently from interoperability standards since they are present on markets which does not show network effects. Only, where there is a market failure in the form of a patent thicket or some other market failure situation should these markets 'naturally' migrate towards one standard.

Competition as a procedure for developing markets and for creating wealth does not seem to be the best procedure for developing some

---

[1] Cf. generally Friedrich A. Hayek, *New Studies in Philosophy, Politics, Economics, and the History of Ideas* (Routledge and Kegan Paul, 1978), 185 et seq. Joseph Schumpeter, *Capitalism, Socialism and Democracy* (George Allen & Unwin 1976 (first published in 1943)), 82 et seq.

[2] Standardization of basic protocols and interfaces was the prerequisite for the development of the internet. Cf. Marcus Glader, 'Open Standards: Public Policy Aspects and Competition Law Requirements', (2010) 6 *European Competition Journal*, 611, 613.

classical infrastructure standards, such as the width and size of railroad track. Implementing such an infrastructure implies selecting one solution for an industry, market or society. Inevitably, infrastructure standards are not most effectively developed through a 'trial and error' method where consumers are exposed to different solutions, and then, through selecting and re-selecting, chose the best alternative. Infrastructure standards are rather developed through a standard-setting process where the relevant stakeholders negotiate and agree on the infrastructure, while conducting R&D to develop the standard. These standards should, therefore, not be considered the sort of goods and services which Hayek and Schumpeter were discussing.[3] These 'heavy-weights' considered, even though abstractly and theoretically, goods and services where consumers and society *de facto* have a choice. In other words, where the consumer may select a good, consume it or try it out, and purchase another good if the first good did not meet his or her satisfaction. Furthermore, the theories on Schumpeter are firmly grounded in the notion of 'one product – one patent'. Not that patents only cover parts of a technology and are tradable to the same extent as goods. Here, as stated above, the fundamental principles of Hayek, Schumpeter and Arrow[4] work, i.e. there is a choice, and innovation, or competition as a process, through 'trial and error'.

However, in the New Economy or 'high-tech' network-driven industries, certain technologies that are currently being standardized are, perhaps short-lived but still infrastructure. Thus, society needs to agree, *de jure*, on a standard, and it is be unlikely that the parties to these standards, including suppliers, content providers and consumers, will be able to 'back-track' when the technology or standard has been selected. They will all have to accept and invest in the new standard. Possibly, a new technology/standard will soon develop that will overtake the old standard, but it is still true that the industry or markets connected to the standard can due to network effects only sustain one standard at a time. For these standards, as well as classical infrastructure standards, competition as a process does not suffice as a theoretical ground for selecting the best technology for society. First, a trial and error method could be a

[3] Cf. Friedrich A. Hayek, *New Studies in Philosophy, Politics, Economics, and the History of Ideas* (Routledge and Kegan Paul, 1978), 185 et seq. Joseph Schumpeter, *Capitalism, Socialism and Democracy* (George Allen & Unwin 1976 (first published in 1943)), 82 et seq.

[4] Kenneth Arrow, 'Economic Welfare and the Allocation of Resources for Invention', in R. Nelson (ed), *The Rate and Direction of Inventive Activity: Economic and Social Factors* (National Bureau of Economic Research, 1962), 620 et seq.

very costly way of selecting infrastructure.[5] Secondly, if these standards are not agreed upon, *de facto* standards will soon emerge. However, *de facto* standards created through network effect and 'tipping' could very well be inferior to a *de jure* standard.[6] In the New Economy, due to such network effects and tipping, a single solution may become a global solution. A trial and error method would imply that a less good solution for society may possibly become the *de facto* standard, and that that solution will be in the hands of one monopolistic firm. Instead, stakeholders must be allowed not only to choose between available technologies, but also to discuss the pros and cons of different technical solutions, while individually continuing their R&D efforts, and to reach a compromise on a technology to standardize. The result will be a compromise between different stakeholders, often including technologies from different sources. In these circumstances the standard-setting process must be understood as a form of collective innovation, and also collective competition, where the end result is a standard that meets the demands of stakeholders as a whole.[7] In theory, what may be created through a standard-setting process is a standard that utilizes technology from several firms (an 'oligopoly' situation), while a *de facto* standard in the New Economy may wind up in the hands of one firm (a 'monopoly' situation).[8]

Until now, we have been discussing infrastructure or interoperability standards. At the other end of the spectrum, where there is room in the market for consumers to choose between different technical solutions, firms should have the ability to compete for that demand. It seems to be an increasing trend for firms to come together in smaller groups, consortia and fora, and agree on a technology, which they then market to

---

[5] Private standard-setting organizations advance consumer welfare on several levels. See, generally, e.g. Mark Lemley, 'Antitrust Intellectual Property and Standard Setting Organizations' (2002) 80 *California Law Review* 1889.

[6] Carl Shapiro and Hal R. Varian, *Information Rules* (Harvard Business School Press 1999), 173 et seq.

[7] Josef Drexl, 'Anti-competitive Stumbling Stones on the Way to a Cleaner World: Protecting Competition in Innovation without a Market', (2012) 8 *Journal of Competition Law & Economics*, 507, 534. See also Steven Anderman and John Kallaugher, *Technology Transfer and the New EU Competition Rules* (Oxford University Press, 2006), 252, fn. 32.

[8] For a very interesting scholarly work on the driving forces of the old and the new economy and on what markets may be created, see Carl Shapiro and Hal R. Varian, *Information Rules* (Harvard Business School Press, 1999), 173 et seq.

SDOs and other stakeholders.[9] Thus, consortia-created standards can represent 'products' on a relevant technology market. Such markets and standards should be developed through a 'trial and error' procedure, where consumers have a choice over selecting from different technical solutions to meet their demand. Where there is room for competition by technical substitution, such competition should prevail and, hence, be protected.

Moreover, interoperability or the virtual infrastructure is created by firms in collaboration, and not by governments. Governments do not have the capacity, or knowledge, nor are they able to decide efficiently on interface technologies for global standards. Instead, firms' ability to create standards is inevitable for the development of global entrepreneurial activity. The prerogative for firms is to decide on standards in global collaborations at a level representing global solutions.

If the above, rather theoretical, discussion is accepted as valid, competition law must be restricted. To what extent are competition law agencies or courts able to review the selection of a technology which will become a global infrastructure? The agencies and courts have very little room to do this, although they have an ability to chaperone the procedure to establish the standards, and terms of access to the standard, when established. 'Misuse of the standard-setting process' may very well constitute competitive harm, as well, also, as non-access to membership of SSOs and the standard, while the substantial result of the standard-setting process in itself, especially if the result is an infrastructure standard, should seldom be scrutinized.

7.2.2 Government and Courts should not Decide on Standards

In the *EMC* case[10] discussed in more detail above[11], EMC Development AB (EMC) challenged the Commission's decision[12] to reject the complaint against European Portland cement producers, the European Cement Association (Cembureau) and the European Committee for

---

[9] The CD, DVD and Blu-Ray technologies/standards are a clear example of consortia-developed standards. These technologies have been extensively discussed. See, for example, Julian Christ and André Slowak, 'Why Blue-Ray v. HD-DVD is not VHS v. BETAMAX: The Co-evolution of Standard Setting Consortia', (2009) *FZID Discussion Papers*, Universität Hohenheim.

[10] Case T-432/05 EMC Development AB [2010] ECR II-01629.

[11] Supra Chapter 4.2.

[12] For the Commission decision, cf. Case COMP/F-2/38.401 EN 197-1 Standard-EMC/European Cement.

Standardization (CEN) in relation to the European cement market for creating a cartel solicited by an industrial standard in order to create barriers to entry to the European cement market. The Commission and the EU courts dismissed EMC's claims one by one, but the interesting feature of the case is not whether the safe harbour was applicable, or not, but the fact that neither the Commission nor the courts analysed the standard from the outset to establish whether there was a cartel in the first place. As stated above, they only established that the safe harbour was applicable. Thus, the Courts (and the Commission) only scrutinized whether the procedural rules, i.e. the by-laws of the association, were in line with the safe harbour rules. They did not analyse whether there was a boycott cartel and a division of the market. Since the Commission had found that the safe harbour was applicable, i.e. the 'good governance' procedural rules fulfilled, the Commission could not find that the effect of the vehicle firmly within the harbour amounted to a cartel, i.e. was anti-competitive.[13]

However, perhaps even more striking, at first glance, of its inability to regulate SDOs, is the fact that the Commission failed to take into consideration the claim that the technology developed and patented by EMC was 'better' than the technologies now agreed under the standard. EMC actually specifically claimed that the technology EMC had developed was superior and the reason why it was not standardized was exactly because of its superiority. Because of its superiority, the other cement producers would have had to license the technology from EMC, had EMC's energetically modified cement technology become the standard.[14] Allegedly, the European standard excluded the superior technology

---

[13] Case T-432/05 EMC Development AB [2010] ECR II-01629.

[14] The EN 197-1 Standard ('the Standard') was adopted in April 2000 by the 19 national standards bodies that were members of CEN at that time. It was developed by a CEN technical committee, CEN/TC 51 'Cement and Building Limes' ('CEN/TC 51'), under mandate M/114 which was granted by the Commission and the European Free Trade Association (EFTA) pursuant to Directive 89/106. That mandate defined the scope of application of the Standard, set out the list of products that had to be taken into consideration and stated that the Standard would be expressed, as far as practicable, in product-performance terms, having regard to the interpretative documents. The Standard defined each of the 27 common cement products, that is to say, the common cements described by the various national standards bodies within CEN as traditional and well tried. Those products were further grouped into five main cement types (CEM I to CEM V), according to the proportions in which the main constituents were to be combined to produce those distinct products in a range of six 'strength classes'. Each main cement type was composed of a certain percentage

from gaining access to the market on equal terms, or to create a level playing field between the standardized technologies and EMC's technology. The Court presumably found this line of argument to be outside the ambit of the proceedings, and did not discuss it in detail.

Even though this is a remarkable conclusion in itself, the Court actually went a step further in the *EMC* case. Neither the Court nor the Commission took seriously into consideration the claim that the standard should at least have been a performance standard rather than a descriptive standard.[15]

If the standard had been drafted so as to encompass all methods that enable cement to reach certain quality thresholds – i.e. a performance standard – EMC's technology, according to EMC's claim, would have been in accordance with that standard, and would have gained access on equal terms to costumers/consumers. The Commission instead distanced itself from this discussion and stated that this assessment was outside the scope of the proceeding.[16] According to the Commission, the discussion whether a standard should be prescriptive or performance based 'cannot be reopened in a framework concerning the application of Article 101 or 102 EC Treaty'.[17]

The Commission and the courts reached in the end the right decision in this case. They should very seldom deal with the substance of the standard. What EMC would have needed to show is that the cement producers 'gamed' or misused the standard-setting process so that a competitor or competition was excluded. Without such a finding of an abuse or misuse, the plaintiff is in reality asking the Commission and the courts to scrutinize the standard-setting process itself. Thus, whether the 'legislative process' put in place to create standards in itself violates competition law.[18]

---

of Portland cement clinker combined with varying levels of constituents. That definition included requirements which the constituents have to satisfy, and mechanical, physical, chemical and durability requirements of the 27 common cement products and 'strength classes'. According to the applicant and Cembureau, 'real' Portland cement corresponded to products of the main cement type CEM I, as defined by the Standard. Blended cements corresponded to the cement of the four other main types, CEM II to CEM V.

[15] The Court did not elaborate on this point. However see Case COMP/F-2/38.401 EN 197-1 Standard – EMC/ European Cement Producers, para 111.

[16] Case COMP/F-2/38.401 EN 197-1 Standard – EMC/ European Cement Producers, para. 107.

[17] Ibid, para. 111.

[18] In EMC, it seemed clear that the dominant position of the involved firms and exclusionary effect of the standard were present, but since the firms involved

The US Justice Department has actually reached similar conclusions. In, for example, a Business Review Letter from 2002, *American Welding Society*, the Justice Department stated that it does not consider whether one standard is better than another, only whether the process of standard-setting has been abused.[19] Likewise in the patent pool Business Review Letters, e.g. MPEG-2, the Justice Department did not analyse the technology as such, but satisfied itself that the technology was standardized by an SDO.[20]

The Court's decision in *EMC,* and the US Justice Departments letter in *American Welding Society,* reflect a decision that reviewing and deciding on the substance of the standard, i.e. what constitutes the 'best' technology is outside the scope and the ability of the government and the courts.[21] This may be a sensible decision. Neither governments directly, nor competition authorities or competition courts indirectly, may have the

---

had followed the by-laws and the good governance rules for standard-setting, there was no misuse or breach of 'competition on the merits'. EMC's only argument to prove that a misuse of the standard-setting process had occurred, was the quality argument, which neither the Commission nor the Court took into consideration. According to Hovenkamp, the courts should be very reluctant to be embroiled in evaluating complex technical concepts, but there are times when the courts are forced to do so. Where an antitrust plaintiff has shown that one standard was chosen over others, that *prima facia* other technologies were rejected for anti-competitive purposes and that this has had relevant economic effects on the market, by making the market less competitive, it is likely that the standard was not selected on technical merits. However, the defendants should be able to argue in their defence that the selected technology is still superior and was selected on its merits. The burden of proof is on the defendant. Hertbert Hovenkamp et al., *IP and Antitrust: An Analysis of Antitrust Principles Applied to Intellectual Property Law* (Aspen Publishers, 2010), § 35.4, 35-35.

19 American Welding Society Business Review Letter from Charles James to Douglas Mcdonald, dated 7 October 2002, where the Justice Department stated that it does not consider whether one standard is better than another, only whether the process of standard setting has been abused. The letters can be found on http://www.usdoj.gov/atr/public/busreview/letters.htm, accessed 19 March 2009. The American Welding Society letter is discussed in Peter Plompen, 'The New Technology Transfer Guidelines (TTG) as Applied to Patent Pools and Patent Pool Licensing: Some Observations Regarding the Concept of "Essential Technologies", in Clause-Dieter Ehlermann and Isabela Atanasin (eds), *European Competition Law Annual 2005: The Interaction between Competition Law and Intellectual Property Law* (Hart Publishing, 2005), 300 fn. 11.

20 See discussion supra.

21 Generally, the majority of commentators seem to agree on this point. See, for example, Steven Anderman and John Kallaugher, *Technology Transfer and the New EU Competition Rules* (Oxford University Press, 2006), 252.

ability to judge and decide on the substantive issues of a technology.[22] Nonetheless, assessing the technical subject matter and the scope of a standard could ultimately be an antitrust issue in situations where, for example, overstandardization limits competition and product variety without benefiting the industry in form of greater interoperability. Traditionally, however, competition authorities have been reluctant to judge the technical merits of standards.[23]

Instead, when dealing with interoperability (or infrastructure) standards, many of the disputes regarding the selection of a standard involve neither a significant effect on prices or output for consumers, nor a significant reduction in incentives for future innovation. The disputed issue in these cases, according to Anderman and Kallaugher, is, instead, which set of rights holders should be able to benefit from rents attributable to a standard. According to these authors, Article 101 or Sec. 1 Sherman Act is not a good platform to judge these issues. Presumably, they are not good platforms because the courts need then to analyse the substance of the standard. It is therefore important to identify a competitive harm and whether the relevant market is able to hold competing technologies or not.[24] Only if a plaintiff shows that several standards could prevail in the market, and that the standard-setting process was misused so as to exclude a competing technology that could prevail side-by-side with the standard now implemented, may the plaintiff be successful in showing a breach of competition on the merits, which may also cause anti-competitive effects under the Anderman and Kallaugher formula.

In light of the above, it is clear that the competition authority and courts need to uphold competition by focusing on the procedural aspects of standard-setting and patent pools. Seldom can a court venture to decide whether the technology selected is the best technology or not.[25] So competition can only be upheld indirectly, by stipulating rules for the

---

[22] Hovenkamp argues that Courts may become involved in a discussion about technology in some cases, if the defendant objectively seeks to show that although the selection of the technology was biased it is still the superior technology. Herbert Hovenkamp et al., *IP and Antitrust: An Analysis of Antitrust Principles Applied to Intellectual Property Law* (Aspen Publishers, 2010), § 35.4, 35–35.

[23] Marcus Glader, 'Open Standards: Public Policy Aspects and Competition Law Requirements', (2010) 6 *European Competition Journal*, 611, 615.

[24] 251 et seq.

[25] See however Hovenkamp's claims. Herbert Hovenkamp et al., *IP and Antitrust: An Analysis of Antitrust Principles Applied to Intellectual Property Law* (Aspen Publishers 2010), § 35.4, 35–35.

standard-setting process and against collusion and exclusion in circumstances of competition by substitution.

However, if the SDOs may now decide on standards that *de facto* are binding on the markets, are they not legislators? Should these standards be judged under competition law at all?

7.2.3 The Interface Between Competition Law and Trade Rules

There seem to be a general consensus among EU public lawyers that, under EU law, there has been a delegation of power to standard development organizations (SDOs) from the public legislators.[26] Public product regulation has had to stand back in the light of an increase in private standards. Especially under the so-called 'New Approach' under EU law, private standards have been promoted to European Standards, implying a delegation of standard-setting authority according to some academics.[27] EU scholars seem also to widely agree that the New Approach falls far short of fulfilling the requirements set up by the CJEU for when the Commission is allowed to delegate to a private body according to the *Meroni* ruling.[28] Under the *Meroni* rule, delegation of discretionary power is prohibited and the decision being delegated shall, among other things, be subject to the same conditions as if the Commission exercised them.

In the US, delegation of Federal power is benign from a constitutional perspective, while state courts may have a different opinion.[29] The heavy use of private standards by public agencies, triggered the so-called non-delegation doctrine, i.e. that public power to legislate cannot be delegated to private parties under (state) constitutions.[30]

---

[26] Harm Schepel, *The Constitution of Private Governance – Product Standards in the Regulation of Integrating Markets* (Hart, 2005), 63 et seq, especially 67 fn. 144. See also 225 et seq and 246 et seq.

[27] Ibid, 63 et seq, especially 67 fn. 144. See also 225 et seq. with several references. The issue was discussed mainly by German scholars in the 80s and 90s.

[28] Ibid. See also Case 9/56 Meroni [1958] ECR 133. Case 10/56 Meroni [1958] ECR 157.

[29] D. E. Lawrence, 'Private Exercise of Governemental Power', (1986) 61 *Indiana Law Journal*, 647, 649.

[30] Harm Schepel, *The Constitution of Private Governance – Product Standards in the Regulation of Integrating Markets* (Hart, 2005), 261 et seq.

Notwithstanding the above, the New Approach did include rules and principles regarding good governance, which the National Standards-Setting Organizations (NSOs) must take into consideration when establishing a standard.[31] The new Regulation on European Standardization (hereinafter sometimes referred to as the Regulation) from 2012 also has rules regarding the standard-setting procedure and the quality of the standard as regards when consortia-created standards should be indentified for incorporation in public procurement procedures.[32] These rules seem somewhat similar to the rules for 'safe harbours' in the EU Horizontal Guidelines. Hence, there might be a concern about regulatory overlap, as to whether standards identified under the Regulation, should conform with good governance rules under the Regulation and the New Approach (i.e. the EU trade rules), or under competition law.

Private standards have, for a long time, been regarded as immune from the reach of e.g. Article 34 TFEU. It should be acknowledged that the CJEU, has however broadened the definition of the state in several cases, e.g. *Buy Irish*, which could imply that NSOs under EU law could benefit from the application of Art. 34 TFEU. Schepel, referring to research conducted in Germany, indicates that standards originating in several NSOs – the Irish, French and the Greek standard bodies – could be capable of being measured under Art 34 TFEU. On the other hand, some NSOs – The German, British and Danish (DIN, BSI and DS) – could not. The respective Member States do not have a dominant influence over these NSOs and the NSOs do not conduct or hold public power in this regard.[33]

---

[31] See Schepel's analysis of several procedural requirements: Harm Schepel, *The Constitution of Private Governance – Product Standards in the Regulation of Integrating Markets* (Hart, 2005), 227 et seq, and 242 et seq. See also Liguo Zhang, *Standardization and Patent Licensing in the European Union* (Oy Nord Print Ab, 2012), 35 et seq.

[32] Regulation (EU) No 1025/2012 of the European Parliament and of the Council of the 25 October 2012 on European standardisation, OJ L 316 of 14 November 2012, Art 13 and Annex II.

[33] Harm Schepel, *The Constitution of Private Governance – Product Standards in the Regulation of Integrating Markets* (Hart, 2005), 43 et seq. A far-fetched approach would be to apply Art 34 in conjunction with the principle of loyalty, not against the SDO but against the Member State directly, i.e. holding a Member State responsible for measures taken by the SDO in line with the existence of a duty for Member States to prevent private parties from erecting barriers to trade. A similar approach would be to use Art. 101 and 102, in conjunction with Art. 10, i.e. the *effet utile* doctrine, according to which Member

A bold approach is to apply Art 34 TFEU directly to the SDOs. In an isolated obiter dictum in *Dansk Supermarked*, the CJEU held in 1981 that 'it is impossible in any circumstances for agreements between individuals to derogate from the mandatory provisions of the Treaty on the free movement of goods.'[34] Even though the CJEU has subsequently ignored this statement, it gives support to a general principle under free trade rules. The CJEU has accepted this reasoning regarding the free movement of workers and services as early as 1974.[35] CJEU has furthermore confirmed the principle in *Bosman*[36], *Wouters*[37] and *Laval*[38]. If this principle also applies to the free movement of goods, it could be applicable to standards, given their ability to inhibit free movement of goods and access to markets. Nonetheless, whether this principle does also apply to the free movement of goods should be judged in the light of the interface between Art. 34 TFEU and the competition rules. The *Dassonville*[39] formula originates from *Consten and Grundig*[40] and *Leclerc,*[41] and the CJEU lays down similar goals for both the rules of free movement of goods and the competition rules.

In the recent *Fr.bo* case,[42] the CJEU therefore took a new, but expected, step and actually found that SSOs, SSO-created standards and certifications can be scrutinized under Art 34 TFEU.

The CJEU considered several factors when analysing whether to use Art. 34 or 101 TFEU in *Fr.bo*. The main thrust of the analysis was on the SSOs' special position because it was mentioned in the German Regulation, was *de facto* the only body able to certify products under the standard, and, thus, was able to exclude the marketing and market for products which were not certified by the body. CJEU concluded, therefore, that Article 34 TFEU was applicable and, if one read between the lines, had also been infringed.

The SSO in *Fr.bo* was organized as a limited company but was structured as a consortium, with members from the relevant industry. It

---

States are required not to introduce or maintain in force measures which aim to render the competition rules ineffective.

34 Case 58/80 Dansk Supermarked v. Imerco [1980] ECR 181, para 17.

35 Case 36/74 Walrave v. Koch [1974] ECR 1415.

36 Case C-415/93 Bosman [1995] ECR I-4921.

37 Case C-309/99 Wouters [2002] ECR I-1577.

38 Case C-341/05 Laval [2002] ECR I-11767.

39 Case 8/74 Dassonville [1974] ECR 837.

40 Joined cases 46 and 58/ 65 Consten and Grundig v. Commission [1966] ECR 299.

41 Case 231/83 Cullet v. Leclerc [1985] ECR 305.

42 Case C-171/11 Fr.bo SpA v. DVGW, not reported yet.

held some powers under German law, especially concerning certification. Nonetheless, it seems that *Fr.bo* could also have been judged under Art 101 TFEU, especially if the plaintiff had included also the members of the organization in the suit.[43]

Fr.bo provides an opening to judge standards, not only in the light of the objectives and aims acknowledged under competition law, but possibly also under other public policy objectives recognized and readily applicable under the free trade rules. In fact, under the free movement of goods regulation, in conjunction with the Regulation on European Standards, it seems clear that a court actually could judge the content, quality, and whether a standard should be implemented in the first place.[44] Moreover, does Art 34 TFEU require a showing of effect in these cases? That is highly unlikely. In fact, Art 34 TFEU utilizes a per se doctrine from a competition law perspective. Clearly, European SDOs risk violating Art 34 TFEU under the *Fr.bo* case, especially if they connect the standard to a certification system.

Furthermore, the new Regulation on European Standardization stipulates rules for the standardization process and, to a limited extent, has regard to the quality and substance of consortia-derived standards.[45]

From a free movement of goods perspective, *Fr.bo* is a natural step for the CJEU to take. Similar cases exist under the free movement of workers, of service, and the right to establish.[46] But from a standard-setting perspective, is it a good development that SDOs should be bound by free trade rules? Was not the whole idea of the New Approach precisely to have standards decided outside the public sphere? The conclusion in the preceding chapter was that competition agencies and courts should not intervene in the substance of the standard, but the courts may precisely intervene under the rules of free trade in these

---

[43] The organizational structure of the SSO in Fr.bo, for example, seems similar to the SSO in the German EU competition law case from the Federal Supreme Court (Bundesgerichtshof) July 13, 2004 – Case No. KZR 40/02 ('Tight-Head Drum') (Standard-Spundfass).

[44] See, for example, the rules in Annex II of the Regulation of European Standards regarding identifying ICT consortia created standards for public procurement procedures. Here, the court clearly can be forced to judge the technical quality of standards.

[45] Regulation (EU) No 1025/2012 of the European Parliament and of the Council of the 25 October 2012 on European standardisation, OJ L 316 of 14 November 2012, Art 13 and Annex II.

[46] Case C-415/93 Bosman [1995] ECR I-4921; Case C-309/99 Wouters [2002] ECR I-1577; Case C-341/05 Laval [2002] ECR I-11767 and Case 8/74 Dassonville [1974] ECR 837.

circumstances. However, from a free trade perspective, the response might be that entities that create infrastructure hold power – perhaps not private power on relevant markets, but public power – and they need therefore to be held accountable for these activities. While their economic conduct should be judged under competition laws, possibly their conduct representing public power should be judged under free trade rules. This sounds good in theory, and given the fact that the scope for scrutiny of standard setting is less under competition law, it is likely that the system will not be held up to closer scrutiny by utilizing only competition law. Some standards, and even firms' conduct in SDOs, can be scrutinized under the free trade rules and, when applicable, the Regulation of European Standards.

Furthermore, the application of free movement of goods rules is different from that of the competition rules. The notions of restriction of trade and discrimination are based on nationality, while the competition rules mainly turn on whether competition has been restricted. Hence, Art 34 TFEU would seldom be applicable to the EU-wide SDOs, e.g. CEN and ETSI. The notion of restriction of trade or discrimination based upon nationality may exist, but more predominant would perhaps be restriction of trade or restriction of access to markets. However, the Regulation on European Standardization may be applicable in these circumstances. For example, SMEs will not be able to get their innovations recognized by SDOs adequately, and this would constitute a breach of stakeholder participation under the Regulation.[47] But these rules are not about discrimination or restriction of trade based on nationality. Instead, they concern restrictions to accessing markets and trade. In other words, they are principles equivalent to the rules and principles regarding 'good governance' found in the Horizontal Guidelines. In fact there may be some overlap in the regulation of SDOs between the Regulation on European Standardization and the rules for the 'safe harbour' in the Horizontal Guidelines. As stated above, the Regulation and the principles making up the rules under that Regulation offer more benefits to private plaintiffs than the competition rules.[48]

---

[47] It must be acknowledge that the Regulation on European Standardization is far from clear.

[48] The public interest exemptions in Art. 36 TFEU, and under the doctrine of mandatory requirements of *Cassis de Dijon*, are furthermore less forgiving than Art. 101(3) TFEU in exempting rules on the basis of the procedure of the organization in question. Art 36 TFEU is focused on public policy exemptions such as the enviroment, public health etc. which are difficult to fit inside a

It seems that the EU legislator needs to make a choice how to regulate SDOs and their members. Clearly, given the *Fr.bo, EMC* and *SELEX*[49] decisions, she will have a difficult choice. The SDOs (and the governments that indentify ICT standards created by consortia under the Regulation) may be scrutinized under the free movement rules, while economic conduct in SSOs, consortia and the members of technical committees, and thereby indirectly the SDOs, may be judged under the competition rules. These entities fulfil the requirement for an 'undertaking', while ETSI, CEN and even IEEE could, presumably, be judged particularly under Art. 34 TFEU.

While it is at best uncertain whether it is possible to use Art 34 TFEU against SDOs, the application of the dormant commerce clause in the US Constitution with reference to SDOs is unlikely, or even alien, to American jurists. Similar case law to *Dassonville* may be found in the US under the dormant commerce clause, see *Minnesota v. Clover Leaf Creamery Co.*[50] and *Bibb v. Navajo Freight Lines*[51]. Furthermore, the 'state action' exemption under US antitrust law, first established in *Parker*[52] immunizes the federal and state government and agencies. This implies that, for these agencies, other rules apply, such as, possibly, the dormant commerce clause.

Actually, very few commentators indeed in the US academic debate have ever approached the dormant commerce clause from this point of view. Nonetheless, in several antitrust standard-setting cases, the *Noerr* defence was raised and the defendants argue that the SSO should be regarded as a public body.[53] The Courts have been reluctant to accept that line of reasoning. However, if courts did allow the *Noerr* doctrine to be applicable, would that imply that the dormant commerce clause might be available vis-à-vis the SDO?

Notwithstanding the above, it is clear the economic conduct that does not fall inside the exemption for conduct that reflects activities in accord with the concept of public power will be scrutinized under competition law. In addition, when deciding when competition law is applicable, the variable that competition law regulates markets needs to be taken into

---

competition law analysis. Cf. Case 120/78, Rewe-Zentral AG vs. Bundesmonopolverwaltung für Branntwein [1979] ECR 649.

49 Case C-113/07, SELEX, [2009] ECR I-2207.

50 Minnesota v. Clover Leaf Creamary Co, 449 U.S. 456 (1981).

51 Bibb v. Navajo Freight Lines, 359 U.S. 520 (1959).

52 Parker v. Brown 317 US 341 (1943).

53 See for example, *Allied Tube*.

consideration. Indeed, pre-competition conduct when selecting technologies, or, for that matter, when construing infrastructure standards should only be regulated under competition law if an anti-competitive harm and potential effect can be identified.[54] Otherwise, a plaintiff needs to utilize other regulations, such as the free trade rules or intellectual property law.

7.3 THE INTERACTION AND INTERFACE BETWEEN STANDARDS, IP ARRANGEMENTS UNDER SSOS/SDOS AND PATENT POOLS AND WHAT SHOULD BE CONSIDERED ANTI-COMPETITIVE

7.3.1 What May be Anti-competitive?

In theory, with a conspiratorial mind and some imagination, the harm that can be done to competition by means of joint R&D, standardization collaboration, and a patent pool, especially the combination of these three collaborations, i.e. IP Banks, can be considerable:[55]

BOX 7.1

(i) The parties may collude over innovation by forming an R&D agreement in order to bilaterally block or exclude research or research avenues from each other or in order to bilaterally limit competition or potential competition in R&D.
(ii) The joint R&D venture may exclude or discriminate against third parties, blocking access to innovation markets or results, denying them essential resources (e.g. access to patents) or facilities by creating blocking patents, i.e. exclusion from innovation such as strategic R&D and patenting.
(iii) Standardization agreements can be too wide or deep, i.e. regulate too much technology or in too minute a detail, so

---

[54] See generally Josef Drexl, 'Anti-competitive Stumbling Stones on the Way to a Cleaner world: Protecting Competition in Innovation without a Market', (2012) 8 *Journal of Competition Law & Economics*, 507.

[55] I do not claim that this list is novel. Earlier commentators have already produced such lists, cf., e.g., the headlines in Joseph Iandiorio, 'Patent Pools and the Antitrust Laws', (1964) *Journal of the Patent Office Society*, 712.

that competition is prevented, or so that the only competition allowed is strictly imitative competition rather than dynamic competition. By encompassing more technology under the standard, more patents become essential to the standard. However, in that case, the patents may not be strictly necessary as part of the solution to the technical problem being addressed. This may be regarded as tying or bundling patents, which bars the technology to new entrants.

(iv) Standardization agreements can raise royalty rates for essential intellectual property rights and create the platform for hold-up and patent ambush situations.

(v) Some patent pools are also joint litigation vehicles for their patentees. This implicitly increases royalty rates and also the ambition and the ability to find violators.[56] Patentees in patent pools use coercive collective patent litigations, where possibly invalid patents may be protected and enforced.[57]

(vi) A pool can reduce the incentive to innovate for the pool members. According to the pool agreement and the standardization agreements, the pool members have agreed on a technology. Since they possibly do not want to intrude or 'cannibalize' their own investment in the pool or standard, the pool members will not invest in new research. This may be true if they are obliged to share any new innovation with the members of the pool.

---

[56] Cf. Hanns Ullrich, 'Patente, Wettbewerb, under technische Normen: Recht- und ordnungspolitische Fragestellungen', (2007) 10 *GRUR* 2007, 817. Damien Geradin has recently published substantially on the topic: see Damien Geradin, 'Standardization and Technological Innovation: Some Reflections on Ex-ante Licensing, FRAND, and the Proper Means to Reward Innovators', (2006) 29 *World Competition*, 511. See also in the US where Mark Lemley and Carl Shapiro have lately been publishing substantially on the topic of royalty rates and standardization agreements. See Mark Lemley and Carl Shapiro, 'Patent Holdup and Royalty Stacking', (2007) 85 *Texas Law Review*, 1991. For case law, see, e.g., German cases such as LG Dusseldorf, WuW 13.12.2007, helft 12, Seite 1278-1288, DE-R 2120-2130, Dutch cases concerning patent ambush, Vonnis, 11 June 2007 LG Electronics v. Philips, zaaknummer 287026, or English cases, Scandisk Corp. v. Sisvel et al 2007 EWHC 448.

[57] There are other cases which state that joint defence funds are per se antitrust violations. See, e.g., United States v. Krasnov, 143 F. Supp 184 (E.D. Pa 1956) aff'd. 355 U.S. 5 (1957).

(vii) A pool reduces the incentive to innovate for the licensees. The grant-back clauses or the reciprocity cross-licensing obligations imply that competitors will be granted access to each other's innovations. The innovating licensees will therefore not be in a better position on the product market after the innovation than before. An innovator will gain certain royalties through the pool, but will not increase its market share on the product market.[58]

(viii) The pools reduce the incentive to innovate for non-members. Even if competing patents emerge, it is by no means certain that the competing, substitute and now non-essential patents will have to exit the pool. As a matter of fact, both under US and EU antitrust law, the plaintiff needs to prove market power. The result is that licensees and other firms would have less incentive to make an extra investment in a competing technology.

(ix) Tying, or bundling, in the sense that non-essential rights are encompassed in a patent pool, excludes competing patents

(x) Patent pools seem to survive until a new breakthrough innovation is on the horizon. This might be beyond the statutory limit of the original essential patents. The expiry of the original patents, however, does not reduce the royalty rates from the licensees to the pools.

(xi) Necessarily, both R&D collaboration and patent pools can create spillover collusion on product markets, e.g., price cartels, geographic or a technical division of a product or geographic market, or exclusion of third parties from product markets.[59]

(xii) Furthermore, the patentees may create marginal squeeze or excessive pricing systems through a patent pool and may exclude new innovation reaching the market.

---

[58] The royalties received can also only be at most fair. The patentee may therefore not receive a royalty reflecting the exclusivity or even gate keeping feature of the patent. Thus, it may not be able to obtain monopolistic profits through the royalty. For pricing patents so that price neutrality is achieved, see Stephen Maurer and Suzanne Scotchmer, 'Profit Neutrality in Licensing: The Boundary Between Antitrust Law and Patent Law', (2006) 8 *American Law and Economics Review*, 476, 480 et seq.

[59] Cf. Andreas Fuchs, *Kartellrechtliche Grenzen der Forschungskooperation* (Nomos Verlaggesellschaft, 1989), 75 et seq. See also Commission, *Report on Competition Policy 1994*, 105 et seq.

(xiii) Finally, creating standards increases the possibility of patent ambush and FRAND ambush incidents.

These antitrust problems are broadly sketched. They represent anti-competitive conduct in reference to competition in innovation, price, output, and market division. Essentially the problems can be boiled down to three material concerns: (i) collusion: (ii) exclusion of inter-technology competition, i.e. elimination of competitors and competing technologies (for example group boycotts); and (iii) the exclusion of intra-technology competition, i.e. the elimination of follow-on innovations. In fact, market-wide standards and patent pools imply that dynamic competition has been eliminated, at least in the short term, and that competition by imitation is promoted.

Before analysing the courts approach to standard-setting procedure and patent pools, the safe harbours of the US and EU for these collaborations, i.a. for the IP Banks, need to be analysed.

7.3.2 Application of Competition Law

(i) A broad and general look at the safe harbours

According to the Commission, where participation in standard-setting is unrestricted and the procedure for adopting the standard in question is transparent, standardization agreements, which contain no obligation to comply with the standard and provide access to the standard on fair, reasonable and non-discriminatory terms, will not normally restrict competition within the meaning of Article 101(1) TFEU. [60] The paragraph indicates that there is a safe harbour for Standard Setting Organizations (SSOs) (and its members), which is described in the new horizontal guidelines, quite recently published by the EU Commission (Horizontal Guidelines). Under US antitrust law, the seldom discussed, but important, National Cooperative Research and Production Act of 1993 (NCRPA) was amended in 2004 by the Standards Development Organization Advancement Act, in order to extend the protection from the antitrust laws to specified activities of SSOs, which had previously been granted to R&D collaborations. If an SSO discloses the scope and

[60] Guidelines on the application of Art 101 of the Functioning of the European Union to horizontal co-operation agreements, OJ C 11, 14/01/2011, 1 (earlier defined as Horizontal Guidelines).

nature of its activities to the Department of Justice, it may take advantage of the NCRPA.

Under the legislation described above, technology standardization agreements and SSOs are *de facto* exempted or per se legal, i.e. immune under EU competition law and US antitrust rules as long as the rules of procedure, good governance and transparency etc. stipulated in either the Horizontal Guidelines or the NCRPA are adhered to.

In addition to this, there are safe harbours for joint R&D collaborations under both EU and US competition law, while the patent pool safe zone was developed in conjunction and was, up until the new TT Guidelines, actually a carbon copy of its counterpart.[61] Indeed, each step of the business model, i.e. joint R&D, standardization agreement and technology pool, is analysed separately under both US and EU antitrust law, with separate safe harbours, whereas the 'larger picture', the actual business purpose or conduct of the firms in the standard-setting business are disregarded.[62] The firms mastering the standard-setting business model are, in fact, seldom found infringing competition law.

But there are firms, for which I use the term 'IP Banks' for the lack of better terminology, that enter into joint R&D agreements with R&D producing firms to obtain intellectual property rights for future standards. They participate in technical committees to adopt the developed technologies into standards. These standard agreements are at the centre of this industry. The IP Banks exploit the standards and their mutual assured destruction (MAD) patent portfolios through unilateral licence agreements under FRAND standard licence agreements or through patent pools.

The black square in the graph below (Figure 7.1) is the industry or market where IP Banks, including firms with MAD capability, often congregate. Interestingly, this area seems semi-exempted from any serious antitrust scrutiny in either of the jurisdictions providing to 'safe harbours' and exemptions, as laid down in the NCRPA, R&D block exemption, and various guidelines. In fact, neither US antitrust law nor EU competition rules (normally) recognize either anti-competitive or pro-competitive conduct where no relevant market can be identified. Yet

---

61 Commission Notice – Guidelines on the application of Article 81 of the EC Treaty to technology transfer agreements, OJ C 101, 27.04.2004, 2.

62 See also *Steven Anderman and Hedvig Schmidt, EU Competition Law and Intellectual Property Rights – Regulation of Innovation* (Oxford University Press 2011), 293 et seq. where the different stages for creating a standard are summarized.

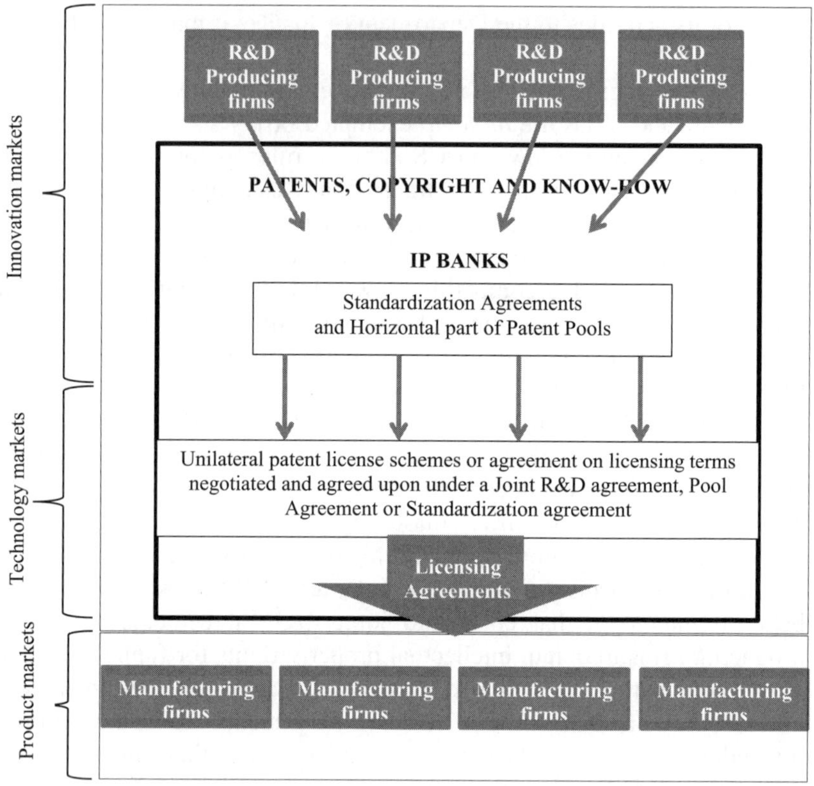

Figure 7.1 IP banks' business model

holders of blocking patents are considered to be non-competitors.[63] These IP Banks, which are the largest holders of patents in the industry, are often therefore formally non-competitors, but *de facto* they are clearly competing and have similar or even equivalent business models. That these firms should be considered non-competitors, while firms with few patents are more likely to be considered to be in competitive relationships, is an antitrust paradox. Moreover, the general trend is that also the large, formally known multinationals, are congrugating in the black

[63] For example, it is clear from the TT Guidelines that two firms holding blocking patents are non-competitors. TT Guidelines, para. 32. See also the definition under the TTBER. For a critique of this definition of a non-competitor, see Hanns Ullrich, 'Patent Pools – Policy and Problems', in Josef Drexl (ed), *Research Handbook on Intellectual Property and Competition Law* (Edward Elgar, 2008), 145, fn 25.

square or box by divesting and outsourcing production and even R&D. The Microsoft/Nokia transaction is only the latest step in that process.

Essentially, the US and the EU regulations, separately and in combination, exempt IP Banks. There are generally, 25 vertical prohibitions[64], and nine horizontal prohibitions that the IP Banks need to abide by to benefit from the exemption. The horizontal prohibitions are:

(i) participation in standard-setting organization may not be restricted;
(ii) the procedure for adopting the standard in question must be transparent;
(iii) standardization agreement must not contain an obligation to comply with the standard; and
(iv) access to the standard and the essential IP connected to the standard must be available at least on [fair], reasonable and non-discriminatory terms.

IP Banks, when agreeing on a technology, may not:

(i) exchange information relating to the cost, sales, profitability, prices, marketing, or distribution of any product, process, or service that is not reasonably required for the purpose of developing or promulgating a voluntary consensus standard, or using such standard in conformity with assessment activities;
(ii) allocate shares in a market with a competitor;
(iii) enter into any agreement or conspiracy that would set or restrain the prices of any good or service;
(iv) enter any agreement aimed at excluding actual or potential competitors; and

---

[64] The vertical prohibitions are the 'black clauses' stipulated in the R&D block exemption and the NCRPA, and the joint list of vertical licence covenants stipulated in the DVD Busines Review Letter and Comfort Letter (cf. relevant Chapters 4.1.5, 4.2.4, 5.4.3. supra) However, IP policies and IP arrangments under SSO may be more lenient then similar terms for patent pools (compare Chapters 3.3. and 5.4.3). Interestingly, comparing the list of prohibitions for patent pools with the more lenient black lists for R&D-only firms, implies that patent banks may control R&D-only firms to a greater degree than manufacturing-only firms. In the DVD 6C pool, the Commission clarified what would become the usual criteria under the TT Guidelines for excempting patent pools under Art. 101(3) TFEU, and even though it was the US Justice Department that first addressed patent pools under the Business Review Letter procedure, the Commission first stipulating the concrete rules in a list (cf. supra).

(v) enter any agreements using the disclosure of the most restrictive licensing terms prior to the adoption of a standard as a cover to jointly fix prices (restricting competition by object).

Interestingly, the broad picture does indicate some difference in the application of the different jurisdictions' competition laws. Generally, the US NCRPA encompasses the whole picture depicted in Figure 7.1 above. Thus, the dotted area in the business model above is *de facto* exempted from private antitrust litigators and semi-immune from antitrust scrutiny by the state and federal enforcement agencies both under Sec. 1 and Sec. 2 Sherman Act.[65] In addition, under the Business Review Letter procedure the Justice Department has defined what it regards as anti-competitive conduct with respect to each collaborative effort.[66]

On the face of it, US antitrust law exempts more behaviour under the NCRPA than the EU does under the block exemptions, but the difference is irrelevant. Private litigation, in light of the US experience, is limited under EU competition law in general. The market share ceilings in the block exemptions are a difference, but the guidelines make the exemptions applicable by analogy also outside the block exemption. Furthermore, by not accepting the concept of the 'innovation market' and by not recognizing that patentees in dynamic competition might invent around each other's blocking patents and, hence, be dynamic competitors, EU competition law clearly takes a narrow view of what constitutes infringement of competition law. It reflects an attitude that anti-competitive conduct on innovation markets (and by potential competitors on technology markets) is exempted under EU competition law. This more narrow view influences not only whether two firms are competing, but generally the very definition of essential patents under EU competition law.

In fact, the size of the safe harbours seen together is somewhat surprising. We clearly have firms today, for example PAEs but also large multinationals, where the patent portfolio is becoming more important than the production of goods for their business models and for acquiring wealth. The standards are the tool that connects their patent portfolios with the production and sale of products that they do not produce in-house anymore. By controlling the standards, they control the firms

---

65 The state enforcement agencies are bound by the NCRPA, see Sec. 3 and 4; however they are not as affected as private litigants by the lack of treble damages and the possible liability for the litigation costs.

66 For Business Review Letters, cf. http://www.usdoj.gov/atr/public/, accessed 1 May 2013.

that produce products. While these firms may be exposed to competition law, since product markets are recognized under competition law, the firms focused on standard setting are only to a limited extend exposed to competition law. This is due to the fact that the antitrust community has difficulty in establishing a relevant market for standard setting: holding large patent portfolios in fact makes firms rather immune to competition law, especially the prohibition against anticompetitive agreements, and the immunity increases with the size of the patent portfolio.[67] This will increase as a problem, because standard setting and the cultivation of large patent portfolios is quickly becoming an industry in itself, but the antitrust community's inability to find a market for this business may cause the whole industry to be lost to competition law all together. Indeed, the current development under US antitrust law is an indication of this. The use of the rule of reason approach under, for example, *Rambus*, the way the *eBay* ruling opened up an intellectual property law exemption to obtain something very close to compulsory licences to access SEPs, and now the FTC's refusal to use antitrust law in reference to the *Google* consent order (FTC used unfair competition rules under Sec. 5 of the FTC Act) imply that US antitrust law only has a marginal influence on the business conducted under and with the use of standards.[68] In fact, US Antitrust law perhaps for the first time since it inauguration will not, or only marginal, be applicable to certain firms' core business conduct (their standard-setting and licensing activities) since the US court do not recognise the anti-competitive effects these conducts materialize.

7.3.3 The Application of Competition Law Outside the Safe Harbour

The scant (and mostly US) case law regarding the horizontal effects of standard-setting can be divided in reference to what sort of technology is scrutinized. In fact, when scrutinizing the standard-setting cases, most of the successful horizontal cases have been brought by plaintiffs regarding

---

[67] Competition law has a problem with the conduct that take place before and during the standard-setting procedure. Several commentators purport that agreement on a research path or on technology may be exclusionary and/or collusive conduct while the problem is that there is no market to show actual market effect. See, e.g. Jonathan J Rubin, 'Patents, Antitrust, and Rivalry in Standard-Setting', (2007) 38 *Rutgers Law Journal*, 509, 520.

[68] Cf. FTC, Statement in the In the Matter of Google Inc., FTC File No. 121-0120, January 3, 2013. http://www.ftc.gov/os/caselist/1210120/130103googlemotorolastmtofcomm.pdf, accessed 11 July 2013.

markets that may hold several different standards/technologies, where competition by substitution may exist, while the SSOs, in these cases, have been misused or misled when selecting one technology as a standard and thereby excluding other technologies.[69] In these cases, there are mechanisms that make the selected technology/standard become dominant and work as a barrier to trade for any other technology to penetrate the market, i.e. there are lock-in effects on the stakeholders. Competition by substitution is prevented where competition by substitution could prevail. The same goes for patent pools. The successful patent pool cases normally revolved around exclusion of competing technologies from markets where the plaintiff and the court agree that the market should be able to hold competing technologies.[70]

The need to show anti-competitive effect, under US Antitrust law, seems to imply that a plaintiff needs to show that the market is able to bear several technologies or standards (or at that the standard is acknowledge by public organs), while thereto the plaintiff needs to show an abuse/misuse of the standard-setting process.[71]

Patent pools or IP policies under standardization agreements, should, thus, generally be divided into at least two groups: (i) patent pools that are created on the basis of an infrastructure or an interoperability technology standard (or otherwise on markets where there are market failures); and (ii) technology pools that are present on markets where there may be alternative technologies or products available for the consumer to choose from. Is there room for competition by substitution or only by imitation?

In other words, as discussed above, one could divide also patent pools in reference to what kind of technology or standard and thereto connected collaborations they adhere too. Thus, the test should start in the safe harbour. If it is not applicable the courts could move on and decide what form of standard/technology is up for scrutiny? Is it an infrastructure, interoperable or product (design) standard? Based on the result of that analysis, the Court may scrutinize the standard or patent pool collaboration.

---

[69] See the Allied Tube case.

[70] See, for example, the VIXS patent pool. Cf. In re Summit Tech. Inc., 127 F.T.C. 208 (1998), In re VIXS Inc., 127 F.T.C. 136 (1999).

[71] See discussion, supra, Chapter 4.1.4. Hertbert Hovenkamp et al., *IP and Antitrust: An Analysis of Antitrust Principles Applied to Intellectual Property Law* (Aspen Publishers, 2010), 35.4, 35–31.

7.3.4 Anti-competitive Agreements under Infrastructure Standards

A basic or infrastructure standard should preferably be derived from an all-inclusive standard-setting process, where the organization's inherent collusive character must be tolerated, but access to membership and results must be open and 'protected' under competition law, since such standards create markets and downstream competition. In fact, under EU competition law this *seems* to be a requirement for SSOs according to the EU Commission.[72]

For these technologies, of which our (virtual) infrastructures are examples for, collaboration so as to create joint solutions is likely to have a better outcome than competition. The reasons for this is that these markets harbour natural monopolies, or are plagued by network effects and tipping, and without a standard-setting effort these technologies can easily be hijacked by the first mover or for that matter the firm with the most developed strategic alliances.[73] Standards may here facilitate the prevention monopolies and the creation of competition.

A patent pool originating out of an infrastructure standard scenario is probably beneficial to competition because input prices in the downstream market can be kept low and non-discriminatory by such an organization.[74] Nonetheless, a patent pool, if it is set up under an infrastructure standard and therefore dominant, should be open and unrestricted. The procedure for adopting the pool should be transparent, and access to the result should be granted on fair, reasonable and non-discriminatory terms. As discussed above, the *Orange-Book-Standard* rule, as well as the exception circumstances doctrine under EU competition law, may be applicable.[75] As a result, a safe harbour for the

[72] It depends on interpretation of the Horizontal Guidelines, para. 295.

[73] Josef Drexl, 'Intellectual property in competition: How to promote dynamic competition as a goal' in Josef Drexl et al (eds), *More Common Ground For International Competition Law?* (Edward Elgar, 2011), 210 et seq.

[74] However, as discussed above, the incentive for a dispersed set of essential patentees to enter into such collaboration can be slight, if not minimal. Motorola for example confesses that royalty rates are lower in a patent pool setting than what might be obtained through bilateral negotiations. Motorola made this statement in reference to the H.264 patent pool ran by MPEG LA. See United States District Court Western District of Washington at Seattle, Microsoft v. Motorola, Case no. C10-1823 JLR, Findings of Fact and Conclusion in Law, 25 April 2013, para 498.

[75] See the discussion regarding Magill, IMS Health and Microsoft in Chapter 6.5.1. See also Horizontal Guidelines, para 280. See also the certification case, Joined cases T-213/95 and T-18/96 SCK and FNK v. Commission

standard agreement and the patent pool will be applicable and the SDO will not risk infringing the antitrust laws.[76] Thus, the standard-setting and pool endeavour needs to be to open to new members and to create a transparent procedure connected to the working of the relevant SDO. In other words, competition law will focus on whether the standard-setting procedure has been abused through the breach or misuse of the procedure, with the effect of excluding memberships or firms from the benefits of the standard.[77] In addition, if an SSO's by-laws allow for the standard-setting procedure to be misused, the SSO may be in breach of the antitrust laws.

However, especially in the US, under the rule of reason laid down in *Rambus* and *Philips I* and *II*, it would be difficult to show an anti-competitive effect of the misuse of a standard-setting procedure to the effect that a technology has been excluded under an infrastructure or interoperability standard. A plaintiff cannot show an anti-competitive effect, since the market only holds one technology and there will be no demand for a competing technology. Moreover, it may not be successful with the argument that the technology selected is suboptimal compared to the plaintiff's technology. These infrastructure or interoperability-standards/pools are difficult to address for their horizontal effects, as regards both exclusion and collusion under the US system.

Under EU Competition Rules, it seems that if the rules of the SSO have been 'gamed', an SSO, which has selected one technology over another when deciding an infrastructure standard, may still have infringed Art 101 TFEU. The EU Commission seems to believe that if participation in the standard-setting process is restricted there is anti-competitive effect if the standard has an infrastructure character.[78] The question is how far this rule applies. Is participation restricted if the vote in the technical committees weighed 45 to 1?

[1997] ECR II-1739, an action against Commission decision IV/34.179 – SCK and FNK, (1995) OJ L 312/79.

[76] The Horizontal Guidelines, para 294, do acknowledge that the existence of competing standards does have a significant effect on how competition law should be applied to the stakeholders to a standard.

[77] The EU Commission has on at least two occacions scrutinized ETSI's rules of intellectual property for whether they violate EU Competition Rules, see discussion in Chapters 4.2.6 and 4.2.7. See also Case No. IV./35.06 – ETSI IPR Policy [1995] O.J. C76/5, para. 1. See also Maurits Dolmans, 'Standards For Standards', (2002) 26 *Fordham International Law Journal*, 163, 181, describing the Commission's preliminary position.

[78] Horizontal Guidelines, para. 295.

It seems clear that some commentators find that this does not cause any anti-competitive effect.[79] It is true that antitrust courts should not select one technology above another, even if the technology selected as standard is the wrong or less developed technology. But the Commission seem to imply that non-access to markets or to the standard-setting procedure is in itself an antitrust violation, but that the remedy is not to select another standard: it is just to ensure that access is granted. The EU Commission implies that non-access to the standard-setting procedure is not considered 'competition on the merits'. The question is how far this rule applies. Is the participation restricted if the vote in the technical committee is weighed 45 to 1 depending on turnover of the participating firms? Is the representative of the small R&D firm having one vote really participating? Perhaps, when we are dealing with infrastructure, standards 'competition on the merits' imply that firms cannot discriminate. The SDO may otherwise consider facilitating the possibility of misusing the standard-setting procedure.

Thus, the vertical effects can be addressed (e.g. non-access to standards, SEPs, standard-setting procedure, price discrimination or marginal squeeze) under infrastructure standards, while the horizontal effects of standard setting (i.e, technical collusion and exclusion), may still be scrutinized under antitrust law, but it is difficult for a court, as a remedy, to declare that a new standard should be selected.

7.3.5 Anti-competitive Agreements under Interoperability Standards

Dealing with interoperable standards is difficult and the courts need to be careful and conduct an analysis of the relevant markets and of innovation competition. The issue, at least under US antitrust law, is whether these standards or patent pools should be analysed only for their vertical effects or for their horizontal effects as well.

Pure interface or interoperability standards are as infrastructural standards often plagued by network effects and their related patent pools are beneficial to competition. Interoperability standards, that originate from an industry initiative, with input from suppliers and consumers (for example, standard setting by an SDO), may be platforms for considerable beneficial externalities for the industry and society as a whole. The issue is, however, whether the relevant market, or the relevant market to be, is

---

[79] Steven Anderman & John Kallaugher, Technology Transfer and the New EU Competition Rules (Oxford University Press 2006), 252.

able to bear competition by substitute, or whether there can only be one solution to the demand.[80]

If the market cannot support competing standards or technologies there will be no anti-competitive effects on the relevant markets, and, thus, there are no real antitrust effects related to a horizontal agreement. This is actually what the courts are telling us when demanding a showing of anti-competitive effect. For example, in the *Philips* cases, the plaintiff had difficulties proving that the substitute technology included in the pool had, or would have, an independent demand.[81] While in *Rambus,* FTC was not able to show that the SDO would have selected a competing technology 'but for' Rambus making it known that it held SEPs to the standard.[82] Thus, if the plaintiff can show that a substitute or a competing technology exists and there would at least potentially be a demand for it in the market, and there was still a demand for the 'incumbent technology', anti-competitive harm (exclusion) and effect can be shown.[83] Thereby, using the division made in this book, such a standard is a product standard rather than an interoperability standard.

Whether a market holds not one but several technologies is a difficult analysis for the courts to conduct, but necessary in determining whether standard-setting ventures and related agreements should be analysed under a raised antitrust threshold for its horizontal effects, and lower antitrust threshold for its vertical effects.[84] In fact, they need to establish whether there is network effect or other circustances, which implies that only one standard may prevail.

The test whether the market would be able to bear more than one technology may include an analysis of the innovation process and relevant innovations in the near future that will compete with the suggested standard. This must be done with great caution so that the court is not too speculative.[85] Perhaps guidance can be found in the R&D

---

80 Ibid., 252.

81 See discussion, supra, Chapters 5.3.4. and 5.5.

82 See discussion, supra, Chapter 6.3.2.

83 Steven Anderman and John Kallaugher, *Technology Transfer and the New EU Competition Rules* (Oxford University Press, 2006), 252, fn. 69.

84 The Horizontal Guidelines clearly indicate that the existence of competing standards implies less of an antitrust obligation to give access to the standard or essential patents under the standards. See Horizontal Guidelines, para. 294. For a similar general division see also Marcus Glader, 'Open Standards: Public Policy Aspects and Competition Law Requirements', (December 2010) 6 *European Competition Journal*, 611.

85 Cf. Steven Anderman and John Kallaugher, *Technology Transfer and the New EU Competition Rules* (Oxford University Press, 2006), 261, fn. 69.

block exemption where the courts are obliged to look three years into the future to see whether any potential competitors are emerging.[86] In the US, the NCRPA seem to indicate that the notion of an innovation market should be applied in these circumstances. However, in *Rambus* and in the *Philips* cases, the appeal courts focused more on current market effects.[87] If the courts agree that this is a network driven standard and the market would not be able to facilitate other options, then one standard with a patent pool would be beneficial. Likewise, if the court agrees that the market has such inherent tipping effects that only one solution would prevail due to market failures, then it should allow for only one standard to prevail and that competitors may access the standard and the SEPs. This analysis includes an analysis of the customers. Are they willing to accept more than one solution or standard on the downstream markets? For example, in *IMS Health*, the petitioner had tried to enter the market of providing pharma information, but could not do so due to the fact that the copyright protected grid (the 'brick-structure') used for providing such information to customers had become a *de facto* standard.[88] The customers would not accept being given the pharma information in any other format. It thus prevented competition by substitution.

In light of the above, the courts should not speculate; often, they should agree with the defendant that the standard is benign and that there is no room for competition except by substitution. However, on the other hand, if the court allows for a collaboration, including all competitors and potential competitors in the industry, and the market would actually have held more technologies than the one standard, then the court has exempted a very powerful anti-competitive venture in the market that most likely will survive for several decades. Such a patent pool with a connected standardization agreement may inhibit dynamic competition, and also set prices to high levels. Thus, the court must be open to analysing the markets and seeing whether they may facilitate competition by substitution, and whether the collaboration scrutinized is, thus,

---

86 The R&D block exemption is discussed, supra Chapter 4.2.4.

87 See discussion, supra, Chapter 4.1.1. Here the notion of an innovation market could come up, but, as discussed before, the court should make a more independent analysis of what innovations may appear in two or three years' time. In other words, the court needs to look into the future and determine whether the plaintiff can establish that competing technologies are likely to develop. If such technologies might exist, they must be taken into consideration. Will such technologies have access to consumers if the market is standardized? Or will the standard exclude these innovations from the market?

88 For discussion of IMS Health, see Chapter 6.5.1.

collusive or will *de facto* or *de jure* exclude competition. If that is the case, the market needs to become open to competition. Because in these situations the 'counterfactual' is a market where different technologies compete and the standard would actually prevent that market from materializing.[89] This would imply restricting the exclusionary effects of the standard and the patent pool.

If the parties put forward an argument that the market can only hold one standard due to tipping effects, the court needs to take this into consideration. It needs to analyse whether the tipping effects are created on the demand side or the supply side. Shapiro *et al* ascertained that the difference between networks-driven markets in the new 'high-tech' economy, and the old industrial market is that they are demand-side driven.[90] The demand creates the tipping effects, while in the old industry, markets were more influenced by the supply side, i.e. whether they could create economies of scale and scope.

However, that does not imply that the firms in the 'New Economy' are not able to influence demand. For example, the network or tipping effects purported to exist as regards the HD standard war between Blu-Ray and HD-DVD, discussed above, seem to originate from exclusive supply arrangements (strategic alliances) rather being driven by consumer demand.[91]

If these exclusive arrangements had been non-exclusive, or the content providers had been open to both technologies, perhaps both competing technologies could have been present on the relevant market, while the consumers would not have been 'afraid' to select the 'wrong' technology: the one that would exit the market. Possibly, the relevant market in the Blu-Ray–HD-DVD war could only support one technical solution, but we do not know how this market would have evolved under competition.[92] If consumer has different preferences and values choice, different systems may survive. Possibly, competition law should then promote interoperability so to facilitate different product systems being selected in the

---

[89] Cf. Steven Anderman and John Kallaugher, *Technology Transfer and the New EU Competition Rules* (Oxford University Press, 2006), 252, fn. 32.

[90] See supra Chapter 2.1.

[91] Christ and Slowak seem to agree that the market would possibly have supported both technologies, but that strategic behaviour – collecting more content providers – tipped the market. Julian Christ & André Slowak, 'Why Blue-Ray v. HD-DVD is not VHS v. BETAMAX: The Co-evolution of Standard Setting Consortia', (2009) *FZID Discussion Papers*, Universität Hohenheim.

[92] Ibid.

market.[93] Only when the court has established that the market has failed because consumers demand only one solution should competition by substitution not be upheld.

Further examples of the dichotomy between interoperability and product standards are the 802.11 (WiFi) standard and the H.264 (video compression) standard.

BOX 7.2

The 802.11 standard and patent pool and the H.264 standard and patent pool are good illustrations of these issues, while one is a prime example of the 'good' way of creating standards (H.264), and the other is not (802.11). There are clear unilateral hold-up problems for these technologies, which are now being investigated by several courts in the US and EU, and by the EU Commission.[94]

The H.264 standard for video coding (also known as MPEG-4 part 10), created jointly by ISO/IEC and the ITU, through two SSOs (MPEG and VCEG). It was created between 1998 and 2001 and was truly an impressive effort of collective joint standard setting. It was the result of 170 entities submitting over 2,300 documents. The largest technical contributor was Telenor. It became very successful and it is estimated that during the period around 2005 it was clearly the dominant (monopoly) technology for video decoding of compressed information. For example, the internet and on Blu-Ray used H.264 (today H.264 is challenged by other technical solutions for the internet).[95]

H.264 seems clearly to facilitate interoperability. While this H.264 standard is an interoperability standard, it should, under the current antitrust law, probably fall outside scrutiny under Art. 101 TFEU or be considered almost per se legal under US antitrust law. H.264 seems to have created new markets in itself and there were network effects that push the technology into a monopoly position, while this network effect was not created by

[93] Cf. Marcus Glader, 'Open Standards: Public Policy Aspects and Competition Law Requirements', (2010) 6 *European Competition Journal*, 611, 613 et seq. with references.

[94] Discussed, supra, Chapter 3.4.

[95] Ibid.

exclusive agreements between content providers and technology providers (like the Blu-Ray and DVD technologies), but by consumer demand for the technology.

The anti-competitive situations that arose under the H.264 standard could be from firms trying to hold up utilizers of the standard by charging excessive royalties or using injunctions under SEPs, i.e. trying to limit competition by imitation. Furthermore, there could be a problem of marginal squeeze or price discrimination, while the horizontal part of the standard and the pool (including FRAND) might escape antitrust scrutiny. Thus, these collaborations have more of a vertical antitrust problem then a horizontal problem (from the perspective of the up-stream standard).

The 802.11 standard is the dominant technology for wireless transfer of data and information in houses and businesses. It should, perhaps, be scrutinized in more detail for the horizontal and vertical effects created by the standards and the connected pool. It seems here that the standard (as discussed above) perhaps included competing technologies. Thus, there are *de facto* competing solutions on the market, in this case within the same class of standards. The competition courts and agencies need therefore to scrutinize it under the effect doctrine or rule of reason to establish whether there might be anti-competitive collusion under the standard in the form of price agreements and group boycott (collusion or exclusion). The patent pool created under the standard could be a collaboration between competing firms including competing technologies, which may be anti-competitive.[96] Furthermore, the discussion during the

[96] According to the EU Horizontal Guidelines, para. 317, this may be in violation of Art. 101 TFEU: 'As a general rule standardization agreements should cover no more than what is necessary to ensure their aims, whether this is technical interoperability and compatibility or a certain level of quality. In cases where having only one technological solution would benefit consumers or the economy at large that standard should, be set on a non-discriminatory basis. Technology neutral standards can, in certain circumstances, lead to larger efficiency gains. Including substitute IPR as essential parts of a standard while at the same time forcing the users of the standard to pay for more IPR than technically necessary would go beyond what is necessary to achieve any identified efficiency gains. In the same vein, including substitute IPR as essential parts of a standard and limiting the use of that technology to that particular standard (that is to say, exclusive use) could limit inter-technology competition and would not be necessary to achieve the efficiencies identified.

pre-standardization phase when the FRAND royalty rate under the IP arrangement were, perhaps, discussed may also constitute price collusion. Finally, if a technology were excluded for the standard, while it includes several other competing technologies, the standard agreement may be regarded as a group boycott, excluding competition.

The 802.11 standard may very well be exempted under Art 101 (3), or fall outside Sec. 1 Sherman Act under the rule of reason, especially since the current set-up seems to have been the only plausible solution to a standard. The courts may therefore weigh the efficiencies of having this standard compared to a situation without any standard. In fact, perhaps having competing technologies under the standard was indispensible to their creation.

As with infrastructure standards, for truly interoperability standards, the vertical effects can be addressed (e.g. non-access to standards, SEPs, standard-setting procedure, price discrimination or marginal squeeze), while the horizontal effects of the standard setting (i.e, technical collusion and exclusion) which could be prevented if a new standard were selected, should nonetheless not be scrutinized under antitrust law. The courts should not, from the viewpoint of an antitrust policy based on defining anti-competitive effect with reference to prices and output, decide on the quality of standards.

Nonetheless, access to the standard-setting procedure must, as with infrastructure standards, be upheld. When deciding interoperability standards, we must perhaps accept weighted voting procedures in the technical committees because these standards do not last as long as infrastructure standards and special treatment must be given to the technology providers that otherwise could create a de facto standard.

7.3.6 Anti-competitive Conduct under Product Design Standards

At the other end of the spectrum, a patent pool under a design standard, implying that members of a SSO have agreed to set a standard for a market that would hold more than one product standard, should be scrutinized more carefully. Is there competition on the market between different technologies? Will this competition be prevented by implementing a standard? That is not certain. The application of a standard is often voluntary, and only if there are some 'lock-in' effects will a standard create anti-competitive effects. There are, *de lege ferenda*, four conditions that need to be met for a product standard to amount to a group boycott or an agreement to exclude: (i) there must be a genuine alternative technology; (ii) the number of firms agreeing on the technology must be sufficient to make the competing technology unviable; (iii) there must be some lock-in effects that make it unlikely that they will switch to the competing technology; and (iv) it must be possible to increases prices to detriment of consumers.[97] An additional requirement, at least under US antitrust law, could be that the standard-setting procedure must have been misused or 'gamed' somehow.[98] The by-laws do not need to have been breached, but the integrity of the standard-setting procedure must have been infringed to the extent that it cannot be considered 'competition on the merits'.[99]

If the standard-connected patent pool contains competing patents and has patentees that are competitors on a relevant market connected to the patent pool, and the standard effectively excludes competing technologies, this collaboration may have anti-competitive effects.[100] Hence, while patent pools under an infrastructure or interoperability standards could be regarded as falling outside Art 101(1) TFEU or Sec. 1 Sherman Act, product standard pools should be scrutinized more carefully. Here competition by substitution can exist and be suppressed.

The issue is whether these standards or pools are anti-competitive and can be exempted under Art 101(3) or under the rule of reason. That depends on their market power and, generally, on the establishment of anti-competitive exclusionary effect. If the members hold market power and the collaboration implies a joint effort to have their innovation standardized, competition law should prevent the standardization effort being merely a contractual vehicle to exclude competition. This would imply misusing the standard-setting procedure even though the parties have adhered to the by-laws and procedural rules of the SDO.

However, under product standards, the court should not be keen to grant access to either standard-setting procedure or standard. Only if the plaintiff can show that the SSO or the standard has market power to the degree that the doctrine of exceptional circumstance would be applicable (under the SEP doctrine or *IMS Health* or the *Microsoft* case) should a

---

[97] See Steven Anderman and John Kallaugher, *Technology Transfer and the New EU Competition Rules* (Oxford University Press, 2006), 250, fn. 30.

[98] See Allied Tube case law and Chapter 4.1.2.

[99] The US cases seem to require this, e.g. Allied Tube. Cf. discussion, supra, in Chapter 4.1.4.

[100] See, e.g., In re Summit Tech. Inc., 127 F.T.C. 208 (1998), In re VIXS Inc., 127 F.T.C. 136 (1999).

court allow for such access. Under US antitrust law, access will not be granted since the US antitrust law community has dismissed the refusal to license/essential facility doctrine.

In contrast to the infrastructure and interoperability standard-setting procedures, the horizontal effects of a products standard-setting procedure shall be scrutinized, but the courts should only very rarely give access to either procedure or standard.

7.3.7 Patent Thicket and other Market Failures

Patent thicket standards are product standards. A standard agreement, if it is entered into and creates competition and a relevant market out of a patent thicket, is acceptable. In other words, as stated above, a joint effort where the standard or patent pool is drafted so to enable trade and competition by creating collaboration between all 'essential' patentees is welcomed. In fact, the standard and the pool are the solution to a market failure and the effect of these collaborations is that a market is created and 'tip' to the advantage of the technology defined in the standard and the pool agreement. It should be permissible to create even all industry-wide collaborations, as long as the SSOs and their members are able to prove that there is a patent thicket problem, or some other form of market failure, that the standard and the patent pool will overcome. The MPEG-2 patent pool is the prime example of this form of pro-competitive collaboration.[101]

7.3.8 Conclusion

In conclusion, any court scrutinizing standards or patent pools should take as its point of departure the kind of market and standard to be analysed. If the underlying market can only hold one standard (there is no competition by substitution), the horizontal result of that standard, i.e. the standard itself, falls outside the ambit of competition law.[102] Thus, it will be very difficult to show anti-competitive effect. In addition, the 'governance' rules regarding access to the SDO, transparency, due process and the possibility of appealing draft standards should be taken

[101] See the MPEG-2 Pool Business Review Letter to Gerrard Beeney dated 26 June 1997, 6. See http://www.usdoj.gov/atr/public/busreview/215742.htm, accessed 3 May 2009.

[102] Likewise, if the standard is not a design standard but more of a performance standard, then the collaborations should fall outside Sec. 1 Sherman Act or Art 101 TFEU.

into account. In other words, if the result of the collaboration falls outside the ambit of competition law, indirect rules regarding access to the collaboration become important from an antitrust perspective (under pain of abusing the dominance rules) These rules are important also for SDOs creating infrastructure, interoperability or patent thicket standards.

However, if the standard and related patent pool is of a product or design type (i.e. the market holds several competing solutions) then courts might want to scrutinize in more detail their horizontal collusive and exclusionary effects.

7.4 PRE-STANDARDIZATION AGREEMENTS AND AGREEMENT ON TECHNOLOGY

At the beginning of the 1990s, patent pools were the hot topic of discussion, and especially, that competitors should be allowed to collaborate in patent pools due the problem of patent thickets and anticommons.[103] Thereafter, the problem of patent ambush under standards emerged, and with that the antitrust community start focusing on standard setting. Patent pools were still discussed but now as a tool for preventing patent ambush. The doctrine of patent pools was somewhat rewritten so that patent pools could also facilitate the PAE, or any holder of SEPs, in making the patent pool an efficient one-stop-shop to access markets under standards. Patent pools would prevent hold-up. However, quite quickly the community realized that the PAEs did not want to enter the patent pools. The patent pools were dictated to by the vertical integrated firms and a PAE must then agree on a royalty rate, which could be lower than hoped under the maverick business strategy of the PAEs.[104]

Nonetheless, the experience with PAEs made it painfully apparent that the patent pools, which had been set up to fight 'patent thickets', were now a licensing tool for many firms focusing on standard setting. Many patent pools use (copy) the definition of relevant technology from technical standards produced by SDOs. Thus, few, if any, pools come up with their own definition of the relevant technology. The idea that patent pools are caused by, and the antidote to, patent thickets may be wrong, since they are rather more derived from agreements on standards.

---

[103] See discussion supra, Chapter 5.2.4.

[104] See for example, Judge Robart's argument that the royalty rates of patent pools are normally belowe the rate agreed in unilateral negotiations. Discussed supra, Chapter 6.7.

But, it is actually the opposite. Successful standards and pools often create patent thickets. For example, in the consumer electronic industry, certain firms seem to have a business strategy of conducting standard setting and patent pooling. The CD-ROM standard and pool, DVD standards and pools, and the HD-DVD v. Blu-Ray standards and pools are just examples of business strategies focusing on developing consumer electronic products, and through these collaborative means get markets to adopt and implement a technology through standards. In hindsight, the DVD Business Review Letters clearly did not recognize patent thicket problems.

From a competition law perspective, perhaps the revelation will soon come that, within the standard-setting process, firms perhaps do not conduct unilateral R&D and then present and discuss their findings in the technical committees of the SDOs. Instead, they often conduct joint R&D under the consortia-driven standard-setting model. It seems clear the standard-setting consortia model may also imply jointly developing the technology to be implemented.[105] As stated in the introduction to this book, standard-setting in this regard is a form of collective innovation.[106] Baron and Pohlmann's recent in depth research also shows that firms with substitutable R&D programs or patent portfolios are more likely to be members of the same pre-standardization consortium.[107] In fact, Baron and Pohlmann's research, based on a database including all ICT standards issued between 1992 and 2009, shows that consortia have been formed for all standards with unusual high number of patent holders.[108] Indeed, through upfront R&D coordination under the consortium, firms that have the same business model can coordinate R&D and better anticipate technology selection decision in SDOs.[109] However, their research shows that R&D specific or technology specialists firms,

---

[105] See Steven Anderman and Hedvig Schmidt, *EU Competition Law and Intellectual Property Rights – Regulation of Innovation* (Oxford University Press, 2011), 293 et seq.

[106] Josef Drexl, 'Anti-competitive Stumbling Stones on the way to a Cleaner World: Protecting Competition in Innovation Without a Market', (2012) 8 *Journal of Competition Law & Economics*, 507, 534.

[107] Justus Baron and Tim Pohlmann, 'Who Cooperates in Standard Consortia – Rivals or Complementors?', (2013) 9 *Journal of Competition Law & Economics*, 905, 921, 928.

[108] Justus Baron and Tim Pohlmann, 'Who Cooperates in Standard Consortia – Rivals or Complementors?', (2013) 9 *Journal of Competition Law & Economics*, 905, 912, 921 et seq., 928.

[109] Ibid.

possibly the SMEs, are not members of the pre-standardization consortia.[110] The firms that Baron and Pohlman have discovered to set up and use consortia seem to be the firms I refer to as IP Banks. Baron and Pohlman also warn that if the major economic function of consortia is to reduce technological rivalry, competition authorities should monitor SDO cooperation with standards consortia carefully.[111]

However, that does not seem to be the general development. As stated above, even ISO promotes collaboration with consortia. Moreover, it seems that ESOs can even get funding from the EU Commission under the art 15 of the Regulation on European standardization to sponsor joint R&D.[112] Moreover, through the European Technology Platforms, the EU Commission promotes joint fora for R&D and standard setting, while the future outlook is for even more intervention by the EU Commission in promoting standard-setting-driven joint R&D.[113] In the US, a similar development may be detected. It seems that specific US research laboratories may also be available to conduct joint research in standard-setting procedures under the National Technology Transfer and Advancement Act of 1995 (NTTAA) and the Stevenson-Wydler Technology Advancement Act of 1980.

Thus, the question is whether there actually is competition *for* a standard, or whether we have standards that are a collaborative effort from innovation to patent pool, with much government support on every level. In fact, the absurd situation may possible arise in which horizontal R&D collaboration including agreement on price will receive support from both the EU and the US government, while possibly the antitrust agencies would find them rather suspicious.

It seems that several antitrust scholars and practitioners defend the collaboration in standard setting and patent pooling because rivalry still exists at the R&D stage. Pre-competition rivalry implies that there is some kind of race in which entrepreneurial skills are matched against each other, but is that really true? In light of the above, it is possibly not. Moreover, in this book several examples of standards that were created by joint R&D collaborations have been given. Actually, one could argue that the consortia model of standard setting includes joint R&D as well. In the future, pre-standardization agreements or 'pre-normative research'

---

110 Ibid.

111 Ibid. 928.

112 Discussed, supra, Chapter 3.2.2.

113 Commission White Paper 'Modernising ICT Standardisation in the EU – The Way Forward', COM(2009) 324 final, 7 et seq.

will increase dramatically due to the support given by different governments.[114] The EU Commission bluntly supports joint exploration and agreement on different research avenues through the European Technology Platforms concept.[115]

Actually, it is perhaps not so surprising that firms seek out collaborations. It even seems clear that firms, after the *eBay* case law in the USA and the *Orange-Book-Standard* case in Europe, will be obliged to give access to their patents under successful standards, so why would they not try to collaborate to conduct the R&D? That would be a way of distributing cost and risk. The firms in the technical committees also conduct joint R&D in the broader sense. They divide the R&D between them and agree to research avenues, and sometimes jointly outsource R&D to R&D-specific firms.[116] If the leading members in an industry collaborated in R&D, standard setting and exploitation, they would have an incentive to create a single *de facto* and *de jure* monopoly technology that reflected their joint R&D. This could in turn cause courts to conclude that the market reflects such a market failure as would warrant that competition law would not protect competition by substitution, only by imitation. Thus, these firms produce a market failure, and also their own exemption for collaborating under competition law.

However, as discussed above, competition law has a problem with the conduct that takes place before and during the standard-setting procedure. Several commentators argue that agreement on a research path or on technology may be exclusionary and/or collusive conduct although the problem is that there is no market yet to show actual market effect.[117] Then it becomes too speculative to be taken into consideration. If the notion of an innovation market is not accepted, there are no relevant markets to establish anti-competitive effects.

Establishing an interoperability standard is furthermore not a rigorous, scientific process driven by identifying the 'best' technology in a particular field.[118] Rather, technology is included in a standard through a collaborative process. It draws heavily on prior R&D, standards, and may

114 Commission, 'Communication from the Commission to the European Parliament, the Council and the European Economic and Social Committees, COM(2011) 311 final, 7.

115 Cordis European Technology Platsforms, http://cordis.europa.eu/technology-platforms. Accessed 6 September 2012.

116 See supra, Chapters 4.1.1 and 4.2.6.

117 See Jonathan J Rubin, 'Patents, Antitrust, and Rivalry in Standard-Setting', (2007) 38 *Rutgers Law Journal*, 509, 520.

118 Ibid.

involve evaluation of, or selection and even compromise among competing technical approaches.[119] While we may analyse, with the help of engineers, whether intellectual properties reflect substitute technologies[120], it is very difficult to establish what constitutes the best technology and what might not be competition on the merits, especially, when it comes to interoperability standards for the New Economy. We just do not know what should be considered pro- or anti-competitive.

Notwithstanding the above, we should still not lose sight of the 'but for' case. For product standards specifically, a situation without a standard would imply competition between technologies on markets. Even with reference to interoperability standards, the 'but for' reality is competition between technologies. Perhaps it is not the competition we want because one firm will probably gain monopoly power due to network effects, but it will, at least, be in competition and rivalry with other firms. Furthermore, maybe these monopolies in the New Economy will not last because new innovations will soon follow.[121] It seems that we are too afraid to allow that to happen. However, to state that standard setting would not take place in a 'market' seem to disregard the fact that standard setting is often the alternative to competition for consumers in a market based on price, quality and design.

Antitrust violations may then be identified as conduct which is not 'competition on the merits', but to do so would be based, rather, on an evaluation that the business practice in question does not match what is considered legitimate business practice, since we cannot establish anti-competitive effect in a market. What is not 'competition on the merits' needs, as our legal method imply, to be derived from the use and the development of case law and on our logical conclusion of what conduct might cause anticompetitive effect. So let us do that.

If the latest imperical research by Baron and Pohlmann is correct[122], it seems to imply that pre-standardization consortia, where competing firms engage in deciding on R&D and technology, with the intent to be able to conclude majority voting blocks when the standard is decided in the more official SDOs, then is that so different from what we saw in *Allied*

---

[119] Ibid.

[120] Identifying substitute technologies may be very difficult, which the analysis of the several pools has shown.

[121] See generally, Carl Shapiro and Hal R. Varian, *Information Rules* (Harvard Business School Press, 1999), 173 et seq.

[122] Justus Baron and Tim Pohlmann, 'Who Cooperates in Standard Consortia – Rivals or Complementors?', (2013) 9 *Journal of Competition Law & Economics*, 905.

Tube? Allied Tube, the plastic electrical conduit manufacturer, that had proposed the inclusion of plastic electrical conduits in the standard and received preliminary approval by the SDO. However, prior to the 1980 meeting, at which the final NFPA vote occurred, the defendant and other steel industry and NFPA members agreed before the meeting to 'pack' the NFPA with new members in order to defeat the proposal.[123] Could not a pre-standardization consortia be a more elegant way to 'pack' the technical committee?

Could it not be a misuse of the standard-setting procedure if *de facto* the procedure in the SDO is irrelevant or a sham, while the larger IP Banks already have decided on what technology to select in the pre-standardization phase in a closed and confidential consortium? Especially, if the voting rights are already twisted to the benefit of larger firms with larger patent portfolios in the technical committees in the SDO, e.g. in ETSI? At least we could agree that it could be a primia facia case of misuse of the standard-setting procedure, while there is still the issue to resolve whether this behaviour effectively excludes competing or rival technologies. Indeed, the issue is still whether the market can sustain several standards or technologies (effectively excluding several interoperability standards) and that the decision on a product standard *de facto* excludes a competitor or potential competitor by excluding a competing or substitute standard or technology from the market. Thus, the plaintiff needs to show at least potentially anti-competitive effect, while the members of the consortia may refute any allegation by provided support for the idea that the collaboration created efficiencies. Of course, consortia increase efficiency in R&D and also eliminate duplicate or wasteful R&D.[124]

7.5 UNILATERAL CONDUCT UNDER STANDARDS

So-called patent ambush was the first kind of unilateral conduct that could amount to abuse or monopolization. It deals with a patentee that is also a member of an SSO, which omits to tell the SSO that it holds a potential SEP. When the standard has been adopted and the members and other firms have invested in the standard, the patentee emerges and, knowing that the exit cost will be large for firms in the industry, charges

---

123 Discussed supra, Chapter 4.

124 Justus Baron and Tim Pohlmann, 'Who Cooperates in Standard Consortia – Rivals or Complementors?', (2013) 9 *Journal of Competition Law & Economics*, 905, 907, 928.

a royalty rate that reflects both the exit costs for the firms and the value of the standard as such, while the SEP may only cover a small part of the standardized technology. The issue was, and is, whether this may constitute abuse of a dominant position under Art 102 TFEU, or monopolization or attempt to monopolize under Sec. 2 Sherman Act (or Sec. 5 FTC Act). The amount of market power gained by the patentee depends on three factors: (i) the level and fairness of the competition before the standard was set; (ii) the level of competition between different technologies after the standard is set; and (iii) the level of lock-in for the stakeholders of the standard.[125]

It is now relatively certain that access to SEPs on fair terms under infrastructure standards and interoperability standards may be granted under *eBay* in the US and under the *Orange-Book-Standard* doctrine or equivalent under EU law. Both the *eBay* and *Orange-Book-Standard* cases go beyond the basic patent ambush scenario and provide access also in other circumstances as long as the technology is vital for the standard or the product. Actually, the latest US and EU case law development seems to suggest that holding an SEP per se implies that injunctive relief is not available.[126] That is a major step in restricting intellectual property to become rights and not property.

However, what about the division between, on the one hand, infrastructure standards or interoperability standards, and, on the other hand, design or product standards? Should access be granted to an SEP when the standard only reflects one technology or standard out of several in a relevant technology market? If there are competing standards should access to an SEP be granted? Or, the other way around, should the SEP defence under patent infringement suits be granted? In the above cases, e.g. *Orange-Book-Standard, In re Dell, Rambus*, it is clear that the court imagined an industry-wide standard. The Motorola cases in the US (Posner and Robart) also deals with infrastructural or interoperability standards (802.11 and H.264). Perhaps, access, without the possibility of injunction should only be granted under these forms of standards when

---

125 Marcus Glader, 'Open Standards: Public Policy Aspects and Competition Law Requirements', (2010) 6 *European Competition Journal,* 611, 614, n. 12. See also Daniel Swanson and William Baumol, 'Reasonable and Nondiscriminatory (RAND) Royalties, Standards Selection, and Control of Market Power', (2005) 73 *Antitrust Law Journal*, 1, 9 and Joseph Farrell et al., 'Standard Setting, Patents, and Hold-up', (2007) 74 *Antitrust Law Journal*, 603, 625 et seq., 646.

126 See the EU Commission statements in the Google/Motorola merger case and in different press releases in reference to Samsung and Google. Discussed, supra, Chapter 6.5.

the market has failed, and competition by imitation is the only competition that may prevail. Access under standards that only represent a competing product in a larger technical market should not be granted.[127]

For standards where the market has failed, the relevant issue becomes defining both these standards and, furthermore, deciding whether the claimed SEPs are truly essential under the standard. The patentee must bear the risk of whether the patent truly is essential or not and run the risk of abusing its dominant position should the patent prove to be essential to the relevant SDO, or breach of contract should it prove otherwise. It could amount to misuse of the standard-setting process, irrespective of what is stated in the by-laws.[128] The firm should probably be considered dominant with reference to the claimed SEP. At least, the firm, *de lege late*, should be perceived as dominant with reference to that SEP until it is proven non-essential.[129]

Moreover, what about accessing the standard-setting procedure and the patent pool? Under EU competition law, the 'exceptional circumstances' doctrine of *IMS Health* and *Microsoft* is possibly in play when the standard being developed is an infrastructure, interoperability standard, or where there is a market failure, or standard derived from a patent thicket. In these circumstances, a third entity may have a claim to join the standard-setting procedure. However, this does not imply that the firm may access the unilateral R&D carried out in connection with the standard-setting procedure. Rivalry in R&D needs to be upheld, and under *IMS Health* and *Microsoft*, EU competition law still upholds somewhat of a 'new' product requirement.[130]

What about pre-standardization conduct? During the development of the 802.11 standard, certain members of the technical committee in IEEE were accused of stalling the process of implementing the new 802.11n standard because implementing that standard would lead to lower sales under the 802.11g and, thus, loss of revenue for these firms. Some

---

127 See, for example, Horizontal Guidelines, para. 294.

128 Many by-laws do not reqire the firms to make a thorough search for essential patents. See discussion, supra, under Chapter 6.

129 See the EU Commission statements in the Google/Motorola merger case and in different press releases in reference to Samsung and Google. Discussed, supra, Chapter 6.5.

130 See discussion regarding whether this requirement is still valid: Josef Drexl, 'Anti-competitive Stumbling Stones on the Way to a Cleaner World: Protecting Competition in Innovation without a Market', (2012) 8 *Journal of Competition Law & Economics*, 507, and Steven Anderman and Hedvig Schmidt, *EU Competition Law and Intellectual Property Rights – Regulation of Innovation* (Oxford University Press, 2011), 102 et seq.

claimed PAEs tried to block the new standard since their SEPs fitted the old, but not a new, standard.[131] Is this anti-competitive? Here, possibly, the good governance rules may apply, but also those customary rules which reflect the integrity of the standard-setting system and process. Thus, if the firms are lobbying and working inside the by-laws of the SDO, this conduct could still be regarded as a breach of 'competition on the merits' under competition law, if they 'game' the standard-setting procedure.[132] To establish a set of rules regarding conduct or good governance rules under competition law seems to be the way that the EU Commission and the Justice Department have indicated competition law should develop.[133]

Where there is competition between different standard-setting consortia, access, outside the serious cases of patent ambush, should not be granted lightly. Possibly, in these cases, consortia are competing over innovation by trying to get at patents inside the competing consortium's standard. Should this sort of competition be restricted, or may it in these

---

[131] Discussed supra, Chapter 3.4.

[132] The VPC manufacturer in Allied Tube did not violate any of the by-laws of the organization by enlisting other steel makers in order to block the PVC standard and by packing the meeting with new members to vote against the proposal. The Second Circuit held anyway that the defendant violated the integrity of the organization's procedure and subverted the organization's standard-setting process for the purpose of achieving an anti-competitive result. Cf. Allied Tube and Conduit Corp. v. Indian Head, Inc. 817 F2.d 938 (2d Cir 1987) aff'd 486 U.S. 492, 500 (1988), 817 F.2d at 947. In Rambus, on the other hand, the Federal Circuit did not venture far from the exact wording of the IP policy and FRAND commitment. However, it did not discuss whether there are business customary rules, which may maintain the integrity of the standard-setting procedure.

[133] See the discussion above regarding the EMC case and the American Welding Society, Case COMP/F-2/38.401 EN 197-1 Standard – EMC/ European Cement Producers, para. 107. American Welding Society Business Review Letter from Charles James to Douglas Mcdonald, dated 7 October 2002, where the Justice Department stated that it does not weigh whether one standard is better than the other, only whether the process of standard setting has been abused. The letters can be found on http://www.usdoj.gov/atr/public/busreview/letters.htm, accessed 19 March 2009. The American Welding Society letter is discussed in Peter Plompen, 'The New Technology Transfer Guidelines (TTG) as Applied to Patent Pools and Patent Pool Licensing: Some Observations Regarding the Concept of "Essential Technologies"', in Claus Dieter Ehlermann and Isabela Atanasin (eds), *European Competition Law Annual 2005: The Interaction between Competition Law and Intellectual Property Law* (Hart Publishing, 2005), 300 fn. 11.

circumstances even be pro-innovative? It pushes consortia to compete in innovation and to work around innovation created by a competitor to the consortium. Thus, where competition by substitution may prevail, access may be limited. As a matter of fact, the monopsony problem may instead occur. As stated above, the argument that PAEs were exposed to anti-competitive monopsonies under SDOs (mainly ETSI) was mainly put forward in Europe, and had no or very limited success with the antitrust agencies. However, this line of argument might be used if the standard is a product standard and there is competition by substitution between different standard-setting consortia. Thus, a design or product standard might be considered anti-competitive if it has been hijacked by certain firms that, by creating a very broad standard, try to 'collect' competing technologies under grant-back clauses and bring them inside the FRAND jurisdiction by increasing the scope of the standard. This may be considered an antitrust harm if the patentee can show that membership and adherence to FRAND is essential to be part of the relevant market.

7.5.1 PAEs

The firms that disturb the business model for the IP Banks are the PAEs. They are the mavericks of the technology markets, and must be regarded as misusing the standard-setting process if carrying out patent ambushes and similar acts.[134] There was a general consensus that patent trolls were abusing the standard-setting system and the larger firms have publically addressed the Commission and EU legislators regarding the effects a unitary patent court system in Europe may have for the power balance between PAEs and vertically integrated firms. The fear is that PAEs would be able to obtain EU wide injunctions through the unitary patent court system and cause EU wide hold up situations.[135]

---

[134] Tom Ewing, 'Indirect Exploitation of Intellectual Property Rights By Corporations and Investors', (2011) 3 *Hastings Sci & Tech Law Journal* 1 and Thomas L. Ewing, 'Practical Considerations In the Indirect Deployment of Intellectual Property Rights by Corporations and Investors', (2011) 4 *Hastings Sci & Tech Law Journal* 109, for a good analysis of privateering. See also Edward Wyatt, 'F.T.C. Turns a Lens on Abuse of Patent System', *NY Times*, 16 July 2013.

[135] Letter dated 26 Sepetmber 2013, https://docs.google.com/file/d/0BwxyRPFduTN2NkpoN29UVm11OWc/edit?pli=1. Accessed 21 February 2014.

But now the lines between PAEs and IP Banks are becoming blurred. Moreover, it seems obvious that PAE and IP Banks are collaborating. Microsoft and Nokia have been accused of setting up their own PAE/ patent pool/troll, Mosaid.[136] Philips has also been accused in other blogs of privateering, i.e. outsourcing patents to PAEs (Sisvel). Even Ericsson was accused of privateering when in January 2013 it sold more than 2,000 patents to Unwired Planet.[137] Unwired Planet had previously sued Apple, Google and RIM.

One reason for 'privateering' is to get a PAE to initiate litigation against a competitor in order to increase costs and uncertainty for that competitor without the competitor being able to effectively counter sue.[138] It is an interesting issue whether this business practice may be considered anti-competitive. The PAEs will presumably suffer under the *eBay* and the *Orange-Book-Standard* rules about the prohibition, or at least increased hurdles, for the use of the injunction tool.

Perhaps, one could argue that the defendant and potential licensee of the PAE may regress, i.e. take recourse against the firm that sold patents to the PAE. Any increased costs due to higher royalties being paid to the PAE should perhaps be charged to this firm, should it have pledge FRAND to the relevant SDO and, even, perhaps previously entered into a licence agreement with the licensee, which included the technology now transferred to the PAE. Furthermore, as discussed above, the assignor may in fact have violated the rules and integrity of the standard-setting procedure when transferring SEPs with the intent of eliminating competition to the PAE.

---

[136] According to Popofsky and Laufert, Nokia transferred patents of nominal value to Mosaid with the agreement that Nokia would receive 2/3 of all royalties collected on those patents by Mosaid. See Mark Popofsky and Michael Laufert, 'Patent Assertion Entities and Antitrust: Operating Company Patent Transfers', (April 2013), *The Antitrust Source*, 1, 7 et seq. According to news articles, Google has submitted a complaint regarding the creation of Mosaid to the EU Commission. See, e.g., Suzanne Tindal, 'Nokia, Microsoft Support Patent Trolls: Google', *ZDnet*,1 June 2012) http://www.zdnet.com/nokia-microsoft-support-patent-trolls-google-1339338945/ Accessed 3 February 2014.

[137] Mark Popofsky and Michael Laufert, 'Patent Assertion Entities and Antitrust: Operating Company Patent Transfers', (April 2013), *The Antitrust Source*, 1, 3.

[138] Thomas L. Ewing, 'Practical Considerations in the Indirect Deployment of Intellectual Property Rights by Corporations and Investors', (2011) 4 *Hastings Sci & Tech Law Journal* 109, 150 et seq; Robin Feldman and Tom Ewing, 'The Giants Among Us' (2012) 1 *Stanford Technology Law Review*, 1.

Under *Singer*[139] and *Krasnov*,[140] joint litigation schemes and defence agreements to prevent new entry were considered to be anti-competitive in certain circumstances.[141] However, these cases may be considered circumvented. MPEG-2 and other patent pools seem to arrange joint litigation on behalf of the licensors of any firm trying to enter the standardized markets.[142] Part of Intellectual Ventures' business idea seems to be joint or proxy litigations for partners.[143] These collaborations are an indication that collective litigation schemes are today left unchallenged by the antitrust agencies.

In addition, Intellectual Ventures seems to have several partners and also acts as a joint defence fund for its partners.[144] Furthermore, certain IP Banks are today not far from being PAEs: the only difference of the latter is their more holistic approach and a well known brand and business culture, which causes them to be portrayed, not as mavericks, but as vertically integrated firms. However, *de facto* they hold MAD patent capability, which is their core business.

7.6 MORE DEVELOPED AND STRINGENT PROCEDURAL RULES WHEN SCRUTINIZING SSOS

Standard-setting is quickly becoming part of the core business strategy of many firms and the antitrust agencies need to develop a policy towards these forms of collaborations.

Such a policy or guidelines must be based on the difference, and interface, between different markets and different standards. Only the framework of such a policy can be outlined here.

Furthermore, competition agencies and courts need to devise indirect rules on how to regulate standard setting, if standard setting is to be regulated at all under competition law. Clearly, the development under

---

139 United States v. The Singer Manufacturing Comp. 374 U.S. 174 (1963).

140 United States v. Krasnov, 143 F. Supp 184 (E.D. Pa 1956) aff'd. 355 U.S. 5 (1957).

141 Cf. Richard Gilbert, 'Antitrust for Patent Pools: A Century of Policy Evolution', (April 2004) *Stanford Technology Law Review*, 3, 33, stating that joint patent defence might be a sign of substitute patents.

142 See discussion, supra, Chapter 5.4.2.

143 Robin Feldman and Tom Ewing, 'The Giants Among Us', (2012) 1 *Stanford Technology Law Review*, 1.

144 Ibid.

US antitrust law is that competition law plays only a minor role when regulating standard setting and unilateral conduct under standards. Furthermore, under EU law, the regulation of free trade and the Regulation on European Standards may shift the focus of how standards should be regulated. Nonetheless, the activity of standard setting is quickly becoming a core business for firms, so competition agencies and courts need to establish tests to evaluate these collaborations, or decide to stay out of the standard-setting arena.

A policy must take its point of departure from the fact that different standards create different competitive effects, which must create different rules, whether the effect creates market failures or not. Furthermore, pre-standardization effects must be taken into consideration. R&D conducted in association with standard setting should be included in the analysis of anti-competitive effect or what constitutes abuse of 'competition on the merits'.

It is clear that courts and governments should be reluctant to decide on standards – this is the prerogative of SSOs – while, to protect competition, 'good governance' rules must be developed within competition law. These rules should protect competition indirectly, by regulating so that the integrity of the standard-setting procedure is upheld. Competition law must be detached from the by-laws of the SSOs, and create its own set of norms on how firms may compete and interact in SSOs. Competition law can develop such rules under the notion of 'competition on the merits'. Such rules should have a firm basis in what may cause anti-competitive effects, while aiming to protect the integrity of standard-setting procedures. These rules must be focused on the transparency of the standard-setting procedure, and access to membership and standards must be upheld, especially when dealing with standards where competition is based on imitation.

The chapter regarding standard agreements in the Horizontal Guidelines is a good start, but, since we are dealing with an area where there are no markets at the time of deciding the standard, and the concept of an innovation market is conceptually wrong, the standard-setting procedure, and as a result, the innovation process must be protected indirectly by stipulating rules about openness and access to the SSO. In fact, the WTO principles for standard setting[145] and the rules derived from them, for

---

[145] See Articles 2, 5 and Annexes III to the WTO/TBT Agreement and related decisions. Annex III of the TBT Agreement is the Code of Good Practice for the Preparation, Adoption and Application of Standards, which is known as the WTO Code of Good Practice. In accepting the TBT Agreement, WTO Members agree to ensure that their central government standardizing bodies accept and comply with

example, the requirements for identifying ICT consortia standards to be used in public procurement procedures under the Regulation, may be used as a point of departure to identify what good governance rules should be used under the competition rules.

Since standards come in such a multitude of different forms, these rules must take into consideration the aim and ambit of the proposed standards and the market being regulated. There may be standards that can be implemented but where there is room for competition by substitution, for example by stipulating performance standard rather than a descriptive product standard. Competition law should then protect such competition, while, if that is not possible, competition law should be used to gain access to the downstream markets regulated by that infrastructure or interoperability standard.[146] Thus, procedural rules under competition law are the only way to uphold competitive pressure.

For example, the FTC *Google* settlement order[147] may be criticized in many ways, but it clearly lays down rules of good governance regarding when an injunction may be applied for. It actually describes quite delicate and detailed procedural rules for identifying FRAND, including arbitration. The Samsung proposal to EU Commission to settle all its cases in Europe is in many ways similar to the FTC Google settlement order. It stipulates a somewhat similar mechanism for a FRAND procedure: five years of immunity for infringement suits, thereafter (i) tvelve

this Code of Good Practice and agree also to take reasonable measures to ensure that local government, non-governmental and regional standardizing bodies do the same. The Code is therefore open to acceptance by all such bodies. In addition, the TBT Agreement is reviewed annually and triennially and the reviews will become important interpretations of the document. Under the TBT, decisions and recommendations setting out criteria defining the principles of an international standards developing organization have been issued. These decisions or principles came out of the Second Triennial Review (23 May 2002) and specify that the WTO-TBT criteria for a 'international standards developing organization' are transparency, openness, impartiality, effectiveness, relevance, consensus, performance-based, coherence, due process and technical assistance. See WTO, Decisions and Recommendations adopted by the WTO Committee on Technical Barriers to Trade since 1 January 1995, G/TBT/1/Rev.10, 46. See http://ec.europa.eu/enterprise/tbt/index.cfm?fuseaction=library.viewLibrary&section_id=6&dspLang=EN, accessed 6 September 2012.

146 Compare the EMC case discussed supra.

147 Cf. FTC, Statement In the Matter of Google Inc., FTC File No. 121-0120, 3 January 2013. http://www.ftc.gov/os/caselist/1210120/130103googlemotorolastmtofcomm.pdf, accessed 11 July 2013.

months negotiations and (ii) court or arbitration to settle FRAND level.[148] These are clearly procedural rules and presumably these procedural rules will be a large and important part of the settlement of all cases in this patent war, which will end in a settlement. Possibly, in the area of standard setting, such detailed and delicate governance or procedural rules need to be developed within competition law, if competition law is to be used to supervise SSOs. Lately, Lemley and Shapiro have also argued for a set of rules for members of SSOs when setting reasonable royalties, which are quite similar to the FTC *Google* consent order.[149] These authors imply that, if there is room for competition law, these rules should be applied and competition law may be left to act as an incentive and threat for adhering to these good governance rules. In fact, as Lemley and Shapiro suggest, when the rules of the SSO are 'gamed' antitrust law should step in.

This applies to both the members of an SSO and the SSO itself. If the SSO does not set clear rules, or rules that can easily be manipulated or 'gamed', the SSO may be in breach of competition law due to the collusive effects these vague rules facilitate. So, patentees that game these rules by patent ambush, FRAND ambush, or by selling SEPs to PAEs with the intention of raising royalty rates or eliminating competitors, may be in breached of competition law. SSOs, on the other hand, can be in breach of competition law if the rules are so vague that they facilitates collusion or patent hold-up.[150] An SSO may and should have, for example stringent IP policies.[151]

On this issue, the *ex ante v. ex post* concept has been raised: SSOs should support, even require, *ex ante* negotiations between the patentees to establish the price for the different technology alternatives to be standardized. The antitrust agencies allow for *ex ante* unilateral statements regarding royalty rates before the standard is set, while not yet

---

148 See EU Commission press realease about Samsung electronic's proposed commitments. http://europa.eu/rapid/press-release_IP-13-971_en.htm and http://europa.eu/rapid/press-release_MEMO-13-910_en.htm. Accessed 28 February 2014.

149 M.A. Lemley and Carl Shapiro, 'A Simple Approach to Setting Reasonable Royalties for Standard-Essential Patents', 20 March 2013, 23 et seq., cf. faculty.haas.berkeley.edu/Shapiro/frand.pdf, accessed 8 August 2013.

150 Ibid.

151 See the VITA and IEEE Business Review Letters, discussed, supra, Chapter 4.1.5.

agreeing to royalty-fixing schemes.[152] *De lege ferende*, the course set out by the FTC in several cases, but most recently in the *Google* Consent Order, is a better development. FRAND should be *ex post* procedure. One part of the analysis could be whether the patentee has unilaterally stated, *ex ante,* the royalty rate for the technology to be included in a standard (or agreed to a certain royalty rate in licence agreements before the standard is set). But that should only be one part of the analysis. Other circumstances may intervene. One reason for having a fixed system for establishing royalty rates *ex ante* is that it should be beneficial to know the price of technologies before one is selected as the standard. This is beneficial to the standard-setting procedure, and a patentee may not know the value of the patent before the standard is set. In fact, perhaps this is a patent law, or a patent application procedural problem. There are certain countries where the patentee can up front state the terms of which it will license the patent to the patent office. This is a conduct that should be greatly encouraged. If this would become a successful business practice, SDOs would not need to state that the patentees are required before the SDOs state their terms and royalty levels. In fact, Patent Exchanges such as the IPXI could also play a roll for establishing terms and royalty rates, and to connect potential licensors and licensees, especially SMEs.[153] However, allowing for patentees and potential licensees to agree on royalty rates beforehand may easily encourage cartels aiming for either monopoly or monopsony prices. Nonetheless, any such royalty agreements under the IP policies of SSOs should be judged under the rule of reason, and if the consortium has no or little market power, and the technology market it is active on can uphold competition between different standards, possibly such an agreement on royalty should be exempted. However, for infrastructure or interoperability standards, FRAND should prevail, as an *ex post* procedure, and as the most benign alternative under competition law.

A different proposition could be, as discussed infra under the conclusion, to interlink the covenants about 'prior art' in the collaboration agreements between certain SDOs and European Patent Office. These collaboration agreements give EPO access to non-confidential information provided and discussed in the technical committees so that this

---

[152] E.g. Horizontal Guidelines, paras. 274, 289 and 299. See the VITA and IEEE Business Review Letters discussed, supra, Chapter 4.1.5.

[153] See IPXI Business Review Letter from William J. Baer to Garrard R. Beeny, dated March, 26, 2013. See http://www.usdoj.gov/atr/public/busreview/, accessed 3 May 2013.

information may be considered 'prior art' when analysing patent application before the EPO. This seems now to be a general accepted rule. The consensus is that utilizing other firms information discussed in the technical committee is not good business practise. It is not 'competition on the merits' to use the information gained in the technical committees as a basis for obtaining patents. It could amount to patent ambush, but, generally, it is not accepted business practise to use the information provided. Perhaps this rule could be extended, so that when a standard is decided, the technical data used in the technical committee and even the technical area the standard covers should be regarded as 'prior art' under patent law. Moreover, filling for patents within the now decided standards should amount to misuse of the standard-setting procedure under competition law if you have been a member of the technical committee or the SDO. This could amount to an abuse or monopolization, and a successful case could possible be construed both under the EU the *AstraZeneca* regulatory fraud doctrine and corresponding US case law, such as *Allied Tube*, but also *Walker Process*.[154]

In fact, given the multitude of different standards and collaborations that the industry supports, joint guidelines for standard setting would certainly benefit the New Economy and the Old Economy as a whole.

[154] Walker Process Equip., Inc. v. Food Mach. & Chem. Corp. 382 U.S. 172 (1965).

8. Conclusion

We need to develop 'antitrust rules and doctrines for the New Economy'.

However, proposing regulations or guidelines for standard setting or coopetition is a challenge. It is clear that competition law alone is not sufficient to handle the whole bundle of agreements and collaborations set in place by the enactment of IP Banks and IP Banks' collaborations, given the set of public interest objectives which might be triggered. In particular, the horizontal effects of these collaborations, i.e. standardization agreements and patent pools, are not regulated sufficiently under competition law.

IP Banks' origins are in the transfer of the power to regulate product and technology standards from the political sector to the markets. SSOs and their members today retain the expertize and the ability to create global standards, which governments do not have. This is the main reason why competition agencies or courts should not intervene in the selection of technology in a standard or a pool. On a more philosophical level, it implies that society has limited competition law so that it regulates only private power and not public power. Or, are the indirect rules referred to above exactly the nascent rules for also regulating the public power gained by SSOs? Or, should they instead be regulated under free trade rules and dormant commerce clauses? Perhaps, at least the infrastructure standards should be regulated under other rules then competition law.

In academic writing at the end of the 1990s and beginning of the 2000s, the solutions that were presented for the problems of patent thickening, 'anticommons' and hold-up were generally two-fold. Either an intellectual property law solution was preferred or the solution was sought in contract law.

The contractual solution, presented by, for example, Robert Merges, was to facilitate the possibility of cooperation between patentees. If they are able to negotiate and enter into agreements, e.g., R&D agreements, patent pools and standardization agreements, they will be able to solve the problems of the patent thicket, hold-ups and anticommons. They are in the best position to mitigate the problems as well as attributing and making use of the market value of the rights. An evolution towards stronger and overlapping intellectual property rights was, therefore, not a problem, since the participants may through contracts mitigate the 'side effects' of patent law and defensive patenting. Part of this solution was, then, to facilitate the possibility of cooperation under competition law.[1] Competition law should stand back to facilitate the possibility of these negotiations and agreements among competitors.

The second broad line of argument was that intellectual property law should facilitate exemptions, for research, prior or fair use, or even discriminatory licensing practices so that firms could, based on intellectual property law, facilitate their access to the technology.[2] This solution implies that competition law should exempt collaborations likely to violate or infringe competition law, such as patent pools.

It should also be noted that several authors, especially in the USA, argued both for more lenient antitrust treatment of standard-setting collaborations, patent pools and joint R&D, and for limiting intellectual property rights. Indeed, there seemed to have been a general consensus

---

[1] Cf., e.g., Robert Merges, 'Institutions for Intellectual Property Transactions: The Case of Patent Pools', in Rochelle Dreyfuss et al. (eds), *Expanding Boundaries of Intellectual Property* Oxford University Press, 2001), 164; Carl Shapiro, 'Navigating the Patent Thicket: Cross Licenses, Patent Pools and Standard Setting', in Adam Jaffe et al. (eds), *Innovation Policy and the Economy* (MIT Press, 2001), 119; and generally the article that started the contemporary more lenient attitude towards patent pools: Roger Andewelt, 'Analysis of Patent Pools under Antitrust Laws', (1985) 53 *Antitrust Law Journal*, 611.

[2] Cf., e.g., Hanns Ullrich, 'Patent Pools: Approaching a Patent Law Problem via Competition Policy', in Claus-Dieter Ehlermann and Isabela Atanasiu (eds), *European Competition Law Annual 2005: The Interaction Between Competition Law and Intellectual Property Law* (Hart Publishing, 2007), 321 et seq., especially 326. Professor Hanns Ullrich argues for making use of the patent law exemptions under Member State patent laws as a means of disabling the problems patent pools are meant to address. See also Robert Pitofsky, 'Antitrust and Intellectual Property: Unsolved Issues at the Heart of the New Economy', (2001) 16 *Berkeley Technology Law Journal*, 535, 543 et seq., 559 making a suggestion for introducing a new 'fair use' exemption under patent law. Cf. Hanns Ullrich, 'Intellectual Property, Access to Information, and Antitrust: Harmony, Disharmony, and International Harmonization', in Rochelle Dreyfuss et al. (eds), *Expanding Boundaries of Intellectual Property* (Oxford University Press, 2001), 383; Graham Dutfield and Uma Suthersanen, 'The Innovation Dilemma: Intellectual Property and the Historical Legacy of Cumulative Creativity', (2004) *Intellectual Property Quarterly,* 378; Robert Pitofsky, 'Antitrust and Intellectual Property: Unsolved Issues at the Heart of the New Economy', (2001) 16 *Berkeley Technology Law Journal*, 535 and John Barton, 'Patent and Antitrust: A Rethinking in Light of Patent Breadth and Sequential innovation', (1997) *Antitrust Law Journal* 449.

that copyright protection regarding software should at least be restricted, especially with reference to interoperability, while technology standards should be tolerated in the software arena under antitrust law.[3]

Within both these propositions, particularly the second, is the call for limiting the strength and breadth of intellectual property laws, for shaping the requirement for granting patents so that only truly new, non-obvious inventions, with utility for mankind, are protected.[4] Indeed, for example, 'discoveries' in the human genome should not enjoy protection at all.[5]

---

[3] Lemley argues for limiting intellectual property rights, at least copyright, over interfaces under standards in connection with the software industry, cf. Mark Lemley and David McGowan, 'Legal Implications of Network Economic Effects', (1998) 86 *California Law Review* 479, 533. Lemley also argues for limitation of patent law, see Mark Lemley, 'Ten Things to Do About Patent Holdup of Standards (and One Not to)', (2008) 48 *Boston College Law Review*, 149, 163 et seq. However, Lemley also argues that SSOs generally should not be held in violation of antitrust law, see Mark Lemley, 'Intellectual Property Rights and Standard-Setting Organizations', (2002) 90 *California Law Review*, 1889, 1969; Mark Lemley, 'Antitrust and the Internet Standardization Problem', (1996) 28 *Connecticut Law Review*, 1041, 1080. For scholars who believe in limiting intellectual property law, cf. e.g., Pamela Samuelson et al., 'A Manifesto Concerning the Legal Protection of Computer Programs', (1994) 94 *Columbia Law Review*, 2308; Graham Dutfield and Uma Suthersanen, 'The Innovation Dilemma: Intellectual Property and the Historical Legacy of Cumulative Creativity', (2004) 8 *Intellectual Property Quarterly*, 379; see also generally scholarly work commenting on biotechnology: Donna Gitter, 'International Conflict over Patenting Human DNA Sequences in the United States and the European Union: An Argument for Compulsory License a Fair-use Exemption', (2001) *New York University Law Review* 1623; Bradley Levang, 'Evaluating the Use of Patent Pools for Biotechnology: A Refutation to the USPTO White Paper Concerning Biotechnology Patent Pools', (2002–2003) 19 *Santa Clara Computer & High Tech Law Journal*, 229.

[4] Even though there are those who argue against such a development, cf. Michael Mireles, 'An Examination of Patents, Licensing, Research Tools, and the Tragedy of the Anticommons in Biotechnology Innovation', (2004) *Fall University of Michigan Journal of Law Reform*, 141, 141 et seq.

[5] This has actually been granted to some extent, see *BCRA gene* case. According to some commentators, genomes (genes) should more accurately be seen as consisting largely of multiple intersecting mini-ecosystems rather than as a single collection of separately functioning 'Lego bricks'. Therefore treating genes as patentable inventions on the basis of a single function is more a reflection of ignorance than of insight, and is essentially anti-innovation, since it potentially hinders opportunities for follow-on researchers to carry out further investigations on genes that a company or university had previously patented on

Interestingly, the courts seem to have heard the call. There has been an overhaul of both the US and EU patent laws, in which several parts of the law and the system to obtain patents have been modernized. From the perspective of intellectual property law theory, both alternatives entail a liability solution to intellectual property law's 'property problem'.[6] Thus, both the inherent obligation to license under the IP policies of SDOs and patent pools, as well as the *eBay* doctrine imply that a patentee may not deny access. From a competition law perspective, the contractual solution now creates a cap to the liability under the liability solution. In fact, individual patentees to successful technologies will now only get a FRAND return. This is a good development. The situation under certain successful standards was very inefficient.

A solution to the FRAND problem but also to, parts of, the patent thicket problems could actually be found in the patent law notion of 'prior art', as discussed above, and the new collaboration agreements between SDOs and European Patent Office. These collaboration agreements give EPO access to information provided and discussed in the technical committees so that this information may be considered 'prior art' when analysing patent application before the EPO. If this is implemented successfully it could have profound effects and solve several problems. Not only would we escape the 'suction effect' where successful standards create an incentive to take out patents under the standard. This would lessen the patent thickets and would diminish patent stacking. The amount of patents would generally lessen in society. Also, with less low quality patents under successful standards, the patents that actually reflect an inventive leap would be more valuable. Only those patents that reflect a genuine R&D efforts on the behalf of the original inventors included in patent application filed before the first meeting in the technical committee would be granted. The royalty fees may for these patents then also be higher then what FRAND normally represents today. The original inventors would receive a larger remuneration.

In fact, the above patent law solution could be backed up with an antitrust abuse rule. It would constitute a misuse of the standard-setting process to file and take out patents based on information received in the

---

the basis that its scientists had discovered one out of possibly numerous functions. See Graham Dutfield and Uma Suthersanen, 'The Innovation Dilemma: Intellectual Property and the Historical Legacy of Cumulative Creativity', (2004) *Intellectual Property Quarterly*, 378, 407.

6 Cf. Robert Merges, 'Contracting into Liability Rules: Intellectual Property Rights and Collective Rights Organizations', (1996) 84 *California Law Review*, 1293.

technical committees, or even in a technology that is covered by a standard.[7]

Notwithstanding this conclusion, it must be acknowledged that intellectual property owners are presumably at less of an advantage than they were before the intellectual property laws were 'beefed-up' and the requirements for obtaining patents were lower in the 1980s. At least then, the average patentee could dream the dream of his or her patent being the 'lottery ticket to wealth'.[8]

However, the competition law solution might create other problems. Collaboration implies an increased risk of collusion. Prices (incl. both IPRs and products) may increase on the whole due to agreements on royalty rates under patent pools. The patent pools become the royalty mechanism for the MAD firms, with large patent portfolios that may move the standardization agreement in their preferred direction.

Of the two solutions to the problems of patent thicket and anticommons, this book generally argues that both the contractual solution and the more 'legalistic' solution predominated. Competition law became more lenient and allowed for patent pools and consortia to flourish, while intellectual property law was restricted to act as liability rules in some specific circumstances.[9] As has been discussed throughout this book, antitrust law on both sides of the Atlantic has had to stand back and allow for collaborations between competitors to a degree that has perhaps never been seen since the very early days of antitrust law.

In the end, I think we must acknowledge that IP Banks, firms with MAD capability, are today a hybrid between undertaking and regulators.

---

[7] Walker Process Equip., Inc. v. Food Mach. & Chem. Corp. 382 U.S. 172 (1965).

[8] Fredric Scherer, 'The Innovation Lottery', in Rochelle Dreyfuss et al. (eds), *Expanding the Boundaries of Intellectual Property* (Oxford University Press, 2000), 4 et seq. Cf. Hanns Ullrich, 'Legal Protection of Innovative Technologies: Property or Policy?', in Owe Granstrand (ed), *Economics, Law and Intellectual Property* (Springer Science+Business Media Dordrecht, 2003), 463 et seq

[9] It should be noted that the threshold for obtaining intellectual property rights has been increasing somewhat under both US and European law. Last year, the US Supreme Court rendered the famous KSR ruling, which makes it easier to meet the requirement for the criteria 'obviousness' under American patent law, see generally KSR International Co. v. Teleflex Inc., 550 U.S. 398 (2007). From a European perspective it is interesting to note that the European Patent Office in Munich granted fewer patents in 2007 than in previous years, even though there were more applications in 2007 than in any previous year. It seems clearly a deliberate strategy of the new EPO president Alison Brimelow, see http://www.epo.org/topics/news/2008/20080401.html, accessed 12 April 2008.

They conduct both public and private tasks and should thus be judged in accordance with both sets of public goals and objectives that regulate these different tasks. However, the best way to do so is indirectly, by stipulating right to access, transparency, possibilities of appeal; and not directly, by having the government and courts deciding on the substance of the technology.

Bibliography

1. REGULATIONS, GUIDELINES AND NOTICES

A. EU Regulations, Guidelines, Notices, Reports and Press Releases

Council Regulation (EEC). No. 2821/71 of 20 December 1971 on the application of Art. 81(3) of the Treaty to certain categories of agreements, decisions and concerted practices, OJ L 285 29.12.1971, 46.

Council Regulation (EEC) No 4064/89 of 21 December 1989 on the control of concentrations between undertakings, OJ L 395, 30.12.1989, 1.

Council Regulation (EC) 1310/97 amending Regulation 4046/89, OJ L 180, 09.07.1997, 1.

Council Regulation (EC) No 1/2003 of 16 December 2002 on the implementation of the rules on competition laid down in Articles 81 and 82 of the Treaty, OJ L 1, 04.01.2003, 1.

Council Regulation (EC) No 139/2004 of 20 January 2004 on the control of concentrations between undertakings (the EC Merger Regulation), OJ L 24, 29.01.2004, 1.

Commission Regulation (EEC) No 418/85 of 19 December 1984 on the application of Article 85 (3) of the Treaty to categories of research and development agreements, OJ L 53, 22.02.1985, 5.

Commission Regulation (EC) No 2658/2000 29 November 2000 on the application of Article 81(3) of the Treaty to categories of specialisation agreements, OJ L 304, 05.12.2000, 3.

Commission Regulation (EU) No 1218/2010 14 December 2010 on the application of Art 101(3) of the Treaty on the Functioning of the European Union to categories of specialisation agreements OJ L 335, 18.12.2010, 43.

Commission Regulation (EU) No 1217/2010 14 December 2010 on the application of Art 101(3) of the Treaty on the Functioning of the European Union to categories of research and development agreements OJ L 335, 18.12.2010, 36

Commission Regulation (EC) No 2659/2000 29 November 2000 on the application of Article 81(3) of the Treaty to categories of research and development agreements, OJ L 304, 05.12.2000, 7.

Commission Notice concerning agreements, decisions and concerted practises in the field of cooperation between enterprises, OJ C 75, 27.07.1968, 3.

Commission Notice – Guidelines on the application of Article 81 of the EC Treaty to horizontal cooperation agreements, OJ C 3, 06.01.2001, 2.

Commission Notice – Guidelines on the application of Article 101 of the Treaty on the Functioning of the European Union to horizontal cooperation agreements, OJ C 11 14.1.2011, 1.

Commission Notice – Guidelines on the application of Article 81 of the EC Treaty to technology transfer agreements, OJ C 101, 27.04.2004, 2.

Commission Notice – Guidelines on the application of Article 101 of the Treaty on the Functioning of the European Union to technology transfer agreements, new/draft guidelines: http://ec.europa.eu/competition/consultations/2012_technology_transfer/index_en.html, accessed 9 January 2013.

B. US Acts, Governmental Guidelines, Business Review Letters and Speeches

Sherman Act of 1890, 15 U.S.C. § 1–7.

Clayton Antitrust Act of 1914, 15 U.S.C. § 12–27, 29 U.S.C. § 52–53.

Federal Trade Commission Act of 1914, 15 U.S.C §§ 41–58.

The National Cooperative Production Amendments of 1993, Pub. L. No. 103–42 [amended the National Cooperative Research Act of 1984, Pub L. No. 98–462, renamed it the National Cooperative Research and Production Act of 1993. The Standards Development Organization Advancement Act of 2004, Pub. L. No. 108–237, extended the provisions of the NCRPA to standards development organizations.], 15 U.S.C § 4301–4307.

U.S DEP'T OF JUSTICE & FED. TRADE COMM'N, 'Antitrust Guide Concerning Research Joint Ventures' (1980).

U.S DEP'T OF JUSTICE & FED. TRADE COMM'N, 'Antitrust Guidelines for the Licensing of Intellectual Property' (1995).

U.S DEP'T OF JUSTICE & FED. TRADE COMM'N, 'Antitrust Guidelines for Collaborations Among Competitors' (2000).

Federal Trade Commission, 'To Promote Innovation: The Proper Balance of Competition and Patent Law and Policy' (2003).

U.S DEP'T OF JUSTICE & FED. TRADE COMM'N, 'Antitrust Enforcement and Intellectual Property Rights: Promoting Innovation and Competition' (2007).

U.S DEP'T OF JUSTICE & PTO, 'Policy Statement on Remedies for Standard-Essential Patents Subject to Voluntary/FRAND Commitments' (January 2013).

2. AUTHORS

ABA, *The Federal Antitrust Guidelines For Licensing of Intellectual Property Origins and Applications* (Chicago, American Bar Association, Section of Antitrust Law, 2002).

ABA, *Intellectual Property and Antitrust Handbook* (Chicago, American Bar Association, Section of Antitrust law, 2007).

Adamsson, Peter et al., *Lagarna inom Immaterialrätten* (Stockholm, Norstedts Juridik, 2008).

Anderman, Steven, 'Technology Transfer and the IP/Competition Interface', in Claus-Dieter Ehlermann & Isabela Atanasiu (eds), *European Competition Law Annual 2005: The Interaction between Competition Law and Intellectual Property Law* (Oxford, Hart Publishing, 2007), 211.

Anderman, Steven and Kallaugher, John, *Technology Transfer and the New EU Competition Rules* (Oxford, Oxford University Press, 2006).

Anderman, Steven and Schmidt Hedvig, *EU Competition Law and Intellectual Property Rights – Regulation of Innovation* (Oxford University Press, 2011).

Andewelt, Roger, 'Analysis of Patent Pools under Antitrust Laws', (1985) 53 *Antitrust Law Journal* 611.

Archibugi, Daniele and Iammarino, Simona, 'The Globalization of Technological Innovation: Definition and Evidence', (2002) 9 *Review of International Political Economy* 98.

Areeda, Phillip and Hovenkamp, Herbert, *Antitrust Law – An Analysis of Antitrust Principles and Their Application,* 2nd ed., Volume XIII (Boston, Aspen Publishers, 2005).

Armentano, Dominick, 'Competition Theory and the Market Economy', in High, Jack and Gable, Wayne (eds), *A Century of The Sherman Act: American Economic Opinion, 1890–1990* (Fairfax, George Mason University Press, 1992), 201.

Arrow, Kenneth, 'Economic Welfare and the Allocation of Resources for Invention', in Groves, Harold (ed), *The Rate and Direction of Inventive Activity: Economic and Social Factors* (Cambridge, Nat'l Bureau of Econ. Research, 1962), 609.

Baldwin, William and Scott, John, *Market Structure and Technological Change* (New York, Harwood Academic Publishers, 1987).

Barton, John, 'Patent and Antitrust: A Rethinking in Light of Patent Breadth and Sequential Innovation', (1997) 67 *Antitrust Law Journal* 449.

Barton, John, 'Antitrust Treatment of Oligopolies with Mutual Blocking Patent Portfolios', (2002) 69 *Antitrust Law Journal* 851.

Baumol, William, 'Horizontal Collusion and Innovation', (1992) 102 *The Economic Journal* 129.

Baumol, William, *Entrepreneurship, Management and the Structure of Payoffs* (Cambridge, MIT Press, 1993).

Baumol, William, *The Free-Market Innovation Machine* (Oxford, Princeton University Press, 2002).

Baron, Justus and Pohlmann, Tim, 'Who Cooperates in Standard Consortia – Rivals or Complementors?', (2013) 9 *Journal of Competition Law & Economics*, 905.

Beeney, Garrard, 'Pro-Competitive Effects of Intellectual Property Pools: A Proposal for Safe Harbor Provisions', submission under the Antitrust Enforcement and Intellectual Property Rights: Promoting Innovation and Competition Hearings (U.S Dep't of Justice & Fed. Trade Comm'n, 2002).

Bekkers, Rudi and Liotard, Isabella, 'European Standards for Mobile Communication: The Tense Relationship Between Standards and Intellectual Property Rights', (1999) 21 *European Intellectual Property Review*, 110.

Bekkers, Rudi et al., 'Intellectual Property Rights, Strategic Technology Agreements and Market Structure. The Case of GSM', *MERIT Research Memoranda* 029, (Maastricht, 2000).

Bekkers, Rudi et al., 'Intellectual Property and Standardization: The Case of GSM', (2002) 26 *Telecommunication Policy* 171.

Bekkers, Rudi, 'Patent Drag and Stacking IPR Fees – Are the IPR policies of Standard Bodies Failing or Should We Better Address Excessive Technology Inclusion?', (2007), Position Paper for High Level Workshop on Standardization, IP Licensing and Antitrust.

Bekkers, Rudi et al., 'Case studies on the interface between research and standardization, and case studies on patent pools as a coordination mechanism ' (INTEREST consortium Priority 8 No. Contract 503 594, EU 6th Specific Targeted Research Project, 2006).

Bekkers, Rudi et al., 'Patent Pools and Non Assertion Agreements: Coordination Mechanisms for Multi-party IRP Holders in Standardization', (2006) *EASST 2006 Conference.*

Bekkers, Rudi and Liotard, Isabella, 'European Standards for Mobile Communication: The Tense Relationship Between Standards and Intellectual Property Rights', (1999) 21 *European Intellectual Property Review* 110.

Bekkers et al., 'Emerging Ways to Address the Reemerging Conflict between Patenting and Technological Standardization', (2012) 21 *Industrial and Corporate Change*, 901.

Bellamy and Child, *European Community Law of Competition,* 5th, 6th, and 7th editions (London, Sweet & Maxwell, 2001, thereafter Oxford, Oxford University Press 2008, and 2013).

Blind, Knut and Gauch, Stephan, 'Trends in ICT standards: The Relationship between European Standardisation Bodies and Standard Consortia', (2008) 32 *Telecommunications Policy*, 503.

Blind, Knut and Gauch, Stephan, 'Research and Standardisation in Nanotechnology: Evidence from Germany', (2009) 34 *Journal Technology Transfer*, 320.

Blind et al., 'How Stakeholders View the Impacts of International ICT Standards', (2010) 34 *Telecommunications Policy*, 162.

Blair, Roger and Harrison, Jeffrey, *Monopsony Antitrust Law and Economics* (Princeton, Princeton University Press, 1993).

Bowman, Ward, *Patent and Antitrust Law: A Legal and Economic Appraisal* (Chicago, University of Chicago Press, 1973).

Brodley, Joseph, 'Joint Ventures and Antitrust Policy', (1981–1982) 95 *Harvard Law Review* 1521.

Brodley, Joseph, 'Antitrust Law and Innovation Cooperation', (1990) 4 *Journal of Economic Perspective* 97.

Brown, Jack, 'Technology Joint Ventures to Set Standards or Define Interfaces', (1992–1993) 61 *Antitrust Law Journal* 921.

Bulow, Jeremy, 'An Economic Theory of Planned Obsolescence', (1986) 101 *The Quarterly Journal of Economics* 729.

Cargill, Carl, 'Intellectual Property Rights and Standard-setting Organizations: An Overview of Failed Evolution', (2002) *FTC/DOJ Hearings on Competition and Intellectual Property Law and Policy in the Knowledge-Based Economy.*

Carlson, Steven, 'Patent Pools and the Antitrust Dilemma', (1999) 16 *Yale Journal of Regulation* 359.

Carrier, Michael A. 'A Roadmap to the Smartphone Patent Wars and FRAND Licensing', (April 2012) *CPI Antitrust Chronicle*, 1.

Caspari, Manfred, 'Joint Ventures – The Intersection of Antitrust and Industrial Policy In The EEC', in Hawk, Barry E. (ed), *Antitrust and Trade Policy in the United States and the European Community, 1985* (New York, Bender, Fordham Corporate Law Institute, 1986), 449.

Cerny, Philip, 'Globalisation, and the Changing Logic of Collective Action', (1995) 49 *International Organization* 595.

Cerny, Philip, 'Globalization, Governance, and Complexity', in Prakash and Hart (eds), *Globalization and Governance* (London, Routledge, 1999).

Chien, Colleen V. and Lemley, Mark A. 'Patent Holdup, the ITC, and the Public Interest', in, *Cornell Law Review; Stanford Public Law Working Paper* No. 2022168 (SSRN, 2012).

Choumelova, Dessy, 'Competition Law Analysis of Patent Licensing Arrangements – The Particular case of 3G3P', (2003) 1 *EU Commission, Competition Policy Newsletter* 39.

Ciborra, Claudio, 'Alliances as Learning Experiments: Cooperation, Competition and Change in Hightech Industries', in Mytelka, Lynn (ed), *Strategic Partnerships and the World Economy* (London, Pinters Publishers, 1991), 51.

Coller, Gillbert, 'Competing, Complementary and Blocking Patents: Their Role in Determining Antitrust Violations in the Area of Cross-Licensing, Patent Pooling and Package Licensing', (1968) 50 *Pat. Off. Soc'y* 723.

Chronopoulos, Apostolos, 'Patenting Standards – A Case for US Antitrust Law or a Call for Recognizing Immanent Public Policy Limitations to the Exploitation Conferred by the Patent Act', (2009) 40 *IIC*, 782.

Crane, Daniel M., 'Joint Research and Development Ventures and the Antitrust Laws', (1984) 21 *Harvard Journal of Legislation* 405.

David, Paul, 'Intellectual Property Institutions and the Panda's Thumb: Copyrights, and Trade Secrets in Economic Theory and History', in Wallerstein, Mitchel et al. (eds), *Global Dimensions of Intellectual Property Rights* (Washington D.C., National Academy Press, 1993), 19.

DeVellis, James, 'Patenting Industry Standards: Balancing the Rights of Patent Holders With the Need for Industry-Wide Standards', (2003) 31 *AIPLY Quarterly Journal* 301.

Dolmans, Maurits, 'Restriction on Innovation: An EU Antitrust Approach', (1997–1998) 66 *Antitrust Law Journal* 455.

Dolmans, Maurits, 'Standards For Standards', (2002) 26 *Fordham International Law Journal* 163.

Dolmans, Maurits and Piilola, Anu, 'The New Transfer Block Exemption: A Welcome Reform, After All', (2004) 27 *World Competition* 351.

Dutfield, Graham and Suthersanen, Uma, 'The Innovation Dilemma: Intellectual Property and the Historical Legacy of Cumulative Creativity', (2004) 8 *Intellectual Property Quarterly* 379.

Drexl, Josef et al., 'Comments of the Max Planck Institute for IP, Competition and Tax Law on the Draft Commission Block Exemption Regulation on R&D Agreements and the Draft Guidelines on Horizontal Cooperation Agreements' (2010) Max Planck Institute for IP, Competition & Tax Law Research Paper No. 10–12.

Drexl, Josef, 'Anti-competitive Stumbling Stones on the Way to a Cleaner world: Protecting Competition in Innovation without a Market', (2012) 8 *Journal of Competition Law & Economics*, 507.

Drexl, Josef, 'Abuse of Dominance in Licensing and Refusal to License: A More Economic Approach to Competition by Imitation and to Competition by Substitution', in Claus-Dieter Ehlermann and Isabela Atanasiu (eds), *European Competition Law Annual 2005: The Interaction Between Competition Law and Intellectual Property Law* (Hart Publishing, 2007).

Drexl, Josef, 'Intellectual property in competition: How to promote dynamic competition as a goal' in Josef Drexl et al. (eds), *More Common Ground For International Competition Law?* (Edward Elgar, 2011).

Epstein, Richard et al., 'The FTC, IP, and SSOs: Government Hold-Up Replacing Private Coordination', in *SSRN Working Paper* (SSRN, 2011).

Ewing, Thomas L., 'Indirect Exploitation of Intellectual Property Rights By Corporations and Investors', (2011) 3 *Hastings Sci & Tech Law Journal* 1.

Ewing, Thomas L., 'Practical Considerations in the Indirect Deployment of Intellectual Property Rights by Corporatiosn and Investors', (2011) 4 *Hastings Sci & Tech Law Journal* 109.

Farell, Joseph and Merges, Robert, 'Incentives to Challenge and Defend Patents: Why Litigation Won't Reliably Fix Patent Office Errors and Why Administrative Patent Review Might Help', (2004) Summer, *Berkeley Technology Law Journal.*

Farrell, Joseph et al., 'Standard-setting, Patents, and Hold-up', (2007) 74 *Antitrust Law Journal* 603.

Feldman, Gabe, 'The Misuse of the Less Restrictive Alternative Inquiry in Rule of Reason Analysis', (2009) 58 *American University Law Review* 561.

Fine, Frank, 'EEC Anti-Trust Aspects of Production Joint Ventures', (1992) 13 *European Competition Law Review* 206.

Fine, Frank, 'The EU's New Antitrust Rules For Technology Licensing: A Turbulent Harbour For Licensors', (2004) 29 *European Law Review* 766.

Fine, Frank, *The EC Competition Law on Technology Licensing* (London, Sweet & Maxwell Ltd 2006).

FTC, *To Promote Innovation: The Proper Balance of Competition and Patent Law and Policy* (FTC 2003).

Fuchs, Andreas, *Kartellrechtliche Grenzen der Forschungskooperation* (Baden-Baden, Nomos Verlaggesellschaft, 1989).

Fuchs, Andreas 'Patent ambush strategies and Article 102 TFEU' in Josef Drexl et al (eds), *More Common Ground For International Competition Law?* (Edward Elgar, 2011).

Gandal, Neil, 'Compatibility, Standardization, and Network Effects: Some Policy Implications', (2002) 18 *Oxford Review of Economic Policy* 80.

Geradin, Damien, 'Standardization and Technological Innovation: Some Reflections on Ex-ante Licensing, FRAND, and the Proper Means to Reward Innovators', (2006) 29 *World Competition* 511.

Geradin, Damien et al., *Elves or Trolls? The Role of Non-Practicing Patent Owners in the Innovation Economy* (SSRN 2008).

Geradin, Damien and Rato, Miguel P., *Can Standard-Setting Lead to Exploitative Abuse? A Dissonant View on Patent Hold-Up, Royalty Stacking and the Meaning of FRAND* (SSRN 2006).

German Institute for Standardization e. V (DIN), *Economic Benefits of Standardization: Summary of Results* (DIN, Beuth Verlag, 2000).

Gilbert, Richard, 'Antitrust for Patent Pools: A Century of Policy Evolution', (2004) April, *Stanford Technology Law Review* 3.

Gilbert, Richard and Newberry, David, 'Preemptive Patenting and the Persistence of Monopoly', (1982) 72 *The American Economic Review* 514.

Gilbert, Richard and Sunshine, Steven, 'Incorporating Dynamic Efficiency Concerns in Merger Analysis: the Use of Innovation Markets', (1995) 63 *Antitrust Law Journal* 569.

Gilbert, Richard and Sunshine, Steven, 'The Use of Innovation Markets: A Reply to Hay, Rapp, and Hoerner', (1995–1996) 64 *Antitrust Law Journal* 75.

Gilbert, Richard and Tom, William, 'Is Innovation King at the Antitrust Agencies? The Intellectual Property Guidelines Five Years Later', (2001) 69 *Antitrust Law Journal* 43.

Ginsburg, Douglas, 'Antitrust, Uncertainty and Technological Innovation', (1979) 24 *Antitrust Bulletin* 635.

Gitter, Donna, 'International Conflict over Patenting Human DNA Sequences in the United States and the European Union: An Argument for Compulsory License a Fair-use Exemption', (2001) 76 *New York University Law Review* 1623.

Glader, Marcus, 'Open Standards: Public Policy Aspects and Competition Law Requirements', (2010) 6 *European Competition Journal* 611.

Gordon, George and Hoerner, Robert, 'Overview and Historical Development of the Misuse Doctrine', in Koback, James (ed.), *Intellectual Property Misuse Licensing and Litigation* (Chicago, ABA Section of Antitrust Law, 2000), 1.

Granstrand, Owe and Holgersson, Marcus, 'The 25% Rule Revisited and a New Investment-based Method for Determining FRAND Licensing Royalties', (2012) 47 *Les Nouvelles*, 3.

Grossman, Gene and Shapiro, Carl, 'Research Joint Ventures: An Antitrust Analysis', (1986) 2 *Journal of Law, Economics and Organization* 315.

Hamilton, Davis, 'Silent Treatment: How Genetech, Novartis Stifled a Promising Drug', *Wall Street Journal*, 5 April 2005, A1.

Hansen, Marc and Shah, Omar, 'The New EU Technology Transfer Regime – Out of the Straightjacket into the Safe Harbour?' (2004) 25 *European Competition Law Review* 465.

Hawk, Barry, *United States, Common Market and International Antitrust: A Comparative Guide* (New York, Law & Business Inc., 1985).

Hay, George, 'Innovations in Antitrust Enforcement', (1995–1996) 64 *Antitrust Law Journal* 7.

Hayek, Friedrich A., *New Studies in Philosophy, Politics, Economics, and the History of Ideas* (London, Routledge and K. Paul, 1978).

Heller, Michael and Eisenberg, Rebecca, 'Can Patents Deter Innovation? The Anticommons in Biomedical Research', (1998) 280 *Science* 698.

Heller, Micheal, 'The Tragedy of the Anticommons: Property in the Transition from Marx to Markets', (1998) 111 *Harvard Law Review* 621.

Hoerner, Robert, 'Innovation Markets: New Wine in Old Bottles?' (1995–1996) 64 *Antitrust Law Journal* 49.

Hovenkamp, Herbert, 'United States Antitrust Policy in an Age of IP Expansion', in Hawk, Barry E. (ed), *International Antitrust Law & Policy 2006* (New York, Juris Publ. Fordham Competition Law Institute, 2007), 230.

Hovenkamp, Herbert, 'Signposts of Anti-competitive Exclusion: Restraints on Innovation and Economies of Scale', in Hawk, Barry E (ed), *International Antitrust Law & Policy 2006* (New York, Juris Publ., Fordham Competition Law Institute, 2007), 409.

Huaiwen, He, 'A Self-Defeating Framework: How Far Could ITU Policy Go', (2009) 31 *E.I.P.R.*, 343.

Iandiorio, Joseph, 'Patent Pools and the Antitrust Laws', (1964) 46 *Journal of the Patent Office Society* 712.

Jacquemin, Alexis and Spinoit, Bernard, 'Economic and Legal Aspects of Cooperative Research: A European View', in Hawk, Barry E. (ed), *Antitrust and Trade Policy in the U.S. and the EC 1985* (New York, Bender, Fordham Corporate Law Institute, 1986), 487.

Jaffe, Adam, 'The U.S. Patent System in Transition: Policy Innovation and the Innovation Process', (2000) 29 *Elsevier Research Policy* 531.

Jaffe, Adam and Lerner, Josh, *Innovation and its Discontents* (Princeton, Princeton University Press, 2004).

Jorde, Thomas and Teece, David, 'Acceptable Cooperation among Competitors in the Face of Growing International Competition', (1989) 58 *Antitrust Law Journal* 529.

Jorde, Thomas and Teece, David, 'Innovation, Cooperation and Antitrust', (1989) 4 *High Tech Law Journal* 1.

Jorde, Thomas and Teece, David, 'Innovation and Cooperation: Implications for Competition and Antitrust', (1990) 4 *Journal of Economic Perspectives* 75.

Jorde, Thomas and Teece, David, 'Innovation, Cooperation, and Antitrust', in Jorde, Thomas and Teece, David (eds), *Antitrust, Innovation, and Competitiveness* (New York, Oxford University Press, 1992), 47.

Jorde, Thomas and Teece, David, 'Rule of Reason Analysis of Horizontal Arrangements: Agreements Designed to Advance Innovation and Commercialize Technology', (1993) 61 *Antitrust Law Journal* 579.

Katz, Michael, 'An Analysis of Cooperative Research and Development', (1986) 17 *Rand Journal of Economics* 527.

Katz, Michael and Shapiro, Carl, 'Systems Competition and Network Effects', (1994) 8 *Journal of Economic Perspective* 93.

Kerber, Wolfgang 'Competition, Innovation and Maintaining Diversity through Competition Law', in Drexl, Josef, Kerber, Wolfang and Podszum, R., (eds), *Economic Approaches to Competition Law: Foundation and Limitations* (Edward Elgar, 2010).

Kirslow, Samuel, *Nations Choose Product Standards and Standards Change Nations* (Pittsburgh, University of Pittsburgh Press, 1997).

Kitch, Edmund W., 'The Nature and Function of the Patent System', (1977) XX *The Journal of Law and Economics* 265.

Kjölbye, Lars and Peeperkorn, Lucas, 'The New Technology Transfer Block Exemption Regulation and Guidelines', in Ehlermann, Claus-Dieter and Atanasiu, Isabela (eds), *European Competition Law Annual 2005: The Interaction between Competition Law and Intellectual Property Law* (Oxford, Hart Publishing, 2007), 161.

Klemperer, Paul, *Auction Theory – A Guide to the Literature* (SSRN 1999).

Koelman, Kamiel J., 'An Exceptio Standardis: Do We Need an IP Exemption for Standards', (2006) 7 *International Review of Intellectual Property and Competition Law* 823.

Korah, Valentine, *R&D and the EEC Competition Rules Regulation 418/85* (Oxford, ESC Publishing Limited, 1986).

Korah, Valentine, 'Critical Comments on the Commission's Recent Decisions Exempting Joint Ventures to Exploit Research that Needs Further Development', (1987) 12 *European Law Review* 18.

Korah, Valentine, *Intellectual Property Rights and the EC Competition Rules* (Oxford, Hart Publishing, 2006).

Lang, John Temple, 'European Community Antitrust Law: Innovation Markets and High Technology Industries', in Hawk, Berry E. (ed), *International Antitrust Law & Policy 1995* (London, Sweet & Maxwell, Fordham University School of Law, 1996), 519.

Layne-Farrar, Anne et al., 'Pricing Patents for Licensing in Standard-Setting Organizations: Making Sense of FRAND Commitments', (2007) 74 *Antitrust Law Journal* 671.

Lee, Nari, 'Patented Standards and the Tragedy of Anti-commons', (2006) *Teollisoikeudellisia Kirjoituksia VII.*

Leiponen, Aija E.,'Competing Through Cooperation: The Organization of Standard Setting in Wireless Telecomminucations, (2008) 54 *MGMT. SCI.*, 1904.

Leistner, Matthias, 'Federal Supreme Court (Bundesgerichthof)', (2005) 6 *International Review of Intellectual Property and Competition Law* 741.

Lemley, Mark, 'Antitrust and the Internet Standardization Problem', (1996) 28 *Connecticut Law Review* 1041.

Lemley, Mark, 'Intellectual Property Rights and Standard-Setting Organizations', (2002) 90 *California Law Review* 1889.

Lemley, Mark, 'Ten Things to Do About Patent Holdup of Standards (and One Not to)', (2008) 48 *Boston College Law Review* 149.

Lemley, Mark and McGowan, David, 'Legal Implications of Network Economic Effects', (1998) 86 *California Law Review* 479.

Lemley, Mark and Shapiro, Carl, 'Patent Holdup and Royalty Stacking', (2007) 85 *Texas Law Review* 1991.

Lemley, Mark and Shapiro, Carl, 'A Simple Approach to Setting Reasonable Royalties for Standard-Essential Patents', (2013) 28 *Berkeley Technology Law Journal* 1135.

Lerner, Josh, 'Patenting in the Shadow of Competitors', (1995) 38 *Journal of Law & Economics* 463.

Lerner, Josh and Merges, Robert, 'The Control of Technology Alliances: An Empirical Analysis of the Biotechnology Industry', (1998) 46 *Journal of Industrial Economics* 125.

Lerner, Josh et al., 'The Structure and Performance of Patent Pools: Empirical Evidence', in *NBER* (Harvard University, 2003).

Levang, Bradley, 'Evaluating the Use of Patent Pools for Biotechnology: A Refutation to the USPTO White Paper Concerning Biotechnology Patent Pools', (2002–2003) 19 *Santa Clara Computer & High Tech Law Journal* 229.

Lim, Daryl, 'Misconduct in Standard-setting: The Case for Patent Misuse', (2011) 51 *IDEA: The Journal of Law and Technology* 557.

Lindemann, Jürgen, 'A Practical Critique of The EEC Joint Research Rules and Proposed Joint Venture Guidelines', in Hawk, Barry E. (ed),

Antitrust and Trade Policy in the U.S. and the EC 1985 (New York, Bender, Fordham Corporate Law Institute, 1986), 343.

Lundin, Pernilla et al., 'International Collaboration in R&D Structure and Dynamics of Private Sector Actors', in *Internationalisation of R&D – Implications to Science and Technology Policy*, ProACT programme, Interim Report 1 (Gaia Group Oy & RAND Europe), 17.

Maciver, Angus, 'EEC Competition Policy in High Technology Industries', in Hawk, Barry E. (ed), *Antitrust and Trade Policy in the U.S. and the EC 1985* (New York, Bender, Fordham Corporate Law Institute, 1986), 701.

Majewski, Suzanne E., *How Do Consortia Organize Collaborative R&D? Evidence from the National Cooperative Research Act* (SSRN 2004).

Majewski, Suzanne E. and Williamson, Dean V., *Endogenous Spillovers, Strategic Blocking, and the Design of Contracts in Collaborative R&D: Evidence from NCRA filings of R&D Joint Ventures* (SSRN 2002).

Martin, Stephen, 'The Evaluation of Strategic Research Partnerships', (2003) 15 *Tech. Analysis & Strategic MGMT* 159.

Martin, Stephen and Scott, John T., 'The Nature of Innovation Market Failure and the Design of Public Support for Private Innovation', (1999) 29 *Research Policy* 437.

Maurer, Stephen and Scotchmer, Suzanne, 'Profit Neutrality in Licensing: The Boundary Between Antitrust Law and Patent Law', (2006) 8 *American Law and Economics Review* 476.

Melamed, A. Douglas, 'Identifying Exclusionary Conduct under Section 2: The No Economic Sense Test Symposium – Identifying Exclusionary Conduct under Section 2', (2006) 73 *Antitrust Law Journal* 375.

Melamed, A. Douglas and Lerch, David, 'Uncertain Patents, Antitrust, and Patent Pools', in Ehlermann, Claus-Dieter and Atanasiu, Isabela (eds), *European Competition Law Annual 2005: The Interaction Between Competition Law and Intellectual Property Law* (Oxford, Hart Publishing, 2005), 273.

Melamed, Douglas, 'Patents and Standard: The Unimportance of Being Essential', (unpublished, 2006).

Merges, Robert, 'A Brief Note on Blocking Patents and Reverse Equivalents: Biotechnology as an Example', (1991) 73 *Journal Pat. & Trademark Off. Soc'y* 878.

Merges, Robert, 'Contracting into Liability Rules: Intellectual Property Rights and Collective Rights Organizations', (1996) 84 *California Law Review* 1293.

Merges, Robert, 'Institutions for Intellectual Property Transactions: The Case of Patent Pools', in Dreyfuss, Rochelle et al. (eds), *Expanding*

Boundaries of Intellectual Property (Oxford, Oxford University Press, 2001), 123.
Merges, Robert and Nelson, Richard, 'Market Structure and Technical Advance: The Role of Patent Scope Decision', in Jorde, Thomas and Teece, David (eds), *Antitrust, Innovation and Competitiveness* (New York, Oxford University Press, 1992), 185.
Meyer, Martin, *Academic Entrepreneurs or Entrepreneurial Academics? Research-Based Ventures and Public Support Mechanisms* (SSRN 2003).
Mireles, Michael, 'An Examination of Patents, Licensing, Research Tools, and the Tragedy of the Anticommons in Biotechnology Innovation', (2004) 38 *University of Michigan Journal of Law Reform* 141.
Monopolkommission, 'Huaptgutachten: Wettbewerbspolitik vor neuen Herausforderungen', (1988/89).
Mortensen, Bent Ole Gram m Standardisering og certifiering som instrument på miljøområdet (JØF, 1999).
Motta, Massimo, *Competition Policy* (Cambridge, Cambridge University Press, 2004).
Narula, Rajneesh, 'Globalisation and Trends in International R&D Alliances', in *MERIT Research Memoranda* Nr 001 (Maastricht Economic Research Institute on Innovation and Technology, 2003),
Narula, Rajneesh, *Globalization and Technology* (Cambridge, Polity Press, 2003).
Narula, Rajneesh and Dunning, James, 'Explaining International R&D Alliances and the Role of Governments', (1998) 7 *International Business Review* 377.
Narula, Rajneesh and Hagedoorn, James, 'Innovating through Strategic Alliances: Moving Towards International Partnerships and Contractual Agreements', (1998) 19 *Technovation* 283.
Nelson, Philip, 'Patent Pools: An Economic Assessment of Current Law and Policy', (2007) 38 *Rutgers Law Journal* 539.
Newberg, Joshua, 'Antitrust, Patent Pools, and the Management of Uncertainty', (2000) 3 *Atlantic Law Journal* 1.
OECD, *OECD Science, Technology and Industry Outlook 2008: Highlights*, (2008).
Ohana, Gil et al., 'Disclosure and Negotiation of Licensing Terms Prior to Adoptation of Industry Standards: Preventing another Patent Ambush', (2003) 24 *European Competition Law Review* 644.
Ogus, Anthony, 'Rethinking Self-Regulation', (1995) 15 *OJLS* 97.
Ostry, Sylvia and Nelson, Richard, *Techno-Nationalism and Techno-Globalism Conflict and Cooperation* (Washington D.C., The Brookings Institute, 1995).

Pál, Szilágyi, 'Bidding Markets and Competition Law in the European Union and the United Kingdom Part I', (2008) 29 *European Competition Law Review* 16.

Patterson, Mark, 'The Role of Power in the Rule of Reason', (2000) 68 *Antitrust Law Journal* 429.

Patterson, Mark, 'Inventions, Industry Standards, and Intellectual Property', (2002) 17 *Berkeley Technology Law Journal* 1043.

Peritz, Rudolph J.R. 'Competition within Intellectual Property Regimes – The Instance of Patent Rights', in Steven Anderman and Ariel Ezrahi (eds), *Intellectual Property and Competition Law: New Frontiers* (Oxford, Oxford University Press, 2013).

Peterson, Scott, 'Consideration of Patents During the Setting of Standards', (2002) *DOJ/FTC* Hearings on Competition and Intellectual Property Law and Policy in the Knowledge-Based Economy.

Peterson, Scott, 'Patent and Standard-setting Process', (2002) FTC/DOJ Hearings on Competition and Intellectual Property Law and Policy in the Knowledge-Based Economy.

Petit, Maria Luise and Tolwinski, Boleslaw, 'Technology Sharing Cartels and Industrial Structure', (1996) 15 *International Journal of Industrial Organization* 77.

Pfeffer and Nowak, 'Patters of Joint Venture Activity: Implications for Antitrust Policy', (1976) 21 *Antitrust Bulletin* 315.

Pitofsky, Robert, 'Antitrust and Intellectual Property: Unsolved Issues at the Heart of the New Economy', (2001) 16 *Berkeley Technology Law Journal* 535.

Plompen, Peter, 'The New Technology Transfer Guidelines (TTG) as Applied to Patent Pools and Patent Pool Licensing: Some Observations Regarding the Concept of "Essential Technologies"', in Ehlermann, Claus Dieter and Atanasin, Isabela (eds), *European Competition Law Annual 2005: The Interaction between Competition Law and Intellectual Property Law* (Oxford, Hart Publishing, 2005), 295.

Popofsky, Mark and Michael Laufert, 'Patent Assertion Entities and Antitrust: Operating Company Patent Transfers', (2013) April *The Antitrust Source*, 1.

Priest, George, 'Cartels and Patent Licensing Arrangements', (1977) 20 *Journal of Law and Economics* 309.

Queen, Thomas W., 'Recent Development in Federal Antitrust Legislation', (1984–1985) 53 *Antitrust Law Journal* 443.

Rapp, Richard, 'The Misapplication of Innovation Market Approach to Merger Analysis', (1995–1996) 64 *Antitrust Law Journal* 19.

Richtel, Matt, 'In Settlement, Nokia Will Pay Royalties to Qualcomm', in *New York Times,* 24 July 2008.

Ritter, Cyril, 'The New Technology Transfer Block Exemption under EC Competition Law', (2004) 31 *Legal Issues of Economic Integration* 161.

Rubin, Jonathan, 'Patents, Antitrust, and Rivalry in Standard-Setting', (2007) 38 *Rutgers Law Journal*, 509.

Salop, Steven C., 'Exclusionary Conduct, Effect on Consumers, and the Flawed Profit-Sacrifice Standard', (2006) 73 *Antitrust Law Journal* 311.

Samuelson, Pamela et al., 'A Manifesto Concerning the Legal Protection of Computer Programs', (1994) 94 *Columbia Law Review* 2308.

Saunders, Kurt M. and Levine, Linda, 'Better, Faster, Cheaper-later: What Happens When Technologies are Suppressed', (2004) 11 *Mich. Telecomm. & Tech. L. Rev* 23.

Schallop, Michael, 'The IPR Paradox: Leveraging Intellectual Property Rights to Encourage Interoperability in the Network Computing Age', (2000) 28 *AIPLY Quarterly Journal* 195.

Scherer, F.M. and Ross, David, *Industrial Market Structure and Economic Performance* (Boston, Houghton Mifflin Company 1990).

Scherer, Fredric, *Industrial Market Structure and Economic Performance* (Chicago, Rand McNelly, 1980).

Scherer, Fredric, 'The Innovation Lottery', in Dreyfuss, Rochelle et al. (eds), *Expanding the Boundaries of Intellectual Property* (Oxford, Oxford University Press, 2000), 3–21.

Schrijver, Steven de and Marquis, Mel, 'Licensing Technology in the EU after the Big Bang: the New Technology Transfer Block Exemption Regulation and Guidelines', (2004) 25 *Business Law Review* 161.

Schumpeter, Joseph, *The Theory of Economic Development* (Cambridge, MA, Harvard Univ. Press 1934, reprinted 1961).

Schumpeter, Joseph, *Capitalism, Socialism and Democracy* (London, George Allen & Unwin, 1943, reprinted 1976).

Scotchmer, Suzanne, 'Standing on the Shoulders of Giants: Cumulative Research and the Patent Law', (1991) 5 *Journal of Economic Perspective* 29.

Scotchmer, Suzanne, *Innovation and Incentives* (London, The MIT Press, 2004)

Scott, John, 'Diversification versus Cooperation in R&D Investment', (1988) 9 *Managerial Decision Economics* 173.

Scott, John, 'The National Cooperative Research and Production Act', in ABA (ed), *Issues in Competition Law and Policy* (Chicago, ABA Section of Antitrust Law, 2008), 1297.

Serafino, David, 'Survey of Patent Pools Demonstrates Variety of Purposes and Management Structures', *KEI Research Note* 2007:6, (2007).

Shapiro, Carl, 'Navigating the Patent Thicket: Cross Licenses, Patent Pools and Standard-setting', in Jaffe, Adam et al. (eds), *Innovation Policy and the Economy* (Cambridge Massachusetts, MIT Press, 2001), 119.

Shapiro, Carl, 'Setting Compatibility Standards: Cooperation or Collusion?', in Dreyfuss, Rochelle et al. (eds), *Expanding The Boundaries of Intellectual Property* (Oxford, Oxford University Press, 2001), 81.

Shapiro, Carl, 'Competition and Innnovation: Did Arrow Hit the Bull's Eye?', in Josh Lerner and Scott Stern (eds), *The Rate & Direction of Inventive Activity Revisted* (Chicago, University Chicago Press, 2012).

Schepel, Harm, *The Constitution of Private Governance – Product Standards in the Regulation of Integrating Markets* (Oxford, Hart, 2005).

Siegel, Donald, 'Data Requirements for Assessing the Private and Social Returns of Strategic Research Partnerships: Analysis and Recommendations', (2003) 15 *Tech. Analysis & Strategic MGMT* 207.

Skitol, Robert A., (2002) *DOJ/FTC Hearings on Competition and Intellectual Property Law and Policy in the Knowledge-Based Economy.*

Skitol, Robert A., 'Buyer Power and Antitrust: Concerted Buying Power: Its Potential for Addressing the Patent Holdup Problem in Standard-setting', (2005) 72 *Antitrust Law Journal* 727.

Smith, Joel, 'EC: Competition – Revised Technology Transfer Block Exemption Rules in Force', (2004) 26 *European Intellectual Property Review* 113.

Sufrin, Brenda, 'The Evolution of Article 81(3) of the EC Treaty', (2006) 51 *Antitrust Bulletin* 915.

Sullivan, Lawrence and Grimes, Warren, *The Law of Antitrust: An Integrated Handbook* (St. Paul, Thomson/West, 2006).

Swanson, Daniel and Baumol, William, 'Reasonable and Nondiscriminatory (RAND) Royalties, Standards Selection, and Control of Market Power', (2005) 73 *Antitrust Law Journal* 1.

Tapia, Claudia, *Industrial Property Rights, Technical Standards and Licensing Practices (FRAND) in the Telecommunications Industry* (Carl Heymanns Verlag – eine Marke von Wolters Kluwer Deutschland GmbH, 2010).

Tassey, Gregory, 'Standardization in Technology-Based Markets', (2000) 29 *Res. Pol'y* 587.

Tindal, Suzanne, 'Nokia, Microsoft Support Patent Trolls: Google', (1 June 2012) *www.ZDnet.com*, http://www.zdnet.com/nokia-microsoft-support-patent-trolls-google-1339338945/. Accessed 3 February 2014.

Tom, William and Newberg, Joshua, 'Antitrust and Intellectual Property: From Separate Spheres to Unified Field', (1997) 66 *Antitrust Law Journal* 167.

Treacy, Pat and Heide, Thomas, 'The New EC Technology Transfer Block Exemption Regulation', (2004) 26 *European Intellectual Property Review* 414.

Ullrich, Hanns, *Kooperative Forschung and Kartellrecht* (Heidelberg, Verlag Recht und Wirtschaft, 1988).

Ullrich, Hanns, 'Intellectual Property, Access to Information, and Antitrust: Harmony, Disharmony, and International Harmonization', in Dreyfuss, Rochelle et al. (eds), *Expanding Boundaries of Intellectual Property* (Oxford, Oxford University Press, 2001), 365.

Ullrich, Hanns, 'Competitor Cooperation and the Evolution of Competition Law: Issues for Research in a Perspective of Globalisation', in Drexl, Josef (ed), *The Future of Transnational Antitrust From Comparative to Common Competition Law* (Berne, Kluwer Law International, 2003), 159.

Ullrich, Hanns, 'IP-antitrust in Context: Approaches to International Rules on Restrictive Uses of Intellectual Property Rights', (2003) 48 *Antitrust Bulletin* 837.

Ullrich, Hanns, 'Legal Protection of Innovative Technologies: Property or Policy?', in Granstrand, Owe (ed), *Economics, Law and Intellectual Property* (Dordrecht, Kluwer Academic Publishers, 2003), 439.

Ullrich, Hanns, 'Expansionist Intellectual Property Protection and Reductionist Competition Rules: A TRIPS Perspective', (2004) 7 *Journal of International Economic Law* 401.

Ullrich, Hanns, 'The Interaction between Competition Law and Intellectual Property Law – An Overview', in Ehlermann, Claus Dieter and Atanasiu, Isabela (eds), *European Competition Law Annual 2005: The Interaction between Competition Law and Intellectual Property Law* (Oxford, Hart Publishing, 2007), xvii.

Ullrich, Hanns, 'Patent Pools: Approaching a Patent Law Problem via Competition Policy', in Ehlermann, Claus-Dieter and Atanasiu, Isabela (eds), *European Competition Law Annual 2005: The Interaction Between Competition Law and Intellectual Property Law* (Oxford, Hart Publishing, 2007), 305.

Ullrich, Hanns, 'Patente, Wettbewerb, und technische Normen: Recht und ordnungspolitische Fragestellungen', (2007) 10 *Gewerblicher Rechtsschutz und Urheberrecht 2007* 817

Ullrich, Hanns, 'Patent Pools – Policy and Problems', in Drexl, Josef (ed), *Research Handbook on Intellectual Property and Competition Law* (Cheltenham, Edward Elgar Publishing Limited, 2008), 139.

Ullrich, Hanns and Heinemann, Anders, 'Competition Policy and Intellectual Property Rights: A Comparative Analysis of the Competition Rules Relating to IPR in the European Union, the USA, Japan and in International Law', Report for UNCTAD1999/2000 (1999).

Ullrich, Hanns, 'Patents and Standards – A Comment on the German Federal Supreme Court Decision, Orange Book Standard', (2011) 41 *IIC*, 337

Ullrich, Hanns, 'Patente under technische Normen: Konflikt under Komplementarität in patent- und wettbewerbsrechtlicher Sicht', in Leistne Matthias (ed), *Europäische Perspektiven des Geistigen Eigentum* (Tübingen, Mohr Siebeck, 2010).

Venit, James, 'The Research and Development Block Exemption Regulation', (1985) 10 *European Law Review* 151.

Venit, James 'Article 82 EC: Exceptional Circumstances – The IP/Antitrust Interface after IMS Health', in Claus-Dieter Ehlermann and Isabela Atanasiu (eds), *European Competition Law Annual 2005: The Interaction between Competition Law and Intellectual Property Law* (Hart Publishing, 2007).

Vollebregt, Erik, 'The New Technology Transfer Block Exemption: From Straightjacket to Moving Targets', (2004) 10 *Computer and Telecommunications Law Review* 123.

Waldman, Michael, 'A New Perspective on Planned Obsolescence', (1993) 108 *The Quarterly Journal of Economics* 273.

Wallace, James H., 'Recent Development in Federal Antitrust Legislation', (1983) 52 *Antitrust Law Journal* 479.

Wallace, Joel, 'Rambus v. F.T.C. in the Context of Standard-Setting Organizations, Antitrust, and the Patent Hold-Up Problem', (2009) 24 *Berkley Technology Law Journal* 661.

Wells, Wyatt, *Antitrust and the Formation of the Postwar World* (New York, Columbia University Press, 2002).

White, Eric, 'Research and Development Joint Ventures under EEC Competition Law', (1985) 16 *International Review of Intellectual Property and Competition Law* 663.

Wyatt, Edward, 'F.T.C. Turns a Lens on Abuse of Patenet System', the *New York Times*, 16 July 2013.

Xiong, Tao and Kirkbride, James, 'Controlling Research and Development Co-operation through EC Competition Controls: Some Concerns', (1998) 19 *Competition Law Journal* 296.

Zain, Saami, 'Suppression of Innovation or Collaborative Efficiencies? An Antitrust Analysis of a Research & Development Collaboration That Led to the Shelving of a Promising Drug', (2006) 5 *John Marshall Review of Intellectual Property Law* 347.

Zhang, Liguo, 'How IPR Policies of Telecommunication Standard-Setting Organizations can Effectively Address the Patent Ambush', (2010) 41 *IIC*, 380

Zhang, Liguo, Standardization and Patent Licensing in the European Union (Oy Nord Print Ab 2012).

Index